NINTH EDITION

CANADIAN DEMOCRACY

STEPHEN BROOKS

OXFORD

UNIVERSITY PRESS

OXFORD
UNIVERSITY PRESS

Oxford University Press is a department of the University of Oxford.
It furthers the University's objective of excellence in research, scholarship,
and education by publishing worldwide. Oxford is a registered trade mark of
Oxford University Press in the UK and in certain other countries.

Published in Canada by
Oxford University Press
8 Sampson Mews, Suite 204,
Don Mills, Ontario M3C 0H5 Canada

www.oupcanada.com

First Edition published in 1993
Second Edition published in 1996
Third Edition published in 2000
Fourth Edition published in 2004
Fifth Edition published in 2007
Sixth Edition published in 2009
Seventh Edition published in 2012
Eighth Edition published in 2015

Library and Archives Canada Cataloguing in Publication

Title: Canadian democracy / Stephen Brooks.
Names: Brooks, Stephen, 1956- author.
Description: Ninth edition. | Includes bibliographical references and index.
Identifiers: Canadiana (print) 20190189916 | Canadiana (ebook) 20190189924 | ISBN 9780199032501
(softcover) | ISBN 9780199032549 (EPUB)
Subjects: LCSH: Canada—Politics and government—Textbooks. | LCSH: Democracy—Canada—Textbooks. |
LCGFT: Textbooks.
Classification: LCC JL65 .B76 2020 | DDC 320.971—dc23

Cover image: © Friend of a Friend Films/Shutterstock
Cover design: Laurie McGregor
Interior design: Sherill Chapman

Brief Contents

Contents

PART I Introduction

1 An Introduction to Political Life   2

PART II The Societal Context of Politics

2 Political Culture   30

3 The Social and Economic Setting   63

4 Diversity and Multiculturalism   82

5 Regionalism and Canadian Politics   109

PART III The Structures of Governance

6 The Constitution   132

7 Rights and Freedoms   166

8 Federalism   197

9 The Machinery of Government   231

10 The Administrative State   269

PART IV Participation in Politics

11 Parties and Elections 292

12 Interest Groups   333

13 The Media   363

PART V Contemporary Issues in Canadian Political Life

14 Language Politics   386

15 Women and Politics   412

Figures and Tables

Figures

Tables

Boxes

Politics in Focus

The Social Fabric

Governing Realities

Media Spotlight

Preface

One might excuse Canadians for feeling self-congratulatory. Every year Canada places towards the top in the global rankings of democracy published annually by the respected Economist Intelligence Unit (EIU). In the 2018 rankings Canada was sixth. Moreover, Canada was one of only 20 countries of the 165 included in the EIU's assessment to achieve the distinction of a full democracy. Indeed, in the category of civil liberties Canada earned the highest possible score. This was not a one-off result. Canada has done very well for as long as the EIU has published its widely cited annual ranking of how democracy fares around the world.

Not everyone agrees with this glowing assessment. Indigenous spokespersons and advocates regularly lament what they believe to be the continuing injustices suffered by Indigenous peoples. Environmental groups in Canada, the United States, and Europe criticize Canadian governments for what they charge is the country's disproportionate contribution to global warming. And there is no shortage of very prominent Canadians who argue that the country's electoral system is fundamentally undemocratic.

The title of this book—*Canadian Democracy*—is not a judgment or a conclusion. It is, rather, a focus. Over the previous eight editions of this textbook, as in the present edition, I have tried to structure my treatment of the key components of Canada's political system around such themes as equality, freedoms, rights, and access. This approach is neither an uncritical celebration of Canadian politics nor a lopsided condemnation of its shortcomings and failures. In using the complex and contested concept of democracy as my touchstone I hope to encourage readers to think about Canadian government and politics in ways that will enable them to assess fairly and realistically the performance of Canada's political system.

The political landscape in Canada has changed remarkably over the past couple of generations. Some of these changes have involved the country's system of government, most notably the Charter of Rights and Freedoms and its profound impacts on the policy process. The Charter has also contributed to change in how Canadians think and talk about politics. At the same time, some of the issues and fault lines that mark the political landscape are recognizably the same as in the past. Whether they are older or newer, all of the central issues in Canadian political life raise questions of fairness, freedom, representation, justice, and dignity. These are values we associate with democracy. We may not agree on the concrete meaning of these values or on the balance among them that best satisfies our ideal of democracy. But hardly anyone would disagree that whether what is at stake is the location of a landfill or revisions to the Constitution, these values and trade-offs are fundamental to democratic politics.

Instructors who have used previous editions of *Canadian Democracy* will see that this ninth edition represents a rather major overhaul of what has gone before. Some chapters, particularly those on Indigenous Canadians, Women and Politics, the Media, and Canada in the World, have been largely rewritten to reflect important changes that have taken place in recent years in the subject matter, but also in the ways in which we think about these issues. These chapters are the ones where the changes are greatest, but all of the chapters have been very substantially revised and updated. Since the last edition, several new podcasts have been added at the book's companion website (www.oup.com/he/Brooks9e) and more are planned for the next few years.

Highlights of the Ninth Edition

While preparing this ninth edition of *Canadian Democracy*, one paramount goal was kept in mind: to produce the most accessible and interesting, yet comprehensive and authoritative introduction to Canadian politics available.

This edition builds on the strengths of the market-leading previous editions, using approachable content and dynamic pedagogy to explore the characteristics and controversies associated with Canadian politics. The following pages outline some of the most significant features of the new edition.

Comprehensive updates throughout *Canadian Democracy*, ninth edition, bring readers the latest data, research, court rulings, and analysis of current events that come to bear on Canadian politics and society. Some specific changes to note:

- ✔ Chapter 2, "Political Culture," includes new content on conflict between Indigenous groups and the Canadian government regarding Indigenous title and land rights.

- ✔ Chapter 3, "The Social and Economic Setting," contains new data and considerations of precarious work and the uncertain economic futures of millennials and Generation Z in Canada.

- ✔ Chapter 9, "The Machinery of Government," includes new content on Canada's "democratic deficit," including a new boxed feature.

- ✔ Chapter 11, "Parties and Elections," provides an expanded exploration of the electoral system, including new content on the popular vote, minority governments, and proportional representation.

- ✔ Chapter 13, "The Media," offers new content on issues of the media and democracy, including the decline of traditional media, the use of social media for news, new media gatekeepers, and updated data on the media habits of Canadians.

- ✔ Chapter 16, "Indigenous Politics," has been updated with significant new material on political organizations within Indigenous communities in Canada, as well as new content on the United Nations Human Rights Council's 2018 review of Canada's treatment of Indigenous Peoples.

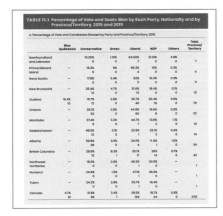

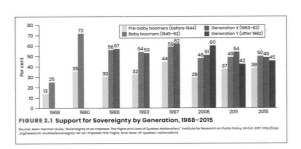

FIGURE 2.1 Support for Sovereignty by Generation, 1968–2015

Source: Jean-Herman Guay, "Sovereignty at an impasse: The Highs and Lows of Quebec Nationalism," Institute for Research on Public Policy, 24 Oct. 2017, http://irpp.org/research-studies/sovereignty-at-an-impasse-the-highs-and-lows-of-quebec-nationalism/.

Updated feature boxes *Canadian Democracy* includes four recurring boxed features scattered throughout every chapter to highlight current issues, show politics at work, and encourage students to think critically.

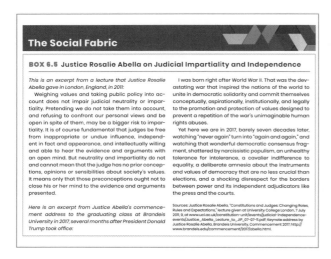

"The Social Fabric" boxes explore social issues that impact—and are impacted by—political developments and concerns.

"Governing Realities" boxes analyze examples of government at work as well as concepts related to the institutions and processes of government.

"Politics in Focus" boxes examine current issues and events through a critical lens.

"Media Spotlight" boxes highlight key media pieces and editorials and consider the media's role in politics.

Revised aids to student learning A rich pedagogical program enhances students' engagement with the material, encouraging critical thinking and further exploration.

✔ **Chapter overviews** outline the main topics covered in each chapter and serve as a quick reference and study tool for students.

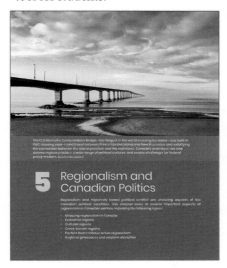

✔ Lists of starting points for research provide readings that serve as a jumping-off point for students looking to do further research for assignments and papers.

✔ Review exercises encourage students to apply what they have learned and use practical research skills.

✔ A glossary of key terms provides students with concise definitions for concepts that are, in many cases, unfamiliar and perhaps a bit specialized for most laypersons. These terms are important to an understanding of the material covered in this book.

✔ An engaging photo and political cartoon program—featuring an extensive selection of both contemporary and historic photos as well as insightful and thought-provoking editorial cartoons from renowned artists such as Michael de Adder and Len Norris—brings a visual dimension to the discussion of Canadian politics.

The reading of a new budget is a ceremonial affair in Ottawa, and though no one knows its origin, there is a long-standing tradition of the Finance minister purchasing and wearing a new pair of shoes for the occasion. Jim Flaherty, Finance minister in the Harper government from 2006 until his sudden death in 2014, always wore new shoes.

Ancillary Resource Center

Updated suite of online resources *Canadian Democracy* is part of a comprehensive package of learning and teaching tools that includes ancillary resources for both instructors and students, all available on the book's Ancillaries Resource Centre (ARC) at **www.oup.com/he/Brooks9e**.

For Instructors

- A robust **Instructor's Manual** provides extensive pedagogical tools and suggestions for every chapter, including objectives for student learning, classroom discussion and debate ideas, class activities, and lists of teaching aids.

- Classroom-ready **PowerPoint Slides** summarize key points from each chapter and incorporate graphics from the book for ease of presentation.

- An extensive **Test Generator** provides instructors with hundreds of questions in multiple-choice, true/false, short-answer, and essay formats.

For Students

- **A Student Study Guide** includes short-answer study questions; self-testing quizzes; an expanded glossary; annotated lists of relevant websites; and suggestions for books, articles, and media resources highlighting political issues in Canada.

- **Podcasts**—many new for this edition—provide mini-lectures that hone in on current issues such as political corruption, the future of Quebec separatism, and Canada-US relations, allowing students to delve more deeply into topics of interest and make further connections between the text and the real world.

- **"Conversations on Canadian Politics" videos** feature interviews with experts on various core concepts introduced in the text, enabling students to go even deeper on key topics such as federalism, political participation, and environmental politics.

Acknowledgements

Since the first edition of this book I have been privileged to work with truly exceptional people at Oxford University Press. I see their fingerprints throughout this latest edition, reaching back to Michael Harrison, who originally approached me about writing a text on Canadian government and politics, to the current team at Oxford. Every person with whom I have worked has helped make this a better book than it would have been without their advice, guidance, and talents. I would like to make particular mention of Richard Tallman's meticulous copy-editing. His advice on points of style and substance has transformed the manuscript for each edition of this book into a much better product. It is always a privilege to work with him.

I join the publisher in thanking the following reviewers, along with those who wish to remain anonymous, whose thoughtful remarks have helped to shape this edition:

Ralph Ashford, Sir Sanford Fleming College
Carey Doberstein, University of British Columbia
Peter Graefe, McMaster University
Royce Koop, University of Manitoba
Andrea Lawlor, King's University College and Western University
J.P. Lewis, University of New Brunswick
Janice Newton, York University
Paul Prosperi, Langara College
Kandace Terris, Dalhousie University
Stephen Tomblin, Memorial University of Newfoundland and Labrador
Kelly Saunders, Brandon University
John Soroski, MacEwan University
Nelson Wiseman, University of Toronto

Over the years I have taught Canadian politics to several thousand students in Canada, the United States, France, and Belgium. I have come to realize what a privilege and responsibility it is to explain to others how politics works, and who it works for. This book is dedicated to my students, past, present, and future.

Stephen Brooks
Windsor, Ontario, and Lille, France

PART I
Introduction

We all have an idea of what politics involves. But the term *political science* may be less familiar and, in some ways, rather puzzling. The problem arises from the word "science." Science evokes images of laboratories, ideas of measurement, and the domain of hard facts on which depend the construction of bridges that do not collapse and medications that cure rather than kill us. The study and understanding of politics, as is true of all forms of human behaviour and organization, would seem to lack the hard edge and to rely on techniques quite different from those characteristic of physics and genetic biology. Can there be such a thing as political *science*?

The answer is, "within limits." Political science expresses the aspiration among those who study politics to do so in an objective way. It involves the attempt to understand why things are the way they are and therefore how they may be changed, rather than how they ought to be. Political science rests on a bedrock of empirical analysis—analysis that seeks to formulate laws about the world of politics and government based on verifiable observation and, in some cases, experimentation—and not on the ideological leanings and personal preferences of the person doing the observing and

explaining. But whereas genes may be spliced and the weight-bearing capacity of a bridge may be tested through a computer simulation, political scientists generally have to make do with observing behaviour and the functioning of institutions in less controlled circumstances. How they undertake their analysis of politics and the certitude of their observations may not look very much like the activities and results of those in the natural and applied sciences. Nevertheless, the aspiration to produce objective, empirical knowledge is the same.

Those who study Canadian politics and government rely on the same concepts and analytical methods used by those who wish to understand these subjects in France, China, Egypt, or any other society. Power, authority, identity, participation, bureaucracy, integration, stability, and equality are just some of the core concepts relevant to an understanding of politics in any country. In this first section of *Canadian Democracy* we will examine some of the concepts that are crucial to an understanding of politics and government in Canada. This will provide the basis for the subsequent chapters that focus on particular features of Canadian political life.

This book aims to explain how the political system works in Canada, and to give you the tools needed to evaluate the processes and outcomes of Canadian politics. Whatever your conclusions, they should include the belief that politics does matter and that your thoughts and actions hold political significance. **ChristopheLedent/iStockphoto**

1

An Introduction to Political Life

To understand politics and government, one requires a tool kit consisting of the fundamental concepts and terms that are useful in analyzing political life. This chapter aims to equip the reader with these tools by examining the following topics:

- What is politics?
- Power
- State and government
- Democracy
- Who gets heard and why?
- Consent and legitimacy
- Political identities
- Political fault lines: old and new

If you want a job that earns you the trust and respect of your fellow citizens, then become a nurse, doctor, scientist, or farmer. Do not become a politician. This, at least, is the conclusion that emerges from a 2017 poll and from many similar polls over the years. Politicians came in twenty-seventh of the 27 professions that were ranked according to the trust that Canadians place in them, only 6 per cent of respondents saying that they had a very positive opinion of them and another 18 per cent saying that they had a somewhat positive opinion.[1] Politicians and their craft have what marketing people would call an image problem.

This image of politicians as untrustworthy, and of their calling as low and dishonest, is not entirely fair. There is no hard evidence that politicians are more likely to be dishonest or have low morals than those in other occupations. Indeed, many if not most people who run for and are elected to public office are motivated by a desire to serve and to improve the lives of those they represent. And popular perceptions notwithstanding, many politicians make significant financial and personal sacrifices by holding public office.

But Canadians do not trust them. To understand why, we need to think about the nature of the politician's craft in societies such as Canada where not everyone shares the same opinions or has identical interests, and where the political system is such that the votes of about 40 per cent or more of those who bother to cast their ballots will be needed for a political party to win a national election. In these circumstances, politicians and political parties—or at least those serious about winning elections—need to appeal to a range of interests and values. Once elected, they must do the same, balancing competing demands and points of view. On top of this, they may find that their ability to do certain things that may be popular or that they believe to be the right things to do, regardless of public opinion, is limited by circumstances beyond their control. The promises they made cannot be kept, or perhaps not quite in the form they were made or according to the timetable that was expected. And perhaps they knew or suspected this all along, saying things and making promises with what some might

EVERY CHRISTMAS YOU MAKE A LOT OF PROMISES YOU NEVER KEEP, WHY DON'T YOU BECOME A POLITICIAN

Alfredo Martirena/Cartoon Gallery

Most Canadians do not follow politics very closely. Surveys show that younger voters tend to be the least interested in politics and less likely to participate than middle-aged and older citizens. A contributing factor to Canadians' political apathy is their lack of trust in their politicians.

characterize as reckless disregard for their truth or prospects of achievement.

It is the messy activity of politics—including the compromises, the occasional evasiveness, the failure to deliver on promises made, and the resulting sense that those elected to public office do not faithfully represent those who put them there—that leads to cynicism about politicians and political parties. Canadians, however, are not alone in their negativity. In fact, in no established democracy do a majority of people say that they have a great deal or quite a lot of confidence in political parties.[2]

A healthy dose of cynicism about politics is probably a good thing, at least if it is cynicism fuelled by knowledge. Cynicism based on ignorance or coupled to apathy, however, can make no such claim. Whether you are a hardened cynic or an enthusiastic fan when it comes to Canadian politics—in fact, if you are like most Canadians your age, you probably do not follow politics very closely and therefore do not feel strongly one way or the other—no judgment about how well the political system works and in whose interests should be uninformed. This book aims to give you that information and the analytical tools needed to evaluate the processes and outcomes of Canadian politics. The conclusions you draw and the judgments you arrive at are, of course, up to you. Whatever your conclusions, they should not include the belief that politics does not matter in your life and that your thoughts and actions are somehow without political significance. The Polish poet and 1996 Nobel Prize laureate, Wislawa Szymborska, has this to say about such ideas:

> All affairs, day and night,
> yours, ours, theirs,
> are political affairs.
>
> Like it or not,
> your genes have a political past,
> your skin a political cast,
> your eyes a political aspect.
>
> What you say has a resonance;
> what you are silent about is telling.
> Either way, it's political.[3]

What Is Politics?

Politics arises from the fact of scarcity. In the real world it is not possible for all of us to satisfy all of our desires to the fullest extent. Limits on the stock of those things that people desire—wealth, privacy, clean air and water, social recognition—ensure that conflicts will take place between rival claimants. These conflicts explain why politics comes about. But politics is about more than the fact of conflict. It is also about how rival claims are settled. What distinguishes politics from the conflicts, struggles, and rivalries that take place in such settings as the family, the workplace, and the economic marketplace, and in social organizations like churches and labour unions, is the *public nature* of political disputes and the use of public authority—embodied in

the state—to deal with them. **Politics**, then, is the activity by which rival claims are settled by public authorities. The boundaries of what is considered to be political are located where the state's authority reaches. Political philosophers sometimes call this the public realm. Beyond this line is the private realm, where the state's authority does not extend.

As Box 1.1 shows, this definition does not have the field all to itself. All of these contending definitions agree that politics is about the exercise of power. They disagree, however, about what power relations count as political ones. Foucault, Marx, and the feminist movement define politics in ways that would include the relations between bosses and workers in a corporation, between parents and children in a family, between teachers and students in schools, and between spiritual shepherd and flock in a faith community. And in a sense they are right. Lasswell and Easton both offer a more limited definition of politics, one that goes back to Aristotle's conception of the Greek *polis*. They argue that what is distinctive about politics is the association of this activity with a system of settling disputes that is both public and binding on the whole community. At the centre of this system is the state, or government, as those raised in the Anglo-American tradition are more likely to call it.

These definitions disagree in another important way. **Marxism**, postmodernism (Foucault), and feminism associate politics with a pervasive pattern of oppression. Politics is, for them, fundamentally about how inequalities are generated and reinforced through the relations that exist between classes (Marxism), gender groups (feminism), or these and other systemically unequal power relations between groups (postmodernism) at all levels of society.

Does it matter, in the end, how we define politics? Or is this mainly a harmless diversion for academic hair-splitters? Some argue that there is a very practical reason for rejecting those definitions of politics that confer on all power relations, wherever they may be located and however limited they may be, the title "political." If politics is viewed as being everywhere and in all social interactions, we lose the ability to see the boundary that separates the public and private realms. This boundary may not be very distinct, but it is crucial for understanding the politics of any society and, in particular, that society's ideas about the acceptable scope of state activity. Limits on the state's legitimate authority are necessary in order to protect the freedoms that most of us believe to be important features of a democratic society. Political conflict in democracies is often about where exactly this boundary between public and private should be drawn, what should be considered a proper matter for public life and decisions by the state, and what should remain private matters. We can agree that power relations are ubiquitous without going the next step to claim that politics, therefore, has no bounds.

Not everyone agrees. Political scientist Jill Vickers echoes many of her feminist colleagues when she argues that the public realm/private realm distinction is fundamentally sexist. It is based, she maintains, on a tradition of political thinking that accepted as natural the domination of the public realm by males and the limitation of women to the private sphere. When women were finally admitted to the public realm it was on identical terms with men, a formal equality that failed to recognize the substantive inequalities in the typical life conditions of males and females.

But whatever sexist biases may have been embedded in the public-versus-private distinction in traditional Western political thought, is it not the case that the contemporary importance of this distinction lies in the value it assigns to individual freedom? This, too, says Vickers, is fundamentally sexist. "The concept of *freedom,*" she writes, "has become an almost totally masculinized idea in Western political thought, meaning *freedom from* constraints—an autonomy in which no dependence on another is required or recognized."[4] According to Vickers, this is a value with little appeal to most women, who have as their goal "interdependence among equals" rather than the freedom to act without constraint.

Politics in Focus

BOX 1.1 Some Important Definitions of Politics and Power

"[A] political system can be designated as those interactions through which values are authoritatively allocated for a society."

David Easton, *A Systems Analysis of Political Life*

"Politics: Who Gets What, When and How"

Harold Lasswell, *Politics: Who Gets What, When and How*

"Political power, properly so called, is merely the organized power of one class for oppressing another."

Karl Marx and Friedrich Engels, *The Communist Manifesto*

"Basically power is less a confrontation between two adversaries or the linking of one to the other than a question of government. This word must be allowed the very broad meaning which it had in the sixteenth century. 'Government' did not refer only to political structures or to the management of states; rather it designated the way in which the conduct of individuals or of groups might be directed: the government of children, of souls, of communities, of families, of the sick. It did not cover only the legitimately constituted forms of political or economic subjection, but also modes of action . . . which were destined to act upon the possibilities of action of other people. To govern, in this sense, is to structure the possible field of action of others."

Michel Foucault, *The Subject and Power*

"The personal is political."

Slogan of the 1960s feminist movement

Power

Power is the ability to influence what happens. It is found in all sorts of settings, not simply political ones. When Facebook makes decisions about when and under what conditions it will share the personal information collected from billions of users, that is power. When the Vatican issues an official proclamation on same-sex marriage or the exclusion of women from the priesthood, elements within the Roman Catholic Church respond. The Vatican has power within the community of Roman Catholics. When a person is persuaded to give up his wallet at gunpoint, his attacker has power. Parents who are able to compel their children's obedience through the threat or fact of punishment, or through persuasive arguments and the offer of rewards, have power. A television network whose programs shape the issues that viewers are thinking about has power. And when a peaceful demonstration of citizens outside the headquarters of a corporation or in front of the legislature changes the behaviour of the targeted institution, that, too, is power. In each of these cases one party affects the behaviour of another, although the reasons for compliance differ.

Social scientists like to unpack the concept of power, breaking it down into species that are distinguished from one another according to the reason why the compliant party obeys. Compliance may result from the threat or use of force (**coercion**); from the ability of A to convince B that a particular action is reasonable or otherwise in B's best interests (**influence**); or from the recognition on the part of the compliant party that the person or organization issuing a command has the right to do so and should be obeyed (**authority**). Politics involves all of these faces of power—coercion, influence, and authority—at various times and in different circumstances. Democratic politics relies primarily on the two non-coercive species of power. But coercion is used, and no democracy is without its system of courts, police, and prisons.

How far coercion and democracy are compatible, however, is an open question. It was posed in a stark manner in October 1970,[5] a few days after the Canadian government responded to the terrorist activities of the Front de libération du Québec

by invoking the War Measures Act. Critics challenged the government's decision, arguing that the use of the military on Canadian streets to deal with the threat of terrorist actions amounted to the imposition of a police state. Prime Minister Pierre Trudeau rejected this view, stating that "it is more important to keep law and order in society than to be worried about weak-kneed people. . . . I think the society must take every means at its disposal to defend itself against the emergence of a parallel power which defies the elected power in this country, and I think that goes to any distance."

Is Trudeau right? It is one of the great ironies of democracy that, unlike other political systems, it requires that dissenting points of view and opposition to those in power be respected. Arresting people suspected of terrorist acts is, most would agree, necessary to protect democratic government. At some point, however, the protection of law and order may exact a high cost in terms of personal freedoms. In a democracy, those in power must justify their use of the state's authority, including resort to coercion, as being necessary to maintain such values as freedom, equality, justice, and the **rule of law**. Inevitably, however, people will disagree over the meaning and relative importance of these values, and over how much coercion, in what circumstances, is acceptable. The practical difficulties that can arise in an *open society*—a society in which individuals are free to speak their minds, associate with whom they wish, and move freely about without having to notify or justify their movements to the public authorities—was brought home to Canadians, and even more so to Americans, after the terrorist attacks on the World Trade Center and the Pentagon on 11 September 2001. Access to public buildings became more restricted, border crossings became more time-consuming and stressful, airport security was tightened, and measures were taken to curb the rights of immigrants. Some of these changes proved to be temporary, but many—such as the air travel security tax that all Canadian travellers have been required to pay since 2002, the Anti-Terrorism Act, which came into effect in December 2001,[6] and a general increase in legal surveillance, both public and private—have been enduring. Among the most significant consequences of 9/11, and of subsequent terrorist plots exposed in Canada and abroad, has been the debate generated regarding the appropriate balance between individual rights and national security in a democratic society. Some believe that Canadian co-operation with the United States in the creation and maintenance of what officialdom calls a "common security perimeter" is necessary to protect the open society from enemies who would take advantage of the freedoms it affords to spread terror. Others see such a policy as being democracy's own "Iron Curtain," and thus a flagrant violation of the principles that the open society is supposed to embody and uphold.

State and Government

The existence of the state is a necessary condition for a social order that allows for the peaceful resolution of conflict. But what is the "state"? To this point we have used the terms "state" and "government" as though they meant the same thing. This failure to make a distinction between them is often harmless, but it can lead to confusion. For example, Henry David Thoreau argues in his famous *Essay on Civil Disobedience* that the state, at its best, is nevertheless an institution that will from time to time perpetrate and perpetuate injustices. This, he maintains, is not due to the imperfections of the

Jesse Winter/StarMetro Vancouver

RCMP and Emergency Response Team tactical unit officers force their way over a reinforced gate set up by the Wet'suwet'en people to prevent the construction of an oil pipeline through their unceded traditional territories. The RCMP broke through the barrier to enforce a court injunction that would allow Coastal Gaslink to access the land, prompting criticism of the perceived abuse of court and police power to infringe on an Indigenous title and the rights of the land protectors.

particular lawmakers and other public officials who comprise the government of the day, although some governments will be better than others. It is due to the nature of the state, the character and function of which is to require that some persons, from time to time, submit to laws that they believe to be unjust or otherwise morally wrong. Thoreau's argument is with the state as such, as when he pushes Thomas Jefferson's dictum a bit further to declare, "That government is best which governs not at all."

Canadian political scientist Leo Panitch provides this definition of the **state**:

> [The state is] a broad concept that includes government as the seat of legitimate authority in a territory but also includes bureaucracy, judiciary, the Armed Forces and internal police, structures of legislative assemblies and administration, public corporations, regulatory boards, and ideological apparatuses such as the education establishment and publicly owned media. The distinguishing characteristic of the state is its monopoly over the use of force in a given territory.[7]

Defined this way, the state has three main characteristics. First, it involves territorial boundaries. States have borders, beyond which their legal authority is either nil or strictly limited. Second, the state consists of a complex set of institutions that wield public authority. The courts, the police, and the educational system are outposts of the state's authority no less than are the elected legislature and the bureaucracy. Third, the state is defined in terms of power, what Weber (see Box 1.2) called its "monopoly of the legitimate use of physical force in the enforcement of its order." For what purposes and in whose interests this power is exercised are important questions.

Some definitions of the state offer answers to these questions. The Marxist definition in Box 1.2 characterizes the state as an instrument of class oppression. Marx argued that the end of class conflict would sound the death knell for the state. It would "wither away," no longer having any function to perform. Contemporary Marxists, except for

Politics in Focus

BOX 1.2 Alternative Definitions of the State

"The executive of the modern State is but a committee for managing the common affairs of the whole bourgeoisie."

Marx and Engels, The Communist Manifesto

"The state is that fiction by which everyone seeks to live at the expense of everyone else."

French economist Frédéric Bastiat, circa 1840

"L'État, c'est moi." [I am the state.]

Louis XIV of France

"[The state is that institution which] successfully upholds a claim to the monopoly of the legitimate use of physical force in the enforcement of its order . . . within a given territorial area."

Max Weber, The Theory of Social and Economic Organization

"All state-based political systems are patriarchal—that is, in no country in the world are women equal participants in the institutions of the state or equal beneficiaries in its distribution of power or in the norms and values sanctioned in law and enforced by those institutions."

Jill Vickers, Reinventing Political Science

a few diehards, no longer predict the state's demise. Feminists view the state as a patriarchal institution, reinforcing and perpetuating the social superiority of men over women. Many political scientists, and probably most economists, would argue that the state is responsive to any group with enough political clout to persuade policy-makers that it is in their interest to meet the group's demands for public actions on private wants.

Any useful explanation of the state must ask on whose behalf and in whose interests the state's authority is exercised. Contemporary political science offers four main answers to these questions: **pluralism**, **class analysis**, **feminism**, and **postmodernism**.

Pluralism. Those who see politics as being fundamentally a competition between different interests are likely to conclude that the state responds chiefly to the demands of those groups that are best organized, have superior financial resources, can credibly claim to speak on behalf of large numbers of voters or segments of the population that are influential for other reasons, and are successful in associating their special interests with the general interests of society. The pluralist model assumes various forms, some of which are society-centred. The *society-centred* variants emphasize the impact of groups in society on the state, while *state-centred* variants place greater emphasis on the ability of public officials to act on their own preferences and according to their own interests, rather than merely responding to the demands of voters and interest groups. Pluralist models of the state do not assume that the competition among groups takes place on a level playing field. On the contrary, many of those who work within this perspective argue that business interests occupy a privileged position within this competition. Many pluralist thinkers argue that those who shape our perception of the world, especially those in the media, tend to lean in a particular ideological direction that favours certain interpretations, values, and interests over others.

Class analysis. Beginning with Karl Marx, class analysis has always seen the state in capitalist societies as an instrument through which the small minorities who control most of a society's wealth maintain their social and economic dominance.

Precisely how this is done has been the subject of enormous debate, but the state's complicity in perpetuating inequalities rooted in the economic system is an article of faith shared by all variants of class analysis. Few of those who analyze politics from a class analysis perspective today would deny that the demands and interests of subordinate classes influence state decision-makers. But this influence, they argue, is sharply limited by the state's vulnerability to a decline in business confidence, the control that the dominant class has over the mass media and popular culture, and a lack of class consciousness among even the least privileged groups in society that stems from the widespread acceptance—what Marx called "false consciousness"—of capitalist and individualistic values as normal and inevitable.

Feminism. Feminists view the state as an inherently patriarchal institution. This means that the state, its structures, and its laws all serve to institutionalize male dominance. Increasing the representation of women in elected legislatures, the bureaucracy, and the courts, and creating governmental bodies and programs that recognize women as a group with interests and needs that are not identical to those of men can attenuate this male dominance. However, much of feminist political theory still insists that a state-centred political system will be patriarchal. "A feminist state that is a structure of authority," says R.W. Connell, "a means by which some persons rule over others, is self-contradictory."[8] It is the hierarchical nature of authority embodied in the state that makes it fundamentally patriarchal. Like Karl Marx's famous prediction that the state would "wither away" once classes were abolished, some feminists argue that if gender discrimination were to be eliminated the state, *as we know it*, would disappear.

Postmodernism. Postmodernism views the state as an essentially oppressive and even repressive institution. But unlike class analysis and feminism, postmodernism is much more eclectic in the forms of oppression that it associates with the state and public authority. That oppression may be targeted at groups based on their race, gender, ethnicity, sexual preference, or some other trait that places them outside the dominant group that controls the levers of state power and whose values and identity are reflected in the institutions, language, and mores of the society. Postmodernism views the state as a repressive institution in that the structures, laws, and activities that constitute the state repress the expression of some values at the same time as they legitimize and nurture others. Those who embrace this approach comprise what is sometimes called the New Left. The Old Left wished to see the overthrow of the capitalist state and its transformation into the vehicle whereby those without property, money, and status would be able to reform society. Postmodernism is more dubious about the revolutionary visions associated with class analysis and the Old Left, believing that the problem of the state is not simply its relationship to economic power but to forms of oppression and repression more generally. This leads some postmodernists, such as the French philosopher Jean Baudrillard, to despair of the possibility of achieving justice and democracy through the state. Others, such as the American philosopher Richard Rorty, are more optimistic.

A distinction can be made between the state and government. **Government** is a term more usefully reserved for those who have been elected to power. It is more personal than the state, being associated with a particular group of people and, usually, with political parties. In democratic political systems governments are chosen and removed through elections. These elections—the rules and procedures by which governments are formed—are part of the state system. And like the rest of the state, they are much less likely to generate political controversy and to undergo change than are the government and its policies, although in some states, notably the United States, the redrawing of electoral districts is done for partisan political advantage and this gerrymandering becomes a contentious issue.

Underlying the distinction between state and government is an important practical difference in how each compels the obedience of citizens, corporations, and associations that fall within its jurisdiction. The willingness of individuals and groups to obey the decisions of government—decisions they may vigorously disagree with, and a government they may not have voted for—is based on their view that the state's authority is legitimate.

By **legitimacy** we mean that the rules and institutions that comprise the state, and which determine how governments are chosen, are accepted by most people as being reasonable (or at least they are not seen as being unfair). The legitimacy of the state is, therefore, based on the *consent* of those who are governed. It does not depend on an ever-present fear of the penalties that follow from disobeying the law. It rests instead on what is usually an implicit acceptance of the rules of the political game. If the state's authority, and ultimately the ability of governments to govern, depended on a sort of constant referendum of the popular will, politics would be a brittle enterprise. In reality, this popular consent is not something that people regularly (if ever!) reflect on or consciously avow (the "Pledge of Allegiance" recited by American schoolchildren in all but a handful of states has no counterpart in most democracies, and certainly not in Canada).

Perhaps the best way to understand the importance of the state/government distinction in a democracy is to imagine what would happen if a government's ability to pass and implement laws depended on its popularity. Assume for a moment that a government's "approval rating" sinks to 20 per cent, according to public opinion polls, and that particular actions of the government are opposed by a clear majority of citizens. Should people simply choose to disobey the law and treat this unpopular government as one that has lost its right to govern? And if polls showed that the leader of another political party was clearly preferred by most voters, would this leader have a better moral claim to govern than the discredited leader of the government?

This is a scenario for chaos and anarchy. Democracy requires some measure of stability and respect for rules, including those rules that determine who has the right to govern and how and when that right ends. A particular government or prime minister may be deeply unpopular, but people continue to obey the law and refrain from storming the legislature (although they may organize protests and even throw some tomatoes) because of their implicit acceptance of the state's legitimacy. Government popularity and state legitimacy are not the same.

The state's authority may be upheld by consent or by force. In fact, it is usually upheld by both. When Indigenous protesters block a highway or access to a proposed development project and are arrested and charged for this act of civil disobedience, they are challenging the authority of the state. When Quebec separatists demand political independence for their province they are registering their belief that the existing boundaries of the Canadian state, and its authority in Quebec society, are not legitimate. And when striking unions ignore back-to-work legislation, and in doing so run the risk of being fined or their leaders being imprisoned, this also goes beyond disagreement with government policy to challenge the legitimacy of the state. The state's authority is sometimes questioned by individuals or by organized interests. When this happens, the public authorities may resort to force in order to crush civil disobedience and maintain their ability to govern.

The question of when citizens may be justified in resisting the law, through either passive disobedience of public authority or violence, is an old one. Two of the world's greatest democracies, the United States and France, trace their modern origins to bloody revolutions undertaken in defence of principles that the revolutionaries believed warranted violence against the state. Some, such as the American writer and libertarian thinker Henry David Thoreau, India's Mahatma Gandhi, and the black civil rights leader Martin Luther King Jr, developed a philosophy of non-violent civil disobedience that has been influential across the world. Others embrace the philosophy of the American black activist Malcolm X, whose slogan was "By any means necessary." A wide range of contemporary movements, including anti-globalists, Indigenous groups, and animal rights activists, embrace Malcolm X's view that violent opposition to the law and those who enforce it is morally justifiable and consistent with democracy when it targets oppression and injustice. "Violence and nonviolence are tools," writes *The Atlantic* editor Ta-Nehisi Coates, and "violence—like nonviolence—sometimes works."[9]

The debate over civil disobedience—when it is justified and what forms it may take in a

The Canadian Press/Ron Poling

In a 1992 Gallup Poll, then Prime Minister Brian Mulroney earned an approval rating of just 11 per cent, making him one of the most unpopular Canadian leaders since the inception of opinion polling. His government's introduction of the Goods and Services Tax, a recession, and the failure of the Meech Lake Accord contributed to the decline in his popularity during his second term in office. It was through the processes of the state that Canadians made their dissent known: in the 1993 federal election, the Progressive Conservatives were reduced from 151 seats to a mere 2 in the House of Commons, losing their official party status.

democracy—has resurfaced in recent years, principally around issues associated with globalization and income inequality. Since what the media dubbed the "Battle in Seattle" in 1999, when the meetings of the World Trade Organization were disrupted by thousands of protesters and scenes of violent confrontations with the police were broadcast live around the world, organized protest has become a standard and expected part of any meeting of policy-makers from the world's wealthiest countries. The street tactics used at anti-globalization protests in Seattle, Genoa (2001), Toronto (2010), Hamburg (2017), and elsewhere have produced a globally oriented service industry that specializes in providing activist groups with advice and training on confrontations with the police, effective use of the media, and, more generally, strategies and tactics for influence through civil disobedience. Training for Change (www.trainingforchange.org) and the Ruckus Society (www.ruckus.org) are examples of such organizations.

It is, of course, perfectly lawful to provide information that one intends will disrupt the status quo. But what about advice or action that involves breaking the law? When should law enforcement officials intervene to enforce the law and when is the public interest, justice, social order, or some other value better served when they remain on the sideline?

These are questions that governments, in Canada and elsewhere, often confront. Here is an example. In January of 2013 an Ontario court judge publicly rebuked the province's police for failing to carry out the terms of two injunctions that he had issued concerning the blockade of the railway line near Kingston, running from Toronto to Montreal. Members of the Idle No More movement had erected the blockades in protest against federal policies. "We seem to be drifting into dangerous waters in the life of the public affairs of this province," Justice David Brown stated, "when courts cannot predict . . . whether police agencies will assist in enforcing court injunctions." He went on to say that "Just as 15 persons would not have the right to stand in the middle of the main line tracks blocking rail traffic in order to espouse a political cause close to their hearts, neither do 15 persons from a First Nation."[10] Who was right, the judge or the Ontario government that instructed the province's police force not to enforce the law by intervening?

Although public opinion in this case and others like it was divided, many Canadians and citizens of other countries believe that such resistance is a justifiable reaction to a history of oppression and a political system and justice system believed by some to be heavily biased against the interests of those who have been marginalized. The oppression and violence that the state may inflict on members of the society, the argument goes, warrant self-defence on the part of victims of this oppression and violence.

Government that relies primarily on threats and violence to maintain its rule is generally unstable. Even the most repressive political authorities usually come to realize that popular consent is a firmer basis on which to govern. In some societies the popular consent that legitimizes political rule may appear to emerge more or less spontaneously from the uncoordinated activities of the media, the schools, the family, governments: from the various social institutions that influence the values and beliefs of citizens. In other societies, the state's legitimacy is deliberately and assiduously cultivated through the organs of official propaganda. The calculated fostering of consent is a characteristic feature of totalitarian rule. **Totalitarianism** is a system of government that suppresses all dissent in the name of some supreme goal. This goal may be tied to the destiny of the "race," as it was in Nazi Germany, or to "class struggle," as it was in the Soviet Union. It survives today in North Korea, where virtually every aspect of the lives of citizens is controlled by the state and where access to and information about the outside world is tightly restricted. Distinctions between the state, government, and society lose all meaning—indeed, they are considered to be subversive—under totalitarianism.

The active mobilization of society by the state, the deliberate manipulation of public attitudes, and the ruthless suppression of dissent by the public authorities are not features that any reasonable person associates with democracy. The way in which legitimacy is generated in political democracies is more subtle than under totalitarian rule, depending primarily on social institutions that are not part of the state system. This gives legitimacy the appearance of being based on the free choice of individuals, an appearance that some argue is an illusion. Marxist critics use the term **cultural hegemony** to signify the ability of society's dominant class to get its values and beliefs accepted as the conventional wisdom in society at large.

Howard Zinn, a prominent American historian and social critic, long argued that Americans were duped into believing that theirs is a society of freedom and equal opportunities. "If those in charge of our society—politicians, corporate executives, and owners of press and television—can dominate our ideas," he wrote, "they will be secure in their power. They will not need soldiers patrolling the streets. We will control ourselves."[11] This was, Zinn maintained, the state of affairs under American capitalism. Noam Chomsky takes this same position in arguing that the privately owned mass media reinforce and perpetuate inequalities in wealth and power by presenting "facts," images, and interpretations that either justify or gloss over these inequalities.[12] Feminists make a similar case, arguing that sexist attitudes of male superiority continue to be pervasive in social institutions—from the bedroom to the boardroom—so that the legitimacy of patriarchal power relations is reinforced on a daily basis. For both Marxists and feminists, government by "popular consent" is a sham that conceals the fundamentally undemocratic character of society and politics.

This may strike you as, at a minimum, an exaggeration of the disconnect that may be created between the reality of people's lives and their beliefs about how the world works and what possibilities exist for them. Or perhaps you find the cultural hegemony argument to be plausible or even convincing. Either way, it directs our attention to something that is quite important in all societies. This is the role played by the various agents of learning. Families, schools, the mass media, governments, and organizations and groups, formal and informal, contribute to the information, ideas, and sentiments that we have about the world around us. Indeed, in many respects the system through which information, ideas, and interpretations are generated and disseminated deserves to be considered the cornerstone of democracy. If our ideas are manipulated, based on falsehoods, and at odds with important aspects of the reality in which we live, no constitution, elections, or grand speeches can turn this sow's ear into a silk purse.

Democracy

"Democracy is like pornography," says classical historian and political commentator Victor Davis Hanson, "we know it when we see it."[13] But as is also true of pornography, what one person may believe to be unredeemed smut, another may think is art. And yet a third may say that it is all a matter of personal judgment anyway, no one's standard being, a priori, superior to anyone else's. At the same time, however, Hanson's observation seems commonsensical. Most of us would agree that a country in which free elections are held is almost certainly more democratic than one where they are not. And where we see egregious and persistent violations of human rights or a serious lack of accountability on the part of those who govern, we are likely to be skeptical about claims that such a country is democratic.

But that does not stop leaders in political systems as different as those of Canada, the United States, the Democratic People's Republic of Korea, Russia, and the Islamic Republic of Iran from all claiming to be democracies. Democracy is a label to which regimes throughout the world try to lay claim. Obviously they cannot all be democratic without our understanding of this concept being diluted to the point that it becomes meaningless.

Is democracy a system of government? Or does democracy connote a type of society? Was Canada "democratic" before the female half of the population received the vote? Do the persistence of poverty and the clear evidence of large inequalities in the economic condition and social status of different groups in Canada oblige us to qualify our description of Canadian society as "democratic"? These are questions that produce sharp disagreements between political philosophers as they also do between friends having a coffee at Tim Hortons.[14]

In recent times the debate over what is and is not democratic has become even more complicated. Some argue that in addition to the familiar Western model of democracy, a Muslim model deserves to be called democratic. Turkey (at least before the 2014 election of President Recep Tayyip Erdoğan) and Indonesia, whose populations are overwhelmingly Muslim, have been pointed to as proof that there is no necessary incompatibility between Islam and democracy. They argue that making room for faith in the public square, such as through laws inspired by religious texts and teachings, may be antithetical to contemporary Western notions of secular democracy. They can, however, coexist with free elections, the rule of law, respect for human rights, and equality.

Critics of such claims point out that none of the major and reputable rankings of democracies in the world consider any majority Muslim country to be democratic. For example, the Economist Intelligence Unit's widely cited annual report ranks only Indonesia and Tunisia in its "flawed democracies" category, placing all the rest in the even less democratic "hybrid regime" or "authoritarian" categories.[15]

In the final analysis, about the only thing that everyone can agree on is that democracy is based on equality. Agreement breaks down over how much equality, in what spheres of life, is necessary for a society to qualify as democratic. Majority rule, government by popular consent, one person–one vote, and competitive elections are the political institutions usually associated with democratic government. But it has long been recognized that the operation of democratic political institutions can result in oppressive government. If, for example, a majority of Quebecers agree that legislative restrictions on the language rights of non-francophones are needed to preserve the French character of Quebec, is this democratic? In order to safeguard the rights and freedoms of individuals and minorities against what Alexis de Tocqueville called "democratic despotism," constitutional limits may be set on the power of the state over its citizens, or the political status of particular social groups may be entrenched in the formal rules and informal procedures of politics.

Perhaps even more important than constitutional guarantees and political practices are the social and cultural values of a society. Tocqueville argued that the best protection against the **tyranny of the majority** is the existence of multiple group identities in society. When individuals perceive themselves as being members of particular social groups— whether a religious denomination, an ethnic or language group, a regional community, or whatever

the group identity happens to be—in addition to sharing with everyone else a common citizenship, the likelihood of the democratic state being turned to oppressive ends is reduced. After all, everyone has a personal interest in the tolerance of social diversity because the rights and status of their own group depend on this.

Some twentieth-century writers agreed that cultural values represented the main bulwark against the tyranny of the majority. In *The Civic Culture*, American political scientists Gabriel Almond and Sidney Verba make the argument that democratic government is sustained by cultural attitudes, including respect for the right of others to hold views different from one's own.[16] According to this political culture approach, the determination of how democratic a society is must be based on an examination of the politically relevant attitudes and beliefs of the population. This, and not the mere fact of apparently democratic political institutions, is argued to be the true test of democracy and the key to sustaining it.

The civic culture thesis has enjoyed a renaissance in recent years through work on what is called **social capital**. This refers to norms of interpersonal trust, a sense of civic duty, and a belief that one's involvement in politics and in the life of the community matters. Where levels of social trust are low, public authorities must invest more in institutions and policies that rely on repression and force to maintain social order. Many argue that social capital also has an economic value, but the main argument made for policies, practices, and institutions that promote social capital is that citizens will be happier and their control over their own lives will be greater. Empirical studies of social capital show that all countries in which levels of social trust and cohesion are highest—a list that includes Canada— are well-established, stable democracies.[17] This may, however, just pose the question: does a high level of social capital contribute to successful democracy or does the experience of successful democratic politics encourage and reinforce high levels of social trust and cohesion? The causal arrows probably point in both directions.

Socialists argue that a society in which a large number of people are preoccupied with the problem of feeding and housing themselves decently cannot be described as democratic. This preoccupation effectively excludes the poor from full participation in political life, and in this way socio-economic inequality translates into political inequality. The formal equality of citizens that democratic government confers, and even the fact that most people subscribe to democratic values, does not alter the fundamental fact that social inequalities produce inequalities in political power. Some critics go even further in dismissing the democratic claims of capitalist societies, arguing that social and political inequalities result from the simple fact that a very small proportion of the population—the capitalist class—controls the vast majority of the means of economic production and distribution. This inequality in property ownership, Marxists have long argued, far outweighs the importance of one person–one vote and competitive elections in determining the real political influence of different classes in society.

Inequalities between bosses and workers, between parents and children, between men and women, between ethnic or language communities—the list could go on—are often claimed to undermine the democratic character of societies whose formal political institutions are based on the equality of citizens. Indeed, if we use any of the all-inclusive definitions of politics examined earlier in this chapter it is impossible to resist the logic of this argument. Inequalities confront us wherever we turn, and true democracy seems to be terribly elusive. Even if we define politics more narrowly to include only those activities that focus on the state, it is obvious that a small portion of all citizens actually dominates public life. This is true even in the most egalitarian societies. For most of us, participation in politics takes the form of short bursts of attention and going to the polls at election time. Is it reasonable to speak of democratic government when the levers of state power are in the hands of an elite?

The short answer is, "It depends on what we expect from democracy." If we expect that all citizens should have the opportunity to participate in the law-making process, we are bound to be disappointed. With some historical exceptions like the Greek *polis* and the township democracies of seventeenth- and eighteenth-century America, examples of direct government of the people by the people are scarce. Direct democracy survives in some tiny New England towns where citizens are given the chance to participate directly in local government.[18] More relevant to the circumstances of modern societies, however, may be the Swiss model of direct democracy. Switzerland's constitution includes provisions for popular initiatives and legally binding referendums on public issues. Indeed, over the past few decades these measures of direct democracy have been used with increasing frequency in that country.[19] Modern technology has created the possibility of direct democracy from people's living rooms in all advanced industrial societies. Everyone who has watched an episode of *American Idol* or the European song competition *Eurovision* knows how this brave new world of participatory democracy could work. Whether through your phone or by tapping the touchpad of your computer, there is no physical or technological reason why this method of popular choice could not be adapted to political decision-making. There may, however, be other reasons for rejecting what modern technology makes possible.

Perhaps the most commonly advanced reason for rejecting direct democracy via the Internet and for being skeptical about the value of public opinion polls is that many citizens are poorly informed about important public issues much of the time, and it occasionally happens that most citizens are grossly uninformed or misinformed about public issues. What sense does it make to ask citizens what the government's policy should be on a matter about which the majority of people know either little or nothing, and where what they think they know may be factually incorrect?

Thomas Jefferson provided a famous answer to this question. "Every government degenerates when trusted to the rulers of the people alone. The people themselves therefore are [democracy's] only safe depositories."[20] Members of the public, Jefferson acknowledged, are often poorly informed or wrong in their opinions on public matters. But the democratic solution to the problem of an ill-informed public is not to exclude it from the

REASONS CANADIANS GIVE FOR NOT VOTING

REASONS SYRIANS GIVE FOR NOT VOTING

LINE-UP HERE

Michael de Adder/Artizans

Unlike other forms of government, democracies do not depend primarily on coercion and violence. In Canada, the promotion of citizen engagement continues to be a challenge and citizen apathy continues to be high.

blames modern education and especially the media for this ignorance. Television, he argues, led the way in what he believes to have been a decline in the general level of knowledge that citizens require in order to make informed and rational decisions about public affairs.

> What is happening here is that television is altering the meaning of "being informed" by creating a species of information that might properly be called *disinformation*. . . . Disinformation does not mean false information. It means misleading information—misplaced, irrelevant, fragmented or superficial information—information that creates the illusion of knowing something but which in fact leads one away from knowing. . . . [W]hen news is packaged as entertainment, that is the inevitable result.[21]

determination of public affairs; rather, it is to educate public opinion. Jefferson placed great stress on the role of the press and public education in producing an informed citizenry.

We often hear that the information explosion generated by satellite communication, television, and the Internet has made us the best-informed generation of all time. But as Neil Postman observed many years ago, this conceit fails to address why most people are unable to explain even the most basic elements of issues that have received saturation coverage in the media. This ignorance does not prevent pollsters from asking people for their opinion on matters they may barely understand, and clearly deprives the results of polls of any meaning other than the signals they send to politicians looking for waves to ride. Postman

Whatever the limitations of direct democracy, Canadians claim that they like the idea. A 2017 survey by the Pew Research Center found that two-thirds of Canadians agreed that "a democratic system where citizens, not elected officials, vote directly on major national issues to decide what becomes law" would be good. The same survey found that almost nine out of ten Canadians believed that "a democratic system where representatives elected by citizens decide what becomes law" would be good.[22] In other words they apparently like representative democracy, the system that they have, but they wouldn't mind a bit of direct democracy too.

All modern democracies are **representative democracies**. Government is carried out by elected legislatures that represent the people. Citizens delegate law-making authority to their representatives, holding them responsible for their actions through periodic elections. In *The Federalist Papers*, No. 10, James Madison provided what is generally thought of as the chief argument in favour of this model of democracy: "The effect of [a representative democracy] is . . . to refine and enlarge the public views, by passing them through the medium of a chosen body of citizens, whose wisdom may best discern the true interest of their country."[23]

Representative democracies sometimes include decision-making processes that provide opportunities for greater and more frequent citizen participation than simply voting every few years, as is the case in Switzerland and the United States. *Plebiscites* and *referendums*—direct votes of citizens on important public questions—frequently held elections, choosing judges and some administrative officials through election, and formal procedures for removing an elected official before the end of his or her term, as through voter petitions and "recall" elections, are democratic institutions that appear to allow for widespread citizen participation in public affairs. Critics level a wide range of charges against these procedures for giving citizens a more direct say in their governance, including what may seem to be the counter-intuitive claim that they lead to undemocratic outcomes. This claim would not, however, have surprised either James Madison or Alexis de Tocqueville. The reality is that any evaluation of direct democracy requires that the other cultural and institutional circumstances of the political system in which it exists be taken into account.[24]

Respect for rights and freedoms is generally considered a distinguishing feature of democratic government. Which rights and freedoms warrant protection, and in what circumstances they may legitimately be limited by government, are matters of dispute. Libertarians, many economists, and conservative philosophers argue that government that levies heavy taxes on citizens is undemocratic. Their reasoning is that individual choice is reduced when government, representing the collectivity, decides how a large share of people's income will be spent. Others argue that the same levels of taxation actually promote freedom by paying for policies that give less advantaged groups opportunities that they would not have in a "free" market. Even a value as central to democracy as freedom of speech is sometimes argued to have undemocratic side effects. For example, some believe that any person or organization should have the right to spend money on advertising a particular political point of view during an election campaign. Others argue that unlimited freedom of speech in these circumstances is undemocratic because some individuals and groups are better endowed than others and, therefore, the points of view of the affluent will receive the greatest exposure.

Rights and freedoms are believed by most of us to be important in democracies, but everyone except extreme libertarians believes that protecting these rights or freedoms can sometimes produce undemocratic outcomes. No surefire test can tell us when democracy is promoted or impaired by protecting a right or freedom. Philosophers, jurists, politicians, and others have long disagreed on the question of when a particular limitation on an individual's freedoms or an abridgement of his or her rights is legitimate. In fact, the answer to this question is very much conditioned by the particular history and culture of the society in which it is posed.

So how democratic is Canada? According to the Freedom House's World Democracy Audit (www.worldaudit.org), Canada is one of the most democratic countries in the world. But it is not the most democratic country, trailing slightly behind some of the Scandinavian and Northern European democracies. In arriving at its ranking of countries, Freedom House **operationalizes** the concept of democracy, defining it in ways that can be measured so that scores can be assigned to each country. This methodology has the advantage of making explicit the criteria used in determining whether a country is more or less democratic. The criteria used in the Freedom House survey of the world's political systems combine measures of political rights, civil liberties, press freedom, public corruption, and the rule of law in arriving at a country's democracy ranking (see Box 1.3).

A country may have free elections, a constitution that protects rights and freedoms, and a media system that permits the expression of diverse points of view and criticism of the powerful. But if individuals and organizations are able to buy special treatment, or nepotism is rampant, or the law applies to different people in different ways, depending on who they are and who they know, this will undermine a society's claim to be democratic. Corruption, including bribery and special treatment based on friendship and family connections, can be found in any political system. In a democracy, however, such behaviour is considered to be unlawful or at least unethical, depending on how egregiously it violates the rule of law. The **rule of law** may truly be said to be the foundation of democratic government, on which all else rests. "It means," writes Eugene Forsey, one of Canada's foremost constitutionalists of the twentieth century, "that everyone is subject to the law; that no one, no matter how important or powerful, is above the law."[25] The rule of law also means that no public official has the legitimate right to exercise any powers other than those assigned to his or her office by the law. And if someone in a position of public trust attempts to go beyond the authority that the law permits? In such circumstances it is up to the courts to check that abuse of power. An independent judiciary is, therefore, a necessary feature of democratic governance and a vital protection for the rule of law.

Listen to the "Political Corruption in Canada: It's Not as Bad as You Think!" podcast, available at: www.oup.com/he/Brooks9e

Who Gets Heard, When, and Why?

Access to political decision-makers and the ability to influence public opinion are not equally distributed in society. If the president of the Royal Bank of Canada places a telephone call to the federal minister of Finance, this call will be returned. Your call or mine probably will not (try it!). For as long as elections have taken place in Canada, individuals and organizations have made financial contributions to political parties and their candidates. For the relatively modest sum of $1,600 per year—the maximum contribution an individual can make to a federal party or candidate as of 2019—you can join the Liberal Party's Laurier Club. Among other things, this buys an invitation to party functions across the country, including the possibility of

some face time with the party leader. Corporations are banned from buying memberships, but their CEOs, presidents, board members, and so on are not, and many of the individual members of the Laurier Club have corporate connections.

Between election campaigns, interest groups of all sorts are active in many ways, trying to influence the actions of government and the climate of public opinion. Much of this activity costs money, often a lot of money. The services of a high-powered, well-connected lobbying firm can easily run into hundreds of thousands of dollars. A public relations campaign that uses polling and focus groups, followed by some combination of electronic and print media advertising, may cost as much or more. Although spending money on such activities carries no guarantee of favourable political outcomes, a widespread and probably well-founded belief suggests that such an investment may yield impressive returns. Spending on such activities is quite unevenly distributed across groups in society. Some people conclude from this that having more money buys, at a minimum, greater access to those in positions of political authority and the ability to get a wider and perhaps more sympathetic hearing for the issues and points of view that matter most to the group spending the money.

But it is not this simple. The issues that get onto the **public agenda**—the matters that have been identified by opinion leaders in the media and in government as ones that warrant some policy response, even if that response is a decision not to act—and the framing of these issues are not determined by the spending of self-interested groups alone. The American journalist H.L. Mencken once said that the proper role of his profession was to "bring comfort to the afflicted and afflict the comfortable." Some in the media, in Canada and elsewhere, take Mencken's counsel to heart. But whether what they report and how they report it "afflicts the comfortable," it is undeniably the case that the values and beliefs of those who shape public opinion—including teachers, journalists, television and radio producers, bloggers and tweeters with larger numbers of followers, researchers, and even, in their minor way, textbook writers!—influence the stories they tell and how they are told.

In Canada, as in other capitalist democracies, there is a long-standing and ongoing debate over whether those in the media—an important segment of the opinion-shaping class—do more to afflict or comfort the privileged and the powerful. On one point, however, the evidence is clear: interests and points of view that are not those of the wealthy and the well-connected do find their way into the public conversation. Getting heard is not only or always a matter of money. If it was, the voices of Indigenous Canadians, environmental advocates, and the LGBTQ+ community would not have been as widely heard as they have been in recent decades.

Is Democracy a Process or an Outcome?

Tocqueville warned about the tyranny of the majority, that the multitude might show little concern for the rights and interests of minorities and see little wrong in imposing their force of superior numbers on those whose values, behaviour, and preferences are different from those of the majority. Most people agree that majoritarianism needs to be tempered by protections for individual and group rights. That is why constitutions like Canada's include express guarantees for rights and freedoms.

But it often happens that when the rights claims of a minority are upheld by the courts, in the face of unsympathetic or divided public opinion and in circumstances where elected officials have shown an unwillingness to legislate such protection, some will argue that this is undemocratic. What is undemocratic, these critics charge, is that unelected public officials—judges in this case—have usurped policy-making prerogatives that, in a democracy, should be exercised by the people's elected representatives. For example, when the Charter of Rights and Freedoms was agreed in 1981 by Ottawa and the provincial governments, its equality section (s. 15) did not include sexual orientation among the banned grounds for discrimination. This omission was deliberate. The case for including a reference to sexual orientation had been made during the hearings on the Charter, but had been rejected by the governments representing Canadians and the 10 provincial electorates. Several years later, however,

the Supreme Court of Canada decided that discrimination under the law on the basis of sexual orientation was *analogous* to discrimination based on religion, race, or colour—forms of discrimination that are expressly prohibited by s. 15 of the Charter—and that sexual orientation should have the same constitutional status under the equality rights provision of the Charter as the forms of discrimination expressly mentioned by those who drafted and agreed to this important part of Canada's Constitution. Almost 20 years after the equality section came into effect, the Ontario Court of Appeal used it as the basis for its decision striking down the federal Marriage Act's definition of marriage as restricted to heterosexual couples. Reform of the law quickly followed. Public opinion was about evenly divided at the time.

You probably agree that this was the right thing to do. Or you may not. The point is, however, that this case and many like it raise contentious issues about what processes are democratic. Is there a problem when unelected public officials, who cannot be removed from office when they make unpopular decisions, determine such matters? Even if public opinion is divided, so that many people support the decisions of judges or other unelected officials, should some issues—by their nature or because of their importance—be resolved only by those who have been elected to govern? Does democracy involve a particular process, and if so what process? Or is it more about particular outcomes being produced—a destination rather than a journey—whether by politicians, bureaucrats, or judges?

On reflection, most of us would probably agree that democracy involves a bit of both. Indeed, the 2017 Pew survey mentioned earlier in this chapter found that while strong majorities of Canadians expressed fondness for both representative and direct democracy, about four out of 10 agreed that a good way of governing the country would be through "a system in which experts, not elected officials, make decisions according to what they think is best for the country." It is entirely possible that the word "experts" did not conjure up judges in the minds of many of those who answered this question. Nevertheless, for some significant share of the

Governing Realities

BOX 1.3 Measuring Democracy

Freedom House is one of a number of well-known organizations that track and attempt to measure the quality of democracy in countries across the world. Its focus is on the state of individual rights and freedoms and some group rights. Transparency International (www.transparency.org) focuses on the degree to which corruption is believed to exist in countries, low levels of corruption being associated with, among other things, respect for the rule of law. The Heritage Foundation's (www.heritage.org) Index of Economic Freedom focuses on those government policies and actions that it believes influence the degree of economic choice available to individuals and businesses. The Varieties of Democracy Project (https://www.v-dem.net/) uses an enormous set of indicators to assess the quality and nature of democracy in countries of the world, and how these have evolved since 1900. What virtually all of these attempts to operationalize and rank order democracies have in common is reliance to some degree on the

assessments of multiple country experts who are asked to evaluate the state of one or another aspect of democracy. All of these assessments rank Canada among the world's leading democracies.

Other organizations provide regular, sometimes annual report cards on the state of democracy in Canada and other countries. Human Rights Watch and Amnesty International are among the best known. The United Nations Human Rights Committee (UNHRC) also provides such evaluations on a periodic basis. Its last evaluation of Canada, issued in 2015, was quite critical of Canada's performance on a number of fronts, particularly the treatment of Indigenous people and counterterrorism measures that, in the view of the UNHRC, placed undue limits on human rights. The annual reports of Amnesty International and Human Rights Watch also tend to paint a less glowing picture of democracy in Canada than emerges from the rankings of Freedom House and the other think-tanks mentioned above.

Canadian population, getting the right outcomes appears to matter more than having a process where decisions are made by the people's elected representatives.

Throughout this book we will argue that formal institutions are only part of what makes a society's politics democratic or not. The activities of the media, interest groups, and political parties are at least as crucial to the quality of democracy. Likewise, the socio-economic and ideological backgrounds to democratic government have important effects on how the formal and informal features of the political system operate. Democracy, then, cannot be reduced to a simple constitutional formula or to some particular vision of social equality. Several complex elements come into play, so that defining the term "democracy" is a perilous task. Someone is bound to disagree, either with what is included in the definition or with what has been left out.

In full recognition of these hazards, we offer the following definition. **Democracy** is a political system based on the formal political equality of all citizens, in which there is a realistic possibility that voters can replace the government, and in which certain basic rights and freedoms are protected.

Political Identities

Identities are ideas that link individuals to larger groups. They are self-definitions, such as "I am a Canadian" or "Je suis québécois," that help us make sense of who we are and how we fit into the world around us. An identity is a state of mind, a sense of belonging to a community defined by its language, ethnic character, religion, history, regional location, gender experiences, belief system, or other factors (see Box 1.4).

Identities perform important psychological and emotional functions. They provide the moorings that connect us to places, beliefs, and other people. People who share an identity are more likely to feel comfortable together and understand one another than they are with those who are not part of their identity group. Often we only become aware of the importance of identity when we find ourselves in a very unfamiliar place or set of circumstances. Responses ranging from disorientation and longing for home—"home" understood both physically and culturally—to hostility and xenophobia are common when we become unmoored from our familiar identities.

By nature, identities are exclusive. If, for example, I think of myself as a member of the working class, I implicitly acknowledge the existence of other groups with which I do not identify. At the same time, it is possible to identify with a number of groups without causing a sort of multiple personality disorder. There is, for example, no reason why a person could not think of himself or herself as a Canadian and a québécois(e) at the same time, and many do. Multiple identities are common—sociologists term this "intersectionality," where various personal identities (e.g., black, female, lesbian) combine to create greater oppression or privilege—but some identities will be more significant in shaping a person's political ideas and behaviour than others.

A shared identity is based on a perception of having common interests. But the fact of some number of people having interests in common does not necessarily generate a shared identity. Most of us have no difficulty in recognizing that corporations in the same industry, or consumers, municipal ratepayers, or university students, have identifiable interests in common. These interests are related to the conditions that promote or impair the material well-being of the members of these groups. They become political interests when they are organized under a collective association that claims to represent the members of the group and attempts to influence the actions of the state. Organization is expected to provide the group's members with more collective influence in politics than any individual member could hope to exercise alone. The number of possible political interests is virtually without limit. Of these, only a finite number

actually become organized for collective political action, and an even smaller number achieve significant political clout.

A political interest brings together individuals who might otherwise have little in common in terms of their attitudes and beliefs. What they often have in common is a material stake in how some political conflict is resolved. Wheat farmers, automotive workers, university students, east-coast fishers, pulp and paper companies, and small business people are all examples of political interests. Their participation in politics as organized groups is based on considerations of material well-being. Indeed, the interests that the members of such groups have in common are primarily economic ones.

The desire to protect or promote one's material well-being, while an important basis for the political organization of interests, is certainly not the only motivating factor. Politically active interests may come together around ideas, issues, and values that have little or no immediate relationship to the incomes, living conditions, social status, or other self-interest of a group's members. Mothers Against Drunk Driving (MADD) is an example of a group whose political involvement is motivated by shared values rather than material self-interest, as is People for the Ethical Treatment of Animals (PETA). The Canadian Abortion Rights Action League and the Canadian Conference of Catholic Bishops are opposing groups whose political involvement on the abortion issue is motivated fundamentally by values.

Interests and identities are not inevitably political. One can be a French Canadian, an Albertan, a woman, or the member of some other social or cultural group, and be conscious of the fact, without this having any special political relevance. Identities such as these become politically relevant when those who share them make demands on the state—or when the state recognizes their group identity as a reason for treating them in a particular way. Some political identities emerge spontaneously in society, while others are forged and promoted by the state. Governments in Canada have come to play an increasingly active role in defining and

The Social Fabric

BOX 1.4 Identity Politics

In Canada, as elsewhere, individuals have long thought of themselves as members of groups with specific traits that set them apart from others. After the French defeat on the Plains of Abraham in 1759 and the final terms of surrender in the 1763 Treaty of Paris, which ceded New France to the British, French-speaking *canadiens* thought of their language and the Catholic religion as defining features of who they were and who they were not. From the late 1800s until the middle of the 1900s, religion was an important marker of identity in Canadian society, separating Catholics from Protestants. Regional identities acquired political significance from the time of Confederation, when it became apparent that the greater population and economic influence of Ontario and Quebec would ensure that their voices would be louder and their values and interests more prominent in Canadian politics.

But since the 1960s the number of identities that matter in Canadian politics, as in other democracies, has proliferated enormously. Part of the reason for this proliferation has been the emergence of a culture of rights—group rights, but also individual rights—that gained irresistible momentum after World War II. Various social movements, involving women's rights, Indigenous rights, gay and lesbian rights, environmentalism, and multiculturalism, have provided the intellectual architecture and the organizational impetus for this culture of group rights. Older identities tied to religion, language, territory, and values systems have not been washed away. But some have faded in significance and all must contend with the fact that newer identities have assumed a social and political importance far beyond what they had a couple of generations ago.

promoting political identities in this country, a role that sometimes has generated controversy.

The **nation** has been a particularly crucial political identity in Canadian politics. It is probably the single most powerful political identity in the world today—although religious identity surpasses it in some societies. The meaning of the term "nation" is a matter of dispute (see Box 1.5). These disputes are not merely academic. Most people would agree that a nation is a community with certain characteristics that distinguish it from other communities. The devil, however, is in the details. What traits are associated with nationhood? Are they racial, as in Hitler's "Aryan nation"? Are they sociological, including the sorts of "objective" and "subjective" attributes referred to in the first definition offered in Box 1.5? Is shared citizenship enough, as former Canadian Prime Minister Pierre Trudeau apparently believed? Or is a nation simply an imagined community—not the same as an *imaginary* community—as Rupert Emerson's definition

suggests? Is nationalism a good and normal state of mind conferring dignity on those who believe themselves to be part of a nation and producing positive social and political consequences? Or is it, on the whole, a negative phenomenon, as Pierre Trudeau and George Orwell believed (see the definitions below)?

In *Blood and Belonging*, Michael Ignatieff describes the consequences that can follow from ideas about who does and does not belong to the nation. His book examines the rise of ethnic nationalism in the former Yugoslavia after the end of the Cold War, leading to the violent breakup of the country and to a long chain of events that ultimately produced several states—Bosnia and Herzegovina, Croatia, Kosovo, Macedonia, Montenegro, and Serbia—out of what had previously been a single country. Ignatieff, one of Canada's foremost intellectuals, reserves a chapter for Quebec and Québécois nationalism. He endeavours to explain how a society whose sons have been Canada's prime ministers for over one-third of the country's history produced a powerful nationalist movement whose goal is nothing less than the independence of Quebec.

Nationalism usually is accompanied by territorial claims. The nation is associated with some particular territory—"the homeland," "la patrie"—that is argued to belong to the members of the nation. Quebec nationalists have asserted such claims, but so, too, have organizations representing Indigenous peoples within Canada, many of which are grouped together under the Assembly of First Nations. The territorial demands of organizations that claim to represent nations boil down to a demand for self-government, a demand that those making it usually justify as the democratic right of any "people" to self-determination.

But a sense of place—a regional consciousness—may produce political demands that stop far short of independence and self-determination. A regional identity may be based on a variety of cultural, economic, institutional, and historical factors that distinguish the inhabitants of one region of a country from those of other regions. This identity may influence the political behaviour of those who share it, but their political demands generally will be less sweeping than those made by nationalist groups. When regionalism enters politics, it usually takes the form of demands for fairer treatment by the national government, better representation of the region in national political institutions, or more political autonomy for regional political authorities—all of which stop short of the usual catalogue of nationalist demands.

Cultural and social identities are not inherently political. The differences that exist between religious, ethnic, language, regional, or gender groups—to name only a few of the most important social-cultural divisions in the world today—may give rise to political conflicts when they are associated with inequalities in the economic status, social prestige, and political power of these groups. In other words, identities acquire political consequences when the members of a group, the "identity-bearers," believe they experience some deprivation or injustice because of their socio-cultural identity and when a "critical mass" of the group's membership can be persuaded to take

political action based on their self-identification as women, French Canadians, westerners, or whatever the identity happens to be. Political identities may not be primarily economic, but they usually have an economic dimension. Even when the stakes appear to be mainly symbolic—for example, the long-standing political debate over special status for Quebec in Canadian federalism—material considerations generally lurk behind the demands that the representatives of a social or cultural group make on the state.

Why particular identities surface in politics, while others remain "pre-political," is a question that can only be answered by looking at the particular history and circumstances of any society. The persistence of regional, ethnolinguistic, and religious identities in the modern world and the emergence of gender inequality onto the political agendas of virtually all advanced industrial societies have confounded the earlier belief of many social scientists, and all socialists, that class divisions would come to dominate the politics of advanced capitalism. The term "class" (like most of the concepts discussed in this chapter) means different things to different people. When used as in the labels "upper class" or "middle class," it refers to a social status determined by such measures as the societal prestige of a person's occupation, an individual's income, or one's lifestyle. Since Karl Marx's time, many social scientists have defined class as being primarily an economic concept. According to this usage, a person's class membership is determined by one's relationship to the means of economic production—the main division in society being between those who control the means of production and those who must sell their labour in order to earn a livelihood.

No one seriously argues that modern-day capitalism is characterized by a simple division between the owners of capital—the *bourgeoisie*—and their workers—the *proletariat*—as Marx predicted would happen. Advanced industrial/post-industrial democracies like Canada all have very large middle-class components, notwithstanding arguments about a shrinking middle class. Moreover, the growth of pension funds and other large institutional investors has given

BOX 1.5 What Is a Nation?

"A nation is a community of persons bound together by a sense of solidarity and wishing to perpetuate this solidarity through some political means. Contributing to this solidarity are common 'objective' factors such as history, territory, race, ethnicity, culture, language, religion and customs and common 'subjective' factors such as the consciousness of a distinct identity, an awareness of common interests and a consequent willingness to live together. Because of the existence of such factors, there is a special relationship among members of a nation which enables them to co-operate politically more easily among themselves than with outsiders."

Canada, *Report of the Task Force on Canadian Unity* (1979)

"A nation . . . is no more and no less than the entire population of a sovereign state."

Pierre Elliott Trudeau, "Federalism, Nationalism, and Reason" (1965)

"Nationalism is not to be confused with patriotism. Both words are normally used in so vague a way that any definition is liable to be challenged, but one must draw a distinction between them, since two different and even opposing ideas are involved. By 'patriotism' I mean devotion to a particular place and a particular way of life, which one believes to be the best in the world but has no wish to force upon other people. Patriotism is by its nature defensive, both militarily and culturally. Nationalism, on the other hand, is inseparable from the desire for power. The abiding purpose of every nationalist is to secure more power and more prestige, not for himself but for the nation or other unit in which he has chosen to sink his own individuality."

George Orwell, "Notes on Nationalism" (1945)

"The simplest statement that can be made about a nation is that it is a body of people who feel that they are a nation; and it may be that when all the fine-spun analysis is concluded this will be the ultimate statement as well."

Rupert Emerson, *From Empire to Nation* (1960)

"That this House recognize that the *québécois* form a nation within a united Canada."

Motion passed by the Canadian House of Commons by a vote of 266 to 16, on 27 November 2006

---

a significant share of the middle class a direct ownership stake in their national economy and the economies of other countries. The last several decades have also seen a proliferation in the number of jobs that, while they involve dependence in the sense of relying on an employer for a salary, also are characterized by considerable personal freedom in terms of how work is done and even the nature of the work. These people—university professors, engineers, consultants of various sorts, physicians, and lawyers, to name a few—cannot seriously be squeezed into a classic definition of the working class.

In recent years, however, the concept of class has experienced a comeback. This comeback has been linked to the phenomenon of globalization, which refers to the unprecedented integration of the world's economies through trade, capital flows, and internationalized production, as well as cultural integration through mass media, marketing, satellite- and computer-based information technologies, and migration. Critics argue that globalization has produced greater polarization between the affluent and the poor, both within advanced industrial democracies like Canada and between the wealthy developed countries and the poor developing countries. "Globalization is creating, within our industrial democracies, a sort of underclass of the demoralized and impoverished," says former United States Secretary of Labor Robert Reich.[26] Moreover, critics argue that the ability of governments to protect the interests of society's poorest and most vulnerable groups, and to pursue policies that are unpopular with powerful corporate interests and investors, has been diminished by globalization.

In some societies class identity is a powerful force in politics. Political parties make calculated appeals to class interests and draw on different classes for their electoral support. This is not particularly true of Canada. The sense of belonging to a class is relatively weak in Canadian society. Other political identities, especially ethnolinguistic and regional identities, have overshadowed class in Canadian politics. Some commentators argue that this should be taken at face value—that the linguistic and regional interests of Canadians are simply more vital to them than class in a society in which recent polls indicate that roughly 60–80 per cent of Canadians see themselves as being part of the middle class.[27] Others maintain that the consciousness of belonging to a class whose interests are at odds with those of other classes has been suppressed in various ways by political parties and elites who have vested interests in preventing the emergence of class awareness and action.

Political Fault Lines, Old and New

Some of the fault lines that shape the topography of Canadian politics extend back to the early years of this country, in some cases to the colonial era of Canada's history. The rift that separates French and English Canada is the oldest, going back to the military conquest of New France in 1759 and the subsequent domination of the francophone population by an English-speaking minority. The demographic balance would soon shift in favour of the anglophone population, a shift that lent even greater urgency to the fundamental issues of whether and how the language and distinct society of French Canada would be recognized and protected. These are fundamental questions of survival for many French-speaking Canadians that remain very much alive today.

A second fault line that reaches back to Canada's colonial past involves this country's relationship to the United States. The American Revolution and the victory of the Thirteen Colonies in the American War of Independence had a profound and enduring impact on Canada. At times this impact has been felt as a territorial threat from the United States. But for more than a century now, the economic, cultural, and political influences of the United States have replaced the fear of American troops and annexation. And over this entire period, from the American Declaration of Independence in 1776 to the present day, a long shadow has been cast over Canadian politics and culture by the simple but primordially important fact of living alongside a much more powerful neighbour that resembles us in terms of historical origins, values, and dominant language but that, very clearly, is not us. David Bell argues that at the root of the identity dilemma in English Canada is a need—a need that goes back to 1776—to explain to ourselves who we are as Canadians and in what ways we are not Americans.

A third fault line of somewhat less ancient vintage than the French–English and Canada–United States ones involves regionalism. In a country as physically vast and diverse as Canada it was unavoidable that the economic and social characteristics of the regions would develop differently. Moreover, the concentration of most of the country's population and wealth in Ontario and Quebec, not surprisingly, led Ottawa to be more sensitive to the needs and preferences of the centre over those of the "hinterland" regions. Inter-regional conflict began to acquire a sharp edge in the late nineteenth century around such issues as high tariffs and railroads. This particular fault line quickly assumed an intergovernmental character, as provincial governments became the spokespersons for aggrieved regional interests in opposition to the federal government.

These three fault lines have been called by Donald Smiley the enduring axes of Canadian politics. They are not, however, the only fault lines that mark the

Canadian political landscape. Some historically prominent ones, such as religious conflict and division between agrarian-rural and urban-industrial interests, have receded in importance (in the former case because of the diminished force of religion in Canadian life, and in the second because the rural and farm populations are today vastly outnumbered by those who live in urban centres and work in non-farm sectors of the economy). But other issues, including gender equality, the rights of Indigenous peoples, environmental protection, and multiculturalism, have traced new lines in Canadian politics.

The evidence of this may be seen in the issues profiled by political parties and their leaders in recent elections. Climate change, social justice, human rights, and environmental protection have become more prominent issues for all of the parties. The older issues associated with political cleavages generated by language, region, and Canada–US relations are still on the agenda, but they must compete for time and attention with these newer issues, particularly among millennials. But even before the millennial generation, baby boomers and those who followed were more likely than previous generations of voters to be interested in issues that

Canadian author, activist, and filmmaker Naomi Klein has become a voice at the forefront of the anti-globalization movement.

have to do with the quality of life rather than the standard of living. This is what Ronald Inglehart and his colleagues refer to as the post-materialist/materialist divide.[28] In recent decades it has emerged as an important political cleavage—social scientists' term for the important lines of political division in a society—in all affluent democracies.[29]

Recent years also have seen the re-emergence of a political fault line that, while quite prominent in the politics of many societies, has generally assumed a rather muted form in Canada and the United States: class conflict and the politics of the distribution of wealth. It is today widely believed that the forces of globalization have widened the gap between the affluent and the poor in Canada and in other advanced industrial societies and, in the process, have undermined democracy. As New Left activist and writer Naomi Klein explains:

> When we're talking about globalization, we're talking about a crisis of democracy. The crisis that we face in many ways has to do with this conspiracy of experts around globalization and this feeling, this message that we've all received that this is really complicated, and . . . you need a degree in international law, in economics, even, so why don't you just go shopping and play your part in the global economy. . . . You have a situation where the vast majority of populations feel that they just don't have the tools to participate in the discussion.[30]

Stories and analyses linking globalization to claims of growing income inequality; increasing poverty, unemployment and homelessness; and a shrinking middle class have been common since the 1990s. Some of these claims rest on stronger empirical foundations than others (we will revisit this issue in Chapter 3). Nevertheless, if they are believed to be true by large numbers of people, then we would expect to find some political fallout. In other words, the class fault line should become a more prominent feature of Canada's political landscape. To this point, however, the class polarization that many argue has taken place in Canadian society has not reached very deeply into the consciousness of most Canadians, nor has it affected very profoundly their political behaviour. Political parties that appeal to voters on class issues, notably the New Democratic Party, have not experienced a surge of support. The NDP's breakthrough in the 2011 federal election, which saw it win the second largest share of the popular vote and number of seats for the first time in its history, had more to do with leadership, the collapse of the Bloc Québécois, and the feckless Liberal campaign than with class politics. Political protest and activism by labour unions and social justice advocacy groups probably have increased since the 1990s, in response to issues like free trade, outsourcing, and the cutbacks to social spending that were front and centre in that decade. It is not clear, however, that such activism reflects an awakening sense of class consciousness on the part of the general population. A more plausible argument can probably be made that the main manifestations of the new politics of class include the explosion in books, articles, blogs, and other social media dealing with globalization, class polarization, and social activism. But if behaviour at the ballot box is the litmus test of how deeply this fault line has cut into Canada's political landscape, one would have to conclude that class inequality remains a comparatively unimportant issue for most Canadians.

Summing Up

The thread that runs throughout this book is democracy. We have seen in this chapter that the meaning of this very familiar word is hotly contested and not at all obvious. In order to arrive at a determination of how democratic Canadian politics is, it is not necessary that we have a rigid definition of this concept. It is important, however, that we be sensitive to the various and often quite different ideas about what processes, institutions, values, and outcomes are necessary before we can say that a society is democratic.

Democracy is not the only contested concept in the study of politics. The definition of power, the state, the nation, and even what counts as politics are all matters of contention. In this chapter we have examined some of the ways in which these key concepts are understood. The disagreements that exist between perspectives alert us to the fact that the enterprise of political science, as is also true of sociology, psychology, and other social sciences, is not free from the analyst's premises about human nature and social relations. Karl Marx wrote, "The philosophers have only interpreted the world . . . the point is to change it." That's a fine slogan for activists and ideologues. Our goal as political scientists—and it is already a tall order—is to understand the political world in as objective a manner as possible.

The questions that we ask about a country's politics arise out of its history, demography, economic system, geopolitical circumstances, and other forces that make certain issues and divisions relevant and others less so or not at all. In the case of Canada, some of the questions asked today have roots that may be traced back to dividing lines that have existed for decades and even centuries. Others are of much more recent vintage. As is true of other affluent democracies, some of these new dividing lines in Canadian politics, and the political conflicts they spawn, are related to forces of globalization and to the rise of what has been called post-materialism.

Listen to the "Nouveau Politics" podcast on parties, branding, and political ideology, available at: www.oup.com/he/Brooks9e

Starting Points for Research

Bernard Crick, *Democracy: A Very Short Introduction* (Oxford: Oxford University Press, 2002). In barely more than 100 pages Crick provides a pithy and engaging exploration of some of the concepts and controversies discussed in this chapter.

Economist Intelligence Unit, "Democracy Index 2018," https://www.eiu.com/public/topical_report.aspx?campaignid=Democracy2018. The London-based weekly, *The Economist*, is read by decision-makers and the politically attentive public around the world. This annual publication assesses and compares the state of democracy in Canada and other countries across the globe. You will have to register online to read it, but registration is free and worth the effort.

Robert Garner, Peter Ferdinand, Stephanie Lawson, and David B. MacDonald, *Introduction to Politics*, 2nd edn (Toronto: Oxford University Press, 2017). This well-written textbook covers the key concepts and issues that students of politics need to know, providing many Canadian examples.

César Hidalgo, "A Bold Idea to Replace Politicians," TED Talk, April 2018, https://www.ted.com/talks/cesar_hidalgo_a_bold_idea_to_replace_politicians. You may already be familiar with online TED Talks. Many of them deal with aspects of politics around the world. This particular talk challenges us to think about whether politicians are still necessary.

Jill Vickers, *Reinventing Political Science: A Feminist Approach* (Halifax: Fernwood, 1997). It is a pity that this important and thought-provoking book has not had a new edition since it was published in 1997. Vickers, one of Canada's most prominent feminist political scientists, invites readers to rethink conventional ways of understanding political life, viewed through a feminist lens.

World Values Survey, www.worldvaluessurvey.org. This ongoing cross-national project includes a number of online publications having to do with modernization and democratization, written by some of the world's foremost political scientists.

Review Exercises

1. Nationalism is a powerful force in the modern world. In 2014 Scotland held a referendum on national independence. After Britons voted in 2016 to leave the European Union, the Scottish Nationalist Party insisted that a new referendum on Scottish independence should be held. The most affluent region of Spain, Catalonia, declared its independence in 2017. Why would these affluent societies want independence? Compare the reasons motivating the Scottish and Catalan independence movements to those offered by separatists for the independence of Quebec.

2. How does identity affect your political behaviour? If you were asked to describe who you are and what aspects of your self-image are most important to you, what would you list? When you see or hear a media person, a politician, or a professor do you notice his or her race, gender, signs of ethnicity, accent, or other features of the person? Do you think other people notice such traits? Should they?

3. Which country is more democratic, Canada or the United States? Canada or Sweden? You probably have a ready answer to the first comparison, but you may not be certain about the second. What criteria have you used in arriving at your conclusions and how would you set about measuring whether a society has more or less of the attributes that you associate with democracy? In order to guide your thinking about how the concept of democracy can be operationalized, go to the website for Freedom House: www.freedomhouse.org. Does Freedom House's ranking of Canada seem reasonable to you?

PART II
The Societal Context of Politics

In every society certain issues and divisions have a more prominent status and are more fundamental to an overall understanding of its politics and government than are others. In the United States, for example, the issue of race and the relations between white and black America are at the centre of that country's political history. In Canada, the fact that English and French are spoken by large portions of the population, and that the French-speaking population is concentrated mainly in one region of the country with a history that predates the emergence of an anglophone majority, continues to influence Canadian political life. The arrival of millions of immigrants from countries outside of Europe has changed Canadian demography in important ways over the last several decades, having a significant impact on Canadian politics. The country's long-standing relationship to the United States, a relationship that involves a complex web of interconnections through trade, investment, population, culture, and foreign policy, has always been a major factor affecting Canadian politics and government. In short, the societal context within which political life unfolds is crucial to understanding any country's politics and its distribution of power and influence.

Some argue, however, that the actions of the state and their impacts on society are at least as important as the effects that societal forces have on the policies and institutions of government, and that sometimes these actions are more important. State actors, including key political leaders and bureaucrats, often have a determining influence on what happens in politics, shaping the contours of the political conversation, the interests and voices that are listened to, and the outcomes that ensue. But only rarely are elected and appointed officials able to ignore the pressure of ideas and interests from the society around them. These ideas and interests, including the significant **political identities** in a society, its economic structure, and the major fault lines that cut across its landscape, provide the broader context within which political behaviour and policy-making take place. These societal factors are the subject of this next section of the book.

Children sit on a float during a Canada Day parade in Scarborough, Ont., on Sunday, July 1, 2018. Many Canadians take pride in the values that they feel distinguish them from other countries, including beliefs in multiculturalism, tolerance, compassion, and collectivity. (THE CANADIAN PRESS/Christopher Katsarov)

2 Political Culture

Ideas constitute an important element of political life. This chapter surveys some of the key issues pertaining to the role of ideas in Canadian politics and discusses the political ideas of Canadians. The following topics are examined:

- Ideologies, values, and institutions
- Explanations of the origins of Canadian political ideas
- The political beliefs and values of Canadians
- The nature of Canadian and American value differences
- Community
- Freedom
- Equality
- Citizen expectations for government

There is no more Canadian pastime than reflecting on what it means to be a Canadian. Unlike the French, the English, the Chinese, the Russians, and the Americans, to name a handful of other peoples, Canadians have long obsessed over what it is in their values and beliefs that makes them distinctive, that sets them apart from others. In recent years some societies that have long been thought of as having quite confident self-identities seem to have acquired the Canadian penchant for introspection. The French government launched its Grand débat sur l'identité française in 2009. It was again a major issue in that country's 2017 presidential election. Issues relating to how demographic change and multiculturalism have affected the American identity have roiled the waters of that country's politics and intellectual life for a generation. But in neither France nor the United States has the question of national identity been asked so urgently and often—and with answers seeming to be so elusive—as in Canada.

In fact, this perennial search for the cultural essence of the Canadian condition has most often been about identifying and explaining the ways in which the values and beliefs of Canadians are different from those of Americans. Various answers have been given over the years. Until the latter half of the twentieth century, these answers more or less boiled down to this: Canadians believe in a more orderly, less individualistic society than that of the United States, in which the state is expected to engage in activities that promote the welfare of society and the development of an independent Canada. The affective tie to Great Britain remained strong well into the middle of the last century, and indeed many Canadians thought of themselves as British and of their country as more British than American in its institutions, values, and heritage.

This answer to the question of what it means to be a Canadian seemed less plausible as immigration changed the ethnic profile of Canada in the latter half of the twentieth century. Even among those of British ancestry, the connection to Great Britain increasingly became a matter of history rather than part of their contemporary identity. Many still believe, however, that Canadian values continue to be less individualistic and less hostile to government than in the United States. Such

words as "tolerant," "compassionate," and "caring" are often used in comparisons between the two countries, always suggesting that Canadians have more of these qualities than Americans. And it is not just Canadians who make this claim. On the American left, Canada, for more than a generation now, has served the function of a sort of "Nirvana to the north," a place that shows what is possible in public policy and social relations and a model to be emulated.[1] As the bonds joining Canada to the United States economically and culturally have multiplied and deepened, the question of what it means to be a Canadian continues to be a sort of national obsession.

This is not true, however, in French-speaking Canada, whose centre of gravity is Quebec, where over 90 per cent of Canadian francophones live. Insulated from American cultural influences by language and for much of their history by the strongly Catholic character of their society, French Canadians have been much less likely than their English-speaking compatriots to define themselves and their history with reference to the United States. They have long worried about anglicizing influences on their language and culture, but they have tended to see the challenge as coming chiefly from within Canada, with its English-speaking majority, rather than from the United States. This perceived challenge has provided the basis for the rise of what was once referred to as French-Canadian nationalism and today as Quebec nationalism. Over the last couple of generations, as non-traditional sources of immigration became increasingly important in Quebec, the question of what it means to be Québécois received greater attention. But in answering it, few French-speaking Canadians would think of using as a starting point the United States and what are believed to be American values and beliefs.

Ideologies, Values, and Institutions

Ideas assume various forms in political life. When they take the form of a set of interrelated beliefs about how society is organized and how it ought to function—an interpretive map for understanding the world—this is an **ideology**. An ideology spills beyond the boundaries of politics to embrace beliefs and judgments about other social relationships, including economic ones. This holistic character of ideologies distinguishes them from more limited political value systems. Although most people are not aware of having ideological leanings, and might be puzzled or even startled at being labelled "conservative," "liberal," or "socialist," this does not mean that ideology is irrelevant to their political beliefs and actions. Instead, it may simply indicate that a particular ideological mindset is so pervasive and dominant—it has become, in other words, the conventional wisdom—that its unexamined premises seem inevitable and obvious.

Someone who regularly and consciously thinks about political matters and other social relationships in ideological terms, and who believes that these realms of life should be organized in specific ways, is an ideologue. Such a person is consciously committed to a particular interpretive map of society. Most people are not ideological in this sense of the word, even if they may be said to have absorbed through the media, the family, schools, and other agents of social learning the main premises of their society's dominant ideology.

If ideology is the currency of the political activist, political culture is the medium of the general population. A political culture consists of the characteristic values, beliefs, and behaviours of a society's members in regard to politics. The very definition of what is considered by most people to be political and an appropriate subject for government action is an aspect of political culture. The relative weight that people assign to such values as personal freedom, equality, social order, and national prestige is another aspect of political culture. The expectations that citizens tend to hold for their participation in public life and the patterns of voter turnout, party activism, social movement activities, and other politically relevant forms of behaviour are part of political culture, as is the pattern of knowledge about political symbols, institutions, actors, and issues. Beliefs about whether government actions tend to be benign or malign, and towards whom, also are part of the political culture.

Obviously, people will not hold identical views on these matters, nor will their participation in politics conform to a single template. It is reasonable, nevertheless, to speak of a society as having certain core values or a belief system that is shared by most of its members. Political culture may be thought of as a cluster of typical orientations towards the political universe. The fact that in one society this cluster may be comparatively dispersed and marked by division between different segments of society, while in another it is relatively compact, is in itself an observation about political culture. In the first case the culture is polarized. In the second it is more coherent.

In Canada, research on political culture has focused primarily on the differences that exist between the politically relevant attitudes and beliefs of French-speaking and English-speaking Canadians, and on the question of whether English-speaking Canada is characterized by regional political cultures. In recent years intergenerational differences in values and beliefs have become another focus of research on political culture. To determine whether significant and persistent differences exist, political scientists have attempted to measure such things as levels of political knowledge and participation, feelings of political efficacy (people's sense of whether their participation in politics matters) and alienation (variously defined as apathy, estrangement from the political system, or the belief that politics is systematically biased against one's interests and values), attitudes towards political authority and the different levels of government, and the sense of belonging to a particular regional or linguistic community.

A third way in which ideas are relevant for politics is through individual *personality*. Historically, one of the most often repeated claims about Canadians has been that they are less likely to question and challenge authority than are Americans. Canadians are said to be more deferential. We examine this claim later in the chapter. Several of the standard questions used in studies of political culture, such as those dealing with political efficacy, trust in public officials, and emotional feelings towards political authorities, tap politically relevant dimensions of personality. Much of the research on the political consequences of individual personality traits has focused on the relationship between a person's general attitudes towards authority and non-conformity, on the one hand, and, on the other, his or her political attitudes on such issues as the protection of civil liberties, toleration of political dissent, the group rights of minorities, and attitudes towards public authorities. The main conclusion of this research is that, to some degree, general personality traits show up in an individual's political ideas and action.

One way of categorizing political ideas—perhaps the most popular way—is to describe them as being *left-wing*, *right-wing*, or *centrist/moderate*. These labels are used to signify the broader ideological premises believed to lie behind an action, opinion, or statement. For example, a newspaper editorial slamming welfare fraud and calling for mandatory "workfare" would be called right-wing by some, as would a proposal to cut the capital gains tax or opposition to affirmative action. Proposals to increase the minimum wage, ban the use of replacement workers during a strike or lockout, or increase spending on assistance for developing countries are the sorts of measures likely to be described as left-wing. Centrist or moderate positions, as these terms suggest, fall between the right and left wings of the political spectrum. They attempt to achieve some middle ground between the arguments and principles of **left** and **right**. The **centre** is, virtually by definition, the mainstream of a society's politics, and those who occupy this location on the political spectrum are likely to view themselves as being non-ideological and pragmatic.

"Right" and "left" are shorthand labels for conflicting belief systems. These beliefs include basic notions about how society, the economy, and politics operate, as well as ideas about how these matters *should* be arranged. Generally speaking, to be on the right in Anglo-American societies means that one subscribes to an *individualistic* belief system. Such a person is likely to believe that what one achieves in life is due principally to his or her own efforts—that the welfare of society is best promoted by allowing individuals to pursue their own interests and that modern government is too expensive and too intrusive. To be on the left, however, is to hold beliefs that may be described

as *collectivist*. A leftist is likely to attribute greater weight to social and economic circumstances as determinants of one's opportunities and achievements than does someone on the right. Moreover, those on the left have greater doubts about the economic efficiency and social fairness of free markets, and have greater faith in the ability of government to intervene in ways that promote the common good. Although those on the left may be critical of particular actions and institutions of government, they reject the claim that the size and scope of government need to be trimmed. Smaller government,

Michael De Adder/Artizans

The right–left political spectrum is one way to map out the ideologies embedded in actions, opinion, and statements. Some would suggest, however, that the ideological gap between the principal "right" and "centre" parties in Canada, the Conservative Party and the Liberal Party, is quite small, and even the main party on the "left," the New Democratic Party, if it ever attained power at the federal level, would drift to the centre, as has most often been the case in recent years with NDP governments at the provincial level. This political cartoon illustrates criticisms that during his time as prime minister, Justin Trudeau has maintained the status quo established by Stephen Harper's Conservatives rather than delivering the changes promised during the 2015 federal election.

they would argue, works to the advantage of the affluent and privileged, at the expense of the poor and disadvantaged.

In reality, the politics of left and right is more complicated than these simplified portraits suggest. For example, while opposition to abortion, same-sex marriage, and physician-assisted suicide generally are viewed as right-wing positions, many who subscribe to all the elements of right-wing politics listed in the preceding paragraph may support these policies. Such people, sometimes labelled **libertarians**, believe that individuals should be allowed the largest possible margin of freedom in all realms of life, including those that involve moral choices. Social conservatives, another group identified with the political right, are distinguished by such stands as opposition to abortion and same-sex marriage, support for stiffer jail sentences, and the rejection of lifestyles and cultures they believe are corrosive of traditional values. The wellsprings of their conservatism are quite different from those of libertarianism, but their shared antipathy for certain aspects of the modern welfare state cause libertarians and social conservatives to be grouped together on the right. The fissures in this alliance, and therefore the limitations of the simple right–left categorization of political ideas, become apparent when the issue is one of personal morality. On such issues libertarians and conservatives are likely not to see eye to eye. Left versus right may also be of limited use, and even misleading, when it comes to environmental issues. It is true that the modern environmental movement and "green" political parties are clearly on the left, as seen in their skepticism towards private enterprise and market forces, their support for state measures, from taxation and regulation to outright bans on certain behaviours, and their general opposition to military solutions to international conflicts. But support for protection of the environment and particularly for conservation of natural habitats and species may also be generated by religious values and beliefs that are usually thought of as conservative. For such persons, human beings have been entrusted by God with the stewardship of nature, given dominion over it but also obliged to protect it and ensure that it is passed on to future generations in a state that

enables those later generations to profit from nature's bounty. This sort of environmentalism derives from a very different source than that based on the premises that there are physical limits to economic and population growth and that capitalist economics is the road to inevitable environmental catastrophe.

The waters separating the ideological categories of left and right are further muddied by the exigencies of governing and what is required for re-election. Different parties may claim to be quite different ideological animals and may be clearly distinguishable during the heat of an election campaign. But once in power the pragmatics attached to future electoral success and to successful governance often result in the governing party moving to the centre to meet the needs and demands of the broader society rather than merely those of their core constituency.

Despite various limitations, and the fact that labels like "right" and "left" are more often used to dismiss and discredit one's opponents in politics than to inform in a dispassionate way, the right–left spectrum taps a crucial and enduring truth of modern politics. This involves the issue of the nature of the good society and how best to achieve it. We have said that the underlying struggle is essentially one between collectivist and individualist visions of the good society. These visions differ in how they view the conditions that promote human dignity and in their conceptions of social justice. For example, it is often said that one of the cultural characteristics distinguishing Canadians from Americans is the greater propensity of Canadians to sacrifice individual self-interest for the good of the community. In this connection Canada's health-care system is invoked whenever Canadian–American cultural differences are discussed, and when fears are expressed that Canada is sliding down the slope towards American values and public policies. What the defenders of Canadian-style health care are really saying is that the more collectivist Canadian health-care model provides greater dignity for individuals and is fairer than the more individualistic American system.

Defenders of the American health-care system often retort that Canadian health policy is a form of socialism (although it must be said that the word "socialism," long an epithet in American politics, seems to have lost some of its sting in recent times). **Socialism** is one of a trio of ideologies that have greatly influenced the politics of Western societies since the American and French revolutions. The other two are **liberalism** and **conservatism**. The idea that Canada's health-care model both reflects and is vital to the protection of Canadian values has often found its way into election campaign advertising, particularly to attack parties and candidates who appear to favour significant reform of the system. They are portrayed as being un-Canadian and, worse, American in their sympathies and values.

The importance of these ideologies in defining the contours of political life is suggested by the fact that major and minor political parties in many Western democracies continue to use the names "liberal," "conservative," and "socialist." In Canada, the two parties that have dominated national politics for most of the country's history are the Liberal Party and the Conservative Party (the Conservative Party was renamed the Progressive Conservative Party in 1942; in December 2003, when it merged with the Canadian Alliance, the federal party dropped the "Progressive" label and is once again the Conservative Party of Canada). These two parties have their roots in the ideological divisions of the nineteenth century. Over time, however, the labels have lost much of their informative value. Today, the ideological distance between a Liberal and a Conservative is far from insignificant, but it tends to be narrower than that separating a Democrat from a Republican in the United States. Indeed, already at the beginning of the twentieth century the astute French observer André Siegfried remarked that the Liberal and Conservative parties were virtually indistinguishable in terms of their ideological principles. They and their supporters shared in the dominant liberal tradition that pervaded Canada and the United States.

At the heart of this liberal tradition was the primacy of individual freedom. *Classical liberalism—* liberalism as it was mainly understood until the middle of the twentieth century—was associated with freedom of religious choice and practice, free enterprise and free trade in the realm of economics,

and freedom of expression and association in politics. These liberal values constituted a sort of national ethos in the United States, where they were enshrined in the Declaration of Independence and in the American Bill of Rights (even as they were denied for much of the population). In the colonies of British North America, which would become Canada in the late nineteenth century, liberalism's dominance was somewhat more tentative than in the United States. This was due to the streak of conservatism kept alive by some of the elites in colonial society, notably the Catholic Church, the Church of England, and the British colonial authorities.

This conservative streak, what we may call classical conservatism, was based on the importance of tradition. It accepted human inequality—social, political, and economic—as part of the natural order of things. Conservatives emphasized the importance of continuity with the past and the preservation of law and order. They were wary of innovation and opposed such basic liberal reforms as equal political rights for all men (even liberals did not come around to the idea of equal political rights for women until the twentieth century). Unlike liberals, who located the source of all just rule in the people, conservatives maintained that God and tradition were the true founts of political authority. Consequently, they supported an established church and were strong defenders of the Crown's traditional prerogatives against the rival claims of elected legislatures.

Although no party having the label "socialist" has ever achieved the status of even an important minor party in either Canada or the United States, socialist ideology has been influential in various ways. *Classical socialism* was based on the principle of equality of condition, a radical egalitarianism that distinguished socialist doctrine from liberalism's advocacy of equality of opportunity. Socialists supported a vastly greater role for the state in directing the economy, better working conditions and greater rights for workers vis-à-vis their employers, and reforms like public health care, unemployment insurance, income assistance for the indigent, public pensions, and universal access to public education that became the hallmarks of the twentieth-century welfare state.

The usefulness of these three "isms" as benchmarks for reading the political map is no longer very great. There are two main reasons for this. First, all three of these classical ideologies, but especially liberalism and conservatism, mean something quite different today from what they meant 100–200 years ago. For example, contemporary liberalism does not place individual freedom above all else. Instead, modern liberals are distinguished by their belief that governments can and should act to alleviate hardships experienced by the poor and the oppressed. They are more likely to worry about the problems of minority group rights than individual freedoms, or at any rate to see the improvement of the conditions of disadvantaged minorities as a necessary step towards the achievement of real freedom for the members of these groups. Modern liberalism also has become associated with support for multiculturalism and openness towards non-traditional lifestyles and social institutions.

The doctrine of classical conservatism has disappeared from the scene in contemporary democracies, leaving what has been called the conservative outlook or "conservative mind."[2] Modern conservatives tend to embrace the economic beliefs that once were characteristic of liberals. And like classical liberals they defend the principle of equality of opportunity. They are more likely to place the protection of personal freedoms before the advancement of minority rights. As in earlier times, today's brand of conservatism is generally viewed as the ideology of the privileged in society. It is worth noting, however, that conservative politicians and political parties receive much of their support from middle-class voters whose hands are far from the levers of economic power and social influence.

Of the three classical ideologies, the meaning of socialism has changed the least. There is today, however, much less confidence among socialists that state ownership of the means of economic production and distribution is necessary or even desirable. Modern socialists, or *social democrats* as they often call themselves, temper their advocacy of an egalitarian society with an acceptance of capitalism and the inequalities that inevitably are generated by free-market economies. The defence of the rights of society's least-well-off elements, which has always been a characteristic of socialism, is today carried out largely under the banner of other "isms," including feminism, multiculturalism, and environmentalism. In Canada and the United States these other collectivist–egalitarian belief systems have more of an impact on politics than does socialism.

A second reason why the traditional trio of "isms" is no longer a reliable guide to politics has to do with the character of political divisions in modern society. The aristocracy of land and title and the deferential social norms that nurtured classical conservatism belong to the past. They live on as the folklore of castles and estates in the once rigidly hierarchical societies of Europe, in the continuing pomp of hereditary royalty, and in the fascination that many have had for the world portrayed in the BBC television series *Downton Abbey*. Otherwise, classical conservatism has no legitimacy in the middle-class cultures of Western societies. In the United States the structures and values that supported classical conservatism never existed, and in Canada they achieved only a precarious and passing toehold.

The struggles of liberalism in the eighteenth and nineteenth centuries, and of socialism in the nineteenth and twentieth, have largely been won. Liberals fought for free-market reforms and the extension of political rights and freedoms, first to the new propertied classes created by the Industrial Revolution and then more widely to the (male) adult population. They fought against conservatives who dug in to protect the political privileges of a hereditary aristocracy and the economic dominance of the traditional land-owning classes. Socialists fought for more government control over the economy, for workers' rights like collective bargaining and limits on the hours of work, and for the welfare state. They fought against both the privileges defended by conservatism and liberalism's emphasis on individualism.

The classical ideologies were formed and evolved in response to one another as well as to the social and economic conditions in which they were rooted. Today, Canadians, Americans, and Western Europeans live in affluent, mainly middle-class societies that bear little resemblance to those of the nineteenth century, when Europe was a tilting ground for the rivalries among conservatism, liberalism, and socialism. As the character of Western societies has changed, so too have the ideologies that slug it out in their politics.

Does this mean, as some have argued, that the traditional ideologies are obsolete, unsuited to the realities of modern society? This is the **"end of ideology"** thesis that American sociologist Daniel Bell put forward in the 1960s. "In the western world," he argued, "there is today, a rough consensus among intellectuals on political issues: the acceptance of a Welfare State; the desirability of decentralized power; a system of mixed economy and of political pluralism."[3] Since then, some commentators have dismissed the traditional "isms" and the left–centre–right ideological grid as outmoded ways of thinking about politics.

Those who would argue that familiar ideological categories and the individualism/collectivism dichotomy have become obsolete and that politics has become largely a debate about means rather than ends underestimate the continuing vitality of the struggle between what we might call competing images of the moral order. Many of the most profoundly felt differences of opinion on issues of importance in contemporary public life, from ideas and policies relating to the family to issues of trade and taxation, are based on the different ideas that people have about what social, economic, and political arrangements are consistent with personal dignity, justice, social order, economic efficiency, and the good society. By and large, those on the right of the modern ideological divide are less likely than those on the left to look to state action for the advancement and protection of the moral order that they prefer. This may be seen in the ongoing debate over the consequences of globalization—a debate in which moral considerations are seldom far from the surface.

Explaining the Origins and Development of Canadian Political Ideas

The pace of change that has characterized modern societies over the past several decades may lead us to believe that what people believed 200 or even 100 years ago, and why they held these ideas, can be of little help in understanding today's ideas about life, including politics. And, indeed, it can happen that once-dominant ideas may quickly become obsolete. For example, between 1997 and 2017 the percentage of Canadians expressing support for same-sex marriage rose from about 40 to 75.[4] Dramatic changes in the dominant ideas of a population, however, are relatively rare, and even when they occur it may often be the case that if we look a bit more closely we find that new ways of thinking continued to be anchored to certain core values and premises that paved the way for change. In the case of the rapid growth in the popular acceptance of same-sex marriage, Canadians have long attached importance to the value of individual choice and to a notion of equality that was already expressed in 1967 by then Justice Minister Pierre Trudeau when he famously said, "There's no place for the state in the bedrooms of the nation."

Consider the following two propositions: "actions are right in proportion as they tend to promote happiness; wrong as they tend to produce the reverse of happiness" and "the only purpose for which power can be rightfully exercised over any member of a civilized community, against his will, is to prevent harm to others."[5] They probably make perfect sense to most of you and if you were told that they appear at a popular political blog or were recently tweeted by a politician, writer, or celebrity you respect, you would not be surprised. In fact, they come from the writings of the British philosopher John Stuart Mill (1806–73). The first is known as Mill's principle of utility and the second as his harm principle. These ideas are foundational in Western thinking and are as influential today as they were when Mill wrote these words over 150 years ago. Thus, in understanding where our current ideas come from, including our ideas about politics, it is often useful and even necessary to reach back many generations and even centuries.

Historical explanations of Canadians' political ideas, and of the institutions that embody them, can be grouped into three main camps: **fragment theory**, the role of formative events, and economic explanations. Each of these perspectives stresses a different set of causes in explaining the origins of

Canadians' political ideas and institutions, and the forces that have shaped their development down to the present.

Fragment Theory: European Parents and Cultural Genes

Canada, along with other New World societies, was founded by immigrants from Europe. Indigenous communities already existed, of course, but the sort of society that developed in Canada had its roots and inspiration in the values and practices of European civilization. Those who chose to immigrate to the New World—or who were forced to, as were the convicts sent from Britain to Australia—did not represent a cross-section of the European society from which they came. They were unrepresentative in terms of their social class (the privileged tended to remain in Europe, although primogeniture traditions forced many of the younger scions of privilege to emigrate), their occupations, and in some cases their religion. Moreover, immigration tended to occur in waves. New World societies were "fragments" of the European societies that gave birth to them. They were fragment societies because they represented only a part of the socio-economic and cultural spectrum of the European society from which they originated, and also because their creation coincided with a particular ideological epoch in European development. The timing of settlement is crucial. Along with whatever material possessions immigrants brought with them, they also brought along their "cultural baggage": values and beliefs acquired in Europe and transplanted into the New World. As David Bell and Lorne Tepperman observe, "the 'fragment theory' sees the culture of founding groups as a kind of genetic code that does not determine but sets limits to later cultural developments."[6]

But why should the ideas of the founders carry such weight that they shape the political values and beliefs of subsequent generations? Fragment theory is rather weak on this point, arguing that the fragment's ideological system "congeals" at some point—the ideology of the founders becomes the dominant ideology—and that immigrants who arrive subsequently have little choice but to assimilate to the dominant values and beliefs already in place. The transmission of the fragment culture from generation to generation presumably depends on social structures and political institutions that date from the founding period, and embody the dominant ideas of the founding immigrants.

Canada has been characterized as a two-fragment society. French Canada was founded by immigrants from France who brought with them their Catholicism and *feudal* ideas about social and political relations. Feudal society is characterized by the existence of rigid social classes, connected to one another by a web of mutual rights and duties based on tradition, and by the exclusion of most people from the full right to participate in politics. According to French-Canadian historian Fernand Ouellet, this was the ideological and social condition of New France when the colony was conquered by British forces in 1759.[7] Cut off from the social and political developments unleashed by the French Revolution (1789)—emigration from France, with the exception of some priests, virtually dried up—French Canada's ideological development was shaped by its origins as a feudal fragment of pre-revolutionary France. Institutions, chiefly the Catholic Church, the dominant social institution in French Canada until well into the twentieth century, operated to maintain this pre-liberal inheritance.

The "cultural genes" of English Canada are, according to fragment theory, very different. English Canada was originally populated mainly by immigrants from the United States. These were the so-called Loyalists; those who found themselves on the losing side of the American War of Independence (1776). They migrated north to British colonies that were overwhelmingly French-speaking.[8] The "cultural baggage" they carried with them has been the subject of much debate, but the general view seems to be that they held predominantly *liberal* political beliefs. The liberalism that emerged in the eighteenth century was built around the idea of individual freedom: freedom in politics, in religion, and in economic relations. One of its crucial political tenets was the idea that government was based on the consent of the people. So why did the Loyalists leave the United States, a society whose political independence was founded on liberal beliefs?

The defenders of fragment theory offer different answers to this question. Some argue that the liberalism of the Loyalists was diluted by *conservative* or *Tory* political beliefs: deference towards established authority and institutions, an acceptance of inequality between classes as the natural condition of society, and a greater stress on preserving social order than on protecting individual freedoms.[9] Others reject the view that Tory values were ever a legitimate part of English Canada's political culture, arguing that this belief system had no roots in the pre-revolutionary Thirteen Colonies and therefore could not have been exported to English Canada through the Loyalist migration.[10] The Loyalists were "anti-American Yankees" who had rejected American independence because of their loyalty to the British Empire and to the monarchy, and their dislike of republican government (or, as they were more likely to put it, "mob rule"). Their quarrel was not with liberal ideology, as shown by the fact that they immediately clamoured for elected assemblies and the political rights they had been used to in America. Bell and Tepperman thus argue that:

Forced to leave their country, the Tories, or Loyalists, suffered profound doubts. Expulsion kept the Loyalist from basing a fragment identity on the liberal principles of John Locke. Made to give up his real identity, the Canadian Loyalist invented a new one. As a substitute, it was not quite good enough, of course. How could it be, when he had continuously to deny its true nature, liberalism? "The typical Canadian," an Englishman observed a hundred years ago, "tells you that he is not, but he is a Yankee—a Yankee in the sense in which we use the term at home, as synonymous with everything that smacks of democracy." The Loyalist in Canada is thereafter always a paradox, an "anti-American Yankee." Only one path leads out of his dilemma: creating a myth that helps him survive. In this myth, he insists that he is British.[11]

The debate over how important non-liberal values were among the Loyalists is not merely academic. For most of Canada's history, analyses of English Canada as a more deferential and conservative society than the United States traced this alleged difference back to the original ideological mixtures of the two societies. A second reason why the debate matters involves the explanation for the greater legitimacy of socialist ideology in Canada than in the United States. Those who contend that conservative values were an important and

The United Empire Loyalist Monument in Hamilton, Ontario, gifted to the city in 1929. What political and social developments in the early twentieth century might have contributed to this interest in the Loyalist myth and Canada's connection to the British Empire?

Library and Archives Canada

legitimate component of English Canada's original cultural inheritance go on to argue that the legitimacy of socialism in Canada was facilitated, first, by the fact that liberalism never achieved the status of an unchallenged national creed (as it did in the United States) and, second, by the fact that social class was not a foreign concept in English Canada.[12] Conservatism had already introduced collectivist ideas into the Canadian political culture and in this way, if no other, resembled socialism's stress on the collectivity over the individual.

Formative Events: Counter-Revolution and the Conquest

Societies, like human beings, are marked by certain major events at critical periods in their development. These events are "formative" in the sense that they make it more probable that a society will evolve along particular lines instead of along others. In the world of politics, these formative events are associated both with ideas and with institutions. For example, the American Revolution was fought in the

TABLE 2.1 Liberalism, Conservatism, and Socialism: Classical and Contemporary Versions

I. CLASSICAL	Liberalism	Conservatism	Socialism
a. Characteristics of the Good Society	Individual freedom is maximized; politics and economics are free and competitive; achievements and recognition are due to personal merit and effort; a capitalist economy will produce the greatest happiness for society and maximize material welfare; personal dignity depends on the individual's own actions.	The traditional social order is preserved; individuals are members of social groups linked together by a web of rights and obligations; those born in privileged circumstances have an obligation to those below them on the social ladder; a natural social hierarchy is based on inherited status; personal dignity depends on one's conformity to the norms and behaviour of one's social group.	Social and economic equality are maximized; private ownership of property is replaced by its collective ownership and management; competition is replaced by co-operation; the welfare of society is maximized through economic and social planning; personal dignity depends on work and one's solidarity with the working class.
b. Nature of Government	All just government rests on the consent of the governed; party system is competitive; the state is subordinate to society; government should be small and its scope limited; the elected legislature is the most powerful component of the state; separation between church and state.	The rights and responsibilities of those who govern derive from God and tradition; the state's fundamental role is to preserve social order; the state is superior to society and is owed obedience by all citizens and groups; the Crown is the most powerful component of the state; the size and scope of government are small by modern standards, but are not limited by liberalism's suspicion of the state; the state recognizes an official church.	All just government rests on the consent of the governed and the principles of social and economic equality; the state should control crucial sectors of the economy; government has a responsibility to redistribute wealth from the wealthy to the less fortunate social classes; government is large and its scope wide; a socialist state is the embodiment of the will and interest of the working class; no officially recognized religion.

II. CONTEMPORARY	Liberalism	Conservatism	Socialism
a. Characteristics of the Good Society	Individual freedom is balanced by protection for disadvantaged elements in society and recognition of group rights; capitalism must be regulated by the state to ensure the social and economic well-being of the majority; social diversity should be recognized and promoted through public education, hiring, and the policies of governments; social entitlements are respected, including a certain standard of living and access to decent education, health care, and accommodation; personal dignity is based on freedom and social equality.	Individual freedom is more important than social equality and should not be sacrificed to the latter; state regulation of capitalism should be kept to a minimum and should not be used to promote any but economic goals; social diversity is a fact, but is not something that should be actively promoted by government; individuals should be responsible for their own lives and policies that encourage dependency on the state should be avoided; personal dignity depends on one's own efforts and is undermined by collectivist policies and too much emphasis on promoting social and economic equality.	Social and economic equality values; individual rights must be subordinated to collective goals; small-scale capitalism has its place, but state economic planning and active participation in the economy are still necessary to promote both economic competitiveness and social fairness; the environmental consequences of all public and private actions must be considered; systemic discrimination based on gender, race, and ethnicity is eliminated through government policies; personal dignity depends on social and economic equality.
b. Nature of Government	The state has a responsibility to protect and promote the welfare of the disadvantaged; the post-WWII welfare state is a necessary vehicle for ensuring social justice; government should reflect the diversity of society in its personnel and policies; the state should not be aligned with any religious group.	The state's primary function should be to maintain circumstances in which individuals can pursue their own goals and life plans; government should be small and the level of taxation low in order to minimize interference with individual choice; government should not remain neutral between different systems of morality, but should promote traditional values through the schools and through support for the traditional family.	The state should redistribute wealth in society and ensure the social and economic equality of its citizens; some modern socialists argue that political power should be decentralized to community-level groups as the best way to ensure democratic responsiveness and accountability; the state should reflect the society in its personnel and policies; traditional value systems are based on systemic discrimination and oppression, and government has a responsibility to eradicate these values.

name of liberal values and was followed by the adoption of a constitution and structures of government that enshrined the victors' preference for dispersed political power, a weak executive, and guarantees for individual rights. The institutions put in place after the Revolution embodied eighteenth-century liberal values of individual freedom and limited government. They shaped the subsequent pattern of American politics by promoting and legitimizing behaviour and issues that conformed to these values.

The main exponent of the formative events theory of political culture is American sociologist Seymour Martin Lipset. He first introduced it by arguing that the political development of the United States has been shaped by its **revolutionary origins**, while that of English Canada has been shaped by its **counter-revolutionary origins**. Lipset writes:

> Americans do not know but Canadians cannot forget that two nations, not one, came out of the American Revolution. The United States is the country of the revolution, Canada of the counterrevolution. These very different formative events set indelible marks on the two nations. One celebrates the overthrow of an oppressive state, the triumph of the people, a successful effort to create a type of government never seen before. The other commemorates a defeat and a long struggle to preserve a historical source of legitimacy: government's deriving its title-to-rule from a monarchy linked to church establishment. Government power is feared in the south; uninhibited popular sovereignty has been a concern in the north.[13]

Many of those who found themselves on the losing side of the American Revolution—the Loyalists—migrated north. They were the founders of an English-speaking society that originated in its rejection of the new American republic. This original rejection would be repeated several times: in the War of 1812; in the defeat of the American-style democratic reforms advocated by the losers in the 1837–8 rebellions in Lower and Upper Canada; in the 1867 decision to establish a new country with a system of government similar to that of Great Britain. Much of Canada's political history, including many of the major economic and cultural policies instituted by Canadian governments, reads largely as a series of refusals in the face of Americanizing pressures.

Is rejection of American political values and institutions proof of the greater strength of conservative values in English Canada? Some of those who agree with Lipset about the importance of formative events do not agree that counter-revolutionary

gestures signify *ideological conservatism*. David Bell and Lorne Tepperman have argued that **Loyalism** concealed an underlying *ideological liberalism*. They acknowledge that the Loyalists were not anti-government, and that Canadians ever since appear to have been more willing to use the state for social, economic, and cultural purposes than have their American neighbours. But, they argue, a fondness for government is not inconsistent with liberal values. It is only in the United States, where the Revolution was directly about the tyranny of government, that liberalism acquired a strongly anti-government character.[14]

If Loyalism was not a conservative ideology, what was it? Bell and Tepperman argue that Loyalism was essentially a self-justification for not being American. Faced with the paradox of being cast out of a society whose political values they mainly shared, the Loyalists had a serious identity crisis. They resolved it by insisting on their Britishness and by constant criticisms of American values and institutions. The insistence on the Britishness of Canada passed away in the 1960s, mourned by George Grant—himself the descendant of Loyalists—in his very influential book, *Lament for a Nation*.[15] But anti-Americanism did not pass from the scene. Today it is anchored to Canadian self-images of multiculturalism and a clutch of other values widely believed by Canadians to make their society and politics superior to those of the United States. Canadian poet Dennis Lee has this to say about the Loyalist narrative of Canada:

> The dream of tory origins
> Is full of lies and blanks,
> Though what remains when it is gone,
> To prove that we're not Yanks?
> "When I Went Up to Rosedale" from
> *The Difficulty of Living on Other Planets*
> (Macmillan 1987)

What 1776 represents for English Canada's political development, the British Conquest of New France in 1759 represents for that of French Canada. As Jocelyn Létourneau and his colleagues write, "In the historical imagination of Quebec—at least in that which remains dominant in the heart of

Quebec society—the Conquest, with an obligatory capital 'C', is not an event that can be relegated to the past. It involves a fundamental turning point, according to most analysts, marking the starting point of a collective catastrophe whose negative consequences are felt down to the present day."[16]

There is no agreement as to exactly how the Conquest has affected the ideological development of French Canada. Some, like historian Michel Brunet and sociologist Marcel Rioux, have argued that the Conquest cut off the development of a French-speaking bourgeoisie—francophones were rarely found in Canada's corporate elite until only a few decades ago—thereby depriving French Canada of the class that elsewhere was the main carrier of liberal political values. The mantle of social leadership, and the task of defining French-Canadian society, eventually fell on the Catholic Church and the ideologically conservative politicians who accepted the clerics' interpretation of that society as Catholic, French-speaking, non-liberal, and agrarian—in about that order of importance.

Others, like historian Fernand Ouellet and political scientist Louis Balthazar, maintain that there was no fledgling bourgeoisie at the time of the Conquest, and therefore no catalyst for liberal political reform. French Canada, they argue, was essentially a feudal society when it passed from French to British rule. It fixated at this pre-liberal/pre-capitalist stage because it was cut off from the future, not because French Canada was deprived of something it once possessed.

History did not, of course, stop at the Conquest. The crushed 1837 rebellion in Lower Canada (Quebec) signalled the defeat of the politically liberal *patriots* and consolidated the dominance of the conservative ideology in French Canada. This ideology would ultimately collapse by the end of the 1950s, finally brought down by the weight of the enormous social and economic transformations that the conservatives had ignored and even denied. Since then, the pre-liberal ideology that dominated in Quebec has lost virtually all of its influence. But the memory of the Conquest continues to cut deep grooves into the dominant narrative that Quebecers tell themselves about their history and their relationship to predominantly English-speaking Canada.

Both the fragment theory and the formative events explanation for the development of Canadian political culture are **path dependency models**. This explanatory framework emphasizes the impact that key historical events and conditions have on the trajectory that will be followed by a society, a value system, or an economy. James Mahoney explains it this way:

[P]ath dependence characterizes specifically those historical sequences in which contingent events set into motion institutional patterns or event chains that have deterministic properties. The identification of path dependence therefore involves both tracing a given outcome back to a particular set of historical events, and showing how these events are themselves contingent occurrences that cannot be explained on the basis of prior historical conditions.[17]

Economic Structures and Political Ideas

An economic interpretation of culture, and of the institutions that embody and reproduce that culture, views political beliefs, values, processes, and laws as being profoundly shaped by class relations. These class relations are themselves rooted in the particular system of economic production and distribution—the *mode of production,* as classical Marxism calls it—found in a society at any point in time. Ideas and institutions change in response to transformations in the economic system and in the class relations associated with this system. What distinguishes this approach from the other two we have examined is the belief that *culture and institutions are the embodiments of power relations whose sources lie in the economic system.*

The questions asked by this class analysis approach to political ideas include the following: How is political culture produced? By whom? For whom? With what effects? How do political institutions embody and reinforce the power relations that characterize society? Those who take this approach argue that the dominant ideas of a society are inevitably those of its most powerful class, i.e., those who control the system of economic production and distribution. Important means of forming and disseminating ideas and information, they note, including the privately owned mass media, are controlled by the dominant class. Others, including the schools, mainstream religious organizations, and the state, accept and propagate the values of this class for reasons more subtle than ownership. Chief among these reasons are their support for *social order* and their rejection of tendencies and ideas that fundamentally challenge the economic status quo. None of these major institutions is in the business of overturning society. They depend on a stable social order to carry out their respective activities and to satisfy their particular organizational needs. But the social order they support, and whose values they accept, embodies a particular economic system and the power relations it produces. Defence of established institutions and values is not, therefore, a class-neutral stance.

Why would the members of subordinate classes embrace values and beliefs that, according to this class perspective, are basically justifications for the self-interest of the dominant class? The answer has two parts. First, those who are not part of the dominant class—and this would by definition include the majority of people—may be the victims of **false consciousness**. This concept, first used by Karl Marx, involves the inability of the subordinate classes to see where their real interests lie. For example, deference to established authority and belief in a hereditary aristocracy's "natural right to rule," ideas that defend the privileges of the dominant class in a feudal society, very clearly reinforce the subordinate social position of those who are not fortunate enough to be born into the ruling aristocracy. In liberal societies, the widespread belief that opportunities to move up the socio-economic ladder are relatively open to those who are willing to work hard is argued by some to reinforce the dominant position of that small minority who control the economy and who account for most of society's wealth. After all, critics argue, abundant empirical evidence shows that significant barriers to socio-economic mobility exist, that a good deal of poverty is passed on from generation to generation, and that those at

the top of the socio-economic pyramid constitute a largely self-perpetuating elite. And yet we learn in school, through the mass media, and in countless other ways that equality of opportunity, not systemic inequality, is a characteristic feature of our society.

The second reason why, according to this class perspective, members of subordinate classes accept the ideas of the dominant class as "common sense" is because these ideas conform, to some significant extent, to their personal experience. Democratic claims about the fundamental equality of all persons have a false ring in societies where some people are denied a share of this equality because they are black or female, for example. But in a society in which, under the constitution, there are no second-class citizens, and where everyone has the right to vote and participate in politics and enjoys equal protection under the law, claims about equality may appear to be valid. Or, consider the liberal belief, discussed earlier, that opportunities to acquire wealth and social standing are relatively open. There is, in Canada and in other liberal societies, enough evidence of this mobility to make the proposition appear true (see Chapter 3 on social mobility). The election of Barack Obama as president of the United States—the son of a Kenyan goatherd!—is evidence of mythic proportions. While some people never escape the socio-economic circumstances they are born into, many others do. There is enough proof that hard work and/or intelligence pays off in terms of material success to make liberalism's claim about what determines a person's socio-economic status a credible one. As Patricia Marchak observes, "the propagation of an ideology cannot occur in a vacuum of experience; there must be a fair amount of congruence between personal experience and ideological interpretation for the propaganda [read, 'dominant ideology'] to be successful."[18]

This idea is important: a certain degree of congruence must exist between the dominant values and beliefs of a society and the lived experience of most of its members, otherwise the ideas of the dominant class will be exposed as pure self-interest. It means that what some have called "false consciousness" cannot be totally false. Ideological systems not anchored to some significant degree to the social and economic realities of those subject to them are just not viable. Propaganda and repression of dissent must be relied upon to maintain the state's authority when the gap between the dominant ideology and the experience of most people is too great.

The Political Ideas of Canadians

In order to understand the nature of Canadian political culture we will organize our analysis under four themes: community, freedom, equality, and attitudes towards the state. These tap crucial dimensions of Canada's political belief system and at the same time allow us to explore the differences and similarities between Canadians and Americans. The evidence we will use is drawn from history, survey research data on attitudes, and measures of actual behaviour of individuals, groups, and policies from which values can be inferred.

Community

Consider these two statements: "There is no core identity, no mainstream in Canada."[19] "Canada is the only country in the world that knows how to live without an identity."[20] The first was made by Prime Minister Justin Trudeau shortly after his party's 2015 election victory. The second was made over 50 years ago by Canadian media theorist Marshall McLuhan. Let us assume for the moment that these statements are correct. It would seem a remarkable achievement that in a country without a core identity Canadians have managed to live together so long and so peacefully. Perhaps it is precisely because there is no core identity that might be seen by some minorities as excluding them that this achievement has been possible. Or it may be that a shared identity is not a precondition for a sense of political community.

These questions about identity and community have preoccupied Canadians, or at least their opinion leaders, for a very long time. Lacking a robust unifying sense of national identity, Canadian society has been buffeted by identity politics and the often irreconcilable definitions of Canada—sometimes proposing the dismemberment of the country as we know it—advanced by various groups. At the same time we should not imagine that Canadians are alone in asking such questions and facing such challenges. "Identity politics throughout the West," argues Will Kymlicka, "have become routinized and domesticated as part of everyday processes of democratic deliberation and negotiation."[21]

The term "political community" implies, quite simply, a shared sense of belonging to a country whose national integrity is worth preserving. This is something less than nationalism, which defines a community by its language, ethnic origins, traditions, or unique history. And it is not quite the same as patriotism, which one associates with a more fervent and demonstrative love of country and its symbols than has usually been considered seemly in Canada (although one would be hard-pressed to believe this when Canada is playing the United States in ice hockey!). Political community is, rather, what historian W.L. Morton once described as "a community of political allegiance alone."[22] National identity, in such a community, is free from cultural and racial associations. Instead, national identity is essentially political—a sense of common citizenship in a country whose members have more in common with one another than with the citizens of neighbouring states and who believe there are good reasons for continuing to live together as a single political nation. The term "political nationality" is used by Donald Smiley to refer to precisely this sort of non-ethnic, non-racial sense of political community.[23]

Canada's sense of community has sometimes seemed terribly fragile, threatened by French–English tensions, western grievances against Ontario and Quebec, and, most recently, conflicts between the aspirations of Indigenous Canadians and the policies of federal and provincial governments. This apparent fragility needs to be viewed alongside evidence suggesting that the country has been relatively successful in managing (repressing, critics would say) challenges to the idea and continuation of a united Canada. The existing

Constitution dates from 1867, making it one of the oldest and most durable in the world. Moreover, the territorial integrity of the country has remained unshaken by either civil war or secession. This is not to understate the importance of the rifts in Canada's sense of community. But the problems of Canadian unity and identity should be viewed from a broader perspective that includes the unity challenges other societies have faced.

Over the years, the Canadian political community has faced two major challenges: the management of French–English relations and Indigenous demands for self-government. Some commentators would include regional conflict as a third challenge to the Canadian political community. Such conflict certainly has deep roots in Canadian history and has generated regionally based movements and parties of protest. But these regional grievances and conflicts have never threatened the territorial integrity of Canada. Westerners and, less stridently, eastern Canadians have long complained about policies and institutions that favour the interests of Ontario and Quebec. They also have complained about an idea of Canada that often has seemed to relegate their regional histories and realities to the margins. But their resentment has never boiled over to produce politically significant separatist movements in these regions, nor widespread popular defection from the *idea* of Canada. The importance of regionalism will be discussed in Chapter 5.

For most of Canada's history, relations between French- and English-speaking Canadians have not posed a threat to the political community. The differences and tensions between Canada's two major language groups were managed through political accommodations arrived at between their political elites. This practice arguably goes back to the Quebec Act of 1774. Official protection was extended to the Catholic Church and Quebec's civil law system just when the British authorities were worried about the prospect of political rebellion in the American colonies spreading north. The tradition of deal-making between French and English Canada acquired a rather different twist in the couple of decades prior to Confederation, when the current provinces of Ontario and Quebec

were united with a common legislature. The practice of dual ministries, with a leader from both Canada East (Quebec) and Canada West (Ontario), quickly developed, as did the convention that a bill needed to be passed by majorities from both East and West in order to become law. The federal division of powers that formed the basis of the 1867 Confederation continued this deal-making tradition. The assignment to the provinces of jurisdiction over education, property, civil rights, and local matters was mainly in response to Quebec politicians' insistence on control over those matters involving cultural differences.

This tradition of elitist deal-making has continued throughout Canada's history at two different levels. Nationally, the federal cabinet and national political parties, particularly the Liberal Party of Canada, have been important forums where the interests of Quebec could be represented. But with the rise of a more aggressive Quebec-centred nationalism in the 1960s, the ability to represent the interests of French and English Canada within national institutions became less important than whether compromises could be reached between the governments of Canada and Quebec.

The modus vivendi that for a couple of centuries prevented French–English conflicts from exploding into challenges to the idea of a single Canada seemed to come unstitched during the 1960s. Quebec independence, which previously had been a marginal idea that surfaced only sporadically in the province's politics, became a serious proposition advocated by many French-speaking intellectuals and supported by a sizable minority of Québécois. The independence option spawned a number of organized political groups during the 1960s. In 1968, most of them threw their support behind the newly formed pro-independence Parti Québécois (PQ). Since then, the debate over whether the province should remain in Canada, and if so on what terms, has been one of the chief dimensions of Quebec political life.

According to public opinion polls, the level of popular support for Quebec independence has ranged between a low of about 20 per cent just after the birth of the PQ to a high of nearly 60 per cent

In Canada to attend Expo 67, then French President Charles de Gaulle roused—and stunned—a crowd assembled at Montreal's city hall on 24 July 1967 when he spoke from a small hotel balcony and exclaimed, "Vive Montréal! Vive le Québec! Vive le Québec libre!" ("Long live free Quebec!"). The slogan became a rallying cry for those organizing around a growing Quebec sovereignty movement at the time.

(see Figure 2.1). In recent years it has hovered around one-third of Quebecers, including just over 4 in 10 of those whose mother tongue is French. Without reading too much into the numbers, we may say that there appears to be a durable core of support for the idea of Quebec independence, but that it may lack the potential for growth (see the discussion in Chapter 14). Not only has the level of support varied over time, it is also influenced by what sort of independence is envisaged by the pollster's question. Support always has been higher for softer options such as "sovereignty-association"—a term generally understood to mean a politically sovereign Quebec that would be linked to Canada through some sort of commercial union or free trade agreement—than for outright political and economic separation. Quebecers have twice been given the opportunity to register popular support for an independent Quebec and, thus, rejection of the Canadian political community. The first of these came in May of 1980, when the PQ government that had been elected four years earlier held its promised referendum on sovereignty-association. The referendum was very deliberately—some said deceptively—worded. It stressed that what was being proposed was not a radical break from Canada, but a

Listen to the "Thoughts on the Future of Quebec Separatism" podcast, available at: www .oup.com/he/Brooks9e

negotiated political independence for Quebec that would maintain economic ties to Canada.

> The Government of Quebec has made public its proposal to negotiate a new arrangement with the rest of Canada, based on the equality of nations; this arrangement would enable Quebec to acquire the exclusive power to make its laws, administer its taxes and establish relations abroad—in other words, sovereignty—and at the same time to maintain with Canada an economic association including a common currency; no change in political status resulting from these negotiations will be effected without approval by the people through another referendum; on these terms, do you give the Government of Quebec the mandate to negotiate the proposed agreement between Quebec and Canada? Yes. No.

Despite the PQ's careful strategy, Quebec voters rejected the sovereignty-association option by a vote of 59.6 per cent ("Non") to 40.4 per cent ("Oui"). Even among francophones, a majority voted against Quebec independence.[24] Advocates of Quebec separatism were quick to point out that sovereignty-association was more popular among younger than older voters. Time, they argued, would turn the tide in favour of independence. Others argued that the greater popularity of the "Oui" option among those who entered adulthood in the nationalist 1960s and early 1970s—Quebec's "baby boomers"—reflected the exceptional politically formative experiences of this generation, and that subsequent generations, not raised in the intensely nationalist ferment that characterized the 1960s in Quebec, would find separatism less appealing.

The second referendum on Quebec independence took place in 1995 and produced a much closer outcome. Those voting "Non," against independence, surpassed those voting "Oui" by a margin of 50.6 per cent to 49.4 per cent, in a referendum in which almost 94 per cent of eligible citizens voted. Quebec society was very clearly and deeply divided on its relationship to the Canadian political community. Among francophones, 55 per cent voted for independence compared to only 7 per cent among non-francophones. Younger Quebecers were considerably more likely than older citizens to vote for independence.[25] Once again, the supporters of Quebec independence, though disappointed with the immediate result, took heart. Time, they believed, was on their side.

But as Figure 2.1 shows, it seems that younger Quebecers can no longer be counted on to be those most enthusiastic about the vision of Quebec independence. The youngest cohort of voters had always been as strongly supportive of independence as any age cohort until about a decade ago.

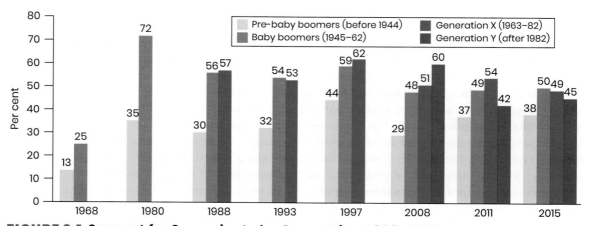

FIGURE 2.1 Support for Sovereignty by Generation, 1968–2015

Source: Jean-Herman Guay, "Sovereignty at an Impasse: The Highs and Lows of Quebec Nationalism," Institute for Research on Public Policy, 24 Oct. 2017, http://irpp .org/research-studies/sovereignty-at-an-impasse-the-highs-and-lows-of-quebec-nationalism/.

Millennials (those born after 1982) are actually less supportive of Quebec independence than any age group except the dwindling numbers of pre-baby boomers. This has led many to conclude that Quebec separatism no longer poses a serious challenge to the Canadian political community, an issue that will be revisited in Chapter 14.

Accustomed to the challenge that Quebec separatism posed to the political community, most Canadians probably were surprised in 1990 when the Oka Crisis revealed the existence of another challenge to the idea of the Canadian political community. During the summer and autumn of 1990 a group of Mohawk Warriors, protesting the planned expansion of a golf course on land they claimed as their own, barricaded a road leading to the golf course. The confrontation eventually escalated, resulting in the death of one Quebec police officer, a sympathy blockade by Mohawks at Kahnawake of the Mercier Bridge leading into Montreal, an important commuter route for the city, and other sympathy blockades of rail lines and roads by other Indigenous people in communities across the country. Eventually, the standoff at Oka, Quebec, led to riots involving the non-Indigenous townspeople and members of the local Mohawk band of Kanesatake, intervention by thousands of Canadian troops, and even United Nations observers.

Although many Canadians may have been taken by surprise by these events, the armed confrontation between Quebec and Canadian authorities and the Kanienkehaka (Mohawk) at Oka had several precedents. Violent confrontations between Indigenous peoples and non-Indigenous Canadians and their political authorities punctuate Canadian history, going back to the colonial era and the extermination of the Beothuk Indians of Newfoundland in the 1700s (the last Beothuk died in 1829). Fears of another Oka were raised in 1995 when small groups of Indigenous Canadians occupied land they claimed was sacred at Gustafsen Lake, BC, and Ipperwash Provincial Park in Ontario. Violence broke out in both cases, and at Ipperwash an un-armed protester from Kettle and Stony Point First Nation was shot and killed by a provincial police officer. Since then a number of violent episodes,

but no deaths, have occurred in several provinces, including British Columbia, New Brunswick, Ontario, and Quebec.[26] Although the circumstances of each case were unique, they all had one element in common: resistance by Indigenous people against laws, policies, or property claims based on what they maintained to be their distinct status and rights. In the case of the standoff at Caledonia, Ontario, some spokespersons for the Six Nations Reserve stated bluntly that the rulings of Canadian courts do not apply to their people. Some non-Indigenous Canadians agree. Such attitudes, regardless of whether we agree with them, represent a significant challenge to the notion of a single Canadian political community.

If the authority of Canadian courts is not recognized on land claimed by Indigenous peoples, what aspects of the Canadian state's authority apply within such territories? The answer given by many Indigenous leaders is "Not much." The following statement on the meaning of First Nations sovereignty, from the Chiefs of Ontario, is widely accepted among the leaders of Indigenous peoples in Canada:

> As distinct and independent Nations, we possess inherent rights to self-determination. These inherent rights were not endowed by any other state or Nation, but are passed on through birthright, are collective, and flow from the connection to the Creator and our lands. They cannot be taken away. Self-determination means we freely and independently determine and exercise our own political, legal, economic, social and cultural systems without external interference. In other words, we have jurisdiction over all aspects of our livelihood.[27]

That's the theory. In practice, major land claim settlements that include structures for self-government, notably the Nunavut Land Claims Agreement of 1993, out of which the eastern Arctic territory of Nunavut and its public government (i.e., a government not ethnicity-based or exclusive to Inuit) were established in 1999, and the Nisga'a Final Agreement that came into effect in British Columbia

The Canadian Press/Geoff Robins

Minister of National Defense Harjit Sajjan, Minister of Indigenous and Northern Affairs Carolyn Bennet, and Chief Thomas Bresette attend a ceremony to commemorate the federal government's agreement to return expropriated land to the Kettle and Stony Point First Nation, twenty years after Dudley George was killed by the Ontario Provincial Police in Ipperwash Provincial Park.

in 2000 (with a government based on membership and Nisga'a citizenship), state explicitly that laws of general application continue to apply to those who inhabit these Indigenous lands and that the Charter of Rights and Freedoms applies to their governments. Where conflicts arise between the laws and regulations of these governments and federal and provincial statutes, Canadian law generally holds sway. Nevertheless, a sort of de facto acceptance of separate communities, defined by their specific Indigeneity, now exists within Canada. The tension between the traditional idea of Canadian sovereignty and ideas of Indigenous community that would limit or even deny the application of Canadian laws to self-governing Indigenous territories has been an important feature of Canadian politics since the 1990s.

Freedom

"Live free or die" reads the motto on licence plates in the state of New Hampshire. Individual freedom is said to be part of the American political creed, symbolized in such icons as the Statue of Liberty, Philadelphia's Liberty Bell, the Bill of Rights, and the Declaration of Independence. Canadians, it often has been claimed, are more willing than Americans to limit individual freedom in pursuit of social order or group rights. Is this true?

On the face of it, freedom does indeed appear to occupy a more central place in the American political culture. Not only are many of the country's iconic symbols linked to the idea of personal freedom, the American creation story is about individuals banding together against a repressive state in defence of their freedom. References to freedom are much more common in the American political conversation than in Canada, and the libertarian movement—for which personal freedom trumps all other political values—is more prominent in the United States than in Canada. Themes of individualism, liberty, and self-reliance, as well as mistrust of the state as the potential enemy of freedom, are woven through the American historical narrative.

For all this, however, the differences between what Canadians and Americans believe when it comes to freedom tend not to be dramatic. Moreover, these differences are almost always narrower than the gap separating the values of Canadians from Western Europeans. There is also evidence that whatever might have been true in the past, today Canadians tend to value certain aspects of freedom more than their neighbours to the south.

Earlier in this chapter we discussed the concept of path dependency. The greater prominence of freedom in the American historical narrative and contemporary political conversation may be traced to the origins of the United States and Canada. As Lipset and others have observed, the American Revolution launched these two countries on different trajectories in regard to personal freedom and the individual's relationship to the state. Mistrust of the state, from the beginning, was an important theme in American political thinking. The constitutional system of checks and balances and divided governmental power, as well as a constitutionally entrenched Bill of Rights, reflected this original preoccupation with protecting the individual's rights and freedoms against encroachments by the state.

English Canada was not founded on an ethos of limited government. Nor did the country experience self-government and then independence until long after the American Revolution that Loyalists rejected. Instead of celebrating what Abraham Lincoln, in the Gettysburg Address (1863), describes as "a new nation, conceived in liberty and dedicated to the proposition that all men are created equal," most of Canada's leaders celebrated the connection to Great Britain and the conservative idea that "freedom wears a crown"[28] until well into the twentieth century. As Lipset observes, "If [Canada] leans towards communitarianism—the

public mobilization of resources to fulfill group objectives—the [United States] sees individualism—private endeavour—as the way an 'unseen hand' produces optimum, socially beneficial results."[29] Canadian writer Pierre Berton made the same point when he maintained that "We've always accepted more governmental control over our lives than . . . [Americans] have—and fewer civil liberties."[30]

Lipset and Berton made these observations almost 40 years ago. They reflected the collective wisdom at the time, as well as the judgment of most scholars who studied Canada–US cultural differences. Today, however, they sound rather outdated and perhaps even inaccurate. And indeed recent surveys show that on some measures of personal freedom Canadians continue to lag behind Americans, but on others they are more likely to embrace personal choice.[31]

One of Lipset's arguments is that the greater American stress on personal freedom is reflected in higher rates of crime in the US than in Canada and in attitudes towards law and order in the two societies. "[E]fforts to distinguish Canada and the United States," he writes, "almost invariably point to the greater respect for law and order and those who uphold it north of the border."[32] Canadians, because of their weaker attachment to personal freedom, have always been more deferential to state authority, including that of the police and justice system, whereas Americans have been likely to resent and resist the state's limits on their freedom. This difference, Lipset argues, has its roots in the American Revolution that created the United States, the revolutionary country whose founding celebrated personal freedom and the mistrust of state authority, whereas Canada is the society of the counter-revolution.

In a recent test of this hypothesis, Nick Baxter-Moore and his colleagues conclude that Lipset's argument is supported by their survey of Canadian and American university students on either side of the Niagara River border. In their 2017 study they presented respondents with five statements, based on Lipset's hypothesis:

- Peace and order are more important than free speech.

- It is better to live in an orderly society than to allow people so much freedom they become disruptive.
- Protests need to occur under police supervision to prevent violence.
- If justice has not been done, citizens have the right to take the law into their own hands.
- Violence is part of life; it is no big deal.

While the results revealed a mixed pattern, on three of the response items Canadians tended to give what would be thought of as a more deferential and less personal freedom-oriented answer. These differences between the Canadian and American samples, while not great, were statistically significant. On the other two items the differences were small and not statistically significant. The study also asked a large number of questions dealing with trust in government, government limits on personal privacy, gun ownership, belief that the justice system will treat one fairly, whether the convicted are treated severely enough, and the treatment of minorities by the police and the justice system. On the whole, the results from these questions supported Lipset's hypothesis. "We found systematic variations in the orientations of our Canadian and American students toward guns, crime, policing, and the criminal justice system that are generally consistent with expectations based on Seymour Martin Lipset's formative events thesis."[33]

More support for the view that Canadians tend to be somewhat less committed to personal freedom than Americans comes from a 2015 survey by the Pew Research Center's Global Attitudes Survey. It found that Americans are the most freedom-oriented of all the populations surveyed and that on the four items shown in Figure 2.2, they tended to give more freedom-oriented responses than did Canadians. These differences were not always very great, but they were all in the same direction.

Freedom also has moral dimension that involves the ability of persons to make individual choices regardless of whether these choices are believed by others to be morally acceptable. When it comes to this dimension of freedom, the evidence suggests that Canadians are more freedom-oriented than

Americans. Surveys conducted by Gallup in the United States and Abacus Data in Canada in 2016 found significant differences between the two societies on a number of issues related to moral choices. In almost every case Canadian responses were more liberal, and in many cases much more liberal, than those of Americans (see Figure 2.3).

We find, therefore, a rather mixed pattern of results when examining Canadian and American values with respect to freedom. It may be, as some have argued, that the explanation lies in an important difference in the way that Canadians and Americans tend to understand freedom. Americans are more likely than Canadians to view freedom as the absence of limitation on individual behaviour, what is sometimes called negative freedom. This, according to critics such as the Canadian philosopher Charles Taylor, actually denies real freedom to many people. Canadians' greater willingness to permit government restrictions on individual behaviour does not mean that they value freedom less. Instead, it means they are more likely than Americans to believe that real freedom often requires that government interfere with individual property rights and economic markets. Moreover, governments should guarantee to all citizens such things as public education and health care in order to help equalize the opportunities available to the well-off and the less-privileged. Canadians, some argue, have what might be characterized as a positive conception of freedom, one that requires governments to act in ways that empower individuals to make choices rather than simply getting out of the way.

Some support for this claim that Canadians and Americans tend to understand freedom and the conditions that nurture it in different ways is found in the results of a 2009 survey on economic mobility in these two countries. Canadians were more likely than Americans to express the belief that government does more to help people move up the economic ladder (46 per cent of Canadians agreeing, compared to 36 per cent of Americans), whereas Americans were more likely than Canadians to believe that government did more to hurt mobility (46 per cent vs 39 per cent). This is, admittedly, not a particularly large gap between the

Publics Worldwide Support Right to Criticize Their Government
People should be able to make statements that publicly

	Criticize the government's policies	Are offensive to minority groups	Are offensive to your religion or beliefs	Are sexually explicit	Call for violent protests
	%	%	%	%	%
US	95	67	77	52	44
Canada	93	52	64	37	29
Europe					
Spain	96	57	54	70	32
UK	94	54	57	31	22
Germany	93	27	38	23	11
France	89	51	53	41	32
Poland	89	41	40	50	60
Italy	88	32	29	36	30
Middle East					
Lebanon	98	1	1	34	6
Israel	93	36	32	41	15
Palest. ter.	74	24	20	17	30
Jordan	64	6	4	7	13
Turkey	52	25	24	20	24
Asia/Pacific					
Australia	95	56	62	33	35
Philippines	73	58	59	42	50
India	72	26	28	22	25
Indonesia	72	23	26	15	22
South Korea	70	42	51	17	24
Japan	67	14	24	10	9
Malaysia	63	27	26	*	25
Vietnam	61	34	37	9	20
Pakistan	54	16	20	11	20
Latin Amrica					
Chile	94	29	26	27	27
Argentina	91	49	40	27	21
Brazil	90	48	43	23	20
Venezuela	89	53	51	37	35
Mexico	84	65	56	36	39
Peru	76	51	50	30	35
Africa					
Burkina Faso	80	16	11	13	11
Tanzania	80	66	40	26	25
Ghana	79	41	27	21	17
Kenya	74	42	43	30	30
Nigeria	71	31	33	22	25
South Africa	64	51	50	36	42
Uganda	61	27	17	13	19
Senegal	60	10	6	13	9
Ukraine	87	18	12	8	8
Russia	72	26	22	16	17

* Question not asked in Malaysia.

FIGURE 2.2 Support for Religious, Media, and Personal Freedom, Selected Countries

Source: Adapted from Pew Research Center, Global Attitudes Survey, Q30a–e, Spring 2015.

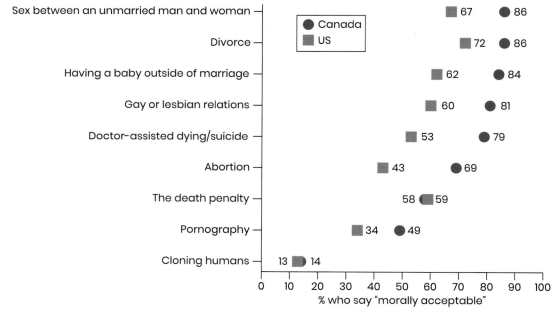

FIGURE 2.3 Freedom and Morality, Canada and the United States, 2016

Note: The Canadian survey was conducted by Abacus Data in June 2016. The American survey was carried out by Gallup in May 2015.

Source: Abacus Data, "Canadians' Moral Compass Set Differently from That of Our Neighbours to the South," 9 June 2016, https://abacusdata.ca/canadians-moral-compass-set-differently-from-that-of-our-neighbours-to-the-south/.

beliefs of Canadians and Americans.[34] Regrettably, subsequent cross-national surveys that have asked questions about perceptions of opportunities for upward mobility and the importance of personal versus systemic factors in shaping a person's chances to achieve his or her life goals, including Pew's Global Attitudes Project, have excluded Canada.

Equality

A long line of sociologists, political scientists, and historians, going back to Alexis de Tocqueville and other Europeans who visited North America in the nineteenth century, agreed that America's political culture was more egalitarian and Canada's more hierarchical. To arrive at this conclusion, of course, one had to conceptualize egalitarianism in a manner that ignored the existence of slavery in the United States until the end of the Civil War, followed by Jim Crow segregation laws that persisted well into the second half of the twentieth century.[35] Nevertheless, the historical evidence suggests very

strongly that Canadian society was somewhat more elitist and socio-economic mobility in Canada was more limited than in the United States.[36]

In more recent times, however, it has been usual for Canadians to think of their society as the more egalitarian one and for some Americans to agree with them![37] A 2017 survey by Gallup and Ipsos Affairs found that Canadians were slightly more likely than Americans to support the idea of a basic annual income (44 per cent vs 38 per cent). Canadians, by relatively small margins, were also less likely than Americans to say that such a policy would tend to make individuals more dependent on the state (60 per cent vs 69 per cent) and discourage them from seeking employment (54 per cent vs 63 per cent).[38]

In Canada, egalitarianism has its roots in a more collectivist tradition; in the United States it draws on a more individualistic tradition. But the value differences between the two societies tend to be shaded rather than starkly contrasting. Nevertheless, these differences help to explain

Canadians' apparently greater acceptance of social spending that redistributes income between groups and even between regions of the country. Lipset's conclusion may still be a fair one: "Canadians are committed to redistribution egalitarianism, while Americans place more emphasis on meritocratic competition and equality of opportunity."[39]

This difference between the two societies, however, should not be exaggerated. If Americans care more about equality of opportunity and Canadians about equality of condition, then we would expect to find greater acceptance of economic inequalities among Americans and less skepticism about the fairness of the economic system. But the evidence is unclear. A survey carried out in 2013 for the Pew Research Center found that almost identical percentages of Canadians (58 per cent) and Americans (61 per cent) agreed that the economic system favours the wealthy.[40] When asked whether they thought it was more important to reduce inequality or to ensure that everyone has a fair chance to improve their economic standing, 71 per cent of Americans and 68 per cent of Canadians chose ensuring a fair chance.[41] If Canadians are truly more oriented towards equality of condition, and if this is an important difference between the values of Canadians and Americans, then one would expect to find a greater gap. Miles Corak observes that "Both Americans and Canadians feel strongly that individual characteristics, like hard work, ambition, and [education], lead to upward economic mobility. In both countries, factors external to the individual, outside of his or her control, rank much lower."[42] Majorities in both countries expressed the view that all of their fellow citizens had a fair chance of moving up the economic ladder. Corak notes that Canadians were about as likely as Americans to support merit-based differences, including the right of hard workers to make more than others, the limited role of luck, gender, and race in determining one's economic fortunes, and the fairness of inequalities when there is equality of opportunity.

Equality is about more than economic opportunities and conditions. It also involves ideas and behaviour about and towards people of other ethnicities, cultures, sexual preferences, religions, and so on. Just as most Canadians believe their society attaches greater importance to economic equality than does their southern neighbour, they also overwhelmingly believe that tolerance of differences, respect for diversity, and the protection of group rights are more likely to be embraced by Canadians than by Americans. At the centre of this narrative of difference is the familiar claim that Canada is a mosaic and the United States is a melting pot. Pressures on newcomers to assimilate to the dominant culture are weaker in Canada than in the United States. Canadian multiculturalism celebrates difference while the culture of *e pluribus unum* (from the many, one) holds up a sort of uniform Americanism as the model that all should aspire to.

In fact, however, Canadian governments have shown themselves to be as capable as their American counterparts of discriminating against ethnic and religious communities. Both countries banned immigration from China for long periods of time, the United States for over a half-century after the 1882 passage of the Chinese Exclusion Act and Canada for more than two decades following passage of the Chinese Immigration Act of 1923. In both Canada and the United States many people of Japanese ancestry were deprived of their property and kept confined to camps during World War II. In Canada, the religious beliefs of Doukhobors, Hutterites, Mennonites, and Jehovah's Witnesses have at various times brought them into conflict with either Ottawa or provincial governments. And in both Canada and the United States immigration policy until the 1960s discriminated against non-white, non-European peoples. Although this is no longer overtly characteristic of policy in either country, some argue that discriminatory practice in immigration has ramped up in recent years, especially as those on the political right seek to hold back the demographic inevitability of the two North American neighbours no longer being white-majority countries. These critics argue that white supremacy has slithered from the political fringes to become a mainstream immigration view in the United States.

Despite evidence that, in Canada, too, tolerance of cultural diversity has known limits, these limits have been less restrictive than in the United States. The treatment of Canada's Indigenous peoples, for example, has been less harsh and less violent than that of America's Native populations, though perhaps no less insidious. Moreover, nothing in Canada's history compares to the official discrimination and the physical violence directed against African Americans for much of that country's history. An official policy of **multiculturalism** has existed in Canada since 1971 and was recognized in the Constitution in 1982.[43] Also, Canada's Constitution appears to provide a firmer basis for affirmative action programs and other state activities that have as their goal "the amelioration of conditions of disadvantaged individuals or groups including those that are disadvantaged because of race, national or ethnic origin, colour, religion, sex, age or mental or physical disability."[44]

Canadians' often unshakeable belief that theirs is the society of the mosaic, characterized by tolerance, accommodation, and respect for diversity, in contradistinction to the cultural blender to the south, is based in part on widespread ignorance of the reality of American society. For several decades a combination of government policies and court decisions has steered the United States in the direction of multiculturalism. An extensive system of bilingual, Spanish–English schools has been created in parts of the United States, particularly California. Some public services, including written driving tests, health care information, and voter registration, are offered in several languages in many American states and cities and American law requires multilingual ballots and poll workers in some circumstances. Affirmative action policies at American universities, intended to increase the representation of targeted groups, and congressional boundary lines drawn to maximize the proportion of minority voters (referred to as majority-minority districts) began earlier and have been taken further in the United States than in Canada. (In Canada, federal and provincial electoral boundary laws allow what are referred to as "communities of interest" to be taken into account in the drawing of these lines. Mainly because electoral boundaries are determined by non-partisan commissioners instead of by politicians, as is common in the US, the process has been less controversial in Canada.) Universities and other schools in the United States pioneered the concept and practice of minority-oriented curricula

(African-American studies, for example), and this dimension of cultural pluralism is well established there, even while education institutions and other aspects of multiculturalism are at the centre of the so-called culture war in America. Indeed, the very intensity of controversy over multiculturalism, identity politics, affirmative action, and ascription-based policies in the United States is to some degree a reflection of just how successful the mosaic model has been in influencing public life in that society. The backlash attests to the inroads it has made.

In view of how deeply the distinction between the Canadian mosaic and the American melting pot is embedded in the collective psyche of Canadians, it seems surprising that there has been little effort to test empirically this article of faith. But perhaps this is not so surprising. Why would one test a proposition that is so self-evidently true? Indeed, it might even seem to border on sacrilege to question a belief that is so central to Canadians' ideas of what distinguishes their society from that of the United States.

Raymond Breton and Jeffrey Reitz risk this sacrilege in what is the most ambitious and systematic attempt to test the proposition that Canadians are more tolerant of diversity than their allegedly more assimilationist neighbours to the south. In *The Illusion of Difference* they review existing studies of the mosaic versus melting pot thesis and examine a number of comparative surveys and census data from the two countries. They conclude that the differences between Canada and the United States are "more apparent than real." The Canadian style, they argue, "is more low-key than the American; moreover, Canadians have a conscious tradition of 'tolerance' that Americans do not have." These differences in the way multiculturalism and ethnic diversity have been thought of in the two societies "have not produced less pressure towards conformity in Canada, or less propensity to discriminate in employment or housing."[45] Comparing rates of language retention, ethnic group identification, participation in ethnically based social networks, and attitudes and behaviour towards racial minorities, Breton and Reitz make the case that almost no empirical data support Canadians' cherished self-image of their society as being more tolerant and less assimilationist than that of the United States. Several years later their conclusion was supported by a study of language retention based on Statistics Canada's 2002 Ethnic Diversity Study.[46] This study found that in both Canada and the United States, one out of five persons spoke a foreign language at least some of the time at home. A recent investigation into social, cultural, and civic aspects of the integration of newcomers into Canadian society concludes that "[i]mmigrants had a lower integration score compared to the Canadian-born but the difference is small." The researchers found that this disparity existed principally because of lower rates of integration among immigrants who were also members of racial minorities.[47]

Gender equality is another dimension of group rights that has acquired prominence in recent decades. In both Canada and the United States attitudes concerning the appropriate roles and behaviour of men and women have changed sharply in the direction of greater equality. The visible signs of this change are everywhere, including laws on pay equity, easier access to abortion, greater female than male participation and graduation rates in universities, increased female representation in male-dominated professions, how females are portrayed by the media, and greater female participation in the political system.

All of the above are indirect measures of attitudes towards gender equality. Although they do not provide a direct indication of cultural values, we might reasonably infer these values from what we observe in the economy, the educational system, and politics. Comparing Canada to the United States on such measures, we come up with a mixed scorecard. The differences between the two societies tend not to be very large, Canada being "more equal" on some counts, the United States on others.

For example, the World Economic Forum's 2017 *Gender Gap Report* found that women did quite a bit better in the United States than in Canada in regard to economic participation and opportunity (19th among 144 countries, compared to 29th for Canada), but Canada did much better in terms of political empowerment for women (20th, compared to 96th for the United States).[48] In both Canada and the United States women hold about one-fifth of seats on the boards of directors of each country's 500 leading corporations.[49] According to recent data collected by the World Values Survey, public opinion is almost identical in the two countries regarding relations between the sexes and the roles appropriate to each.

When it comes to attitudes on race, however, most Canadians are quite convinced that their society does better than the United States. There is little doubt that racism and racial violence have been less prominent in Canadian history. Although it is tempting to infer from the statistics on racial segregation, income differences associated with race, crime and sentencing data, and a host of other measures that Americans tend to be more racist than Canadians, such an inference may not be warranted. The enormous differences in the social and economic circumstances that have shaped race relations in the two societies and the much greater relative size of the black population in the United States are two reasons to be wary of drawing such conclusions. The fact is that demography and history ensure that race and racism are far more central to American political life than to politics in Canada.

According to data from the World Values Survey, Canadians and Americans are among the most racially tolerant populations in the world. Under 5 per cent of respondents in both countries choose "people of a different race" from a list of kinds of people they would not want as neighbours. But a 2016 Gallup poll found that 18 per cent of Canadians and 23 per cent of Americans agreed with the statement that some races are superior to others.[50] A 2010 survey carried out for the Canadian Race Relations Foundation found that Americans are more than twice as likely as Canadians to say that they would not want their child to marry someone of another race (32 per cent vs 14 per cent; the figures were 33 per cent in Spain and 20 per cent in Germany).[51] At the same time, however, the percentage of interracial couples in the United States is about twice that in Canada, although black–white couples are less common in the United States than in Canada and Asian–white couples are more common in the United States than in Canada. Are any of these observed differences related to ideas about race? According to some researchers, ideas about race may be much less important in explaining these

lev radin/Shutterstock

In Canada, all citizens' health care is administered via a public system in which a pool of funds provides for medical costs. Those funds are collected via taxation and are managed and paid out by government. During the ongoing health-care debate in the United States, many have protested proposed reforms for a similar universal system, claiming that health-care management should be determined by a private system composed of users, medical providers, and insurers—not governments. However, views on health care may be changing in the United States. Vermont Senator Bernie Sanders's progressive campaign for universal health care brought him widespread support during the 2016 campaign for the Democratic Party's presidential nomination, and this remained a key platform issue for his 2020 bid.

differences than the relative size of racial communities in marriage markets.[52] The bottom line is this: comparing ideas about race in Canada and the United States is not as straightforward and predictable as one might imagine.

Citizen Expectations for Government

Canadians, it has often been argued, are more likely than Americans to look to government to meet their needs. Moreover, they are more likely to accept state actions that they dislike, instead of mobilizing against such policies and the governments that institute them. Thomas Jefferson's declaration, "That government is best which governs least," has an oddly foreign tone to Canadians. The mistrust of government and implicit celebration of individualism that inspired Jefferson's aphorism have not resonated in Canada the way they have throughout American history.

The belief is firmly entrenched that Canadians expect their governments to do more than do Americans, and are more passive in the face of state action, including government policies they may not like. It may once have been an accurate characterization of an important difference between the political cultures of Canada and the United States. The inconvenient reality, however, is that the two countries have converged considerably, such that a sweeping generalization about Canadians being more statist and deferential than Americans is simply not supported by the evidence. Canadian governments have been resistant to the expansion of a private presence in health care and post-secondary education, although this resistance has weakened over the past couple of decades. They own corporations whose activities range from producing electricity to television broadcasting, while American governments have generally been content to regulate privately owned businesses in these same industries. Canadian governments are much more actively involved in promoting particular cultural values, especially those associated with bilingualism and multiculturalism, than are most governments in the United States. In Canada the public sector historically has accounted for a larger share of gross national expenditure than in the United States, although the difference between the two countries is today very small. Similarly, although governments in Canada used to spend a greater share of GDP on social programs, now the difference between the two countries is quite negligible.[53] One difference that remains involves taxation. Canadian governments collect a somewhat larger share of total national income in taxes than do governments in the United States.[54] All in all, this adds up to a rather mixed picture, but certainly not one that allows us to confidently say that Canada is a more statist society than the United States.

What about the evidence for Canadians' alleged passivity in the face of government actions they dislike? Is it true that Canadians are more deferential to authority, including political authority, than their American counterparts? It was once fairly common to hear Canadian political experts intone that ours is a more orderly society. The stability that Canadians experienced through this country's parliamentary system and constitutional monarchy, compared to the rather chaotic "mobocracy" to the south, was seen to provide a sort of protective mantle under which citizens were better able to enjoy their democratic rights and freedoms. Canadians' apparent greater faith in government, compared to the more skeptical attitudes of Americans, owes a good deal to a collectivist ethos that sets Canadians and their history apart from the United States. It is this ethos that Canadian nationalists are invoking when they argue that Canada's public health-care system and more generous social programs reflect the "soul" of this country, and that their dismemberment would send Canadians down the allegedly mean-spirited path of American individualism. Some of Canada's most prominent thinkers, including George Grant and Charles Taylor, have argued that the collectivist ethos and greater willingness of Canadians than Americans to use the state to achieve community goals are central to the Canadian political tradition.

In *Lament for a Nation*, Grant argued that the Canadian political tradition was marked by a communitarian spirit that rejected the individualism of American-style liberalism. He traced the roots of this spirit to the influence of conservative ideas and the British connection, which helped to keep alive a benign view of government as an agent for pursuing the common good. This distinctive national character, Grant believed, was doomed to be crushed by the steamroller of American liberalism and technology, homogenizing influences that would ultimately flatten national cultures throughout the capitalist world. Grant's "lament" was in the key of what has been called **Red Toryism**. Red Tories are conservatives who believe that government has a responsibility to act as an agent for the collective good and that this responsibility goes far beyond maintaining law and order. In Canada today, Red Tories are an endangered political species. Indeed, for practical purposes the label has come to mean little more than a sort of ideologically centrist Conservative politician or brand of conservatism and is often used to distinguish such a person or political orientation from a harder-edged variety of contemporary conservatism.

Unlike George Grant, Charles Taylor is firmly on the left of the political spectrum. He agrees with Grant about the importance of collectivism in Canada's political tradition. Taylor has always been extremely critical of what he calls the "atomism" of American liberalism, a value system that he believes cuts people off from the communal relations that nurture human dignity. Like most Canadian nationalists, he believes implicitly in the moral superiority of Canada's more collectivist political tradition.

Taylor is one of the leading thinkers in the contemporary movement known as **communitarianism**. This is based on the belief that real human freedom and dignity are possible only in the context of communal relations that allow for the public recognition of group identities and that are based on equal respect for these different identity groups. Taylor argues that the key to Canadian unity lies in finding constitutional arrangements that enable different groups of Canadians to feel they belong to Canada and are recognized as constituent elements of Canadian society. "Nations . . . which have a strong sense of their own identity," says Taylor, "and hence a desire to direct in some ways their common affairs, can only be induced to take part willingly in multinational states if they are in some ways recognized within them."[55] He calls this the recognition of "deep diversity." The realization of deep diversity would require, at a minimum, official recognition of Quebec as a distinct society and probably constitutional acknowledgement of an Indigenous third order of government. To some this might sound like a recipe for dismantling whatever sense of Canadian community currently exists. Taylor insists, however, that one-size-fits-all notions of community do not work in the modern world.

The characterization of Canada as a deferential society, or at least one where citizens are less likely to question political and other sources of established authority than in the United States, has been challenged in recent decades. In *The Decline of Deference*,[56] Neil Nevitte agrees that Canadians are less deferential today than in the past. He attributes this to the post-materialist values of those born in the post–World War II era. **Post-materialism** attaches comparatively greater importance to human needs for belonging, self-esteem, and personal fulfillment than does **materialism**, which places greater stress on economic security and material well-being. Such issues as employment and incomes matter most to materialists, whereas post-materialists are likely to place higher value on so-called quality-of-life issues such as the environment, human rights, and group equality. Materialists are more likely than post-materialists to have confidence in public institutions and to trust the judgments of elites.

Nevitte shows that Canadians' confidence in government institutions, a category that included the armed forces, police, Parliament, and public service, declined during the 1980s and that high levels of confidence are much less likely to be expressed by those between the ages of 25–54 than among older citizens. He also finds that Canadians are, if anything, slightly more skeptical of government institutions than are Americans—not what one would expect to find if the traditional stereotype of deferential Canadians versus defiant Americans holds true.

The fact that Canadian data are not included in the latest rounds of the World Values Survey (2010–14 and 2015–19) or in the International Social Survey Program (ISSP) since 2004 deprives us of the ability to extend Nevitte's analysis to the present. With this caveat in mind, survey data from the 2004 ISSP Citizenship Survey and the 2005–9 wave of the World Values Survey suggest that, for the most part, Canadians and Americans are not particularly different when it comes to attitudes and behaviours towards the state. Figure 2.4 shows very little to no difference between the two populations in terms of citizens' confidence in government and in such behaviours as having contacted a politician or taken part in a demonstration. The differences, however, are more significant in regard to the belief that citizens should be involved in political decision-making, respect for authority, whether a good citizen is one who always obeys the laws, petition signing, and whether individual citizens have any influence on what government does. With the exception of petition signing, where Canadians are more likely to say that they have done this in the past year, Americans are more likely to respond in ways that suggest a greater willingness to challenge authority.

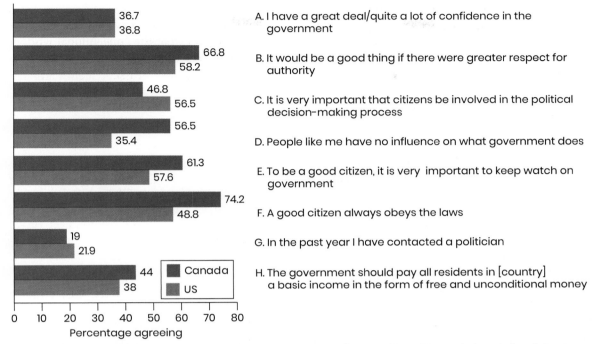

Figures (bar chart data):

- A. I have a great deal/quite a lot of confidence in the government — Canada 36.7, US 36.8
- B. It would be a good thing if there were greater respect for authority — Canada 66.8, US 58.2
- C. It is very important that citizens be involved in the political decision-making process — Canada 46.8, US 56.5
- D. People like me have no influence on what government does — Canada 56.5, US 35.4
- E. To be a good citizen, it is very important to keep watch on government — Canada 61.3, US 57.6
- F. A good citizen always obeys the laws — Canada 74.2, US 48.8
- G. In the past year I have contacted a politician — Canada 19, US 21.9
- H. The government should pay all residents in [country] a basic income in the form of free and unconditional money — Canada 44, US 38

Percentage agreeing

FIGURE 2.4 Attitudes towards Citizen–State Relations, Canada and the United States

Sources: The responses to questions A and B are based on World Values Survey data collected in 2006. The responses to questions C through G are based on data collected by the International Social Survey Program in 2004. Responses to question H are based on an international survey conducted by Ipsos Global Advisor in 2017.

Summing Up

We began this chapter with a discussion of the various forms that ideas take in political life. In particular, a distinction was made between ideology and political culture. The first involves a set of ideas about how society, politics, and economics work and how society should be organized. Liberalism, conservatism, and socialism have been the three most influential ideologies in Western democracies over the past couple of centuries. We saw that the meaning of each has evolved over time and that they continue to be useful in understanding political divisions and the manner in which issues are framed.

Political culture, by contrast, involves the norms, premises, beliefs, and attitudes held by the general population concerning political life. Our analysis of Canada's political culture began with an examination of various theoretical explanations of the origins and development of the political ideas of Canadians. These explanations have in common the fact that they attempt to explain Canada's political culture by comparing it to that of the United States. Canadians have always made such comparisons. Indeed, it is virtually impossible to say anything meaningful about a country's political culture without comparing it, even if implicitly, to some other society or societies, or some idealized model. In the case of Canada, comparison to the United States has always come naturally.

The analysis of the political ideas of Canadians was organized under four headings: community, freedom, equality, and citizen expectations for the state. We saw that the sense of community in Canada has been challenged over the years by Quebec separatism and by the demands of Indigenous peoples for a different and more autonomous relationship to the Canadian state. The analysis of ideas about freedom, equality, and expectations for the state compared Canada to the United States. We found that the historical image of Canada as a less freedom-oriented, less egalitarian, and more deferential society than that of the United States is no longer accurate. We also found that the contemporary Canadian self-image, which sees Canadians as being more attached to freedom and equality than their southern neighbours, is not as obvious as many believe. Instead, we found a mixed picture of two societies whose political cultures are similar in many ways and whose differences are not always what the conventional wisdom would lead us to expect.

Starting Points for Research

Katherine Fierlbeck, *Political Thought in Canada: An Intellectual History* (Toronto: University of Toronto Press, 2006). Explores political thought over the course of Canadian history, including the forces that have shaped the political ideas of Canadians.

Gad Horowitz, "The Deep Culture of Canadian Politics," *Inroads: The Canadian Journal of Opinion* (Winter/Spring 2017), http://inroadsjournal.ca/the-deep-culture-of-canadian-politics/. Horowitz's 1966 article, "*Conservatism, Liberalism and Socialism in Canada: An Interpretation*," was a seminal and contested analysis of Canadian political culture for decades. In this 2017 article he argues that his analysis of that culture is still relevant.

Philip Carl Salzman, "Yes, Canada Does Have a Culture," *Inside Policy: The Magazine of the Macdonald-Laurier Institute*, https://www.cbc.ca/radio/ideas/the-2018-cbc-massey-lectures-all-our-relations-1.4763007. A thought-provoking essay written by an internationally renowned anthropologist at McGill University.

David Thomas and David Biette, eds, *Canada and the United States: Differences That Count*, 4th edn (Toronto: University of Toronto Press, 2014). This collection includes many insightful essays on differences in Canadian and American values, behaviour, institutions, and policies, ranging from health care to crime.

Review Exercises

1. Where would you place each of the parties represented in the federal Parliament on a political ideology scale ranging from far left to far right? What are your criteria and how would you measure them? Where would you place the party that governs your province? Where would you place yourself?
2. Choose any three organizations from the following list. From the information included at their websites, decide whether each organization advocates mainly collectivist or mainly individualistic ideas. Explain whether and why, or why not, you think these organizations represent the ideas of significant numbers of Canadians.
    Fraser Institute: www.fraserinstitute.ca

    Centre for Social Justice: www.socialjustice.org
    Canadian Centre for Policy Alternatives: www.policyalternatives.ca
    Canadian Labour Congress: www.clc-ctc.ca
    Ecojustice Canada: www.ecojustice.ca
    Canadian Taxpayers Federation: https://www.taxpayer.com/en/
    Council of Canadians: www.canadians.org
3. Watch the CBC story "What Canadians Think of Americans," based largely on interviews at Ryerson University in Toronto: https://www.youtube.com/watch?v=P-u3o2hvdUg. Do you share the views of the students interviewed and some of the experts interviewed for this story? Why or why not?

Lobster traps in Josephine's Cove fishing harbour, Newfoundland. Fishing has long been an important industry for Canadians, both economically and culturally. More than one thousand communities across the country rely heavily on fishing as their primary business. Though less than 4 per cent of Canadians work in the fishing industry, Canada is one of the world's largest fish and seafood exporters, with the Arctic, Atlantic, and Pacific Oceans and Great Lakes giving Canadians a wide fishing diversity. (john t. fowler/Alamy Stock Photo)

3 The Social and Economic Setting

Politics unfolds against a backdrop of social and economic conditions. This chapter focuses on the following aspects of Canadian society:

- Material well-being
- Equality
- Quality of life

As Yogi Berra would have said, it was déjà vu all over again. In the weeks before the 2016 American presidential election, social media were abuzz with posts from American celebrities claiming that if Donald Trump won, they would be packing their bags and heading to Canada. Among them were Snoop Dogg, Miley Cyrus, Cher, and Samuel L. Jackson. Several years earlier, after President George W. Bush's 2004 re-election, many Canadians were gratified to read stories claiming that thousands of Americans were inquiring into the possibility of moving to Canada. This seemed to them to be the surest confirmation of their belief—a belief shared by most Canadians—that Canada is superior in important ways to the powerhouse to the south, the benchmark against which we always compare ourselves and our achievements. The Canadian self-image is one of compassion, tolerance, and prosperity. Canadians tend to see themselves as being more abundantly endowed with these qualities than Americans. Their neighbours may be richer, but most Canadians believe that their country's prosperity is more equally shared. And they believe that this is as it should be.

Canadians are indeed fortunate. But that good fortune is not shared by all Canadians. Roughly five million Canadians fall below what is conventionally called the "poverty line," the low-income point established by Statistics Canada and defined as individual or household earnings that are less than half the national median. In recent years, anti-globalization protesters, poverty activists, Indigenous people and their allies, and spokespersons for the homeless have all been critical of conditions in Canada and the performance of government in this country.

In this chapter we will examine the social and economic setting of Canadian politics. At various points comparisons will be made between Canada and other countries, between regions in Canada, between various points in Canada's history, and between actual conditions and some idealized standards that have been applied to the performance of Canada's political system. Our goal in this chapter is not, however, chiefly to judge. Instead, our main purpose is to understand the socio-economic context that influences, and is influenced by, politics and public policy. In doing so we will be selective, focusing on aspects of Canadian society and the economy that are closely associated with several values that most Canadians consider to be important.

Obviously, such values as material well-being, equality, and quality of life will be interpreted differently by different people. Disagreements aside, these values are of special importance for two related reasons. First, they represent public purposes that most of us expect governments to preserve or promote. Second, political controversies are frequently about one or more of these values—disagreements over how to achieve them; over what value(s) should give way, and by how much, when they conflict; about whether they are being adequately met; and so on. It makes sense, therefore, to focus on these dimensions of the social and economic setting of Canadian politics.

Political issues and outcomes are not determined in any simplistic manner by such things as the extent and nature of inequalities in Canadian society or the level of material well-being, any more than political ideologies and institutions translate directly into political behaviour and public policy. Like ideology and institutions, the social and economic settings of politics establish boundaries to political life. They do so by determining the sorts of problems a society faces, the resources available for coping with these problems, the nature and intensity of divisions within society, and the distribution of politically valuable resources between societal interests.

Material Well-Being

Canada is an affluent society. This simple fact is sometimes obscured by the news of layoffs, plant closings, slipping competitiveness, and pockets of poverty. For much of the late twentieth century, the average real purchasing power of Canadians was the second highest in the world, topped only by that of Americans. In the last couple of decades Canada has slipped significantly. As of 2017, 13 industrialized democracies ranked ahead of Canada in terms of average real purchasing power, or **purchasing power parities**.[1] This does not mean that Canadians have become, on average, poorer in any absolute sense. It means, rather, that other countries have grown richer more quickly and moved ahead of Canada.

On a global scale, however, Canadians remain relatively wealthy. Affluence affects both the opportunities and problems faced by policy-makers. The problem of poverty, for example, assumes a very different character in an affluent society like Canada from that in a poorer society like Mexico or a destitute one like Sudan. Not only does Canada's poverty problem look rather enviable from the standpoint of these other countries, but the means that governments in Canada have available to deal with this problem are far greater than those that can be deployed by the governments of poorer societies. The very definition of what constitute public problems, warranting the attention of government, is also influenced by a society's material conditions. Environmental pollution, a prominent issue on the public agendas of affluent societies, tends to be buried under the weight of other pressing social and economic problems in less affluent societies.

Within the elite club of affluent societies, cultural and institutional differences are probably more important as determinants of the public agenda and government response to them than country differences in material well-being. But the particular characteristics of a national economy, factors upon which material affluence depends, are significant influences on the politics and public policies of any society. These characteristics include the sectoral and regional distribution of economic activity, the level and distribution of employment, characteristics of a country's labour force, the profile of its trade with the rest of the world, and so on. Despite enjoying one of the highest standards of living in the world, Canadians have seldom been complacent about their affluence. Fears that Canada's material well-being may rest on fragile footings have long been expressed. They have mainly involved anxiety

over the outsourcing of jobs and the restructuring of the Canadian economy, anxiety that has been exacerbated by perceptions of globalization's impact on Canada, as well as worry that the country's economic prosperity may be too dependent on international demand for natural resources with little or no value-added processing or manufacture done in Canada.

The economy and unemployment are perennially towards the top of the issues Canadians identify as the most important facing the country. Indeed, since the global financial crisis of 2008 they have been the top two issues.[2] Compared to other advanced industrialized democracies, Canada has done fairly well when it comes to unemployment and job creation. Over the past 30 years the national level of unemployment has fluctuated between a low of just under 6 per cent (2018) and a high of 13 per cent (1983), averaging about 7–9 per cent during most of this period. In the United States, by comparison, the rate over this same period has fluctuated between a low of 4 per cent (2018) and a high of about 10 per cent (1983 and 2010), averaging about 6 per cent over the last three decades. The long-term unemployment rate in Canada (i.e., the percentage of the unemployed who have been out of work for at least 12 consecutive months) is about half the OECD average and one of the best in the world. The rate of job creation is directly related to the rate of growth in the economy. Since the mid-1990s, Canada has had the highest annual growth rate of any G7 economy, which has translated into the best record of job creation among this small group of leading capitalist economies.[3] Indeed, only Australia, which is not a member of the G7, has had a better rate of job growth among affluent democracies. Looking at the distribution of employment across sectors of the Canadian economy, one finds that Canada closely resembles the world's other major capitalist economies. Close to four-fifths of workers are in the service or tertiary sector (education, finance, insurance, hospitality, retail, health care, etc.) and about one-fifth are employed in industry (the primary and secondary sectors of farming, fishing, forestry, mining, and manufacturing and construction). These shares are broadly similar to those of our major trading partner, the United States, and those of other leading capitalist democracies.[4] Over time, the service sector's share of total employment has grown dramatically, from about 40 per cent in the mid-twentieth century to the current level of about 8 in 10 jobs. The shares in the primary and secondary sectors have obviously declined, more sharply in primary industries than in manufacturing. These employment trends have led many to worry that the Canadian economy is "deindustrializing." But Canada is not alone in experiencing such dramatic change. Broadly similar changes have occurred in all of the world's major capitalist economies over the last several decades.

The fact that manufacturing jobs are fewer, less secure, and, in many cases, lower-paying than they were in the past has caused much concern in Canada, as in the United States, France, and other wealthy societies whose prosperity, not so long ago, seemed to be based on this sector. Economists, however, are not in agreement on the question of whether a shrinking manufacturing sector and greater reliance on service-sector employment is necessarily a bad thing from the standpoint of incomes and general prosperity. Some, including Harvard economist Michael Spence, argue that globalization is directly responsible for a dearth of well-paying industrial jobs in the American and other Western economies. Others, including another Harvard economist, Robert Lawrence, and business writer Richard Katz, maintain that a shortage of jobs and flat incomes have much more to do with government policies and internal factors than with the outsourcing of jobs.[5] A consensus among serious economists today is that automation has been a much more significant factor contributing to the decline of manufacturing in developed economies than globalization.[6]

Fears over the export of low-skill manufacturing jobs have been replaced in more recent years by worries that more highly skilled jobs, including those requiring a good deal of education, have been moving abroad to some developing countries. Some of the work in computer programming, financial services, and even accounting and legal services has moved to India. An increasing share of the production of machine tools, dies, and moulds for manufacturing has relocated to China (although not without problems and certainly less than was feared a decade ago). These are more recent forms of **outsourcing**. Unlike the earlier movement of textile, footwear, and repetitive low-skill jobs to developing countries, some of these newer forms of outsourcing involve the loss of more highly skilled and highly paid jobs. Examples are easy enough to find, from the telephone call that you receive from India on behalf of a Canadian bank or other financial services company trying to sell you new products to the software design that contributed to the latest app you downloaded onto your phone.

These fears may be unfounded. Canada's job creation rate has been one of the best in the developed world for over a decade and virtually all labour economists project that as the country's population continues to age, the supply of workers, including those needed to fill highly skilled and well-paying jobs, will not meet the projected demand.[7] But even if it could be shown that outsourcing has and will continue to result in a hemorrhage of jobs, one could still make the case that sharing employment opportunities with people in less affluent parts of the world is preferable to providing them with foreign aid. If Canadians truly believe that the world's wealth should be shared more equally—which is what they regularly tell pollsters—then they should applaud the redistribution of economic activity from the rich countries of the world to those that aspire to a higher standard of living. But most do not.

Equality

Class can be an elusive concept. It is often operationalized on the basis of self-identity and measured by responses to surveys asking respondents whether they think of themselves as belonging to one or another class, as in lower, middle, or upper class. But it may also be thought of in terms of one's relationship to the means of production, the classic and rather *démodé* Marxist concept of class. Or it may be thought of in terms of values and aspirations. What is certain, however, is that for most of

Media Spotlight

BOX 3.1 Generation Jobless?

You are part of the first generation in modern times that will not do as well as their parents. You are more likely to have precarious employment throughout your lifetime. The market value of your university degree is not what it would have been in the past. Home ownership? Better forget that dream.

It would be surprising if you have not heard one or all of these claims, and heard them often. Indeed, they are repeated so often that they have almost become banal. "Generation Jobless" was the title of a 2013 CBC documentary that is fairly representative of this rather depressing genre of social analysis. Here is a summary of its analysis:

> There was a time when a university degree assured you of a good job, good pay and a comfortable life. Not anymore. Today, the unemployment rate for young people in this country is close to 15 per cent—double that of the general population. But the real crisis is the increasing number of university and college grads who are *underemployed*—scraping by on low-paid, part-time jobs that don't require a degree. Although there are no official statistics in Canada, it's estimated that after graduating, one in three 25 to 29 year olds with a college or university degree ends up in a low-skilled job. And to make things worse, 60 per cent graduate with an average debt of $27,000. Mired in debt, and working in dead end jobs, their launch into adulthood is being curtailed.[8]

"The New Underclass" was how a *Maclean's* article published at about the same time described this generation. "University Graduates Juggle Jobs of Varying Certainty" was the title of a *Globe and Mail* article published in 2016, and "Precarious Work and the Passage to Adulthood" was the theme of a 2017 article in *Policy Options*, the respected digital magazine published by the Institute for Research on Public Policy. In these and many other commentaries and analyses of the economic prospects of younger Canadians, the picture tends to be bleak.

The good news is that this analysis is wrong. In his direct response to the "Generation Jobless" documentary, but more generally to the conventional wisdom that it represented, Léo Charbonneau, editor of *University Affairs*, had this to say:

I *do* think it is tough for young adults entering the workforce right now, due partly to the lingering aftereffects of the world financial crisis of 2008. But this is not the first generation to graduate into a bum market—just ask those who graduated in the early 1980s or the early 1990s. In fact, the share of job losses among youths under age 25 was higher during both those past recessions compared to today.

On the other hand, it does seem, anecdotally, that the nature of employment is changing, with fewer of those coveted full-time, long-term, benefits-paying jobs of the type the previous generation took for granted. However, even if that is true, I doubt that would have anything to do with Canadians being overeducated or mis-educated. I would argue, in fact, that higher education is a buffer for individuals against those trends, providing them with a greater chance of meaningful long-term employment.[9]

Serious empirical studies support Charbonneau's much more optimistic assessment of the economic prospects for recent and future university graduates. A study by University of Ottawa economist Ross Finnie and his team concludes, "The data show that while the number of post-secondary graduates has grown in recent years, the benefits of a degree in terms of more stable employment and higher earnings have not diminished."[10] A 2018 study by the Pew Research Center in Washington, DC, concludes that, "After bottoming out in 2011, incomes are rising for American households—and those headed by a Millennial (someone age 22 to 37) now earn more than young adult households did at nearly any time in the past 50 years."[11]

Millennials making *more* than their parents? That's a headline that you probably haven't come across. Indeed, in all likelihood stories of how this generation's prospects are more dismal than those of their predecessors will continue to grab the headlines, just as they did in the early 1980s and early 1990s. They were wrong then and the data seem to indicate that they may be wrong now.

Canada's history, certainly during the era of industrialization and greater affluence that began in the 1950s, most Canadians have thought of themselves and their society as predominantly middle class. Moreover, they have not been inclined to think of classes, to the extent that they have thought of them at all, as being in some sort of antagonistic relationship.

Some believe that this has changed. A 2017 poll conducted by Ekos found that only 43 per cent of Canadians surveyed self-identified as middle class, barely more than the 37 per cent who self-identified as working class.[12] In 2002 Ekos had found that roughly 70 per cent of Canadians identified with the middle class. For many years now, and especially since the financial crisis of 2008, it has been common to read and hear headlines proclaiming that the Canadian middle class is shrinking, is already smaller than it was not so long ago, and is in jeopardy. Indeed, this was the main message of the Liberal Party of Canada's successful 2015 election campaign.

It is not obvious that this is true, or at least not in the unqualified and often apocalyptic manner in which this claim is often presented. First of all, not all surveys suggest that Canadians' predominantly middle-class self-image is a thing of the past. A 2017 Canada Project poll by *Maclean's* magazine, taken at about the same time as the Ekos poll, found that over 70 per cent of Canadians considered themselves to be middle class, and that 76 per cent of those outside of Ontario and 81 per cent of those not born in Canada self-identified as middle class.[13]

At the same time, however, Canadians are aware of and concerned by inequalities based on income. A 2017 Nanos poll found that 6 out of 10 Canadians said they were concerned by the gap between the rich and the poor in their country, a figure that rose to over four out of five when those who said they were somewhat concerned were included.[14] Surveys taken between 2008 and 2017 show that about half of all Canadians strongly agree with the statement, "Government should implement strong policies to reduce income inequality."[15] Perceptions aside, how great is income and wealth inequality in Canada, has inequality increased over time, and

what groups are most likely to experience lower incomes? Is the middle class smaller today than it was a generation ago? And are Canadians right to be as concerned about the state of the economy as polls perennially show them to be?

There is no doubt that income and wealth inequality are greater today than in the past. At the same time, the majority of Canadians on most rungs of the income ladder, with the exception of those at the bottom, are better off than was the case a generation ago. The data on change in real disposable income show growth for all groups except those with the lowest incomes. Those towards the top of the income ladder have experienced the greatest improvements in their income situation. The top 1 per cent of income earners, and even more so the among the top 0.1 per cent, have seen much greater increases in their incomes over time than have other groups. But it is not true that the middle class, defined here as those within the middle 60 per cent of the total income distribution, have experienced a decline in their incomes.[16]

In 2017 the top-earning 20 per cent of Canadian households accounted for about 41 per cent of all income, while the poorest one-fifth accounted for slightly less than 7 per cent.[17] These shares are not very different from what they were a couple of generations ago. In 1960, the bottom quintile of Canadians accounted for just over 4 per cent of all money income compared to about 41 per cent for the top fifth of income earners. The gap between the top and the bottom is somewhat larger if one looks at household wealth, which includes earnings but also home equity, savings, investments, etc. In 2017 the top 20 per cent of households accounted for 49 per cent of all wealth and the bottom 20 per cent for slightly less than 6 per cent. Despite the widespread belief that the Canadian middle class has experienced relative losses over the last decade or so, the data on the distribution of income do not support this assertion. The relative shares of both household income and wealth across quintiles were essentially unchanged over the period from 2010 to 2017.

The change over time looks a bit more dramatic if one focuses on the very wealthiest of Canadians. The top 1 per cent of tax filers accounted for just under 10 per cent of income in 1960 and just over 12 per cent in 2006, falling slightly to just over 11 per cent in 2015. Perspective is sometimes everything. Before World War II, the top 1 per cent of income earners in Canada accounted for about 18 per cent of income, a share that declined dramatically during the war and then more gradually in the following decades, reaching a low of about 8 per cent in the late 1970s. All of these figures include social transfers such as public pensions, social security payments, and employment insurance. State spending narrows the gap between those at the top and bottom of the income ladder from what it would be in the absence of redistributive policies. Government transfers account for roughly half of the income for the lowest 20 per cent of households and roughly one-quarter of all income for the second lowest quintile. At the same time, those at the top of the income ladder account for a greater share of government revenue. In 2015 the top 1 per cent of income earners—those who earned at least $232,400—paid 22.2 per cent of federal, provincial, and territorial income taxes, compared to 13.4 per cent in 1982.

In recent years, news stories and academic studies purporting to show a growing gap between the rich and the poor in Canada have contributed to a widespread belief that inequality has increased. It has, but probably not as much as or in the ways that most Canadians imagine. Most of the increase in inequality occurred during the decade of the 1990s. This trend has flattened in recent years. Both the increase in inequality and the more recent levelling off are due to the share of income going to the very wealthiest Canadians. If we look at the income shares of quintiles of the Canadian population or at the change in the Gini index of income inequality over time, the message that emerges is mainly one of stability. If, instead, we focus on the gap between those at the very top of the income and wealth ladder and the rest of Canadian society, the message appears rather different. At the same time, most Canadians are better off today than they were about 40 years ago.

Compared to the distribution of income in other advanced capitalist societies, Canada's is fairly typical. The distribution of income is more equal than in some countries, such as the United States and the United Kingdom, but less equal than in others, including France and the Scandinavian democracies (see Figure 3.2). Although surveys appear to show that Canadians are concerned about income inequality, such polls always include a prompt mentioning income inequality among other problems or matters that should be priorities for the government. When Canadians are not prompted in this manner, but are simply invited to identify a couple of areas they think ought to be priorities for the government, few mention inequality. A 2016 Nanos poll found that on an open-ended question regarding what Ottawa's two leading priorities ought to be in an upcoming budget, 73 per cent mentioned

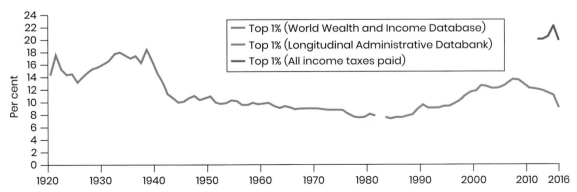

FIGURE 3.1 Income Share and Share of Income Taxes Paid by Top 1 Per Cent of Tax Filers, 1920–2016

Sources: Statistics Canada, "The Rise and Fall of Canada's Top Income Earners," https://www150.statcan.gc.ca/n1/pub/11-630-x/11-630-x2016009-eng.htm; Statistics Canada, "High Income Tax Filers in Canada," https://www150.statcan.gc.ca/t1/tbl1/en/tv.action?pid=1110005501.

health care as either number one or two, 59 per cent infrastructure, 18 per cent public safety, 13 per cent the military, and 11 per cent the economy and jobs. Other priorities, including closing the income gap, were mentioned by only very small numbers of respondents.[18]

The distribution of income is only part of the story in any assessment of equality. The other part involves the extent of poverty. Poverty is to some degree a relative concept, meaning something different in an advanced industrialized society like Canada than in a developing country like Nigeria. In Canada, poverty is usually measured using Statistics Canada's definition of what constitutes an income that is so low that an individual or household lives in "straitened circumstances." Statistics Canada's low-income cut-offs (LICOs) are generally referred to by the media, academics, politicians, and others as the **poverty line**. This low-income threshold, with some variation depending on family size, region of the country, and city (or rural) population, is reached by a household that spends over 20 per cent more of their annual family income on the basic necessities of living (food, clothing, and shelter) than does the national average household. To give an example of the variation due to different costs of living in different parts of

the country, the LICO for a four-person household in 2017 was estimated to be $39,701 in a metropolitan area with a population of more than 500,000 and $25,970 for such a household in rural Canada. Statistics Canada also reports data on poverty using other measures of low income, including its market basket measure and low-income measure.[19]

The term "poverty line" has become an established part of Canada's political vocabulary, evoking images of need and destitution in the minds of many if not most Canadians. There is, however, nothing magical or inevitable about the particular definition of "low income" used by Statistics Canada or any other agency or expert measuring poverty. Statistics Canada acknowledges the limitations of its low-income cut-offs. These limitations are that all poverty lines are relative and are not absolute measures of need or deprivation; and they are all arbitrary to some degree, based on value judgments about what constitutes poverty in a particular society.

Although the number of Canadians whose incomes fall below the poverty line varies from year to year, the figure has fluctuated over the past few decades between a high of about 16 per cent (1996) and a low of 9–10 per cent, being roughly 13 per cent in recent years. The likelihood of being poor is

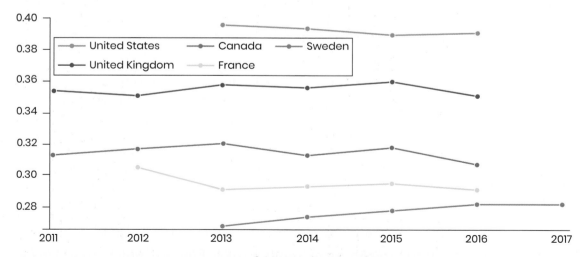

FIGURE 3.2 Distribution of Income (Gini Coefficient) in Selected Countries, 2011–17

Note: Gini coefficient: 0 = complete equality; 1 = complete inequality.

Source: Based on data at OECD Data, "Income Inequality," https://data.oecd.org/inequality/income-inequality.htm.

not, however, evenly distributed across the population. Rates of low income are significantly greater for some groups, being greatest among lone-parent families headed by females (44 per cent), those over the age of 65 living alone (34 per cent), and individuals living on their own (28 per cent). The poverty rate for Indigenous Canadians was about 24 per cent and just over 30 per cent for Indigenous children, which was slightly more than twice the rate for non-Indigenous children. All of these figures are for 2016, when the percentage of the entire population below the Statistics Canada LICO was 13 per cent.[20]

Although it is widely believed that the extent of poverty in Canada has grown over time, this is not the case. It is lower today for virtually all groups in the population than it was in the mid-1990s. The rate for children in single-parent families, one of the most vulnerable groups in the population, fell from almost 60 per cent in 1995 to about 30 per cent in 2014. For all children it fell from almost 20 per cent to 8.5 per cent over that same period. The rate for seniors fell from about 8 per cent to 4 per cent (although it is higher, at closer to 8 per cent, for single seniors). For women it fell from between 15–16 per cent to 8–9 per cent over this period. The percentage of the population falling below the LICO line for at least three of the previous six years fell from about 12 per cent between 1993 and 1998 to 6 per cent between 2005 and 2010.

Social assistance or welfare, as it is commonly referred to, is the principle income maintenance program for those who have exhausted other means of financial support. Although some of the money that pays for the program comes from Ottawa through transfer payments, each province administers its own program and therefore rules regarding eligibility, benefit levels, and categories of assistance vary between provinces. In every province, however, eligibility is subject to a means test that examines an applicant's income and assets. In no province does the value of social assistance reach the poverty line.

The Caledon Institute of Social Policy, which wound down in 2017, and, before it was disbanded by the federal government, the National Council on Welfare, tracked welfare incomes in relationship to the poverty line for decades. The Institute's 2017 report[21] shows that social assistance and related benefits (GST and PST credits, and additional benefits that may be available to some categories of social assistance recipients) fall far short of Statistics Canada's LICO and even farther below the agency's market basket income (MBI) measure of poverty. For example, in Ontario (2016), a single employable person would receive an income worth about 44 per cent of the LICO and the same percentage of the MBI. A couple with two children would receive social assistance payments worth about 75 per cent of the LICO and 70 per cent of the MBI. Although it is widely believed that social assistance payments have declined in real terms over time, this is not true. The same Caledon Institute study shows that in all provinces except Alberta and British Columbia the real value of social assistance increased between 1986 and 2016. In most provinces and for most recipient categories, the increases were quite small. The increases were greatest in Quebec.

Why are certain groups particularly susceptible to poverty? There is no single or simple answer. A few of the contributing causes are fairly clear, however. In the case of Indigenous people in Canada, prejudice has long played a role in explaining their higher jobless rate and lower incomes. Without suggesting that prejudice and its legacy no longer affect the economic circumstances and opportunities of Indigenous people in Canada, it is certain that systemic factors play a greater role in explaining the income gap between Indigenous people in Canada and non-Indigenous Canadians. One of these factors is education, which is strongly related to income. Indigenous people in Canada, and especially those living on reserves, tend to have lower levels of education than non-Indigenous Canadians. Only 40 per cent of Indigenous people living on reserves have completed high school, compared to about 60 per cent for those living off-reserve and close to 80 per cent for non-Indigenous Canadians. The employment rate among those living on reserves is only about 70 per cent that of Indigenous people living off-reserve in Canada and only about 60 per cent that of non-Indigenous Canadians. Those living on reserves have incomes that, on average, are about 60 per cent of what Indigenous people off-reserve make, and only

40 per cent of what non-Indigenous Canadians make. Close to 30 per cent of the income of those living on reserves involves government transfers of one sort or another, compared to just under 20 per cent for those living off-reserve and slightly more than 10 per cent for non-Indigenous Canadians. The conclusion is inescapable: a person who lives on a reserve is far more likely than one who does not, whether Indigenous or not, to be unemployed and poor. Of significance here is the geographic marginalization of Indigenous peoples set in motion by the Indian Act and the creation of the reserve system. Many people living on-reserve or in rural Indigenous settlements and northern communities simply do not have the employment opportunities of Canadians living in urban areas in southern Canada. According to Statistics Canada, less than 52 per cent of Indigenous people living within Canada in 2016 were located in urban areas, far below the more than 81 per cent of all Canadians who reside in urban areas.[22]

One of the important dimensions of equality, and one of the chief influences on it, is **socio-economic mobility**. This refers to the ability of individuals, families, and groups to move from one rung on the socio-economic ladder to another. Where socio-economic mobility is high, movement up and down the ladder is more common and the barriers to entry into high-paying occupations, prestigious status groups, or powerful elites are relatively low. This is what students of mobility call an open society. In a closed society there is relatively little intergenerational movement on the social ladder and barriers to entry into privileged social and economic groups are high.

Most Canadians believe that theirs is a relatively open society, and compared to most rich countries it is. Miles Corak has examined how closely sons' rankings on their society's income ladder are related to the earnings of their fathers.[23] He reports that intergenerational mobility in Canada is surpassed by that in only a small number of Scandinavian democracies, and then just marginally, but that it is greater than in such countries as Australia, Sweden, Germany, and France, and significantly greater than in Italy, the United Kingdom, and the United States. At the same time, most Canadians doubt that their children will grow up to be better off financially than they are, a view that a 2015 Pew Center survey found to be widespread across wealthy democracies. Their skepticism may prove to be well-founded, but in the meantime the empirical research suggests quite a lot of movement, both up and down the ladder. Corak observes that:

> Earnings mobility for children from the very broad middle—parents whose income ranges from the bottom 10 percent all the way to the cusp of the top 10 percent—is not tied strongly to family income. These children tend to move up or down the income distribution without regard to their starting point in life. This may be one element of insecurity among the middle class: in spite of their best efforts, their children may be as likely to lose ground and fall in the income distribution as they are to rise.[24]

So the good news is that upward economic mobility in Canada is reasonably high and intergenerational social mobility in Canada appears to be higher than in the United States, Great Britain, France, and most other wealthy democracies. Moreover, Canada does a better job than many other societies in terms of how quickly immigrants and their children are able to climb the socio-economic ladder. Smooth integration into the labour force often does not happen immediately, despite the fact that the Canadian economy has needed highly skilled immigrants for decades. Immigrants' job prospects and incomes do, however, improve over time, something that will be discussed at greater length in Chapter 4. Indeed, Statistics Canada observes that "[i]mmigrants who come to Canada as children achieve similar labour market outcomes as their Canadian-born counterparts."[25] For example, those who arrived between 1980 and 1991 and who were under 20 at the time of their arrival in Canada today have average earnings that are slightly higher than those of their Canadian-born counterparts. In addition to earning more, the sons and daughters of immigrants tend to be more educated than their Canadian-born counterparts, and are more likely to hold managerial or professional jobs. This is not true in such countries as France, the United Kingdom, Germany, and the Netherlands, where those who have been born in the country to immigrant parents continue to lag far behind the native-born in education and income.

Quality of Life

Canadians are happy and satisfied with their lives. Not all of them, of course, and not all of the time. But compared to populations across the world, Canadians regularly score towards the top of the table of countries in terms of self-reported happiness and satisfaction with their lives.[26] Moreover, when asked whether they would prefer to live elsewhere, only a small percentage of Canadians say yes. The high regard in which they hold life in Canada appears to be shared by others. Canada routinely places among the top countries in the world in international surveys asking respondents which country would be the best place to live and surveys of experts asked to rank countries according to various measures of the quality of life.[27] Gallup polls regularly find that, after the United States, Canada is generally the second or third most desired destination for potential emigrants worldwide.[28]

But Canada's high standard of living and enviable **quality of life** (QOL) are not shared by everyone. Some segments of the population, as we have seen in this chapter, are more likely than others to experience conditions that may undermine QOL. In some cases government policies are blamed for having caused or contributed to a QOL problem. For example, Indigenous groups and those sympathetic to their demands argue that the appallingly bad QOL experienced by many Indigenous Canadians is due to unjust and discriminatory policies. Perhaps surprisingly—and this might alert us to the limitations of survey results as a measure of QOL—Indigenous Canadians also express high levels of satisfaction with their lives, not very different from those of the general population.[29]

The fact that people report being happy and satisfied with their lives needs to be taken seriously. But so, too, should objective measures of the health and living conditions that they experience and that need to be taken into account in any serious assessment of the QOL. Organizations that measure QOL, including the Conference Board in the case of Canada and the OECD for its member states, include a wide range of such measures.[30] We will focus on mortality, crime, suicide, drug addiction, and destitution.

Compared to other advanced industrialized societies, Canada does relatively well on all of these measures. Average life expectancy is about 82 years, 11 years longer than it was in 1961, at about 80 years for males and 84 years for females. This is above the average for OECD countries, being somewhat lower than in such countries as Japan, Sweden, and Spain, but higher than in the United States, the United Kingdom, and Germany. At about 10.5 per cent of GDP spent on health care, Canada is about average for the wealthier members of the OECD. There is, however, little evidence of a correlation between life expectancy and spending on health care among these countries. The United States and Germany both spend a considerably greater share of GDP on health care without having longer life expectancies than in some wealthy countries that spend considerably less. Among wealthy members of the OECD, France, Japan, Italy, and Spain all spend less on health care than does Canada but have longer life expectancies. The elderly tend to consume more health-care services than younger cohorts of the population, so one might imagine that differences in the age profiles of these countries explain much of the differences in the level of health-care spending. This is not the case. Japan, France, Italy, and Spain all have older populations than Canada and all spend less on health care.[31]

Another indicator often used to account for quality of life is health-adjusted life expectancy, or HALE. This represents the average number of years a person can expect to live in good health. Instead of considering all years of life as equal, as in the conventional life expectancy indicator, HALE weights years of life according to health status. HALE is calculated by subtracting from life expectancy the average number of years in ill-health weighted for severity of the health problem. In 2016, the most recent year for which HALE data are available, the average number of years that Canadians could expect to live in full health was slightly more than

70. The countries where people stay healthiest the longest are Sweden, at almost 75 years, and Japan at almost 74 years.[32]

In terms of violent crime, Canada is unexceptional. Canada's homicide rate is 1.4 per 100,000 population, compared to rates of well under one per 100,000 in many European countries and to a rate of about five per 100,000 in the United States (2016). Although rates vary marginally from year to year, the statistics certainly do not support the popular assumption that murders have become more common. Canada's homicide rate is actually about half of what it was two decades ago.[33]

Differences between countries in reporting procedures make it difficult to compare rates of violent and non-violent crimes across countries. Culture is also a factor, particularly in the case of sexual offences where the reported number is generally much lower than the actual number of offences because of reluctance on the part of victims to come forward. Victimization surveys, while they have their own limitations, may sometimes provide a more reliable picture of the real extent of crime. Unfortunately, what was perhaps the most reliable international comparison of crime statistics, the International Crime Victim Survey, has not been updated since it reported data for the period 1989–2005.[34] A 2012 survey found that 13 per cent of Canadians and 12 per cent of Americans said they had been the victim of a crime during the previous year. That same survey found that Canadians and Americans are also about as likely to feel safe in their neighbourhoods, 35 per cent of Canadians and 40 per cent of Americans saying that they felt very safe.[35]

Notwithstanding widespread belief to the contrary, probably born of the "if it bleeds, it leads" approach taken by much news reporting, crime has fallen across virtually all categories of offences since the 1990s.[36] Although the overall crime rate has levelled off and even increased marginally in the last few years (see Figure 3.3), it is still much lower than it was in previous decades. According to one study, however, the rather sharp decline in crime in Canada over the last generation has not been accompanied by less spending on those state activities linked to criminal behaviour. On the contrary, these costs appear to have increased significantly.[37]

Suicide, Drugs, and Alcohol

Suicide and drug abuse are social pathologies that are symptomatic of a low QOL. Suicide is the ninth leading cause of death among Canadians and the second leading cause of death among young adults,

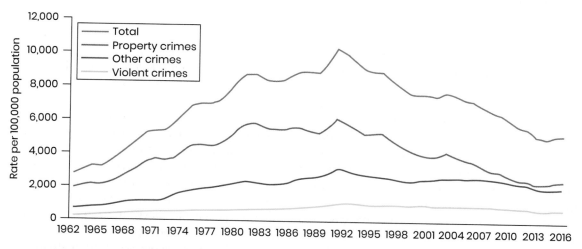

FIGURE 3.3 Police-Reported Crime Rates in Canada, 1962–2016

Source: Statistics Canada, "Police-Reported Crime Statistics in Canada, 2016," 24 July 2017, Chart 3: https://www150.statcan.gc.ca/n1/pub/85-002-x/2017001/article/54842-eng.htm.

The Social Fabric

BOX 3.2 Why Are Danes the Happiest People in the World?

In April of 2012 the United Nations held the Conference on Happiness, which commissioned the *World Happiness Report*. Every year since then Danes are either at the top or within the top three in self-reported happiness. Denmark has been ranked the happiest country by the annual Eurobarometer survey almost every year since 1973. What is the secret to the Danes' happiness?

The answers vary. Harvard economist Jeffrey Sachs, one of the editors of the annual *World Happiness Report*, says that happiness is produced by a combination of factors. "Political freedom, strong social networks and an absence of corruption," he writes, "are together more important than income in explaining well-being differences. . . . At the individual level, good mental and physical health, someone to count on, job security and stable families are crucial." Political scientist Ronald Ingelhart, director of the World Values Survey, answers the question a bit differently, arguing that Denmark's secret involves a combination of prosperity, democracy, and high levels of social tolerance. Philip Greenspun, a computer science professor at MIT, suggests that one of the key factors is lower material expectations and less of a keeping-up-with-the-Joneses mentality of the sort that characterizes

societies where conspicuous consumption leads to greater competitiveness and anxiety.[38]

Before we conclude that the Danes have discovered something we all need to emulate, keep in mind that the populations of countries quite different from Denmark that don't have much in the way of a welfare state or job security, and where political freedom may not be particularly impressive and corruption is common, also score very high in terms of happiness. Mexicans and Colombians always finish towards the top of surveys of national happiness, and neither of these countries has these attributes. It seems, therefore, that there are different pathways to national happiness.

Finally, it may be worth noting that alcohol consumption and abuse, including among teenagers, are higher in Denmark than in most of its European neighbours. Close to half of all Danish marriages end in divorce (a fact that some point to as positively related to happiness, because divorce is very easy and inexpensive in Denmark and females find it easier than in many other countries to combine work and single parenthood). The country's leading film director, Lars von Trier, is a self-confessed depressive whose *oeuvre*, whatever its artistic merits, is quite disturbing. Perhaps, after all, something is rotten in the state of Denmark!

---

ages 15–34, after accidents and unintentional injuries.[39] As in other countries, the rate of successful suicide is considerably higher among men than women, at about 18 per 100,000 population for men compared to 6 per 100,000 for women. There is enormous international variation even when levels of national wealth are controlled for, suggesting that suicide is more closely related to culture than level of economic development. For example, Mexico's rate is about 5 per 100,000, Italy and the United Kingdom have rates of about 6 and 10 per 100,000, respectively, while Japan (20 per 100,000) and South Korea (about 30 per 100,000) have among the highest rates. Canada's rate of

about 12 per 100,000 falls in the middle for affluent democracies.

Although there is some variation between provincial suicide rates, what stands out is the much higher rate in Nunavut. If Nunavut were a country, its suicide rate of about 65 per 100,000 would place it well above such countries as Lithuania, South Korea, Japan, and Russia, which have among the highest rates in the world. Across Canada, Indigenous people have much higher suicide rates than the non-Indigenous Canadian population. The rates are about six times higher among Indigenous persons ages 15–24 compared to those for non-Indigenous Canadians in this age cohort.[40]

The Social Fabric

BOX 3.3 Is Loneliness a Public Health Problem?

In early 2018 British Prime Minister Theresa May appointed a Minister for Loneliness. The appointment raised some eyebrows and was the occasion for some jokes. But the circumstances that prompted this appointment are serious and the consequences of loneliness, or social isolation as it is more likely to be called in the scientific literature, have been known for some time. A recent article in *Scientific American* cites a Harvard study that has followed people over a period of 75 years and finds "the quality of people's relationships as the single clearest predictor of their physical health, longevity and quality of life."[41] Social isolation is identified by the study as a major contributor to the quality of these relationships. Psychology professor Julianne Holt-Lunstad agrees, arguing that the physical and emotional damage from loneliness is even worse than obesity or being sedentary.[42] A recent review of the scientific literature on the health consequences of social isolation arrives at this conclusion: "The findings support the view that loneliness poses a significant health problem for a sizeable part of the population with increased risks in terms of distress (depression, anxiety), suicidal ideation, health behavior and health care utilization."[43]

As in many other countries, it appears that an increasing number of Canadians experience social isolation. Simon Fraser University's Andrew Wister, one of Canada's foremost experts on social isolation, says that about one in five Canadians experiences loneliness.

Seniors are more likely than other Canadians to have intense feelings of loneliness, but as more and more Canadians live on their own—close to 30 per cent of Canadian households currently consist of one person, up from about 20 per cent 40 years ago, and the number is expected to continue to rise—the problem of loneliness may become more widespread in younger cohorts of the population. A 2016 survey of 43,000 Canadian university students found that two-thirds of them reported feeling very lonely at some point over the past year. Why is this the case? Some attribute it to digital technologies that, while promising unprecedented connectivity, are said to reduce non-virtual forms of human contact that are important for our well-being.[44] Others, including psychologist Bruce Alexander in *The Globalization of Addiction*, blame modern globalizing free market societies. Alexander writes: "[P]eople around the world are being torn from the close ties to family, culture, and traditional spirituality that constituted the normal fabric of life in pre-modern times. This kind of global society subjects people to unrelenting pressures towards individualism and competition, dislocating them from social life."[45]

What do you think? Is it Alexa, Instagram, and ATMs, or globalized capitalism and the cultural and social changes that have accompanied it? Or is it something else? Or perhaps we were always lonely—some of us most of the time, and even more of us some of the time—and we just didn't think of it as a public health problem.

Estimating alcohol and other forms of drug abuse is difficult, but a high level of drug use in a population carries high personal and social costs. In the case of alcohol, the most consumed drug in Canada and other affluent democracies, how much is judged to be too much from the standpoint of one's health differs widely across jurisdictions and according to experts. A study published in 2018 in the highly respected scientific journal *The Lancet* placed the acceptable number of drinks per week at 10.[46] Some countries in Europe recommend a maximum consumption level of 3–4 drinks per day. Guidelines for low-risk consumption set by the Canadian government in co-operation with the provinces are 10 drinks per week for women and 15 for men. According to a 2015 survey, about 20 per cent of the Canadian population exceed these limits, including about one-quarter of 18–24-year-olds.[47] Rates of heavy drinking, as defined by the Health Canada guidelines, and reported hospitalizations

The epidemic of suicide in Nunavut, particularly among young people, is a complex issue with roots in Canada's residential school system, the economic deprivation of northern communities, and ongoing colonialism. Here, students from the Nunavut Sivuniksavut program raise awareness of this epidemic by marking World Suicide Prevention Day with a Celebration of Life on Parliament Hill.

due entirely to alcohol are highest in the Canadian territories.

Hospitalizations due to alcohol represent an obvious cost both to the person suffering from excessive alcohol consumption and to the society that pays all or part of the costs for his or her treatment. We may also assume that there are costs to the economy such as work absenteeism and lost productivity, as well as financial costs to families. There are also insurance and law enforcement and justice system costs related to behaviours that may be linked to alcohol consumption. In addition, of course, family members and the victims of alcohol-driven behaviour experience various other social and physical costs, including injury or deaths resulting from drunken rages or drunk driving. The Canadian Institute for Health Information is one among many organizations that has attempted to estimate the costs of excessive consumption of alcohol.[48]

Without in any way defending alcohol abuse, it must be said that estimates of the economic costs of alcohol consumption typically ignore or grossly understate the value of tax revenues received by governments, jobs created, and other "benefits" associated with the production, distribution, and consumption of alcohol. The same may be said of tobacco. In fact, however, rather serious and persuasive cost–benefit analyses of these industries purport to show that the economic benefits outweigh the economic costs associated with these drugs.[49] Of course, this does not mean that the social and human costs of their use should not cause people and their governments to regulate these industries and even discourage consumption. It is simply to say that when one hears an argument that rests entirely on economic grounds, skepticism may be warranted.

Falling through the Cracks

Advanced industrial societies all have in place a "safety net" of social programs intended to protect individuals and households from destitution. Nevertheless, some people fall between the cracks.

When the safety net fails to catch a significant number of those who, for one reason or another, cannot make ends meet, this is surely an indication that the QOL experienced by some people falls below acceptable standards of human decency.

Homelessness and the demands placed on food banks are two indicators of holes in the social safety net. The extent of homelessness is difficult to pin down for the obvious reason that the homeless, unlike those who have a fixed address, cannot easily be enumerated, telephoned, or otherwise kept track of with any accuracy. Statistics Canada's first attempt to count the homeless came up with the implausibly low figure of 14,145, based on the number of people nationwide sleeping in emergency shelters the night of 15 May 2001. The 2008 Senate report *Poverty, Housing and Homelessness* acknowledged the difficulties and did not even

THE CANADIAN PRESS/Frank Gunn

For years the Gardiner Expressway has provided shelter for the homeless residents of these makeshift camps. In March 2019, the city of Toronto served residents with notices to leave and began to demolish the camps, citing safety concerns. With shelters at capacity and one of the most expensive rental markets in Canada, it remains unclear how Toronto will address its growing issue of homelessness and affordable housing going forward.

attempt to attach a number to this problem. A 2016 report of the Canadian Observatory on Homelessness estimates that about 235,000 persons use homeless shelters each year, a number that does not include street people who do not use shelters or those who use some other shelter such as women's shelters, but this total does include the "hidden homeless" who stay with friends or family or who perhaps live in their cars when they have nowhere else to go.[50]

The Canadian government's *National Shelter Study 2005–2014* arrives at somewhat different numbers. It finds that the number of unique individuals who used shelters in 2014 was about 147,000 and that the number of occupied shelter beds that year was 5,057,813. Some individuals used shelters for many more than a single night. Moreover, the study found that the number of shelter users was down from about one in 207 Canadians in 2005 to one in 260 Canadians in 2014. "Demand for shelter beds has increased due to longer stays," the report states, "especially by families and people aged 50 and over.[51] The study also found that less than 2 per cent of all individuals who used a shelter during the 10 years covered by the study used a shelter at some point in every one of those years. Whatever the precise numbers happen to be is obviously less important than the fact that a significant demand for shelter exists across the country, and this is most visible and acute in such metropolitan areas as Toronto and

The Social Fabric

BOX 3.4 Vancouver Counts Its Homeless

In March of 2018 Vancouver did what cities across Canada and elsewhere do from time to time. It attempted to get a clearer picture of how many people are homeless and the characteristics of this destitute segment of the city's population. The two-day count found 2,181 homeless persons, 659 of whom were living on the street and 1,522 in shelters. Here are some of findings that emerged from the homeless count, as reported by the CBC:

- The homeless in Vancouver comprised 0.3 per cent of the city's total population.
- Seventy-eight per cent of those counted were living in Vancouver when they became homeless and over half had been homeless for less than a year.
- Indigenous people represented about 40 per cent of those counted, but only 2.2 per cent of Vancouver's total population.
- Thirty-five per cent of homeless people said they had no addictions, 28 per cent said they were addicted to cigarettes, and 25 per cent said they were addicted to opioids.

- Thirty-eight per cent said they were on income assistance, 29 per cent received disability benefits, and 20 per cent were employed.
- Forty-four per cent said they had some sort of medical condition or illness, 43 per cent had a mental health issue, and 38 per cent had a physical disability.[52]

Low incomes and unaffordable housing are commonly cited as the chief causes of homelessness. Matters are not this simple. Various studies have pointed to addiction as either the number-one cause or among the top three factors contributing to homelessness in cities across Canada. Family conflict, domestic abuse, and having spent time in jail are among the other contributing factors regularly identified in surveys of the homeless. Of course, some of these factors may also contribute to the likelihood of having a low income, or it may be that chronically straitened economic circumstances may increase the likelihood of experiencing one or more of these non-economic conditions. In any event, the problem of homeless is complicated and the solution is not simply increasing the number of shelters and beds, although this is often a good start.

Vancouver where rising prices have increased the pressure on the stock of affordable housing.

Like homelessness, the growing need for and use of food banks reflect the precarious living circumstances of many Canadians. Food Banks Canada estimates that in a typical month in 2016 almost 900,000 persons used food banks. Some individuals and some families use more than one food bank during a month. Food bank policies regarding how often a person or family may use their services, whether and what income requirements are imposed, and whether people need to register in order to use the food bank's services vary a good deal. These factors make the calculation of how many separate individuals use food banks during any given period an imprecise science, but if the Food Banks Canada estimate is reasonably accurate, then close to 3 per cent of the Canadian population rely on this charitable service. The number of food bank users appears to have increased over the period from 2005 to 2016.

Single-person households accounted for close to half of all food bank users, but represent only about 30 per cent of Canadians. The percentage of food bank users who are Indigenous is about four times their share of the Canadian population.[53]

Summing Up

Homelessness, food banks, and the gap between social assistance and the cost of making ends meet, discussed earlier in this chapter, all focus our attention on neediness and suggest that Canada faces challenges in providing opportunity for and taking care of those at the lower end of the income scale. This is certainly true. It is also true, however, that most Canadians, on the whole, are better off today than they were a generation ago or even just 10 years ago. The distribution of income and wealth are more unequal today than in the past, but this is almost entirely due to the disproportionate gains made by those at the top of the income/wealth ladder and not due to an absolute decline in the incomes of those lower on the socio-economic ladder, nor is this a result of a shrinking middle class.

The OECD's Better Life Index and other international rankings of this sort regularly rank Canada among the countries in the world where the QOL is highest. Its most recent annual report concludes that "Canada ranks above the average in housing, subjective well-being, personal security, health status, social connections, environmental quality, jobs and earnings, education and skills."[54] None of this, however, provides grounds for complacency. Indeed, one of the greatest failings of public policy in Canada involves the persistence of poverty and serious social pathologies among certain more vulnerable groups in the population. Foremost among these groups are Indigenous Canadians. Their circumstances and the politics and policies associated with Indigenous people living within Canada will be examined in Chapter 16.

Starting Points for Research

Conference Board of Canada, *How Canada Performs,* www.conferenceboard.ca/hcp/default.aspx. A report card on a wide range of social and economic indicators. It was last updated in 2019.

Miles Corak, "Canada's Official Poverty Line: What Is It? How Could It Be Better?" 21 Aug. 2018, https://milescorak.com/2018/08/21/canadas-official-poverty-line-what-is-it-how-could-it-be-better/. A stimulating discussion of poverty and its measurement by one of Canada's foremost researchers on inequality.

Julie McMullin and Josh Curtis, *Understanding Social Inequality: Intersections of Class, Age, Gender, Ethnicity, and Race in Canada,* 3rd edn (Toronto: Oxford University Press, 2016). A widely used textbook that explores the complex relationships among various dimensions of inequality in Canada.

Social Progress Imperative, "Social Progress Index," **https://www.socialprogress.org/index/global/** **results.** The Social Progress Index score includes three broad dimensions: basic human needs, foundations of well-being, and opportunity, each of which in turn includes several measures. The Index provides the basis for interesting comparisons between Canada and other countries.

Statistics Canada, www.statcan.gc.ca/start-debut- **eng.html.** Springboard to census and National Household Survey data on various characteristics of Canadian society. Click on headings found under "Browse by subject."

Review Exercises

1. What are the characteristics of the richest 1 per cent of the Canadian population? You may want to start with the information at: https://www.theglobeandmail.com/news/canada-1-per-cent-highest-paid-workers-compare/article36383159/. To what degree do gender, class background, education, and ethnicity affect the likelihood of getting into the top 1 per cent?

2. How many homeless people are in your community, and how many people in your community regularly rely on food banks? How would you go about finding answers to these questions? (Suggestions: Call a member of your city or town council and ask for the names of persons or organizations that operate food banks and shelters. Alternatively, you might call your local office of the United Way or a religious organization like the Salvation Army to ask about these matters.)

3. How would you define poverty? Calculate a monthly budget for a single person—including expenditures for food, shelter, clothing, transportation, and entertainment—that you think is the minimum necessary to ensure a decent standard of living. What annual income is necessary to maintain this standard of living? Ask two friends or family members to do the same exercise (don't give them any hints about your own calculations) and compare your estimates.

4. On 28 April 2014, Pope Francis tweeted, "Inequality is the root of social evil." Thinking about Canada, do you agree? Why or why not?

Torontonians stand outside the US Consulate to protest Donald Trump's signing of Executive Order 13769, popularly known as his "Muslim ban." While the rise of isolationist politics in North America and Europe has emboldened some to express xenophobic ideas publicly, many continue to view multiculturalism and diversity as Canada's key strengths. As Canadian society continues to become more diverse, there is a need to reflect the experiences and issues of all Canadians in public institutions such as schools and the political arena nationwide. (arindambanerjee/Shutterstock)

4 Diversity and Multiculturalism

Diversity is both a part of the social reality of Canada and one of the leading values associated with Canadian politics. In this chapter we examine the politics of diversity in Canada, paying special attention to issues of multiculturalism and equality. Topics include the following:

- The changing ethnic character of Canadian society
- Increased awareness of diversity
- The institutionalization of diversity
- The political representation of ethnic groups
- Other models of integration and accommodation
- The economic integration of immigrants

Over the last 40 years respect for diversity has joined equality and freedom as one of the core values of Canadian politics. Indeed, many would go so far as to say that it has become *the* pre-eminent Canadian cultural trait, the quality that more than any other defines Canada and how our society and political life are different from those of other countries, but particularly from the United States. As long ago as 1979, Progressive Conservative Party leader Joe Clark described Canada as "a community of communities."[1] His characterization of the country was greeted with quite a lot of criticism, including from Pierre Trudeau, who was then prime minister and Clark's chief opponent in the 1979 election campaign. The current prime minister, Justin Trudeau, is on a rather different wavelength from his father. He has often stated that diversity and inclusiveness are Canada's two major values.[2] Canadians, we are routinely told, are united by their differences. This claim appears to be at least paradoxical and possibly even contradictory. What it means, however, is that tolerance, respect, the recognition of group rights, and a belief in the equal dignity of different cultures are central to the Canadian ethos. Indeed, the very idea of such a thing as a Canadian ethos is comparatively recent, emerging at the same time as this image of Canada as the pluralistic society par excellence and a model of cultural coexistence.

This image of Canada is not without its ironies and skeptics. Foremost among the ironies is the fact that separatist sentiment in Quebec—support for which is far from extinguished—challenges this rosy picture of Canada as a model of cultural coexistence. On the skeptical side, many people maintain that the diversity-centred image of Canada, and policies and institutions based on it, do more to undermine Canadian unity than strengthen it. While most Canadians avow support for multiculturalism in principle, evidence suggests that many of them also harbour doubts about how it has worked in practice.

Ironies and skepticism aside, there is no denying that the politics of diversity has moved to the centre of Canada's political stage in recent decades. The evidence ranges from official recognition of multiculturalism in the law and under the Constitution to occasional controversy over the accommodation of cultural practices that many Canadians may find unfamiliar and that some find objectionable. While diversity is nothing new in Canada, the idea that it should be recognized, protected, and even promoted through the actions and institutions of the state has existed for only the last couple of generations.

In this chapter we will look at the politics of diversity and the policy of multiculturalism in Canada. The issues that will be considered include the following:

- how Canada's population characteristics have changed over time;
- the ways in which diversity politics has been institutionalized in state institutions and policies;
- controversies associated with the Canadian multicultural experience and comparisons to policies in other pluralist democracies.

From Founding Nations to Multiculturalism: The Changing Ethnic Demography of Canada

The Canada we know today was built on two premises: the displacement and marginalization of Indigenous peoples and the settlement and development of the land by European immigrants. Not only were the vast majority of the immigrants who settled in Canada during the country's formative years European, they were overwhelmingly of French and British Isles origins. Many of the latter came to Canada via the United States in the wave of Loyalists and non-Loyalists who left America during the three decades after the War of Independence. The languages these immigrants established in Canada were mainly French and English. With very few exceptions their religion was Christian, either Roman Catholic or Protestant. For much of Canada's history they would be referred to without hesitation as the founding nations or *charter groups*, the founding partners in the Canadian enterprise. One was French-speaking and Catholic and the other English-speaking and primarily Protestant.

British emigrants gather on the deck of a boat preparing to leave Liverpool for Canada in 1925. After declining during World War I, immigration to Canada increased in the 1920s as the economic situation in Europe worsened.

At the time of Confederation the virtual monopoly of those of French and British ancestry on Canadian public life was symbolized in the partnership of John A. Macdonald, the leading English-Canadian advocate of an independent Canada, and George-Étienne Cartier, the major spokesperson for French Canada. The first Canadian government under Macdonald did not include anyone who was *not* a member of these so-called charter groups (not to be confused with today's Charter groups!). This image of Canada as a partnership—albeit an unequal one—of two European charter groups survived well into the twentieth century. It was not until the 1960s and, more specifically, the work of the Royal Commission on Bilingualism and Biculturalism (the B&B Commission) that the two-nations image of Canada experienced any serious competition. Spokespersons for non-French and

non-British groups in Canada argued that this image of Canada and the policies based on it excluded them from the Canadian picture. These groups, in the main, also represented Canadians of European origin. Ukrainian spokespersons, for example, were prominent among those who were critical of the two-nations, bicultural image of Canada. The demands of these dissenting groups stopped well short of equality of status with English and French for their groups and languages. What they demanded and won was that the bicultural image of Canada be replaced by official recognition of Canada as a *multicultural society*. This was achieved through the 1971 passage of the Multiculturalism Act and the creation of a new federal Ministry of State for Multiculturalism. Today, the role and responsibilities that began in 1971 fall under the rubric of the Department of Canadian Heritage.

The image of Canada as a sort of New World extension of two European peoples and their value systems came under challenge from some Canadian intellectuals during the 1960s. John Porter's influential book *The Vertical Mosaic*[3] drew attention to the stratified nature of Canada's pluralistic society, in which English Canadians dominated virtually all of the important elites and controlled the channels of recruitment into them. The picture he painted was of a Canada in which influence, status, and wealth were held disproportionately in the hands of one of Canada's two charter groups and where the members of other groups were largely blocked from access to the opportunities monopolized by Anglo-Canadians. This situation of a **corporate elite**, Porter argued, was inconsistent with the democratic values of openness, socio-economic mobility, and equality preached by Canadian politicians and believed in by the general population. His analysis of the systemic inequality and discrimination that characterized Canadian society would provide much of the inspiration for a generation of social critics who, unlike their predecessors, did not take for granted the domination of the British charter group and the exclusion of increasing numbers of Canadians who were not of French or British Isles ancestry from what was essentially a bicultural image of Canada.

The challenges launched by intellectual critics such as Porter and by the groups that wanted the biculturalism in the B&B Commission to be replaced with multiculturalism would not have had much of an audience or impact had it not been for the changes to Canada's population characteristics that were well underway by the 1960s. These demographic changes have accelerated since then, as the share of Canada's population with neither French nor British Isles ethnic origins has increased dramatically. Immigrants from Eastern and Southern Europe became increasingly important within Canada's overall immigration picture between the 1950s and 1970s. They have been joined in recent decades by increasing numbers of non-European immigrants, many of whom come from non-Christian cultures.

The 1871 census, Canada's first, reported that 61 per cent of the population was of British Isles ancestry, 31 per cent of French ancestry, and only 8 per cent of other ancestries, mainly other European countries of origin and Indigenous Canadians (3 per cent). The 1971 census found that the non-French and non-British European ancestry share of the population had increased significantly to over one-fifth of the population. Those of British and French ancestry continued to dominate, however, at 44 per cent and 29 per cent of the population, respectively. The ethnic ancestry picture painted by the census is now much more complicated, but also more realistic because of the fact that since 1981 Canadians are able to report multiple ancestries. In 1991, about 29 per cent of Canadians reported multiple ancestries, increasing to 41 per cent in 2016. About one-third of all Canadians claim British Isles origins as at least one of their ancestries. The proportion claiming French ancestry has fallen to only about one in seven Canadians, a much lower figure than the percentage of those who have French as their mother tongue. This may be explained by the fact that some French Canadians, and indeed many Canadians, give simply "Canadian" as their ethnic origin. Indeed, roughly 20 per cent of respondents to the 2016 census gave "Canadian" as their only ethnic ancestry and about one-third gave "Canadian" and one or more other ancestries. About 17 per cent of Canadians claim an Asian ancestry, alone or in combination with some other ethnic origin.[4]

The changes in Canada's ethnic demography are seen most strikingly in the largest metropolitan areas, magnets for immigrants. It is here where most new Canadians of neither British nor French ethnic origins have settled and where the **visible minority** population has increased significantly in recent decades (see Figure 4.1). The 2016 census found that visible minorities comprise about 22 per cent of the Canadian population. In Toronto the percentage was 51 per cent, in Vancouver 50 per cent, in Ottawa 25 per cent, in Montreal 22 per cent. In every case the figure was significantly higher than a couple of decades ago. Change in the ethnic distribution of Canada's population has been brought about by shifting patterns of immigration. For most of Canada's history the major sources of immigration were Europe and the United States. In recent

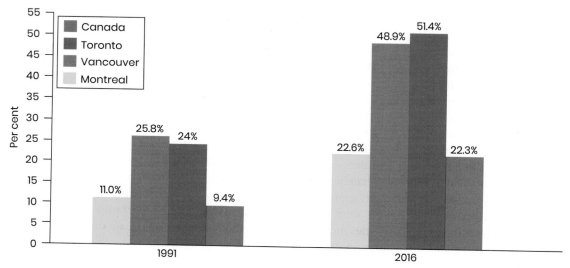

FIGURE 4.1 Visible Minorities in Canada and in Main Metropolitan Areas, 1991 and 2016

Sources: Statistics Canada, *Canada's Ethnocultural Portrait: The Changing Mosaic*, Catalogue no.96F0030XIE2001008; Statistics Canada, Data Tables, 2016 Census.

decades the leading sources of immigration have been Asian countries, including China, Pakistan, India, and the Philippines (Statistics Canada includes the Middle East under Asian immigration). Immigration from Africa, the Caribbean, and Latin America also has comprised a much greater share of total immigration than was the case before the 1970s. Whereas just under 95 per cent of all immigrants to Canada before 1961 were born in Europe or the United States, that figure was only 22.3 per cent for the period 1991–2001 and fell to about one in five of those who immigrated between 2001 and 2011 and to 15 per cent between 2011 and 2016. Immigrants from Asia, the Middle East, Africa, Latin America, and the Caribbean, who together accounted for only 5.5 per cent of all immigrants prior to 1961, grew to about 77.5 per cent of all immigration during the 1991–2001 decade, three-quarters for the years 2001–11, and well over 80 per cent for the period 2011–16. The dramatic change in the sources of immigration to Canada may be seen in Figure 4.2.

Canada remains, even after recent waves of immigration from non-European countries, a predominantly Christian society. About two-thirds of Canadians claim an affiliation with either the Catholic Church or a Protestant denomination.

This is down from all but a sliver of the population at the time of Confederation and even represents a considerable drop since 1971, about the time the profile of Canadian immigration began to shift away from traditional European sources. This decline in the percentage of the population claiming a Christian religious identification has been due chiefly to a sharp increase over the last generation in the number of people without a religious affiliation. As of 2011, they constituted 24 per cent of the population. People belonging to non-Christian religions continue to constitute a rather small minority, at about 9 per cent of the population. Their presence in particular cities, however, such as Sikhs and Hindus in Vancouver and Muslims, Hindus, and Buddhists in Toronto, is much greater than it is nationwide. The question on religious identity is asked every 10 years, so data from the 2016 census is not available. It is very likely that the 2021 census will show a bit of an uptick in the percentage of the population with non-Christian religious affiliations and an even greater increase in the percentage of Canadians reporting no religious affiliation.

The growth of the non-European and non-Christian elements of Canadian society has not been entirely free from tensions and unease on the

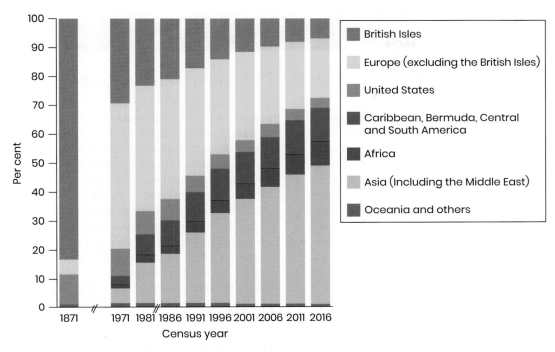

FIGURE 4.2 Region of Birth of Immigrants, 1871–2016

Source: Adapted from Statistics Canada, "Distribution of Foreign-born Population, by Region of Birth, Canada, 1871 to 2036," https://www.statcan.gc.ca/eng/dai/btd/othervisuals/other009.

part of some. Canadians are overwhelmingly supportive of multiculturalism in principle, but specific cases have suggested that their tolerance for accommodating difference has limits (see Boxes 4.1 and 4.2). Public opinion polls also indicate that many Canadians have reservations about some aspects of multiculturalism and that, in this respect, they are not so different from some other Western populations as the dominant Canadian self-image would have one believe. A 2013 survey found that about one-third of Canadians said they felt their identity is threatened when they see a turban, hijab, or kippa. The percentage was 46 per cent in Quebec and 27 per cent in the rest of Canada. It was also higher among French-speakers, at 52 per cent, than among English-speakers, at 27 per cent.[5]

A survey carried out by the Angus Reid Institute in 2016 and two surveys carried out in 2017, one by Montreal-based CROP for Radio-Canada and the other by the Pew Research Center in Washington, DC, suggest that Canadians' support for multiculturalism is not unqualified.[6] The Angus Reid survey found that while two-thirds of Canadians expressed satisfaction with how well new immigrants were integrating into their communities, two-thirds also agreed that "minorities should do more to fit in better with mainstream Canadian society." Almost six out of 10 respondents said that it should be a higher priority to encourage minorities to be more like most Canadians. About a third said that a higher priority should be given to encouraging Canadians to accept minority groups and their customs and languages. Interestingly, Americans were considerably more likely than Canadians to agree that "We should encourage cultural diversity with different groups keeping their own customs and languages" (47 per cent vs 32 per cent).

The CROP/Radio-Canada survey painted a mixed picture of Canadian attitudes towards diversity and new immigrants, but much of what it found runs counter to the dominant narrative about

Governing Realities

BOX 4.1 The Kirpan, Religious Freedom, and Canadian Multiculturalism

Beliefs and behaviours that are unfamiliar may or may not generate controversy. The fact that many Canadians of Ukrainian, Russian, and Serbian ancestry are members of the Orthodox Church and celebrate Christmas and Easter several days after the dates of these statutory holidays is probably unknown to many Canadians. Once known, most people will be indifferent. They might not be indifferent, however, if members of the Orthodox Church demanded forms of public recognition for their religious holidays, such as the right to a paid holiday.

Something of the sort was at issue in 2001 when a young Sikh male attending public school in Quebec was told that he could not bring his kirpan to school. The kirpan is a metal ceremonial dagger that Sikh males are required to wear at all times after being baptized. It symbolizes religious loyalty. The parents of the boy in question were told by the school authorities that he would be permitted to wear a kirpan made of wood or plastic, some material that would eliminate or at least reduce its capacity to be used as a weapon. His parents refused, arguing that their son's religious freedom, guaranteed by the Charter, was violated by the school board's policy. Eventually the dispute reached the Supreme Court. In March 2006 the Court ruled that the wearing of a kirpan in schools for religious reasons is indeed protected by the Charter.

This case was about both religious freedom and multiculturalism. Indeed, the two values are intertwined, as the Court said in its ruling:

> Religious tolerance is a very important value of Canadian society. If some students consider it

unfair that G may wear his kirpan to school while they are not allowed to have knives in their possession, it is incumbent on the schools to discharge their obligation to instil in their students this value that is at the very foundation of our democracy. A total prohibition against wearing a kirpan to school undermines the value of this religious symbol and sends students the message that some religious practices do not merit the same protection as others. Accommodating G and allowing him to wear his kirpan under certain conditions demonstrates the importance that our society attaches to protecting freedom of religion and to showing respect for its minorities.[7]

As noted above and demonstrated in January 2011, this might be especially true in Quebec, where four members of the World Sikh Organization, who had been invited to testify before a legislative committee examining a proposed law on reasonable accommodation of ethnic minorities, were denied entry to Quebec's National Assembly because they wore kirpans. As one of the four, Balpreet Singh, said: "Unfortunately, we weren't allowed to enter because we wear the kirpan, which is a bit ironic because we were here to speak upon the issue of accommodation and we weren't accommodated."[8] Within weeks, the members of Quebec's National Assembly voted unanimously to ban the wearing of the Sikh ceremonial dagger from the province's legislative buildings.

Canadians' embrace of multiculturalism. Here are some of what might be characterized as pro-multicultural findings from the survey:

- The vast majority of Canadians agree that other cultures have a lot to contribute and their influences enrich us (78 per cent in Quebec, 84 per cent in the rest of Canada [ROC]) and agree with the statement "I like to have very different people around me; it's

stimulating and I always learn something" (79 per cent in both Quebec and the ROC).

- If ethnic groups keep their cultural identity our country will only be more interesting (52 per cent agreeing in Quebec and 64 per cent in the ROC).
- The fact of having a growing number of different ethnicities and nationalities makes Canada a better place to live (more respondents agreed than disagreed: 33 per

Governing Realities

BOX 4.2 Becoming Canadian

Late in the 2015 federal election campaign the Federal Court of Canada (FCC) cleared the way for Zunera Ishaq to take her oath of Canadian citizenship while wearing a niqab. The niqab is worn for religious reasons and covers a female's body and hair, leaving the eyes visible. The Conservative government had argued in court on three occasions that the requirement that one's face be visible "enhances the integrity of obtaining citizenship and promotes the broader objective of having the oath recited publicly, openly and in community with others. These are important Canadian values and an integral part of becoming a Canadian citizen." The FCC disagreed, ruling that the requirement violated the Charter of Rights and Freedoms and the Citizenship Act's requirement that respect be shown for religious beliefs and practices.

Polls showed that a strong majority of Canadians, both French- and English-speaking, agreed with the government's position. Conservative Party leader Stephen Harper, who was prime minister at the time, had characterized the practice of wearing a niqab as "contrary to our own values" and "rooted in a culture that is anti-women." His position was supported by the Bloc Québécois, but vigorously opposed by the Liberal Party and the NDP. It is probable that the NDP's position damaged its support in Quebec and that the Conservative Party's position helped it in English-speaking Canada. The degree to which either of these tendencies in voter support occurred is a matter of conjecture. Despite the blustery assertions of some pundits, it is unlikely that the issue was decisive in the election and it most certainly was less important than voter anxiety about the economy and what the Liberal Party framed as the precariousness of the middle class.

cent agreeing and 26 per cent disagreeing in Quebec; 46 per cent agreeing and 21 per cent disagreeing in the ROC).

Other findings suggest more qualified support for multiculturalism, or even reservations:

- Immigrants should have to take a test for "anti-Canadian" values (in Quebec 75 per cent agreed, 74 per cent in the ROC).
- Significant percentages of the population in both Quebec and the ROC said that they did not favour the construction of non-Christian places of worship. The percentages were greatest for mosques, 60 per cent being unfavourable in Quebec and 44 per cent in the ROC. A majority of Quebecers also were unfavourable towards the construction of synagogues (52 per cent, compared to 32 per cent in the ROC).
- Many Canadians outside Quebec, and majorities in Quebec, expressed support for a ban on the wearing of religious clothing (turbans and veils were specifically mentioned in the question) in the case of teachers, persons in

positions of authority, and public service employees (see Figure 4.3).

- Asked whether they perceived the wearing of the veil as more of a personal choice or a sign of submission, 62 per cent of Quebecers saw it as a sign of submission, compared to 48 per cent of those in the ROC.
- The gap between Quebecers and Canadians in other provinces was even greater when respondents were asked about whether and when the niqab or burqa should be allowed. Large majorities of Quebecers said that it should be banned in public places, including in the street (62 per cent), when voting (79 per cent), and when taking the oath of Canadian citizenship. In the ROC, support for a ban was 35 per cent, 49 per cent, and 51 per cent, respectively.

Canadians, it turns out, are not significantly different from the populations of several other wealthy democracies when it comes to what it takes to be "truly Canadian" (or American, Australian, Japanese, or any of the other nationalities surveyed).

The Canadian Press/Patrick Doyle

Zunera Ishaq speaks with reporters outside the Federal Court of Appeal after a hearing on whether or not she would be allowed to wear a niqab while taking her citizenship oath. While the Federal Court of Appeal ruled in Ishaq's favour, Stephen Harper's government aimed to advance the case to the Supreme Court. Jody Wilson-Raybould, then newly appointed as Prime Minister Justin Trudeau's minister of Justice, withdrew the Supreme Court challenge in November 2015.

This, at least, is the conclusion that emerges from the Pew Research Center's 2017 cross-national survey of what people believe is most important to national identity. Respondents in 13 countries were asked whether they believed that speaking our national language, sharing national customs and traditions, and being a Christian (this was not asked in Japan) were important for being truly Canadian, American, British, etc. Figure 4.3 shows that Canadians are slightly less likely to say that speaking either English or French is very or somewhat important to being truly Canadian, but are slightly more likely than those in most other countries to agree that sharing national customs and traditions is important. Canadians, as is true of all the populations in the survey with the exception

of the United States, Greece, Poland, Italy, and Hungary, tend not to believe that being a Christian is important in order to truly belong. Only about one in five Canadians agrees that having been born in Canada is important to being truly Canadian. Australians, Swedes, Germans, and the Dutch are even less likely to believe that this is important.

The conversation on diversity in Canada and across much of the world is not only about aspects of culture and behaviour linked to ethnicity, nationalism, and religion. It also includes such matters as family structure, sexual identity, and physical, mental, and emotional abilities. In all of these respects, Canadians and their governments recognize greater diversity than was the case in the past. Indeed, under Prime Minister Justin Trudeau a

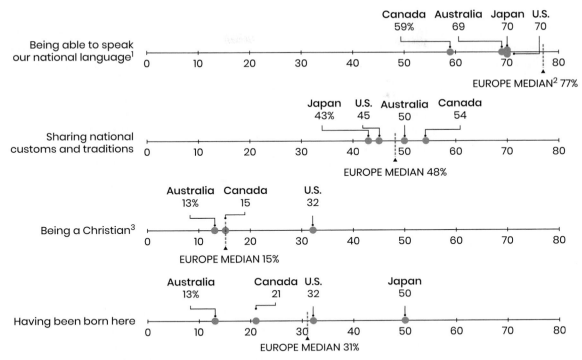

¹In Canada, national language asked as "either English or French."
²European median based on 10 countries.
³In Italy, Poland, and Spain asked "Catholic." Not asked in Japan.

FIGURE 4.3 **What Is at the Core of National Identity?**

Sources: Adapted from Bruce Stokes, "What It Takes to Be One of Us," Pew Research Center, 1 Feb. 2017, http://assets.pewresearch.org/wp-content/uploads/sites/2/2017/04/14094140/Pew-Research-Center-National-Identity-Report-FINAL-February-1-2017.pdf, p. 4; Pew Research Center, Spring 2016 Global Attitudes Survey.

Cabinet Committee on Diversity and Inclusion was created, a first in Canadian history.

The idea of inclusion is not a new one. Fundamentally, it involves identifying and breaking down barriers in social, political, and economic institutions and settings that impede the participation of the members of specific groups. What is different about the contemporary conversation about diversity and inclusion is threefold. It has moved much closer to the centre of the conversation about politics and society than was true in the past. It focuses on the exclusion and unjust treatment of more groups and different types of groups than was once the case. And it has become embedded in processes and institutions at all levels of government, in many corporations, throughout the educational system, and in the media. In sum, awareness of diversity and of the under-representation of some groups has become more widespread, and measures to promote greater inclusion have multiplied.

Opinions differ regarding how successful these efforts have been.

Official Recognition and the Institutionalization of Cultural Diversity

Multiculturalism was given its own minister—albeit a minister of state, which is a rung down from a departmental minister—in 1972. But the official recognition of groups of Canadian citizens according to their group characteristics and the institutionalization of diversity go back much further. We have already mentioned that the Quebec Act of 1774 represented the first official confirmation of the status and rights of a particular segment of the population, in this case French-speaking Catholics. But the distinction of "first" probably ought to be conferred upon the Royal Proclamation of 1763. This document recognized the presence and rights of "the several Nations or Tribes of Indians with whom we are connected, and who live under our protection." Indigenous peoples were recognized by the Proclamation as distinct rights-bearing peoples under the protection of the British Crown. This relationship continues to the present day—although the Canadian government long ago assumed the obligations that originally belonged to Britain—perpetuated and institutionalized through the Indian Act and s. 35 of the Constitution Act, 1982, which recognizes the "treaty rights of the aboriginal peoples of Canada."

There is, therefore, a long history of recognizing diversity in Canada. But until the 1960s that recognition extended principally to the French- and English-language communities (s. 133 of the Constitution Act, 1867), to the Catholic and Protestant religions for schooling purposes (s. 93 of the Constitution Act, 1867), and, arguably, to Indigenous Canadians. This changed as a result of the emergence of feminism as a political force in the 1960s and 1970s and the increasing popularity—first among some elites, spreading later to the general population—of multiculturalism and group-oriented thinking about rights.

Leslie Pal argues that the institutionalization of diversity in Canadian public life was leveraged during the late 1960s and throughout the 1970s and 1980s by the activities of a small organization, the Citizenship Branch of the Department of Secretary of State (SOS).[9] The grants disbursed by the Citizenship Branch through its Official Language Minority Group, Women's Program, and Multiculturalism section helped finance thousands of organizations that, in time, made group-related policy demands on government, raised the profile of diversity issues, and reinforced the idea that government should be protecting and promoting group interests. SOS played a pivotal role in financing diversity advocacy. "Measured in dollars," Pal concludes, "the programs were insignificant. Measured in increased tolerance for minorities and women, they were at best marginally successful."[10] But their enduring significance, Pal argues, was to help reshape the structures of government and the relationship of the state to groups of citizens in ways that institutionalized diversity.

This process of recognizing and promoting diversity did not stop at SOS. Human rights commissions at both the federal and provincial levels have played an important role in expanding the concept of minorities. The earlier emphasis on language, religion, and ethnic origins has been joined in recent years by other forms of minority status and group identity, including gender identity and sexual orientation and disabilities. Human rights commission officials, as R. Brian Howe and David Johnson argue, have been at the forefront of the movement to extend the recognition of diversity through expanding the number of rights-bearing groups. They write:

> By providing education about rights, and by publicizing the existence of a system of rights protection, human rights programs and institutions politicized Canadian society in the direction of making demands for wider rights. Rights consciousness and awareness of human rights commissions encouraged more and more groups to pressure for more and more rights. The result was a steady expansion of human rights protections, the entrenchment of human rights legislation, and the institutionalization of human rights commissions, embedded in an increasingly politicized society in which rights-conscious human rights interest groups demanded ever-wider rights.[11]

At the federal level, the activities of the Canadian Broadcasting Corporation, including its Indigenous news service, the National Film Board, and Telefilm Canada all have contributed to the public projection of images of Canadian society that reflect the diversity of the country's population and history. The Canadian Radio-television and Telecommunications Commission (CRTC) plays a major role in promoting diversity through its licensing activities, in accordance with the requirements of the Broadcasting Act.[12] The Department of Canadian Heritage inherited the functions pioneered several decades ago by the Citizenship Branch of SOS, providing grants to an enormous array of groups and operating as the leader within government for the promotion of

Canadian pluralistic identity. Its grant budget was roughly $1.1 billion in 2017, not all of which was spent on programs and activities that had as their aim the recognition and promotion of diversity. But much of this spending was in fact linked to the goals of multicultural policy. It went towards supporting hundreds of groups and projects, ranging from relatively smaller one-time grants, such as $25,000 to the Iranian-Canadian Centre for Art and Culture and $48,500 to Caribbean Promotions Arts and Culture (towards the cost of a festival in Brampton), to larger multi-year grants such as $98,066 over two years for the Aboriginal Languages Initiative of the University of Alberta's Department of Elementary Education, $550,000 over two years to Alliance des femmes de la francophonie canadienne, and a two-year grant of $250,000 to the Ukrainian Canadian Congress as part of the Commemoration Canada program. The Department of Canadian Heritage also provides funds for provincial departments and agencies that spend the money on cultural and diversity activities.[13]

At the same time, many of the activities and organizations funded by Canadian Heritage have nothing to do with ethnic and cultural communities and the promotion of diversity. It provides money for athletic organizations such as the Canadian Soccer Association and cultural activities such as the Canadian Opera Foundation, as well as special events and celebrations such as those associated with the 200th anniversary of the War of 1812 and Canada's *sesquicentennial*. Indeed, over time the balance of spending by Canadian Heritage has clearly shifted in the direction of activities not linked to particular ethnic and cultural communities, representing quite a change from the priorities of its predecessor department, the Department of Multiculturalism and Citizenship (1991–6).

Diversity and Political Representation

The 1878 cabinet of Sir John A. Macdonald had 14 members. All but one were born in Canada. About 80 per cent (11 of 14) had British Isles ethnic origins and the others were of French ancestry. All were either Catholic (4 of 14) or Protestant. The 2018 cabinet of Justin Trudeau looked very different from that of Sir John A. Of its 31 members, four were born outside of Canada (two in India, one in Lebanon, and one in Somalia). About 80 per cent had European ancestry (in some cases in combination with another ancestry). The religious affiliation of MPs is today more difficult to ascertain from public records than it was in the past,[14] but it seems that about 20 per cent of the members of cabinet may have had a non-Judeo-Christian religious affiliation. It is probable that some members of the 2018 cabinet had no religious affiliation. Members of visible minorities comprised about 20 per cent of the 2018 cabinet. The concept of visible minority did not exist when Sir John A. was prime minister. The most striking difference between the cabinets of 1878 and 2018 is that Macdonald's contained no women (they could not vote or run for office) and Justin Trudeau's included 15. There were no Indigenous persons in the 1878 cabinet, but Jody Wilson-Raybould, a member of the We Wai Kai Nation, served on Trudeau's cabinet until her resignation in 2019.

The diversity found in the Trudeau government may also be seen in the House of Commons. Prior to the 2015 federal election there were 28 visible minority and seven Indigenous MPs, together representing 11 per cent of all members of the House. These numbers increased to 47 and 10 after the 2015 election, comprising 17 per cent of all MPs. "On average," observes Erin Tolley, "visible minority MPs were elected in ridings where visible minorities made up 45 per cent of the population. . . . Indigenous MPs, meanwhile, were elected in ridings where Indigenous peoples make up, on average, 33 per cent of the population."[15] About one-quarter of MPs are female. Canada's unelected Senate is somewhat more diverse than the House of Commons, including a greater percentage of females, Indigenous persons, persons with disabilities, and about the same percentage of visible minority persons.[16] A comparison of the representation of these groups in the Senate and the House, as well as in the population as a whole, may be seen in Figure 4.4.

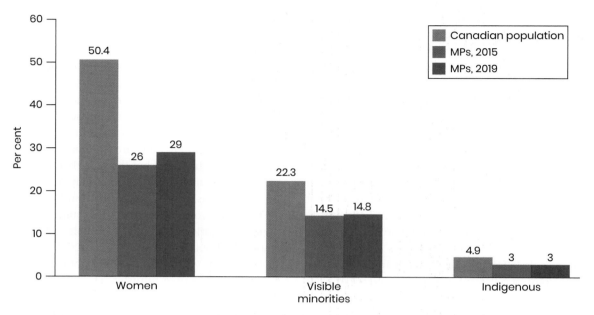

FIGURE 4.4 Representation of Women, Visible Minorities, and Indigenous Canadians in the House of Commons, 2015 and 2019, and in the Canadian Population

Source: Adapted from data reported in Jolson Lim and Victoria Gibson, "Gender, minorities, parenthood: Here's how the next Parliament compares to Canada today," iPOLITICS, October 24, 2019: https://ipolitics.ca/2019/10/24/gender-minorities-parenthood-heres-how-the-next-parliament-compares-to-canada-today/. The percentages of the Canadian population for each group are based on the 2016 census.

The situation is not different in the case of the judicial elite and the highest ranks of the federal bureaucracy. If we look at the 88 individuals who have been members of the Supreme Court since its creation, all but a handful have had British or French ethnic origins and all have had Judeo-Christian backgrounds. A 2016 study by Andrew Griffith found just a handful of visible minority and Indigenous persons among the 65 justices on the four federal courts (Supreme Court of Canada, Federal Court of Canada, Federal Court of Appeal, and Tax Court). The representation of these groups was no greater among the almost 1,000 provincial judges appointed by Ottawa. The percentages of visible minority and Indigenous persons were somewhat greater in the case of provincially appointed judges.[17] In the year after Griffith's study (October 2016 to October 2017), Ottawa made 74 judicial appointments. Half of the appointees were

women, about 12 per cent were members of visible minority groups, and 4 per cent were Indigenous Canadians. Some critics charged that this progress was too slow. Others pointed out that the pool of applications from visible minority and Indigenous candidates was limited.[18]

The greater representation of visible minorities and Indigenous Canadians in the federal bureaucracy has been an avowed goal of Canadian governments for decades. Between 2006 and 2016 the percentage of positions in the federal public service held by Indigenous persons increased from 4.2 to 5.2 per cent and for visible minority persons from 8.6 to 14.5 per cent. These 2016 figures were judged by the Treasury Board to be slightly above the workforce availability of these two groups. This was not the case, however, among the roughly 5,000 federal bureaucrats in the executive category of the public service. These are the most responsible and

Media Spotlight

BOX 4.3 The Portrayal of Cultural Diversity through Canadian Television

In 2017 the CRTC organized a series of focus groups to determine Canadians' reactions to the portrayal of cultural diversity in Canadian television programming. At least two-thirds of each focus group consisted of visible minorities, women, people with disabilities, or members of the LGBTQ+ community. Here is a summary of participants' perceptions of how various groups are portrayed:

- *Women*: On the whole the perception is that women tend to be adequately portrayed, and it was routinely observed that women often play lead roles. However, despite a widespread impression that the portrayal of women is generally good (e.g., they are more likely to be portrayed as independent, confident, and successful), there was also a sense that portrayal is still "stereotypical" or "unrealistic" at times. The most common criticism in this regard is that women are still sexualized at times or portrayed as men want them to be (e.g., as tall, slim, beautiful, and well dressed).
- *Visible ethnocultural minorities*: Assessments of the portrayal of visible ethnocultural minorities tended to be mixed. Despite the widespread sense that they are more visible on screen, there was also general agreement that, while roles have improved, there is still stereotyping at work (e.g., blacks portrayed as criminals, Hispanic and Latino people as religious, Muslims only being shown in traditional dress, people of Middle Eastern descent as terrorists).

- *LGBTQ+ community*: There was a relatively widespread sense that the portrayal of members of this community tends to be good, though it was also often suggested that the portrayal can be stereotypical in the sense that they are depicted as extravagant or their character traits are exaggerated.
- *People with disabilities*: Participants tended to agree that the depiction of people with disabilities is better in terms of portrayal than representation. In other words, there are very few characters or personalities with a disability, but when there are they tend to be well portrayed. Some added that the inclusion of a person with a disability on TV shows tends to be "thematic" or "episodic." In other words, a show will have an episode that includes a person with a disability, but the focus tends to be on how the main characters react to the disability per se, not on developing or exploring the character of the person with a disability.
- *Indigenous peoples*: Indigenous peoples were consistently described as faring poorly in terms of portrayal. There was a widespread impression that when they are portrayed the depiction tends to be stereotypical (e.g., depicted as poor, alcoholic, sniffing glue or gas).

Source: Phoenix Strategic Perspectives, *Cultural Diversity in Canadian Media*, a report prepared for the CRTC, 22 June 2017, http://epe.lac-bac.gc.ca/100/200/301/pwgsc-tpsgc/por-ef/crtc/2017/063-16-e/report.html.

influential positions in the bureaucracy. As of 2016, 9.4 per cent of these positions were held by visible minorities and 3.7 by Indigenous persons.[19] In the case of heads of missions, the senior positions representing Canada abroad, as of 2017 about 14 per cent were held by visible minority persons and none were held by Indigenous persons.[20]

Models of Integration and Accommodation

Canada is a very diverse society. But it is certainly not the world's most diverse society[21] and whether it is the most accommodating is a distinction that

Swedes might claim belongs to them.[22] At slightly more than 20 per cent, Canada's population born outside the country is greater than that of any other G7 country, although somewhat lower than Australia where almost 3 out of 10 persons were born outside that country. Among the world's major cities, Dubai and Brussels have larger foreign-born populations than either Toronto or Vancouver, although it is fair to point out that in at least the case of Dubai many of the foreign-born are there for reasons related to work and have no intention or even possibility of becoming citizens. Close to six out of 10 residents of Miami were not born in the United States and such cities as New York and Sydney, Australia, are not far behind Canada's major metropolitan areas in terms of their foreign-born populations.

Measuring diversity is a tricky business. The size of the foreign-born population is, obviously, a rather crude measure. One might argue that if almost all of the foreign-born come from countries that share the same language and the same general culture, which is true of the foreign-born Latino population in Miami, that this represents less diversity than a case like Toronto, where there is no single dominant language or cultural community within the city's foreign-born population. Demographers are quick to point out that ethnic diversity is not the same as cultural diversity. Nevertheless, ethnically and culturally, Canada is always towards the top of developed countries in rankings of diversity.[23]

The Canadian model of multiculturalism represents one possible regime for the accommodation and recognition of the ancestral cultures of minorities, including their languages and religious beliefs. Other models exist and it would probably surprise most Canadians to learn that some Western democracies have taken group recognition and the protection of cultural rights considerably further than in Canada. Table 4.1 shows a range of models for the accommodation and recognition of minority cultures. At one end is what we might call *deep diversity multiculturalism*, represented by the Netherlands until about a decade ago. At the other end of the spectrum is *integration without major or official accommodation*, as found in France. Between these extremes fall Canada and the United States. Quebec has its own rather different regime of integration and accommodation that also falls between these extremes. The Canadian version of multiculturalism is towards the middle of this scale in terms of the degree to which the state is obliged to protect and promote minority cultures and identities.

The Dutch Experiment with Deep Diversity Multiculturalism

To understand how multiculturalism is viewed by a particular society and why certain institutions and policies exist, one needs to examine the historical circumstances and demographic conditions of that society. In the case of the Netherlands, increasing wealth and a shortage of unskilled labour led to an increase in immigration during the 1970s. "Guest workers"—immigrants who were not given citizenship rights and who were expected to return to their countries of origin after a certain number of years in the Netherlands—arrived from Morocco and Turkey, along with non-European immigrants from former Dutch colonies. They were followed by refugees from Sri Lanka, Iran, Iraq, and Somalia in the 1980s and 1990s and by the relatives of Moroccan and Turkish workers already living in the Netherlands. This influx of non-European immigrants took place against the historical backdrop of World War II and the Holocaust, and a sense of what has been called "Dutch guilt." This involves a widespread feeling, the Anne Frank story notwithstanding, that the country's population did not do enough to resist the Nazi occupation and the deportation of Dutch Jews. Therefore, the adoption of multiculturalism, mainly in the 1990s, was inspired by a constellation of factors. It was, in a sense, compensation for what was seen as a failure to stand up for minorities during the Nazi occupation. It was also a practical response to a labour market situation where guest workers were expected to return to their countries of origin eventually, so providing them and their children with education and public services in their own languages, and in various ways making it unnecessary for these immigrants to integrate into Dutch society, appeared to make sense. But the policy also accorded

TABLE 4.1 Models of Cultural Accommodation

	Deep Diversity Multiculturalism	Interculturalism	Official Multiculturalism	De Facto but Contested Multiculturalism	Universalism with Skeptical Acceptance of Some Aspects of Multiculturalism
Characteristics	• Allows and encourages groups to maintain their languages, religions, and identities • Provides public support for schools, religious organizations, community centres	• Advocates the official recognition of minority cultures and state measures to protect their rights and sustain their practices and beliefs	• Allows and even encourages the retention of minority cultural identities through state support for cultural organizations, heritage language instruction, inclusion in state symbols, ceremonies, etc.	• Allows for the retention of minority cultural identities with some state support • Opposed by some as divisive	• Discourages the official recognition of group cultural identities • The public space and state institutions are based on a universal set of values and a single national identity
Guiding principles	• "The larger society is obliged to support the institutions symbolizing and sustaining the identity of the majority."*	• Mutual respect between the cultural majority and minorities and a willingness from both sides to accommodate the other and adapt	• Minority cultures deserve respect and recognition • Based on concept of reasonable accommodation	• Cultural pluralism is positive, but citizens should be encouraged to share a common civic identity	• Pragmatic recognition of cultural minorities exists • Cultural minorities should be discouraged from retaining separate identities and should be encouraged to identify with the universal values of the society
Countries	• The Netherlands during the 1990s, until roughly 2004	• Recommended for Quebec by the Bouchard-Taylor Commission, 2008	• Canada	• United States	• France

*Paul Sniderman and Louk Hagendoorn, *When Ways of Life Collide: Multiculturalism and Its Discontents* (Princeton, NJ: Princeton University Press, 2007), 5.

with the liberal politics that was ascendant among Western intellectuals and was particularly strong in secular, tolerant Holland.

The result was a multicultural regime based on a principle that the Canadian philosopher Charles Taylor has called "deep diversity." It involves the idea that in a pluralistic society no single national identity is possible or even desirable without depriving some minority or minorities of equal status, recognition, and dignity. Taylor argues that different communities can belong to a country in different ways and that competing loyalties are not necessarily destabilizing for a society. This ethos underpinned the Dutch experiment with multiculturalism. Paul Sniderman and Louk Hagendoorn summarize the results as follows:

> In the Netherlands, as much as can be done on behalf of multiculturalism has been done. Minority groups are provided instruction in their own language and culture; separate radio and television programs; government funding to import religious leaders; and subsidies for a wide range of social and religious organizations; "consultation prerogatives" for community leaders; and publicly financed housing set aside for and specifically designed to meet Muslim requirements for strict separation of "public" and "private" spaces.[24]

In short, Dutch multiculturalism went considerably beyond the Canadian model in the extent to which it supported and promoted minority cultural identities.

Although diagnoses of what went wrong vary, there is a general consensus that the Dutch model failed. The fact that immigrant communities were not integrated into the wider Dutch society—on the contrary, the incomes of Muslims, Turks, and Moroccans remained the lowest in the country—permitted a situation to develop where members of these groups saw themselves, and were seen by the majority group, as being *in* the country without being *of* the country. A 2013 study by the Netherlands Institute for Social Research found that social contact between white native-born Dutch and the country's main immigrant groups had diminished over the preceding 17 years.[25] In 2011 the Dutch government announced its abandonment of its long-standing multicultural policy in favour of integration: "The government shares the social dissatisfaction over the multicultural society model and plans to shift priority to the values of the Dutch people. In the new integration system, the values of the Dutch society play a central role. With this change, the government steps away from the model of a multicultural society."[26]

American Multiculturalism: Contested Institutionalization

Canadians, conditioned as they often are to believe that the United States is an assimilationist melting pot that actively discourages immigrants from retaining their ancestral cultural identities, are likely to be perplexed by the suggestion that there is any sort of multiculturalism regime in that country. In fact, however, the main difference between Canadian and American multiculturalism may be that in Canada it is enshrined in law, referred to in the Constitution, and has become, since the 1970s, a central aspect of the story that Canadians tell themselves and others about who they are and what they are about culturally. Not coincidentally, this narrative serves the culturally and politically important function of establishing a frontier of difference between Canada and the United States.

What public authorities across the United States do to protect and in some ways even to promote minority cultural identities is not very different from policies and programs in Canada. Laws providing rights to public services in languages other than English—Spanish, for the large Latino population in the United States, but other languages, too—are common across the country. In California, the code governing state services requires that state agencies employ persons who speak minority languages, provide interpreters for non-English-speaking citizens needing state services, and offer information about government services in minority languages. In practice, the minority language usually is Spanish, but the law does not limit this requirement to Spanish and services in many other languages are provided by some agencies. Most states offer driver examinations in foreign languages, many of them in multiple languages. New York is one of many states that provide publicly paid interpreters for all litigants and witnesses in both criminal and civil law proceedings.

When it comes to the incorporation of minority ethnic identities and cultures into their public life, Americans can hardly be said to lag behind Canadians. There may be less celebration of diversity in the institutions and activities of the US federal government than in Canada, but many state and local governments across the United States, as well as community activities that do not depend on government funding and initiatives, recognize and celebrate ethnic diversity. An important difference is that there is less agreement in American society that multiculturalism—which usually is referred to as "diversity"—is a good thing. In Canada the idea of multiculturalism is widely accepted. In the United States it is a hot-button issue that divides liberals from conservatives in that country's culture wars. The area of American life where multiculturalism is most evident, institutionalized, and contested involves the country's educational system. Ethnic studies exploded onto American university campuses at the end of the 1960s. Even the most casual perusal of curricula, programs, and research centres in American higher education shows that diversity education is at least as pervasive in that system as in Canada. In words that most Canadian educators would find comforting and familiar, the latest curricular standards created for the National Council for the Social Studies state:

> The civic mission of social studies demands the inclusion of all students—addressing cultural, linguistic, and learning diversity that includes similarities and differences based on race, ethnicity, language, religion, gender, sexual orientation, exceptional learning needs, and other educationally and personally significant characteristics of learners. Diversity among learners embodies the democratic goal of embracing pluralism to make social studies classrooms laboratories of democracy.[27]

On the other hand, in May 2010 the state legislature of Arizona passed a law prohibiting courses in public schools that "advocate ethnic solidarity instead of the treatment of pupils as individuals." The target of this ban was Mexican-American studies courses. It was overturned by the courts in 2017. Although other states did not go as far as Arizona, the controversy over whether ethnic studies should be required in public schools has been divisive in a number of states, including California and Texas. Clearly, the institutionalization of ethnic studies has not gone unchallenged.

Although Americans are less likely than Canadians to mention multiculturalism as a defining or even *the* defining characteristic of their society, their attitudes towards cultural minorities and immigrants are not, in some important respects, very different from those of Canadians. We have already seen that Canadians are more likely than Americans to agree with the statement, "Minorities should do more to fit in better with mainstream Canadian/American society" (68 per cent vs 53 per cent: 2016). Canada scores slightly higher that the United States on the Gallup Migrant Acceptance Index, a composite measure based on three questions asking whether it is good or bad to have immigrants living in the country, being one's neighbours, and marrying into one's family. But the difference is small and both countries fall within the top 10 of all 138 countries surveyed.[28] A 2017 survey by Université du Québec à Montréal political scientist Allison Harell found that Canadians were more supportive than Americans of a ban on the wearing of Muslim headscarves in public places (47 per cent vs 30 per cent) and more likely to agree that what happens in mosques should be monitored (51 per cent vs 46 per cent).[29]

In short, it is not at all clear that Americans are less supportive of multiculturalism than are Canadians. What is clear is that the idea of multiculturalism is much less central to the dominant narrative of American society than is true in Canada and, second, that the concept is more polarizing south of the border than it is in Canada.

France: Where Multiculturalism Exists but Is Not Officially Embraced

When you step out of the exit of Paris's Gare du Nord train station you immediately see that the capital of France is a place where races and cultures meet. But they do not always mix. If you take the metro to the city's perimeter, where *les banlieux* (the suburbs) begin, you immediately sense that Paris is a highly segregated place. In Montreuil, for example, at Paris's eastern edge, the vast majority of the population is non-white and a significant portion is Muslim.

What percentage is non-white and what percentage is Muslim? No one knows for sure because French law prohibits state authorities from asking people their race, ethnicity, or religion. This prohibition exists because the official ideology of the French state, enshrined in the constitution, is based on universalist values of *liberté, égalité, et fraternité* (freedom, equality, and social solidarity). These values are at the heart of the French civic identity. Along with the French language they define what it means to be French.

Like many other countries of Western Europe, France has become culturally more diverse as a result of non-European immigration over the last several decades. The most reliable statistics show that just over 10 per cent of the population is foreign-born. Immigrants from France's former colonies in Africa and elsewhere have arrived in large numbers, some originally as guest workers, some as refugees, some because they had a right to residence and citizenship in France as a result of their colonial relationship to the métropole, and others illegally. Today it is estimated that about one-tenth of the French population is Muslim. The official ideology enforced by the state sees only citizens, regardless of their skin colour, religion, and ethnic ancestry. But the reality of French society is multicultural. And in response to that fact the state has grudgingly and to a limited degree provided some recognition of the existence and importance of minority cultural identities. It has done so within the framework of a classically liberal approach, focusing on cases of discrimination on the basis of ethnic origin, race, religion, and so on. The Haute autorité de lutte contre les discriminations et pour l'égalité is the key institution in this regard, operating much as a human rights commission does in Canada.

Tensions between the evolving multicultural reality of French society and the universalist ideology of the state and the dominant ideology have been increasingly evident in recent years. In the autumn of 2009 the government of President Nicolas Sarkozy launched what it called *le grand débat sur l'identité nationale*, creating a commission and soliciting input from individuals across the country. The idea that France, of all countries, would create a commission to study the *problem* of national identity would have been unthinkable a couple of decades earlier. Although some dismissed the national identity initiative as a politically motivated attempt to pander to the prejudices of right-of-centre voters, this interpretation ignores the widespread unease, cutting across the French ideological spectrum, regarding what are seen as challenges to the principles of gender equality and secularism in France. The debate about national identity was, in fact, a debate about the compatibility of Islam—or some forms of Islam—and the French civic culture.

Two of the measures taken by the French government, and widely supported by the French public, include what might be called "citizenship-values contracts" for newcomers (Le Contrat d'Intégration Républicaine) and a ban on the wearing of the burqa and the niqab in public places (schools, government offices, public transportation, etc.). It should be said that France was not alone in enacting such measures. Citizenship-values contracts were also mandated in Germany, the Netherlands, the United Kingdom, and several other Western European democracies and have been advocated in recent years by the Parti Québécois for newcomers to Quebec. Likewise, laws banning face veils exist in Belgium and at the regional and local levels in a number of European countries and have been upheld by the European Court of Human Rights.

The dominant view in France on the matter of multiculturalism is probably that held by the current president, Emmanuel Macron. He has said "I am against multiculturalism, but I'm for integration that is not assimilation." During the 2017 French presidential debates Macron was asked whether he believed that France was a multicultural nation. He replied, "The answer is no. France has a history, a language and a culture. That culture and that language are enriched by what foreigners bring to our country, but they remain the foundation of our identity."[30]

Quebec: Interculturalism

Since the 1960s, when the preference of immigrants for the English language caused Quebec demographers to predict, and nationalist spokespersons to fret, that the French language and distinctive culture of Quebec would be placed under increasing pressure, immigrants have been an important part of the debate about language and cultural policy in Quebec. For decades, Quebec's birth rate has been below the level needed to reproduce the population. Immigration has long been crucial for population and labour market growth, as is also the case in the rest of Canada. Immigrants accounted for about 10 per cent of Quebec's population in 2001 and almost 14 per cent in 2016. And as is true of the rest of Canada, the sources of immigration to Quebec have shifted from Europe to other parts of the world. According to the 2016 census, about two-thirds of immigrants in Quebec came from countries outside of Europe and the United States. The figure is closer to 80 per cent among those who immigrated between 2006 and 2016. North Africa, Asia, the Middle East, the Caribbean, and Latin America have become major sources of immigration to the province.[31]

The debate in Quebec has shifted somewhat from the impact of immigrants on the French language—after all, many of these immigrants come from former French colonies and speak French—to the integration of newcomers into Quebec culture and society. Tensions in the province were crystallized in the highly publicized case of Hérouxville, a small town 180 kilometres north of Montreal, whose local government adopted a declaration of cultural standards by which newcomers were expected to abide.[32] These standards were targeted mainly at what the town councillors believed to be typical forms of Muslim behaviour, stating that immigrants were unwelcome in their community of less than 2,000 if they covered their faces, carried weapons to school (a reference to the Sikh kirpan), practised genital mutilation, stoned or burned women to death, and so on. The furor that the publication of this code of behaviour incited—the story was widely covered throughout the world, including in France, Great Britain, and the United States—eventually led the Quebec government to appoint a consultative commission on "reasonable accommodation," under the leadership of philosopher Charles Taylor and sociologist Gérard Bouchard.

In the eyes of some, their report seemed to recommend that the Quebec government and Quebec citizens embrace a form of multiculturalism within the province rather similar to that which has been embraced by the federal government for decades.

The report's reception was not enthusiastic. Most French-speaking Quebecers, and not simply the folks in Hérouxville and communities like it, felt that the emphasis in the Bouchard-Taylor report leaned too far in the direction of accommodation and openness to change on the part of old-stock Québécois—sometimes called *les québécois de souche*—and not enough on the need for newcomers to adapt and accept not only the language of the French majority, but their culture and mores as well.

What the Bouchard-Taylor report recommended was called **interculturalism**. This was proposed as an alternative to the Canadian multicultural regime, about which Quebecers are more skeptical than their compatriots in the rest of the country. Multiculturalism is about accommodating the different values and practices of minorities. It imposes an obligation of cultural tolerance on the majority. Interculturalism, on the other hand, as explained by the Bouchard-Taylor Commission, is about reconciliation and mutual adaptation on the part of both the dominant majority and minorities: both sides must be prepared to make cultural concessions. The difference may appear to be rather nuanced and, in fact, it is not always obvious.[33] Quebec nationalism has always been uneasy with the Canadian concept of multiculturalism, which is often seen to be in competition with the notion that Canada ought to be viewed as a partnership between two founding peoples, one French-speaking and the other English-speaking. The separatist Parti Québécois argued that the emphasis of interculturalism on compromise and mutual adaptation sidestepped what for most Quebecers is the real problem: the protection and preservation of their French identity. "It is not necessary to be born here to be part of our collective journey," said then PQ leader Pauline Marois, "but you have to get on the train."[34] The Quebec Liberal government immediately distanced itself from the Bouchard-Taylor report of 2008 and subsequent Quebec governments, while sometimes expressing support for the concept of interculturalism, have done little to implement the ambitious and extensive recommendations of the report.

On the contrary, actions taken subsequently by PQ, Liberal, and Coalition Avenir Québec (CAQ) governments in Quebec have been premised on what can only be characterized as a rejection of the spirit of the Bouchard-Taylor Commission. In 2013 the PQ government introduced legislation called the Charter of Quebec Values that would have denied public employment and government services to women wearing face coverings such as the burqa or the niqab. It went further than this to prohibit the wearing of religious attire and "conspicuous" symbols on the part of public employees. Before the province's National Assembly could vote on the bill, the PQ was defeated by the Liberal Party in Quebec in the April 2013 provincial election. Despite having been critical of the Charter of Quebec Values, the new the Liberal provincial government proceeded to introduce rather similar legislation banning Muslim face veils in the public sector, including schools, as well as the chador, which exposes the face. It also proposed to amend the Quebec Charter of Human Rights to include mention of the religious neutrality of the state and to create a hierarchy of rights in which gender equality would take precedence. Whereas the PQ's Charter of Quebec Values was framed as

While proponents of the Charter for Quebec Values argued that the bill would promote the secularism of the state, a majority of Canadians outside Quebec, including cartoonist Michael de Adder, saw the bill as a violation of Canada's Charter of Rights and Freedoms.

a policy imposing secularism on the state and its interactions with Quebec citizens, the Liberal policy has been framed as one of religious neutrality on the part of the state. The bill, An Act to Foster State Religious Neutrality (short title), was passed in October 2017.[35] Although the bill was widely reviled outside Quebec as intolerant, Islamophobic, and contrary to the spirit and letter of Canadian multiculturalism, polls taken at the time of its passage found that 87 per cent of Quebecers supported it, 62 per cent being strongly in favour and 25 per cent somewhat in favour. Among francophones, 92 per cent supported the bill. Even among Quebec anglophones support was high, at 67 per cent.[36] Quebec's two main opposition parties voted against the bill because they believed that it did not go far enough in establishing Quebec as a secular state in the manner of France. Guidelines regarding the application of the law were issued by the Quebec Liberal government in April 2018.

The story did not end at this point. Court challenges to the Act to Foster Religious Neutrality cast doubt on its constitutionality. The Liberal government lost the October 2018 election to the Coalition Avenir Québec, led by a one-time member of the PQ. The new provincial government lost no time in introducing Bill 21, An Act Respecting the Laicity of the State, which retained all of the main features of the Liberal government's Act to Foster Religious Neutrality. The CAQ government's bill also invoked the notwithstanding clause of the Charter of Rights and Freedoms that would protect the law from Charter-based challenges. Teachers, police officers, and other state officials are prohibited from wearing clothing, headwear, or other symbols of their religion. Those who receive government services are required by the law to make their faces visible. Defending the law against a wave of criticism from the English-language media, Christopher Skeete of the CAQ government replied, "When you exercise the power of the state, we are asking that you leave your religion at the door." Opinion in predominantly English-speaking Canada and among immigrant communities in Quebec was overwhelmingly negative. But as had also been true of the previous government's Act to Foster Religious Neutrality, a strong majority of Quebecers supported the law.

Immigration and Economic Integration

Immigration has long been a crucial factor contributing to the growth of Canada's population. At various points in the country's history (the late nineteenth century and during the Great Depression) more people left Canada than entered, but the balance over time has strongly favoured immigration over emigration. As the fertility rate in Canada has fallen over the last several decades to the current rate of about 1.6 (it has not been at the replacement rate of 2.1 since 1971), immigration has become crucial for population maintenance and growth. Indeed, since 2001 immigration has contributed a greater share to overall population growth than natural increase.[37] Demographers project that it will account for virtually all of Canada's population growth by about 2040.

We have seen that the sources of immigration to Canada have changed dramatically since the 1970s. This is partly due to the fact that several of the European countries that previously had been major sources of immigration were becoming more affluent. Economics has always been a main driver of population migrations, with people fleeing impoverished circumstances and moving towards places they believed would provide them and their families with a better life and more opportunities. The economic recovery and increasing affluence of Western Europe in the decades following World War II reduced the incentives for people to leave for Canada, the United States, and Australia, all of which were main destinations for European immigrants.

But another factor contributing to the change in the pattern of immigration to Canada was the reform of immigration law. Prior to the 1960s the law had discriminated in favour of European nationals and essentially held the door wide open to immigrants from the United Kingdom. Moreover, immigration policy actively discriminated against certain non-European groups at various points in Canada's history, notably against Chinese immigrants beginning in 1885 through the imposition of a head tax. The tax began at $50 per person but was increased 20 years later to $500. The head tax was abolished in 1923 and replaced with a ban on Chinese immigration that was not repealed until 1947.

The Immigration Act, 1967 eliminated racial discrimination and ethnic favouritism and established a points system that has been used since then. Immigrants who apply under the economic category—the law also recognizes family reunification and refugee status as grounds for immigration, as well as business-class immigrants who bring capital and entrepreneurial skills—receive points for their level of proficiency in one or both of Canada's official languages, years of formal education, years of work experience, age (most points are awarded to those between 20 and 50 years of age), having arranged employment in Canada, and adaptability (this includes having family already in Canada and a number of other factors). In virtually every year over the past couple of decades, economic-class immigrants have constituted about half or more of the annual intake of immigrants (Figure 4.5).

Canada is not the only country to use such a point system. Australia and New Zealand, countries that, like Canada, have relatively high levels of immigration, also use this system (see Box 4.4). Immigrants who arrive under the points system are much more likely than family-class immigrants or refugees to have the education, language skills, and job-related qualifications that enable them to integrate more quickly into the labour force and the Canadian middle class.[38] Language proficiency, which is linked in subtle and not so subtle ways to familiarity with cultural norms in the host society, is a key factor affecting employment prospects and earnings.[39] Immigrants who mainly or always use a language other than French or English at work are essentially trapped in a lifetime of much lower incomes.[40]

In view of the criteria required to qualify as an economic-class immigrant, it is not surprising that these new Canadians tend to be more educated than Canadian-born citizens of the same age. But education, professional certification, and years of work experience abroad do not necessarily produce easy entry into the Canadian labour force, at least not right away. Longitudinal studies of immigrant employment in Canada have found that a much greater percentage of prime working-age

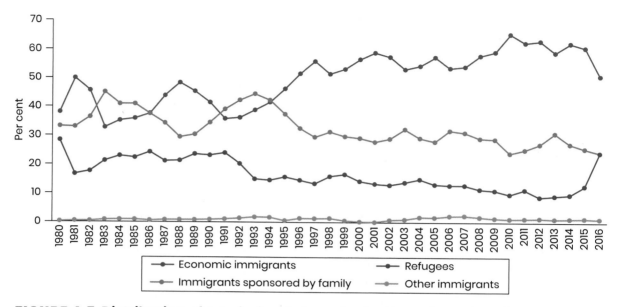

FIGURE 4.5 Distribution of Admission Categories by Year of Immigration, 1980–2016

Source: Statistics Canada, Focus on Geography Series, 2016 Census, Figure 1.4.

Governing Realities

BOX 4.4 What Should Determine Who Gets In?

In recent years roughly 60 per cent of annual immigration to Canada has been under the economic category, whereby prospective immigrants must score a certain number of points to qualify for entry to Canada. This system for determining who gets in is referred to by economists as a human capital model, emphasizing as it does the attributes of immigrants most likely to contribute positively to the economy and less likely to place a burden on state spending. The system is not without its critics. The criteria include education, fluency in the language of the country applied to, having a skill or profession for which there is labour market demand, relevant work experience or arranged employment, age (applicants in prime working years receive more points), and adaptability (this is often determined by whether an applicant already has family members in the country to which he or she has applied). Canada was the first country to adopt such a system in 1967. It also exists in Australia, New Zealand, and the United Kingdom, as well as a handful of other countries.

A bill that would mandate a points system in the United States was introduced in Congress in 2017. Although it has considerable support, including the backing of President Donald Trump, it also faces tough opposition. The arguments against this model are expressed by the American Immigration Council: "[T]he proposed points system likely would put some categories of people at a tremendous disadvantage. These groups include women, people who work in the informal economy (including those who do unpaid work), individuals with family ties to US citizens but without formal education and employment history, middle age and older adults, and applicants from less-developed countries."[41]

immigrants (25–44) who arrive in the economic class compared to other immigrant classes found work within their first two years in the country, roughly half found work in their intended occupation, 40 per cent within their first year in Canada, and their incomes were considerably higher than those of other immigrants.[42] At the same time, however, a significant number of those who arrive as economic-class immigrants do not find work in their intended occupation, at least not for a number of years, and experience lower earnings than is typical for those in the economic class. Why?

The answer sometimes given is discrimination, in systemic forms and in subtle and more overt forms. In fact, the explanation is far more complex than this and raises the question, "What do we mean by discrimination?" Research by Jeffrey Reitz and others[43] points to four main factors that slow or even block the entry of highly educated, skilled immigrants into the professions they held in their countries of origin. They include the following:

- *Language proficiency.* Being proficient in the official language of one's community of residence and workplace is positively correlated with the likelihood of being employed in one's intended occupation. Not being fluent in one of the official languages—and this can include having an accent that interferes with the ability of clients, patients, or co-workers to understand the speaker—can limit an immigrant's employment prospects. Focus group sessions commissioned by the federal government in 2014 found that inadequate English language skill was one of the factors most often mentioned by immigrant professionals in explaining the challenges they had faced in getting career-related work.[44]
- *Cultural norms.* This is often associated with language proficiency. Communication is not only about understanding the words spoken by someone else. It is also about the unspoken meanings and messages transmitted in everything from a face-to-face conversation to an e-mail message. Not having been raised in the language community and associated culture of the majority may be a

disadvantage in terms of communications skills. At any rate, there is little doubt that some Canadian employers will believe this to be the case and may be reluctant to hire an immigrant worker for fear that customers, clients, or patients may not "connect" with him or her as well as with someone who is more fluent in the mainstream culture.
- *Work experience.* Having worked for 14 years with two employers in Lahore (Pakistan) or for seven years with an employer in Posdan (Poland) may not be viewed seriously by a Canadian employer who has never heard of these places. Even if the places of previous employment are recognized, it would not be surprising if an employer in, say, Calgary placed more confidence in work experience with a company that he or she knows, in Toronto or Victoria, than in a company that he or she has not heard of, in a market far away. The 2014 focus groups conducted by Environics Research group for the Canadian government found that many of the economic-class immigrants who participated believed that lack of Canadian experience was a coded form of discrimination.[45] This Catch-22 situation often is the experience of highly educated, skilled immigrant workers. To get the job in Canada one needs experience. But the experience one has may not be recognized in Canada.
- *Credentials.* Degrees and professional certification are usually required for a professional or other skilled occupation; however, degrees and certification earned abroad are often not recognized in Canada (sometimes those earned in one province are not recognized in another!). Once in Canada, a highly educated immigrant may have to return to school to acquire a degree, certification, or training that will qualify him or her for the anticipated job. These barriers to the recognition of foreign degrees and certification are not always, and perhaps not even usually, arbitrary and without reasons associated with the competencies expected of a person in a given profession in this country. But

in some cases they may be. Ottawa and the provinces have taken steps in recent years to improve the process whereby degrees and qualifications earned abroad are evaluated.[46]

Do these four factors add up to discrimination? This may depend on what one means by discrimination. If one means norms and rules that have as their consequence the differential treatment of individuals on the basis of characteristics that tend to be associated with a person's country of origin, including the likelihood of speaking English or French proficiently and of having the social capital more likely to be acquired by those who have grown up in a culture than by those who have not, and the probability that one will have degrees and work experience that are not as readily acknowledged as those earned in Canada, then this certainly amounts to discrimination. Some might argue, however, that these criteria are relevant to a person's ability to perform a job at a high or even reasonable level of competence or in a manner satisfactory to some customers, clients, or patients. Is it discriminatory, they might ask, to place more confidence in one person over another because one understands him or her better or is familiar with the background and credentials of one person but not at all with those of the other? We make choices on the basis of these sorts of considerations all the time. Indeed, in a world of imperfect information, where we cannot

The Social Fabric

BOX 4.5 Multiculturalism and Canadian Exceptionalism?

Prime ministers from Jean Chrétien to Justin Trudeau have told Canadians that their country is the world's first post-national society and a model of cultural tolerance that is admired throughout the world. Canadian schoolchildren learn early on that multiculturalism and the acceptance of difference are part of the warp and woof of Canadian life and something that distinguishes Canada from its southern neighbour. Surveys have long shown that Canadians are overwhelmingly supportive of the idea of multiculturalism. As right-wing populism appeared to be on the rise across the world, Toronto-based writer Stephen Marche called Canada "the last cheerful country on earth," with a unique identity rooted in acceptance of otherness and without the fear of immigration that existed in so many Western countries.[47]

The reality is a bit more complicated. Yes, Canadians embrace multiculturalism, at least in principle. But a 2017 study by the McGill Institute for the Study of Canada found that this embrace was neither as strong nor as exceptional as Canadians may believe. In "Canadian Exceptionalism: Are We Good or Are We Lucky?," Michael Donnelly compares Canadian attitudes towards immigration and diversity to those of populations in dozens of countries across the world. He finds that when it comes to perceptions of the economic and cultural impacts of immigration, whether the government should be generous in accepting refugees, and whether Canada should accept immigrants from poorer countries, Canadians' views are quite similar to those of the average for European countries.

Donnelly also found that only 46 per cent of Canadians said that they would oppose an end to immigration. While only 19 per cent said that they would support such a policy, 35 per cent responded that they neither supported nor opposed an end to immigration. Almost six in 10 respondents agreed with the statement, "Too many immigrants don't seem to feel connected to Canadian society," and close to seven in 10 agreed that, "People who come to Canada should change their behaviour to be more like Canadians." Donnelly concludes that "Whatever is driving Canada's exceptionally positive history of immigration and integration over the last half century, it does not appear to be an exceptionally tolerant public."

Source: Michael Donnelly, "Canadian Exceptionalism: Are We Good or Are We Lucky?" *Policy Options*, http://policyoptions.irpp.org/fr/po-events/canadian-exceptionalism-are-we-good-or-are-we-lucky/.

know everything that might be relevant to a decision that we need to make and where the costs of acquiring such information may be high, we necessarily rely on what is familiar to us. Just because a decision is based on what does and does not fall into our comfort zone—the range of what we think we know and that is familiar to us—does that make it discriminatory? Here, the answer will depend in part on ideology—conservative or liberal; individualist or communitarian—and in part on which side of the hiring desk one is seated.

Whatever one concludes about the human capital model used to determine who is permitted into Canada as an economic-class immigrant, and whether or not one believes that even highly educated and well-qualified immigrants face unfair and unreasonable barriers in the Canadian workforce, one thing is certain. The fact that immigration is comparatively uncontroversial in Canada and that the country lacks the sort of immigrant, low-income enclaves found in many Western countries may be ascribed to the Canadian immigration system. Canadians' overwhelming support for multiculturalism and the generally high level of support for current immigration levels that has existed for most of the past couple of decades have surely been influenced by the fact that immigrants tend to integrate into the middle class more rapidly and more often in Canada than in such countries as France, Germany, the Netherlands, the UK, and even the United States.[48]

Summing Up

Multiculturalism is a prominent feature of Canadian society. By some measures Canada has the highest level of ethnocultural diversity among the world's affluent democracies. A country in which persons of French and British Isles ancestry accounted for about 90 per cent of the population in the years after Confederation has become much more diverse because of changing patterns of immigration. Canada's shifting ethnocultural demography has been accompanied by important changes in the country's political conversation and self-image. Today, most Canadians are likely to identify multiculturalism and respect for diversity as foremost political values and as markers that distinguish their society from that of the United States.

This general embrace of multiculturalism is not without some reservations and occasional friction. Francophone Quebecers are less likely to support this image of Canada, seeing it as being in competition with the view that the primordial facts about the country are its linguistic duality and the idea of Canada as a partnership between two founding nations. Moreover, the more precarious position of the French language, including the fact that newcomers integrate into Quebec's francophone majority less quickly and at a lower rate than they integrate into the anglophone majorities of the other provinces, is a factor that contributes to a somewhat lower level of support for multiculturalism in Quebec. The quite different reactions of French-speaking Quebec and the rest of Canada to the 2015 Federal Court of Canada ruling on the wearing of the niqab during a citizenship ceremony was a flash point that illustrated this more general difference regarding multiculturalism.

At the same time, it appears that Canadians as a whole have some reservations about multiculturalism. National surveys carried out in 2016 and 2017 found that majorities across the country expressed dissatisfaction with the extent to which they believed newcomers were integrating into Canadian society. These surveys painted a mixed picture of Canadian attitudes towards diversity and new immigrants. A cross-national survey carried out in 2017 found that Canadian views on the integration of newcomers were not particularly different from those found in most other wealthy democracies.

Whether or not the views of Canadians are very different from those other national populations, there is no doubt that Canada has experienced less social and political friction associated with increasing ethnocultural diversity and immigration. The political polarization and anti-immigrant sentiment observed in recent years in these other countries have been largely absent from Canada. Most Canadians probably believe that this is due to their country's values. It may be, however, that Canada's immigration model, a model under which in most years about 60 per cent of newcomers have been accepted based on what is determined to be their economic suitability, deserves much of the credit for this.

Starting Points for Research

Gérard Bouchard, *Interculturalism: A View from Quebec,* translated by Howard Scott (Toronto: University of Toronto Press, 2015). An explanation of Quebec's alternative to multiculturalism, written by one of the creators of the concept. Charles Taylor, Bouchard's colleague as co-chair of the Quebec government's Consultation Commission on Accommodation Practices Related to Cultural Differences, contributes an introduction to the English translation of this book.

Will Kymlicka and Kathryn Walker, eds, *Rooted Cosmopolitanism: Canada and the World* (Vancouver: University of British Columbia Press, 2012). As in Kymlicka's earlier book, *Multicultural Odysseys: Navigating the New International Politics of Diversity* (Toronto: Oxford University Press, 2007), this collection discusses Canadian multiculturalism in relation to global trends in the understanding of citizenship, identity, and belonging.

Queen's University, Multiculturalism Policy in Contemporary Democracies: https://www .queensu.ca/mcp/. Interesting and regularly updated information on diversity and policies affecting multiculturalism in Canada and many other countries.

Phil Ryan, *Multicultiphobia* (Toronto: University of Toronto Press, 2010). A lively analysis of Canadian multiculturalism and its critics.

Review Exercises

1. Ethnic and racial profiling involves the practice of singling out people for different and disadvantageous treatment because of their ethnicity or race. Find two or three cases where this has been alleged to be a systematic practice in Canada. You might start by going to the websites of the Canadian Race Relations Foundation (www.crr.ca), the Canadian Bar Association (www.cba.org), and the Canadian Civil Liberties Association (www.ccla.org).

2. Canadians and their leaders usually attribute the comparatively good relations between ethnic communities in Canada to the country's policy of multiculturalism. But some experts on immigration, diversity, and integration argue that Canada's immigration policy, which for several decades has favoured immigrants with higher levels of education and job skills, is the main factor explaining why Canada's pluralist model appears to work better than those in some other democracies. How would you set about testing these claims? Where would you find the data needed to test these propositions?

3. In recent decades quite a lot of research has been done on the question of whether cultural diversity may, in fact, contribute to lower levels of social trust. One of the major researchers in this field is Harvard's Robert Putnam. See the following *Guardian* article, at: www.theguardian .com/society/2007/jul/18/communities .guardiansocietysupplement, and, optionally, listen to the interview with Putnam at the link found at this webpage. Follow this by reading the 2016 *Scientific American* article "Does Diversity Create Mistrust?": https://www .scientificamerican.com/article/does-diversity-create-distrust/. Do you think there is any basis for concern about what some social scientists have argued is a possible negative relationship between diversity and levels of social trust?

The 12.9 kilometre Confederation Bridge—the longest in the world crossing ice water—was built in 1997, allowing year-round travel between Prince Edward Island and New Brunswick and solidifying the connection between the island province and the mainland. Canada's enormous size and diverse regions produce a wide range of political cultures, and create challenges for federal policy-makers. (benedek/iStockphoto)

5 Regionalism and Canadian Politics

Regionalism and regionally based political conflict are enduring aspects of the Canadian political condition. This chapter looks at several important aspects of regionalism in Canadian politics, including the following topics:

- Mapping regionalism in Canada
- Economic regions
- Cultural regions
- Cross-border regions
- Factors that continue to fuel regionalism
- Regional grievances and western alienation

"Canada has too much geography," declared the country's longest-serving prime minister, Mackenzie King. By this he meant that the vastness of the country and the diversity in the natural endowments and interests of its regions produced conflicts that would either not exist in a more compact country or whose resolution would be less difficult. Canadians have always accepted the truth of King's dictum, believing that the challenges of **regionalism** and inter-regional conflict are a central part of the Canadian story. These challenges have been at the root of major political divisions and controversies throughout Canada's history and continue to be a prominent feature of Canada's political landscape.

As a concept, regionalism is a bit murky. It refers to a territory, as in the Arctic region of Canada, the Basque region of Spain, or the Pacific Northwest region of the United States. What is special about such a region, what sets it apart from contiguous or other regions in a country and why one should apply the label "region" to a particular territory, is often less obvious. It could be for economic, demographic, cultural, environmental, geopolitical/strategic, or other reasons, or for some combination of these. The term is rendered even murkier by the fact that what is distinctive about some regions is the concentration of a particular community defined by language, culture, and history—in short, a nation, as many would define this term—and the presence of a nationalist movement that makes political claims on behalf of this community. Another layer of complication is added by the fact that regions sometimes overlap with political jurisdictions, such that regional interests, identities, and relations with other parts of the country and with the central government may take the form of intergovernmental conflicts. Federalism, the division of constitutional powers between a central government and some number of regional governments, does not necessarily fuel regionalism (think of Switzerland). But it may, and it appears to have done so in Canada.

In politics, the conversation on regionalism and debates about protecting and promoting regional interests, identities, and autonomy arise out of a dynamic relationship with forces that tug in a centralizing direction. Historically, Ontarians have been less likely to think of themselves and their province in regional terms than, say, British Columbians, Albertans, or Nova Scotians, because their interests and issues seemed to them identical to those of Canada. Indeed, surveys have long shown that Ontarians have been more likely than Canadians in other parts of the country to believe that their province "is treated with the respect it deserves in Canada," less likely than other Canadians to agree that their province "has less than it deserves in Canada," and considerably less likely than Canadians in other regions to identify with their province more than with Canada (although there is evidence that Ontarians have become more like other provincial populations in recent years).[1] They were less likely than other Canadians to have a regional self-image and to think of their interests in regional terms for the simple reason that, for most of Canada's history, these interests were well represented and protected by the central government in Ottawa. Regional populations that have not shared this assumption that their interests and values would be well represented and promoted in Ottawa have been more conscious of their regional identity in ways that affect their politics.

Regionalism in politics may emerge in response to a sense of being disconnected from, under-represented in, or exploited by the national government. But it may also arise in response to larger forces of centralization. Many national populations in the member-states of the European Union have responded to what some of their citizens believe to be excessive control from Brussels at the expense of their country's own values, traditions, and interests by supporting anti-EU parties and populist movements. Globalization, by its very nature, represents a challenge to territorially based differences and local control over matters of culture, economics, and politics. It has also spawned reactions in the form of regional efforts to protect cultural distinctiveness, social institutions, and economic interests, and to reassert local control.

Mapping Regionalism in Canada

How many regions does Canada have? The answer depends on our definition of "region." A map with boundaries drawn along economic lines will look different from one drawn along lines of demography or history. Some have argued that the only sensible way to conceive of regions in Canada is along provincial and territorial lines, such that each province and territory constitutes a separate region. More commonly, however, political observers have tended to combine certain provinces and the territories into the same region, particularly the western and eastern provinces and the three northern territories. But here, too, there are difficulties. The justification for lumping Manitoba and British Columbia into a common region designated the "West" is not obvious. Aside from both being west of Ontario they may appear to have no more in common than Manitoba and Nova Scotia. Difficulties aside, it has been common to speak of four or five main regions in Canada: the West (or British Columbia and the Prairies), Ontario, Quebec, and the Atlantic provinces. From the point of view of both physical and cultural geography, as well as economics, the Canadian North comprises another significant region.

There are three principal ways of determining the boundaries of regions, all of them useful. They involve economics, values and identity, and politics.

Canada's Economic Regions

Common economic interests, often linked to physical geography, may provide a basis for the classification of regions. Atlantic Canada's greater dependence on fisheries, the significant manufacturing base of Ontario and Quebec, and the West's comparatively greater reliance on grain production and natural resources are economic interests that have provided a basis for thinking of these parts of Canada as constituting distinctive regions. As Table 5.1 shows, the economic characteristics of Canada's provinces vary considerably.

The regional variation in Canada's industrial structure has often been at the root of major political conflicts between regions of the country and between Ottawa and the provinces. Historically, some of the federal government's major economic policies have been slanted towards the interests of central Canada. On occasion the discrimination against and even exploitation of other regions of the country, particularly the West, has been egregious. Examples include the following.

Tariffs. For most of Canada's history a cornerstone of economic policy was high tariffs on manufactured imports, the costs and benefits of which were distributed unequally between the country's regions. The cost for western farmers to ship grain by rail to the Fort William railhead (today's Thunder Bay), despite federal subsidies, always

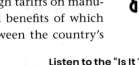

Listen to the "Is It Time to Redraw the Regional Map of Canada?" podcast, available at: www.oup.com/he/Brooks9e

seemed greater than it should have been to those in the West, and shipment of eastern manufactures to the West made prices higher than they might have been if trade, protected by the high tariffs of the National Policy beginning in 1879, could have followed more natural north–south lines to contiguous American states and regions. The extensive prime lands controlled by the Canadian Pacific Railway as part of its original agreement with the government in the nineteenth century also rankled western sensitivities.

One study of tariff impacts prior to the 1989 Canada–US Free Trade Agreement concluded that the per capita benefits for Ontario were about equal to the per capita costs imposed on the West and Atlantic Canada. Quebecers were also net beneficiaries, but the decline of that province's manufacturing base by the 1980s reduced the level of these benefits from what it had been for most of the previous century.[2]

Terms of entry into Confederation. Outside of Alberta and Saskatchewan, few Canadians know, and probably even fewer care, that when these provinces entered Canada in 1905 they did not immediately receive all of the law-making powers held by the other provinces. This was also true of Manitoba when it entered Confederation in 1870. Specifically, these provinces did not have control over public lands and natural resources within provincial borders, a power that sections 92 and 109 of the Constitution Act, 1867 assigns exclusively to the provinces. The reason for this discriminatory treatment involved, quite simply, Ottawa's desire to retain control over the economic development of the Prairies, a part of the country that was being settled rapidly in the early 1900s and whose expansion was essential to the National Policy goal of building a larger domestic market for the manufacturers of Ontario and Quebec.

TABLE 5.1 Selected Economic and Population Characteristics, by Province

Province or Territory	Median Family Income (2015) ($)	Unemployment Rate (average for 2013–17) (%)	Share of Total Merchandise Exports Accounted for by Exports to the US (2017) (%)	Key Industries	Population Growth, 1997–2017 (%)	Per Capita Federal Transfers (2017) ($)
Newfoundland and Labrador	67,272	12.9	53.0	Fishing, mining, oil & gas	–4	3,298
Prince Edward Island	61,163	10.6	73.7	Agriculture, tourism, fishing	12	5,072
Nova Scotia	60,764	8.7	64.4	Forestry, agriculture, tourism, fishing	2	3,866
New Brunswick	59,347	9.5	90.4	Forestry, mining, agriculture	1	4,386
Quebec	59,822	7.2	70.6	Manufacturing, mining, hydroelectric power, agriculture (especially dairy)	15	2,714
Ontario	74,287	6.8	82.2	Motor vehicles & parts, manufacturing, finance	26	1,871
Manitoba	68,147	5.6	64.0	Manufacturing, agriculture, mining	1	4,187
Saskatchewan	75,412	5.1	55.3	Agriculture, mining, oil & gas	14	2,955
Alberta	93,835	6.2	87.1	Oil & gas, agriculture	52	2,027
British Columbia	69,995	6.0	50.1	Forestry, tourism, mining, fisheries	22	1,980
Yukon	84,521	14.6	94.4	Mining	21	28,377
Northwest Territories*	117,688	7.5	0.3*	Mining, energy	7	32,335
Nunavut	97,441	14.7	0.4*	Mining	47	42,927
Canada	70,336	6.8	75.9		5.9	2,464 (national average)

Note: The fact that median incomes in the territories, and particularly in the Northwest Territories, are considerably higher than the Canadian average is mainly due to the incomes of the non-Indigenous populations in these parts of Canada. They hold many of the well-paying federal public-sector positions and jobs in the extractive industries. Indigenous incomes in the territories are, on average, about half those of the non-Indigenous population.
*European countries are by far the major export destinations for merchandise from these territories.

Source: Various online publications of Statistics Canada, www.statcan.ca.

The National Energy Program (1980). Almost two generations after it was abolished by the Progressive Conservative government of Brian Mulroney in 1984, the **National Energy Program** (NEP) remains iconic in the memory of many Albertans. It involved, they quite reasonably believed, an enormous transfer of wealth from Alberta to the rest of Canada, and chiefly to the consumers and industries of Canada's industrial heartland. It was perpetrated by a Liberal government they saw as being hostile to western, and especially Alberta's, interests. The NEP placed a limit on the price that could be charged in Canada for oil and gas from Canadian sources. This price was considerably below the going world price. Canadian producers'

ability to export their petroleum at the higher world price was limited by the fact that any energy exports had to be approved by the National Energy Board. Albertans saw the NEP as a thinly disguised subsidy their province was made to pay to central Canada. These fears were rekindled when the price of oil and gas rose dramatically in 2005, leading to proposals from some eastern Canadian politicians that Alberta's energy "windfall" be shared more equitably with the rest of Canada.[3]

Energy and the environment. When world oil prices doubled in 2007–8, there was somewhat less talk about the rest of Canada getting a slice of Alberta's growing revenue pie. Part of the reason for this change was probably the fact of a Conservative

Malcolm Mayes/Artizans

Government responses to climate change have become a major political issue internationally as well as within Canada. Here, the provincial premiers are shown pressuring Trudeau to drop his carbon tax by borrowing the tactics of France's yellow vest protesters, who took to the streets in November 2018 to pressure President Macron to drop his proposed hike in fuel taxes.

Governing Realities

BOX 5.1 Neighbours at Odds over Pipelines

Historically, Alberta and British Columbia have generally been on the same page when it comes to natural resource issues, if only because they found themselves in opposition to policies of the federal government. When bumper stickers reading "Let the eastern bastards freeze in the dark" proliferated in Alberta after Ottawa's imposition of the NEP, many British Columbians agreed with the underlying premise. Federal policies, including energy policies, seemed to be based on what was good for Ontario and Quebec, with little thought for the interests of the West. The prosperity of Alberta, BC, and Saskatchewan has always been tied to the export of natural resources, another factor that has usually made them good neighbours when it comes to resource issues.

This changed in 2012–13. The issue was the proposed Northern Gateway oil pipeline that would transport oil from northern Alberta to the inland port at Kitimat, BC, from where it would be shipped by tankers to markets in Asia. Public opinion polls in BC showed that a majority of the province's citizens opposed the pipeline and, moreover, that many more people strongly opposed the pipeline than strongly supported it. Environmental groups and some First Nations also opposed the pipeline's construction. Hearings on whether Enbridge, the pipeline proponent, would receive a permit for construction were held before a federal review panel under the authority of the National Energy Board Act and the Canadian Environmental Assessment Act. Shortly after her re-election in May 2013, BC Premier Christy Clark announced that her government was officially opposed to the pipeline.

For its part, the Conservative government in Ottawa supported the proposal, allying itself with the Alberta government and in opposition to that of BC. The collision of environmental concerns with energy interests has created circumstances that were almost unthinkable a generation ago. Albertans were used to eastern Canadian criticism of the oil sands, which appeared to them to be simply another chapter in a long-standing story of eastern Canadian insensitivity to western interests. Criticism and, worse, active opposition from a resource-dependent neighbour were something rather new. The federal Liberal government that replaced the Conservatives in power after the 2015 elections vetoed the Northern Gateway in late 2016.

Fast forward to 2018 and the issue of a pipeline to move Alberta oil to tidewater on the Pacific coast was still on the table. Kinder Morgan's Trans Mountain pipeline expansion proposal had the support of both the federal Liberal government and the government of Alberta. The Liberal government of BC had come around to supporting the pipeline's expansion, but that government lost the 2017 provincial election and was replaced by an NDP government that was steadfastly opposed to the Trans Mountain proposal. What ensued was a war of words and threats between the NDP governments of Alberta and BC, many legal challenges, and, ultimately, a federal government decision in May of 2018 to try to break the logjam by purchasing the existing Trans Mountain pipeline and its expansion project, followed by a large purchase of tanker cars by the Alberta government to transport that province's oil to market by rail.

Throughout this saga it was clear that the economic interests, environmental concerns, and public opinion in the duelling provinces mattered more than which party held power in BC and Alberta. These were the principal drivers of the positions taken by these provincial governments. They are features of the regional landscape that any party must respond to if it wants to win and hold onto power. While they do not necessarily tie a government's hands, ensuring that any party will behave in the same way on an issue as important to provincial interests as petroleum pipelines, they establish limits to what is possible. And they help to explain how it is that the federal wing of the NDP, which is firmly opposed to new petroleum pipelines, and the party's Alberta organization are on such different pages when it comes to this issue.

government in power, holding all 28 of Alberta's seats in the House of Commons and led by a prime minister from that province. But another part of the explanation was that the energy issue was now framed largely in environmental terms. How to wean consumers and industry from dependence on fossil fuels and reduce CO_2 emissions had become a far more prominent issue than whether the good fortune of some provinces meant that they should be expected to share the wealth (see Box 5.1)

This shift in how the energy issue, and particularly Alberta oil, was framed did not put an end to inter-regional conflict. Criticisms of Alberta the greedy were replaced by those of Alberta the despoiler of the environment and major source of global warming. The issue of greenhouse gas emissions and policies to limit and reduce them, including a tax on carbon, pitted Ottawa against Alberta from the late 1990s. This changed during the four years of NDP government in Alberta (2015–19). With the 2019 election of the Conservatives in Alberta and Conservative governments in power in Saskatchewan, Manitoba, Ontario, and New Brunswick, provincial opposition to the federal carbon tax regime spread beyond western Canada.

Canada's Cultural Regions

In one of the first studies of regional political cultures in Canada that drew upon survey research data, Richard Simeon and David Elkins concluded in 1974 that "there are strong differences among the citizens of Canadian provinces and those of different language groups in some basic orientations to politics."[4] They go on to argue that these regional variations cannot be totally explained by demographic and socio-economic differences between Canada's regions. The sources of these differences in basic political orientations, Simeon and Elkins admit, are unclear. But their existence, they insist, is undeniable.

In the decades since this seminal article was published, researchers have arrived at very different conclusions about the nature and extent of regional political cultures in Canada. Indeed, if

there is anything approaching a consensus on this question—and it is a shaky consensus at best—it is that regional variations in basic and enduring political values and beliefs are not very great in English-speaking Canada, and while the differences between French-speaking Quebec and the rest of Canada appear to be more significant, they are not enormous.

One of the most thorough examinations of political ideology in Canada corroborates the conclusion that, Quebec aside, the regional variations in political culture in the rest of Canada are not very great.[5] Based on a large national survey, Michael Ornstein and Michael Stevenson measured Canadians' support for social programs, redistributive policies, foreign investment, labour unions, and large corporations. Their examination of the variation in the ideological profiles of the provinces reveals that the differences are, for the most part, small and that Quebec stands out as the one province that is clearly to the left of the others. Moreover, contrary to the findings of Simeon and Elkins 25 years earlier, Ornstein and Stevenson did not find any significant variation between the provinces, Quebec included, in levels of political efficacy or political participation. "Not one province," they argue, "differs significantly from the national mean for the measure of efficacy,"[6] and the small provincial variations in participation do not conform to the pattern found by Simeon and Elkins. Several recent surveys support Ornstein and Stevenson's conclusion. They include the following:

- *Free speech and the Charter.* A 2017 survey by Abacus Data found very small differences between provincial populations on the issue of whether speech that might be considered controversial should be protected by the Charter's guarantee of free speech. Respondents were asked whether the Charter's guarantee of free speech should protect "so-called hate speech," whether it should protect speech that "praises terrorists or acts of terrorism," or speech that "criticizes specific religions." Levels of agreement were broadly similar in all of the provinces, the sole exception being with respect to speech that supports terrorism. In this case the range was from 19 per cent agreement in BC to 33 per cent in Quebec, the other provinces clustering very close to the national average of 28 per cent.[7]

- *Ideological self-placement.* The conventional wisdom, as found in the media, is that Canada's most left-leaning province is Quebec and the most right-leaning is Alberta. The rest fall somewhere in between. A 2012 survey by Ekos provided only tepid confirmation for this claim. Asked to place themselves on a 7-point scale where 1 was most liberal and 7 was most conservative (respondents were told that the question referred to their political beliefs or ideology, not support for political parties), Quebecers were very clearly the least likely to place themselves towards the conservative end and were more likely than the citizens of other provinces to place themselves at the liberal end of the spectrum, although just barely ahead of citizens in British Columbia. There was quite a lot of variation among the other provincial populations. Those in Saskatchewan and Manitoba—these provinces were combined because of the relatively small sample sizes from each—were the most likely to self-describe as ideologically conservative, more likely than Albertans.[8]

  A 2017 Environics survey asked Canadians to place themselves on a 10-point scale from left (1) to right (10). It found that 60 per cent of Canadians placed themselves in the middle (4–7) and that the range between the regions was from 55 per cent in the Atlantic provinces and in Alberta to 67 per cent in Manitoba/Saskatchewan. The dispersion was only slightly greater among those who self-identified on the right of the ideological scale (8–10). It ranged from 15 per cent in Manitoba/Saskatchewan to 30 per cent in Alberta. There were only small regional variations from the national result in the case of those who self-identified on the left (1–3).[9]

- *Morality and policy.* A 2016 survey by Abacus Data found very small differences, generally within a range of five percentage points, between the provincial populations on such matters as the morality of birth control, divorce, unmarried sex, recreational marijuana use, doctor-assisted dying, suicide, medical testing on animals, wearing clothing made of fur, and cloning animals and humans. While there were somewhat greater provincial differences on the morality of such behaviours as gambling, abortion, and the death penalty, the range was generally only 10–12 per cent.[10]

- *Canadian identity.* The 2013 General Social Survey, conducted by Statistics Canada, found very similar levels of agreement in all of the predominantly English-speaking provinces on the importance of the Charter, the Canadian flag, the national anthem, the RCMP, and hockey as national symbols. The outlier was Quebec, where respondents were significantly less likely than in the rest of Canada to believe that these are very important to Canadian national identity. Provincial levels of pride in being Canadian, in the Constitution, in the way Canadian democracy works, in Canadian history, and in a list of Canadian achievements were high and quite similar in all provinces with the exception of Quebec.[11]

- *Trust and confidence.* A 2013 survey by Ekos Politics found that, for the most part, only small variations exist between provincial populations in the level of trust they have in various groups and institutions. Respondents were asked to indicate how much trust they had in government, nurses, doctors, teachers, newspapers, journalists, television news, pollsters, social media, and bloggers. If there was any discernible pattern at all, Quebecers appeared to be somewhat more trusting than other provincial populations.[12] The General Social Survey of 2013 asked a rather similar question, asking respondents how much confidence they had in a number of institutions, including the police, school system, banks, the justice system and courts, the media, Parliament, and major corporations. The interprovincial range tended to be quite small for all these institutions. Quebec did not stand out from the other provinces.[13]

- *Faith and religious authority.* Quebec, once thought to be the most traditionally religious province, now appears to be the least. Variations among other provincial populations are small. A 2012 survey found that Quebecers are less likely than other provincial populations to say that religion is important in their lives, that God exists, that bad deeds are punished, and that a higher power governs the world. The provincial populations, including Quebec, are not very different in levels of trust in people who are very religious or not very religious, but Quebecers are much less trusting of clergy and religious leaders than are Canadians in other provinces.[14] It may be, however, that Quebec is losing the distinction of being the most secular province. A 2017 survey by CROP presented Canadians with the statement, "My religious beliefs are very important to me." Quebecers and British Columbians, at 43 per cent, were the least likely of the provincial populations to agree totally or somewhat.[15]

Despite the rather impressive number of studies that fail to corroborate the Simeon and Elkins argument that all of the provinces have distinctive political cultures, the belief that region must possess some independent explanatory power in Canadian politics lives on and researchers continue to test this claim. In a recent study based on survey data from the Comparative Provincial Elections Project, McGrane and Berdahl compare provincial populations in regard to political efficacy, belief in the honesty of politicians, feeling that government is wasteful, support for free markets, and post-materialist values. They find that the differences between provincial populations are not particularly significant, but that the differences between regions of Canada are more striking. "Overall, the data suggest that Canadian political culture has stronger *inter-regional* variations than *inter-provincial* variations.[16]

In another recent analysis of differences in provincial political cultures, Maxime Héroux-Legault compares the explanatory power of three models that explain political values. The first relies on socio-demographic factors, the second used province as the independent variable, and the third uses both socio-demographic factors and province. He concludes that the explanatory power of

socio-demographic variables far exceeds that of province in explaining attitudes relating to moral traditionalism, pluralism, immigration, and individual responsibility. Only in the case of attitudes towards egalitarianism is province a somewhat stronger explanatory factor than socio-demographic variables. Moreover, in the four cases where socio-demographic variables have the strongest explanatory power, the influence of province adds very little to the ability to predict political values. Héroux-Legault concludes, "Despite the importance of the literature published on questions of provincial and regional cleavages in political values in Canada, they are generally better explained by socio-demographic characteristics rather than province or region of residence."[17]

A similar conclusion is reached by Nelson Wiseman. He observes: "Surveys suggest that Canadians outside Quebec have remarkably similar tastes, values, opinions, and beliefs, but their political behaviour—as opposed to their popular culture—differs remarkably when we examine their political preferences regionally. Institutional walls—provincial boundaries, provincial administrations, and the configuration of party systems and social forces they contain—reinforce these differences."[18]

Cross-Border Regions

An alternative method of mapping regions is suggested by Debora VanNijnatten and her colleagues in their work on **cross-border regions** (CBRs). They define a CBR as a distinct grouping of neighbouring and nearby provinces and states with economic, cultural, and institutional linkages that create commonalities between the members of this binational (Canada–US) grouping and set it apart from other regions. Dense ties of trade and investment between the provinces and states that comprise a CBR are fundamental to such regions. They give rise to physical infrastructure such as roads, rail lines, bridges, tunnels, and shared water routes. They also provide the impetus for cross-border institutions and processes—both public, between subnational governments, and between non-governmental groups—whose functions are to co-ordinate, plan, promote, and resolve conflicts related to the economic linkages between the members of a CBR. A significant degree of shared values and even a sense of regional identity characterize some of the CBRs that span the Canada–US border.

Based on an analysis of the density of economic, institutional, and socio-cultural ties between adjacent and nearby provinces and states, VanNijnatten and her colleagues propose a rather different map of regionalism (see Figure 5.1). It includes the following regions:

- *The West.* This CBR consists of British Columbia, Alberta, Yukon, Alaska, Washington, Idaho, Oregon, and Montana. It is characterized by a feeling of remoteness from the central governments of each country and a strong sense of regional identity, such that residents may be more alike in their values than they are with their compatriots in other regions of their respective countries. A dense network of private and public institutional linkages spans the Canada–US border and more emphasis is placed on shared environmental issues than characterizes other regions.

- *The Prairie–Great Plains.* This CBR includes Alberta, Saskatchewan, and Manitoba on the Canadian side, and Montana, Wyoming, North Dakota, South Dakota, and Minnesota on the US side (Alberta and Montana were identified by the CBR project as belonging to both this CBR and the West). Although the institutional linkages between these relatively sparsely populated and natural resource-dependent provinces and states are less deeply entrenched than is true of the other CBRs, the economic ties between them are extensive and strong linkages exist based on shared management of common watersheds.

- *The Great Lakes–Heartland.* The shared waters of the Great Lakes and the enormous volume of trade and daily flow of vehicles and people across the Canada–US border are the most obvious features of this CBR. A dense network of cross-border institutions, public and private, links these states and provinces. But unlike the West, there is no strong sense of shared regional identity.

- *The East.* Although Quebec and Canada's Atlantic provinces have some significant trade and institutional linkages, their ties to adjacent and nearby American states are rather different. Quebec is part of a CBR that includes Vermont, Maine, New Hampshire, and New York, while the Atlantic provinces belong to a CBR that includes Maine, New Hampshire, Massachusetts, Rhode Island, and Connecticut. The Quebec–New England CBR is characterized by strong ties of history, trade, transportation, and institutions, but nothing much in the way of a shared regional identity. The Atlantic–New England grouping within the East is based on ties of history, trade, environmental and energy co-operation, a rich network of institutional linkages, and a strong sense of regional identity.

Thinking about Canadian regions in a way that takes into account these cross-border linkages is useful in various ways. First, it enables us to better understand the causes and nature of integration between Canada and the United States, much of which has taken place through regionalized networks. Canada–US economic integration is perhaps more accurately described as integration between the states and provinces of each of these four CBRs. As VanNijnatten puts it, North American integration has been and continues to be largely a bottom-up phenomenon.[19] Second, the significant powers held by provincial, state, and local governments on both sides of the border, and the fact that transportation, environmental, security, energy supply and distribution, and many other matters tend to be regional in nature, ensure that these subnational governments and private regional organizations and institutions will be important players in the management of cross-border issues. This is nowhere more apparent than in the case of environmental issues (see Box 5.2). Several recent studies of the cross-border management of issues, ranging from the regulation of river flows to schemes for the promotion of renewable energy sources for regional electricity grids, highlight the key role played by subnational governments and organizations.

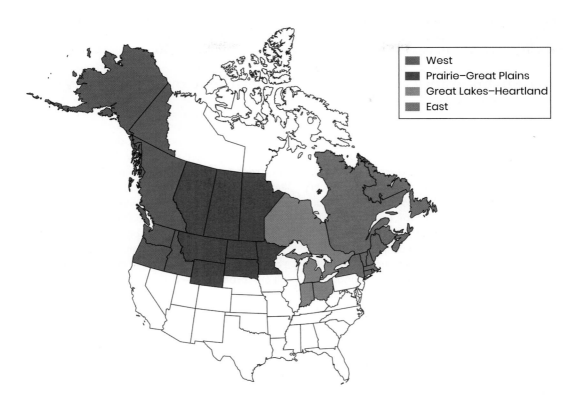

FIGURE 5.1 Cross-Border Regions

Source: Adapted from Debora VanNijnatten, "Canada–US Relations and the Emergence of Cross-Border Regions," Government of Canada, Policy Research Initiatives, 2006, www.policyresearch.gc.ca.

At the same time, the CBR concept has clear limitations. Some states and provinces are easily or logically placed in one CBR rather than another; others are not. Most of New York, for example, could be included in the Great Lakes–Heartland region rather than the East and Pennsylvania could reasonably be added to either of these regions; similarly, Alberta and Montana are inconveniently but at the same time quite reasonably included in both the West and Prairie–Great Plains regions. Another problem with this scheme is that it seeks to fit entire political jurisdictions into particular regions. But the economic and cultural linkages across the international border may be much more localized than this. For example, southwestern Ontario has very strong ties to Michigan and Ohio, but these ties are not experienced by northern or eastern Ontario, or at least not in the same ways or to the same degree. Limitations aside, this method of mapping regions

alerts us to the fact that political boundaries are far from being the final word when it comes to understanding regionalism.

The Factors That Continue to Fuel Regionalism in Canada

In view of the fact that the evidence for distinctive provincial political cultures is rather weak, the case of Quebec being an exception in some important ways, one might well ask why regionalism continues to be an important force in Canadian politics. The answer has several parts, some of which have been alluded to earlier in this chapter. They include the following.

The party system. For most of Canada's history the two historically dominant parties, the Liberals and Conservatives, competed with each

Governing Realities

BOX 5.2 Transboundary Environmental Governance and the Reality of Cross-Border Regions

National and provincial borders are only part of the story regarding the management of many environmental issues. The Great Lakes region is a major case in point: two countries; two Canadian provinces and eight American states. Several major cities of each country border the lakes and the rivers that connect them. Many more are part of the watershed of the Great Lakes. The Assembly of First Nations estimates that 75 Indigenous communities inhabit the coastlines of the Great Lakes and many more fall within the regional watershed. Transportation infrastructure, industry, agriculture, energy generation and transmission grids, pipelines, and municipal water and waste activities on both sides of the Canada–US border affect the environment of the Great Lakes region. On top of this, the legal authority to regulate all of these matters is not only divided between two countries, it is divided between national and subnational governments. The transboundary nature of so many environmental issues ensures that their management will require the involvement of multiple stakeholders representing different political jurisdictions and interests. The Great Lakes region is not unique in this regard. A couple of decades ago the International Joint Commission, a binational body with representation from Canada and the United States, launched what it called its International Watersheds Initiative. Its map of the Canada–US border shows a string of 12 transboundary watersheds from the Pacific to the Atlantic, and also includes the basin that includes much of Alaska and Yukon (http://www.ijc.org/en_/Transboundary_Basins). For environmental management purposes, these are all cross-border regions. Addressing issues of pollution, water management, species protection, fisheries, and energy requires the engagement and co-operation of multiple governments, First Nations communities, industries, and environmental groups. The structures and processes through which this issue management may occur may be state-to-state, as through treaties and other binational agreements. But they are as likely to take place through networks of subnational governments and to include the representatives of non-state interests and Indigenous communities.[20]

other across Canada. Although they did not draw equally well from all regional segments of the electorate—the Liberal Party did much better than the Conservatives in Quebec for most of the twentieth century and continues to do better in the current century, and the Conservative Party has tended to be stronger than the Liberals in the West since the 1950s—both were very clearly national political parties with significant support across Canada.

During much of the time since the 1993 general election, the character of Canada's party system has appeared to be more regionally than nationally based. This was most obvious in the case of the Bloc Québécois, which only runs candidates in Quebec and which elected more MPs from that province than any other party in every national election between 1993 and 2008, and running a close second to the Liberals in 2019. The Canadian Alliance, formerly the **Reform Party**, won almost all of its seats west of Ontario and received the greatest share of the popular vote of any party in the combined four western provinces during the 1993, 1997, and 2000 federal elections. The Progressive Conservative Party, long a truly national party in terms of the regional breadth of its support, elected more of its MPs from the Atlantic provinces in these three elections than from any other part of the country. The Alliance and the Progressive Conservatives merged into the Conservative Party of Canada before the 2004 election, a union that delivered less than a handful of seats in Ontario and none from Quebec in that election. Only the Liberal Party appeared capable of claiming significant support in all regions of the country over these four national elections, although even its regional levels of support were very uneven.

The 2006 and 2008 elections saw a continuation of very weak Liberal support west of Ontario, but a resurgence of Conservative support in Ontario and even, to a lesser degree, in Quebec. Nevertheless, recent elections, including those of 2011, 2015, and 2019, produced party representation in Parliament that is strikingly fragmented along regional lines. The Liberal Party won more seats nationally than any other party in 2019, but won only 15 of the 104 seats in the four westernmost provinces and not a single seat in either Alberta or Saskatchewan. *The unevenness in the historically dominant political parties' regional support reduces their ability to represent the diverse regional interests of the country.*

Regionalism is also apparent when one looks at the provincial party systems across Canada. Unlike in some federal countries, such as Germany, the United States, and Australia, the parties that compete to form a government at the provincial level in Canada are often different from those that compete for seats from that province in federal elections. Quebec is an obvious case in point, where the Parti Québécois was one of the two dominant provincial parties from the 1970 provincial election until the 2018 election, when it elected only 10 members and lost official party status in the National Assembly. The PQ is a political party that exists only in Quebec. In British Columbia, provincial elections since 1991 have been mainly competitions between the NDP and the province's Liberal Party. Although the Conservative Party does well in federal elections in BC, its provincial counterpart almost disappeared in the 1990s and in recent elections has received only a handful of votes and no seats in provincial elections. Since 1999, elections in Saskatchewan have been contests between the NDP and the Saskatchewan Party. The provincial Liberal Party has been very weak in recent elections and there is no provincial Conservative Party (instead, there is a Progressive Conservative Party that runs candidates in a handful of ridings and won just over 1 per cent of the vote in the province's 2016 election). In Quebec, the provincial Conservative Party essentially exists in name only. Its candidates have received a fraction of 1 per cent of the popular vote in recent provincial elections. On the other hand, in addition to the PQ, the Action démocratique du Québec, which merged with the Coalition Avenir Québec (CAQ) in 2012 (both being parties that do not exist at the federal level), received significant voter support in recent

provincial elections. Indeed, the CAQ was elected the government of Quebec in 2018.

In short, in many provinces considerable asymmetry exists between provincial party systems and the pattern of party competition in federal elections. *Canada's decentralized party system does not play a role in attenuating regional divisions in the country.*

Western alienation. Western grievances against Ottawa and the Ontario–Quebec axis have existed for as long as the western provinces have been part of Canada. But in the 1970s there was a sharp upward ratcheting in the rhetoric associated with these grievances. At this point the term "western alienation" entered the lexicon of Canadian politics. As had always been the case, economics was at the root of the discontent. Spokespersons for the western provinces argued that Ottawa treated the resources with which the West was well endowed, and which formed the basis for western prosperity, differently and less favourably than those located primarily in provinces like Ontario and Quebec. Although Albertans were the most vocal in making this case, politicians and industry leaders in British Columbia and Saskatchewan provided a supportive chorus.

During the years of Conservative federal government (2006–15), when the West was well represented in Ottawa, talk of western alienation subsided. The region's historical sense of grievance, however, was only dormant. As we will see later in the chapter, it has re-emerged in recent years.

Intergovernmental conflict. The pendulum of federal–provincial power has swung from Ottawa to the provinces and back again several times since Confederation. Prime Minister John A. Macdonald hoped that the provincial governments would become little more than "glorified municipalities," deferring to Ottawa on all matters of national importance. His vision was stymied from the beginning by provincial politicians who had other ideas and by judges whose interpretation of the division of powers in Canada's Constitution did not accord with Macdonald's. In recent years intergovernmental conflict has been alive and intense on a number of fronts, including environmental policy, health care, taxation, energy and pipelines, cities, and post-secondary education. Judging from these conflicts, regionalism continues to mark the Canadian political landscape.

Brian Gable/*The Globe and Mail*

The historical positions of provinces in relation to one another are always changing. In February 2019, the Conference Board of Canada predicted only modest growth for Quebec and Ontario, with larger growth in British Columbia, PEI, and Newfoundland and Labrador. Long considered a "have-not" province, household incomes in Saskatchewan are now about as high as in Ontario.

The persistence and even resurgence of regionalism, in Canada and elsewhere, took many by surprise. One of the few points of agreement among most twentieth-century social and political observers was that as the conditions of people's existence became more alike, their values, beliefs, and behaviour would converge. Modern transportation, mass media, public education, and consumer lifestyle habits would break down the barriers that previously separated regional communities and nurtured their distinctiveness, such that regionalism would become a weaker force in social and political life. Those on the left predicted that region, like religion and ethnicity, eventually would be replaced by class as the dominant fault line in the politics of modernized societies. Indeed, some went so far as to argue that only the obfuscations and manipulations of the dominant class, exercised through their control of the mass media and political parties,

kept alive the fiction that region, and not class, was more important in shaping the interests and identities of average people.

Contrary to these expectations, and despite the undeniable fact that in many important ways the lives of people across the rich industrialized societies of the world are more alike today than two or three generations ago, regionalism and its even more robust cousin—nationalism—continue to be important forces in political life. This certainly is true in Canada, as the signs of the vitality of regionalism discussed above attest, and as the persistence of a significant nationalist movement in Quebec demonstrates. Three principal factors help to explain the attraction and persistence of regionalism.

First, traditional thinking underestimated the degree to which regionally based states and elites may invest in regionalism—and regionally based nationalism too, as in the case of Quebec—when this investment either serves their own interests or, more charitably, promotes their vision of what is in the best interests of the regional community they purport to represent. During the 1970s Canadian political scientists began to use the term **province-building** to describe the phenomenon of powerful provincial governments using the various constitutional, legal, and taxation levers available to them to increase their control over activities and interests within their provincial borders and, in consequence, their stature vis-à-vis Ottawa. Alberta and Quebec were the two provinces most often cited as illustrations of this drive on the part of provincial state elites to extend the scope of their authority. In recent years the concept of province-building has continued to be relevant. Mirelle Paquet uses it to analyze the increasing role that provincial governments have assumed in immigration policy.[21] Wilder and Howlett argue that the concept is as relevant today for an understanding of the dynamic of intergovernmental relations and provincial pushback against Ottawa as at any time in the past.[22]

A second factor not anticipated by those who predicted the demise of regionalism involves the failure of national institutions—political, cultural, and economic—to produce levels of national integration and identity that would overcome regionally based ways of thinking and acting in Canadian politics. To put this a bit differently, many Canadians, particularly in Quebec and in the West, have remained unconvinced that the institutions of the national government and its policies have their best interests in mind. Students of federalism have made a distinction between *inter*-state federalism, where conflict and co-operation are played out between the national and regional governments, and *intra*-state federalism, where the regions are represented and their voices heard within the institutions of the national state. There certainly has been no shortage of national structures and policies intended to accommodate regional interests and perspectives. A short list of these, past and present, would include the following:

Structures

- The Senate incorporates the principle of regional representation, with Ontario, Quebec, the four western provinces, and the three Maritime provinces all being assigned 24 seats. Newfoundland and Labrador has six seats and each of the three territories is assigned one seat. Senators are appointed from specific provinces and territories and are, as such, representatives of the region from which they have been selected. Whether they see themselves as regional spokespersons is another matter.
- The Supreme Court Act requires that at least three of the nine justices be members of the Quebec bar. Moreover, the custom has developed over time whereby it is expected that three of the judges will be from Ontario, two from the western provinces, and one from Atlantic Canada.
- The federal cabinet has always been at the centre of attempts to ensure regional representation in federal decision-making. Every prime minister has given careful consideration to the representation in cabinet of each region and, insofar as possible, each province.
- Section 36 of the Constitution Act, 1982 commits the federal government to the principle of "making equalization payments to ensure that provincial governments have sufficient revenues to provide reasonably comparable levels of public services at reasonably comparable levels of taxation." Although the practical significance of this constitutional commitment is far from clear, the spirit of it clearly involves a federal obligation to assist the less affluent provincial governments in paying their bills.

Policies

- For several decades, and in response to criticism that the Canadian media and federal cultural policy were strongly biased towards central Canada, Ottawa has attempted to "regionalize" its cultural activities in various ways. One of these involves regional programming through the Canadian Broadcasting Corporation and a conscious policy of ensuring that regional points of view are expressed in its national programming, as required by the Broadcasting Act, 1991. Another involves the programs and spending activities of the Department of Canadian Heritage, which, like the CBC, has a mandate to express the diversity of Canada, including its regional diversity and histories.
- Federal support for regional economic development has a long and much-criticized history in Canada. These activities were given an organizational focus and a major spending boost through the 1968 creation of the Department of Regional Economic Expansion, which has morphed into departments and agencies by other names over the years. Today, Ottawa's support for the economies of the less affluent provinces is channelled mainly through five regional development agencies under Innovation, Science and Economic Development Canada.
- When making decisions that have important regional spending and employment implications, from the awarding of contracts to the location of government offices, Ottawa is always sensitive to the probable reactions of citizens and their spokespersons in regions competing for a share of the federal pie.

Although it would be unfair to write off these structures and policies as amounting to a complete and abject failure, they clearly have not succeeded in neutralizing regionalism. It is always possible, of course, that regional grievances and the acrimony that often accompanies intergovernmental relations in Canada might have been worse in the absence of these efforts to represent and respond to regional interests and preferences through structures and processes of the federal state.

A third factor that has always fuelled regionalism, and whose importance remains undiminished, involves the persistence of differences in the economic interests of Canada's regions. For example, about one-quarter of Alberta's GDP is accounted for by the petrochemical industry, a level of dependence on this particular industry unrivalled in Canada. Ontario is far more dependent than any other province on the automobile industry, with just over 20 per cent of provincial GDP accounted for by automotive vehicle and parts production and about 30 per cent of provincial exports, close to 95 per cent of which go to the United States. British Columbia accounts for over half of all Canadian lumber and wood product exports, most of which go to the United States, China, and Japan. As these few examples suggest, the economic issues that will capture the attention of politicians and the public differ considerably among the provinces.

Of course, the regional economic differences that exist within provinces, for example, between northern Ontario and the southwest of that province, are easily as great and in some cases greater than those between provinces. Nevertheless, it makes sense to focus on provinces as the regional unit of analysis. Provinces, not regions within provinces, possess the constitutional powers and the political means to represent and respond to the economic interests within their borders.

Regional Identities and Western Alienation

If, instead of looking for significant and enduring regional differences in fundamental political values and beliefs, we ask whether citizens of Canada's regions view their history in different ways and hold different aspirations for their country and their region's role in it, we then find rather compelling evidence for the existence of important regional differences, if not regional political cultures. In particular, the West has long been characterized by sentiments of resentment towards and alienation from Ottawa and what many westerners have perceived to be the political preoccupations of central Canada. These sentiments vary in intensity across the western provinces and also fluctuate in response to specific circumstances and events. Gibbins and Arrison argue that it is reasonable to speak of "national visions" in the West that, in their words, "address not simply the place of the West within the Canadian federal state, but also the nature of *Canada* as a political community."[23] These visions are not merely reactions to citizens' sense of being unfairly treated and marginalized within Canadian politics—the resentment captured in the Reform Party's founding slogan, "The West wants in." Rather, these western visions of Canada are deeply rooted in regional histories and memories that are not the same as those of central and eastern Canada.

Starting in a major way in the 1950s with W.L. Morton, western Canadian historians began to react against what they saw as a narrative of Canadian history told from a central Canadian perspective, with little allowance for the distinctive experiences and cultures of the West. This perspective, said Morton, "fails to take account of regional experience and history and makes coherent Canadian history seem an 'imperialist creed,' an imposition on Maritime, French-Canadian, Western and British Columbian history of an interpretation which distorted local history and confirmed the feeling that union with Canada had been carried out against local sentiment and local interest."[24] Morton and many others have attempted to counter the centralist bias of Canadian history writing, but the belief lives on that the West's stories are not given fair weight by a Canadian academic and cultural establishment whose centre of gravity is in the Toronto–Ottawa–Montreal triangle.

In a broadly similar vein Barry Cooper, a Calgary-based political scientist, argues that a distinctive political tradition exists in western Canada, the roots of which lie in the history of that region. "[D]ualism," he observes, "is not the political issue in the West that it is in central Canada. Moreover, multiculturalism does not mean the same thing to a third or fourth generation non-French, non-British Westerner as it does to someone from the Azores or Calabria living on College Street in Toronto."[25] What is referred to as **western alienation**, Cooper argues, is not in fact a psychological, sociological, or economic condition experienced by those in the West. Rather, it is the awareness that the public realm—whose voices are heard and what counts as legitimate political discourse—belongs to others. These others are the citizens of central Canada and the elites who purport to speak on their behalf.

Of course, the history of the West and the political traditions that have evolved in western Canada are not disconnected from those of the rest of Canada. Likewise, as Gibbins and Arrison observe, "western visions" of the nature of the Canadian political community and that region's place in it are not restricted to the West. They identify a set of core values they believe are more solidly anchored in the West than in other regions of Canada, but the same values also find support among Canadians in other regions, including French-speaking Quebec. The difference is one of degree. Western visions of Canada, Gibbins and Arrison argue, are more likely to embrace the *individual* equality of all Canadians, the equal status of all provinces, and a populist style of doing political business.

Regarding the first of these values—individual equality—Gibbins and Arrison rightly note that reservations about the official recognition and even constitutionalization of multiculturalism and a group rights concept of Canada have come largely from such popular western spokespersons as John Diefenbaker, Preston Manning, and Stephen Harper. Such visions of Canada are part of what Alberta political scientist Barry Cooper refers to as the "Laurentian Canada" perspective that projects the history, preoccupations, and preferences of Ontario and Quebec onto the rest of the country.[26] The election of ideologically conservative provincial governments in the 1990s and early twenty-first century, such as those of Ralph Klein, followed by Ed Stelmach in Alberta and Gordon Campbell in British Columbia, and the impressive support in western Canada for Reform/Alliance and then the Conservative Party in federal elections, are factors that appear to corroborate this argument that westerners are more receptive to what might be characterized as a classically American conception of equality. This involves the equal treatment of all individuals, without taking group membership into account, and formal equality of opportunity. On the other hand, little in the way of survey evidence supports the claim that westerners are significantly different from their compatriots in other regions in what they think about equality. Moreover, the quite different histories of the western provinces—compare that of Saskatchewan to neighbouring Alberta, for example—should give pause to anyone who wishes to generalize about a *western* conception of equality.

The second core value of the western vision that Gibbins and Arrison identify is provincial equality. This really has two components. One is the sense that Canadian federalism would operate more fairly if the West had more influence on decisions taken by Ottawa. The idea of an elected Senate in which each province has an equal number of senators is one that has been spearheaded by western spokespersons since the 1980s. The other component of this core value involves opposition to any arrangement that appears to treat Quebec differently from and more favourably than the western provinces. Opposition to the Charlottetown Accord in the 1992 referendum was significantly higher in the four western provinces than in the rest of English-speaking Canada. Constitutional recognition of Quebec as a distinct society and other provisions that may well have been interpreted as providing special status for Quebec were, of course, among the most controversial sections of the Charlottetown Accord. Observers of the western political scene know that westerners have often felt resentment against Quebec, believing it to be the "spoiled child" of Confederation. The West's enthusiasm for the idea that the provinces are all equal in their rights and powers clashes with Quebecers' preference for a binational vision of the country in which Quebec, as the home of 90 per cent of French-speaking Canadians, and English-speaking Canada are conceived of as equal partners. In recent years the resentment that some westerners have felt towards Quebec has been generated by differences over pipeline construction and what is desirable when it comes to the future of fossil fuels. Quebecers and their provincial government have led the way in questioning projects that many westerners believe to be indispensable to their region's prosperity.

The third component of the western vision involves a populist style of politics. **Populism** arose in the American West and Midwest in the late 1800s out of the perception that economic and political elites, often far from where the people affected by their decisions lived, were too powerful and unsympathetic to the people's interests. The western Canadian version of populism was a combination of imported ideas and homegrown conditions that made the American message resonate in a farm and resource-based economy where people were constantly reminded by the railroads, the banks, the tariffs, and the grain elevator companies that they did not control their own destiny.

Politics in Focus

BOX 5.3 The West as Canada's Internal Colony

John W. Dafoe was a journalist and editor with the Winnipeg Free Press, *back in an era when newspapers were still the dominant medium whereby people learned about public affairs and the* Winnipeg Free Press *was considered one of Canada's leading dailies. The foundation that bears Dafoe's name annually awards a prize to what it judges to have been the non-fiction book that contributes most to the understanding of Canada. In 2013 the prize went to Mary Janigan's* Let the Eastern Bastards Freeze in the Dark: The West Versus the Rest Since Confederation. *As a staunch defender of western interests he believed were regularly ignored by Ottawa, Dafoe most certainly would have approved of this selection. Here is Janigan's summary of the story that she tells:*

The struggle over resource control twines through the nation's history as vividly as those wrenching debates over language and culture. The political actors who were once larger than life are now forgotten. But the legacy of their fights with the Rest of Canada, which played out in furious time across the decades, lingers in the language and the airy assumptions of today's politicians. Those battles have created an edgy regional identity. Even first-generation Westerners bristle at the mere mention of federal regulatory incursions. Canadians in other provinces still suspect Westerners of abusing the national patrimony—when they would never assert the same control over the hydro resources of Quebec or Newfoundland and Labrador.

These attitudes are bred in the bone, integrated after generations of political struggles between the West and the Rest of Canada. While Quebec struggled to maintain its status as one of the founding peoples of Canada, the West fought for the same constitutional right of resource control that other provinces possessed. The ingredients for trouble were woven into the very founding fabric of the nation. In the late 1860s when Ottawa purchased Western lands and resources from the Hudson's Bay Company, it viewed the West as a colonial space that it could span with a railroad and settle with immigrant farmers. The unexpected resistance of Louis Riel and the Métis to this second-class status was the first in a long line of objections to the West's limited powers and Ottawa's oblivious intrusions. In response, Ottawa and the other provincial governments countered that they had bought the West: the Rest owned the West. The most strident clash occurred on that cusp of time when the Great War ended and the First Ministers gathered to remake their world. By the time that tempers cooled, regional identities had solidified. The narratives of mutual suspicion were set.

This is *not* a regional story. It is the story of Canada. And it is still playing out in real time whenever Canadians ponder the privileges and the challenges of the West's resource wealth.

Source: Excerpt from Mary Janigan, *Let the Eastern Bastards Freeze in the Dark: The West Versus the Rest Since Confederation* (2013). Reprinted with permission from Mary Janigan: http://maryjanigan.ca/.

Populism, in its simplest form, seeks to return power to the common people. It sees elected politicians as delegates of those who elected them and therefore is hostile to party discipline and aspects of parliamentary government that reduce a public official's ability or willingness to be a direct tribune of his or her constituents' preferences. Populists favour recall votes to remove unfaithful public officials from office, plebiscites and referendums to give people a more direct say in the decisions that affect them, short terms of office, and term limits for public officials. In what is probably the best study of referendums in Canada, Patrick Boyer shows that this favoured instrument of populist democracy has been used far more extensively in the West than in other parts of Canada.[27] About 60 per cent of all provincial referendums held since Confederation have been in the four western provinces. The Reform Party's original platform placed a heavy emphasis on referendums and recall votes, although this became a less prominent feature of the Alliance Party's platform and essentially disappeared after the 2003 merger of the Alliance and the Progressive Conservatives to form the Conservative Party of Canada.

The greater popularity in western Canada of referendums and other measures that give citizens a direct say in their governance may be seen in a number of measures enacted by western provincial governments. British Columbia passed a recall law in the 1990s—the first province to do so—and the British Columbia government of Gordon Campbell held a 2002 referendum on the highly contentious question of Indigenous title and treaty negotiations in the province. BC held another referendum in 2005 and again in 2009 and 2018 on proposals to change the province's electoral system. In 2011 a mail-in referendum asked about changing the province's sales tax. British Columbia is also the only province to provide for the possibility of a citizen initiative whereby a new law may be proposed if a petition receives the signatures of at least 10 per cent of registered voters in each of the province's electoral districts (more difficult than it may sound!). The current United Conservative government in Alberta supports legislation requiring that a referendum be held before any carbon tax may be introduced in the province. Alberta law also requires that a referendum

be held in order to impose a sales tax in the province. All of the four western legislatures have laws requiring that proposals for constitutional amendment be submitted to the people in a referendum, although Canada's Constitution does not require this. In short, there have been strong indications that populist values are more solidly rooted in the West than in the rest of Canada. The Conservative Party's string of victories in the 2006, 2008, and 2011 federal elections was accompanied by a sharp decline in western Canadians' belief that their region was treated unfairly by the national government. The prime minister was from Alberta, several of his most influential cabinet ministers were from the West, and the Conservative Party had won a majority of seats in the four western provinces in every election since 2006. Was western alienation finally dead?

In an analysis of western Canadians' perceptions of their treatment by Ottawa, Loleen Berdahl notes a sharp decline between 2004, when the Liberals were still in power, and 2008 in the percentage of westerners who say that the federal government treats their province worse than the others. The decline was most dramatic in British Columbia and Alberta. Data from the 2011 Canadian Election Survey confirmed that westerners appeared to be much less alienated from the federal government than prior to the Conservative victory of 2006. Berdahl notes that westerners who identified with the Conservative Party were, not surprisingly, most likely to feel that their province is treated fairly by Ottawa, but the decline in the percentage of respondents saying that their province is treated worse than other provinces was found among supporters of other political parties too.[28] More recently, however, polling carried out by the Angus Reid Institute in 2016 and 2019 found that the sense of being treated unfairly by the federal government and the belief that the province contributes more to the country than it receives in return have increased in Alberta and Saskatchewan. The 2019 survey found that only 17 per cent of Albertans and 23 per cent of those in Saskatchewan agreed that their province is treated fairly by Ottawa, compared to a figure of 44 per cent nationally and 56 per cent in Ontario.[29]

Notwithstanding this recent uptick in resentment towards the federal government in Alberta and

Saskatchewan, a demographic trend may already have weakened the traction of the western alienation narrative in the politics of the West. It involves immigration. Neil Nevitte and his colleagues find that immigrants from non-European source countries tend to be "more federally oriented than the local population in their province." After Ontario and Quebec, British Columbia and Alberta have had the highest levels of immigration since the 1980s. Much of it has been from Asian countries. At almost 30 per cent in British Columbia and roughly 22 per cent in Alberta, only Ontario, where three out of 10 residents were born outside Canada, has a higher share of immigrants. The historical memory of grievances that has long fuelled western alienation is, presumably, less likely to exist among the non-native born.[30] Moreover, a sense of grievance may be less likely among those who moved to the West from other parts of Canada. The share of both the Alberta and British Columbia populations born in other provinces is considerably greater than is the case in other provinces.[31] Most of these interprovincial immigrants come from parts of the country where people are less likely than native-born westerners to have heard the story of western grievances against Ottawa and the purported domination of Canadian politics by central Canada.

The anger and vituperation that existed in the West at the time of the NEP and the birth in 1987 of the Reform Party have cooled. Western alienation, however, should not be dismissed as mere history. The sense of regional grievance, with roots reaching back to the nineteenth century, can resurface very quickly and with real political consequences. In 2018, the leader of Alberta's United Conservative Party, Jason Kenney, said, "The hypocrisy in this country is driving a level of alienation here I haven't seen in my whole life. People are angry, and they should be." The hypocrisy he was referring to involved what he argued was a double standard in how Ottawa treated the interests of Alberta compared to those of Quebec. "In the past year," Kenney went on, "I have heard more expressions of support for Western or Alberta separatism than I've heard in my whole life."[32] This, of course, could be dismissed as the sort of thing a party leader might say to mobilize voter anger and support in the lead-up to a provincial election, as occurred in 2019 when Kenney's party was elected with a majority government.

Professor Jack Mintz puts the matter in more measured tones. He argues that regional alienation is indeed on the upswing in the West. In words that could have been written during the 1980s heyday of western alienation, Mintz explains this upswing:

> [It] arises from a sense that the federal government's professed support for resource provinces is hollow. . . . Regulatory rules have changed to make approvals slower, more complicated and less certain, hurting the industry's international competitiveness. The government has raised taxes on resource firms but its subsidies for Central Canada's manufacturing and aerospace firms continue unabated. Where Ottawa provided emergency aid to Ontario's manufacturers in the 2009 recession, it can barely lift a finger to help Alberta and Saskatchewan with their brutal recessions.[33]

As Canada's poorest region with its own list of grievances against the federal government and central Canada, one might have expected that the Atlantic provinces would have generated an eastern version of western alienation. Over the years the easternmost provinces have indeed produced leaders, such as Newfoundland premiers Joey Smallwood (1949–72), Brian Peckford (1979–89), and Danny Williams (2003–10), who have taken a back seat to none in being outspoken critics of what they saw as unjust treatment of their province by Ottawa. Secession from Canada dominated the political conversation in Nova Scotia just two decades after Confederation. The Maritime Rights movement[34] swept the region in the 1920s, and proposals for Maritime union have existed since before Confederation, continuing to surface from time to time as ideas, though with little political support. But the dissatisfaction of Atlantic Canadians has never produced a major political vehicle for the expression of regional alienation and resentment, such as the Progressive movement of the 1920s, the Social Credit Party from the 1930s to the 1970s, and the Reform Party in the late 1980s and 1990s in western Canada. Why not?

The answer is complex, but two elements are certainly crucial. First, the populist values linked to western alienation from its beginnings over a century ago have been comparatively weak in the Atlantic provinces. The reasons for this involve a combination of demographic and economic differences between the eastern and western regions of Canada, but also differences in the political histories of the two regions. Whereas Alberta and Saskatchewan did not achieve provincial status until 1905—and then, without control of their natural resources for 25 years—Nova Scotia and New Brunswick, despite some loud and articulate anti-Confederation voices in the region, were original members of the Confederation pact, and PEI soon followed. The historically dominant parties have deep roots in the Maritime provinces, stretching back to Confederation. **Protest parties** have always found it difficult to break through the two-party domination in the East. The Progressives failed to win a single seat from the region even in 1921, when they emerged from the general election as the official opposition. Social Credit and the Reform Party did no better. It was not until 1974 that the NDP won a seat from the region, breaking the party duopoly that had existed for more than a century. Economically and demographically the Maritimes have been in decline, relative to the rest of Canada, since the late nineteenth century. The region's population as a share of the national population has plummeted since Confederation. As shown in Table 5.1, the economies of the eastern provinces are among the weakest in Canada. This remains true despite Newfoundland and Labrador's impressive resource-fuelled growth of recent years. (The province's population has barely changed over the last decade and it continues to lose highly educated and skilled workers to other parts of the country, notwithstanding increases in its provincial GDP and government revenues.) All of the eastern provinces except Newfoundland and Labrador depend on money redistributed by Ottawa from more prosperous regions of the country to pay for public services.[35] This stands in stark contrast to the prosperity that Alberta and British Columbia have experienced during most of the last half-century, and that Saskatchewan now enjoys as a result of higher world prices for natural resources found in the province. As well, the dramatic population growth experienced in the West is in direct contrast to the demographic stagnancy in the East.

The much more assertive attitude of western than eastern Canadians and their greater willingness to reject the traditional political parties in favour of protest parties surely is linked to confidence in the economic future of their region. "The West wants in," the founding slogan of the Reform Party, was not the plea of a weak and supplicant region. Rather, it was the demand of a region whose population believed that Canadian politics needed to adjust to the reality of their economically powerful and growing provinces. Pollster Darrell Bricker and journalist John Ibbitson argue that the traditional political elites of Ontario and Quebec have failed to recognize this new reality. "The provinces that mattered most don't matter as much anymore," they write. "The country's centre has shifted west, and power has shifted with it."[36] The 2016 census found that for the first time in Canadian history about one in three Canadians lives west of Ontario. The West also accounts for a larger share of Canada's economic activity than at any point in the past, at about 36 per cent of GDP (2016). This disconnect between the growth and prosperity of the region and what is perceived as Ottawa's greater concern with the interests and preferences of central Canada continues in large measure to fuel western resentment.

Summing Up

It would be surprising—in a country as vast and geographically varied as Canada, where settlement in different parts of the country took place at different points in time and with a federal constitution that recognizes the importance of regions by assigning legislative and revenue-raising power to provincial governments—if regionalism was not an important part of politics. And indeed no account of Canadian politics, past or present, can ignore the importance of regional differences and conflicts. At the same time, the causes of regionalism and even the boundaries of politically relevant regions continue to be matters of dispute. Some point to what are believed to be important differences in political culture between Canada's regions. Others emphasize variations in the economic interests that predominate in the regions. Yet others point to federalism and the importance of provincial governments in Canadian politics.

With the exception of Quebec, the cultural differences between the provinces do not appear to be so great or of a nature that provides a very robust explanation for regionalism. Economic differences, however, combined with Canada's rather decentralized model of federalism (more on this in Chapter 8), provide a much more persuasive explanation for the political differences that exist between the provinces and the intergovernmental disputes that occasionally roil the waters of Canadian politics. The historical domination of federal politics by Ontario and Quebec is another factor that has fuelled regionalism, generating resentment in what have sometimes been called the peripheral regions of the country, most significantly in western Canada.

Starting Points for Research

Loleen Berdahl and Roger Gibbins, *Looking West: Regional Transformation and the Future of Canada* (Toronto: University of Toronto Press, 2014). Berdahl and Gibbins's earlier book, *Western Visions, Western Futures*, was the best short survey of the special characteristics of western Canada's political value system and the roots and consequences of western alienation. In *Looking West* they provide an updated picture of western Canada and argue that the future of Canada is powerfully influenced by developments in the West. See also the January 2019 report by the Angus Reid Institute on Western Canadian Attitudes, http://angusreid.org/wp-content/uploads/2019/01/2019.01.10-Identity-Release.pdf.

Environics Institute for Survey Research, "Canada: Pulling Together or Drifting Apart?" Apr. 2019, https://www.environicsinstitute.org/docs/default-source/confederation-of-tomorrow-2019-survey—report-1/confederation-of-tomorrow-survey-2019—report-1-pulling-together-or-drifting-apart---final-report.pdf?sfvrsn=9abc2e3e_2. Based on surveys conducted between 1977 and 2019, this report examines public opinion in the provinces and territories on a range of political issues.

Jared Wesley, ed., *Big Worlds: Politics and Elections in the Canadian Provinces and Territories* (Toronto: University of Toronto Press, 2016). An excellent collection of essays on each of the provinces that includes a chapter on the territories. The book concludes with the editor's interpretation of the differences that exist between these jurisdictions.

Nelson Wiseman, *In Search of Canadian Political Culture* (Vancouver: University of British Columbia Press, 2007). Wiseman examines the distinctiveness of regional political cultures and emphasizes their importance in Canadian politics. This is a must-read book for those who wish to understand the long-standing debate on regional political cultures in Canada.

Review Exercises

1. How well do you know other regions of Canada? Make a list of the personal connections that you have outside of your province. Have you lived in or visited other provinces? Which ones? Do you have friends or family members in other provinces? In which ones? Do you know which parties form the governments of other provinces? Can you name their premiers? Their capitals? Have you spent more time travelling or living in the United States or other countries than in other provinces? Do you ever think that you might move to another part of Canada for employment? Where?

2. Who were Amor de Cosmos, Henry Wise Wood, Louis Robichaud, and Joseph Howe? What is the significance of each for his region of the country?

3. In a Canada in which a handful of the largest metropolitan areas have larger populations and economies than almost half the provinces, is the concept of regionalism and the idea of the provinces as the proper voices for what are typically referred to as regional interests and perspectives still relevant?

PART III
The Structures of Governance

The root of the word *government* is the Latin verb *gubernare*, meaning to guide or direct. And, indeed, what government does is to provide direction for a society through the management of the public's business. This general function is performed through a number of more specialized institutions, including a country's legislature, head of state and head of government, system of courts, and bureaucracy. Their authority and roles within a country's structure of government will depend in large part on the constitution. Laws are made, implemented, and enforced, and redress is provided to aggrieved citizens on the basis of the written and unwritten rules embodied in a country's constitution. This, at any rate, is the ideal of democratic governance.

Constitutions and structures of government are reflections of the societies in which they are embedded. In the case of Canada, the Constitution adopted in 1867 and the country's parliamentary system of government may be understood as responses to particular societal and historical circumstances. The same is true for the important revisions that took place as a result of the Constitution Act, 1982. But once in place, constitutions and institutions of government tend to have what political scientists call an *independent effect* on political outcomes. In other words, the issues that get onto the political agenda, how they are framed, what voices are listened to, and what ultimately happens are influenced to some degree by the structures of government. Societal factors are important—the environment of ideas and interests that press on those who exercise public authority—but political outcomes will be shaped by the nature of the constitutional and governmental systems through which they are processed.

One of the most difficult challenges in political analysis is to distinguish between the influence of *societal factors* and that of *structural factors* on politics and policy. There is no one-size-fits-all answer to this question. The balance between structural and societal factors depends on the issue in question. But most of the time governmental structures play an important role in the determination of political outcomes.

Prime Minister Pierre Elliott Trudeau and HRH Queen Elizabeth II look on as future Prime Minister Jean Chrétien—then serving as Minister of Justice and Minister of Energy—signs the 17 April 1982 constitutional proclamation that patriated Canada's consitution, giving the country full political independence from the United Kingdom. The Constitution of Canada outlines the country's system of government and the rights of citizens. (© Government of Canada. Reproduced with the permission of Library and Archives Canada [2019].)

6 The Constitution

Constitutions are at the heart of democratic politics. This chapter examines key features of the Canadian Constitution. It includes the following topics:

- Functions of a constitution
- Rights and freedoms
- Parliamentary government
- Responsible government
- Ministerial responsibility
- Parliamentary and constitutional supremacy
- Judicial independence
- The House of Commons and the Senate
- Changing the Constitution
- Citizen participation in constitutional reform
- Does Quebec have the right to secede?

Most Canadians have only a vague and often inaccurate idea of what is included in their country's Constitution. In view of the fact that little attention appears to be paid to these matters in elementary and secondary school, this is perhaps not so surprising. A 2018 Ipsos poll for the Canadian Constitutional Foundation (CCF) found that only four out of 10 respondents remembered being taught about the Constitution at school. A CCF poll conducted a year earlier found that just over one-third of respondents were able to pass a six-question quiz about what is in the Constitution and only 4 per cent answered all six questions correctly. A CCF survey from 2012 found that only half of Canadians surveyed could identify from a list of choices the date when Canada's Constitution came into force (1 July 1867), four out of 10 could list some of the rights and freedoms in the Charter of Rights and Freedoms, and fewer than one-third knew that French and English are the official languages of Canada.[1]

Perhaps ignorance on this scale does not matter. After all, does knowledge of dusty facts, some of which go back to the nineteenth century, make one a better person? Will your ability to earn a living be impaired if you cannot identify Canada's official languages? Are people likely to find you less interesting if you don't know what is in the Charter of Rights and Freedoms, let alone when Confederation took place? The answer to all of these questions may well be "no."

What is certain, however, is that you cannot truly claim to understand Canadian politics and government without having some basic knowledge of what is in the Constitution. You may be able to identify the political parties and their leaders (although if you know nothing about the Constitution then it is unlikely that you have this other knowledge); you may have passionate opinions on climate change, income inequality, and health care; and you may have ideas about who exercises power in society and on what basis. But you will not truly understand why things happen the way they do in Canada's system of government, nor will you know who to hold to account when and for what. This understanding requires a knowledge of the Constitution, in Canada as in any other democracy.

A **constitution** is the fundamental law of a political system. It is fundamental because all other laws must conform to the constitution in terms of *how they are made* and in terms of their *substance*. A constitution is a necessary condition for democratic politics. Without it there is no civilized way of resolving conflicts and no way of predicting either the powers of government or the rights of citizens.

A constitution is expected to establish order, allowing for the peaceful settlement of differences. Early liberal thinkers like Thomas Hobbes and John Locke used the concept of the "state of nature" to explain why people consent to be governed and why constitutional government is important. The state of nature, wrote Hobbes, was a state of chaos in which no individual could feel secure in the possession of his property or life. This insecurity leads people to accept the authority of government and the rules embodied in a constitution. The alternative is anarchy, chaos, and civil strife, where there are no generally accepted rules for resolving the differences between factions of the population. A constitution does not ensure democratic government—Hobbes was not a democrat and he certainly was not advocating for a democratic constitution—but it is a first and necessary step towards a system of rules that allows for the peaceful resolution of differences in society.

The rules that make up a constitution deal with two sets of relations. One of these involves the relationship between citizens and the state. A constitution empowers the state to act, to pass laws on behalf of the community. At the same time a democratic constitution will limit power. It does this by identifying those freedoms and individual rights, and in some cases group rights, that the state cannot infringe or that it may be required to promote. The other set of relations encompassed by a constitution involves the distribution of functions and powers between different parts of the state. Modern government is, after all, a complex mechanism. This mechanism is often analyzed under three main functional headings: the legislature (making the law); the executive (implementing the law); and the judiciary (interpreting the law). The reality of the modern state is more complicated than this tripartite division of powers suggests.

But whatever the degree of complexity is, the rules that govern the relations between the various parts of the state are an important component of the constitution.

In a federal state like Canada, where the Constitution divides law-making powers between a national government and regional governments, the rules governing the relations between these two levels are also part of the Constitution. This third aspect of the Constitution overshadowed the other two for most of Canada's history. Indeed, before 1982, when the Charter of Rights and Freedoms was adopted, the relations between individuals and the state in Canada were defined by the courts mainly in terms of federal and provincial legislative powers.

A constitution, then, is a set of rules that govern political life. These rules may take three forms: written documents, the decisions of courts (called the **common law**), or unwritten conventions. **Constitutional conventions** are those practices and understandings that emerge over time and are generally accepted as binding rules of the political system. An example would be the convention that the leader of the party that wins the most seats in a House of Commons election is called on to form a government. This rule is not set down in the written constitution. In Canada the first two components of the Constitution—written documents and the common law—together comprise *constitutional law*. Conventions, while part of the Constitution, do not have the status of constitutional law, at least not in Canada. This distinction was made by the Supreme Court of Canada in a 1981 ruling (see Box 6.1). It should not be interpreted to mean that constitutional law is more important than constitutional conventions. What it does mean, however, is that the rules of constitutional law are enforceable by the courts, whereas constitutional conventions are not.

Constitutional Functions

A constitution does more than provide a basis for the non-violent resolution of differences. It also performs several more specific functions that include the following.

Representation

All modern democracies are representative democracies, in which politicians make decisions on behalf of those who elect them. But this still leaves enormous room for variation in how the population is represented, who is represented, and how the people's representatives are selected.

A constitution prescribes both the *basis* of political representation and the *method* by which representatives are chosen. The basis of democratic representation may be by population, by territory, or by group. Representation by population is based on the principle of "one person, one vote." Under such a system, all elected members of the legislature should represent approximately the same number of voters. This arrangement is most likely to allow the preferences of a simple majority of the population to be translated into law. Although virtually all modern democracies incorporate some form of "rep by pop" in their constitutions, many temper majority rule by representing regions as well. For example, the American Constitution gives each state the right to two senators, despite the fact that the population of the largest state is about 60 times that of the smallest. Representation in Canada's Senate is also by region: Ontario, Quebec, the western provinces, and the Maritime provinces each have 24 seats; Newfoundland and Labrador has six; and the northern territories are represented by three senators. Federalism is a form of government that embodies the principle of territorial representation. It does so by giving regional governments the exclusive right to pass laws on particular subjects.

A constitution may also accord representation to groups. New Zealand's constitution, for one, guarantees seven seats in that country's legislature to representatives of the Maori minority. Singapore has guaranteed seats for official ethnic minority groups. Pakistan reserves 60 seats in the national legislature for women and 10 for non-Muslims. In Canada, suggestions for Senate reform have sometimes included proposals to guarantee seats for women and for the representatives of Indigenous peoples. The defeated 1992 Charlottetown Accord would have ensured that Quebec, whose share of Canada's population has been falling steadily, would maintain one-quarter of all seats in the House of Commons. This was, one might argue, a thinly disguised guarantee for francophone group representation. Proposals like that in the Charlottetown Accord and the various guarantees of group representation that exist in some countries are based on premises about democracy that are quite different from those that underpin one person/one vote.

A constitution also establishes the methods by which the holders of public office are selected. Election and appointment are the two basic methods, but each allows for a wide variety of procedures that affect who is represented and how responsive public officials are likely to be to the popular will. For example, it is typical for members of the judiciary to be appointed for life, a practice expected to insulate them from popular passions and the partisan preferences of elected governments. An elected legislature is a standard feature of democratic political systems and, for that matter, of non-democratic ones. But many constitutions divide the legislative power between an elected chamber and an appointed one, as in Canada, the United Kingdom, and Germany.

Finally, the electoral process itself has a crucial influence on representation. As we will see in Chapter 11, the single-member, simple plurality constituency system used in Canada discourages political parties from directing their appeals at a narrow segment of the national electorate. Unless that segment happens to be concentrated in a particular region, such a strategy will not pay off in elected members. A system of proportional representation, whereby a party's percentage of the popular votes translates into a corresponding share of seats in the legislature, has a very different effect. It promotes a splintering of the party system and allows for the direct representation of such interests as ardent environmentalists in Germany, orthodox Jews in Israel, and anti-immigration elements in the Netherlands. In a system like Canada's, these groups would have to rely on whatever influence they could achieve within one of the larger political parties or else turn to non-electoral strategies to influence public opinion and government policy.

Power

The simple fact of constitutional government means that the state is empowered to act and that its actions may be backed up by the full weight of public authority. A constitution, therefore, provides the basis for the legitimate exercise of state power. But it also *limits* and *divides* power, at least under a democratic constitution. For example, a constitutional requirement that elections periodically be held restrains state power by making those who wield it accountable to, and removable by, the electorate. The existence of separate branches of government under the constitution, or of two levels of government as in the case of federalism, divides state power between different groups of public officials. How power is divided among the various parts of the state, or between the national and regional governments, is not determined solely by the constitution. But constitutional law and conventions affect both the extent and distribution of state power.

Rights

A right is something that a person is entitled to, like the right to vote or the right not to be held against one's will without a reason being formally given. Constitutions vary greatly in the particular rights they assign to individuals and to societal groups. At a minimum, a democratic constitution establishes the basic right of citizens to choose their government. But most constitutions go beyond this to guarantee—although not without limit—such rights as the individual's right to free speech, freedom of association, and freedom of religion and conscience, as well as legal rights such as freedom from arbitrary detention and unreasonable search and seizure. These rights limit the state's power vis-à-vis the individual.

Rights may also empower individuals by requiring the state to either protect or promote their interests. For example, a right to equal treatment under the law provides individuals with a constitutional remedy in cases where they have been discriminated against because of their sex, race, ethnic background, or whatever other basis of discrimination

Governing Realities

BOX 6.1 What Is a Constitutional Convention?

. . . [M]any Canadians would perhaps be surprised to learn that important parts of the Constitution of Canada, with which they are the most familiar because they are directly involved when they exercise their right to vote at federal and provincial elections, are nowhere to be found in the law of the Constitution. For instance it is a fundamental requirement of the Constitution that if the Opposition obtains the majority at the polls, the Government must tender its resignation forthwith. But fundamental as it is, this requirement of the Constitution does not form part of the law of the Constitution. . . .

The main purpose of constitutional conventions is to ensure that the legal framework of the Constitution will be operated in accordance with the prevailing constitutional values or principles of the period. . . .

The conventional rules of the Constitution present one striking peculiarity. In contradistinction to the laws of the Constitution, they are not enforced by the courts. . . .

It is because the sanctions of convention rest with institutions of government other than courts, such as the Governor General or the Lieutenant-Governor, or the Houses of Parliament, or with public opinion and, ultimately, with the electorate that it is generally said that they are political.

Source: Supreme Court of Canada, *Attorney General of Manitoba et al. v. Attorney General of Canada et al.*, 28 Sept. 1981. Canada Supreme Court reports: http://publications.gc.ca/site/eng/112454/publication.html.

is prohibited by the constitution. The state is obliged to protect their interests. As a practical matter this may be interpreted in a manner requiring the state to act—to pass a law, create a program, spend money, or in some other way take steps that will provide redress for those who fall into the category of persons who have been judged to experience unequal treatment under the law. The protection of equality may see the state involved in sweeping and ongoing activities like affirmative action or racial desegregation on the grounds that such steps are necessary to alleviate discrimination.

Constitutions may also recognize the special status of particular groups, thereby giving special rights to their members that are not enjoyed by others. For example, Canada's Constitution declares that both French and English are official languages with "equality of status and equal rights and privileges as to their use in all institutions of the Parliament and government of Canada."[2] This is a *positive* right in the sense that it obliges the state to assume particular linguistic characteristics, and, therefore, to protect actively the rights of French- and English-speakers—at least in matters that fall under Ottawa's jurisdiction. At a minimum, a constitution that recognizes the special status of a particular religious denomination, as the Israeli constitution recognizes the Jewish religion, the Iranian constitution the religion of Islam, or as the Danish constitution recognizes the Lutheran Church as the state religion, gives members of that faith community a status and special relationship to the state that others do not have. This matters more in a country like Iran than it does in Denmark.

Community and Identity

When Pierre Trudeau wrote that "A nation is not more and no less than the entire population of a sovereign state,"[3] he was arguing that a constitution establishes a political community. And in an obvious sense it does. A constitution is the set of fundamental rules that govern political life *in a particular territory*. Its rules apply within that territory and not elsewhere. Individuals in Rimouski, Quebec, and in Kitimat, British Columbia, fall under the same constitutional system and share a formal political status as Canadians. Even if they perceive their differences to be more important than what they share, this does not diminish the fact that they have legal membership in the same constitutional community.

Carrying the same national passport and being eligible to vote in the same elections may seem a rather weak basis for a *sense of community*, a sentiment that transcends the formal ties of common citizenship. The fact of being citizens of Spain, for example, does not erase the strongly nationalist sentiments of many Catalonians. Indeed, it probably sharpens their resentment and fuels their nationalism. For nationalist Catalonians, the Spanish constitution and the political community it created are things to regret, not to celebrate. Similarly in Canada, a significant minority of the population—Quebec separatists—rejects the Canadian political community and would prefer to live under a different constitution creating an independent Quebec.

A constitution, therefore, may inspire negative or positive feelings among the members of a political community. Or it may leave them feeling indifferent. These feelings may be associated with the political community that a constitution creates, but they may also be associated with the particular institutions, values, and symbols embedded in a constitution. For example, the monarchy and other institutions and symbols redolent of Canada's British colonial past have historically been an aspect of the Canadian Constitution dividing Canadians of French and British ancestry. On the other hand, some features of the Constitution unite, rather than divide, Canadians. There is, for example, overwhelming support among all regions and social groups for the Charter of Rights and Freedoms. In general, we may say that a constitution generates a shared identity among the citizens of a country to the extent that most people have positive feelings towards the political community it creates and the values it is perceived to embody. On these counts, Canada's Constitution has had a mixed record of successes and failures.

National Purpose

When the first permanent white settlement was established in 1608 at what today is Quebec City, it operated under a royal charter that proclaimed the Catholic mission of the French colony. Aside from being an outpost of political and economic empire, it was to be a beachhead of Christianity from which Catholicism would spread to the rest of the continent. The constitution of New France, if we may call it that, was therefore linked to a communal goal, to a sense of purpose and direction for society.[4]

This is not so rare. The constitution of the People's Republic of China starts with a very long preamble that describes the country's path to socialism. The constitutions of the Islamic Republic of Iran and of Pakistan both declare that society should conform to Muslim religious teachings. The short preamble to the United States Constitution includes this statement of national purpose: "in Order to form a more perfect Union, establish Justice, insure domestic Tranquility, provide for the common defence, promote the general Welfare, and secure the Blessings of Liberty to ourselves and our Posterity"; Brazil's constitution starts with a preamble that sets forth national goals that probably most Canadians would think of as their own.[5] The constitutional document that created Canada, the Constitution Act, 1867, also included a number of provisions that embodied a national purpose. This purpose was the building of a new country stretching from the Atlantic to the Pacific oceans and an integrated economy tying together this vast territory. The nation-building goal is evident in the anticipation that other parts of British North America eventually would be admitted into Canada,[6] in the prohibition of barriers to trade between provinces,[7] and even in the constitutional commitment to build the Intercolonial Railway, a project described as "essential to the Consolidation of the Union of British North America, and to the assent thereto of Nova Scotia and New Brunswick."[8]

The Constitution Act, 1982 commits Ottawa and the provinces to the promotion of equal opportunities for Canadians and the reduction of economic disparities between regions of the country.[9] Some argue that this represents at least one of Canada's national purposes, namely, the equitable treatment of its citizens regardless of their province of residence. Such declarations of national purpose may be symbolically important, but they do not always have teeth. By way of illustration, the fact that the Constitution Act, 1867 prohibits internal barriers to trade between the provinces has not prevented the proliferation of a dense thicket of provincial protectionist measures, many of which continue to exist today.

Canada's Constitution

As constitutional documents go, Canada's is fairly lengthy. In fact, it is not one document but a series of laws passed between 1867 and 1982. Together they are both longer and more detailed than the United States Constitution. Even so, the written documents of Canada's Constitution provide only a fragmentary and in many important ways misleading picture of how the Constitution actually works. Some of the most basic features of the Constitution—including most of those that deal with the democratic accountability of government to the people—are nowhere to be found in these documents. On the other hand, some of what is included in the written Constitution, if acted on, would probably result in a constitutional crisis! For example, Queen Elizabeth II is formally the head of state in Canada and has the constitutional authority to make decisions of fundamental importance, such as when an election will take place and who will be appointed to cabinet. No one expects, however, that she will actually make such decisions.

Canada's Constitution, like all constitutions, embodies values and principles central to the political life of the country. In its 1998 decision on the constitutionality of Quebec separation, the Supreme Court of Canada referred to these values and principles as the "internal architecture" of the Constitution,[10] or what, in an earlier ruling, the Court had called the "basic constitutional structure."[11] These basic principles, although not necessarily part of the written Constitution, "form the very foundation of the Constitution of Canada."[12] The principles that the Supreme Court identified as making up the internal architecture of Canada's Constitution include federalism, democracy, constitutionalism and the rule of law, and respect for minority rights.

Federalism

"The principle of federalism," declares the Supreme Court, "recognizes the diversity of the component parts of Confederation, and the autonomy of provincial governments to develop their societies within their respective spheres of jurisdiction."[13]

In other words, provinces are not constitutionally subordinate to the federal government and Ottawa is not dependent on the provinces for the exercise of those powers assigned to it by the Constitution. The written Constitution distributes law-making and revenue-raising authority between the central and regional governments. This distribution reflects the underlying federal principle that some matters properly belong to provincial societies and their governments to decide, while others are national in scope and properly decided by the Parliament and government in Ottawa. We will explore more fully the nature and development of Canadian federalism in Chapter 8.

Democracy

Democracy has always been one of the fundamental, if unwritten, givens of Canada's constitutional system. A literal reading of Canada's written Constitution before the inclusion of the Charter of Rights and Freedoms in 1982 might well have led someone who knew nothing of Canada's history and culture to draw a very different conclusion. Aside from the fact that periodic elections were required under the Constitution Act, 1867, there were few other explicit indications that the Constitution adopted by the founders was democratic. On the contrary, while the authority of governments was detailed painstakingly, the Constitution was remarkably silent when it came to the rights of citizens. Why was this so?

In explaining the silence of the pre-Charter Constitution, the Supreme Court states that to have declared explicitly that Canada was a democracy, and to have specified what that entailed, would have seemed to the founders "redundant" and even "silly." "The representative and democratic nature of our political institutions," the Court writes, "was simply assumed."[14] This assumption was suggested in the preamble to the Constitution Act, 1867, which states that Canada has adopted "a Constitution similar in Principle to that of the United Kingdom." The very centrality of the democratic principle and the fact that it was simply taken for granted as the baseline against which government would operate explain why the framers of the written Constitution did not perceive the need to state what all assumed to be obvious.

But the precise meaning of the democracy principle, as we saw in Chapter 1, is not obvious and has evolved over time. Women did not have the vote for more than 50 years after Confederation, and only a minority of the population found anything undemocratic in this exclusion. Even when the meaning of democracy is specified in a written constitution, as it was to a very considerable degree in the United States Constitution and the Declaration of Independence that preceded it, expectations and understandings change over time, as they have over the course of American history. What meaning is properly attributed to the democratic principle of Canada's Constitution today?

The Supreme Court's 1998 decision answers this question by distinguishing between process and outcomes. On the process side, the Court observed that majority rule is a basic premise of constitutional democracy in Canada. The fact that Canada has a federal constitution means, however, that "there may be different and equally legitimate majorities in different provinces and territories and at the federal level."[15] In other words, a nationwide majority does not trump a provincial majority if the matter in question belongs constitutionally to the provinces or requires the approval of some number of provincial legislatures (which is true for most constitutional amendments).

In a 1986 Charter decision,[16] the Supreme Court expressed the view that the democratic principle underlying the Charter and the rest of Canada's Constitution is also linked to substantive goals. Among these are the following:

- respect for the inherent dignity of every person;
- commitment to equality and social justice;
- social and cultural diversity, including respect for the identities of minority groups' social and political institutions that enhance the opportunities for individuals and groups to participate in society.

This view was echoed in the Supreme Court's 1998 ruling. In words directly relevant to the issue of Quebec separation, the Court said that "The consent of the governed is a value that is basic to our understanding of a free and democratic society."[17] Democratic government derives its necessary legitimacy from this consent. Moreover, the legitimacy of laws passed and actions taken by a democratic government rests on "moral values, many of which are imbedded in our constitutional structure."[18] The Supreme Court did not elaborate on what these moral values might be.

Constitutionalism and the Rule of Law

"At its most basic level," declares the Supreme Court, "the rule of law vouchsafes to the citizens and residents of the country a stable, predictable and ordered society in which to conduct their affairs."[19] It guarantees, therefore, that all public authority must ultimately be exercised in accordance with the law and that there will be one law for all persons. When it comes to light that some public official has overstepped the bounds of his or her office, regardless of the office-holder's intentions, or that someone has been accorded preferred treatment under the law because of personal connections, we rightly are offended, an issue that arose in 2018–19 in regard to the SNC-Lavalin case (Box 6.2). Such actions violate the premise of the rule of law, namely, that ours is a government of laws, not of men and women, and that everyone is entitled to equal treatment under the law.

Like the rule of law, the constitutionalism principle involves predictable governance that has its source in written rules rather than in the arbitrary wills of individuals. The constitutionalism principle is expressed in s. 52(1) of the Constitution Act, 1982, which states that the Constitution is the supreme law of the land and that all government action must be in conformity with the Constitution. Before the Charter was entrenched in the Constitution and the constitutionalism principle was expressly stated, the final authority of the Constitution was less certain. The pre-Charter era was one of **parliamentary supremacy.** This meant that, in essence, so long as one level of government

Listen to the "SNC-Lavalin Affair and the Rule of Law" podcast, available at: www.oup.com/he/ Brooks9e

Governing Realities

BOX 6.2 From the Classroom to the Front Pages: The SNC-Lavalin Affair and the Rule of Law

SNC-Lavalin is a major Montreal-based engineering and construction firm that employs about 50,000 persons in Canada and countries across the world. It generates

Jody Wilson-Raybould, former minister of Justice, attorney general, and minister of Veterans Affairs.

billions of dollars in annual revenues from projects on virtually every continent. In 2015 the company was charged with fraud and corruption under Canadian law for allegedly having bribed Libyan officials from 2001 to 2011 in order to receive construction contracts in that country. In 2018 Canada followed the lead of several other Western democracies in passing a law that would enable a corporation to avoid a criminal prosecution on charges such as those levelled against SNC-Lavalin through what is called a deferred prosecution agreement (DPA). Companies found to be in violation of laws on fraud and corruption could still be fined and face various punishments, but they would not go through the process of a criminal prosecution. A DPA would have to be recommended by the attorney general of Canada and a judge would have to approve the agreement.

Very few Canadians outside of the legal community and the corporate world had heard of DPAs until 27 February 2019. At that point the former minister of Justice and attorney general of Canada, Jody Wilson-Raybould, testified before the House of Commons Justice Committee. Wilson-Raybould had been relieved

did not trespass onto jurisdictional turf that the Constitution assigned to the other level, it was free to do as it liked. The principle of parliamentary supremacy is captured in the aphoristic statement attributed to the eighteenth-century Swiss-English constitutional theorist Jean-Louis de Lolme that "Parliament can do anything except change a man into a woman and a woman into a man." The constitutionalism principle, by contrast, places certain matters relating to rights and freedoms beyond the reach of any government.

Constitutionalism and the rule of law temper and modify the principle of majority rule in a democracy. They do so by ensuring that the mere fact that a majority of citizens—even an overwhelming majority—supports a particular government action does not mean that such an action will be either lawful or constitutional. Together, these

principles constitute a sort of bulwark against what Tocqueville called the "tyranny of the majority."

Protection of Minorities

The recognition of group rights has a history in Canada that goes back to the beginnings of British colonial rule. The Royal Proclamation of 1763 includes considerable detail—the meaning of which is a matter of dispute—on the rights of the "several Nations or Tribes of Indians . . . who live under our protection." The Quebec Act of 1774 recognized the rights of Catholics in Quebec and guaranteed the overwhelmingly French-speaking population the enjoyment of their "Property and Possessions, together with all Customs and Usages relative thereto, and all other [of] their Civil Rights," concessions that most historians agree were intended to ensure the support of these responsibilities by Prime Minister Trudeau several weeks earlier and reassigned to the much less influential position of minister of Veterans Affairs. She argued that as the attorney general of Canada she had been the target of repeated and high-level pressure from the PMO and the PCO in regard to SNC-Lavalin. All of the pressure, Wilson-Raybould stated, was in order to persuade her to agree to a DPA for the company. This pressure, she argued, was a violation of the rule of law. The role of the attorney general, everyone concedes, is rather different from that of other members of cabinet. This person is the government's chief law officer, a function that has been described as similar in its independence and non-partisanship to that of the judiciary. Just as it is considered inappropriate for a government to interfere in any manner with the decisions of judges, so too, it is argued, they should not attempt to influence the decisions of the attorney general regarding prosecutions.

Questions about the rule of law did not stop there. Some weeks after her testimony to the Commons Justice Committee both Wilson-Raybould and Jane Philpott, the latter of whom had resigned from the Liberal government in solidarity with Wilson Raybould, were expelled from the Liberal Party caucus. Citing rather technical rules from the 2015 Reform Act dealing with the procedures for caucus expulsions and readmissions, these former Liberal cabinet ministers argued that their expulsion from the party caucus was unlawful. The Speaker of the House refused to render an opinion of the matter of whether the law had been violated, arguing that this was not part of his role.

Many in the media and on the opposition benches in Parliament did not share the Speaker's reticence. These critics argued that both the government's attempts to influence Wilson-Raybould and the prime minister's expulsion of her and Philpott from the Liberal Party caucus were flagrant and serious violations of the rule of law. This rather dusty but important constitutional principle moved from university classrooms and law textbooks to centre stage of Canadian politics for a time. But not everyone agreed that the rule of law had been violated or that Wilson-Raybould and Philpott had been treated inappropriately. Legal and constitutional principles aside, there was some short-term decline in the Liberal Party's popularity and approval of Prime Minister Trudeau, but most of this was among those expressing a preference for the Conservative Party. It is not clear that the brouhaha over the rule of law had much of an effect on the 2019 federal election. Jody Wilson-Raybould ran as an independent candidate and won in the riding of Vancouver Granville.

of the Catholic Church authorities in Quebec at a time when rebellion was simmering in the American colonies. Group rights were recognized again through the "double majority principle" that operated when Canada East (Quebec) and Canada West (Ontario) were joined together through a common legislature during the period 1841–67. Under this principle any bill touching on matters of language or religion in either Canada East or Canada West had to be approved by majorities of legislators from both Canada East—mainly French and Catholic—and Canada West—mainly English and Protestant. In practice this gave a veto to each ethnolinguistic community in regard to legislation affecting minority rights.

The Constitution Act, 1867 entrenched the principle of minority rights through the section 93 guarantee of minority religious education rights and the section 133 declaration that French and English were to have official status in the Parliament of Canada, the legislature of Quebec, and courts created by either of those bodies. "The protection of minority rights," declares the Supreme Court, "was clearly an essential consideration in the design of our constitutional structure even at the time of Confederation."[20] The principle acquired a new level of prominence as a result of the Charter of Rights and Freedoms. The Charter enlarges the scope of official-language minority rights, explicitly recognizes Indigenous rights, opens the door to a multitude of group rights claims through the equality section of the Charter (s. 15), and provides a basis for a variety of minority rights claims through other sections, including the legal rights and democratic rights provisions of the Charter.

A useful way of analyzing a constitution is to approach it from the angle of each of the relationships governed by constitutional rules. As noted earlier, these relationships include: (1) those between individuals and the state; (2) those between the various institutions of government; and (3) those between the national and regional governments. The first category involves rights and freedoms, the second deals with the machinery and process of government, and the third category is about federalism. A constitution also includes a fourth category of rules that establish what procedures must be followed to bring about constitutional change. Federalism is dealt with in Chapter 8. We turn now to an examination of the other three dimensions of Canada's Constitution.

The Charter of Rights and Freedoms

Since 1982 Canada's Constitution has included formal distinctions between fundamental political freedoms, democratic rights, mobility rights, legal rights, equality rights, and language rights. These are the categories set down in the Charter of Rights and Freedoms. Most of the rights and freedoms enumerated in the Charter were part of Canada's Constitution before 1982. In some cases they can be found in the Constitution Act, 1867. In others, they were established principles of the common law. Some were set down in the Criminal Code. The inclusion of these rights and freedoms in the Charter, however, has made an important difference in Canadian politics. Groups and individuals are far more likely today than in the pre-Charter era to reach for the judicial lever in attempting to protect their rights. Second, these rights have been more secure since the Charter's passage. This has been due to the courts' willingness to strike down laws and practices on the grounds that they contravene the Charter's guarantees of rights and freedoms. Prior to the Charter, Canadian courts were reluctant to strike down a law on the basis that it was an infringement of human rights.

Fundamental Freedoms

Fundamental political freedoms are guaranteed in section 2 of the Charter. These include freedom of religion, belief, expression, the media, assembly, and association. During the pre-Charter era these freedoms, or *political liberties* as they are sometimes called, were part of the common law and of Canada's British parliamentary tradition. Individual freedoms were part of the British constitution and thus became part of Canada's. Even before the Charter, then, political freedoms occupied a place in the Canadian Constitution. Their protection by the courts, however, was rather tenuous. Except in a few instances, the courts were unwilling to rule that a freedom was beyond the interference of government. Instead, political liberties were defended using the federal division of legislative powers as the basis for striking down a particular government's interference with individual freedom.

Democratic Rights

The basic democratic right is the opportunity to vote in regular elections. This right predated Confederation. It was embodied in the Constitution Act, 1867 through those sections that establish the elective basis of representation in the House of Commons and in provincial legislatures (ss. 37 and 40), through the requirement that the legislature meet at least once a year (ss. 20 and 86), through the right of citizens to vote (s. 41), and through the five-year limit on the life of both the House of Commons and provincial legislatures, thereby guaranteeing regular elections (ss. 50 and 85). All of these sections are now "spent," having been superseded by ss. 3–5 of the Charter.

Mobility Rights

Mobility rights were not explicitly mentioned in Canadian constitutional law before 1982. Section 121 of the Constitution Act, 1867 prohibits the provincial governments from imposing tariffs on commodities coming from other provinces, but there is no mention of restrictions on the movement of people. Such restrictions are now prohibited by section 6 of the Charter. This guarantee of individual mobility rights was prompted by Ottawa's fear that some provincial governments were undermining the idea and practice of Canadian citizenship by discriminating in favour of their own permanent residents in some occupational sectors and by imposing residency requirements as a condition for receiving some social services. The Charter does not, however, categorically ban these types of discrimination. It allows "reasonable residency requirements as a qualification for the receipt of publicly provided social services"[21] and permits affirmative action programs favouring a province's residents "if the rate of employment in that province is below the rate of employment in Canada."[22] The impact of section 6 on provincial practices limiting the mobility of Canadians between provinces has been marginal.[23]

Legal Rights

Most rights-based litigation, both before and since the Charter's passage, has been based on individuals' and corporations' claims that their legal rights have been violated. Legal rights involve mainly procedural aspects of the law, such as the right to a fair trial, the right not to be subjected to unreasonable search and seizure, the right not to be held without a charge being laid, and the right to legal counsel. Before these rights were entrenched in the Constitution through the Charter, they were recognized principles of the common law and constitutional convention. For example, the field of administrative law was based largely on the principles of *natural justice*: hear the other side, and no one should be a judge in his own case. These were accepted parts of Canada's democratic tradition and constitutional tradition even before they were entrenched in section 7 of the Charter. And like political freedoms, democratic rights, and equality rights, these legal rights were included in the Canadian Bill of Rights passed in 1960. In addition, the rights of accused parties were set forth in Canada's Criminal Code.

It is apparent, however, that the constitutional entrenchment of legal rights has made an important difference. The courts have been much bolder in striking down parts of laws and in overturning administrative and police procedures than they were in the pre-Charter era. For example, a successful legal challenge to Canada's abortion law became possible only when the right to "security of the person" was explicitly recognized in section 7

of the Charter.[24] More generally, Charter decisions have expanded the legal rights of the accused, prisoners, and immigrants.

Equality Rights

Equality rights are entrenched in the Constitution through section 15 of the Charter. They embody the *rule of law* principle that everyone should be treated equally under the law. But the Charter extends this principle to expressly prohibit discrimination based on race, national or ethnic origin, colour, religion, sex, age, or mental or physical disability.[25]

The particular headings in this list are important, given that Canadian courts historically have preferred to base their rulings on the precise text of laws and the Constitution. Women's groups and those representing the physically and mentally disabled clearly believed that the wording of the Charter made a difference, and both fought hard—and successfully—to have the original wording of section 15 changed. The 1960 Canadian Bill of Rights, which applied only in areas of federal jurisdiction, did not include age or mental and physical disability in its catalogue of equality rights.

The Charter explicitly declares that affirmative action is constitutional.[26] Thus, the equality rights section of the Canadian Constitution is designed to cut two ways. It provides individuals with grounds for redress if they believe the law discriminates against them. But it also provides a basis for laws that treat different groups of people differently in order to improve the condition of disadvantaged individuals or groups.

Equality rights also are important features of provincial human rights codes. Between 1962 and 1975 every province adopted such a code. Quebec's is probably the most extensive, including even certain economic and social rights. These rights are administered and enforced by provincial human rights commissions.

Language Rights

At Confederation, the issue of language rights was dealt with in three ways. Section 133 of the Constitution Act, 1867 declares that both English and French are official languages in the Parliament of Canada and in the Quebec legislature, and in any court established by either the national or Quebec government. Section 93 of that same Act declares that rights held by denominational schools when a province became part of Canada cannot be taken away. As a practical matter, Catholic schools in Manitoba or even Ontario were often French-speaking, and most English-language schools in Quebec were Protestant. Consequently, what were formally denominational rights in section 93 were, in many cases, effectively language rights as well. This did not help when it came to their protection—or non-protection. The third approach—and in practical terms the most important language rights provision of the Constitution Act, 1867—is put forth in section 92. This assigns to the provinces jurisdiction over "all Matters of a merely local or private Nature in the Province" (s. 92.16). Combined with exclusive provincial jurisdiction over education (s. 93), this has given provincial governments the tools to promote or deny, as the case may be, the language rights of their anglophone or francophone minorities.

The Constitution Act, 1982 extends language rights in several ways. These include the following:

- The declaration of the official equality of English and French, found in section 133 of the Constitution Act, 1867, is repeated and broadened to encompass "their use in all institutions of the Parliament and government of Canada" (s. 16.1) and services to the public (s. 20).
- The New Brunswick legislature's earlier decision to declare that province officially bilingual is entrenched in the Constitution Act, 1982. The official status of English in the legislature and courts of Quebec and Manitoba is reaffirmed (s. 21).
- The right of anglophones and francophones to have their children educated in their mother tongue is entrenched, subject to there being sufficient demand to warrant the provision of such services out of public funds (s. 23).

Language rights would have been given an additional twist if the Meech Lake Accord (1987) or Charlottetown Accord (1992) had become constitutional law (see Chapter 8). The most controversial feature of both accords was the recognition of Quebec as a "distinct society." The "distinct society" clause would have obliged Quebec's legislature and government to "preserve and promote the distinct identity of Quebec." Some critics, including former Prime Minister Pierre Trudeau, argued that this would have promoted the concentration of French in Quebec, with harmful consequences for the status of the French-speaking minorities in the other provinces and for the English-speaking minority in Quebec.

Indigenous Rights

Indigenous rights are also included in Canada's Constitution. Their explicit recognition dates from the passage of the Charter in 1982. Section 25 declares that the rights and freedoms set forth in the Charter "shall not be construed so as to abrogate or derogate" from whatever rights or freedoms the Indigenous peoples in Canada have as a result of any treaty or land claim settlement. It also entrenches in the Constitution "any rights or freedoms that have been recognized by the Royal Proclamation [of 1763]." Section 35(1) of the Constitution Act, 1982 may appear to limit Indigenous rights to the status quo that existed in 1982, stating that "The *existing* **aboriginal and treaty rights** of the aboriginal peoples of Canada are hereby recognized and affirmed" (emphasis added). In fact, however, this has been less a limit than a boost for Indigenous rights, which have been effectively constitutionalized by the 1982 Constitution Act. We examine this in greater detail in Chapter 16.

Parliamentary Government in Canada

The whole edifice of British parliamentary government rests on a foundation of unwritten traditions and rules. These traditions and rules touch on the most fundamental principles of democracy and on practices that are essential to the orderly functioning of government. Such matters as the selection of the prime minister, which party has the right to form a government and when it loses that right, the relationship between the Crown and the government and between the government and the legislature, the rights of the political opposition, and the role of the judicial branch of government cannot be understood from a simple reading of the Constitution. Nevertheless, for all of these matters certain rules are generally agreed upon and are vital parts of the Constitution—so vital, in fact, that when they are challenged the political system faces a crisis.

British parliamentary government was exported to Canada during the nineteenth century. Its main features have remained largely unchanged since then, when the British North American colonies achieved the right to self-government in their domestic affairs. As we have seen, the Constitution Act, 1867 explicitly reaffirms this British parliamentary inheritance. While the declaration that Canada has adopted "a Constitution similar in Principle to that of the United Kingdom" might appear to be somewhat nebulous, Canada's founders understood very clearly what it meant. The Constitution of the United Kingdom was, and remains today, a set of political traditions without a core constitutional document similar to those found in other Western democracies. Those who founded Canada took these traditions as their starting point and grafted onto them certain institutions and procedures—particularly federalism—for which British parliamentary government provided no guide.

Parliament

The distinguishing feature of British-style parliamentary government is the relationship between the various institutions that together comprise Parliament. Parliament consists of the monarch and the legislature. The monarch, currently Queen Elizabeth II, is Canada's head of state. According to the strict letter of the Constitution, the monarch wields formidable powers. These include which party will be called upon to form the government, when Parliament will be dissolved and a new election held, and the requirement that all legislation—federal and provincial—must receive royal assent before it becomes law. In fact, however, these powers are almost entirely symbolic, and the role is essentially a ceremonial one. When the monarch is not in Canada (which is most of the time), her powers are exercised by the governor general. At the provincial level, the lieutenant-governors are the Queen's representatives.

The power that resides formally in the monarchy is in reality held by the Crown's advisers, the Privy Council. The **Privy Council** formally includes all members of the present and past cabinets. However, only present members of cabinet exercise the powers of the Privy Council, and these people are usually elected members of the legislature. At the head of the cabinet is the prime minister. The structure of Canada's Parliament is shown in Figure 6.1.

Parliament comprises, then, both the *executive* and *legislative* branches of government. Those who actually exercise the executive power are drawn from the legislature. In deciding who among those elected members of Parliament (MPs) and appointed senators will become members of the government,

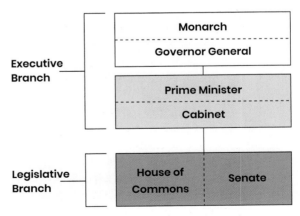

FIGURE 6.1 The Structure of Parliament in Canada

Note: The structure is basically the same at the provincial level, with two differences. The monarch's powers are exercised by a lieutenant-governor and the legislature consists of a single elected chamber.

the rule is quite simple. The leader of the political party with the most seats in the elected House of Commons has the right to try to form a government that has the support of a majority of MPs. He or she is the person who chooses members of the cabinet. If at any time the government loses its majority support in the House, tradition requires that it resign. At this point a fresh election would be called or, if another party could put together a government that would be supported by a majority of MPs, the governor general could call on the leader of that party to try to form a government.

Responsible Government

In order to govern, therefore, the prime minister and cabinet require the confidence of the elected House of Commons. This constitutional principle is called **responsible government**. If a government loses the confidence of the House—through a defeat either on an important piece of legislation (i.e., the annual budget or legislation related to government spending) or on a motion of non-confidence proposed by an opposition party—it loses the right to govern. This may appear to place enormous power in the hands of MPs, capable of making and breaking governments at will. It does not. The reason

THE CANADIAN PRESS/Chris Young

In January 2010, faced with the second prorogation of Parliament since 2008, some Canadians voiced their displeasure at the premature shutdown of government, claiming the decision was politically, rather than practically, motivated.

why the constitutional theory of responsible government does not translate into government tremulous before the legislature is **party discipline**. This is another tradition of British parliamentary government, according to which the MPs of a party generally vote as a unified bloc in the legislature. Few aspects of Canada's system of government are less popular and more poorly understood than party discipline (see Box 6.3).

Of the 42 governments elected between 1867 and 2015 only six fell because of a defeat in the legislature. In all six cases these were *minority governments*: governments that depended on the support of another party's MPs to win votes in the legislature. But even in these apparently precarious circumstances, it was usually the government that finally determined when an election would occur. On only one occasion has a government been defeated in the Commons and then had its request for dissolution of Parliament and a fresh election denied. That was in 1926 when Governor General Lord Byng said "no" to Prime Minister Mackenzie King, provoking a constitutional crisis over the appropriate role of the governor general. There was at least the chance of history repeating itself when the Progressive Conservative government's budget was defeated in 1979. The government had been in office a mere nine months and the possibility of a minority Liberal government, supported by the NDP, was not totally outrageous. As it happened, however, Governor General Ed Schreyer granted Prime Minister Clark's request for a new election, although Schreyer claimed afterwards that he seriously considered asking the leader of the opposition to try to form a government.

The possibility that MPs, and not Canadian voters, might bring about a change in government appeared very real in the late autumn of 2008, just weeks after a federal election produced a Conservative minority government. The three opposition parties reached an agreement to bring down the government and replace it with a Liberal–NDP coalition that would have been led by then Liberal leader Stéphane Dion. The Conservative government cried foul, pointing out that an election had been held only weeks before and that it had won a significantly greater share

Politics in Focus

BOX 6.3 Does Party Discipline Undermine Democracy?

The Samara Centre for Democracy is a think-tank that focuses on issues related to Canadian government, elections, and the quality of democracy. In 2018 it released its second report based on exit interviews with some former MPs. The report was very critical of party discipline and made a case for much greater independence for MPs in the activities of the House of Commons, including its committees. Here is some of what it said:

Parliament [is a sort of] fire drill: Everyone takes their designated places and carries out a performance of their roles. But there is an emptiness in the display, a pervasive sense that it is all just getting in the way of the real work.

This story is not especially new. But nor has life and work at Parliament remained the same. Samara's interviews with former MPs from the 41st Parliament find that the decline of parliamentarians as actors with agency and influence seems to have sped up. The danger is that with each passing Parliament, the shrunken role for MPs becomes more normalized. Without change, future exit interviews may find that MPs experience their own variation of something like Stockholm syndrome, as they become resigned to or even content with a system that simultaneously undermines them and their responsibilities as representatives.

Many of the former MPs we interviewed see and feel this danger, especially in the face of rising distrust and greater risk of authoritarianism around the world. . . . A growing populism in Canada and elsewhere is linked to both who our representatives are and how they work within our representative democracy. MPs should be empowered not for their own sake, nor for the sake of a Gothic Revival building next to a river—but because MPs are and will remain a critical link between citizens and the state. Citizens need to see public life as a worthwhile pursuit, to see themselves in their political leaders and to see their political leaders do the work they are elected to do.[27]

Leaving aside the fact that the Samara study was based on a very unrepresentative sample of MPs from

the Parliament that ended in 2015, Canadians have long said that they don't like party discipline. A 1983 Gallup poll found that half of Canadians thought MPs should vote according to the preferences of their constituents and that only 8 per cent said they should vote as their leader requires them to do. The 1991 Citizens' Forum on Canada's Future reported that party discipline was believed by most of those who engaged in this process to be "a major constraint on the effectiveness of elected officials in representing constituents' views and in controlling a government agenda which may be out of touch with citizens' concerns." An Environics poll taken in the spring of 2013 found that seven out of 10 Canadians surveyed favoured legal restrictions on the ability of party leaders to control their parties' candidates and MPs. The 2017 Electoral Reform consultation carried out by the Liberal government (an online survey whose methodology would set any serious pollster's teeth on edge) found that 83 per cent of respondents somewhat or strongly agreed with the statement, "Members of Parliament should always act in the interests of their constituents, even if it means going against their own party."

Party discipline, it seems, has few friends and is widely seen to be undemocratic. So why does it continue to exist? Senator Eugene Forsey, one of Canada's foremost experts on parliamentary government, argues that without it Canadian government would be less accountable. It enables voters to know where each party stands on the issues and to hold the parties accountable at the next election. He contrasts this to the American tradition of weak party discipline, which, he argues, results in legislators and even the president being able to say "I wasn't responsible. I did (or did not) support that law. Blame the others, not me." This may result in lawmakers who are seen to be more responsive to their constituents, but at the cost of voters not being able to hold the parties collectively responsible for policy choices.[28]

Defenders of party discipline argue that abolishing or even significantly relaxing the practice would result in a chain reaction of consequences for Canada's parliamentary system, including the likely end of majority governments and the weakening of party leaders. Critics agree, and say that this is precisely why such reform is needed.

of the popular vote than any of the opposition parties. Rather than turn over the reins of power to a Liberal–NDP coalition, backed by the Bloc Québécois, the Conservatives would have requested a dissolution of Parliament and fresh elections. The governor general, Michaëlle Jean, was saved from being a twenty-first-century Lord Byng by the government's decision to prorogue Parliament, preventing a vote that could have brought down the government. Opponents of the government now had their opportunity to cry foul, but public opinion showed that most Canadians opposed the idea of a Liberal–NDP coalition propped up with BQ support. The constitutional take-away from this episode is that these important matters concerning who has the right to govern and when that right is lost are determined by the unwritten rules of the Constitution.

Responsible government is not some dusty constitutional relic. It operates today, but not in the narrow sense of legislatures making and defeating cabinets. Instead, it suffuses the parliamentary process in the form of the *rights of the legislature* and the corresponding *obligations of the government*. The legislature has the right to scrutinize, debate, and vote on policies proposed by the government. To carry out these activities the legislature has the general right to question the government and to demand explanations for its actions and for those of bureaucratic officials who act in the government's name. The government, for its part, has a constitutional obligation to provide opportunities for legislative scrutiny of its policies and to account for its actions before Parliament. These rights and obligations are to a large extent codified in the *standing orders*—the rules that govern parliamentary procedure.

Listen to the "Perspectives on Proroguing" podcast, available at: www.oup.com/he/Brooks9e

Responsible government, then, is part of the living Constitution. But its formal definition bears little resemblance to the reality of modern parliamentary government. Disciplined political parties and dominant prime ministers ensure that governments seldom are at risk of being defeated by rebellious legislatures. Indeed, this possibility really only exists during periods of minority government.

Ministerial Responsibility

The accountability of the government to the legislature is the reason behind another principle of British parliamentary government, that of **ministerial responsibility**. It entails the obligation of a cabinet minister to explain and defend policies and actions carried out in his or her name. This individual accountability of cabinet ministers rests on a combination of constitutional law and parliamentary tradition. Section 54 of the Constitution Act, 1867 gives to cabinet the exclusive right to put before the legislature measures that involve the raising or spending of public revenue. In practice, such measures are introduced by particular members of the government. For example, changes to the tax system are proposed by the minister of Finance. The Constitution also requires that any legislation that involves raising or spending public money must originate in the elected House of Commons. This reflects the democratic principle of no taxation without accountable representation. Only the people's elected representatives, legislators who can be removed in a subsequent election, should have the right to propose laws that affect voters' pocketbooks. The accountability of ministers, therefore, is to the people's elected representatives.

Two fundamental principles of British parliamentary government, i.e., strong executive authority and democratic accountability, come together in the concept of ministerial responsibility. Strong executive authority is a tradition that dates from an era when the monarch wielded real power and the principle that these powers depended on the consent of the legislature was not yet established. When the legislature finally gained the upper hand in seventeenth-century Britain, the tradition of strong executive power was not rejected. Instead, it was tamed and adapted to the democratic principle that government is based on the consent of the governed. Since then, individual ministers and cabinet as a whole have exercised the powers that, symbolically, continue to be vested in the Crown. But they do so in ways that enable the people's elected representatives to vote on their proposals and to call them to account for their policies (see Figure 6.2).

In recent times the constitutional principle of ministerial responsibility has come under increasing pressure. The enormous volume of decisions taken in a minister's name and the fact that much of the real power to determine government policy has passed into the hands of unelected officials mean that no minister can be well informed about all the policies and actions undertaken in his name. According to some, the solution is to locate accountability where decision-making power really lies. This strategy is reasonable for most actions and decisions. But elected members of the government must remain directly accountable for the general lines of policy and for major decisions; otherwise, a vital link in the chain of accountability that joins the people to those who govern is lost (see Box 6.4).

Parliamentary Supremacy versus Constitutional Supremacy

Another central feature of British parliamentary government is that of **parliamentary supremacy**. In concrete terms, this means that the courts will not second-guess the right of Parliament to pass any sort of law, on any subject. Parliament embodies the popular will, and unpopular laws can always be defeated by changing the government at the next election. In a federal system such as Canada's there is one complication. Law-making powers are divided between the national and regional governments. But so long as Ottawa acts within its spheres of constitutional authority, and the provincial governments within theirs, both the federal and provincial parliaments are supreme.

Such was the situation in Canada until 1982. When called on to determine whether a law was constitutional or not, the courts almost always referred to the federal division of powers set down in the Constitution Act, 1867. If a legislature was not intruding onto the constitutional territory of the other level of government, its actions were by definition constitutional. The only exception to this rule was in the case of laws or actions that ran afoul of procedural rules of the common law, like the principles of natural justice. The substance of laws, on the other hand, would not be questioned.

Parliamentary supremacy was dealt a death blow by the Charter. Those who opposed the Charter argued that entrenching rights and freedoms in the written Constitution would result in a transfer of power from legislatures to the courts. This, indeed, is what has happened. Since 1982 the Supreme Court has struck down provisions of numerous federal and provincial laws on the grounds that they violate the guarantees set forth in the Charter. The defenders of parliamentary supremacy claim that a system of court-protected rights and freedoms is fundamentally undemocratic. Their reasoning is that it substitutes the decisions of non-elected judges for those of the people's elected representatives.

Parliamentary supremacy has been replaced in Canada by **constitutional supremacy**. The Constitution Act, 1982 makes this very clear. Section 32 declares that the Charter applies to both the federal and provincial governments and to all matters under their authority. Section 52(1) is even more categorical. It states that "The Constitution of Canada is the supreme law of Canada, and any law that is inconsistent with the provisions of the Constitution is, to the extent of the inconsistency, of no force or effect." A vestige of Parliament's former superiority is retained, however, through s. 33 of the Charter. This is the so-called "notwithstanding clause." It enables either Parliament or a provincial legislature to declare that a law shall operate even if it violates the fundamental freedoms, legal rights, or equality rights sections of the Charter. Such a declaration

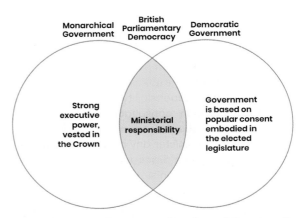

Monarchical Government

British Parliamentary Democracy

Democratic Government

Strong executive power, vested in the Crown

Ministerial responsibility

Government is based on popular consent embodied in the elected legislature

FIGURE 6.2 The Constitutional Roots of Ministerial Responsibility

must be renewed after five years; otherwise, the Constitution reasserts its supremacy.

As a footnote, it is perhaps worth noting that even in Westminster, the "mother of parliaments," the principle of parliamentary supremacy has been limited over the past few decades. This began with the UK's entry into the European Union in 1972, making some British legislation subject to decisions made in Brussels. The devolution of some of the British Parliament's powers to the legislatures of Wales and Scotland, the passage of the 1998 Human Rights Act, and the establishment of a Supreme Court for the UK in 2009 (this function was exercised previously by a committee of the House of Lords) have in practice limited parliamentary supremacy.[29]

Judicial Independence and the Separation of Powers

The role of the judicial branch of government is based in large measure on constitutional convention rather than law. The Constitution Act, 1867

Politics in Focus

BOX 6.4 The Evolution of Ministerial Responsibility

The Commission of Inquiry into the Sponsorship Program and Advertising Activities (also known as the Gomery Commission) was created by the Liberal government in 2004. It arose out of numerous allegations that funds provided under a federal program intended to raise the visibility of the Canadian government in Quebec had been used fraudulently. Liberal cabinet ministers from Quebec refused to take responsibility for the corruption that had taken place, claiming that they had not authorized the acts in question nor did they have any knowledge of them at the time. In other words, they said that ministerial responsibility did not apply. Justice Gomery saw the matter differently:

I believe that the proposition that Ministers and their political staff have no responsibility for the proper implementation and administration of government programs and policies is an inadequate and incomplete expression of the principle of ministerial responsibility. The Minister should take steps, in consultation with the Deputy Minister, to see that trained personnel are available to administer any new initiatives and to establish proper procedures and oversight mechanisms. The Minister should give sufficient directions to the Deputy Minister so that the latter will be able to properly supervise the actions of the subordinate personnel. *Willful ignorance of administrative inadequacies will not absolve a Minister from responsibility for failures within the department.*[30]

A few years later the Conservative government appeared to embrace the Gomery Commission's rather hard line on ministerial responsibility. A 2007 PCO document stated: "Ministers are individually responsible to Parliament and the prime minister for their own actions and those of their department, including the actions of all officials under their management and direction, *whether or not the Ministers had prior knowledge*" (emphasis added). In fact, however, this uncompromising principle has never been the practice in recent times. Only a few years after the PCO issued its 2007 guidelines, the chief spokesperson for the PCO "clarified" what is meant by ministerial responsibility. He stated, "Ministers are required to attend to all matters in Parliament concerning their portfolio organizations, including answering questions. . . . [They] must also take appropriate corrective action to address any problems that may arise within their portfolio organizations, which includes problems arising from the actions of officials. . . . [T]here has always been a distinction between actions deemed blameworthy and the idea that ministers must answer questions in Parliament."[31]

includes several sections that deal with the system of provincial courts, including how judges shall be selected, how they may be removed, when provincial Superior Court judges must retire (age 75), and who will determine judicial salaries.[32] But there is no mention of the Supreme Court of Canada or of any other federal courts. Instead, section 101 authorizes Parliament to establish a "General Court of Appeal for Canada," which it did in 1875 (the Supreme Court of Canada) and again in 1970 (the Federal Court of Canada).

Canadian constitutional law is silent on the powers, indeed on the very existence and composition, of this country's highest court of appeal. Nor is the relationship between the judicial and other branches of government described in much detail. This stands in sharp contrast to the United States Constitution, in which lengthy descriptions of the powers of Congress (the legislative branch) and the president (the executive branch) are followed by Article III on the judicial branch of government. In Canada, however, the role of the judiciary is based largely on constitutional convention and statute law. The fundamental principles that underlie that role are judicial independence and separation of powers.

Judicial independence means that judges are to be free from any and all interference in their decision-making. Former Chief Justice Brian Dickson declared that the core of this principle involves "the complete liberty of individual judges to hear and decide the cases that come before them."[33] It is particularly important that judges be protected from interference by the government. Despite the fact that the principle of judicial independence is deeply embedded in Canada's political culture and enshrined in laws on contempt of court and in guidelines for ministerial conduct, doubts have been raised over whether these protections are adequate. The fact that court budgets are determined by governments represents, in the eyes of some, a potential limitation on judicial autonomy.

The principle of **separation of powers** guarantees the special role of the judiciary. This role is to interpret what the law and the Constitution mean when disputes arise. As in the case of judicial independence, this principle relies more on cultural norms, statute law, and constitutional convention than it does on constitutional law. There is, however, at least one important reference to the role of the judicial branch in the Constitution. This is section 24 of the Constitution Act, 1982, which declares that the enforcement of the Charter shall be through the courts. The perception that the courts represent a check on the powers of Parliament and the provincial legislatures—a perception that has become universal since the Charter's passage in 1982—involved an Americanizing trend in Canadian politics. The concept of checks and balances between the three branches of government is basic to the American Constitution. It is not, however, part of British parliamentary democracy, although the independence of the judiciary is.

The separation of the judiciary's role from that of Parliament is not watertight. The ability of the federal and provincial governments to refer a resolution or draft legislation to the courts for a decision on its constitutionality—a practice called a "reference"—does not, strictly speaking, respect the principle of separation of powers. These constitutional reference cases enable governments to use the provincial and Canadian supreme courts to receive advisory opinions before acting or to thrust a politically volatile issue into the hands of judges. But as former Supreme Court Justice Ian Binnie points out, the Court may decline to hear such a case or, more often, choose not to answer specific parts of the reference made to it.[34]

The separation of powers may be breached when judges step outside their role as interpreters of the law's meaning to advocate some position or reform. Since the mid-1980s the justices of Canada's highest court, in public speeches and interviews, have occasionally weighed in on matters of public controversy, including the funding of bilingualism, gender bias in the law and justice system, multiculturalism, the appropriate role of the judicial branch in Canada's parliamentary system, and even contemporary American politics (see Box 6.5).

The Social Fabric

BOX 6.5 Justice Rosalie Abella on Judicial Impartiality and Independence

This is an excerpt from a lecture that Justice Rosalie Abella gave in London, England, in 2011:

Weighing values and taking public policy into account does not impair judicial neutrality or impartiality. Pretending we do *not* take them into account, and refusing to confront our personal views and be open in spite of them, may be a bigger risk to impartiality. It is of course fundamental that judges be free from inappropriate or undue influence, independent in fact and appearance, and intellectually willing and able to hear the evidence and arguments with an open mind. But neutrality and impartiality do not and cannot mean that the judge has no prior conceptions, opinions or sensibilities about society's values. It means only that those preconceptions ought not to close his or her mind to the evidence and arguments presented.

Here is an excerpt from Justice Abella's commencement address to the graduating class at Brandeis University in 2017, several months after President Donald Trump took office:

I was born right after World War II. That was the devastating war that inspired the nations of the world to unite in democratic solidarity and commit themselves conceptually, aspirationally, institutionally, and legally to the promotion and protection of values designed to prevent a repetition of the war's unimaginable human rights abuses.

Yet here we are in 2017, barely seven decades later, watching "never again" turn into "again and again," and watching that wonderful democratic consensus fragment, shattered by narcissistic populism, an unhealthy tolerance for intolerance, a cavalier indifference to equality, a deliberate amnesia about the instruments and values of democracy that are no less crucial than elections, and a shocking disrespect for the borders between power and its independent adjudicators like the press and the courts.

Sources: Justice Rosalie Abella, "Constitutions and Judges: Changing Roles, Rules and Expectations," lecture given at University College London, 7 July 2011, 9, at www.ucl.ac.uk/constitution-unit/events/judicial-independence-events/Justice_Abella_Lecture_to_JIP_07-07-11.pdf; Keynote address by Justice Rosalie Abella, Brandeis University, Commencement 2017, http://www.brandeis.edu/commencement/2017/abella.html.

Relations between the House of Commons and the Senate

When the founders designed Canada's Parliament, they took the bicameral structure of Britain's legislature as their model. Accordingly, the legislative branch was comprised of two bodies, an elected House of Commons (the lower house) and an appointed Senate (the upper house). A literal reading of the Constitution suggests that their powers are roughly equal. The major difference is that money bills must be introduced in the House of Commons. In fact, however, the superiority of the elected House of Commons has been clear to most observers (except for some senators) from day one. The unelected character of the Senate has always sat uneasily in Canada's democratic political culture, even when the right to vote was much more limited than it is today. This fact, along with the obvious patronage of most government appointments to the Senate, undermined its legitimacy.

The superiority of the House of Commons over the Senate is reinforced by several constitutional conventions. Probably the most important of these involves the selection of the prime minister and other members of the government. Constitutional law does not require that they be drawn from the House of Commons, but it is unthinkable today that the prime minister not be an elected MP. Occasionally, one or two senators have been appointed to cabinet, but this often has been because the party in power had few (or no) MPs from a particular region of the country. The appointment of Michael Fortier to the Senate after the Conservatives' 2006 election victory (with the promise that he would run for a seat in the House of Commons in the next federal election) was such a case. Fortier was an influential lawyer and financier from Montreal, a city in which the Conservatives did not win a seat in 2006, and was immediately appointed to the cabinet position of minister of Public Works and Government Services. Occasionally, the prime minister has appointed to cabinet someone who is neither an MP nor a senator. By tradition, however, this person will very soon afterwards seek election to the House of Commons. The whole system of democratic accountability would crumble if the prime minister and other members of the government were not elected officials, answerable in Question Period and removable by voters in the next election.

Another convention that reinforces the superiority of the House of Commons is found in the legislative process itself. All bills must pass both the Senate and the House of Commons before they become law. Moreover, the stages through which a bill must pass are identical in both houses of Parliament. For most of Canada's history it was generally accepted that the Senate ought not to obstruct or reject the will of the elected House of Commons. On occasion, the Senate would suggest minor revisions to legislation, sending it back to the House of Commons for reconsideration. However, after the 1984 election of the Progressive Conservative government the Senate—dominated by people appointed during over two decades of almost unbroken Liberal government—became more recalcitrant. On important legislation dealing with such matters as drug patents, government spending, Employment Insurance, the Goods and Services Tax, and the Canada–United States Free Trade Agreement the Senate delayed and in some cases rejected bills coming from the House of Commons. Senate unwillingness to pass bills sent to it by the elected House put the two chambers at loggerheads again in 2010. Opposition members of the Senate Finance Committee deleted several sections from an omnibus budget bill that had been passed by the House of Commons. A few days later the bill was passed by the full Senate. In the spring of 2018 it looked as though the Senate might vote to defeat Bill C-45, legalizing the recreational use of cannabis. Senator Peter Harder, the Liberal government's spokesperson in the Senate, stated that a "little-known custom holds that senators do not defeat Bills implementing promises made in campaigns won by the government party."[35] As is so often the case, however, constitutionalists (and many senators!) are not in agreement on this.

Changing the Constitution

Constitutions are meant to last a very long time, but they seldom do. Among the 47 countries whose independence predates 1900, only about a third have constitutions that date from before 1950. Canada's Constitution Act, 1867 is one of the oldest and most durable. Only the United States (1789), Norway (1814), the Netherlands (1815), Luxembourg (1865), and the United Kingdom (although what date should be used for the UK occasions disagreement) have older constitutions.[36]

A *coup d'état* is one way of changing a constitution. More peaceful means may also accomplish dramatic change, including the wholesale replacement of one constitution by a fundamentally different one. Radical alteration of the fundamental rules and structures of government is, however, much less common than is constitutional reform. Reform aims at changing some aspect(s) of the existing constitution, leaving the basic constitutional structure intact. Limited change of this sort is generally accomplished through a formal procedure set down in the constitution. Reforms that result from such a process are called *constitutional amendments*.

When does constitutional reform become constitutional upheaval? This is difficult to pinpoint, but the line has certainly been crossed when, as a result of change, a constitution is no longer recognizable as what it was. For example, the 1982 Constitution Act did three main things: (1) transformed Canada's written Constitution from a set of British laws into Canadian constitutional laws that could be changed without recourse to the British Parliament, a process known as patriation; (2) entrenched the Charter of Rights and Freedoms in the Constitution; and (3) established formal mechanisms for changing the Constitution in Canada. As important as these changes are, they did not amount to a new Constitution. Most features of parliamentary government and of federalism remained the same. On the other hand, the replacement of parliamentary government by American-style congressional government, the elimination of federalism, or—perhaps least far-fetched of all—the political independence of Quebec would in each case represent a radical transformation of Canada's Constitution.

Constitutional change may also come about through the gradual evolution of principles and practices. For example, the principle that the governor general should accept the advice of the prime minister on when Parliament should be dissolved and a new election called was one that emerged gradually as Canada shook off the vestiges of its colonial relationship to Great Britain. It was only when this principle was breached by Governor General Lord Byng in 1926 that it became clear that this relationship between the prime minister and the governor general was part of the Constitution. The clear superiority of the House of Commons over the Senate on matters of legislation is another constitutional convention that became clearer with the passage of time. Those appointed to the Senate in 1867 primarily were prominent politicians from the new provinces. It was during this early period that the Senate became known as the chamber of "sober second thought." Over time, however, the practice of patronage appointments, the emergence of assertive provincial governments as spokespersons for regional interests, and changing ideas about democracy and representation all contributed to the Senate's decline vis-à-vis the Commons.

Amending the Constitution before 1982

The Constitution Act, 1867 gave Ottawa a very modest power to amend the Constitution of Canada regarding matters that concerned only the federal government.[37] In practical terms, all this power amounted to was the ability to change electoral districts and boundary lines. The Act gave the provincial governments a similar power.[38] Canada's founders, however, did not establish an amending procedure that could be used to change the division of powers between Ottawa and the provinces, nor could other important provisions of the Constitution be changed using the very limited amendment powers conferred by sections 91(1) and 92(1). Indeed, the founders did not even discuss such a procedure, a curious oversight in view of the fact that the federal Constitution of the United States—the only federal model that existed at the time—was very clear on the amendment procedures that had to be followed. In Canada, the only clear requirement was that a request would have to be made to the British Parliament to change the Constitution. The reason for this was, of course, that the Canadian Constitution was a British law, originally passed as the British North America Act, 1867.

What was not clear was who would have to agree here in Canada before a resolution could be sent to London. Would all provincial governments have to agree if a proposed amendment affected their powers? Did Quebec or Ontario or any other province enjoy a special right to veto amendments? Just how much provincial consent was needed to change the Constitution? It was not even clear what would happen if all 10 provincial legislatures and the House of Commons agreed to an amendment, but the unelected Senate rejected it. Formally, at least, the Senate appeared to have the power to block constitutional change.

After decades of uncertainty, the issue was decided by the Supreme Court in 1981. The background to this decision was the stalemate in constitutional negotiations between Ottawa and the provinces. The Liberal government of Pierre Elliott Trudeau wanted to patriate the Constitution, entrench in it a Charter of Rights and Freedoms, and establish a formal procedure for future constitutional amendments. Only the governments of Ontario and New Brunswick supported Ottawa's proposal. The conflict ended up in the courts when the governments of Manitoba, Newfoundland, and Quebec each decided to ask their provincial supreme courts whether Ottawa's actions were constitutional. There was some variation in the questions and wording of these provincial references.

Nonetheless, they all asked: (1) whether Ottawa's proposed amendments affected provincial powers; and (2) if provincial consent was constitutionally required in order to make such changes. Quebec's reference also asked if that province had a special veto over amendments. These decisions were then appealed to the Supreme Court of Canada.

In its *Reference on the Constitution*[39] the Court made the following points:

- Some level of provincial consent was required for changes affecting provincial powers. This requirement was a constitutional convention, not part of constitutional law. It could not, therefore, be enforced by the courts.
- The level of required provincial consent was not at all clear. It was the Court's view that a majority of the provinces certainly had to agree, but unanimous consent was not necessary.
- In constitutional law, no province had a special right of veto over constitutional change. The Court did not give an opinion on whether such a right existed as a matter of constitutional convention.
- Ottawa did not need provincial consent before requesting the British Parliament to change Canada's Constitution in ways affecting provincial powers. If the federal government chose to act without the consent of the provinces, or with the support of only a few of them, this would be legal—but at the same time unconstitutional!

Both Ottawa and the dissenting provinces claimed victory as a result of the Court's decision. Legally, the way was clear for Ottawa to act with or without the consent of the provinces. Politically, unilateral action remained a very risky option, particularly in light of the Court's acknowledgement that some level of provincial consent was required by constitutional convention. All 11 governments returned to the bargaining table, each side conscious of the constitutional turf occupied by itself and its opponents. In November of 1981, 10 of them were able to reach agreement on a compromise document that became the Constitution Act, 1982. Only the Parti Québécois government of Quebec rejected the proposed changes. Despite Quebec's refusal to sign the 1981 agreement, the Constitution Act, 1982 is constitutional law in that province just as it is elsewhere in Canada. A 1982 Supreme Court decision confirmed this.[40]

Amending the Constitution since 1982

The uncertainties surrounding constitutional amendment have been largely dispelled by the Constitution Act, 1982. Part V of the Act sets out the amendment procedures. In fact, it establishes four different procedures, each of which applies to certain types of constitutional change. These procedures and when they are used are explained in Table 6.1.

Any of the four amendment procedures may be set in motion by either Ottawa or a provincial government (s. 46[1]). But because intergovernmental agreement is crucial to the success of most amendments, the most likely scenario is that the prime minister and the provincial premiers will first reach an agreement that will then be submitted to their respective legislatures. This procedure led to the Meech Lake Accord, the first proposal for constitutional amendment under the 1982 rules. Negotiations and deal-making between governments—the pre-legislative stage of the amendment process—are as crucial now as when the amendment process was governed by convention. The new procedures have not formally expanded the opportunities for public participation, nor have they enlarged the legislature's role in the process.

Not content with the distinction of having four different procedures for amending the Constitution, the 10 governments that agreed to the 1982 Constitution Act included another extraordinary feature in the amendment rules. This is the "opting-out" section (s. 40). Under this provision, a provincial government that does not agree to an amendment that transfers powers relating to education or other cultural matters from the provinces to Ottawa is not obliged to give up this power. Moreover, Ottawa is required to provide "reasonable compensation" to any dissenting province.

TABLE 6.1 Amending the Constitution

Procedure	Requirement	Application
1. **General (ss. 38, 42)**	• Resolution passed by the House of Commons and the Senate* • Two-thirds of the legislatures of the provinces that together comprise at least half the population of all the provinces	• Reduction or elimination of powers, rights, or privileges of provincial governments or legislatures • Proportionate representation of the provinces in the House of Commons • Senate • Supreme Court of Canada (except its composition) • Extension of existing provinces into the territories • Creation of new provinces
2. **Unanimous consent (s. 41)**	• Resolution passed by the House of Commons and the Senate* • Resolution passed by every provincial legislature	• Queen • Governor general • Lieutenant-governors • Right of each province to at least as many seats in the House of Commons as it has in the Senate • Use of the English or French language (except changes that apply only to a single province) • Composition of the Supreme Court • Changing the amending procedures of the Constitution
3. **Ottawa and one or more provinces (s. 43)**	• Resolution passed by the House of Commons and the Senate* • Resolution passed by the legislature of each province where the amendment applies	• Alteration of boundaries between provinces • Use of French or English in a particular province or provinces
4. **Ottawa or a province acting alone (ss. 44, 45)**	• If Ottawa, a resolution passed by the House of Commons and the Senate* • If a province, a resolution passed by its legislature	• Executive government of Canada, the Senate, and the House of Commons, subject to the limits established by ss. 41 and 42 of the Constitution Act, 1982

*If after 180 days the Senate has not passed a resolution already passed by the House of Commons, Senate approval is not necessary.

The Meech Lake and Charlottetown Accords would have expanded the opting-out section, guaranteeing a dissenting province the right to reasonable compensation in the case of any transfer of legislative powers from the provinces to Ottawa. In fact, this would only have enshrined in the Constitution as a provincial right and federal obligation a practice that has existed in Canada since 1964.

The first effort at amending the Constitution using the 1982 rules ended in acrimonious failure. The proposed amendment was in fact a group of changes collectively known as the Meech Lake Accord. The Accord was a 1987 agreement between Prime Minister Brian Mulroney and the 10 provincial premiers. It was a response to a series of five demands that the Quebec Liberal government of Robert Bourassa wanted met before it was willing to sign the 1981 agreement that produced the Constitution Act, 1982. The main changes proposed by the Meech Lake Accord included recognition of Quebec as a distinct society; constitutional recognition of a provincial (i.e., Quebec) right to control its own immigration policy (something Quebec had under a 1978 agreement between Ottawa and Quebec); provincial power to nominate Quebec's three justices on the Supreme Court of Canada; constitutional entrenchment of a provincial right to opt out of federal–provincial shared-cost programs and to be reimbursed for running parallel programs of their own; and certain changes to constitutional amendment procedures and categories (see Table 6.1).

After three years of wrangling marked by both an anti-French backlash in parts of English Canada and a revival of separatist nationalism in Quebec, the Accord expired. The legislatures of Manitoba and Newfoundland failed to ratify it by the 23 June 1990 deadline imposed on the process by the Constitution.

Both the birth and the death of the Accord suggested that not much had changed as a result of formalizing the amendment process. The proposed changes that made up the Accord represented a deal struck by 11 heads of government with no public participation or legislative debate. In fact, the prime minister and some of the provincial premiers were very insistent that their agreement could not be altered in any respect. It was submitted to their legislatures for ratification, not for open debate and possible modification. Public participation was solicited very late in the process, and then only because the Accord seemed destined for defeat. Indeed, there was little to suggest that any of the governments saw public participation as anything more than a resource to use when convenient. Groups and individuals opposed to the Accord's provisions denounced this process as being undemocratic.

The critics may have been right. But it was also clear that any change to the 1987 first ministers' agreement would have required that a new resolution be submitted to Parliament and all the provincial legislatures, and the ratification process would have to start over again. Serious debate and popular participation *after* an amendment resolution has been agreed to by governments are almost certain to prolong the amendment process and probably reduce the chances of reaching an agreement.

The death of the Meech Lake Accord seemed to indicate that the political process of constitutional amendment remained largely as it was before 1982. The final several months leading up to the ratification deadline were marked by acrimonious debate and some ad hoc efforts to salvage the Accord, and finally ended with Quebec being largely isolated from the other provinces. There was a sense of déjà vu about the whole affair. Quebec had been similarly isolated in 1971 when the government of Robert Bourassa suddenly withdrew its acceptance of the Victoria Charter amendments, and then again in 1981 when Quebec Premier René Lévesque claimed to have been betrayed by a last-minute deal concocted between the other provinces and Ottawa. In each case agreement ran aground because the Quebec government and some of the governments of English Canada were unable to settle their differences on Quebec's status within Canada. Meech Lake came to grief because of the same obstacle that had blocked previous efforts at constitutional change.

The next two years saw dozens of government-organized public hearings on the Constitution and hundreds of conferences and forums organized by academics, political parties, and interest groups. Ottawa and the provinces were determined to avoid the charges of elitist deal-making that had been levelled at the Meech Lake process. In this they failed. Although there were ample opportunities for citizens and groups to express their views on constitutional reform, the proposals presented to Canadians in the 26 October 1992 referendum were widely viewed as yet another instance of the elites cutting a deal and trying to foist it on the public.

The Charlottetown Accord, as these proposals were called, represented the culmination of what the federal government rather misleadingly called the "Canada round" of constitutional negotiations (the period leading up to Meech Lake having been labelled the "Quebec round"). In fact, however, the desire to get the Quebec government's political agreement to the constitutional changes of 1982 and the worry over the post-Meech Lake resurgence of support for separatism were the chief reasons why the constitutional issue dominated Canadian politics with a vengeance between 1990 and 1992. Moreover, the deal ultimately struck at Charlottetown in August 1992 bore a striking

Left: Demonstrators in Ottawa show their support for the Meech Lake Accord during the constitutional talks in Ottawa on 6 June 1990 with signs threatening Quebec secession. Right: Art commemorating Elijah Harper, who, as the only Indigenous MLA in the Manitoba legislature at that time, opposed the bill over multiple readings on the grounds that First Nations peoples affected by the Accord had not been consulted in the constitutional discussions. The failure of the Meech Lake Accord is a testament to the difficult realities of amending the Constitution.

resemblance to the Meech Lake Accord in some important respects. Besides certain carry-overs from Meech, such as Quebec's "distinct society" status, Supreme Court nominations, and provinces' ability to opt out of shared-cost programs without financial penalty, the main features included:

- a Canada clause listing the fundamental characteristics of Canadian society;
- entrenchment of the right to Indigenous self-government;
- an elected Senate with equal representation from the provinces and, eventually, special seats for Indigenous representatives;
- francophone veto in the Senate regarding bills affecting the French language or culture;
- a guarantee to Quebec of at least 25 per cent of the seats in the House of Commons;
- confirmation of the provinces' exclusive jurisdiction in several policy areas, and some decentralization of constitutional powers to the provinces in the areas of immigration and labour policy.

A sense of the potentially far-reaching changes proposed in the Charlottetown Accord is conveyed by the Canada Clause (see Box 6.6). This provision sought to express the fundamental values of Canadians. Had the Accord been passed the Canada Clause would have been included as section 2 of the Constitution Act, 1867 and would have given the courts guidance in their interpretation of the entire Constitution, including the Charter of Rights and Freedoms. It is impossible to know how judges would have interpreted many of the provisions of the Canada Clause. What is certain, however, is that it would have given to the courts a whole new field of opportunity, on top of that already provided by the Charter, to involve themselves in the policy-making process. It requires little imagination to predict that subsection 1(f) of the proposed Canada Clause, committing Canadians to "respect for individual and collective human rights and freedoms of all people," could have become the legal basis for challenges to social spending cuts, or that subsection 1(b) on the Aboriginal peoples of Canada could have become the basis for legal claims on tax resources and distinctive legal rights for Indigenous peoples in Canada. The Canada Clause, whatever its impact on Canadian society might have been, would certainly have produced a constitutional lawyer's paradise.

In the national referendum on the Charlottetown Accord, a majority of Canadians (54.5 per cent) rejected the proposed reforms, including provincial majorities in British Columbia, Alberta, Saskatchewan, Manitoba, Quebec, and Nova Scotia, as well as Yukon. The result in Ontario was virtually a dead heat. During the impassioned referendum campaign it was clear that many English Canadians said "no" to the Charlottetown Accord because they thought it gave Quebec too much, while many francophone Quebecers rejected the deal because they believed it gave them too little! Indeed, the only serious question asked by members of the Quebec media and the province's politicians during the campaign was "Did Quebec get enough in the Charlottetown Accord?" Although the 1992 agreement provided the Quebec government with more than had been proposed by the Meech Lake Accord, this was not enough in the province's nationalist political climate that prevailed in the post-Meech years.

On the other hand, a further decentralization of powers to the provinces and special status for Quebec proved to be more than most English Canadians could stomach. While it is always treacherous and somewhat misleading to talk about Quebec or any society as though it has a single set of aspirations, the failure of the Meech Lake and Charlottetown Accords confirmed that a wide gap existed between those of francophone Quebecers and their compatriots in the rest of the country.

Citizen Participation in Constitutional Reform

For most of Canada's history the only direct actors in constitutional reform were governments. This changed during the negotiations and debates that led to the Constitution Act of 1982, when a number of citizens' interest groups played an active role through lobbying government and attempting to influence public opinion. These groups, and many others inspired by the opportunities created by the Charter, were instrumental in bringing about the death of the 1987 Meech Lake Accord, which had been agreed to by the 11 first ministers in the old pre-1982 decision-making style. During the two years of consultation and negotiation that preceded the signing of the 1992 Charlottetown Accord these citizens' interest groups were very much part of the process. Informally, at least, Ottawa and the provincial governments appeared to have conceded the legitimacy and necessity of a more inclusive style of constitution-making.

What they did not concede, however, was a direct and formal role for public participation and consent. Under the old elitist policy-making style, popular consent was mediated by the heads of government. Under the more inclusive policy-making style that emerged in the early 1980s, popular consent was mediated by these heads of government *plus* certain citizens' interest groups claiming to speak on behalf of women, ethnic and racial minorities, Indigenous peoples, the disabled, official-language minorities, and so on. But not until the decision was taken in the late summer of 1992 to submit the Charlottetown reforms to the people in a national referendum was the public given a direct role in the constitutional amendment process. This represented a remarkable break from Canada's elitist tradition of constitution-making. With few exceptions, mainly from western Canada, the idea of a referendum to approve constitutional change had been rejected throughout Canada's history. When a formal procedure for constitutional amendment was being debated in the 1930s one of the country's most prominent constitutionalists dismissed the suggestion of a referendum as being inconsistent with cabinet government and a device for "passing the buck."[41] Frank Underhill, expressing the views of most intellectuals, argued that average citizens were generally incompetent to decide matters of constitutional change and that their elected representatives usually held more advanced views on public affairs. Legislatures, not citizens, he argued, should be required to ratify constitutional reforms.[42]

The idea of a referendum on the Meech Lake Accord had surfaced from time to time in the English-language media. It was dismissed, however, by Prime Minister Mulroney and most of the provincial premiers as being alien to Canada's political tradition. This view was as likely to be expressed by those on the social democratic left, such as the national New Democratic Party leader Ed Broadbent and Manitoba's NDP Premier Howard Pawley, as by those to the right of the political spectrum.

But in the flood of condemnation that followed the death of the Meech Lake Accord the idea gathered force that popular ratification should be sought in any future attempt to change the Constitution. Quebec's provincial government committed itself to holding a provincial referendum on whatever agreement it reached with Ottawa. British Columbia also passed a law requiring provincial ratification of reform proposals. However, most politicians remained steadfast in their opposition. Ottawa's decision, after much hesitation and obvious reluctance, to introduce legislation enabling Parliament to authorize a referendum (more precisely, a plebiscite, in that the vote would be formally non-binding) reflected practical necessity more than principled conviction. The powerful Quebec caucus of the governing Conservative Party opposed such legislation. The minister of Intergovernmental Affairs, Joe Clark, had often expressed serious reservations about a referendum. But the governments of Quebec and British Columbia were committed to holding a referendum and there was a good chance that the reform proposals would be rejected in both provinces. A national referendum campaign and a favourable vote in most regions was a possible way of legitimizing reform proposals in this divisive climate.

The decision to hold a referendum on the Charlottetown Accord and the willingness to abide by what was, legally speaking, a non-binding popular vote, appeared to mark the beginning of a new era in Canadian constitution-making. Most commentators believed so, arguing that governments in the future would find it impossible to ignore the 1992 precedent of a popular ratification vote.

Such predictions may be premature. A country's political culture and ways of conducting politics seldom change abruptly as a result of a single experience. First ministers will continue to be the key players in any future effort at constitutional reform. Both political tradition and the formal amendment procedure ensure their dominance. But a repeat of the Meech Lake process—an accord negotiated and agreed to without public consultation—has become virtually unthinkable. It is fair to say that a process of consultation and opportunities for public participation in some form have become necessary preconditions for any future agreement.

It remains to be seen, however, whether governments will feel obliged to submit future agreements to the electorate for ratification or whether the Charlottetown experience was an aberration that has left no mark on Canada's political culture. In British Columbia and Alberta, where populism runs a bit deeper than in most of the rest of the country, the political pressure for constitutional referendums may be irresistible. In the case of Quebec, the idea that any major change in that province's constitutional status must be approved by the electorate is now firmly established. These provinces are the ones most likely to insist on popular ratification of constitutional reform. If they do, it becomes very awkward for Ottawa not to concede a role for direct public participation through a national referendum, as happened in 1992.

Does Quebec Have the Constitutional Right to Secede? (And Does It Matter?)

On 20 August 1998 the Supreme Court of Canada handed down its much awaited decision on the constitutionality of Quebec separation. In the eyes of some, the most remarkable aspect of the ruling was that it was made at all. The separation of Quebec, if and when it comes about, is a political matter that will be determined by politicians and the people, not by nine appointed judges in Ottawa. This was certainly the view of most Quebec nationalists and of Quebec's Parti Québécois government, whose disdain for the process was such that it refused to send lawyers to argue the case for the constitutionality of Quebec secession. Indeed, the Supreme Court's involvement in this matter was widely

Governing Realities

BOX 6.6 The Canada Clause of the Proposed Charlottetown Accord

1. The Constitution of Canada, including the *Canadian Charter of Rights and Freedoms*, shall be interpreted in a manner consistent with the following fundamental characteristics:

    a) Canada is a democracy committed to a parliamentary and federal system of government and to the rule of law;

    b) the Aboriginal peoples of Canada, being the first peoples to govern this land, have the right to promote their languages, cultures and traditions and to ensure the integrity of their societies, and their governments constitute one of three orders of government in Canada;

    c) Quebec constitutes within Canada a distinct society, which includes a French-speaking majority, a unique culture and a civil law tradition;

    d) Canadians and their governments are committed to the vitality and development of official language minority communities throughout Canada;

    e) Canadians are committed to racial and ethnic equality in a society that includes citizens from many lands who have contributed, and continue to contribute, to the building of a strong Canada that reflects its cultural and racial diversity;

    f) Canadians are committed to a respect for individual and collective human rights and freedoms of all people;

    g) Canadians are committed to the equality of female and male persons; and,

    h) Canadians confirm the principle of the equality of the provinces at the same time as recognizing their diverse characteristics.

viewed by francophone Quebecers as unwarranted meddling in the internal affairs of the province.

Ottawa's decision to refer the issue of the constitutionality of Quebec secession to the Supreme Court was prompted by the actions of Montreal lawyer Guy Bertrand. A one-time separatist, Bertrand had already begun legal proceedings in Quebec challenging the constitutionality of unilateral secession by Quebec. Ottawa's 1996 decision to refer the question to the Supreme Court of Canada was, in part, due to the simple fact that Bertrand's private action had already released the genie from the bottle. Nonetheless, political risks were associated with Ottawa's involvement in a court challenge to Quebec secession. The Liberal government's decision to push forward, despite these risks, was consistent with what had come to be known as the "Plan B" approach to Quebec separatism. Whereas Plan A had involved efforts to satisfy moderate Quebec nationalists with promises of distinct society status for Quebec and some decentralization

of powers to the provinces, Plan B was a hard-line approach that relied on convincing Quebecers that separation would carry significant economic costs and that some parts of the territory of Quebec might not fall under the authority of an independent Quebec state (this was the partition threat, made by predominantly anglophone communities and Indigenous groups in Quebec, and occasionally expressed by Stéphane Dion, the Liberal minister of Intergovernmental Affairs). The court challenge to Quebec secession became a major component of the Plan B strategy.

In the reference submitted by Ottawa to the Supreme Court, three questions were asked:

- Question 1: Under the Constitution of Canada, can the National Assembly or government of Quebec effect the secession of Quebec from Canada unilaterally?

- Question 2: Does international law give the National Assembly or government of Quebec the right to effect the secession of Quebec from Canada unilaterally? In other words, is there a right to self-determination in international law that applies to Quebec?

- Question 3: If there is a conflict between international law and the Canadian Constitution on the secession of Quebec, which takes precedence?

The Court decided that there is no conflict, and so only the first two questions were addressed.

The Court's answer to the first question was a model of ambiguity that provided both federalists and separatists with congenial arguments. In strictly legal terms, said the Court, the secession of Quebec involves a major change to the Constitution

of Canada that "requires an amendment to the Constitution, which perforce requires negotiation."[43] However, the Constitution of Canada consists of more than the Constitution Acts passed between 1867 and 1982. "Underlying constitutional principles," said the Court, "may in certain circumstances give rise to substantive legal obligations . . . which constitute substantive limitation upon government action."[44] These underlying constitutional principles provided the basis for the Court's argument that if a clear majority of Quebecers voted "yes" to an unambiguous question on Quebec separation, this would "confer legitimacy on the efforts of the government of Quebec to initiate the Constitution's amendment process in order to secede by constitutional means"[45] (see Box 6.7). These underlying

Politics in Focus

BOX 6.7 Where's the Door? Is There a Door?

By far the most common method whereby a territory and its population break away from an existing country is through civil war or the collapse of a state. Peaceful breakups are less common. Some constitutions, including those of Australia, Spain, Afghanistan, and Russia, are clear in declaring secession to be unconstitutional. Very few include an explicit provision that anticipates and allows the constitutional departure of part of the country's territory. France's constitution is one that does in the case of New Caledonia, which in a November 2018 referendum rejected independence from France. A different outcome occurred in the case of Montenegro. The constitution of Serbia and Montenegro permitted Montenegro's independence and included very detailed provisions regarding what needed to be done in order to achieve it. After a referendum in 2006, Montenegro became independent. Such cases, however, are rare. Most constitutions are silent on the question of secession, such that whatever constitutional ground rules exist have to be inferred.

Though a constitution appears to be silent on the matter, courts may nonetheless decide that a constitutional right to secession does or does not exist. After

the American Civil War the Supreme Court of the United States decided that such a right did not exist, and instead that "The Constitution, in all its provisions, looks to an indestructible Union composed of indestructible States" (*Texas v White*, 1869). The Supreme Court of Canada's 1998 ruling on Quebec secession is often pointed to by experts as an example of how, given a country's particular history and constitution, a right to secession may exist even though the written constitution appears to be silent on the matter. Another possibility is that a right to secession may come to be agreed upon by the national government and spokespersons for the territory and population where a nationalist/separatist movement exists, as happened in 2012 between the UK government and that of Scotland (although Scots rejected independence in the 2014 referendum that followed).

So there are lots of different doors that disgruntled parties may try in order to get out of what they find to be an unhappy union. The carpenters who built Canada's structure were the nine Supreme Court justices who decided the 1998 *Reference re the Secession of Quebec*.

constitutional principles also impose on Ottawa and the provincial governments outside of Quebec an obligation to negotiate the terms of secession, if and when Quebecers and their provincial government express the democratic will to separate.

So who wins on the first question? The answer is that both federalists and separatists found enough in the Supreme Court's ruling to allow them to claim victory. Federalists emphasized that Quebec has no constitutional right to secede unilaterally unless a "clear majority" of Quebecers, on an "unambiguous" question, expressed their will to do so, presumably through a referendum. Separatists—or at least those who were even willing to acknowledge the Court's ruling—emphasized that the Court had agreed that the democratically expressed will of Quebecers was decisive in determining whether unilateral secession was constitutional, and that if Quebecers were to express their clear support for separation the rest of Canada would be constitutionally bound to respect this decision and negotiate the terms of secession.

The Court's answer to the second question—whether international law gives Quebec the right to secede—was both shorter and less ambiguous. The Court said "no." While acknowledging that the right of self-determination of peoples exists in international law, the Supreme Court held that this right did not apply to Quebec.

The Court did not answer the contentious question of whether the Quebec population, or a part of it, constitutes a "people" as understood in international law. It argued that such a determination was unnecessary because, however the Quebec people might be defined, it is clear that Quebecers are neither denied the ability to pursue their "political, economic, social and cultural development within the framework of an existing state,"[46] nor do they constitute a colonial or oppressed people (a claim that is a staple of contemporary Quebec historiography).

Does the 1998 Supreme Court ruling make a difference? Probably not, or at least not much of one, as even the Court seemed to acknowledge at various points in its decision. On the issue of what would constitute a "clear majority" and an "unambiguous question" in a referendum on Quebec independence, the Court admitted that "it will be for the political actors to determine what constitutes a 'clear majority on a clear question'."[47] Likewise, the practical meaning of what the Court said was that the constitutional obligation of the rest of Canada to negotiate the terms of separation with Quebec, if Quebecers express the democratic will to secede, would be for political actors to settle. Finally, in response to the argument that a unilateral declaration of independence by Quebec would be effective regardless of whether the Court's test of a clear majority on a clear question was met, the judges could say only that this might well be true, but the action would be unconstitutional nonetheless. One suspects that separatists would not lose much sleep over the constitutionality of such a declaration, particularly if various countries reacted by recognizing the new Quebec state.

Ottawa's response to the 1998 Supreme Court ruling was to pass the Clarity Act in 2000. This law empowers Parliament to review the wording of any future referendum question to determine whether it complies with the Supreme Court's requirement that such a question be "unambiguously worded." It also empowers Parliament to review the margin of victory for the separatism option in a referendum to ensure that it meets the "clear majority" standard required by the 1998 ruling. Under this law the Parliament of Canada could, conceivably, refuse to enter into negotiations on separatism with Quebec if it determined that one or both of these conditions were not met. "Conceivably" is the key word here. There are strong reasons to think that Ottawa's rejection of a referendum question designed by a sovereignist Quebec government, or of a fairly narrow margin of victory for those in favour of independence, could well backfire. Such action might play into the hands of separatists who would be quick to accuse the federal government and the rest of Canada of meddling in Quebec's affairs. The aim of the Clarity Act was doubtless to strengthen the federalists' hand in a future Quebec referendum, but the actual result could prove to be quite the opposite.

In the end, the most interesting thing about the Clarity Act is surely the questions it forces us to ask about when and how it is politically legitimate to break up a country. The issue came to the fore in early 2013 when a Bloc Québécois MP introduced a private member's bill proposing that the Clarity Act be repealed. This placed the NDP, most of whose Quebec MPs had strong nationalist sympathies, in a bind. If the party supported the bill, it would be seen in the rest of Canada as tight with the separatists. If it opposed the bill, many Quebecers who voted NDP in the 2011 election would be displeased. The party reacted by introducing its own private member's bill that clarified the Clarity Act by stating that a vote of 50 per cent plus 1 in a referendum would constitute the "clear majority" referred to in the 1998 Supreme Court ruling and in the Clarity Act. In fact, not only was this the position of Quebec separatists, it is also the official position of all the major provincial parties in Quebec. But it is a position with little support outside of Quebec, among Canadians who believe that a stronger majority ought to be necessary to break up a country.

Summing Up

Canada's Constitution includes both written and unwritten components. Some of the written provisions of the Constitution, such as those associated with the powers of the Queen, who is Canada's head of state, are quite misleading when it comes to understanding where power lies and how government works. On the other hand, many of the most important aspects of Canada's governmental system are regulated by unwritten constitutional rules, including such crucial matters as which party has the right to form a government after an election and when it loses the right to govern. Since 1982, when Canada's Constitution was patriated and changed to include the Charter of Rights and Freedoms and a formal process for constitutional amendment, Canadians have become more aware of the role that the Constitution plays in their country's politics.

The 1982 reforms did not put an end to debate on the Constitution. The federal and provincial governments tried unsuccessfully on two occasions to make additional changes. Their failure led to a resurgence of separatist sentiment in Quebec and to the 1995 referendum on Quebec independence, defeated by a very narrow margin. Canada's Supreme Court weighed in on the independence question in 1998, ruling that if certain conditions are met, Quebec does in fact have the constitutional right to secede. Since then both the desire to revisit the issue of constitutional change and support for Quebec independence have cooled somewhat. Whether this will continue is for seers and fools to predict.

Starting Points for Research

Peter W. Hogg, *Constitutional Law of Canada: 2018 Student Edition* (Scarborough, ON: Thomson Reuters, 2018). This is perhaps the leading text on Canadian constitutional law, widely used in political science and law courses alike, first published in 1977.

Christian Leuprecht and Peter H. Russell, eds, *Essential Readings in Canadian Constitutional Politics* (Toronto: University of Toronto Press, 2011). Classic and contemporary writings on various aspects of the Canadian Constitution.

Kathleen Mahoney, "The Rule of Law in Canada 150 Years after Confederation: Re-Imagining the Rule of Law and Recognizing Indigenous Peoples as Founders of Canada," 29 Mar. 2017, https://ablawg.ca/wp-content/uploads/2017/03/Blog_KM_Indigenous_Founders.pdf. Mahoney argues that the rule of law and the Canadian Constitution are based on lies about the founding of the country that omit recognition of the country's Indigenous founders.

Peter Oliver, Patrick Macklem, and Nathalie Des Rosiers, eds, *The Oxford Handbook of the Canadian Constitution* (Toronto: Oxford University Press, 2017). In 50 chapters contributed by a who's who of the Canadian constitutional law community, this book is an excellent reference work on Canada's Constitution.

Review Exercises

1. What are the pros and cons of the comparatively strict form of party discipline practised in Canada's House of Commons? How does it compare to the practice of party discipline in the British House of Commons? In what ways would Canada's system of government change if all votes in the House of Commons were free votes?

2. Draft a "Canada Clause" to be added at the beginning of the Constitution Act, stating in no more than 100 words (roughly twice the length of the preamble of the United States Constitution) the core principles and values that Canada stands for and that should guide interpretation of the Constitution. Compare yours to those drafted by other members of your class and to similar sorts of clauses at the beginning of the United States and French constitutions.

3. The Canadian and American constitutional systems are compared in Chapter 4 of Eugene Forsey's *How Canadians Govern Themselves*, at www.parl.gc.ca/about/parliament/senatoreugen eforsey/book/chapter_4-e.html. What, according to Forsey, are the main differences? Explain why you mainly agree or mainly disagree with his argument about which system is better.

The crowd waves the Canada Pride flag at the 2016 Toronto Pride Parade, where Prime Minister Justin Trudeau became the first sitting Prime Minister to march in a Pride parade. In the same year, Trudeau also raised a Pride flag above Parliament Hill for the first time in Canadian history and introduced legislation to include the terms "gender identity" and "gender expression" in the Canadian Human Rights Act and the Criminal Code. (Heather Jones Photography)

7 Rights and Freedoms

In modern democracies political demands often are expressed in the language of rights and freedoms. This chapter examines some of the controversies associated with rights and freedoms, and discusses the impact of the Canadian Charter of Rights and Freedoms on Canadian politics. Topics discussed include:

- What do "rights" and "freedoms" mean?
- The origins and meanings of rights
- The pre-Charter era: 1867–1981
- The Charter and constitutional supremacy
- The "reasonable limits" clause
- The "notwithstanding" clause
- The Charter's scope and authority
- Individual rights and freedoms
- Equality and the Charter
- Has the Charter Americanized Canadian politics?

Few things unite Canadians more than their support for human rights. At the same time, some of the most profound divisions in Canadian society and politics have to do with rights. This is no coincidence. When we use the language of rights and make an argument about how things ought to be using that language, we fall very easily, almost inevitably, into the realm of moral absolutes. Morality involves our ideas of how things ought to be, grounded on notions having to do with human dignity, individual worth, and, if we are of a religious turn of mind, the sacred. Absolutes are, of course, just that. They are propositions that are not open to compromise, limitation, or infringement of any sort. When rights are understood as moral absolutes there is no room for compromise. Moral absolutes, by their nature, are non-negotiable. This creates a potential dilemma when different segments of the population do not share the same moral values, or when some people think that an issue ought to be resolved simply on the basis of whatever rights claims might be involved and others think that non-rights considerations such as national security, economic prosperity, or bureaucratic efficiency should weigh heavily in the balance.

In reality, no right or freedom is absolute. There are two reasons for this. One is that rights and freedoms may and often do come into conflict, necessitating some compromise. For example, should freedom of expression protect the right of an individual to shout "Fire!" when there is none in a crowded theatre? This hypothetical case was used by American Supreme Court Justice Oliver Wendell Holmes to explain when and why limits on free speech are justified. Holmes established the "clear and present danger" test,[1] according to which freedom of speech could legitimately be curtailed when it posed an unmistakable and immediate danger to others. Falsely shouting "Fire!" in a crowded theatre obviously endangers the safety of those in the room. To guarantee an individual's freedom of expression in such circumstances is unreasonable because it could jeopardize the right of other individuals to be protected from unnecessary danger.

The trade-offs between competing values are seldom as simple as in the preceding example. Should freedom of expression protect people who publicly communicate statements that "willfully promote hatred"[2] against some group distinguished by race, ethnicity, language, or religion? When do national security considerations or society's interest in preventing trafficking in drugs warrant wiretaps and other violations of the individual's right to privacy? How far should the public's interest in minimizing fraudulent claims on the public purse be allowed to justify intrusions into the homes and lives of welfare recipients or of those in public office? Is affirmative action a legitimate means for promoting social equality, or is it reverse discrimination against those who are not members of the groups targeted for special consideration? When does one right or freedom trump another? And who should determine these trade-offs: the courts or the people's elected representatives?

A second reason why no right or freedom can be treated as an absolute is because to do so often would be impractical. If, for example, a constitution guarantees the right of official-language minorities to public education or services in their mother tongue—as Canada's does—does that mean that all government services everywhere in the country should be available in each of the official languages? Does it mean that minority-language education should be provided in a community where only a handful of families are demanding such a school? Common sense suggests there may be limits as to how far, and in what circumstances, the principles of linguistic equality and minority rights should apply.

What about administrative procedures determined by budget and personnel restrictions, but that may impose hardship on individuals and perhaps even limit their rights if these procedures are curtailed? The Supreme Court has addressed this question on a number of occasions when a government whose procedures or rules were challenged on Charter grounds argued that they were necessary for financial reasons. The courts have not been sympathetic to budgetary arguments. "Budgetary considerations in and of themselves cannot justify violating a *Charter* right, although they may be relevant in determining the appropriate degree of deference to governmental choices based on a non-financial objective."[3] Some taxpayers may view the matter differently.

Even in what may appear to be the most straightforward of circumstances, in which no compromise seems possible, the reality is that a balancing act between rights and other values may take place. Consider the case of human life and the measures that should be taken to preserve it. A 30-year-old person who needs a liver transplant to stay alive is more likely to receive this organ than an 80-year-old. Most, but not all of us, may find this preference for the younger person to be entirely reasonable.

We might be even more likely to approve it if we learn that the 30-year-old is the mother of two young children and her family's main breadwinner, whereas the 80-year-old has a history of serious health problems and is considered unlikely to survive very long after a liver transplant operation. For most people, at least, the determination of whether one person's right to life ought to be protected more vigilantly than another's will be influenced by knowledge of surrounding circumstances like these.

Dilemmas await us at every turn. Despite this, and despite the passions unleashed by such controversies, rights and freedoms have had a low profile in Canadian politics for most of this country's

Len Norris/© Simon Fraser University

"I'm trying to see you, Albert, in the light of our new Charter of Rights and Freedoms . . ."

No right or freedom is absolute. Questions such as *When should one individual's rights and freedoms be diminished to protect those of others?* and *Should one right or freedom supersede another?* are raised when applying a document such as the Charter to everyday situations.

history. Reflecting on her time as a law student, Supreme Court Justice Rosalie Abella says that the question of the role of the courts in developing and protecting rights was hardly ever discussed when she graduated in 1970. But since the passage of the Charter of Rights and Freedoms in 1982, she says, rights and the role of the courts in their interpretation have been very much in focus on Canada's political radar screen.[4] The Charter entrenched various rights and freedoms in the Constitution. Moreover, by establishing the principle of constitutional supremacy (sections 32 and 52[1] of the Constitution Act, 1982), the 1982 constitutional reforms placed these rights more or less beyond the interference of governments. "More or less" because section 1 of the Charter states that these rights and freedoms are "subject only to such reasonable limits prescribed by law as can be demonstrably justified in a free and democratic society," and section 33(1) enables either Parliament or a provincial legislature to declare that a particular law or provision of a law shall operate even if it violates rights or freedoms guaranteed in sections 2 or 7 to 15 of the Charter. Together, sections 1 and 33 appear to maintain some measure of parliamentary supremacy over the courts and the Charter.

There is little doubt, as Justice Abella and so many others have observed, that the Charter has decisively changed the face of Canadian politics. The authority of elected legislatures has receded before the authority of the Constitution and the courts. A transformation has taken place in the venues and language of Canadian politics. The discourse of "rights," always a part of the political scene, has assumed much greater prominence since passage of the Charter. Individuals, organized interests, and even governments have turned increasingly to litigation as a means of influencing public policy. During the first decade after the Charter's passage, about 1,000 Charter cases a year were decided by Canadian courts,[5] reflecting the increased importance of the judiciary as a forum for the resolution of political conflict. About 20–30 Charter rulings were handed down by the Supreme Court each year, including many that had major effects on public policy. The pace

of such judicial interventions has slowed somewhat in recent years. Between 2012 and 2017 the Supreme Court decided roughly 60–80 cases per year, about 20 per cent of which dealt with Charter issues.[6]

Does the Charter matter? The answer may seem to be obvious. But expert opinion on this matter is not in agreement. Most political scientists argue that the Charter has profoundly transformed Canadian politics and society. But some commentators, including Harry Arthurs, a former dean of Osgoode Hall Law School and one of Canada's most distinguished lawyers, argues that the Charter "has not . . . significantly altered the reality of life in Canada."[7] With all due respect to Professor Arthurs, this is, frankly, an unsupportable conclusion. It is, however, fair to ask which groups (leaving aside lawyers) have won as a result of Charter politics and which may have lost ground. Clearly, the processes, venues, and outcomes of Canadian politics have changed in significant ways as a result of the Charter. Some observers may believe that the result has not been a more democratic Canada— this is Professor Arthurs's conclusion—but the weight of the evidence, as we will see, surely suggests otherwise.

To determine how the Charter has affected Canadian democracy we need a baseline that will enable us to assess developments over the almost four decades since its passage. Let us begin by examining the concepts of rights and freedoms. We will then examine the history of rights and freedoms in Canada, pre- and post-Charter, before turning to some Charter decisions and their impacts.

Coming to Terms: What Do Rights and Freedoms Mean?

Although there is a long tradition in Western constitutional law of distinguishing between rights and freedoms, often the practical distinction is rather blurred. An individual's freedom to believe something or to behave in a particular way may be expressed in terms of a right. "I have a right to picket this employer" (freedom of assembly), or "I have a right to distribute pamphlets explaining that the [you fill in the blank] are responsible for most of the evils that beset the world" (freedom of expression). Likewise, the right to fair and equal treatment by the law is often framed in terms of the conditions necessary to ensure a personal freedom. For example, an accused person's right to be tried within a reasonable time—a right guaranteed by section 11(b) of the Charter—may well be violated if he or she has to spend a year in prison before being tried or "free" but under onerous bail restrictions. Obviously, this individual's personal freedom is seriously compromised in such circumstances. Or consider the case of abortion. Those who argue against legal restrictions on a woman's access to abortion claim that such laws violate a woman's right to control her body, an important dimension of the right to privacy. In this case the right being claimed is nothing less than freedom from interference by the state or, as US Supreme Court Justice Louis Brandeis famously expressed it, "the right to be let alone."

Rights and freedoms are not, therefore, entirely distinct and watertight compartments. Nevertheless, constitutional experts usually reserve the term "rights" for those individual and group **entitlements** that "are considered so fundamental to human dignity that they receive special protection under the law and usually under the constitution of a country."[8] Freedoms involve an individual's liberty to do or believe certain things without restraint by government. Whereas the defence of rights often requires some government action, the protection of freedoms requires that government refrain from interfering in certain matters. Under the influence of the United Nations **Universal Declaration of Human Rights** (1948), the term **human rights** has become the commonly used designation for this bundle of rights and freedoms. Included among them are the following:

- *Political rights/fundamental freedoms.* These include freedom of association, assembly, expression, the media, conscience, and religion, and the right to privacy.

- *Democratic rights.* Among these are the rights of all adult persons to vote and stand for public office. Requirements that elections periodically be held and that the law apply equally to those who govern and those who are governed are also important democratic rights.

- *Legal rights.* These are essentially procedural rights intended to ensure the fair and equal treatment of individuals under the law. They include, *among others*, the right to due process of law, freedom from arbitrary arrest, the right to a fair hearing, the right to legal counsel, and the right not to be subjected to cruel or unusual punishment.

- *Economic rights.* Although they usually are not listed as a separate category of entrenched rights, economic rights occupy an important place in all capitalist democracies. They include the right to own property and not to be deprived of it without fair compensation, the right to withhold one's labour, and freedom of contract.

- *Equality rights.* This is the most recent and probably the most controversial category of rights. The American Constitution, the first modern constitution to include an entrenched guarantee of equality rights, refers only to every person's right to "equal protection of the laws."[9] The more recent tendency, however, has been to enumerate the proscribed bases of legal discrimination, such as race, religion, ethnicity, gender, and age. Canada's Charter also includes mental or physical disability and has been interpreted by the courts to prohibit discrimination based on sexual orientation.

These five categories by no means exhaust the rights that may be protected by law. *Language rights* represent an important category of group rights in many societies, Canada included. Other group rights, such as for religious minorities or Indigenous peoples, may also be protected by law. Some argue that *social rights*, or what are sometimes called *entitlements*, including the right to a job, economic

Governing Realities

BOX 7.1 Should Trees, Rivers, and Endangered Species Have Constitutionally Protected Rights?

David Suzuki is Canada's best-known environmentalist and the foundation that bears his name is one of Canada's most influential environmental advocacy groups. For many years Suzuki has argued that Canada's Constitution should be changed to include rights for the ecosystem. By this he does not mean that the Constitution should merely include a reference to the state's duty to promote a healthy environment for citizens and future generations, as is found in Article 2 of Sweden's constitution: "The public institutions shall promote sustainable development leading to a good environment for present and future generations." Nor does he mean that it should include a commitment to sustainable development, as in Article 110(b) of Norway's constitution: "Every person has a right to an environment that is conducive to health and to natural surroundings whose productivity and diversity are preserved. Natural resources should be made use of on the basis of comprehensive long-term considerations whereby this right will be safeguarded for future generations."

Instead, Suzuki would like to see something along the lines of the ecosystem rights that are included in the constitutions of Ecuador and Brazil. Speaking of Ecuador's ecosystem rights, he says, "[They are based on] the principles of 'Buen Vivir'. This means 'good living', a concept that emphasizes living in harmony with other people and nature. It reflects the idea that nature or 'pachamama' is a mother that needs to be respected and celebrated. *It asserts that nature is not property and puts ecosystems on equal footing with humans.*"[10]

Including such protections in a constitution involves a fundamental shift in thinking about rights. Historically, rights have been based on ideas about human dignity and happiness. The notion that non-human life forms should be invested with rights that do not depend on the needs and desires of human beings is radically different. It is based on a rejection of what are referred to by the advocates of plant and animal rights as anthropocentric—human-centred—and species-specific notions of justice that unfairly privilege human beings. This standpoint derives from the same spiritual world view of Canada's Indigenous peoples: that we share responsibility for and must look after "all our relations," including plants, animals, bodies of water, and Mother Earth herself.

To get a better sense of the reasoning and world view on which such arguments rest, visit the Assembly of First Nations webpage "Honouring Earth" (https://www.afn.ca/honoring-earth/) and, for a less inclusive non-Indigenous view, the website of People for the Ethical Treatment of Animals (https://www.peta.org).

security, public education, decent housing, and adequate health care, should also have the status of entrenched constitutional rights. *Environmental rights*, including citizens' rights to clean air and water, to the preservation of wilderness areas, and to the protection of species diversity, are advocated by some groups, including the Canadian Bar Association. Some go even further, calling for the protection of animal rights and the dignity of plant life (see Box 7.1).

In Canada, many of the main categories of human rights are entrenched in the Charter. Table 7.1 identifies the sections of the Charter that correspond to each of them.

On the Origins and Meanings of Rights

There is no inevitability to either the precise rights recognized by a constitution or the meanings that come to be associated with them. Rights, like a society's notions of justice, are constructed out of concrete historical circumstances. Some of the rights claimed in present-day Canada and the rights discourses that emerge around these claims and reactions to them are quite different from those of even a couple of generations ago. And much of Canadian rights discourse would be unrecognizable in a society

TABLE 7.1 Human Rights and the Charter

Rights Category	Pre-Charter Protections	Charter Protections
1. Political rights/fundamental freedoms	Common-law protections implied in the preamble of the Constitution Act, 1867	s. 2
2. Democratic rights	Constitution Act, 1867, ss. 41, 50, 84, 85	ss. 3–5
3. Legal rights	Common law; Criminal Code	ss. 7–14
4. Economic rights	Common-law rights re: contract, property, mobility, etc.	s. 6 (and implied under some other sections)
5. Equality rights	Common law; s. 93 of Constitution Act, 1867, guaranteeing educational rights of religious denominations	ss. 15, 28
6. Language rights	Constitution Act, 1867, s. 133	ss. 16–23
7. Indigenous rights	Treaties	s. 25, plus s. 35 of Constitution Act, 1982
8. Social rights	None	Although not mentioned directly, some court rulings suggest that certain limited social rights are implied

like Iran, where very different religious, cultural, and economic forces have contributed to the recognition of and meaning ascribed to rights. There are, therefore, no absolute rights that may be adduced from human history. What may appear to be the most obvious and uncontroversial rights claims—for example, the right to vote or the right to express one's personal beliefs—are denied in many societies.

Rights come from political struggles. A claim made by an individual or a group will be expressed as a right only when it is denied or placed in jeopardy by the words or actions of some other party. For example, the claim that a woman has a right to abort her pregnancy arises because of legal and practical restrictions on access to abortion. The experience of limitations on freedom of speech, religion and conscience, or association produces calls for their constitutional protection. Groups and individuals come to the defence of the right to privacy precisely because they perceive it is threatened by state actions. Likewise, when a linguistic group claims the protection or promotion of their language as a right, this is an indication that conflict exists between linguistic groups in that society.

Political struggle is a necessary condition for rights claims. It is not, however, a sufficient condition. Only some political conflicts acquire the character of rights issues. To be recognized as legitimate, a rights claim must be successfully linked to one or more of a society's fundamental values. These fundamental values operate as limits on rights discourse.

This may be seen in the case of same-sex marriage. Before the 1970s, sexual relations between persons of the same sex constituted a punishable offence under the Criminal Code. Change began when the minister of Justice, Pierre Trudeau, famously stated in 1967 that "the view we take here is that there's no place for the state in the bedrooms of the nation. I think that what's done in private between adults doesn't concern the Criminal Code." Although Trudeau certainly was not the first to take the position that consenting adults had a *right* to privacy in their sexual relations, his statement was important in shaping the political conversation about homosexuality and helping to shift public opinion from a view that considered such behaviour to be deviant and criminal, to the idea that this was a matter of personal choice or of inherent orientation that should not be regulated by the state. Trudeau's comment and the legislation he introduced to decriminalize sexual relations between persons of the same sex were important steps in changing the political and cultural conversation and transforming same-sex relations into a rights issue.

Decriminalization, however, was only the first step. Canadian public opinion was still opposed to homosexuality in some circumstances and certainly did not accept the idea that homosexuals should be allowed to be teachers or to have the same rights under family law as heterosexual couples. Surveys showed that the percentage of Canadians saying that two adults of the same sex having sexual relations is always wrong was high until the 1990s (63 per cent in 1975; 62 per cent in 1985; 59 per cent in 1990; falling to 32 per cent in 2000).[11] At the same time, however, polls showed that by the end of the 1970s a strong majority of Canadians agreed that "homosexuals are entitled to the same rights as other Canadians" (1980, 70 per cent; 1990, 81 per cent; 2000, 71 per cent).[12] But when asked about more specific rights, such as the right of homosexuals to marry, Canadian public opinion was a bit slower to change. Polls showed that before the mid-to late 1990s, just over one-third of Canadians supported same-sex marriage. Between 1998 and 2005 public opinion changed from being fairly evenly divided on this issue to being supportive of legal recognition of same-sex unions.[13]

The idea of homosexuality, long relegated to the illegitimate margins of Canadian society and even deemed criminal in some circumstances, was becoming more widely accepted in Canadian society. This opened the way for legislative change, including the decriminalization of sexual relations between persons of the same sex and, by the 1970s, the inclusion in provincial human rights codes of prohibitions against discrimination on the basis of sexual preference. Although the Charter did not explicitly mention sexual preference in s. 15 on equality rights, court rulings very soon recognized this as an analogous form of discrimination that, like discrimination based on race, religion, disability, and so on, was proscribed by the Charter. The decline of traditional religiosity in Canada and the boost provided by the Charter to the general conversation on rights combined to produce growing popular receptivity to the argument that recognition of same-sex marriage was a matter of human rights.

The fact that Canadians are much more likely to be receptive to rights arguments today than in the past, finding them normal, appropriate, and often convincing, does not mean that issues must be framed in a manner that draws on the language and conceptual architecture of rights. Indeed, political conflict often is over how an issue should be framed and whether it should be thought of as involving rights or as an issue that pits interests and values against one another. Take the case of immigration. It is possible to frame this issue entirely in the language of economics, demography and social integration, national security, and other concerns. But it is also possible to frame the issue as a matter of human rights. The Canadian Conference of Catholic Bishops, among other groups, takes this latter approach. "The Church supports the right to migrate," it states, "however, this is not seen as an absolute right of individuals. Instead, it is to be subject to the requirements of the common good. This means that states can exercise a certain control over immigration, although it is not to be inspired by selfish attitudes or 'restrictive policies'."[14]

Rights talk—framing issues in the language of rights and anchoring the discourse to rights documents, including the Charter—is often difficult to oppose. Who wants to be seen as being "against" or at least unsympathetic to human rights? But as Michael Ignatieff observes, this may not always be the appropriate way to view and resolve an issue. "Human rights activism," he writes, "likes to portray itself as an anti-politics, in defense of universal moral claims designed to delegitimize 'political,' i.e., ideological or sectarian, justifications for the abuse of human beings. In practice, impartiality and neutrality are just as impossible as universal and equal concern for everyone's human rights."[15] The advocacy of human rights, Ignatieff argues, often involves a sort of idolatry of human rights. By this he means that rights may be treated as universal moral absolutes, brooking no opposition and permitting no compromise. Ignatieff argues that a pragmatic approach to the defence and advocacy of rights is often more effective politically and appropriate in a world in which ideas of justice and what constitutes a good life vary between cultures. His

Stacey Newman/Shutterstock

Canadians wait at Pearson Airport in Toronto to welcome the first Syrian refugees to Canada on 10 December 2015. Immigration and accommodation of refugees and asylum-seekers was increasingly framed as a human rights issue in 2015 as the dangers of the refugee crisis became front-page news with the death of three-year-old migrant Alan Kurdi.

argument is chiefly against what he sees as a sort of rights imperialism that westerners sometimes engage in when they lecture other societies and cultures about how things ought to be. But what Ignatieff calls the idolatry of human rights, the failure to imagine that any other way of understanding and resolving an issue might be legitimate and helpful, is as likely to exist at home as on the international scene.

Rights and Their Protection

During the 1980–1 debate on constitutional reform, critics of a constitutionally entrenched charter of rights warned that such a step would lead to the Americanization of Canadian politics. Since then,

they have lamented that their prediction has come true. The "Americanization" they warned of, and that some still regret, has two main aspects. One involves a more prominent policy role for unelected judges and a related decline in the status of elected legislatures. The other is an increase in recourse to the courts to solve political disputes.

Some of those who opposed entrenched rights argued that rights and freedoms are better protected by elected legislatures that are accountable to the electorate for their actions, than by unelected judges. By "better," they meant that the decisions of elected politicians are more likely to correspond with the sentiments of citizens—or at least that if they do not there exists a democratic mechanism, i.e., elections, to hold politicians accountable for their choices. Rights, the opponents of entrenchment argued, should not be interpreted independently of popular opinion. Nor should important political controversies be determined by unelected officials.

What the critics denounced as the undemocratic flaws of entrenchment, advocates of the Charter acclaimed as its virtues. Rights, they argued, should not be subject to the vicissitudes of public opinion as these are reflected in the legislature. The fact that judges are not elected and are virtually immune from removal before the age of 75 serves to protect, not undermine, democracy. It does so by insulating judges from the winds of partisanship and the vagaries of public opinion. What sort of democracy, entrenchment advocates ask, would permit rights and freedoms to depend on shifting popular sentiments and politicians' calculations of political expediency?

The difference between the opponents and advocates of entrenchment is not over the importance of rights. It is not even primarily about the appropriate balance between the rights of individuals and minorities versus those of the majority. The difference between these two positions is over how best to *protect rights*. Those who advocate the American model of entrenched rights prefer to put their faith in the Constitution and the judges who interpret it. Those who prefer the traditional British model of parliamentary supremacy are more dubious about judge-made law and more inclined to place their trust in the prudence and democratic responsiveness of elected governments.

The Pre-Charter Era: 1867–1981

There is not a single reference to the subject of rights in R. MacGregor Dawson's *Constitutional Issues in Canada, 1900–1931*, published in 1933.[16] In Dawson's *The Government of Canada* (1947), the first textbook on Canadian government, one finds a mere handful of references to fundamental rights and liberties.[17] J.A. Corry and J.E. Hodgetts's *Democratic Government and Politics* (1946)[18] pays greater attention to rights, devoting an entire chapter to a comparison of civil liberties in Britain, the United States, and Canada. Generally, however, rights issues occupied a distinctly marginal place in

Canadian political science and even in legal circles until the middle of the twentieth century.

A couple of factors were responsible for what might appear to be a puzzling silence on questions of rights and their protection in Canada. The most important undoubtedly was federalism. The Constitution Act, 1867 contains very few references to the rights and freedoms of Canadians. It does, however, include a very detailed catalogue of the "rights" of governments, i.e., the legislative and fiscal powers of Ottawa and the provinces. Faithful to the principle of parliamentary supremacy, the courts were unwilling to overrule the authority of elected legislatures. This is why Alan Borovoy, at the time the general counsel of the Canadian Civil Liberties Association and Canada's foremost civil libertarian, originally opposed the Charter of Rights and Freedoms. "The truth is," he argued, "that we have had far more success [in advancing rights] in the political and legislative arenas than in the judicial. . . . [T]he courts have shown a monumental reluctance to apply the protections for civil liberties that exist in our present Bill of Rights."[19] Borovoy and other civil libertarians lamented the fact that throughout most of Canada's history, issues that clearly involved the protection of rights and freedoms were dealt with by the courts as questions of which level of government had jurisdiction. To have a chance at success, therefore, rights claims had to be packaged in the constitutional categories of federalism. In retrospect, the resulting jurisprudence seems bizarre, to say the least. Consider the following cases:

- *Reference re Alberta Statutes* (Alberta Press case, 1938).[20] The law in question was the Accurate News and Information Act, passed by the Alberta legislature in 1937. It imposed censorship restrictions on the province's newspapers, based on the Social Credit government's belief that the press was unfairly critical of its policies. Ottawa referred this and two other pieces of Social Credit legislation to the Supreme Court for a ruling on their constitutionality. The Court was unanimous in striking down the press censorship law. Two of the judgments in this case referred to the "right of free public discussion of public affairs" as being a right fundamental to parliamentary democracy and implied under the preamble to the Constitution Act, 1867, which states that Canada is adopting "a constitution similar in principle to that of the United Kingdom." But both of these judgments, although using somewhat different reasoning, suggested that the federal government possessed the authority to impose restrictions on freedom of the press. The Alberta law was, therefore, struck down essentially on federalism grounds.

- *Saumur v. City of Quebec* (1953).[21] Quebec City had passed a bylaw forbidding the distribution in the streets of any printed material without the prior consent of the Chief of Police. Without explicitly singling out any group, this bylaw was intended to curb proselytizing activities by the Jehovah's Witnesses sect, whose activities and teachings strongly offended Catholic Church authorities. In a five-to-four decision, the Court struck down the bylaw. An analysis of the judges' reasoning reveals how disinclined they were to place the protection of fundamental freedoms over the authority of government. On the majority side, four of the five justices decided that the bylaw was **ultra vires** (i.e., beyond the legal authority of the government in question). The fifth was willing to concede that the regulation fell within provincial jurisdiction, but felt that the right to disseminate religious material was protected by Quebec's Freedom of Worship Act. On the dissenting side, two of the judges argued that the bylaw fell within the province's jurisdiction over civil rights. No one suggested that freedom of religious expression ought to be protected from interference by any and all levels of government.

- *Switzman v. Elbling* (Padlock Case, 1957).[22] In 1937 the Quebec government had passed a law declaring illegal the use of a house for the propagation of Communism, authorizing the Quebec police to put a padlock on premises where such activities were suspected. The Supreme Court of Canada ruled that the

impugned Act had the effect of making the propagation of Communism a crime. But criminal law is under the exclusive jurisdiction of Ottawa and so the "Padlock Law" was struck down as being ultra vires. The issue of political censorship was raised by a couple of justices, but this was not the basis for the Court's ruling.

- *Attorney General of Canada and Dupond v. Montreal* (1978).[23] This case involved a Montreal bylaw that restricted freedom of assembly in public places. The bylaw was used during the 1960s to prevent public demonstrations during a period of political turmoil and occasional terrorist incidents. By a five-to-three vote the Supreme Court upheld the constitutionality of this restriction. The majority argued that the impugned bylaw regulated matters of a local or private nature and therefore came under the authority of the province. Interestingly, the dissenting judges did not focus on the issue of freedom of assembly. Instead, they argued that the Montreal bylaw was ultra vires because it represented a sort of "mini-Criminal Code" and thus intruded upon Ottawa's exclusive authority to make criminal law. As a final note, the judgment in this case was unequivocal in dismissing the relevance of the Canadian Bill of Rights (1960). "None of the freedoms referred to," wrote Justice Beetz, "is so enshrined in the constitution as to be above the reach of competent legislation."[24]

Federalism was not the only factor responsible for the relatively low profile of rights issues until well into the twentieth century. Public opinion was generally sanguine about the treatment of rights and freedoms in Canada. A Gallup Poll taken in 1957 found that 63 per cent of Canadians agreed that "personal rights are being fully protected" and only 19 per cent disagreed. University graduates were as likely as school drop-outs to hold this view.[25] The thinking of most informed Canadians was probably that rights were best protected by legislatures, the common law, and a vigilant public: the system that Canada had inherited from the United Kingdom.

But increasing doubts about the adequacy of these guarantees were being expressed by civil libertarians during the 1940s and 1950s. These doubts were sown by apparent rights violations like Quebec's infamous "Padlock Law" (1937), the Alberta government's attempt to censor the press (1937), the threatened deportation of Japanese-Canadians in 1945–6, and the arbitrary measures taken during the Gouzenko spy affair of 1946. These constituted, according to political scientist Norman Ward, "disturbing signs of a weakening concern by Dominion and provincial governments for personal rights and liberties."[26] Corry and Hodgetts agreed, arguing that the protections provided under British parliamentary government were not sufficient in a young country facing the challenge of absorbing large numbers of persons of diverse ethnic origins and cultural backgrounds.[27]

This growing concern over civil liberties was shared by some influential groups, including the Canadian Bar Association. The solution, they argued, was a bill of rights that would be entrenched in the Constitution. Canada's participation in the United Nations, and the human rights commitments entered into through the UN, reinforced the voices of those calling for constitutionally entrenched rights. When the Conservative Party came to power in 1957 under the leadership of John Diefenbaker, who had long been an outspoken advocate of entrenched rights, the timing for a Bill of Rights seemed propitious.

But there was a major snag. A constitutional Bill of Rights would affect the powers of both Ottawa and the provinces and, it was believed, would therefore require provincial consent. It was clear that some of the provinces would oppose entrenchment. For this reason the Conservative government chose to introduce the Bill of Rights as a statute, requiring only the approval of the House of Commons and the Senate. The **Canadian Bill of Rights** became law on 10 August 1960.

The Bill of Rights proved to be a major disappointment for civil libertarians. The first Supreme Court decisions on its application were very cautious. In a case involving a challenge to the federal Lord's Day Act, the Court took the position that the Bill of Rights only reaffirmed the rights and freedoms status quo that existed at the time it became law

(1960). Speaking for the majority, Justice Ritchie declared that the Canadian Bill of Rights "is not concerned with 'human rights and fundamental freedoms' in any abstract sense, but rather with such 'rights and freedoms' as they existed in Canada immediately before the statute was enacted."[28]

After nearly a decade of judgments that, to paraphrase Saskatchewan Chief Justice Emmett Hall, whittled away at the Bill of Rights,[29] the Supreme Court in 1970 suddenly abandoned its cautious approach. The case involved an Indigenous man, Joseph Drybones, who was convicted under section 94(b) of the Indian Act. This provision of the Act made it an offence for Indigenous persons to be intoxicated off a reserve. In challenging this provision, Drybones's lawyer argued that it conflicted with the Canadian Bill of Rights guarantee of "equality before the law," subjecting Indigenous people to criminal sanctions to which other people were not exposed. This was obviously true. But if the Court remained faithful to its earlier interpretation of the Bill of Rights' application, this would not be sufficient to render the discrimination unconstitutional.

By a five-to-three vote the Supreme Court used the Bill of Rights to strike down section 94 of the Indian Act.[30] This proved, however, to be a one-off decision. Perhaps realizing the Pandora's box they were opening through this more activist interpretation of the Bill of Rights, a majority of the judges retreated from this position after *Drybones*. This became crystal clear a few years later in the *Lavell* case of 1974,[31] where the majority upheld the constitutionality of another provision of the Indian Act against a challenge that it denied equality before the law for Indigenous women who married non-Indigenous men and consequently lost their Indian status.

Another nail was hammered into the Bill of Rights' coffin by the Court's decision in *Hogan v. The Queen* (1975).[32] In *Hogan*, a person suspected of driving while intoxicated refused to take a breathalyzer test before seeing his lawyer. He ultimately was coerced into taking the test and this evidence proved to be decisive in his conviction. The question before the Supreme Court was whether evidence should be excluded if it has been obtained in an improper manner. Under the common law, Canadian judges had followed the rule that such evidence would be admitted so long as it was relevant to the case at hand. But the Canadian Bill of Rights included a number of legal rights, including the right of an accused or detained person "to retain and instruct counsel without delay" (s. 2[c][ii]).

The Supreme Court was unwilling to apply the Bill of Rights in this case. It appeared, therefore, that not only could the Bill of Rights not be used to strike down conflicting federal legislation—at least not laws on the books before 1960—it did not take precedence over established rules of the common law. Chief Justice Laskin's dissenting argument that the Bill of Rights should be interpreted as a "quasi-constitutional instrument" was never supported by a majority of his colleagues. The glimmer of hope that the *Drybones* decision had sparked was extinguished during the 1970s, producing renewed calls for constitutionally entrenched rights.

Before passage of the Charter, the only rights entrenched in Canada's Constitution were associated with democratic elections, religion, and language. Section 41 (now spent) of the Constitution Act, 1867 specified who was qualified to vote and section 50 indicates that no House of Commons may sit for longer than five years (thus ensuring elections). Section 93 of the Constitution Act, 1867 declares that the educational rights of denominational minorities may not be diminished from what they were when a province entered Confederation. Section 133 establishes the equal standing of French and English in Parliament and in federal courts, and in the Quebec legislature and the courts of that province. Neither of these latter two sections proved to be very effective in protecting minority rights.[33]

Life under the Charter

It probably is fair to say that the changes generated by the Charter have far exceeded the expectations of all but a few of the politicians and experts who presided at its birth. On a quantitative level, the Charter has been the direct stimulus for explosive growth in the number of rights cases that come before the courts. Hundreds of Charter cases are decided by Canadian courts each year, and in recent years about 12–20 of these have been rulings by the Supreme Court or one of the provincial superior courts. Whereas the Bill of

Rights was used only once in the pre-Charter era to strike down a part of a federal law (the *Drybones* decision) the Charter has been used to strike down over 80 federal and provincial laws or parts of laws. The Court is, however, more likely to uphold the validity of a challenged law, as it has about two-thirds of the time over the past two decades. In the case of some laws, for example, the Immigration Act, the Income Tax Act, and the Criminal Code, dozens of Charter-based rulings have been handed down by the Supreme Court. An even greater number of provincial laws have been the subject of Supreme Court Charter rulings.

In terms of "quality," the change produced by the Charter has been no less pronounced. The previous pattern of deciding rights issues as federalism cases, asking only whether a government was transgressing the jurisdictional turf of the other level of government, has been abandoned. Rights issues are now dealt with head on, argued by litigants and decided by judges on the basis of the Charter. Moreover, the courts have shed most of their traditional reluctance to question the substance of duly enacted laws and regulations. Emboldened by the Charter's unambiguous declarations that the "Constitution is the supreme law of Canada" and that the courts have exclusive authority to interpret and enforce the Charter's guarantees, judges have struck down provisions in several dozen federal and provincial statutes. Although judges are quite aware of the expanded role they play in the political process, most of them insist that there is nothing undemocratic in this and that it is quite incorrect to assert, as some critics do, that judges engage in policy-making from the bench and have too much power. Retired Supreme Court Justice John Major speaks for most of his colleagues on the bench and in the legal profession when he says that "there is no such thing as judicial activism in Canada."[34] Former Chief Justice Beverley McLachlin has said that "there is no clear demarcation between applying the law, interpreting the law, and making the law."[35] She did not mean this as a criticism of what critics call judicial activism, but instead as an explanation and justification for what critics see as too vast a role for judges.

Looking back from the present, it probably seems obvious that the Charter would come to play a transformative role in Canadian politics and that the influence of the courts would be enhanced significantly as they applied and interpreted its provisions. In fact, however, this was not at all clear when the Charter was passed. On the occasion of her retirement from the Supreme Court, Chief Justice McLachlin recalled those early days: "As a new judge I listened to the debates swirling around me about what the document about to be adopted would mean for the law in general and judges in particular. . . . Seminars were held and lectures were given, but nobody knew how it would play out." The prevailing expectation, she says, "was nothing much would change. By and large, this is how most of the judges with which I worked thought it should be. They were fearful of a wholesale challenge to the existing laws and procedures that they thought had served the country quite well."[36] There were a number of reasons why things worked out quite differently. One of the most important was the Supreme Court's interpretation of the Charter's "reasonable limits" clause.

Reasonable Limits and the Charter

It may appear that the opening words of the Charter invite the courts to exercise self-restraint, commonly called **judicial restraint**. Section 1 declares that the guarantees set forth in the Charter shall be "subject only to such reasonable limits prescribed by law as can be demonstrably justified in a free and democratic society." What are these **reasonable limits**? The Supreme Court established a two-part test in the case of *The Queen v. Oakes* (1986).[37] The first part of this test asks whether a government's objective in limiting a right is of sufficient importance to warrant such an encroachment. The second part of the test asks whether the extent of the limitation is proportionate to the importance of the government's objective. In order to satisfy this second criterion, a limitation must meet three conditions: (1) it must be rationally connected to the government's objective; (2) it should impair the right in question as little as is necessary to meet the government's objective; and (3) the harm done to rights by a limitation must not exceed the good that it accomplishes.

In *Oakes*, the Court was called upon to determine whether a "reverse onus" provision in the Narcotic Control Act violated the presumption of innocence set forth in section 11(d) of the Charter. Under that Act, a person found guilty of possessing drugs was automatically considered guilty of trafficking unless he could prove his innocence on this more serious charge. The Court did not question the importance of the objective associated with this provision of the Act, i.e., to prevent drug trafficking. But in applying the second part of the test that they developed in *Oakes*, the justices decided that the means, in this case placing the onus on the accused to prove his innocence, was disproportionate to the end.

Separating the goals of legislation, part one of the ***Oakes* test**, from an assessment of the means used to accomplish them may appear to be a way around the thorny problem of judges second-guessing the decisions of duly elected governments. In fact, however, it is not possible to answer such questions as whether a right is impaired as little as possible in the circumstances, or whether the means are proportionate to the ends, without wandering into the realm of political value judgments. Since *Oakes*, the courts have been reluctant to question the ends associated with laws and regulations limiting rights. But they have not been shy about using the second part of the *Oakes* test to dismiss governments' section 1 justifications.

This was apparent in the Supreme Court's decision in *Ford v. Attorney General of Quebec* (1988).[38] The case involved a challenge to those sections of Quebec's Bill 101 that prohibited commercial advertising in languages other than French. The Quebec government argued that this limitation was necessary to preserve the economic value of the French language and the predominantly French character of the province. The Court accepted that this was a perfectly legitimate policy goal (it passed part one of the *Oakes* test), but argued that the Quebec government had not shown that "the requirement of the use of French only is either necessary for the achievement of the legislative objective or proportionate to it."[39] Not content to let matters rest here, the Court suggested what the Quebec government perhaps should have done to accomplish its

buzbuzzer/iStockphoto

Since the Charter of Rights and Freedoms was entrenched in the Constitution, the Supreme Court of Canada has assumed a much more prominent role in our political system.

legislative purpose in a way acceptable under section 1 of the Charter. "French could be required," it suggested, "in addition to any other language or it could be required to have greater visibility than that accorded to other languages."[40]

In fairness to judges, why shouldn't they give legislators an idea of how the law needs to be changed to bring it into line with their interpretation of the Constitution? The point is, however, that means and ends are not neatly separable in the real world of politics and policy. Moreover, a requirement that means be proportionate to the ends just asks *who* should determine how much or little is enough? Were the judges who decided the *Ford* case in a better position to know what measures would best protect the economic value of the French language and the francophone character of Quebec? These questions resurfaced with a vengeance when the Supreme Court ruled on 21 September 1995 that the federal ban on tobacco advertising violated the Charter's guarantee of

freedom of expression. The total ban did not, in the eyes of the majority of the Court, satisfy the second part of the *Oakes* test. "The government had before it a variety of less intrusive measures when it enacted the total ban on advertising," observed Justice Beverley McLachlin. Commenting on the government's refusal to allow the Court to see documents pertaining to advertising and tobacco consumption, including one on the alternatives to a total ban on advertising, she added, "In the face of this behaviour, one is hard-pressed not to infer that the results of the studies must undercut the government's claim that a less invasive ban would not have produced an equally salutary result."[41] Anti-smoking groups responded to the decision by calling on Ottawa to use the "notwithstanding" clause to override Charter protection for tobacco advertising. Many staunch Charter boosters became skeptics overnight. They were awakened by the tobacco advertising decision to a basic truth of constitutionally entrenched rights: the

Governing Realities

BOX 7.2 Are Judges More Likely Than Elected Officials to Make the Right Decisions Regarding Scientific Evidence?

One of the earliest and most famous court decisions to rely significantly on scientific evidence was *Brown v. Topeka County Board of Education* (1954). This is the United States Supreme Court ruling that declared laws requiring racial segregation in schools to be unconstitutional. Evidence from social psychologists was cited by the Court in explaining the harm created by such segregation and why it violated the 14th Amendment's guarantee of equal protection under the law.

Since then it has become quite normal, depending on the nature of the case, for courts to accept and assess scientific testimony. Sometimes the evidence provided by scientific experts has a decisive bearing on how a case is resolved. In 2015 the Supreme Court of Canada had to decide whether the prohibition in Canada's Criminal Code against physician-assisted suicide violated a person's Charter rights under s. 7 guaranteeing security of the person.[42] The federal government argued that this was a justifiable infringement under s. 1, the reasonable limits section of the Charter. The trial judge in this case disagreed on the basis of her assessment of the scientific literature from other jurisdictions that allowed physician-assisted suicide. "My review of the evidence . . . on the experience in permissive jurisdictions," she wrote, "leads me to conclude that the risks inherent in permitting physician-assisted death can be identified and very substantially minimized through a carefully-designed system imposing stringent limits that are scrupulously monitored and enforced."

On appeal to the Supreme Court the Canadian government argued that the trial judge's assessment was incorrect and strongly implied that she, and perhaps judges more generally, were not necessarily competent to make such determinations. The Supreme Court of Canada disagreed. In previous decisions, it stated, "this Court [has] affirmed that a trial judge's findings on social and legislative facts are entitled to the same degree of deference as any other factual findings." The Court went on to consider fresh evidence from Belgium, which had recently expanded access to physician-assisted suicide, and determined that there was nothing in this evidence to suggest that the trial judge was incorrect in her original conclusion that the scientific evidence from jurisdictions outside Canada did not support the government's view that a total ban on physician-assisted suicide was a reasonable infringement on a person's rights under the Charter.

What do you think? Who is better qualified to make these sorts of decisions, where scientific evidence needs to be assessed and may be at the crux of whether a law is thought to be reasonable, even if it limits Charter rights? And what should happen when there is no clear consensus in the scientific literature?

price of entrenchment is that judges assume a more important role in political life and one may not always agree with their reasoning or like their rulings (see Box 7.2)

No other provision of the Charter and no Charter decision are cited as often in cases involving constitutional rights and freedoms as the reasonable limits clause and the 1985 *Oakes* ruling. As Ontario court justice James Stribopoulos has written, *"Oakes* is a much more than a test of reasonable limits. It is iconic and a symbol of the *Charter's* goal of maintaining balance between the rights of individuals and the demands of democratic society, and equilibrium between the institutional roles of the legislatures and the courts."[43]

The "Notwithstanding" Clause: Section 33

"What the Charter gives, the legislature may take away." This appears to be the meaning of section 33 of the Charter, the **"notwithstanding" clause**. It states that either Parliament or a provincial legislature "may expressly declare" that a law "shall operate notwithstanding a provision included in section 2 or sections 7 to 15 of this Charter." This clause was not part of Ottawa's original Charter proposal, but was inserted at the insistence of several provinces. Indeed, it appears that federal–provincial agreement on the constitutional deal that produced the Charter would have died without this concession.[44]

Although the "notwithstanding" clause appears to provide governments with a constitutional escape hatch from much of the Charter, it has rarely had this effect. It has been resorted to on only a handful of occasions. At the time of the Charter's passage, civil libertarian Alan Borovoy explained why he thought there was little danger that the "notwithstanding" clause would be used to avoid the Charter's guarantees: "The mere introduction of a bill to oust the application of the Charter would likely spark an enormous controversy. . . . Without solid support in the legislature and the community, a government would be very reluctant to take the heat that such action would invariably generate."[45]

Borovoy's confidence that public support for the Charter and vigilant media would provide adequate protection against government recourse to section 33 was not shared by everyone. Civil liberties groups and the legal profession were, by and large, outspokenly critical of the "notwithstanding" clause, to the point that a court challenge was launched against it immediately after the Charter was proclaimed.[46] The basis of this challenge was that if the Constitution is the supreme law of the land, as the Constitution Act declares, then no part of it should be placed beyond the powers of judicial review. By this reasoning, a legislature's decision to invoke section 33 should itself be reviewable, and therefore able to be overturned by the courts. In a 1985 ruling, the Quebec Court of Appeal agreed. This decision, however, was overruled by the Supreme Court of Canada in *Ford v. Attorney General of Quebec* (1988). The Court pronounced in favour of a literal interpretation of section 33—which also happens to correspond to the intentions of those provincial governments that insisted that the "notwithstanding" clause be included in the Charter—requiring only that a legislature expressly declare its intention to override the Charter.

It is clear, therefore, that no serious legal roadblocks stop a government from using section 33 to circumvent sections of the Charter. Apart from the PQ policy, between 1982 and 1985, of automatically inserting the "notwithstanding" clause into all laws passed by the Quebec legislature and retroactively into all existing provincial statutes, it has been invoked on only a few occasions. The Quebec government actions were part of a symbolic and legal strategy against the constitutional reforms of 1982, to which the PQ government had not agreed. As Borovoy predicted, governments do not want to give the appearance of denying rights to their citizens. There are, however, circumstances where the denial of rights may inflict little political damage on government and may even produce political dividends.

This was certainly true of the Quebec Liberal government's 1989 decision to use the "notwithstanding" clause to re-pass, with some modifications, the provisions of Quebec's Charter of the French Language that had been ruled unconstitutional by the Supreme Court. Public opinion, the province's francophone media, and the opposition PQ all were strongly supportive of legislative restrictions on the use of languages other than French. Although the government's move precipitated the resignation of three anglophone cabinet ministers and drove many English-speaking voters into the arms of the newly formed (and short-lived) Equality Party in the next provincial election, there is no doubt that the political costs of not overriding the Charter would have been far greater.

Likewise, the political costs were negligible when Saskatchewan's Conservative government inserted section 33 in a 1986 law passed to force striking public servants back to work. The government feared that, without the "notwithstanding" clause, the courts might rule that back-to-work legislation infringed the freedom of association guaranteed by section 2 of the Charter. Rather than run this risk, it chose to act pre-emptively to override this right. Denying government employees the right to strike is often popular with the public. Some analysts suggested that the Saskatchewan Conservatives' use of section 33 against public servants may even have produced a net gain in votes for the party in the election that followed about a year later.[47]

In 2000 the Alberta legislature invoked the "notwithstanding" clause when it passed the Marriage Amendment Act. This law reasserted the legal definition of marriage as a union between a man and a woman, at a time when pressure to recognize same-sex marriage was increasing and it appeared that the courts might rule that the Charter required a redefinition of marriage. By invoking section 33 the intention was to protect the traditional definition of marriage in Alberta against a Charter challenge. This was popular with most Albertans at the time. As it happened, however, a subsequent Supreme Court decision ruled that the legal definition of marriage can only be determined by the federal government, so Alberta's law was struck down on that basis.

It is not impossible to imagine circumstances in which politicians and the public might support the use of the "notwithstanding" clause to counter an unpopular Supreme Court decision. In 2005, when Parliament changed the legal definition of marriage to include same-sex couples, the official position of the Conservative Party, then in opposition, was that as a government it would introduce legislation to re-establish the traditional definition of marriage. Given what the courts had said on the matter, it was clear that such a law would have to include the "not-withstanding" clause to circumvent the equality

rights section of the Charter. The Conservatives were elected a year later and, despite what had appeared to be their promise, no such law was introduced during their 10 years in power. Public opinion had swung in favour of same-sex marriage and continued to do so. Thus, a major condition for even the possibility that a government would consider invoking the "notwithstanding" clause, the strong wind of public opinion at its back, did not exist.

More recently, the Ontario government of Doug Ford used the clause in September 2018 to continue with its plan to reduce the size of Toronto's city council in the run-up to municipal elections across the province. In what most Charter scholars recognized was a seriously flawed decision, an Ontario court judge had ruled that this action would have violated the freedom of expression guarantee in section 2 of the Charter. It was not so much that

People gather outside the Legislative Assembly of Ontario to protest Premier Doug Ford's proposed cuts to education in April 2019. While Ford's policies have continued to face vocal opposition within Toronto, Ford has historically enjoyed higher support outside of the city itself.

Premier Ford believed that he had public opinion at his back when he decided to invoke section 33 of the Charter. In all probability most Ontarians, at least outside of Toronto, did not care particularly about how many municipal councillors represented Torontonians. Rather, he knew or at least believed that the law was on his side and that, aside from the rather small number of lawyers, professors, and Charter *aficionados* who care about and follow such matters, the downside of his actions was short. In any event, this episode led to renewed speculation about whether governments might feel more confident reaching for the "notwithstanding" clause in the future. This would seem to be unlikely.

Applying the Charter

During the almost four decades since the Charter's passage hundreds of appeal court rulings have fleshed out the meaning of the rights and freedoms it guarantees. Some of these meanings were established early on and have remained unchanged. Others continue to evolve. And yet others have changed from what the Supreme Court decided at an earlier stage in its interpretation of the Charter. Speaking of the Canadian Constitution, Lord Sankey once characterized it as "a living tree capable of growth and expansion within its natural limits." This may also be said of the Charter. Precisely how the tree will grow in the future is not entirely predictable. Looking back, however, we are able to discern the main tendencies in the courts' interpretation of its provisions.

We will focus on three of these tendencies that are of particular significance. First, how have the courts interpreted the Charter's scope and authority? Second, what difference has the Charter had on the relationship between the state and individuals? Third, what have been the Charter's effects on equality in Canada? The last two issues are, of course, fundamental to our assessment of Canadian democracy.

Scope and Authority

In its first Charter decision, *Law Society of Upper Canada v. Skapinker* (1984), the Supreme Court made clear that it intended to take seriously its new, or at least expanded, responsibility for the protection of rights and freedoms. In this case, Joel Skapinker, a South African citizen living in Canada, had sought admission to the Ontario bar but had been denied because he was not a Canadian citizen. After an appeal court in Ontario ruled that he had been wrongfully denied on the basis of the mobility rights section of the Charter (s. 6), the case moved on to the Supreme Court, which, taking a cautious approach, ruled against Skapinker. While a disappointment for Skapinker, this aspect of the ruling was far less important than what the Court had to say about its own relationship to the Charter. Consciously modelling its position along the lines of *Marbury v. Madison* (1803), the landmark American Supreme Court ruling that established that Court's supervisory role over the US Constitution, the Supreme Court of Canada declared its intention to assume a similar role in applying the Charter. "With the Constitution Act 1982," wrote Justice Willard Estey, "comes a new dimension, a new yardstick of reconciliation between the individual and the community and their respective rights, a dimension which, like the balance of the Constitution, remains to be interpreted and applied by the Court."[48]

Skapinker was more an intimation of things to come than a full-bore broadside at parliamentary government and the tradition of judicial deference to legislatures. A year later the Court was given the opportunity to show how activist it was prepared to be in applying the Charter. The case, *Singh v. Canada (Minister of Employment and Immigration)*, involved a challenge to procedures under Canada's Immigration Act, whereby applicants for political refugee status were not given an automatic right to a hearing. By a 6–0 vote, the Supreme Court decided that this violated fundamental principles of justice. Three of the justices based their ruling on a section of the Canadian Bill of Rights that guarantees the "right to a fair hearing," while the other three went further in arguing that the right to a hearing is implied under section 7 of the Charter, guaranteeing "the right to life, liberty and security of the person and the right not to be deprived thereof except in accordance with the principles of fundamental justice." Justice Bertha Wilson took the most aggressive approach to the Charter, arguing that "the guarantees of the Charter would be illusory if they could be ignored because it was administratively convenient to do so."[49] *Singh* was followed by a series of 1985 rulings that defined in sharper tones the Supreme Court's approach to the Charter's application. In *The Queen v. Big M Drug Mart* (1985), the Court struck down the federal Lord's Day Act on the grounds that it violated the Charter's guarantee of freedom of religion. From the standpoint of the interpretive rules being developed by judges in applying the Charter, the most significant feature of the *Big M* case was the willingness of all of the justices to inquire into the purposes associated with the rights and freedoms set forth in the Charter. The Court signalled its readiness to go beyond the simple words of the Charter and the stated intentions of those who drafted it to interpret the historical meaning and social purposes of a concept like, in this particular case, freedom of religion. This approach is the very hallmark of judicial activism.

The issue of what the Charter's drafters actually intended was raised in *Reference re B.C. Motor Vehicle Act* (1985).[50] In this case, British Columbia's attorney general argued that section 7 protection for the "principles of fundamental justice" was meant by the governments who agreed to the Charter to be a guarantee of procedural fairness. It was not, he argued, intended to enable the courts to assess the fairness of the "substance" of laws. In rejecting the government's argument, the Court quite correctly reasoned that it is not always possible to separate substance and procedure. For example, a law whose substance is the denial of a procedural right associated with the principles of fundamental justice is both procedurally and substantively unfair. The majority was quick to add, however, that judicial review under section 7 should be limited to the criminal law and legal rights, and should not extend to all matters of public policy.

On the question of what the Charter's drafters had intended for section 7, the Court ruled that arguments about intentions could not be binding for two reasons. First, it is not possible to state categorically what legislative bodies intended for the Charter as a whole or for particular provisions of it. Second, if the original intentions were treated as binding on the courts, then "the rights, freedoms and values embodied in the Charter in effect becomes [*sic*] frozen in time to the moment of adoption with little or no possibility of growth, development and adjustment to changing societal needs."[51] This implies, of course, that judges will determine what constitute "changing societal needs."

As reasonable as arguments about the uncertainty surrounding legislative intentions and the need to allow for flexibility in response to changing societal conditions and public opinion may sound, it should be pointed out that the Court has sometimes taken lawmakers' intentions very seriously. This was true in the *Quebec Protestant School Boards* (1984)[52] ruling, where the Court relied on the drafters' intentions for section 23 of the Charter in striking down the education provisions of Quebec's Bill 101. It has also been evident in other decisions, including *Re Public Service Employee Relations Act* (1987).[53] In denying that the right to strike is protected by the Charter, the Court argued that the drafters of the Charter were deliberately silent on economic rights. (The Court has since changed its mind on the right to strike, discussed below.)

The issue of the Charter's scope was the focus of another of the Court's 1985 decisions, *Operation Dismantle v. The Queen*.[54] A coalition of groups opposed to testing the cruise missile in Canada argued that these tests violated the Charter's guarantee of the right to life and security of the person by making nuclear war more probable. The Court rejected this argument on the grounds that the alleged facts in the plaintiff's claim were unprovable speculations. But the other question before the Court was whether cabinet decisions—the decision to allow cruise missile tests was taken by cabinet—and foreign policy and defence issues are reviewable by the courts. The federal government argued that cabinet decisions are "Crown prerogatives" and therefore off limits to the courts. The Supreme Court disagreed. It argued that section 32 of the Charter should be interpreted to apply to all government actions. On the precise question of whether foreign policy and defence issues are inherently political and beyond the reach of judicial review, the Court did not express an opinion. Twenty-five years later, confronted with a somewhat similar question, the

Supreme Court ruled that when it comes to foreign policy and defence issues, "the government must have flexibility in deciding how its duties under the royal prerogative over foreign relations are discharged [but] *the executive is not exempt from constitutional scrutiny*" (emphasis added; see Box 7.3).

An additional feature of the Court's approach to the Charter's scope deserves mention. This involves its insistence that the Charter applies only to relationships between the state and citizens, not to private-sector relationships. Thus, the Charter cannot be used by someone who believes he has been denied a job or an apartment because of his race, or by a person whose private-sector employer requires that she retire at the age of 65. Forms of discrimination like these are pervasive throughout society, but they are not inequalities that can be overcome using the Charter (they can be challenged, however, under provincial human rights codes). The Supreme Court has on several occasions articulated this distinction between public (covered by the Charter) and private, as it did early on in *Dolphin Delivery* (1986).[55]

Politics in Focus

BOX 7.3 When the Charter and Crown Prerogatives Collide

The case of Omar Khadr is well known in Canada. Khadr is a member of a family that immigrated to Canada from Egypt in 1977. The family had ties to Osama bin Laden and several members fought against the NATO forces in Afghanistan. Omar Khadr was 15 years old when he was captured by American troops after allegedly having killed a soldier with a grenade. After recovering somewhat from severe wounding he suffered in the firefight with NATO forces, Khadr was sent to the Guantánamo Bay detention camp in Cuba, where he remained from 2002 until 2012. During much of this time he was not provided with legal counsel. His demands that the Canadian government intervene on his behalf and request his repatriation to Canada were rejected by successive Canadian governments.

Khadr's case eventually reached the Supreme Court of Canada. Here are some key excerpts from its June 2010 ruling:

Canada actively participated in a process contrary to its international human rights obligations and contributed to K's ongoing detention so as to deprive him of his right to liberty and security of the person, guaranteed by s. 7 of the *Charter*, not in accordance with the principles of fundamental justice. . . . While the US is the primary source of the deprivation, it is reasonable to infer from the uncontradicted evidence before the Court that the statements taken by Canadian officials are contributing to K's continued detention. The deprivation of K's right to liberty and security of the person is not in accordance with the principles of fundamental justice. The interrogation of a youth detained without access to counsel, to elicit statements about serious criminal charges while knowing that the youth had been subjected to sleep deprivation and while knowing that the fruits of the interrogations would be shared with the prosecutors, offends the most basic Canadian standards about the treatment of detained youth suspects.

K is entitled to a remedy under s. 24(1) of the *Charter*. . . . The appropriate remedy in this case is to declare that K's *Charter* rights were violated, leaving it to the government to decide how best to respond in light of current information, its responsibility over foreign affairs and the *Charter*.

Khadr was awarded costs by the Court, but challenging the government's prerogative to make foreign policy decisions was a step that the justices were unwilling to take. After a plea bargain before an American military tribunal to avoid lifetime imprisonment by the US, Omar Khadr remained incarcerated at Guantánamo until his transfer to Canada in September 2012, to complete the remainder of an eight-year prison sentence.

Source: Judgments of the Supreme Court of Canada: *Canada v. Khadr*, 2010 S.C.C. 3.

The Charter, it stated, "was set up to regulate the relationship between the individual and the government. It was intended to restrain government action and to protect the individual."[56] This position is, in fact, faithful to the intentions of those who framed and agreed to the Charter.

Every major Supreme Court ruling on the Charter serves to clarify the scope and authority of judicial review. In focusing on several early Charter decisions the point has been to demonstrate that the Court very quickly abandoned the tradition of judicial deference and assumed, instead, an activist stance in applying the Charter. How far judges go in using the Charter to strike down laws and administrative practices is really up to them. There are, of course, two provisions of the Charter that may be seen as potential brakes on the courts' authority. One is the "reasonable limits" clause (s. 1) and the other is the "notwithstanding" clause (s. 33). In practice, however, neither of these has been very effective in limiting the scope of judicial activism.

Individual Rights and Freedoms

Some individual rights and freedoms are better protected today as a result of the Charter. Court decisions have limited certain police powers, expanded the rights of those accused of crimes and of prisoners, women seeking abortions, and gays and lesbians. On the other hand, Supreme Court decisions upheld the constitutionality of provincial and federal anti-hate laws that, at least according to some critics, place vague and overly broad restrictions on freedom of expression; upheld the constitutionality of mandatory publication bans in certain criminal trials; and upheld restrictions on the ability of individuals and organizations other than political parties and their candidates to spend money during an election campaign. In cases involving individual rights and freedoms, the courts are called upon to balance these Charter guarantees against such interests as national security and community safety and standards, as well as other democratic and social values.

This balancing act may be seen in the case of *R. v. N.S.* (2012), in which the issue was whether a person wearing a niqab (a full face veil that reveals only the eyes) for religious reasons should be required to show her face when testifying in a criminal trial. The defendant in this case argued that she should be allowed to wear the niqab when giving testimony against her uncle and cousin in a sexual assault trial. She maintained that her religious beliefs required her to wear the niqab in the presence of male strangers and that this belief ought to be protected by the right to religious freedom in the Charter. The accused persons in this trial argued that their ability to receive a fair trial was undermined by the inability of the judge and jury to see their accuser's face while she was giving testimony. In seeking to reconcile these conflicting rights claims, the Court ruled that "A witness who for sincere religious reasons wishes to wear the niqab while testifying in a criminal proceeding will be required to remove it if (a) this is necessary to prevent a serious risk to the fairness of the trial, because reasonably available alternative measures will not prevent the risk; and (b) the salutary effects of requiring her to remove the niqab outweigh the deleterious effects of doing so."[57] The justices' awareness of the larger social context of their ruling may be seen in Box 7.4.

The courts' rulings on legal rights challenges to Canada's criminal law illustrate the generally more liberal treatment of individual rights in the Charter era. Charter decisions have produced many important changes in law enforcement practices, including the following:

- "Reverse onus" provisions, requiring a defendant to prove his innocence of a charge, have been ruled unconstitutional.
- Evidence obtained by inappropriate means, such as confession obtained without informing an accused person of his or her right to legal counsel or evidence gotten from a workplace computer without a warrant, cannot be used to help convict that person.
- Writs of assistance, under which the police were able to enter premises at any time without a search warrant, have been ruled unconstitutional.

The Social Fabric

BOX 7.4 Multiculturalism, Religious Freedom, and the Justice System

[The case involving the right of a witness in a criminal trial to wear a niqab while testifying] illustrates the tension and changes caused by the rapid evolution of contemporary Canadian society and by the growing presence in Canada of new cultures, religions, traditions, and social practices. This case is not purely one of conflict and reconciliation between a religious right and the protection of the right of the accused to make full answer and defence, but engages basic value of the Canadian criminal justice system. The Charter protects freedom of religion in express words at s. 2(a). But fundamental, too, are the rights of the accused to a fair trial, to make full answer and defence to the charges brought against him, to benefit from the constitutional presumption of innocence and to avert wrongful convictions. Since cross-examination is a necessary tool for the exercise of the right to make full answer and defence, the consequences of restrictions on that right weigh more heavily on the accused, and the balancing process must work in his or her favour. A defence that is unduly and improperly constrained might impact on the determination of the guilt or innocence of the accused.

The Constitution requires an openness to new differences that appear within Canada, but also an acceptance of the principle that it remains connected with the roots of our contemporary democratic society. A system of open and independent courts is a core component of a democratic state, ruled by law and a fundamental Canadian value. From this broader constitutional perspective, the trial becomes an act of communication with the public at large. The public must be able to see how the justice system works. Wearing a niqab in the courtroom does not facilitate acts of communication. Rather, it shields the witness from interacting fully with the parties, their counsel, the judge and the jurors. Wearing the niqab is also incompatible with the rights of the accused, the nature of the Canadian public adversarial trials, and with the constitutional values of openness and religious neutrality in contemporary democratic, but diverse, Canada. Nor should wearing a niqab be dependent on the nature or importance of the evidence, as this would only add a new layer of complexity to the trial process. A clear rule that niqabs may not be worn at any stage of the criminal trial would be consistent with the principle of public openness of the trial process and would safeguard the integrity of that process as one of communication.

Source: *R. v. N.S.*, 2012 SCC 72, [2012] 3 S.C.R. 726, scc.lexum.org/decisia-scc-csc/scc-csc/scc-csc/en/12779/1/document.do›, 7–8.

- Search and seizure powers have been restricted.
- Limits have been placed on the length of time that those accused of criminal offences may wait before their trial.[58]

In striking the balance between individual rights and freedoms and other societal interests and values, the Supreme Court has not hesitated to come down on the side of the latter. This may be seen in the Court's decision to uphold hate speech provisions of Canada's Criminal Code in the case of *R. v. Keegstra* (1990).[59] James Keegstra was an Alberta high school teacher who taught his students that the Holocaust was a hoax and that an international Jewish conspiracy pulled much of the world's political, economic, and cultural strings. He was charged under s. 319(2) of the Criminal Code, which makes it a punishable offence to communicate statements, other than in private conversation, that wilfully promote hatred against any identifiable group. In a 4–3 ruling the majority on Canada's highest court held that the content of speech, in and of itself, could be considered so offensive as to place it outside the free speech guarantee of the Charter. They reasoned that the "pain suffered by target group members," Canada's "international commitments to eradicate hate propaganda," Canada's "commitment to the values of equality and multiculturalism in ss. 15 and 27 of the Charter," and "our historical knowledge of the potentially catastrophic effects of the promotion of hatred" combined to make section 319(2) of the Criminal Code a reasonable limit on freedom of expression.

The Supreme Court's ruling in *Keegstra* paid virtually no attention to the question of whether the messages communicated by the accused placed anyone or any group of persons in imminent peril. Such a test was considered to be wholly unnecessary. Instead, the majority accepted the argument that some speech is quite simply inconsistent with the sort of society that Canada is or ought to be and therefore should not be tolerated by law and protected by the Constitution. The Court repeated this reasoning in *Saskatchewan (Human Rights Commission) v. Whatcott* (2013), in which it stated that it was not necessary to show a clear connection between speech and harm to the members of the group targeted by that speech. "The difficulty of establishing causality," the Court said, "and the seriousness of the harm to vulnerable groups justifies the imposition of preventive measures that do not require proof of actual harm. The discriminatory effects of hate speech are part of the everyday knowledge and experience of Canadians."[60]

Individual freedom of expression, as guaranteed by section 2 of the Charter, was again the issue in *Harper v. Canada* (2004).[61] The case originated as a challenge brought by Stephen Harper in 2000, when he was president of the National Citizens' Coalition, to legislated restrictions on the right of so-called "third parties"—groups and individuals other than registered political parties and their candidates—to spend money on political advertising during election campaigns. In its 2004 ruling the Supreme Court upheld these restrictions by a 6–3 majority. The decision is particularly interesting because of the conception of democracy that underpins the majority's ruling, one that sees unfettered freedom of speech as a danger to the equality rights of citizens (see Box 7.5). In stark contrast, a US Supreme Court decision in *Citizens United v. Federal Election Commission* (2010) opened the floodgates for big-money and corporate political advertising during elections, which has led to

a further skewing of influence in favour of the rich and powerful in that country.

Four years after *Harper v. Canada* the Supreme Court returned to the issue of free speech in the case of *WIC Radio Ltd. v. Simpson* (2008). A radio talk show host and former British Columbia politician, Rafe Mair, compared the ideas of a local conservative activist, Kari Simpson, to those of Hitler and the Ku Klux Klan. Mair made the comparison in a radio broadcast that attacked Simpson's views opposing the use of school materials and lessons that conveyed a positive portrayal of homosexual lifestyles. Simpson claimed that Mair's comments were defamatory and not protected by section 2 of the Charter.

Defamation—the impugning of someone's character or actions in a manner that results in real damage being done to that person's reputation, including such consequences as impairment of his or her ability to earn a living—is a private law matter. Like slip-and-fall accidents on private property or odours from a pig barn that a neighbour claims reduce his enjoyment of his property and its market value, defamation does not fall directly under the Charter. Such matters are covered by the common law that emerges from judicial rulings on actual cases. However, as the Supreme Court stated in the *Simpson* decision, "the evolution of the common law is to be informed and guided by Charter values."[62] Mair argued that the doctrine of fair comment protected him against the charge of defamation. The Supreme Court agreed. Its ruling used the Charter values of freedom of expression and freedom of the media to broaden the defence of fair comment and limit the ability of plaintiffs to intimidate those who would make controversial public statements. The result of this 2008 ruling is that it is more difficult for public figures or organizations to successfully sue, arguing that their reputation has been damaged, and therefore less likely that journalists and broadcasters will censor themselves out of fear of incurring such lawsuits.

Is there an identifiable pattern in the Court's interpretation of the individual rights guaranteed by the Charter? Aside from what most commentators characterize as a moderately activist approach, the

Politics in Focus

BOX 7.5 Does the Ability to Spend Money during an Election Campaign Jeopardize Democracy?

The majority said...

In the absence of spending limits, it is possible for the affluent or a number of persons pooling their resources and acting in concert to dominate the political discourse, depriving their opponents of a reasonable opportunity to speak and be heard, and undermining the voter's ability to be adequately informed of all views. Equality in the political discourse is thus necessary for meaningful participation in the electoral process and ultimately enhances the right to vote.

[Third-party advertising spending limits] prevent those who have access to significant financial resources, and are able to purchase [an] unlimited amount of advertising, to dominate the electoral discourse to the detriment of others; they create a balance between the financial resources of each candidate or political party; and they advance the perception that the electoral process is substantively fair as it provides for a reasonable degree of equality between citizens who wish to participate in that process. . . . The limits set out in [the law] allow third parties to inform the electorate of their message in a manner that will not overwhelm candidates, political parties or other third parties while precluding the voices of the wealthy from dominating the political discourse.

The minority said...

The effect of third-party limits for spending on advertising is to prevent citizens from effectively communicating their views on issues during an election campaign. The denial of effective communication to citizens violates freedom of expression where it warrants the greatest protection—the sphere of political discourse. Section 350 [of the Canada Elections Act] puts effective radio and television communication beyond the reach of "third party" citizens, preventing citizens from effectively communicating their views on election issues, and restricting them to minor local communication. Effective expression of ideas thus becomes the exclusive right of registered political parties and their candidates.

There is no evidence to support a connection between the limits on citizen spending and electoral fairness, and the legislation does not infringe the right to free expression in a way that is measured and carefully tailored to the goals sought to be achieved. The limits imposed on citizens amount to a virtual ban on their participation in political debate during the election period, except through political parties . . . the Attorney General has not demonstrated that limits this draconian are required to meet the perceived dangers.

Source: *Harper v. Canada* (2004).

Court has shown few clearly pronounced tendencies. Moreover, the Court is sometimes sharply divided in its approach to individual rights, as it was in the 1990 *Keegstra* ruling (4–3) on hate speech, in its 1995 ruling on Ottawa's tobacco advertising ban (5–4), and in the 2004 *Harper* ruling on election spending by third parties (6–3). The Court has also been divided on a number of important cases dealing with legal rights. Some critics accuse it of having been too sympathetic to the protection of individual rights over other values and interests, but others view the Court as too timid in its rulings.

Equality and the Charter

In an article on what she has described as the unfulfilled promise of s. 15 of the Charter, Martha Jackman concludes that "the Supreme Court has not fulfilled the expectations of marginalized groups that government action and inaction would be subject to Canadian Charter scrutiny. Instead it has perpetuated exclusion, disadvantage and discrimination against the poor. . . . the Court has knowingly endorsed interpretations of the Charter that are injurious to the rights of poor people."[63] She is not alone in reaching this conclusion.[64] It is, of course, difficult to determine what independent impact Charter rulings may have had on the state of equality. Public opinion, social activism, legislative action not prompted by the Charter, demographic change, and other factors must also be part of the mix in any such assessment. The Charter is only one of the factors influencing issues of equality in Canadian society. But to suggest that the courts' interpretation of the Charter equality rights provisions, particularly sections 7 and 15, has been of no or little consequence is more of an ideology-driven conclusion of how judges and Canadians should view the Charter than an assessment of the differences that court rulings have had on the lives of many Canadians.

One of the complaints made by those who believe the Charter has not made enough of a difference when it comes to equality involves the courts' unwillingness to treat equality rights as superior to other rights in the Charter or to other parts of the Constitution. How to strike this balance was the issue before the Supreme Court in *Re Education Act* (1987),[65] dealing with the constitutionality of an Ontario law extending full public funding to that province's Roman Catholic schools.[66] The Supreme Court ruled that the equality of religion guaranteed by section 15 did not override provincial governments' authority to grant special educational rights to Catholics and Protestants under section 93 of the Constitution Act, 1867. Indeed, the Supreme Court has stated categorically that the Charter does not establish a hierarchy of rights, to the dismay of those who believe the Charter should be seen and used as a tool for the advancement of equality.

Nevertheless, in some cases the equality guarantees of the Charter have provided the basis for fairly dramatic and controversial reversals of long-standing public policy. This was true of the Supreme Court's ruling in *M. v. H.* (1999), a case that involved a challenge to the heterosexual definition of spouses in the Family Law Act. In earlier decisions the Court had ruled that discrimination on the basis of sexual orientation is analogous to the enumerated grounds for discrimination proscribed by s. 15 of the Charter (*Egan v. Canada*, 1995). It came as no surprise, therefore, when the

Supreme Court decided that the heterosexual definition of a cohabiting couple under the Family Law Act was unconstitutional, because it denied the same status and rights to same-sex couples. The Court determined that the exclusion of same-sex relationships from the spousal support provisions of the Family Law Act was not rationally connected to the objectives of the Family Law Act and thus could not be justified under the reasonable limits section of the Charter. The federal government had already announced its intention to change the law so as to provide same-sex couples with the same status as heterosexual ones. The ruling in *M. v. H.* simply made this revision to the law inevitable.

After a decade and a half of considering equality cases without a systematic and consistent framework for assessing s. 15 claims, the Supreme Court developed just such a framework in *Law v. Minister of Human Resources Development (1999)*.[67] At its heart is the question of whether the differential treatment of the members of a group under the law is demeaning to human dignity. The Supreme Court has been very clear and consistent since its first section 15 rulings that the rights and freedoms guaranteed by the Charter should not become tools that the advantaged and wealthy can use to protect their status. In the Charter, especially its equality sections, the Court has elaborated what might be described as an "ameliorative" or "progressive" purpose. "In general terms," the Court stated in the *Law* decision, "the purpose of s. 15(1) is to prevent the violation of essential human dignity and freedom through the imposition of disadvantage, stereotyping, or political or social prejudice, and to promote a society in which all persons enjoy equal recognition at law as human beings or as members of Canadian society, equally capable and equally deserving of concern, respect and consideration."[68] In their interpretation of s. 15 of the Charter, judges have been sensitive to the social and economic context of the inequalities that appear before them as Charter claims. Indeed, many of the major Charter rulings on equality read like sociological or historical treatises. This is precisely what alarms those among the Charter's critics who recoil at what they see as judicial usurpation of the legislature's function.

Judicial sensitivity to the broader societal and historical context of their interpretations of equality rights was very clear in the Supreme Court's 2008 ruling in *R. v. Kapp*. The case involved a group of non-Indigenous fishermen who were charged with salmon fishing during a 24-hour period reserved under federal law to three Indigenous bands. The non-Indigenous fishermen claimed that the law violated their equality rights under the Charter by making legal distinctions based on race. The Supreme Court agreed that this law made such distinctions, but held that they were constitutionally protected by the affirmative action clause, s. 15(2), of the Charter. In arriving at this decision the Court reiterated its long-held view that s. 15 guarantees **substantive equality** for Canadians, not identical treatment. This decision opens the door to the judicial consideration of evidence and arguments based on history, economics, and sociology. Indeed, the decision in *Kapp* included references to over 50 books, articles, and other publications on equality matters.

Returning to the conclusion of Jackman and other critics who maintain that the Charter has not made much of a difference when it comes to equality in Canada, a more accurate way of expressing this might be that it is impossible to determine how much of the change in the direction of equality in such matters as women's reproductive rights, the marriage and other statutory rights of same-sex couples, and more broadly for lesbian, gay, bisexual, and transgender Canadians and for Indigenous rights would have happened, or happened when it did, in the absence of the Charter. The Charter's impact, including the influence that the equality rights provisions have had on Canadian society and law, operates in many and diffuse ways. At all levels of government those who draft legislation and guidelines and regulations under the authority of laws are aware of the need for such rules to comply with the Charter and the manner in which the courts have interpreted its equality guarantees. In the conversation on rights that takes place in the courtroom, but also in the classroom, in the media, in faith communities, and throughout Canadian society, the Charter and its equality guarantees

have made a difference. Social activists frame their demands and often their political strategies with the Charter and the possibility of judicial rulings in mind (Box 7.6).

Has the Charter "Americanized" Canadian Politics?

Early critics of the Charter said that it would "Americanize" Canadian politics. By this they meant that it would do three things they believed were regrettable. First, it would elevate the importance of unelected judges and the courts, giving them a much more prominent role in determining important policy matters. Second, it would undermine the operation of parliamentary government in Canada by diminishing the authority of Parliament to determine the law and to be held accountable to the people, not to the courts, for its decisions. Third, it would generate a more litigious society in which individuals and groups are more likely to base their claims and political arguments on rights, making compromise more difficult and bypassing such political processes as elections and lobbying in preference for the courts. If a victory can be won in court, the critics charged, there will be less need to worry about winning victories in the court of public opinion. The end result of all this, they lamented, would be the Americanization of Canadian politics.

For better or for worse—and there are many people on both sides of this divide—much of this prediction has come to pass. Judges are far more prominent in policy-making than they were in the pre-Charter era. Parliamentary supremacy has been replaced by constitutional supremacy, with the Supreme Court as chief arbiter. And important and controversial issues are often decided in the courts or as a result of court decisions pushing governments in a particular direction. Despite these important changes, the Charter has not resulted in a wholesale Americanization of Canadian politics. Judges in Canada have tended to interpret the Charter's guarantees in distinctively Canadian ways, anchored in aspects of Canada's political

The Social Fabric

BOX 7.6 Homelessness and the Charter's Equality Guarantees

Canada's Charter of Rights and Freedoms makes no explicit mention of social or economic rights, including the right to shelter. For many years some lawyers and social critics have argued that s. 7 of the Charter on the right to life, liberty, and security of the person and s. 15 on equality rights ought to be interpreted in a manner so as to impose a positive obligation on governments to provide what they consider to be adequate shelter. The courts have refused to do so. But as Linda McKay-Panos writes, these sections of the Charter have provided the basis for successful challenges to bylaws and police actions intended to prevent people from sleeping or living in parks or on public property. She notes that the ruling of the BC Court of Appeals in *Victoria v. Adams* (2009) "recognized that while governments do not necessarily create the state of homelessness, they cannot legislate in a way that is indifferent to homeless persons' *Charter* rights."[69]

In another BC court ruling, that of *Abbotsford (City) v Shantz* (2015), that province's Supreme Court was presented with an interesting argument. Indigenous Canadians, persons with mental disabilities, and the members of various other minorities are disproportionately represented among the homeless. The failure to provide adequate social housing for the homeless affects the members of these groups to a greater degree than others and thus perpetuates and worsens

substantive inequality, in violation of s. 15 of the Charter. While acknowledging that certain groups are more likely to experience homelessness than others, the Court did not accept the argument that this was a s. 15 violation.

Disappointed with the courts' unwillingness to find in the Charter a right to shelter, homeless advocates have invoked the UN International Covenant on Economic, Social and Cultural Rights (ICESCR), to which Canada is a signatory. Article 11 of the Covenant states, "The States Parties to the present Covenant recognize the right of everyone to an adequate standard of living for himself and his family, including adequate food, clothing and housing, and to the continuous improvement of living conditions." The treaty is legally binding, but in reality the human rights obligations that Canada and many other countries assume when they sign such international agreements tend to be treated by the courts as "relevant and perhaps persuasive, but not as determinative or, dare we say, obligatory."[70]

What do you think? Is state-provided shelter of a certain quality a right that should be guaranteed by the Charter, and should the obligation to provide it be imposed on governments by the courts? Or is this an issue that ought to be left to elected governments and non-profit organizations, as is currently the case in Canada?

culture that are different from those of the United States (Box 7.7).

This is demonstrated by the case of hate speech that targets a particular group. In Canada, the law and judicial interpretation of section 2 of the Charter stress the *content of speech*, whereas in the United States the test of whether hateful speech directed at the members of a group is protected by the First Amendment is the *probability that actual harm may result*. Judges in Canada and the United States have taken significantly different approaches towards hate speech and its relationship to the

guarantee of freedom of expression found in the constitutions of their respective countries. That difference boils down to this. In the United States, just because you say something demonstrably false and odious about the members of a group does not mean that you lose the Constitution's protection to speak your mind. If, however, this speech becomes what lawyers call "fighting words," liable to incite violence, then it loses the protection of the First Amendment. But in Canada, some speech is considered to be so nasty that, by its very nature, it promotes hatred and is undeserving of constitutional

BOX 7.7 Is Hate Speech Protected by Free Speech?

Canada

Hate propaganda contributes little to the aspirations of Canadians or Canada in either the quest for truth, the promotion of individual self-development or the protection and fostering of a vibrant democracy where the participation of all individuals is accepted and encouraged. . . . Consequently, the suppression of hate propaganda represents impairment of the individual's freedom of expression which is not of a most serious nature. . . .

Indeed, one may quite plausibly contend that it is through rejecting hate propaganda that the state can best encourage the protection of values central to freedom of expression, while simultaneously demonstrating dislike for the vision forwarded by hate-mongers. In this regard, the reaction to various types of expression by a democratic government [and the criminalization of certain forms of speech] may be perceived as meaningful expression on behalf of the vast majority of citizens.

Source: *R. v. Keegstra*, [1990] 3 S.C.R. 697.

United States

The First Amendment generally prevents government from proscribing speech, or even expressive conduct, because of disapproval of the ideas expressed. Content-based regulations are presumptively invalid. From 1791 to the present, however, our society, like other free but civilized societies, has permitted restrictions upon the content of speech in a few limited areas, which are "of such slight social value as a step to truth that any benefit that may be derived from them is clearly outweighed by the social interest in order and morality."

. . . One must wholeheartedly agree . . . that "it is the responsibility, even the obligation, of diverse communities to confront [hateful] notions in whatever form they appear," but the manner of that confrontation cannot consist of selective limitations upon speech. . . . The point of the First Amendment is that majority preferences must be expressed in some fashion other than silencing speech on the basis of its content.

. . . [T]he reason why fighting words are categorically excluded from the protection of the First Amendment is not that their content communicates any particular idea, but that their content embodies a particularly intolerable (and socially unnecessary) mode of expressing whatever idea the speaker wishes to convey.

Source: *R.A.V. v. St Paul*, 505 U.S. 377 (1992), www.findlaw.com.

protection, as is demonstrated by the majority opinion in *Keegstra*. Embedding protection for free speech in Canada's Constitution has not resulted in Canadian judges simply aping the interpretations of their American counterparts, at least not when it comes to hate speech. Moreover, the greater willingness of Canadian courts—as well as legislatures—to restrict hate speech on the grounds that some ideas and their expression contribute nothing to democratic life, and therefore can be restricted without doing any harm to freedom, is consistent with a cultural difference between these countries that predates the Charter era.

The difference between Canada and the United States in how particular rights are interpreted may also be seen in how their respective courts have dealt with the matter of campaign spending by individuals and groups other than parties and their candidates. In Canada this spending is tightly restricted by law, restrictions that the Supreme Court has said are reasonable limits on free speech because of their importance in helping to level the playing field between those who have plenty of resources to formulate and communicate their point of view and policy preferences, and those who do not. Money distorts access to the marketplace of ideas, said the majority in *Harper*, and this distortion undermines democracy.

In the United States the Supreme Court has expressed an entirely different view on this question. "Premised on mistrust of governmental power," the Supreme Court said in *Citizens United*, "the First Amendment stands against attempts to disfavor certain subjects or viewpoints. Prohibited, too, are restrictions distinguishing among different speakers, allowing speech by some but not others. . . . Speech restrictions based on the identity of the speaker are all too often simply a means to control content."[71] The fact that inequalities in the marketplace of ideas may be created or magnified by the fact that some groups and individuals are better able than others to afford the costs of communicating their ideas and preferences, is not seen to be a justification for limiting the free speech rights of those who have more.

On other matters, too, including prisoners' democratic rights and the principles to be followed in drawing electoral boundaries, the highest courts of Canada and the United States have followed very different paths.[72] The judicial understanding of the separation of church and state is also quite different in the two countries, a difference that the Charter has perhaps diminished but has not erased.[73] Scholars disagree on whether the rights traditions of Canada and the United States are diverging or converging. It is clear, however, that in some important respects at least, entrenchment of the Charter in Canada's Constitution has not led to the disappearance of important cultural differences between Canada and its southern neighbour.

Summing Up

No other event over the course of Canada's political history has had as great an impact on Canadian politics as the passage of the Charter of Rights and Freedoms. It has been transformative in four main ways. First, it has changed the manner in which Canadians think about themselves and their relationship to the state. Second, it very quickly became a foremost symbol of Canadian identity and values for large majorities in all provinces (albeit somewhat less among francophone Quebecers). Third, it opened the door to a significant increase in the role of the courts in Canada's system of government. Finally, and related to the previous point, Charter rulings have been the basis for important changes in public policy on issues that include abortion, physician-assisted death, police powers, Indigenous rights, LGBTQ+ rights, rights for francophones outside Quebec, acceptable limits on free speech, and others.

This transformation in Canadian politics has not been without controversy. Although the Charter is a source of pride for most Canadians, some are critical of certain aspects of its impact on Canadian society and politics. The increased influence of unelected judges, say some critics, has been at the expense of elected legislatures that may be held accountable to people for their decisions. The courts have not shown enough deference to governments in their application of the reasonable limits section of the Charter, say the critics. Moreover, by encouraging groups, opinion leaders, and even average Canadians to frame political issues in the language of rights, the Charter promotes what Mary Ann Glendon, in the context of the United States, has described as an exaggerated fascination with rights that, she argues, "promotes unrealistic expectations, heightens social conflict, and inhibits dialogue that might lead toward consensus, accommodation, or at the least the discovery of common ground."[74]

Criticisms such as these are heard in liberal democracies across the world. They are in reaction to the elevation of human rights in the politics of the West, and to a sense that rights talk and judicial activism have gone too far. But the genie is out of the bottle, in Canada as in other Western democracies, and there is no putting it back. Canadians love the Charter, they respect the courts, and they hold judges in much higher regard than they do politicians. The Charter era in Canadian politics and government may have its detractors, but they appear to be on the wrong side of history.

Starting Points for Research

Tom Bateman, Janet Hiebert, Rainer Knopff, and Peter Russell, eds, *The Court and the Charter: Leading Cases*, 2nd edn (Toronto: Emond Publishing, 2017). Includes 36 abridged Supreme Court rulings, each with a brief introduction. An excellent reference work.

David R. Boyd and Emmett Macfarlane, "Should Environmental Rights Be in the Constitution?" *Policy Options*, 3 Mar. 2014, http://policyoptions.irpp.org/fr/magazines/opening-eyes/boyd-macfarlane/. In this engaging pair of articles, Boyd makes the case for including such rights in the Constitution and Macfarlane argues that such matters ought to be decided by legislatures.

Emmett Macfarlane, *Governing from the Bench: The Supreme Court of Canada and the Judicial Role* (Vancouver: University of British Columbia Press, 2013). Macfarlane's focus is on the inner workings of the Supreme Court and its relationship to the other branches of government, the media and Canadian society.

Emmett Macfarlane, ed., *Policy Change, Courts, and the Canadian Constitution* (Toronto: Oxford University Press, 2017). This edited volume includes many chapters on how court interpretation of the Charter has affected the policy process and outcomes.

Review Exercises

1. Find a story in the media that deals with the Charter. Summarize it, covering as many of the following points as are relevant:
   (a) What are the circumstances?
   (b) Who are the people or organizations involved?
   (c) What law/regulation/action/practice is being challenged?
   (d) At what stage is the challenge?
   (e) Are lawyers or other experts interviewed? Who are they?
   (f) What right or freedom of the Charter is at stake in this story?
2. In 2017 the Liberal government launched a new process for the selection of Supreme Court justices. Information on that process may be found at http://www.fja-cmf.gc.ca/scc-csc/index-eng.html. How were Supreme Court justices selected before this process was adopted? Do you believe that the new process is an improvement? Explain your reasons.
3. Compare the Charter of Rights and Freedoms to some of its counterparts in other democracies (simply type into your search engine the words "constitution" and the countries that you are interested in—for example, France, Germany, and the United States—and you will find websites that provide this information). What are the main similarities among them? Are there any aspects of these other rights documents that you think should be adopted in Canada?

The Centennial Flame, located at Parliament Hill, was first lit for Canada's centennial celebrations on January 1, 1967. Originally intended as a temporary monument, the Flame was so popular with Canadians that it became a permanent feature in Ottawa. The flame, a symbol of Canada's unity, is surrounded by the shields of Canada's provinces and territories, reflecting Canada's multiple levels of government. (Reimar/Shutterstock)

8 Federalism

Canada's Constitution establishes two levels of government—national and provincial—both of which have important law-making and taxation powers. This system of divided jurisdiction is known as federalism. In this chapter some of the major issues associated with federalism are discussed, including the following:

- What is federalism?
- The origins, maintenance, and demise of federal states
- The origins of Canadian federalism
- The federal division of powers
- The courts and federalism
- Quebec's impact on federalism
- Intergovernmental relations
- Fiscal federalism
- Federalism and democracy

When the proposal to create an independent Canada was discussed at Charlottetown (1864) and Quebec (1867), the main subject of debate was the relationship between the new national and regional governments. Two decades of self-government and the constitutional traditions imported from Britain provided the colonies with ready guideposts for most other features of the Constitution. Federalism, by contrast, was uncharted territory. Most of the founders' practical knowledge of the principles and operation of federalism was based on their observation of the United States. The lessons they took from the American experience were mainly negative. Secession of the Confederacy and the bloody Civil War of 1861–5 did not inspire much confidence in the American model. Despite all this, Canada's founders opted for a federal system of government.

What Is Federalism?

In a federal system of government the constitutional authority to make laws and to raise revenue is divided between a national government and some number of regional governments. Neither the national government acting alone nor the regional governments acting together have the authority to alter the powers of the other level of government. They are co-ordinate and independent in their separate constitutional spheres. Citizens in a federal state are members of two political communities, one national and the other coinciding with the boundaries of the province, state, canton (the name given to the regional units of a federal state vary between countries) in which they reside.

Federalism is a legal term and its existence is based on the constitution. If a single government controls all legislative and taxation powers in a country, then no amount of administrative decentralization or variation in the economic, social, or cultural characteristics of its regions will make it a federal state. Federalism is chiefly a property of constitutions, not of societies. Nonetheless, some political scientists refer to "federal-type" societies, a tendency that has been labelled the *sociological approach* to federalism. This approach began with American political scientist William S. Livingston's

argument that "the essence of federalism lies not in the constitutional or institutional structure but in the society itself."[1] "Federalism," Livingston declares, "is a function of societies."[2] By this he means that in a society characterized by important ethnic, language, or other cultural divisions, and where different cultural communities tend to predominate in different parts of the country, federalism is likely to be seen as a means of accommodating diversity at the same time as it provides for unity.

Despite the popularity that this idea of federalism has enjoyed, it is fundamentally wrong. It is true enough that some federal political systems, such as those of Canada, Switzerland, and Belgium, are found in societies that conform to Livingston's model of a federal society. But others do not. The United States, which pioneered modern federalism, did not opt for what was an essentially untried political system because of important cultural differences between its founding states.[3] Austria, Germany, and Argentina all have federal constitutions, but they all rank rather low in terms of cultural diversity and none has a large regionally concentrated minority cultural community within its borders. Some of the world's most culturally diverse countries, including ones where a large cultural minority or minorities are concentrated in particular regions of the country, do not have federal constitutions. Indeed, if one looks at the world ranking of countries' ethnic diversity, there is absolutely no correlation between the level of diversity and the likelihood that a country has a federal constitution.[4]

If federalism is understood as a characteristic of societies rather than of their constitutions, then most of the world's countries would seem to qualify. After all, most countries have politically significant ethnic or linguistic minorities that often are concentrated in a particular region or regions. This is true of dozens of countries across Africa, Asia, Eastern Europe, and the Middle East. But only a handful of these countries have adopted federal constitutions. The mere fact that a country is culturally pluralistic and has one or more spatially concentrated cultural minorities may be quite important in understanding that country's politics. But it does not make that country federal.

Cultural diversity can be reflected and managed in a country's politics in many ways. Federal institutions are only one possibility among many. The idea and concept of federalism cannot, therefore, be detached from the institutions of government. *A federal constitution institutionalizes regional divisions by associating them with different governments.* The regionalism responsible for the adoption of a federal constitution in the first place is reinforced by political and administrative rivalries between the national and regional governments. Regional politics can certainly take place in the absence of a federal constitution. But the political significance of regional differences tends to be elevated under federalism by associating them with different political jurisdictions and the governments that preside over them.

Federalism divides political authority along territorial lines. It is not, however, the only form of government to do so. Important policy-making and administrative powers may be exercised at the regional level even in a unitary state. The extent to which these activities are *decentralized*, i.e., placed in the hands of regional officials, or remain *centralized* at the national level, is determined by the particular histories and social, geographic, and political conditions of a country. This is also true of federal states, where the constitution provides only a partial and sometimes very misleading guide to the real division of powers between governments. Political authority is also linked to territory in *confederations and economic and military associations.* These are formal groupings of independent states that have agreed to assign certain policy-making and administrative functions to a common institution or set of institutions. All member states have a say—though not necessarily an equal say—in the decision-making of such a body, while at the same time retaining their ultimate sovereignty (see Box 8.1).

Governing Realities

BOX 8.1 Territory and Political Authority

Under a *unitary* form of government, even when there is a significant measure of administrative or legislative devolution or decentralization, sovereignty or competence resides exclusively with the central government, and regional or local governments are legally and politically subordinate to it. (Examples include France, Japan, China, and Turkey.)

Under the *federal* form of government, sovereignty or competence is distributed between central and provincial (or state) governments so that, within a single political system, neither order of government is legally or politically subordinate to the other, and each order of government is elected by and exercises authority directly on the electorate. (Examples include Canada, the United States, Belgium, Australia, and Germany.)

Under the *confederal* form of government, even where there is a considerable allocation of responsibilities to central institutions or agencies, the ultimate sovereignty, including the right to withdraw from this form of association, is retained by the member-state governments. Furthermore, the members of the major central institutions are delegates of the constituent state governments. (The most prominent example is the European Union, although it has features that resemble the federal form of government, including a parliament whose members are elected directly by the citizens of the EU countries rather than being selected by member-state governments.)

An *economic or military association*, when it has common organizing institutions, is a confederal type of organization in which the functions assigned by the participating states to the common institutions are limited mainly to economic or military co-operation and co-ordination. (Examples include the Canada–United States–Mexico Agreement and the North Atlantic Treaty Organization.)

Source: Adapted from Canada, Task Force on Canadian Unity, *Coming to Terms: The Words of the Debate* (Hull, QC: Supply and Services Canada, 1979), 21–2; emphasis, updates, and examples are added.

The Origins, Maintenance, and Demise of Federal States

Only about two dozen of the 193 member states of the United Nations have a federal system of government (see Figure 8.1). This is an estimate rather than a precise number because the determination of whether a political system is federal is not an exact science. For example, Mexico and Russia generally are included in the club of federal states, but the central governments of these countries have sometimes interfered with the autonomy of state governments. How many countries actually belong to the federalism club is less important than the fact that the club is a small one, although it does include some of the world's largest and most powerful countries. Unitary government is far more popular, even in countries where regionally based internal divisions are strong.

"Federalism," declared Pierre Trudeau, "has all along been a product of reason in politics. . . . it is an attempt to find a rational compromise between the divergent interest groups which history has thrown together; but it is a compromise based on the will of the people."[5] This is why federal unions often are referred to as "pacts," "contracts," or "bargains." The

North America Central America Caribbean	South America	Africa	Europe	Asia-Pacific
Canada	Venezuela	Nigeria	Germany	Pakistan
United States	Brazil	Ethiopia	Belgium	India
Mexico	Argentina	Comoros	Austria	United Arab Emirates
St. Kitts and Nevis		South Africa	Switzerland	Malaysia
			Bosnia and Herzegovina	Micronesia
			Spain	Australia
			Russian Federation	

FIGURE 8.1 Federalism in the World

Source: European Parliament, "Understanding Federalism" (2015), http://www.europarl.europa.eu/cyprus/resource/static/files/understanding-federalism--advantages-and-disadvantages.pdf.

key role of consent may be seen in the case of the former Soviet Union, where it never really existed. As part of the post-World War II deal between the Soviet Union and the US-led Western democracies, the countries of Estonia, Latvia, and Lithuania were made members of the Soviet "federal" state against their will. Their unwilling entry into the Soviet Union, combined with the fact that Moscow dominated the regional republics through the Communist Party's monopoly on power, exposed the hollowness of the Soviet Union's federal pretensions. But with the 1989 abolition of the Communist Party's legal monopoly on power and the greater autonomy enjoyed by the regional republics, the Soviet Union very quickly fell apart. Without even a minimal consensus on the desirability of maintaining the central government, and without the Communist Party and Red Army to keep them in check, republic after republic declared national independence. Force and fear, not consent, had kept the Soviet "federal" system of government together.

Many who have studied the emergence of federal political systems agree with Trudeau's argument that federalism is the product of reason. It is, however, a bit idealistic and does not tell us very much about the precise reasons why federalism is adopted, much less why it persists. In what he calls a theory of circumstantial causality,[6] Michael Burgess identifies a list of common interest factors and external or internal threats that may contribute to the choice of federalism. The precise mix varies, he argues, across particular cases (see Table 8.1).

Federal democracies originate in compromise. The fact that some regions are more enthusiastic than others about the federal compromise—indeed, some may enter it or stay in even though they are dissatisfied only because the alternatives seem even less satisfactory—does not diminish the voluntary consent of the regions forming the basis of a federal union. Once established, however, a federal state may achieve a new dynamic. The existence of a national government and the idea of national citizenship can be centralizing factors that offset the decentralizing pull of regional interests. Market forces—the movement of goods and services and people across the regional borders within the federation—may also offset and diminish the

---

TABLE 8.1 Factors Contributing to the Choice of Federalism

Common Interests	External and/or Internal Threats
Shared political values.	A sense of military insecurity, real or imagined.
Expectations of stronger economic ties and associated benefits.	A sense of economic insecurity, real or imagined.
A multiplicity of ranges of communications and transactions.	A sense of cultural insecurity, real or imagined.
The desire for political independence.	A perceived threat to the stability of the existing political order.
Prior political association.	
Strategic (territorial) considerations.	
Geographical proximity.	
Common cultural and ideological factors, such as nationalism, religion, and inherited traditions and customs.	
Political leadership and a broadening of the political elite.	
Similarity of social and political institutions.	
The appeal of federal models.	
The culmination of historical processes that were founded upon prior political commitments.	

Source: Michael Burgess, *Comparative Federalism: Theory and Practice* (New York: Routledge, 2006), 100.

tug of regionalism. Federalism is sustained, then, not simply on the basis of rational calculations on the part of regional populations and politicians. It may indeed be sustained by a *sense of political nationality*. According to Donald Smiley, one of Canada's foremost experts on federalism, political nationality "means that Canadians as such have reciprocal moral and legal claims upon one another that have no precise counterparts in their relations with others, and that Canadians as such have a continuing determination to carry out a significant number of important common activities together."[7] In short, a sense of political community transcends regional, ethnic, and linguistic identifications, although it does not replace or necessarily overshadow the other identities citizens may have.

Federalism ultimately is sustained by the sense of political nationality—or community—that develops around the national state. By the same token, the breakup of a federal state is sure to be presaged by the deterioration of this sense of community. Sometimes a sense of political nationality is never solidly established in the first place, as it was not in post-independence Nigeria, whose federal system immediately came under stress and collapsed from within shortly after having been adopted. In other cases a sense of political nationality may be destroyed, or fail to develop, because of a particularly divisive regional conflict, as American federalism was split asunder by the slavery issue. The most stable federal systems are those where regional communities share in a sense of political nationality that dampens the decentralizing tendencies produced by regional differences. Switzerland, the contemporary United States, Germany, and Australia are good examples of such stability. The Swiss case in particular demonstrates that regionally based ethnolinguistic divisions do not necessarily prevent the development of a durable political nationality.

If the citizens of a particular region feel strongly that existing federal structures discriminate against their interests economically and politically, and if this sense of grievance is mobilized politically through a social movement or political party, the federal bargain will come under strain. History seems to indicate, however, that the likelihood

of regional grievances threatening the stability of federalism is greatest when they are expressed on behalf of a nation, as in the Catalan nation or *la nation québécoise*. Nationalism usually is accompanied by territorial claims. These claims can range from demands for outright independence to more moderate calls for greater autonomy for the region where members of the national community are concentrated. Nationalism is also likely to be associated with a historical narrative in which the nation is seen to have been unfairly treated by the central government and those who control it. Flemish nationalists in Belgium, Scottish nationalists, Catalan nationalists in Spain, Corsican separatists in France, and Québécois separatists in Canada all share such a narrative. What Smiley called a sense of political community is difficult to sustain when this sort of nationalism is widespread among the members of a spatially concentrated cultural community (see Box 8.2).

The Origins of Canadian Federalism

Canada's federal Constitution was a compromise. Most of the anglophone Fathers of Confederation favoured a unitary system of government under which all power would be in the hands of a new national parliament. They were opposed, however, by two groups. The strongest opposition came from the French-Canadian representatives of Canada East, what today is Quebec. This group, led by George-Étienne Cartier, insisted on constitutional protection for their cultural community. They believed that the most effective way to protect their interests was through a federal union that gave exclusive jurisdiction over linguistic and cultural matters to the provincial governments. Federalism was also the preferred constitutional option of Maritime politicians. Maritimers had developed strong local identities they were unwilling to see submerged under unitary government. They also realized that their regional interests would be swamped if there were to be a single national legislature in which much more populous Ontario and Quebec would dominate.

Politics in Focus

BOX 8.2 Language, Nationalism, and Federalism

This country has two major language communities that have coexisted, sometimes on uneasy terms, since the country achieved independence in the nineteenth century. One of these communities has a significant nationalist movement that includes a couple of political parties committed to independence for their national community. Many of this country's citizens believe that their language community and region has subsidized public services and incomes in the other community for decades and they feel resentful. This resentment is deepened by historical memories of social and political inequality between the two communities. As of 2019, the prospects for their continued cohabitation seem fair, but the prospects for anything more than a rather chilly *modus vivendi* seem poor. The country described here is Belgium.

Over the years Belgium has been compared frequently to Canada, facing some rather similar challenges and attempting to manage conflict between its two main language communities, French and Flemish (Belgium also has a very small German-speaking official-language community), through a federal constitution. Unlike Canada, however, the nationalist movement, a part of which aspires to

break up the country, is associated with the wealthier majority community—the Flemish-speaking north of the country. In the national elections of 2010, 2014, and 2019 the most popular political party in the Flemish region of the country was the Flemish Nationalist Party (NVA), a party committed to independence.

Comparisons between Belgium and Canada can be misleading. Nevertheless, political scientists and constitutionalists from each country have looked to the other to find answers about what does and does not work in managing inter-community relations in a federal state. If recent developments in Belgium hold any lessons for Canada, the main one probably is this: when the ties of identity and shared cultural values that bridge the language gap between communities are weak, and when one group believes that existing state institutions treat it unfairly, federalism is in trouble. The compromise at the heart of federalism's viability ultimately depends on the sentiment of the people or, more precisely, the *peoples* who live together under a federal constitution. This is what the French historian Ernest Renan meant when he said that federalism is a daily referendum of the popular will.

Besides, in an era when politics and patronage were virtually synonymous it was only reasonable that regional politicians would want to retain control over such important sources of contracts as roads and public works, as well as bureaucratic sinecures.

Although the anglophone politicians of Ontario and Quebec tended to be much less enthusiastic about federalism, some of them saw merit in the idea of dividing legislative powers between two levels of government. For example, Ontario's George Brown expressed the view that conflict between the English Protestant and French Catholic communities—conflict that had produced government instability and political deadlock in the

legislature of the United Canadas and that was one of the reasons behind the Confederation movement—would be reduced by assigning local matters to the provincial legislatures.[8] Ottawa would deal with matters of national interest, like trade and commerce, immigration, defence, and transportation. The presumption that sectarian rivalries and local interests would not enter into deliberations on these national issues proved to be naive, to say the least.

The forces pushing the colonies of British North America towards political union required a strong national government. Commercial interests, particularly railroad promoters, wanted unification because their ability to raise investment capital abroad was linked to Canada's creditworthiness. A larger union with a wider revenue base and an integrated national economy were crucial to the railroad promoters' interests and to those of the Canadian financial institutions linked to them. Likewise, a strong central government was needed if British North America was to assume the burden of its own military defence and if expansion into the sparsely populated region between Ontario and British Columbia was to be accomplished. Tugging in the opposite direction were the facts of cultural dualism and the existence of colonial administrations and regional societies that were unwilling to be completely submerged in a unitary state that would inevitably be dominated by Ontario and Quebec. Federalism was a necessary compromise between these contradictory tendencies.

What sort of federal union did the founders envisage? Obviously, politicians had various expectations. Some, such as Canada's first prime minister, John A. Macdonald, anticipated that the provincial governments would be little more than glorified municipalities, subordinate to Ottawa. Others, including Oliver Mowat, who as Ontario's premier led the movement for provincial rights during the 1870s and 1880s, clearly did not share this centralist vision.[9] Individual expectations aside, the agreement the founders reached gave the most important legislative powers and sources of public revenue of the time to the federal government. Ottawa was given authority over trade and commerce, shipping, fisheries, interprovincial transportation, currency and banking, the postal service, and several other areas of endeavour related to managing the economy. Responsibility for immigration and agriculture was divided between the federal and provincial governments, but in the event of a conflict Ottawa's legislation would prevail. The federal government was assigned the duty to build an intercolonial railway connecting Montreal to Halifax. Together, these powers appeared to establish Ottawa's clear superiority over the provinces in economic matters. When we consider that promoting economic growth and military defence (also a federal responsibility)

were two of the chief functions of the nineteenth-century state—maintaining public order was the third, and responsibility for this was divided between Ottawa and the provinces—there is little doubt that Ottawa was assigned the major legislative powers of that era.

Ottawa's superiority also was clear on the taxation front. Donald Smiley notes that customs and excise taxes—indirect forms of taxation—accounted for about three-quarters of colonial revenues prior to Confederation. The Confederation agreement made these the exclusive preserve of the federal government, which could "[raise] Money by any Mode or System of Taxation" (s. 91[3]). The provinces were restricted to the less developed field of "Direct Taxation" (s. 92[2]), as well as royalties on provincially owned natural resources (s. 109). Not only were provincial revenue sources meagre compared to those of the federal government, the Confederation agreement also established the practice of federal money transfers to the provinces (s. 118, repealed in 1950). The dependence of the economically weaker provinces on subsidies from Ottawa began in 1867 and continues to this day (see the discussion later in this chapter).

In addition to all this, the Confederation agreement included several provisions that have been described as *quasi-federal*. They appear to establish a nearly colonial relationship between Ottawa and the provinces by permitting the federal government to disallow laws passed by provincial legislatures. Sections 55, 56, and 90 of the Constitution Act, 1867 give provincial lieutenant-governors, appointees of Ottawa, the authority to reserve approval from any Act passed by a provincial legislature for a period of up to one year, or to disallow the Act at any time within a year of its passage. These were widely used powers during the first few decades after Confederation and were used periodically during the first half of the twentieth century. In most instances Ottawa was reacting to provincial economic policies that challenged its own priorities and jurisdiction. Moreover, section 92(10c) gives the federal government the authority to intervene in a provincial economy by declaring that the construction of a "public work" (this could be anything from a road to an oil field) is in the national interest. This power has been used 470 times, but has not been used since 1961. Finally, section 93(3)(4) actually gives Ottawa the power to pass laws respecting education, an area of provincial jurisdiction. It may do so where education rights that denominational minorities held when a province entered Confederation are abrogated by provincial law. This power has never been used.

Assuming that it is even possible to sort out the founders' intentions, do they really matter? Legally, no. In interpreting the federal division of powers the courts have generally been unreceptive to arguments about what the Fathers of Confederation really had in mind.[10] Indeed, the Supreme Court of Canada's ruling in the 1981 Patriation Reference, *Re Constitution of Canada*, declared flatly that "arguments from history do not lead to any consistent view or any single view of the nature of the British North America Act. So, too, with pronouncements by political figures or persons in other branches of public life. There is little profit in parading them."[11]

Politically, however, arguments about intentions can matter. Quebec politicians and opinion-makers regularly argue that Canadian federalism ought to be seen as a compact between French and English Canada, a partnership between equal communities that goes back to the Confederation agreement. To give but one example, the compact theory or **two-nations theory** as it is sometimes called, is the premise of the Quebec Liberal government's 2017 blueprint on the way forward in relations between Quebec and Ottawa, *Quebecers: Our Way of Being Canadian*.[12] Another perspective on Canadian federalism that has been influential over the years, although not particularly so in more recent times, involves the view that federalism is a contract among provinces that agreed to give up certain powers to a new national government of their creation and that it cannot be changed in any fundamental way without the consent of the parties to this federal bargain. Some of the premiers of the predominantly English-speaking provinces invoked this contract theory of

Library and Archives Canada

The Fathers of Confederation at Charlottetown. Canada's entrance into federalism was far from a unanimous decision; rather, the system of divided jurisdiction was a compromise that made Ottawa the seat of national power to control collective issues such as defence, immigration, and trade, while leaving the provinces to preside over issues of a more local nature, such as culture and education.

federalism at the time of the 1980–1 negotiations on constitutional reform.

The Federal Division of Powers

Whatever the intentions of the founders when they drafted the Constitution Act, 1867, it has long been clear that both levels of government exercise wide-ranging legislative and taxation powers. Their ability to do so ultimately rests on the responsibilities assigned to them by the Constitution. Canada's founders took exceptional pains to specify the responsibilities of each level of government. But a literal reading of the division of powers they decided and of the formal changes that have been made to it since then provide at best a partial and at worst a misleading guide to Canadian federalism. In some cases policy areas were unimagined when the federal division of powers was framed—electronic communications, air transportation, and environmental protection would be examples—and so these legislative powers are not explicitly assigned either to Ottawa or to the provinces. In other cases what were minor responsibilities in the nineteenth and early twentieth centuries have assumed greater importance as a result of economic and societal changes, and of changes in the nature of and expectations for government.

The heart of the federal division of powers is found in sections 91 and 92 of the Constitution Act, 1867. Each of these sections contains a detailed list of enumerated powers that belong exclusively to Parliament (s. 91) or the provincial (s. 92) legislatures. Combined with several other sections that also deal with the division of powers, this is the constitutional foundation of Canadian federalism. An examination of who holds what powers reveals that both Ottawa and the provinces have the capacity to act in most of the major policy fields (see Table 8.2 and Box 8.3).

Some of the constitutional powers listed in Table 8.2 could reasonably have been placed under more than one policy heading. The authority to tax, for example, has been used to promote economic growth, to redistribute income between groups, and to subsidize all sorts of special interests. Unemployment insurance is both an economic policy, tied to manpower retraining and a claimant's job search activities, and a social policy that has the effect of redistributing income to less affluent regions of the country where unemployment is higher. Immigration policy has always been harnessed to the needs of the Canadian economy and has also been tied to cultural policy through citizenship services and language training for immigrants.

At the same time, governments have sometimes found the authority to legislate through powers that are implied, rather than stated, in the Constitution. The most important example of this involves the federal government's *spending power*. Ottawa spends billions of dollars annually on programs that fall under the jurisdiction of provincial and municipal governments. The feds also provide money to universities (for research and student scholarships) and to school boards (for language instruction), even though these organizations fall under the constitutional authority of the provinces, and to individuals for purposes that might appear to fall under provincial jurisdiction (e.g., tax benefits for child care). Ottawa's constitutional "right" to spend money for any purpose has never been definitely established in the courts.[13] Nevertheless, the spending power today provides the constitutional basis, such as it is, for such major federal grants to the provinces as the Canada Health Transfer (CHT), Canada Social Transfer (CST), and equalization payments.

The Courts and Federalism

Laypersons might imagine that such constitutional terms as "trade and commerce," "property and civil rights," and "direct taxation" have straightforward meanings. This view has not been shared by constitutional lawyers, governments, and the private interests that have challenged federal and

TABLE 8.2 The Federal Division of Powers under the Constitution Acts

	Ottawa	Provinces
Public finance	(1867) • 91(3): authority to raise money by any "Mode or System of Taxation" • 91(4): authority to borrow money (1982) • 36(2): commits Ottawa to the principle of equalizing public revenue levels in the provinces (although the degree to which this is enforceable in the courts is moot)	(1867) • 92(2): authorizes direct taxation within the province • 92(3): authority to borrow money • 92A(4): permits provinces to use "any mode or system of taxation" in the case of non-renewable natural resources, forestry resources, and electrical energy
Managing the economy	(1867) • 91(2): regulation of trade and commerce • 91(2A): unemployment insurance • 91(5): post office • 91(10, 12): navigation, international waters, and offshore resources • 91(14, 15, 16, 18, 19, 20): national monetary system • 91(17, 22, 23): commercial standards • 92(10.c): authority to intervene in a provincial economy by declaring a public work to be in the national interest • 95: agriculture • 121: prohibits provincial taxes on imports from other provinces, thus reinforcing the concept of a national economic union (1982) • 6(2): guarantees the economic mobility of citizens anywhere within Canada, reinforcing the concept of a national economic union	(1867) • 92(9): authority to issue commercial licences • 92(10): public works within the province • 92(11): incorporation of companies with provincial objects • 92(13): property and civil rights • 92A: reaffirms provincial authority over natural resources within their borders • 95: agriculture, but federal law takes precedence • 109: establishes provincial ownership of natural resources within their borders (1982) • 6(4): permits provinces to favour provincial residents in hiring if the rate of unemployment in that province is above the national average
Social policy and the quality of life	(1867) • 91(24): "Indians, and Lands reserved for Indians" • 91(26): marriage and divorce • 93(3, 4): authority to protect the educational rights of denominational minorities • 94A: old age pensions, but provincial law prevails • 95: immigration	(1867) • 92(7): hospitals • 92(12): solemnization of marriage • 93: education • 94A: public pensions • 95: immigration, but federal law prevails
Cultural policy	(1867) • 133: official bilingualism of Parliament (1982) • 16(1), 19, 20: establishes official bilingualism in all institutions of the federal government	(1867) • 92(16): all matters of a merely local or private nature • 93: education • 133: official bilingualism of Quebec legislature (1982) • 16(2), 17(2), 18(2), 19(2), 20(2): establishes official bilingualism in all institutions of the New Brunswick government

Continued

	Ottawa	Provinces
TABLE 8.2 Continued		
Administration and enforcement of law	(1867) • 91(27): criminal law • 91(28): penitentiaries • 96: appointment of judges of provincial courts • 100: authority to set judicial salaries • 101: authority to establish a general court of appeal for Canada, and other federal courts	(1867) • 92(14): administration of justice and the organization of courts within the province • 92(15): authority to establish penalties for violations of provincial laws
International relations and defence	(1867) • 91(7): military and defence • 132: authority to enter foreign treaties and perform obligations under them	(1867) • Since the Supreme Court's decision in the *Labour Conventions* case of 1937, it appears that provincial consent is required to implement foreign treaty obligations involving matters of provincial jurisdiction. There is, however, no consensus on this.
Other legislative authority	(1867) • 91 (preamble): authorizes Parliament to make laws for the "peace, order, and good government" of Canada • 91(29): matters not falling under the enumerated powers of the provinces come under Ottawa's jurisdiction	(1867) • 92(8): municipal institutions • 92(16): all matters of a local or private nature in the province
Environmental policy	(1867) • 91: peace, order, and good government of Canada (this basis for federal power is suggested in the Canada Water Act) • 91(10): navigation and shipping • 91(12): sea coast and inland fisheries • 91(27): criminal law • 95: agriculture • 132: foreign treaties	(1867) • 92(5): management and sale of public lands • 92(10): local works and undertakings • 92(13): property and civil rights • 92(16): matters of a merely local or private nature (1982) • 92A: non-renewable natural resources, forestry resources, and electric energy

provincial laws. For these groups the federal division of powers is a dense thicket of contradictory and contested meanings and opportunities, and the interpretation attached to a particular enumerated power is often a matter to haggle over in the courts. The judicial decisions that have resulted from these disputes have played an important role in shaping the evolution of Canadian federalism. Among the many contentious sections of the Constitution, Ottawa's authority to "make laws for the peace, order, and good government of Canada" (POGG) and the federal government's trade and commerce power have been among the most significant in their impact on the division of powers.

A word of warning: Many of the decisions examined in the next two sections may seem to you to be rather old and therefore of questionable relevance. Indeed, some of them go back more than 100 years! In matters of law, however, including constitutional law, age is irrelevant. What matters is whether a ruling is pertinent and therefore has value as a precedent that can and ought to be taken into account in deciding the case at hand. Thus, no lawyer appearing before the Supreme Court of Canada need ever apologize for invoking a case that may have been decided when Canada's population was about 4 million persons, most people worked on farms, and people still moved around in horse-drawn buggies. Relevance, not age, is the test of whether a ruling from the past will be used to decide cases in the present.

Peace, Order, and Good Government

The courts have tended to place a narrow interpretation on the federal Parliament's general authority to make laws for the "**peace, order, and good government of Canada.**" This power has been reduced over time to one that may provide the constitutional basis for federal actions in emergency circumstances. It cannot, however, be used to justify federal laws during "normal" times. This narrow interpretation of POGG began with the *Local Prohibition* case (1896). The Judicial Committee of the Privy Council ruled that POGG could not be used by Ottawa to override the enumerated powers of the provinces. The decision also marked the introduction into Canadian constitutional law of the "national dimensions" test. Lord Watson wrote:

> Their Lordships do not doubt that some matters, in their origin local or provincial, might attain such dimensions as to affect the body politic of the Dominion, and to justify the Canadian Parliament in passing laws for their regulation or abolition in the interest of the Dominion.[14]

When does a matter acquire "national dimensions"? This question was dealt with in a series of three decisions handed down in 1922, 1923, and 1925. In *Re Board of Commerce Act and Combines and Fair Prices Act 1919* (1922), the JCPC struck down two federal laws introduced after World War I to prevent monopolistic business practices and hoarding of essential commodities. For the first time the "emergency doctrine" was articulated, according to which Parliament could pass laws under the authority of POGG only in the case of a national emergency. Writing for the majority, Viscount Haldane declared that:

> Circumstances are conceivable, such as those of war or famine, when the peace, order and good Government of the Dominion might be imperilled under conditions so exceptional

that they require legislation of a character in reality beyond anything provided for by the enumerated heads in either s. 92 or s. 91.[15]

Essentially, the JCPC ruled that some national crisis must exist before federal laws can be based on POGG. The fact that a matter has acquired "national dimensions" would not, by itself, be sufficient to justify such exceptional legislation.

Despite the JCPC's admission that peacetime circumstances could conceivably warrant Ottawa acting under the authority of POGG, subsequent rulings suggested that POGG was really a wartime power. In the first of these decisions, *Fort Frances Pulp and Power Co. v. Manitoba Free Press* (1923), the JCPC declared that war-related circumstances were sufficient to warrant legislating under POGG. Moreover, Viscount Haldane's opinion in *Fort Frances* indicated that the courts should be reluctant to question Parliament's judgment that a war-related emergency exists. Rulings in 1947 by the JCPC and in 1950 by the Supreme Court of Canada repeated this view.[16]

In those cases where the courts have rejected POGG as a valid basis for federal legislation, the impugned laws were intended to deal with peacetime circumstances. The first of these was the decision in *Toronto Electric Commissioners v. Snider* (1925). Relying on the "emergency doctrine" it had developed in the *Board of Commerce* case, the JCPC struck down Canada's major industrial relations law, the Industrial Disputes Investigation Act, 1907. The JCPC again rejected peacetime recourse to POGG in the 1937 reference decision on Ottawa's Employment and Social Insurance Act, 1935.[17] The federal government's attempt to justify this law under POGG, on the grounds that unemployment was a matter of national concern and, moreover, that it threatened the well-being of the country, was considered inadequate by the JCPC.

Confronted with broadly similar reasoning in the 1970s, the Supreme Court of Canada found that POGG could be used to justify federal laws during peacetime. The Court was asked to rule on the constitutionality of Ottawa's Anti-Inflation Act, 1975. A majority of the Court accepted the federal government's argument that mounting

Governing Realities

BOX 8.3 Who Has Authority over Water?

When the Constitution Act of 1867 came into force, water was considered to be significant in three main ways. It was important for navigation, as a source of fish, and for irrigating farmland. In fact, the third of these was not yet particularly important in Canada, although the building of dams and the diversion of rivers for irrigation had begun to be a contentious issue in the United States. The supply of fresh water for drinking was taken for granted. Water pollution was not an issue. No one had heard of invasive species. The issues surrounding hydroelectric power did not yet exist. And the idea that Indigenous rights and interests should be taken into account when it came to water would have been greeted with incredulity.

It is hardly surprising, then, that water is not one of the enumerated legislative powers under sections 91 and 92 of the Constitution Act, 1867. Over time, however, it acquired enormous importance and the question of which level of government held the constitutional authority to regulate its use was asked more often and with greater urgency. Ottawa based its case on a clutch of constitutional provisions, including the "peace, order, and good government" clause, the trade and commerce provision, jurisdiction over coastal and inland fisheries, as well as over navigation and shipping, and its authority to enter into foreign treaties (though not necessarily to implement the terms of such treaties). More recently the federal government's exclusive jurisdiction over criminal law has been advanced as a basis for a federal role in water policy.

The provinces have had their own list of constitutional claims to authority over water. These have included jurisdiction over property and civil rights, municipal institutions, local works and undertakings, the authority conferred by s. 92(5) regarding the management of public lands, and "all matters of a merely local or private nature in the province" (s. 92[16]). Conflict over who has jurisdiction has occasionally led to court battles over pollution, the building of dams, and the management of fisheries.

In the 1960s and 1970s governments in developed economies throughout the world, Canada included, became more active in matters concerning water pollution, passing laws and creating environmental bureaucracies to manage this issue. What Ottawa immediately discovered was that provincial and local governments already claimed responsibility for providing clean water, dealing with sewage, regulating agricultural, industrial, and residential activities that influence water supply and quality, and managing recreational and commercial fishing in their lakes and rivers. Some things, of course, these provincial and local governments could not do, including negotiating water treaties with foreign governments, regulating water that flowed across provincial boundaries, and managing the waters off Canada's coasts. But most of the key regulatory functions related to water supply and quality, which have immediate impacts on Canadians' lives and on their communities, were and continue to be under the control of provincial and local governments.

Some water experts lament the decentralized and divided reality of authority over water in Canada and believe that a more robust federal presence and national standards would be preferable. Whether or not they are right—and it is not obvious that a dominant federal role would produce better water policy, whatever "better" might be understood to mean—the fact is that the constitutional authority to regulate water is divided and overlapping. The "watertight compartments" metaphor of Canadian federalism, proposed by the Judicial Committee of the Privy Council in the 1930s, is never leakier than when applied to water.

inflationary pressures constituted an emergency justifying legislation that encroached on provincial jurisdiction. Not only was the "emergency doctrine" liberated from war-related circumstances, the Court also indicated its reluctance to challenge Parliament's judgment on when emergency circumstances exist. The result, according to constitutionalists like Peter Russell, was that Ottawa now appeared to have fairly easy access to emergency powers under this doctrine.[18] Constitutionally, this may have been so. Politically, however, any federal government would think twice before legislating in a manner that interferes with provincial constitutional authority and invoking the emergency powers doctrine as the basis for such interference. This is as true today as when the Court's 1975 decision was handed down.

The national dimensions test, first expressed in the 1896 *Local Prohibition* case, has come to be the more practically important aspect of POGG. In several cases since the 1950s the federal government has defended legislation that treads upon provincial turf by arguing that the matter in question had national dimensions, thereby justifying federal legislation under the authority of POGG.[19] The key ruling in this regard was handed down by a divided court (4 to 3) in a 1988 ruling. In *R. v. Crown Zellerbach Canada*, a case that involved a challenge to the federal Ocean Dumping Control Act, the Supreme Court upheld the constitutionality of Ottawa's authority on the basis of the "national dimensions" test. The criteria used by the Supreme Court in deciding whether a matter has "national dimensions" should not be approached by the faint of heart and routinely lead to disagreements between justices of the Court.

Trade and Commerce

On the face of it, Ottawa's authority over the regulation of trade and commerce (s. 91[2])[20] appears rather sweeping. Any economic activity or transaction would seem to fall within its scope. In fact, however, court decisions have construed the trade and commerce power to be much narrower than this, limited largely to interprovincial and international trade. At the same time, provincial jurisdiction over property and civil rights in the provinces (s. 92[13])[21] has been interpreted as the provinces' own version of the trade and commerce power. This line of judicial interpretation began with the decision in *Citizens' Insurance Co. v. Parsons* (1881). Based on its view that a broad, literal interpretation of s. 91(2) of the Constitution Act, 1867 would bring any and all aspects of economic life under the authority of Ottawa, leaving the provinces powerless

to affect business, the JCPC interpreted "regulation of trade and commerce" to include "political arrangements in regard to trade requiring the sanction of parliament, regulation of trade in matters of interprovincial concern, and it may be that they would include general regulation of trade affecting the whole Dominion."[22] To construe Ottawa's trade and commerce power otherwise, the JCPC argued, would be to deny the "fair and ordinary meaning" of s. 92(13) of the Constitution Act, 1867, which assigns property and civil rights in the provinces to the provincial governments.

The legacy of *Parsons* has been that Ottawa's authority to regulate trade and commerce has been limited to interprovincial trade, international trade, and general trade affecting the whole of Canada. But even this definition of federal jurisdiction has presented problems of interpretation. For example, what about a federal law whose principal goal is to regulate trade that crosses provincial borders, but which has as an incidental effect the regulation of some transactions that occur wholly within a province? Is such a law constitutional under s. 91(2)? Until the 1950s the courts' answer was "no."[23]

A series of Supreme Court decisions since then, culminating in *Caloil v. Attorney General of Canada* (1971), signified a broader interpretation of Ottawa's power to regulate interprovincial trade.[24] In *Caloil*, the Court acknowledged that a federal law prohibiting the transportation or sale of imported oil west of the Ottawa Valley interfered with local trade in a province. Nevertheless, the Court upheld the federal law on the grounds that its "true character" was "the control of imports in the furtherance of an extraprovincial trade policy."[25] Ottawa's authority was given an additional boost by a 1971 reference decision of the Supreme Court. In *Attorney General for Manitoba v. Manitoba Egg and Poultry Association* the Court ruled unconstitutional a provincial egg-marketing scheme that restricted imports from other provinces on the grounds that it encroached on Ottawa's trade and commerce power. Justice Bora Laskin, who would later become Chief Justice of the Supreme Court, referred specifically to the trend towards a more balanced interpretation of federal and provincial jurisdiction over trade.[26] Laskin argued that "to permit each province to seek its own advantage . . . through a figurative sealing of its borders to entry of goods from others would be to deny one of the objects of Confederation . . . namely, to form an economic unit of the whole of Canada."[27] An answer to the question, raised in the 1881 *Parsons* ruling, as to what constitutes general trade affecting the whole of Canada came a couple of decades later. In *General Motors of Canada v. City National Leasing* (1989), the Supreme Court laid down five criteria that must be met before Ottawa may regulate commerce under the "general trade" provision of s. 91(2) of the Constitution:

1. the impugned legislation must be part of a general regulatory scheme;
2. the scheme must be monitored by the continuing oversight of a regulatory agency;
3. the legislation must be concerned with trade as a whole rather than with a particular industry;
4. the legislation should be of a nature that the provinces jointly or severally would be constitutionally incapable of enacting; and
5. the failure to include one or more provinces or localities in a legislative scheme would jeopardize the successful operation of the scheme in other parts of the country.[28]

In May 2010 the federal government referred the proposed Canadian Securities Act to the Supreme Court for an advisory opinion on its constitutionality. Prompted by the financial crisis that swept across the United States and other capitalist economies in 2008–10, the Act was intended to strengthen Ottawa's regulatory role in Canadian capital markets. The case was particularly interesting due to the fact that the federal government relied entirely on the trade and commerce power in arguing that it had the constitutional authority to regulate the national securities trading market. In December 2011 the Supreme Court ruled against the federal government. "While the economic importance and pervasive character of the securities market may, in principle, support

federal intervention that is qualitatively different from what the provinces can do," said the Court, "they do not justify a wholesale takeover of the regulation of the securities industry which is the ultimate consequence of the proposed federal legislation."[29]

At the same time as Ottawa was experiencing this setback, new rules established by the US Congress to regulate a securities industry that was largely responsible for dragging the global economy to the verge of disaster were being implemented. The irony is that simple words of the United States Constitution—and certainly the founders' intentions—give Congress less scope for the regulation of trade and commerce than the Canadian Constitution appears to give to Parliament. Whereas court rulings in the United States have produced a situation where very few serious obstacles stand in the way of Congress regulating any economic transaction, no matter how local it may appear to be, judicial interpretation in Canada has had the opposite effect. Comparing the evolution of the trade and commerce power in these two countries provides a textbook example of the importance of the courts when it comes to the division of powers under federalism (see Box 8.4).

Court rulings seldom put an end to conflicts between Ottawa and the provinces. Instead, they typically become part of the bargaining process between governments, as has been true in the case of the Supreme Court's 2011 rebuff of Ottawa's efforts to establish a national system of securities regulation. In its ruling the Court indicated what needed to be done to establish a federal regulatory role in this field. Co-operation with the provinces in a joint regulatory regime, the Court indicated, would pass constitutional muster. Negotiations between Ottawa and the provinces have been ongoing since 2013, but so far only half of the provinces and one territory have agreed to a co-operative regime with the federal government.[30] In any event, the issue has shifted from the courts to the playing field of intergovernmental relations.

Governing Realities

BOX 8.4 Is Canada a Single Market? Within Limits, Says the Supreme Court

Those who believe that the courts have not done enough to establish Ottawa's superiority over the provinces when it comes to management of the economy were given additional cause for lament by a 2018 Supreme Court ruling. The constitutional provision at stake was not trade and commerce or POGG's "national dimensions" test. It was section 121 of the Constitution Act, 1867, and the economic activity at stake involved beer and wine.

Section 121 states that "All Articles of the Growth, Produce, or Manufacture of any one of the Provinces shall, from and after the Union, be admitted free into each of the other Provinces." This has generally been understand as prohibiting provincial tariffs against goods imported from another province. In fact, however, there is every reason to interpret this section as prohibiting any barrier to trade between provinces and as the basis for a Canada-wide economic union. At the time of Confederation there were no provincial farm marketing boards, no provincial liquor monopolies, very few licensing restrictions for professions, and no formal purchasing policies whereby provincial governments were required to favour their province's businesses over those from out of province. Consequently, there was no reason to include an express prohibition against these barriers to interprovincial trade. There are very good reasons to believe that s. 121 was intended by those who agreed to it as establishing a national economy. Nevertheless, for complicated reasons best known to those who have studied the jurisprudence on s. 121, this provision has been interpreted as a ban on interprovincial tariffs and not as the basis for prohibiting other forms of provincial protectionism.

This brings us to Gerard Comeau, who in 2012 was stopped by the RCMP at the New Brunswick–Quebec border and fined $292.50. Mr. Comeau's offence was transporting across provincial lines, in violation of New Brunswick law, 14 cases of beer, two bottles of whisky, and one bottle of liqueur that he had purchased in Quebec. To add insult to injury, in addition to the fine all of his purchases were confiscated.

In a unanimous decision that upheld the constitutionality of provincial restrictions on the free movement of beer, wine, and spirits, and in support of a very narrow reading of s. 121, the Supreme Court had this to say:

In this case, the federalism principle is vital. It recognizes the autonomy of provincial governments to develop their societies within their respective spheres of jurisdiction and requires a court interpreting constitutional texts to consider how different interpretations impact the balance between federal and provincial interests. Reading s. 121 to require full economic integration would significantly undermine the shape of Canadian federalism, which is built upon regional diversity within a single nation. The need to maintain balance embodied in the federalism principle supports an interpretation of s. 121 that prohibits laws directed at curtailing the passage of goods over interprovincial borders, but allows legislatures to pass laws to achieve other goals within their powers, even though the laws may have the incidental effect of impeding the passage of goods over interprovincial borders.

It was reasoning that would have warmed the hearts of the British law lords of the JCPC, whose narrow interpretations of the federal government's economic powers and generous interpretations of provincial powers allowed such a situation to arise during the several decades when they were the final umpires of Canada's Constitution. The Supreme Court's apparent acceptance of New Brunswick's argument that the intention of its restrictions on the entry into the province of alcohol purchased in another province is to "control the supply and use of liquor within the province," and to "prohibit holding excessive quantities of liquor from supplies not managed by the province," cannot be taken seriously. As everyone knows, the intention of such restrictions, in every province, is to protect provincial producers of beer and wine and to protect the profit margins at provincially regulated retailers from cheaper out-of-province competition.

The decision in *R. v. Comeau* may be read at https://www.scc-csc.ca/case-dossier/info/sum-som-eng.aspx?cas=37398.

Evolving Federalism

It is generally believed that judicial decisions decentralized Canadian federalism in a way that the Fathers of Confederation had not planned, but that this tendency has been attenuated since 1949 when the Supreme Court became Canada's highest court of appeal. Some bemoan the judiciary's decentralizing influence, particularly that of the JCPC during Canada's first half-century. Others maintain that the limits placed on Ottawa's general legislative authority (POGG) and trade and commerce power, and the broad interpretation of provincial authority over property and civil rights, have reflected the political reality of Canada. As Pierre Trudeau observed, "it has long been the custom in English Canada to denounce the [Judicial Committee of the] Privy Council for its provincial bias; but it should perhaps be considered that if the law lords had not leaned in that direction, Quebec separatism might not be a threat today: it might be an accomplished fact."[31]

Judicial review is only one of the factors that have shaped the evolution of Canadian federalism. Among the other factors, two stand out as having been particularly important: (1) the constitutional status of Quebec and the powers of the Quebec state; and (2) the political and administrative needs of provincial governments.

Quebec

"What does Quebec want?" The question has been asked countless times over the years by English Canadians, some of whom genuinely wanted to know and others who asked it out of exasperation, believing all along that the answer would be unacceptable. The complementary question, "What does English Canada want?" has been posed less often. Yet neither question makes sense in isolation from the other. To understand what Quebec wants from Canada it is also necessary to consider what the rest of Canada expects from, and is willing to concede to, Quebec. Quebec's unique role in Canadian federalism derives from two factors. One is its predominantly French-speaking character. About 80 per cent of the provincial population claims French as their mother tongue and roughly 90 per cent of all Canadian francophones reside in Quebec. The second factor is Quebec's size. At Confederation it was the second most populous province and Montreal was the hub of Canada's commercial and financial industries. Although its weight relative to the rest of Canada is much less today, Quebec is still Canada's second most populous province, accounting for just under 23 per cent (2018) of Canada's population. Neither Ontario nor Quebec is as economically dominant as in the past, but as a centre for finance and manufacturing Quebec continues to be surpassed only by Ontario.

Quebec's distinctive social and cultural fabric explains why it has made special demands on Canadian federalism. Because it is a large province with the second largest bloc of seats in the federal Parliament and because francophones have always been able to control Quebec's provincial legislature, the demands of Quebec have had a significant impact on the evolution of Canadian federalism. This impact has been experienced on two main fronts: (1) the Constitution, and (2) the financial and administrative practices of federalism. We will examine Quebec's impact on the financial and administrative dimensions of federalism later in this chapter.

Quebec's influence on the Constitution predates the Confederation agreement. Between 1848 and 1867 Ontario and Quebec formed the United Canadas, governed by a single legislature in which the two colonies held equal representation. This was Canada's first experience with the federal principle of regional representation. Predominantly francophone Quebec and predominantly anglophone Ontario were joined in a legislative partnership that required the agreement of both regional communities. It turned out to be a failure. Quebec's influence on the Constitution was also strongly evident in the Confederation agreement. Its representatives were the most insistent on a federal constitution for Canada, under which the provincial government would have authority over those matters considered vital to the preservation of the language, religion, and social institutions of Quebec. The clerical and political leaders of French Canada were unanimous in viewing Canadian federalism as a pact between two peoples. "Canadian Confederation," declared Henri Bourassa in 1902, "is the result of a contract between the two races in Canada, French and English, based on equality and recognizing equal rights and reciprocal duties. Canadian Confederation will last only as long as this equality of rights is recognized as the basis of the public right in Canada, from Halifax to Vancouver."[32]

The equality Bourassa had in mind did not last very long. It had already been violated in Manitoba, where the status of French in the provincial legislature and the educational rights of francophone Catholics were swept away a couple of decades after that province entered Confederation. It was also violated in Ontario, where Regulation 17 (1913) banned instruction in French from the province's public schools. These developments contributed to the identification of French Canada with Quebec, the only province in which francophones were in the majority and where they could effectively defend their rights and preserve their culture.

The constitutional consequences of limiting French Canada to the boundaries of Quebec became apparent by the middle of the twentieth century. As Ottawa became increasingly involved in areas of provincial jurisdiction, particularly through its spending power but also by monopolizing the field of direct taxation between 1947 and 1954 under a tax rental agreement with the provinces, the Quebec government became more and more protective of what it argued were exclusive provincial powers under the Constitution. Indeed, the Quebec government of Maurice Duplessis was the first among the provinces to reject Ottawa's exclusive occupation of the personal income tax field, imposing its own provincial income tax in 1954. But not until the Quiet Revolution of the 1960s, marking the eclipse of the conservative anti-statist nationalism that had dominated Quebec politics for more than a century, was Quebec's resentment towards Ottawa's encroachment onto provincial territory matched by aggressive constitutional demands. The first major indication of this occurred during the federal–provincial negotiations on a public old-age pension scheme (1963–5). Quebec Premier Jean Lesage stated that his government would only agree to a constitutional amendment giving Ottawa the authority to pass pension legislation if Quebec were able to opt out of the federal plan. Ottawa agreed, and thus was born the Canadian practice of provinces being able to opt out of a federal shared-cost program without suffering any financial loss.

Quebec's constitutional demands appeared to become even more ambitious a few years later. The 1966 provincial election saw the Union Nationale party run on the slogan "Québec d'abord!" (Quebec first!) The party's leader, Daniel Johnson, had authored the book *Egalité ou indépendance* and in the election campaign the Union Nationale called for major constitutional reform that included the transfer of virtually all social and cultural matters to the province, constitutional recognition of Canada's binational character, and exclusive provincial control over the major tax fields then shared with Ottawa. In fact, however, these demands were not pursued with much vigour during the party's five years in power (1966–70).

Despite the lack of substantive change in Quebec's constitutional status and powers during this period, the province's nationalist undercurrent was gaining momentum. The creation of the Parti Québécois (PQ) in 1968, under the leadership of René Lévesque, brought under one roof most of the major groups committed to the political independence of Quebec. The Liberal Party of Quebec remained federalist, but advocated what amounted to special status for Quebec within Canadian federalism. "Un fédéralisme rentable" (profitable federalism) was the passionless way in which Liberal leader Robert Bourassa explained Quebec's commitment to Canada.

Constitutional negotiations between Ottawa and the provinces had been ongoing since 1968. The 1970 election of a Liberal government in Quebec appeared to provide an opportunity to bring these talks to a successful conclusion. But when the 11 governments got together at Victoria in 1971, it became apparent that Quebec's price for agreeing to a constitutional amendment formula and a charter of rights was higher than Ottawa was willing to pay.[33] The impasse was over social policy. Quebec demanded constitutional supremacy in an area in which Ottawa operated several major programs, including family allowances, unemployment insurance, manpower training, and old-age pensions. Moreover, the Quebec government wanted the fiscal means to pay for provincial policies in these fields. Ottawa went some way towards meeting these demands. The Trudeau government refused, however, to concede the principle of provincial supremacy over social policy and would not provide a constitutional guarantee that provinces would receive financial compensation for operating their own programs in these areas. The federal–provincial compromise reached in Victoria fell apart days later in Quebec, where the deal was widely seen as constitutional entrenchment of an unacceptable status quo.

After Quebec's rejection of the Victoria Charter, the Bourassa government adopted a piecemeal strategy for changing federalism, negotiating with Ottawa on single issues like family allowances, social security, and telecommunications. It was unsuccessful, however, in extracting any major concessions from a federal government that believed provincial powers were already too great, and that was staunchly opposed to special status for Quebec.

A rather different strategy was followed by the PQ government of René Lévesque after it came to power in 1976. The PQ was committed to holding a provincial referendum on its option of political sovereignty for Quebec, combined with some form of economic association with the rest of Canada. But instead of simple confrontation with Ottawa, the Lévesque government pursued an *étapiste* (gradualist) strategy of providing "good government"— which required some degree of co-operation with Ottawa because of the intricate network of intergovernmental programs and agreements—while attempting to convince the Quebec population that its best interests lay in **sovereignty-association**. The two governments co-operated on dozens of new capital spending projects, on management of the economy, and on immigration policy. The PQ government even participated in federal–provincial talks on constitutional reform in 1978–9. All of this occurred against the background of the looming referendum on the PQ's separatist option.

Sovereignty-association was rejected by Quebec voters in May 1980. But they re-elected the PQ to office in 1981. It was thus a PQ government that participated in the constitutional negotiations towards "renewed federalism" that the federal Liberal government had initiated after the Quebec referendum. But it was also a PQ government that refused to sign the final product of these talks, the November 1981 accord that became the Constitution Act, 1982. The PQ's refusal was hardly surprising in light of the fact that none of the demands that Quebec governments had made since the 1960s were included in the 1981 constitutional accord. Indeed, the province's Liberal opposition also found the accord to be unacceptable. The Constitution had undergone its most dramatic reform since its passage in 1867, but the provincial government of the country's second largest province and home to 90 per cent of Canada's francophones had not agreed to these changes. Although the legality of the Constitution Act, 1982 was not in doubt, its political legitimacy was.

This was the situation when Robert Bourassa and the provincial Liberals were returned to power in 1985. Their election appeared to reflect the muted tenor of Quebec nationalism in the post-referendum era. Change had also taken place in Ottawa. Prime Minister Brian Mulroney, elected in 1984, did not share Pierre Trudeau's view that the provinces were already too powerful for the good of the national economy and political unity. Nor was he viscerally opposed to some form of special status for Quebec, as Trudeau was. Conditions seemed propitious, therefore, for a new arrangement that Quebec would accept.

It was not to be. The Quebec government put forward a package of five demands that had to be met before it would agree to the constitutional reforms passed in 1982. These proposals were agreed to by Ottawa and all of the provincial premiers on 30 April 1987, forming the basis for what became known as the Meech Lake Accord. As we have seen in Chapter 6, these constitutional proposals died on the drawing board, and two years later, in 1992, the Charlottetown proposals for constitutional reform, which offered Quebec even more and also brought Indigenous peoples to the table, were rejected in a national referendum, including by a majority of Quebecers.

Only a few years later, and despite widespread fatigue with the issue of constitutional reform, the Liberal government of Jean Chrétien was forced to revisit the issue as a result of the 1994 election of the PQ in Quebec. The PQ was committed to holding a referendum on Quebec independence within a year of their election. When the referendum campaign began in September 1995, the *indépendantiste* side got off to a sputtering start. About halfway through the campaign, however, leadership of the "yes" side passed from Quebec Premier Jacques Parizeau to Bloc Québécois leader Lucien Bouchard. Support for independence took off, due in large measure to Bouchard's charismatic style and unsurpassed ability to connect emotionally with francophone Quebecers, but also because of what in retrospect can be seen to have been a terribly uninspired campaign by the federalists. Prime Minister Jean Chrétien chose to stay on the sidelines until the last couple of weeks of the campaign, when polls showed the "yes" side to be leading. His previous refusal to make any concrete constitutional offer to Quebec wavered during the period before the vote, when he suggested that he supported constitutional recognition of Quebec as a distinct society and a Quebec veto over any future constitutional reform. On 30 October 1995, the "no" side emerged with the narrowest of victories: 49.6 per cent against independence, 48.5 per cent for, with spoiled ballots accounting for the rest.

The federal government's reluctance to deal with the issue of constitutional reform and with Quebec's demands before the 1995 referendum forced its hand was due in great measure to its realization that, outside Quebec, Canadians' reactions to the constitutional issue tended to range from indifference to deep hostility. But as their uncertain performance in the Quebec referendum campaign showed, the Liberals' silence may also have been due to their inability to formulate a response to the sovereignty option that was not simply Meech Lake or Charlottetown redux.

This inability can be traced to the Liberal model of federalism that took shape during the Trudeau era. Although not centralist in any absolute sense—Canada has surely been among the least centralized federal systems in the world for many decades—it

assumes that a strong central government is essential to the maintenance of Canadian unity. Moreover, this model is in general opposed to what is called "asymmetrical federalism," i.e., the constitutional recognition of differences in the status and powers of provincial governments; in particular, it is against constitutional entrenchment of special status for Quebec. The Constitution Act of 1982, particularly the Charter and the denial of a right of constitutional veto to any single province, embodies this vision of federalism.

This model is, of course, hotly contested. The main challenge comes from Quebec nationalists, not only from separatists but also from Quebec's nationalist-federalists. This latter group, which includes the Liberal Party of Quebec, maintains that constitutional reforms, including, at a minimum, recognition of Quebec's special responsibility for the protection and promotion of the French language in Canada and a Quebec veto over constitutional change, are necessary to keep Quebecers interested in Canadian federalism. These demands, all of which go back to the ill-fated Meech Lake Accord, were restated by Quebec's Liberal government in its 2017 policy paper on Canadian federalism and the constitution.[34] Although Prime Minister Justin Trudeau had a mainly cordial relationship with the Liberal government of Quebec, led by Philippe Couillard, he very quickly and very publicly expressed his government's lack of interest in reopening a conversation on Quebec's place in the federation.

State Interests and Intergovernmental Conflict

The fact that Quebec is overwhelmingly francophone gives it a special set of interests that any Quebec government feels bound to defend. Likewise, grain farming and resource extraction in Saskatchewan, petroleum in Alberta, the automotive industry in Ontario, and forestry in British Columbia shape the positions taken by the governments of these provinces on taxation, trade, and other policies affecting these interests. Each province comprises a particular constellation of economic, social, and cultural interests that together

"Oui" supporters rally on the floor of the Palais des congrès in Montreal as they wait for the results of the 1995 referendum vote (left); "Non" supporters react to poll results as the pro-Canada vote inches up to 50 per cent en route to a slim victory in the 1995 sovereignty referendum (right).

influence the demands its provincial government makes on federalism. Intergovernmental conflict, then, is to some extent the clash of conflicting regional interests.

This is, however, only part of the explanation. Governments do not simply reflect societal interests. They actively shape these interests through their policies, sometimes deliberately and other times inadvertently. Moreover, governments have their own political and administrative interests, the pursuit of which may have nothing to do with the interests of those they represent. "Canadian federalism," Alan Cairns has argued, "is about governments, governments that are possessed of massive human and financial resources, that are driven by purposes fashioned by elites, and that accord high priority to their own long-term institutional self-interest."[35] This state-centred interpretation of federalism maintains that conflicts between governments are likely to be generated, or at least influenced, by the "institutional self-interest" of politicians and bureaucrats.

The evidence in support of this view is overwhelming. Intergovernmental turf wars, over their respective shares of particular tax fields and over which level will have jurisdiction over what policy areas, often seem remote from the concerns of Canadian citizens. A recent example, mentioned earlier in this chapter, involves the ongoing impasse between Ottawa and most of the provincial governments over the regulation of the securities industry in Canada. The federal government has a perspective on this issue that reflects its national responsibilities and goals for Canada's capital markets and financial industries. The provinces have their own interests that are tied to their existing systems of securities market regulation. Provincial governments have tended to see Ottawa's ambition to create a national system of securities regulation as, in Kendrick Lo's words, "a 'power grab' in which the provinces are poised to lose control over important levers that impact their economic growth. There is also concern that a 'national' regulator may, in fact, serve to prioritize the interests of select provinces (e.g. Ontario)."[36] One suspects most Canadians, including many who have investments through their financial institutions or employment pension funds, probably don't care very much, or at all, about whether Ottawa or the provinces regulate securities markets. But looked at from the state's point of view, having regulatory authority matters in terms of government's ability to promote its particular goals.

Cairns's argument directs our attention to the institutional motivations that might be expected to influence the preferences and behaviour of politicians and bureaucrats, motivations that are not simply their responses to public opinion and the demands made on them by organized interests. The dynamic of federalism, he argues, is in large measure shaped by intergovernmental rivalries—turf wars, one might even say—over control of revenue sources, legislative authority, and credit in the public eye for programs and spending that are popular with at least some segments of the population. His argument contributed to the concept of *province-building*. This involves the process of developing larger and more sophisticated provincial states, whose governments are more assertive in their relations with Ottawa. The concept is premised on Cairns's argument that elected governments and their bureaucracies, possessed of significant legislative and revenue-raising powers under the Constitution and supported by province-oriented economic interests, will attempt to shape economic and social development in their province in accordance with their own preferences and needs. Historically, analyses of province-building focused mainly on the provincial governments of Quebec and Alberta. For their different reasons—a nationalist agenda in the case of Quebec and conflict with Ottawa over the management of petroleum resources in the case of Alberta—these provinces were more likely than others to aggressively pursue greater control over their respective economies and provincial societies. Some commentators have argued that the concept of province-building might once have been useful in explaining the behaviour of some provincial governments and their conflicts with Ottawa, but that it was no longer particularly relevant by the 1980s.[37]

Others disagree. In a 2015 analysis, Wilder and Howlett argue that the concept has never been more useful than in recent times. They note that there has been an increasing realization that subnational governments play a major role in political systems, like Canada's, characterized by multi-level governance. They recast the concept in the following manner: "'Province-building' is primarily an attitude and secondarily a programme pursued on the part of provincial governments to fulfill provincial goals within established constitutional limits, but limits that may nevertheless be pushed. Critical to the concept is the notion that governments truly engaged in province-building will, if necessary and if resources permit, pursue provincial goals regardless of the frictions that may be produced between levels of government."[38]

Understood in this manner, the concept of province-building directs our attention to the motivations and resources—institutional, constitutional, and in terms of revenue capacity—that may shape the priorities and positions of provincial states in their relations with Ottawa. The earlier work on province-building was influenced by the specific historical circumstances that led to some provinces, notably Alberta and Quebec, developing more assertive postures towards the federal government and building their own state capacities to better control economic and other activities within their provincial borders. Wilder and Howlett's reformulation of province-building does not rely on these or other contingent historical circumstances. Moreover, it appears to help explain what they describe as "recent patterns of policy development indicat[ing] that the influence of provincial governments is once again on the rise . . . , as initiatives in primary resource extraction, transportation, and technological and knowledge-based sectors are demonstrative of provincial leadership in many high profile and emergent policy areas."[39]

Intergovernmental Relations

The Constitution, we have seen, does not establish a neat division of legislative and taxation powers between Ottawa and the provinces. All of the chief sources of public revenue—personal and corporate income taxes, payroll taxes, sales taxes, royalties on natural resources and public-sector borrowing—are shared between the two levels of government. Likewise, both the federal and provincial governments are involved in all the major policy fields. Defence and monetary policy come closest to being exclusive federal terrain, although provincial governments do not hesitate to express their views on such issues as the location of armed forces bases, major defence purchases, and interest rates. On the provincial side, snow removal, refuse

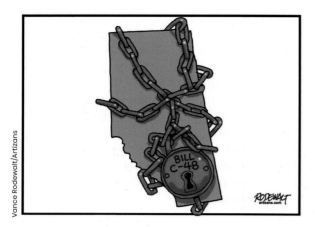

Vance Rodewalt/Artizans

With falling oil prices and a declining oil industry, Albertans like this cartoonist have come to see federal initiatives like Bill C-48 as a constraint on their provincial economy. Bill C-48, the Oil Tanker Moratorium Act, intended to prevent the transport of crude oil along British Columbia's north coast following an oil spill in a major fishing area off the coast of the Great Bear Rainforest, illustrates how provincial governments can find themselves at cross-purposes not only with the federal government, but with each other.

collection, and sidewalk maintenance are the sorts of local activities that supposedly are free from federal involvement. But not entirely: the money that Ottawa transfers annually to the provinces affects the amounts that provincial governments pay to their municipalities, thereby having an impact on municipalities' ability to carry out these local functions.

Divided jurisdiction has given rise to a sprawling and complicated network of relations linking the federal and provincial governments. This network has often been compared to an iceberg, only a small part of which is visible to the eye. The "visible" tip of intergovernmental relations involves meetings of the prime minister and provincial premiers (first ministers' conferences) and meetings of provincial premiers. These meetings, which have become less frequent in recent years, always generate considerable media attention and some part of their proceedings usually takes place

before the television cameras (see Figure 8.2). Less publicized, but far more frequent, are the hundreds of annual meetings between federal and provincial cabinet ministers and bureaucrats. Many of these meetings take place in the context of ongoing federal–provincial structures like the Continuing Committee on Economic and Fiscal Matters, established in 1955, and the Economic and Regional Development Agreements negotiated between Ottawa and the less affluent provinces. Others are generated by the wide range of shared-cost activities that link the two levels of government, from major spending programs such as the Canada Health Transfer and Canada Social Transfer to smaller federal subsidies such as for official minority-language education. In the 2017–18 fiscal year, 138 federal–provincial meetings took place at the level of ministers, deputy ministers, and other senior officials, including one first ministers' meeting.[40]

Executive federalism is a term sometimes used to describe the relations between cabinet ministers and other high-ranking officials of the two levels of government. The negotiations between them and the agreements they reach are usually undertaken with minimal, if any, input from either legislatures or the public. The lack of transparency characteristic of this decision-making process, combined with the fact that the distinction between federal and provincial responsibilities is often blurred by the deals it produces, has generated charges that executive federalism is undemocratic. First, it is undemocratic because it undermines the role of elected legislatures whose role, if they have one at all, is usually limited to ratifying *faits accomplis*. Second, an agreement to finance jointly the cost of a program or to share a particular tax field or legislative power makes it difficult for citizens to determine which level of government should be held responsible for what policies. Third, executive federalism provides no meaningful opportunities for public debate of intergovernmental issues that affect the standard of health-care services, environmental conditions, post-secondary education, energy and natural resources, and other matters of real concern

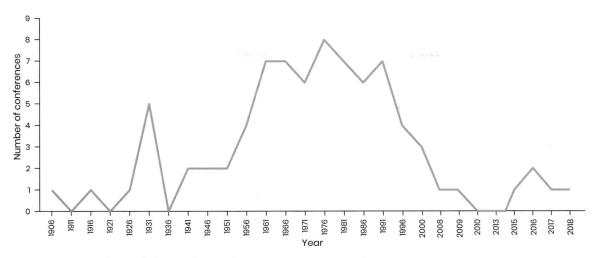

FIGURE 8.2 First Ministers' Conferences, 1906–2018

Source: Adapted with author updates from Canadian Intergovernmental Conference Secretariat, "First Ministers' Conferences, 1906–2004," www.scics.gc.ca/CMFiles/fmp_e.pdf.

to citizens. Political parties, interest groups, and individual Canadians generally are excluded from a decision-making process dominated by cabinet ministers and intergovernmental affairs specialists of the two levels of government.

While these criticisms ought to be taken seriously, it is hard to imagine how intergovernmental affairs could operate in Canada without the architecture and processes of executive federalism. Overlapping authority is an unavoidable fact of life under Canada's federal Constitution. In light of this, is it realistic to imagine that complex administrative and financial agreements can be negotiated in public forums? And besides, much of policy-making is carried on in a closed fashion, dominated by cabinet ministers and bureaucratic elites. Nevertheless, the characteristics of executive federalism are out of sync with the expectations many Canadians have about how governance should be conducted. Governments will continue to conduct much of their negotiations behind closed doors and the constitutional division of powers will continue to be characterized by overlap, competition, and ambiguity. But public acceptance of this and other elitist forms of policy-making is today much weaker than in decades past.

Fiscal Federalism

From the beginning, money has been at the centre of intergovernmental relations. The Confederation agreement included an annual per capita subsidy that Ottawa would pay to all provincial governments.[41] Moreover, the new federal government agreed to assume liability for the debts of the provinces as they stood in 1867.[42] Taxation powers were divided between the two levels of government, with Ottawa receiving what were at the time the major sources of public revenue.

These financial arrangements have never been adequate. Over time, the provinces' legislative responsibilities became much more extensive and expensive than the founders had anticipated. This has been referred to as the **fiscal gap**. Provincial governments attempted to fill this gap between their revenues and their expenditure requirements through an increasing array of provincial taxes. Licence fees, succession duties, and personal and corporate income taxes all were used to increase provincial revenues. In addition, the provinces pressed Ottawa for more money. Indeed, only two years after Confederation the federal subsidy paid to Nova Scotia was increased. An important precedent was thereby established: federal–provincial financial relations are determined by governments, not by the Constitution.

Today, combined provincial and local revenues and expenditures surpass those of Ottawa. This was not always the case. In 1950 combined provincial and local revenues were about half those of the federal government. Seventy years later, combined provincial and local own-source revenues—excluding transfers from Ottawa—exceed those of the federal government by about 25 per cent.[43] The revenue position of the provinces improved steadily between the 1950s and the 1970s, as Ottawa conceded *tax room*—i.e., an increasing share of particular revenue sources such as the personal income tax—to provincial governments that were keen to improve their fiscal capacity. But at the same time, provincial dependence on transfer payments from Ottawa remains high in several provinces. Annual federal transfers to the provinces range from a high of about $4,500 in the case of PEI to roughly $1,700–$1,800 per person for BC and Alberta. These sums do not include federal transfers to persons, which also range widely between provinces and are sensitive to the state of economic conditions in a province. These range from a high of over $4,000 per person in Newfoundland and Labrador to less than half that in Alberta.[44]

To an important degree this provincial dependence has been encouraged by Ottawa through **shared-cost programs**. These are provincially administered programs where Ottawa's financial contribution is geared to the amount that a province spends. In the 1960s, when many of the most expensive shared-cost programs were being put in place, it was common for Ottawa to match provincial spending dollar for dollar and without a limit on Ottawa's financial commitment to the total cost of the program. This was true of the Canada Assistance Plan (CAP), created in 1966 to help finance welfare and other provincial social services. Beginning in 1991 Ottawa placed a cap on the annual increase in its contribution to provinces under this plan. Four years later the federal government replaced CAP with the Canada Health and Social Transfer to the provinces, the amount of which was not geared to provincial spending.

Federal grants to the provinces for health care and post-secondary education also were launched on a shared-cost basis, but were converted by Ottawa into **block funding** programs through the Federal–Provincial Fiscal Arrangements Act of 1977. The federal government argued, reasonably enough, that the shared-cost formula did not encourage the provinces to control program costs. Under block funding, Ottawa's financial contribution is geared to the previous year's subsidy plus an amount calculated on the basis of growth in the recipient province's gross product. Ottawa is not obliged to match provincial spending; indeed, the effect of the switch to block funding has been to transfer an increasing share of the burden of health care and post-secondary education costs onto the shoulders of the provinces.

But perhaps this is where the burden belongs. After all, these social programs fall under the constitutional jurisdiction of the provinces. For their part the provincial governments argued that Ottawa encouraged them to spend more on social services by offering to share program costs on a matching basis without a limit on total spending. It was unfair, they claimed, for the federal government to try to back out of financing policy areas whose growth it encouraged. In fact, the government of British Columbia launched a court challenge in response to Ottawa's 1991 cap on the annual increase in federal transfers for social assistance. The Supreme Court ruled, however, that Ottawa had acted within its constitutional authority.[45] The provinces' second complaint was that their ability to increase their own-source revenues to compensate for reduced federal transfer payments is limited because they share all of the major tax fields with Ottawa. Unless the federal government is willing to give up some tax room (i.e., some of its share of total tax revenue from a particular source) to the provinces, provincial governments face the hard choice of increasing the total tax burden on their citizens, charging or increasing user fees (e.g., tuition fees), or cutting back on program expenditures. A third grievance came from the less affluent provinces. They argued that any reduction in Ottawa's commitment to financing provincial social services hurts the poorer provinces more than it does the wealthier ones. The Maritime provinces in particular have been and continue to be dependent on federal transfers to maintain a level of social services comparable to that in other provinces. Figure 8.3 shows the difference between per capita federal revenues raised in each province and per capita federal transfers to each province in 2017. To express this a bit differently, Ottawa's contribution to provincial budgets typically ranges from a low of about one-tenth of total provincial spending to over one-third in the case of the Maritime provinces. The territories are far more dependent on federal transfers, at 75, 80, and 90 per cent for Yukon, NWT, and Nunavut, respectively, in 2017–18.

Some funding Ottawa transfers to the provinces carries conditions as to how it must be spent. These are called conditional grants. Transfers with no strings attached are called unconditional grants. Important examples of both include the following:

Conditional

- Provincial social assistance programs, financed in part by the Canada Social Transfer, must be based exclusively on need, and must

not make previous residency in the province a condition for receiving benefits.

- The block transfers that Ottawa makes to the provinces under the Canada Health Transfer (CHT) must be spent on health care and the Canada Social Transfer (CST) must be spent on post-secondary education and social services.

- The Canada Health Act, 1984 includes a provision that reduces Ottawa's payment to provincial governments that permit physicians to extra-bill their patients. The terms of the CHT and CST also specify that provinces must respect the principles of the Canada Health Act, 1965 (portability of coverage between provinces, comprehensiveness of provincial plans, universality, public funding, and public administration). Ottawa's contribution to provincial healthcare spending, therefore, is subject to some conditions (see Box 8.6).

Unconditional

- Equalization grants are paid to provincial governments whose per capita tax revenues (according to a complex formula

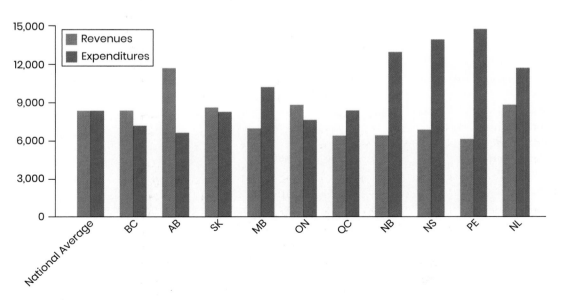

FIGURE 8.3 Federal Per Capita Revenues and Expenditures by Province, 2017

Source: © Library of Parliament.

negotiated between Ottawa and the provinces) fall below the average of the two most affluent provinces. **Equalization** accounts for about one-quarter of all federal cash transfers to the provinces and about one-fifth of the total revenue of the least affluent provincial governments. It carries no conditions as to how it must be spent (see Box 8.5).

Table 8.3 provides a breakdown of federal transfers to the provinces.

The adequacy of federal transfers is not the only issue that has set Ottawa against the provincial governments. Another long-standing complaint of the provinces is that shared-cost programs distort provincial spending priorities because of the enticement of federal grants. Ottawa's spending power, they argue, permits undue federal interference in matters of provincial jurisdiction. Over the years the government of Quebec has been most insistent about this. Indeed, during the 1950s the provincial government of Maurice Duplessis refused to accept federal money for the construction of Quebec's portion of the Trans-Canada Highway and for universities, and was not even compensated for the fact that Canadian taxpayers residing in Quebec were paying for these programs in the other provinces. In 1965 the Quebec government of Jean Lesage opted out of the newly created Canada Assistance Plan (although Quebec has never been freed from the fairly minimal program standards that Ottawa sets) and some other conditional grant programs,

TABLE 8.3 Federal Transfers to Provinces and Territories, 2010–11 to 2019–20

Major Transfers	(millions of dollars)									
	2010–11	2011–12	2012–13	2013–14	2014–15	2015–16	2016–17	2017–18	2018–19	2019–20
Canada Health Transfer	25,672	26,952	28,569	30,283	32,113	34,026	36,068	37,150	38,584	40,373
Canada Social Transfer	11,179	11,514	11,859	12,215	12,582	12,959	13,348	13,748	14,161	14,586
Equalization	14,372	14,659	15,423	16,105	16,669	17,341	17,880	18,254	18,958	19,837
Offshore Offsets	869	787	443	350	196	125	44	36	–72	–64
Territorial Formula Financing	2,664	2,876	3,111	3,288	3,469	3,561	3,603	3,682	3,785	3,948
Total Transfer Protection	525	952	680	56						
Total—Federal Support	55,281	57,739	60,085	62,297	65,029	68,013	70,943	72,870	75,416	78,680
Per Capita Allocation (dollars)	*1,628*	*1,683*	*1,731*	*1,774*	*1,832*	*1,900*	*1,959*	*1,997*	*2,038*	*2,097*

Source: Reproduced with the permission of the Department of Finance, 2019 https://www.fin.gc.ca/fedprov/mtp-eng.asp.

BOX 8.5 Equalization: Is It about Fairness and Sharing, or Politics and Buying Votes?

Equalization grants have often been described as a reflection of the Canadian soul. Here is what the Honourable Howard Pawley, former premier of Manitoba, says in their defence:

> No Canadian should have his or her life chances determined solely by geography. Canadians enjoy a political culture much like a family; we are all responsible for each other. These principles, enshrined in our Constitution, differentiate us from our friends in the United States where no such program exists. The vehicle for leveling the national playing field is the country's equalization program. Because of equalization, the gap between richer and poorer provinces has been reduced. The Canadian people understand the principle. [Polls demonstrate] that overwhelming majorities in each province support equalization.[46]

Some critics of equalization view matters differently. A recent study by Marcelin Joanis argues that, notwithstanding the fact that equalization and other federal transfers to the provinces are based on agreed formulas, politics appears to influence who gets how much and when. He writes:

> [B]oth equalization payments and social transfers are, inevitably, arranged by federal politicians, and politicians have a natural tendency to behave politically. An analysis shows that, in many cases, the amount of money a province receives in federal transfers is correlated with the way that province voted during federal elections. In other words, when a province exhibited dominant support for the national party that controls the federal purse strings, that province often received a greater share of federal transfers. Where provinces were largely unsupportive in a federal election for the victorious party, they were more likely to see their share of federal transfers shrink.[47]

Joanis's conclusions about the role of politics find some support in another recent study of equalization in Canada. Observing that Quebec annually receives most of the total amount of this money transferred to the provinces, Daniel Béland and his colleagues write: "Equalization has most likely helped federalists in Quebec make the case against independence. . . . The economic arguments in favour of Quebec remaining part of Canada have often featured reference, sometimes explicit and other times implicit, to the equalization program as important to the financing of the province's social programs."[48] They add that this may not be a bad thing if equalization has the effect of contributing to national unity by blunting arguments for Quebec independence.

Of course there is no reason to conclude that equalization is all about fairness and a compassionate ethic of sharing, or just about politics and electoral considerations. It can be, and has been, about both.

receiving compensation in the form of tax room surrendered by Ottawa to the province. Both the Meech Lake and Charlottetown Accords included a provision that would have obligated Ottawa to provide "reasonable compensation" to any provincial government choosing not to participate in a new national shared-cost program, so long as the province's own program was "compatible with the national objectives." Critics argued that this opened the door for an erosion of **national standards** in social policy. Defenders claimed that this provision would simply have constitutionalized a long-standing practice in Canadian federalism.

Governing Realities

BOX 8.6 Health Care and Federalism: Canada's Second Longest-Running Soap Opera

After the issue of Quebec's constitutional status, health care has a reasonable claim to being Canadian federalism's second longest-running soap opera. Elements of intrigue, betrayal, and good and evil intermingle in a story that reveals much about the nature of intergovernmental relations.

It may seem odd that there is a story to be told, given the frequent claim that health is an area of exclusive provincial jurisdiction under the Constitution. But the reality is much more complicated. As the Supreme Court observed in a 1982 ruling, "'health' is not a matter which is subject to specific constitutional assignment but instead is an amorphous topic which can be addressed by valid federal or provincial legislation, depending on the circumstances of each case on the nature or scope of the health problem in question."[49] Although the provinces reject the Court's reasoning, Ottawa has been able to enter the field of health care through its spending power, its authority over criminal law, POGG, and several other constitutional levers that include authority with respect to Indigenous affairs, patents, some aspects of the environment, and sports and fitness.[50]

A "soap opera digest" summary of how the story has unfolded might go something like this. Ottawa and the provincial governments co-operated during the 1960s to create a national health-care system that would be administered by the provinces, but where they would share the costs with the federal government. Ottawa, flush with revenue in the 1960s and disposed to encourage provinces to spend money on social programs under provincial jurisdiction, agreed to match provincial spending on health care, a formula that provided little incentive for the provinces to control costs. The feds began to back away from this open-ended commitment to health care in the late 1970s. Over the next 20 years the federal contribution to health care, as a share of total public spending on health, would drop dramatically from about 50 per cent to 20 per cent.

Provincial cries of betrayal were met with federal accusations of provincial treachery, as Ottawa accused some of the provinces of allowing creeping privatization and the importation of "American-style" health care. No one could agree on the numbers. Ottawa protested that its contribution was much greater than the provinces claimed, if the mysterious phenomenon of "tax points" were included. Ottawa threatened to withhold dollars from Alberta in a struggle characterized by some as nothing short of good, compassionate Canadianism versus evil, individualistic conservatism.

By the end of the 1990s Ottawa and several of the provinces launched major studies of the health-care system, producing duelling reports on what was wrong and

Federalism and Democracy

Federalism has often been seen as a system of government that arises from and protects democratic values and processes. It is, wrote Pierre Trudeau, "an attempt to find a rational compromise between the divergent interest groups which history has thrown together; but it is a compromise based on the will of the people."[54] Trudeau was influenced by, among others, the French philosopher Ernest Renan, a great admirer of the Swiss federation. Renan called Switzerland "la nation la plus légitimement composée" (the most legitimately formed nation). It was comprised of communities that differed ethnically, linguistically, and religiously, but these diverse groups shared political values that enable them to come together and support the national state while retaining their autonomy in local and cultural matters.

James Madison, one of the founders of the American Republic, also saw democratic virtue in federalism. In *The Federalist Papers*, No. 51, what we what to do about it. Alberta's Mazankowski Report recommended greater room for private elements to operate alongside the public health-care system. Ottawa's Romanow Report recommended more spending—much more spending—as a major part of the solution to the system's woes. In early 2004, Ottawa and the provinces agreed to a deal whereby $41.3 billion in new health-care funding would be transferred to the provinces over the following 10 years. This ensured that the federal contribution to provincial health-care spending did not decline during the period of the agreement and, to some degree, reduced the intergovernmental tension associated with health-care spending.[51]

But not entirely. Half a century after its first episode, there is little likelihood that the Canadian health-care soap opera will disappear from the prime-time schedule anytime soon. It was an important campaign issue in the 2004 and 2006 federal elections, and could easily become so again. In 2012 the Parliamentary Budget Officer, Kevin Page, issued a report in which he stated that Ottawa's contributions to health care would keep pace with provincial spending until 2016–17, after which they would be tied to the rate of economic growth.[52] Assuming that increases in health-care spending continue to outstrip the rate of increase in the economy, which has been the case for years, this means that Ottawa's share of total health-care spending will begin to fall. This would be good for Ottawa, Page notes, giving it more leeway to cut taxes and pay down its debt, but would leave the provinces with harder choices about cutting spending, increasing taxes, or both. Page's successor, Jean-Denis Fréchette, estimates that demographic change alone will add almost 2 per cent per year to public health-care spending over the period from 2017 to 2042, which will account for about 43 per cent of projected growth in what is already the most expensive category of government spending.[53]

Faced with these numbers, the Trudeau government chose to follow the announced policy of its predecessor, the Harper Conservative government, reducing the annual increases in the value of CHT transfers to the provinces from 6 to 3 per cent. By 2017, after one-on-one negotiations with all the provincial and territorial governments, individual deals were struck between Ottawa and all of these governments, taking into account provincial variations in demographics and certain other factors. The ball has been placed squarely in the court of the provinces to manage their health-care spending in ways that will bring the drivers of health-care cost increases within the limits that Ottawa has now set on its contribution increases to the CHT.

If there is a federalism lesson to be learned from the last 40 years of intergovernmental co-operation and conflict in health care it is this: sharing the costs of an expensive policy area is a prescription for political and bureaucratic rivalry, muddied accountability, and mutual recriminations. This soap opera can be expected to run for many more seasons.

might today consider a rather erudite op-ed piece advocating adoption of the United States Constitution, Madison makes the case for federalism as a means for reducing the likelihood that a majority may emerge and impose its will on minority interests. By dividing political authority between two levels of government, he argued, local interests are better protected from national majorities. Moreover, the division of authority also ensures that the power of each level of government is limited, thereby providing another layer of protection for the rights and freedoms of citizens (see Box 8.7).

In more recent times federalism has been advocated as a means for managing and ultimately eliminating the factors that historically have led to conflict and even war between traditional nation-states. The construction of the European Union since the 1950s has been premised precisely on the idea that bringing nation-states together in a union that over time has acquired more and more of the features associated with federalism (EU-wide elections and a common EU parliament, a common currency used in most of the EU, and various institutions, including the European Commission and

Politics in Focus

BOX 8.7 James Madison on the Democratic Virtues of Federalism

In a single republic, all the power surrendered by the people is submitted to the administration of a single government; and the usurpations are guarded against by a division of the government into distinct and separate departments. In the compound republic of America, the power surrendered by the people is first divided between two distinct governments, and then the portion allotted to each subdivided among distinct and separate departments. Hence a double security arises to the rights of the people. The different governments will control each other, at the same time that each will be controlled by itself. Second. It is of great importance in a republic not only to guard the society against the oppression of its rulers, but to guard one part of the society against the injustice of the other part. Different interests necessarily exist in different classes of citizens. If a majority be united by a common interest, the rights of the minority will be insecure.

Source: *The Federalist Papers*, No. 51.

the European Court of Justice, whose rulings apply to all member states), while retaining member-state autonomy with respect to many important matters. In a part of the world where nation-state rivalries had produced two world wars and had seen the emergence of authoritarian nationalism, the idea of European federalism has been seen as the best protection against these dangers.

In recent decades federalism has been heralded as a democratic answer to the problem of some identity groups not being provided with adequate recognition by the state. Thus, such philosophers as James Tulley, Charles Taylor, and Amy Gutmann[55] have argued that federalism may be one of the most effective ways through which multi-nation states may provide recognition to such groups as the *québécois* or Indigenous peoples, enabling them to exercise what federalism scholar Daniel Elazar has called self-rule within a larger context of shared rule.[56]

Not everyone, however, is convinced that federalism has the democratic properties ascribed to it by its advocates. Madison's argument that, other things being equal, federalism will help to prevent majorities from imposing their will is seen as undemocratic by those who believe that majoritarianism is at the core of democratic governance. By making regions the basis for representation, and in many cases over-representing the smaller populations of some regions, this may increase the

influence of these smaller regional populations and even give them a veto in national decision-making. Some will see this as a good thing, but there is no *a priori* reason to assume so. Moreover, and as we have seen in the preceding pages, intergovernmental processes and agreements under federalism are often very complicated, conducted and agreed to by elites, and therefore lacking in democratic transparency.

In addition to these complaints is another that comes particularly from the left. Turning Madison's reasoning on its head, this criticism of federalism argues that by making it more difficult for the will of a national majority to emerge, democratic reforms will more easily be thwarted by interests that are able to express their objections through regional governments or, in a case such as the United States Senate, through regional representation at the national level of government. A related criticism is that by recognizing and even amplifying the importance of regions in politics and governance, other interests and issues, particularly those associated with social class, may receive less attention than they warrant. This argument has been made by the Canadian left since the Great Depression of the 1930s, when those on the left lamented what they saw as federalism's obstruction of the reforms they believed necessary to deal with the economic and social problems of the times. It continued during the 1960s when the influential Canadian sociologist John Porter argued that "Federalism can provide an excuse for federal politicians not acting against the interest of the corporate economy," and that "federalism has imposed a conservative tone on the Canadian political system and political parties, and has inhibited creative political leadership."[57] The criticism continues to the present day. What many saw as the Harper Conservative government's preference for a more decentralized model of federalism that involved a somewhat diminished policy role for Ottawa was routinely criticized by those on the Canadian left as a cover for a conservative political agenda.[58] Today, whether the issue is environmental protection, health care, addressing poverty, or promoting equality rights, Canada's comparatively decentralized model of federalism is likely to be seen by those on the left as an obstacle to democratic progress.

It is probably fair to conclude that there is nothing inherent in federalism that makes it more or less likely than unitary government to protect and promote democracy. It could be, as some argue, that in a multi-national country such as Canada, Belgium, or Switzerland, federalism is more likely than unitary government to provide meaningful opportunities for ethnolinguistic communities to control those policy matters that matter most for the protection of their culture. It could also be that in those federal countries that are not characterized by these sorts of multi-national divisions, such as the United States, Australia, Germany, and Austria, federalism provides democratic benefits in the sense that it places power over some matters in the hands of representatives who are closer to and accountable to the regional communities most directly affected by these matters.

Whether federalism helps or hinders the achievement of the sorts of outcomes that one associates with democracy depends in large measure on what one means by democracy. These outcomes are likely to be affected by many factors that are unrelated to whether the country has a federal or unitary constitution. Canada has a federal constitution, but its welfare state is less generous and economic inequality is greater than in unitary Sweden or Denmark.

If we take seriously any of the many international rankings of democracy, such as The Economist Democracy Index,[59] states with federal constitutions are not more likely to be found among the most democratic countries than those with unitary ones. Federalism can make a difference in the democratic health of a country. It is likely to be less important, however, than a number of other factors.

Summing Up

For most Canadians, the Constitution evokes the Charter and the rights and freedoms that it protects. This is an important part of the Canadian Constitution. But so, too, is federalism. Indeed, the division of powers between Ottawa and the provinces has had more of an impact on the day-to-day lives of Canadians than has the Charter, as important as that latter addition to the Constitution has been. Federalism has shaped matters of taxation, health care, post-secondary education, economic and cultural regulation, interprovincial trade, environmental regulation, transportation, and much more. And yet most Canadians are hard-pressed to correctly identify what level of government is responsible for what policies.

To some degree they can't be blamed. Canadian federalism is characterized by a high degree of overlapping jurisdiction between the powers of Ottawa and the provinces. Some of the policy fields that we believe to be important today were not even anticipated when the division of powers was enshrined in the Constitution Act, 1867. The fact that Ottawa influences provincial legislative domains through what has come to be known as its spending power is something unknown to most Canadians and unmentioned in the written Constitution. Moreover, surveys show that most Canadians have little idea of whether the financing of their hospitals, schools, roads, and other services and infrastructure are dependent on tax revenue raised in other parts of Canada and transferred to their provincial governments by Ottawa. While the Charter is often the subject of media headlines and stories, federalism and its intricacies tend to be framed as personal feuds between the prime minister and premiers or in some other manner that overlooks the role of the constitutional division of powers.

The reality of governance in Canada is such that a knowledge of federalism is indispensable. It is necessary in order to understand which level of government has responsibility of what policy functions, who has what revenue-raising powers, and how conflicts between their sometimes rival claims have been resolved. Federalism complicates the citizen's task in determining government accountability. All the more reason why some knowledge of these matters is needed.

Starting Points for Research

Herman Bakvis and Grace Skogstad, eds, *Canadian Federalism: Performance, Effectiveness, and Legitimacy*, 3rd edn (Toronto: Oxford University Press, 2012). This is an excellent collection on Canadian federalism and intergovernmental relations.

Daniel Béland, André Lecours, Gregory P. Marchildon, Haizhen Mou, and M. Rose Olfert, *Fiscal Federalism and Equalization Policy in Canada: Political and Economic Dimensions* (Toronto: University of Toronto Press, 2017). The best recent analysis of the financial dimensions of Canadian federalism.

Mowat Centre, https://mowatcentre.ca/research/intergovernmental-economic-social-policy/; Queen's University, Institute of Intergovernmental Relations, https://www.queensu.ca/iigr/links/organizations. Both of these research institutes carry out research on federalism and intergovernmental relations, the Mowat Centre (now closed) focusing principally on Ontario. Excellent resources may be found at their websites.

David E. Smith, *Federalism and the Constitution of Canada* (Toronto: University of Toronto Press, 2010). A marvellous history of Canadian federalism from its origins by one of Canada's foremost experts on the subject.

Review Exercises

1. What is the Council of the Federation (http://www.canadaspremiers.ca/about/)? Do you think it plays an important role in intergovernmental relations? Should its role be strengthened and perhaps even included in the Constitution? Why or why not?
2. Visit the website for one of the provincial or territorial governments. Make a list of the main public issues discussed at the site. What information is provided about the relationship of the province's/territory's finances and programs to Ottawa?
3. Does it matter which level of government pays for what share of health-care costs and which government or governments set the rules for health policy? In answering this question be sure to address the issues of constitutionality, political accountability, Canadian values, and taxpayer interests.

Members of Parliament pose for a group photo in the newly renovated West Block of Parliament Hill, which will serve as the temporary home for the House of Commons until at least 2029 as the Centre Block undergoes renovation. (THE CANADIAN PRESS/Sean Kilpatrick)

9 The Machinery of Government

Modern government is a vast and complicated affair. This chapter examines the key components of the machinery of government, including the following topics:

- The monarch and governor general
- The prime minister and cabinet
- Central agencies
- The legislature
- The influence and activities of MPs
- A democratic deficit?
- The courts
- How a law is passed

One frequently hears that Canada's machinery of government is broken, or at least in need of a serious overhaul. Several of the country's most respected political scientists and journalists have complained that power has become too concentrated in the hands of the prime minister and his closest advisers. This, they say, undermines democratic accountability. Some critics charge that the courts have become too powerful, going well beyond their traditional role in interpreting the law to significantly influence policy. It seems that everyone, to one degree or another, agrees that Parliament is dysfunctional. Proposals to reform Question Period, revamp the committee system, loosen party discipline, and make the Senate elected or abolish it entirely are among the many solutions that have been proposed for what are seen to be the legislature's shortcomings. Talk of a democratic deficit has been ongoing for many years, much of this linked to what are believed to be the broken or worn-out parts of the machinery of government.

Before we can judge whether these claims have merit, we need to understand how Canada's system of government operates. The formal organization of the government of Canada is shown in Figure 9.1. Portrayed this way, the structure appears to be quite simple—deceptively simple, as it turns out! The three branches of government coincide with three major functions of democratic governance: the legislature makes the laws; the executive branch implements the laws; and the judicial branch interprets the laws.

In reality, however, these compartments are not watertight. The legislature does indeed debate and pass laws, but these laws typically originate in the executive branch as bills that are seldom expected to change much, if at all, as they make their way through the legislative mill. The legislature, in fact, is dominated by a small group of its members—the prime minister and cabinet—who oversee the executive branch. The judicial branch of government does not, strictly speaking, involve itself in the making of laws. In recent times, however, Canadian courts have played a major role in the determination of policy on such matters as physician-assisted suicide, abortion, Indigenous landownership, the collective bargaining rights

of workers, and same-sex benefits such as pension rights for gays and lesbians and the legal definition of marriage. The courts may truly be said to have made policy, or at least shaped it in decisive ways, on many important public issues. As we saw in Chapter 7, critics of the courts argue that through their responsibility for interpreting the law judges become involved in what amounts to policy-making. The bureaucrats whose job it is to implement the laws passed by Parliament often have enormous discretion in determining the actual meaning of legislation that provides them with only very general guidelines about how the law is to be applied. When elected officials delegate such discretion to non-elected bureaucrats are they not also delegating part of their law-making function?

While the actual operations of the machinery of Canadian government are more complex than its formal organization in Figure 9.1 suggests, nevertheless, the respective roles of the legislative, executive, and judicial branches are significantly different and their differences are rooted in our expectations for democratic government. These expectations can be briefly summarized as follows:

The legislative branch shall . . .
- represent the people and be accountable to them through periodic elections;
- debate public issues and provide a forum for competition between political parties;
- make laws.

The executive branch shall . . .
- implement the laws;
- ensure that the public's business is carried out efficiently, accountably, and in accordance with the law;
- be non-partisan at the bureaucratic level, such that non-elected officials faithfully carry out the policies of whatever party forms the government of the day.

The judicial branch shall . . .
- be non-partisan and free from interference by the government;
- interpret the law's meaning;

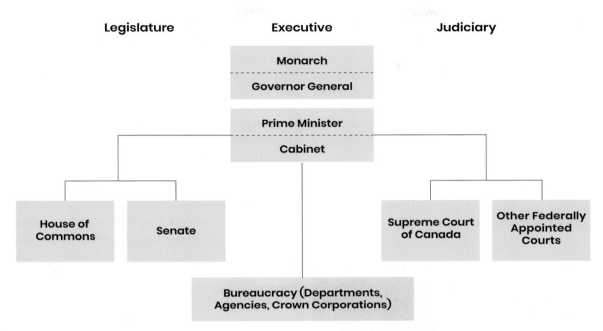

FIGURE 9.1 The Formal Organization of Canadian Government

- not substitute its preferences for those of elected public officials in matters of public policy, as distinct from legal and constitutional interpretation.

Democratic expectations are not, however, immutable. Today, many people expect that the bureaucracy should be representative of the population it serves, an expectation that may affect bureaucratic recruitment and promotion policies. Some argue that it is neither realistic nor desirable to expect non-elected officials to be politically neutral and that accountability for policy (as distinct from its implementation) should be shared between politicians and bureaucrats. The elevated status of Canadian courts in the political process since the Charter of Rights and Freedoms was passed in 1982 has been welcomed by those who see judges as more likely than politicians to protect rights and promote democracy. Others lament that the courts now trespass on turf that properly belongs to the people's elected and accountable representatives. The courts are also expected by many to be representative, instead of being dominated by white males. The under-representation of women and

minorities on the bench, these critics say, undermines the courts' ability to reflect the diverse interests and values of Canadians.

Expectations for our institutions of government are not chiselled in stone. In this chapter we will discuss the main characteristics and functions of the institutions that comprise the machinery of Canadian government, including the changes that have taken place in their roles and the controversies associated with these changes.

The Executive Branch

The Monarch and Governor General

Canada is a constitutional monarchy. The monarch, currently Queen Elizabeth II, embodies the authority of the Canadian state. Any action of the government of Canada is taken in the Queen's name.[1] The monarch is responsible for appointing the prime minister and for deciding when Parliament will be dissolved and a new election held. When she is not in Canada, which is, of course, most of the time, her duties are carried out by the governor general, currently Julie Payette, an engineer and astronaut. Although the strict letter of the Constitution suggests that the role of the monarch in Canada's system of government is a formidable one, most Canadians realize that the Queen and governor general perform mainly symbolic functions. The real decision-making powers of the executive are exercised by the prime minister, who is the head of government, and cabinet.

In matters such as the selection of the prime minister and the dissolution of Parliament, constitutional convention is infinitely more important than the discretion of the monarch. For example,

The Right Honourable Lord Byng of Vimy, pictured in 1921 at the beginning of his tenure as governor general of Canada. William Lyon Mackenzie King used Lord Byng's refusal to dissolve Parliament on his request to push for constitutional changes at the 1926 Imperial Conference, a move that has had a lasting impact on the role of the governor general in Canada and elsewhere in the British Commonwealth.

when one party wins a majority of the seats in an election, the choice of prime minister is automatic. Even when no party has a majority, it is understood that the leader of the party with the most seats will be given the first opportunity to try to form a government that has the support of a majority in the legislature. If, however, it becomes clear that the members of the other parties will not support a government led by this person, the monarch's representative may turn to the leader of the party with the second largest number of seats to try to form a government that has the support of a majority in the legislature. This happened in Ontario after the 1985 provincial election. Whatever the legislative scenarios appear to be, it is understood that a newly elected legislature must at least be given the opportunity to meet. The monarch's representative cannot simply decide that there is no point in convening the legislature and that a new election should be held straightaway.

Likewise in the case of dissolving Parliament, the monarch's discretion is limited by constitutional conventions that have developed over time. Normally, the prime minister's request that Parliament be dissolved and a new election held will be granted automatically. It is remotely conceivable, although highly improbable, that in circumstances of minority government the monarch's representative could refuse such a request and instead ask the leader of another party to try to form a government. The last time this happened was in 1926, when Governor General Lord Byng refused Prime Minister Mackenzie King's request for a new election. This refusal provoked a minor constitutional crisis. Since then, the view of most constitutional experts has been that the monarch's representative is required to accept the "advice" given by the prime minister.

The Byng precedent suddenly and rather unexpectedly became relevant several weeks after the federal election of 2008, which produced a Conservative minority government. The three opposition parties agreed to bring down the government on a motion of non-confidence in the House of Commons. They also agreed to a pact whereby the Liberals and NDP would form a Liberal-led coalition government for a period of at least two years, supported by the BQ. Before they could replace the Conservatives as the government, the governor general would have to refuse Prime Minister Harper's request for a new election. Constitutional experts were divided on the question of whether the governor general would be breaking an important unwritten rule of the Constitution in turning down such a request. In the end, the question became moot when Prime Minister Harper decided to request a prorogation of Parliament until late January 2009, when the government planned to introduce a budget.

The monarch and governor general play no significant role in setting the government's policy agenda or in the subsequent decision-making process. Royal assent to legislation is virtually automatic. It has never been withheld from a law passed by Parliament. On the occasions when the monarch's provincial representatives, the lieutenant-governors, used the disallowance and reservation powers, this was almost always at the behest of the elected government in Ottawa.[2]

What role, then, does the monarchy play in Canada's system of government? We have said that the monarch's role today is primarily a symbolic one. This does not mean that the functions performed by the Queen and governor general—and lieutenant-governors at the provincial level—are unimportant. The ceremonial duties that are part of government must be performed by someone, and it may be that assigning them to a head of state who is above the partisan fray reduces the possibility of too close an association between the political system itself—the state—and the leadership of particular political factions within it. As James Mallory argues, the monarchy "denies to political leaders the full splendor of their power and the excessive aggrandizement of their persons which come from the undisturbed occupancy of the centre of the stage."[3] Perhaps, but it must be admitted that these state functions are performed by an elected president in countries such as the United States and France without there being much evidence that this has imperilled those democracies. On the other hand, both the American and French political systems have legislative checks on executive power that do not exist in a British parliamentary

system. Mallory may be correct, therefore, in his belief that a non-elected head of state serves as a buffer against the self-aggrandizing tendencies of elected politicians. Paradoxically, a non-democratic institution, i.e., an unelected head of state, may contribute to the protection of a democratic social order.

Listen to the "Who Is Canada's Head of State? (And Does It Matter?)" podcast, available at: www.oup.com/he/Brooks9e

But the monarchy has not always been an uncontroversial pillar of stability in Canadian politics. Despite the constitutional fact that the monarch's status in Canada's system of government is that of the King or Queen of Canada, not of the United Kingdom, the institution of monarchy has been perceived by some as an irritating reminder of Canada's colonial ties to Britain and of the historical dominance of Anglo-Canadians in this country's politics. This was particularly true during the 1960s, when royal visits to Quebec acted as lightning rods for the anti-federalist grievances of Quebec nationalists. Ancient memories of English domination and French subordination have faded, but they have not disappeared. The summer 2010 tour of Canada by Queen Elizabeth II avoided Quebec entirely. This may have been due to the fact that the November 2009 visit to Montreal of Prince Charles and Lady Camilla Parker-Bowles occasioned egg-throwing, chants of "le Québéc pour les québécois," and several arrests of demonstrators who were mainly associated with the ultra-nationalist/leftist Réseau de résistance du québécois. The incident suggested that the institution of the monarchy had not entirely lost its power to excite passions in Canada.

Controversy also has arisen from time to time with respect to those who have held the position of governor general. The most important instance of this, discussed in Chapter 6, involved Governor General Lord Byng's refusal to grant Prime Minister Mackenzie King's request for a dissolution of Parliament and the calling of new elections. More recently, some occupants of this role have made public statements that, according to some critics, are not consistent with the expectation, expressed at the official website for the office, that she will "bring Canadians together in a non-partisan way" (see Box 9.1).

Listen to the "Who Should Represent Canada and Why?" podcast, available at: www.oup .com/he/Brooks9e

The Prime Minister and Cabinet

In contrast to the passive and principally symbolic roles of the monarch and governor general, the prime minister (PM) and cabinet are at the centre of the policy-making process. One of the PM's first duties is to select the people who will be cabinet ministers. In the vast majority of cases these will be other elected members of the House of Commons. It has occasionally happened that a senator or two has been appointed to cabinet to give the government representation from a region where the governing party had elected few or no members, or because of the special abilities of a senator. In the British parliamentary tradition, cabinet members are drawn from the same political party as the PM (although the UK had a genuine coalition government from 2010 to 2015, with Liberal-Democratic Party cabinet ministers in a government led by the Conservative Party under Prime Minister David Cameron). In recent decades the size of the federal cabinet has ranged from a low of 20 to a high of almost 40 members. Provincial cabinets are somewhat smaller.

The power of the PM and cabinet rests on a combination of factors. One of these is the written Constitution. Section 11 of the Constitution Act, 1867 states that "There shall be a Council to aid and advise in the Government of Canada, to be styled the Queen's Privy Council for Canada." Section 13 of that Act goes even further to specify that the actions of the monarch's representative in Canada, the governor general, shall be undertaken "by and with the Advice of the Queen's Privy Council for Canada." The Privy Council is, of course, the cabinet, under the leadership of the PM. Formally, anyone who has ever been a member of cabinet retains the title of privy councillor after leaving government. But only those who are active members of the government exercise the powers referred to in the Constitution.

These powers include control over the budget. Section 54 of the Constitution Act, 1867 requires that any legislation or other measure that involves the raising or spending of public revenue must be introduced by cabinet. In fact, cabinet dominates the entire legislative agenda of Parliament, not just money matters. MPs who are not members of the cabinet have the right to introduce private members' bills. But the meagre time allocated to considering these bills and the operation of party discipline combine to kill the prospects of most of these initiatives.

More important than these written provisions of the Constitution, however, are constitutional conventions relating to the PM and cabinet. Although the position of prime minister is not even mentioned in the written Constitution, it is understood that the person who leads the dominant party in the House of Commons has the power to decide the following matters:

- who will be appointed to, or removed from, cabinet;
- when a new election will be held;
- the administrative structure and decision-making process of government;
- the selection of persons to a wide array of appointive positions, including deputy ministers, judges of all federal and provincial courts, senators, members of federal regulatory agencies and of the boards of directors of federal Crown corporations, ambassadors, etc. The Trudeau government introduced what it described as a merit-based, non-partisan appointment for the Senate and for hundreds of administrative positions. Nevertheless, the prime minister must still approve the recommendations of the advisory bodies that propose senators, regulatory commissioners, and judges.

These are formidable powers. They help to explain why the PM is always the pre-eminent figure in Canadian government, even when his or her decision-making style is a collegial one that encourages the participation of other members of cabinet. The PM's pre-eminence is reinforced by constitutional conventions on accountability. Although individual cabinet ministers are separately accountable to Parliament for the actions of their departments and other organizations that fall under their nominal authority, and the entire cabinet is collectively accountable for government policy, the PM cannot

Politics in Focus

BOX 9.1 The Governor General Mocks the Beliefs of 40 Per Cent of Canadians*

On 1 November 2017, only a month into her term as Canada's governor general, Julie Payette made the following statement to the Canadian Science Policy Conference in Ottawa:

> Can you believe that still today, in a learned society and in houses of government, unfortunately, we are still debating and still questioning whether humans have a role in the earth warming up, or whether the earth is even warming up, period? That we are still debating and still questioning whether life was a divine intervention or whether it was coming out of a natural process or let alone, my goodness, a random process?

The governor general was defended by some, including Canada's minister of the Environment and Climate Change, Catherine McKenna. She was criticized by others for mocking—if you listen to her speech at YouTube you will agree that she was incredulous that anyone could hold the views that she derided—not only people who question the role of human activities in contributing to climate change, but those whose faith causes them to believe in the divine origins of life. The governor general's role, these critics said, is not to wade into such waters and in the process ridicule millions of people who do not share her faith in science.

Governor General Payette is not the first occupant of this role to be criticized for overstepping what some consider to be the proper functions of the office. Former Governor General Adrienne Clarkson (1999–2005) showed occasional signs of wanting to reshape the governor general's role in public life. For example, in 2001 she sent a message of congratulations to a gay couple in Ontario who were wed in Toronto's Metropolitan Community Church. This occurred at a time when there was much public controversy over the legal definition of marriage and before Parliament, prodded by the courts, had changed this definition to include same-sex marriages. Her successor, Michaëlle Jean (2005–10), also was not averse to wading into potentially controversial waters: in a speech before the Alberta legislature she urged Albertans to share the "unprecedented prosperity in your province" with other Canadians. Albertans, of course, thought that they had been doing precisely that to the tune of billions of dollars per year for decades.

What do you think? Is it appropriate for the Queen's representative in Canada, appointed by the prime minister, to make public pronouncements on issues that divide Canadians?

---

*A CROP poll released at about the same time as Governor General Payette gave her speech found that 40 per cent of Canadians agreed that the earth was created by God in six days: https://www.crop.ca/en/blog/2017/138/.

---

avoid personal accountability for the overall performance of government and for all major policies. The opposition parties and the media ensure that the PM takes the heat for these matters.

Responsible government is another constitutional convention that strengthens the power of the PM and cabinet. As we noted in Chapter 6, responsible government encourages party discipline. This means that the elected members of a party will tend to act as a unified bloc on most matters, particularly when voting on budget measures and important government legislation. If the members of the governing party break ranks, the government could fall. Party discipline, therefore, ensures that members of the governing party will normally be docile in their support of the government's policies. And when the government has a majority in the House of Commons, the automatic backing of the government party's

Listen to the "SNC-Lavalin Affair and the Rule of Law" podcast, available at: www.oup .com/he/Brooks9e

backbenchers (i.e., MPs who are not cabinet ministers) enables the PM and cabinet to move their legislative agenda through the elected chamber of Parliament without serious impediment. Cabinet dominance may be attenuated, however, during periods of minority government. In such circumstances the PM and cabinet must necessarily be more sensitive to the preferences and manoeuvres of the opposition parties, given the greater risk of being defeated on a vote in the House.

For most of Canada's history the Senate posed no significant obstacle to the legislative dominance of the PM and cabinet. Until the election of Justin Trudeau it was usual for prime ministers to appoint persons from or at least sympathetic to their party when filling vacancies. Some of these senators would eventually decide to sit as independents, but the vast majority sat as Liberals or Conservatives. Prior to the Liberal election victory of 2015, however, Trudeau announced that no senators would formally represent the Liberal Party of Canada and they would not be part of the Liberal caucus, and consequently, appointments made since 2016 are designated as independent. By April 2019 independent senators comprised well over half of all senators. At that time, 59 caucused as the Independent Senators Group, 30 represented the Conservative Party, nine were in the Senate Liberal Group (but with no affiliation to the Liberal Party), and six were unaffiliated. Many believed that this would result in a less supine Senate, one in which those in the Independent Senators Group would be more likely to challenge the PM and cabinet on legislative and budget measures coming before them. In fact, however, Independents have voted with the Liberal government about 95 per cent of the time and have proven to be considerably more reliable in their support of the government than the nominally Liberal senators![4]

The weakness of Canada's political party organizations is another factor that reinforces the dominance of the PM and cabinet. Parties, particularly the Liberal and Conservative parties, are geared primarily towards fighting election campaigns and raising the money needed to do so. Neither party is what one would consider a social movement party with extensive ties to and dependence on organizations and groups in civil society. They are much more concerned with raising money, selecting candidates, and contesting elections than they are with formulating policy positions expected to tie the hands of the government if they win power. Statute law is not an important source of prime ministerial power. It provides, however, a significant legal basis for the authority and responsibilities of individual cabinet ministers. The statute under which a government department, agency, or Crown corporation operates will always specify which minister is responsible for the organization's actions. Legislation may also assign to a particular minister special powers over a part of the bureaucracy, such as a right of approval or veto of all or some category of the organization's decisions, or the right to order an agency or Crown corporation to base its decisions on particular guidelines or to act in a specific way. In fact, however, this sort of intervention is much more likely to come from the PM and cabinet acting collectively rather than being the initiative of an individual minister.

The dominance of the PM and cabinet in Canada's parliamentary system is reinforced by the relationship between the government and the media. This relationship is close—although not necessarily friendly—and mutually dependent. The PM and members of cabinet regularly communicate to the Canadian public, or to narrower segments of the public, via the media. When presenting or defending the government's policies in the House of Commons, they are aware of the wider audience to whom their words and behaviour are communicated by the parliamentary press corps and their cameras. Journalists typically turn first to the PM and the responsible ministers when reporting on politics. In doing so the media contribute to the popular identification of government with the PM and cabinet. The focus on the PM and members of his or her cabinet team, and the ability of the government to communicate directly with the public via social media and the careful orchestration of interactions with the media, have weakened the role of the legislature and political parties. When public sentiment can be gauged through public opinion polls and focus groups and when the PM and cabinet ministers can speak to either the general public or targeted groups via social media and stage-managed appearances and events, the government is unlikely to feel the need to rely on its MPs and the party organization to communicate its message.

The result of this shift in communications strategy is that Parliament may sometimes appear to be little more than a procedural sideshow. This infuriates some constitutional purists, for whom Parliament is the proper conduit between the state and society. They argue that the practice of responsible government, the bedrock of the British parliamentary system, is subverted by direct communications between the government and the people. MPs, they argue, should be the linchpin between Parliament and the people. This rather old-fashioned sounding argument is joined by another that has a more contemporary ring. PMs and governments that bypass Parliament and MPs and, instead, communicate directly with the people are thereby contributing to an excessive and dangerous concentration of power. Canada's system of parliamentary government already concentrates power in the hands of the PM. Anything that allows him or her to sidestep accountability in Parliament simply adds to the aggrandizement of his role and weakens parliamentary checks on the government's power.

Another factor that contributes to the dominant role of the PM and cabinet involves representation. From the beginnings of self-government in Canada, cabinet formation has been guided by the principle that politically important interests should, whenever possible, be "represented" by particular cabinet ministers. Historically, adequate representation of different regions and even particular provinces has always been considered important, as has representation of francophones.

The numerical dominance in Canada of English-speakers has always ensured that they would be well represented in any government. Representation

Prime Minister Trudeau holds a press conference with his new cabinet in 2015. Creating a cabinet that adequately represents all of the country's regions and citizens is a formidable challenge for any prime minister. Trudeau's cabinet appointments reflected his government's stated commitment to reflect the diversity of Canada.

from the business community—the minister of Finance has often been a person with professional connections to either the Toronto or Montreal corporate elite—and the inclusion of ministers perceived to be spokespersons for particular economic interests, particularly agriculture and occasionally labour, have also been significant factors in making appointments to particular cabinet positions. Some representational concerns, such as an adequate balance of Catholics and Protestants, have disappeared over time, while others, such as the representation of women, non-French and non-British Canadians, and visible minorities have become increasingly significant.

Representational concerns also surface in the case of the PM. These concerns are particularly important when a party is choosing its leader. Candidates are looked at, by party members and the media, in terms of their likely ability to draw support from politically important regions and groups. At a minimum, an aspiring leader of a national political party cannot be associated too closely with the interests of a single region of the country. Moreover, he or she must be at least minimally competent in French. In practical terms, this means being able to read parts of speeches in French and answer questions in French. Given the numerical superiority of anglophone voters, it goes without saying that any serious leadership candidate must be able to communicate well in English.

A prime minister whose party's representation in the House of Commons from a key region is relatively weak can attempt to convey a message of inclusion by appointing a high-profile cabinet minister from that region. This is precisely what Prime Minister Trudeau did after the 2015 election. His party won only one of Saskatchewan's 14 seats. That person, long-serving MP and one-time Finance Minister Ralph Goodale, was appointed Deputy House Leader and then moved to the high-profile position of minister of Public Safety. The Liberals won only four of Alberta's 38 seats in that same election. One of those Liberal MPs, Kent Hehr, was immediately appointed to cabinet as minister of Veterans Affairs. Representation is expected to translate into influence. The PM and cabinet have always been at what political

scientist and one-time MP Thomas Hockin called "the apex of power" in Canada's system of government.[5] This power is based on the agenda-setting role of the PM and cabinet and on their authority within the decision-making processes of the state. For this reason, representation in the inner circle of government is valued by regional and other interests.

Each new session of Parliament begins with the Speech from the Throne, in which the governor general reads a statement explaining the government's legislative priorities. This formal procedure is required by the Constitution.[6] Although a typical Throne Speech will be packed with generalities, it will also contain some specific indications of the agenda that Parliament will deal with over the ensuing months. This is one of the main ways in which the PM and cabinet are able to telegraph their policy priorities and set the legislative agenda for the next year.

Budgets represent a second way in which the PM and cabinet define the policy agenda. Every winter, usually around late February, the minister of Finance tables the **estimates** in the House of Commons. This is what students of public finance call the *expenditure budget*.[7] It represents the government's spending plans for the forthcoming fiscal year (1 April–31 March). Given that most public policies involve spending, changes in the allocation of public money provide an indication of the government's shifting priorities. The government can use the expenditure budget to signal its overall fiscal stance as well as its ideological leanings. Increased spending may be part of an expansionary fiscal policy, as was true of the Trudeau government's first budget in 2016, or it may signify a belief that justice, fairness, or other considerations warrant such an increase. Spending restraint and cutbacks, as occurred under the Conservative government beginning in 2012, may signal the government's concern that the total level of public spending and the size of the public-sector deficit are damaging the economy, or that they require levels of taxation and borrowing that are politically undesirable.

From time to time, usually every couple of years, the minister of Finance will present in Parliament a **revenue budget**. Sometimes this is referred to as an *economic statement*. It outlines the government's forecast for the economy and its plans to change the tax system and to introduce other changes intended to influence growth, employment, investment, and competitiveness. Revenue budgets are major opportunities for the government to shape the economic policy agenda.

Even when a government's budget proposals have not originated in cabinet—they sometimes have been generated within some part of the bureaucracy—or when they appear to be inevitable reactions to politically or economically pressing circumstances, these initiatives must still be accepted and sponsored by the government. In deciding which initiatives will be placed before Parliament, the priorities among them, and the strategies for manoeuvring policies through the legislature and communicating them to the public, the government influences the policy agenda. As Figure 9.2 shows, cabinet and cabinet committees, particularly the Treasury Board, are central players in the annual expenditure budget process.

Agenda-setting is part of the decision-making process in government. It is a crucial part, being that early stage during which public issues are defined and policy responses are proposed. The role of the PM and cabinet at this and other stages of the policy process is institutionalized through the formal structure of cabinet decision-making. Between 1968 and 1993 the key committee of cabinet for establishing the government's policy and budget priorities was the Priorities and Planning (P&P) Committee. It was chaired by the prime minister and included only the most influential members of cabinet. This formal distinction between a sort of inner and outer cabinet was abolished under Prime Minister Kim Campbell (1993). Gone, too, was the elaborate system of formal committees created during the Pierre Trudeau years. The structure of cabinet decision-making was streamlined under the Liberal government of Jean Chrétien (1993–2003) to include only five permanent subcommittees of cabinet: Economic Union, Social Union, Treasury Board, the Special Committee of Council, and Government Communications. Under Stephen Harper, the Committee on Priorities

and Planning, chaired by the prime minister, was reinstituted. There were, moreover, five additional committees: Operations (day-to-day co-ordination of the government's agenda and issue management); Social Affairs; Economic Prosperity and Sustainable Growth; Treasury Board; and Foreign Affairs and Defence. But the most significant changes in the cabinet committee system since the revamping under Pierre Trudeau have been made under his son, Prime Minister Justin Trudeau. The Cabinet Committee on Agenda, Results and Communications is, in terms of its functions, broadly similar to the Priorities and Planning Committee created by his father almost 50 years earlier. The Treasury Board, which has existed since Confederation, continues to exist. In addition, however, there are nine other cabinet committees, many of which are quite different from past committees not only in their names but also in their focus.[8]

The formal structure of cabinet decision-making, including its committee structure, has never been more than an imperfect guide to who has influence over what within the government of the day. Under Pierre Trudeau, the Priorities and Planning Committee was a true inner cabinet with final decision-making authority. But its membership ranged from about 15 to 20 cabinet ministers, not all of whom could be placed in the Marc Lalonde or Donald Macdonald category of government heavyweights. Under Justin Trudeau, it is fair to say that all 11 members appointed to the Committee on Agenda, Results and Communications are widely recognized as the most prominent members of the government.

The one reliable rule of thumb is this: ministers are influential to the degree that the prime minister allows them to be influential and supports their favoured projects and initiatives. A minister who has a reputation for having the PM's ear and for being part of his inner circle acquires enhanced status among his or her colleagues in Parliament and in the eyes of the media. Other factors may also contribute to a minister's influence, such as having a base of support within the party or being in charge of a powerful part of the bureaucracy. Nevertheless, the personal relationship between the PM and a

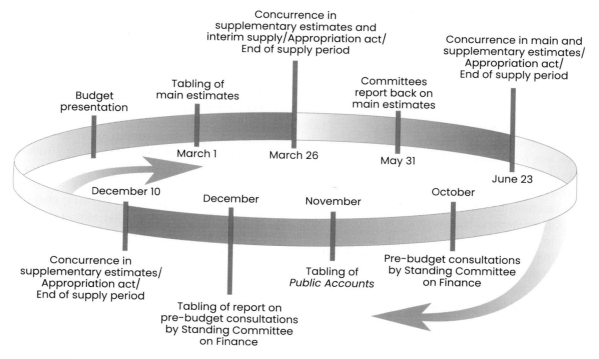

FIGURE 9.2 The Annual Financial Cycle

Source: Parliament of Canada, House of Commons Compendium of Procedure and Practice, https://www.ourcommons.ca/About/Compendium/FinancialProcedures/c_d_financialcycle-e.htm. © Library of Parliament.

minister is always a significant determinant of a minister's influence. The decision-making process in cabinet does not occur only through formal committee meetings. One-on-one conversations in the corridors of the Office of the Prime Minister and Privy Council (formerly the Langevin Building until it was renamed in 2017), in the PM's office in the West Block of Parliament, over the phone, or however and wherever they may take place have always been crucial in the decision-making process. No organization chart can capture this informal but crucial aspect of ministerial influence. Nor can it convey the extent to which the prime minister is the dominant player in this decision-making process. Political observers have long characterized the PM's status in cabinet as *primus inter pares*—first among equals. But as Donald Savoie notes, it has been a long time since there was any *inter* or *pares*. There is only *primus*, the PM, when it comes to setting the government's agenda and taking major decisions.[9]

Ministerial control over the bureaucracy is another dimension of cabinet's decision-making authority. The word "control" should be used carefully, however. Ministers are virtually never involved in the day-to-day running of the departments that fall under their nominal control. Moreover, policy initiatives are more likely to be generated within the bureaucracy, often through ongoing dialogue with interests with whom they interact in the course of administering their programs, than to spring from the fertile imagination of the responsible minister. There are, of course, exceptions. Stéphane Dion, when he was the federal minister of Intergovernmental Affairs, was the principal author of the 2000 **Clarity Act**, an idea he had championed from the time of the 1995 Quebec referendum. Chrystia Freeland, Foreign Affairs minister in the Justin Trudeau government, was well versed on international trade and NAFTA before assuming her role as Canada's chief representative in these matters, as was Dr Jane Philpott, the first minister of Health in the Trudeau government, on health-care issues. Neither of these cabinet ministers was a mere conduit for the ideas of the bureaucrats beneath them. Nevertheless, as Donald Savoie has argued, as a general rule most ministers, most of the time, do not have the expertise or the inclination to exercise this sort of independence. They are much more likely, Savoie says, to act as cabinet advocates for the interests of their department, its budget and programs, and the groups that depend on them. More recently Savoie has revised this generalization, arguing that in some circumstances ministers often rely more heavily on advisers outside of the state than on senior bureaucrats in deciding policy.[10] This appears to have been the case during the Conservative government of Stephen Harper. It is not clear whether this trend, which was fuelled in large part by a mistrust of the permanent bureaucracy, will continue.

Central Agencies: "Where the Public Service Meets Politics"

Cabinet has always been a decision-making body. But when John A. Macdonald and the first cabinet met in 1867, they dealt with a workload that was a fraction of that facing government today. There were only a handful of departments and no publicly owned corporations or regulatory agencies. Moreover, federal–provincial relations were still relatively uncomplicated (although this would not last long!). The scope and complexity of contemporary government are much greater today. To deal with the sheer volume of information that comes before cabinet and the hundreds of separate decisions that it takes annually, cabinet needs help. This help is provided by central agencies.

Central agencies are parts of the bureaucracy whose main or only purpose is to support the decision-making activities of cabinet. More concretely, this means they perform such functions as providing cabinet with needed information, applying cabinet decisions when dealing with other parts of the federal bureaucracy, and communicating cabinet decisions and their implications to the public, provincial governments, or other organizations within the federal state. Unlike other parts of the federal bureaucracy they do not administer programs, with exception of the Department of Finance, which is responsible for the administration of equalization payments to the provincial governments. Instead, their influence rests on their direct support for and involvement in cabinet decision-making and their ability to intervene in the affairs of departments. Those in central agencies occupy the crucial space where, in the words of one official interviewed by Donald Savoie, "the rubber meets the road, where the public service meets politics, and all . . . that means."[11]

The main organizations usually considered to have central agency status are the Department of Finance, the Privy Council Office (PCO), the Treasury Board Secretariat, and the Prime Minister's Office.

Department of Finance

The Department of Finance plays the leading role in the formulation of economic policy. Its formal authority is found in the Department of Finance Act, 1869, the Financial Administration Act, and several other statutes. The authority that the law confers on Finance is reinforced by the department's informal reputation within the state. Although comparatively small—it employs about 750 persons (2018)—Finance has always been a magnet for "the best and the brightest" within the public service because of its unrivalled status in all aspects of economic policy-making.

The Finance Department has what amounts to almost exclusive authority over the preparation of the revenue budget, budget speeches, and economic statements delivered in Parliament by the Finance minister. Whatever input other parts of the bureaucracy and interests outside of government have is at the discretion of the minister of Finance and the department, and, of course, the prime minister. New initiatives in taxation and trade policy and in managing the level of government spending and debt will often be generated within Finance. Even when a new policy idea originates elsewhere, it is unlikely to reach the legislation stage if Finance is steadfastly opposed.

Finance officials are able to influence the entire spectrum of government policy through their role in the annual formulation of the expenditure budget. They are involved at the very beginning of the expenditure budget process, providing projections on the future state of the economy and the fiscal framework within which spending choices will have to be made. A Finance forecast of weak economic activity and lean taxation revenues may impose across-the-board restraint on departments jostling for scarce funds. But in addition to this macro-level influence on policy, Finance officials may also be involved in micro-level decisions about programs and in setting the policy agenda.

The dominant status of Finance can be traced back to the 1930s, when Keynesian economic policies were being embraced by Western governments, including Canada.[12] This importance was reinforced during the 1990s when deficit reduction and debt management became Ottawa's overriding priorities. Once Ottawa turned the corner on the deficit issue and began to accumulate considerable budget surpluses during the late 1990s, many believed that Finance's stranglehold on the government's agenda would loosen under pressure from those who believed that Ottawa could afford to restore spending on some of the programs that had been cut during the mid-1990s. In fact, however, Finance lost none of its authority at the centre of the policy-making universe. As Donald Savoie observes:

> [T]he budget has come to dominate policy and decision-making in Ottawa as never before. This holds significant advantages for the centre of government. It enables the prime minister and the minister of finance to introduce new measures and policies under the cover of budget secrecy and avoid debate in Cabinet—and perhaps, more importantly, long interdepartmental consultations and attempts to define a consensus.[13]

In other words, what has long been the unrivalled status of Finance within the federal bureaucracy is one of the factors that has reinforced the power of the PM, who, along with his or her minister of Finance, is the only member of the government to be intimately involved in the process that leads up to the making of a budget or economic statement

in the House of Commons. The point is made in a rather understated way by a Library of Parliament analysis of the minister of Finance's role: "the minister of Finance's control over the allocation of spending makes him or her one of the most powerful ministers in Cabinet."[14]

More recently, Savoie has suggested that Finance now has rivals in providing economic advice likely to influence the government's actions. He notes that the chief economists of some of Canada's banks and some Canadian think-tanks with interests in fiscal policy, particularly the Fraser Institute and the C.D. Howe Institute, have acquired high profiles in the media and that the views of some of these nationally prominent economists appear to have carried weight with governments in Ottawa.[15] Moreover, the Parliamentary Budget Officer, a position created by the Conservative government in 2008, has come to be a rival source of advice on economic matters. As Brooke Jeffrey writes, "the role of the PBO is one that has the potential to threaten some of the most important vested interests and departments of the federal government, namely Finance, Treasury Board and Privy Council. Certainly this new watchdog can be seen as a direct challenge to their hegemony."[16]

The Privy Council Office

The Privy Council Office is the cabinet's secretariat and a principal source of policy advice to the prime minister. It employs close to 1,000 persons but, as is also true of Finance and the Prime Minister's Office (PMO), the PCO's influence cannot be gauged from its size. The PCO was formally created by Order-in-Council in 1940. The position of chief clerk of the Privy Council, the foremost bureaucrat in the federal government, was put on a statutory basis in 1974 without any specification of the duties associated with this position. The authority of the chief clerk and the influence of the PCO derive mainly from their intimate and daily involvement in cabinet decision-making. Indeed, the chief clerk has been aptly described as the deputy minister to the prime minister.[17]

Unlike government departments, the PCO does not administer programs and its budget is comparatively small. Its influence does not depend,

The Canadian Press/Nathan Denette

The reading of a new budget is a ceremonial affair in Ottawa, and though no one knows its origin, there is a long-standing tradition of the Finance minister purchasing and wearing a new pair of shoes for the occasion. Jim Flaherty, Finance minister in the Harper government from 2006 until his sudden death in 2014, always wore new shoes.

therefore, on the support of large or otherwise influential groups that benefit from its spending. Instead, its influence in Canada's system of government rests on its ability to speak on behalf of the prime minister and cabinet. As Alex Smith puts it:

The PCO does not have formal authority over line departments, but its roles in assisting the prime minister and Cabinet give it substantial influence. Line departments must consider the advice of the PCO very carefully because the advice generally reflects the wishes of the prime minister or Cabinet. In addition, because the PCO acts as a gatekeeper for the information that is made available to Cabinet, departments must ensure that their

submissions reflect the PCO's guidance. The PCO often filters or summarizes information provided by departments to ensure that the prime minister and Cabinet have adequate supporting information to make informed decisions.[18]

In terms of its organization, the PCO is divided into a number of secretariats that provide support services for the various committees of cabinet. These services range from such mundane functions as scheduling and keeping the minutes of committee meetings to activities that carry the potential for real influence, such as providing policy advice and dealing directly with government departments. Perhaps more than any other single component of the bureaucracy, the PCO is capable of seeing "the big picture" of government policy. This picture embraces policy *and* political concerns. As Donald Savoie observes, "the office briefs the prime minister on any issue it wishes, controls the flow of papers to Cabinet, reports back to departments on the decisions taken, or not taken, by Cabinet, advises the prime minister on the selection of deputy ministers . . . on federal–provincial relations and on all issues of governmental organization and ministerial mandates."[19] If the government of Canada is a railway, the PCO is Union Station.

Savoie argues that the title "clerk of the Privy Council" is in some ways a misnomer as this most senior member of the federal bureaucracy in fact serves and reports to the PM, not to cabinet as a whole. Along with the PM's chief of staff in the PMO, the clerk of the PCO is the only official who meets almost daily with the PM when he is in Ottawa. "The clerk," Savoie observes, "has direct access to the prime minister as needed."[20] Little wonder that the occupant of this role is virtually always among the top 10 persons in the *Hill Times* list of the "100 Most Powerful & Influential People in Government & Politics," and always towards the top of its list of the most influential unelected persons in the federal government.[21]

The Treasury Board Secretariat

The Treasury Board Secretariat (TBS) supports the functions of the Treasury Board. The Treasury Board is the only cabinet committee that has a statutory basis, going back to 1869. It is, in a sense, guardian of the purse strings, but it performs this function in more of a micro fashion compared to Finance's macro authority in relation to spending matters. The Treasury Board is also the government's voice on employment and personnel matters and on administrative policy within the federal government. Its authority is, in a word, extensive. But although the responsibilities of the TBS are wide-ranging and important, it occupies the shadows of the policy-making and agenda-setting process when compared to Finance and the PCO. Donald Savoie quotes a senior federal official who compares the roles of Finance, the PCO, and the TBS this way: "PCO looks after the broad picture and

resolves conflicts between ministers and departments. Finance looks after the big economic and budgeting decisions. The Treasury Board looks after the little decisions."[22]

"Little," however, should not be confused with "unimportant." Particularly from the standpoint of program managers within the federal bureaucracy, the activities and decisions of the Treasury Board and TBS are quite significant. The TBS includes the Office of the Comptroller General of Canada (OCG), whose functions include departmental audits, establishing and enforcing accounting standards in government, and the evaluation of particular programs. As government employer, the Treasury Board negotiates with federal public-sector unions, establishes the rules for recruitment and promotion, is involved in implementing the terms of the Official Languages Act relating to the representation of francophones in the public service and the availability of services to the public in both official languages, and is responsible for equity matters, including setting rules for increasing the representation of women, visible minorities, disabled persons, and Indigenous people in the Canadian public service. These clearly are important functions.

TBS officials formulate the expenditure outlook that, along with the economic outlook and fiscal framework developed by Finance, is the starting point in the annual expenditure budget exercise. The expenditure forecasts provided by TBS are used by cabinet in making decisions on the allocation of financial resources between competing programs. The involvement of TBS officials does not stop here. Along with the spending committees of cabinet, they assess the spending proposals and plans that departments are required to submit each year. Preparation of the main estimates, the detailed spending plans that the government tables in the House of Commons each winter, is the responsibility of the Treasury Board. Given the range of its activities it is not surprising that TBS is the largest of the central agencies, with almost 1,900 employees. Because the TBS has the deepest ongoing knowledge of government spending programs of all central agencies, it is often turned to by the PCO and Finance—its more muscular and glamorous cousins—for information and advice.[23]

The Prime Minister's Office

As the Library of Parliament's description of the PMO rather laconically, if aptly, states, "The precise role of the PMO depends on the wishes of the prime minister."[24] At some moments under some prime ministers, the PMO has been viewed as the power centre of government. At other times it has assumed a lower profile. But at all times it plays an indispensable, important and rather unique role as the agency entrusted with the task of maintaining what is hoped to be a favourable public image of the prime minister and his or her government.

Unlike the other central agencies, the Prime Minister's Office is staffed chiefly by partisan appointees rather than by career public servants. These officials are the prime minister's personal staff, performing functions that range from handling the PM's correspondence and schedule to speech-writing, media relations, liaison with ministers, caucus, and the party, and include providing advice on appointments and policy. In its relations with other parts of the federal government the PMO serves as the PM's political eyes and ears, and has the added distinction of being able to speak on behalf of the PM. The PMO is headed by the PM's Chief of Staff and by the Principal Secretary. The distinction between these two roles is not watertight. It is usual to place the Chief of Staff above the Principal Secretary in the PMO hierarchy and to think of the Chief of Staff as having primary responsibility for internal matters within the PMO and the Principal Secretary as the PM's lead adviser for strategy and political advice. Under Prime Minister Justin Trudeau this distinction has not been clear and the occupants of these positions, Chief of Staff Katie Telford and Principal Secretary Gerald Butts, regularly referred to one another as "co-CEOs" until Butts resigned in February 2019. No other non-elected officials are in such regular contact with the PM. Since the expansion in the PMO that took place under Pierre Trudeau four decades ago, the size of the prime minister's staff has varied enormously. Trudeau more than doubled the staff from the 40 persons who worked in the PMO under Prime Minister Pearson. Under Prime Minister Mulroney the staff reached just under 200. Today the PMO employs about 90 persons. This may seem to be a rather large number of people to serve the needs of one person, even a very important person such as the prime minister. But the demands on the prime minister's time are enormous and the process of coordinating his activities, providing him or her with briefing and advice, organizing his travel schedule, and dealing with the volume of communication that flows into and from the Prime Minister's Office are daunting, to say the least. The bottom line for all staffers in the PMO, from the Chief of Staff to those who deal with correspondence, is summed up by a former PMO staff member in these words: "Our job is quite simple really, we make the PM look good."[25] This can, on occasion, be a challenge.

Although the PMO is clearly the most partisan of the central agencies, it would be quite wrong to think of the PMO as being unconcerned with policy matters. Protecting the prime minister and making him look good necessarily involve PMO officials in issues of policy, large and small. "Senior PMO staff," says Savoie, "will get involved in whatever issue they and the prime minister think they should."[26] It simply is not possible to draw a line between the drafting of a speech for the prime minister, a function that typically will take place in the PMO, and providing policy advice. Moreover, officials in the PMO work regularly and closely with those in the PCO to push forward the PM's agenda. But how involved PMO officials are in shaping policy and what their influence is vis-à-vis other central agency officials and departmental managers will, as always, depend on the prime minister. Ultimately, the prime minister decides from whom to seek advice and who will be a player on any particular issue.

One of the criticisms levelled at the PMO over the years has to do with the fact that persons who have not been elected to office and who are not part of the public service—"exempt staff" is the technical term for these employees—may appear to have an exceptional influence on the prime minister and government policy. Principal secretaries and chiefs of staff, in particular, have sometimes been portrayed by the media or the opposition parties as *des eminences grises*, unaccountable partisan operatives behaving in some Machiavellian manner behind the scenes.[27] During the prime ministership of

Stephen Harper a somewhat related criticism was often heard, namely that the government's determination to ensure disciplined messaging resulted in a centralization of communications within the PMO. The government of Justin Trudeau came to power promising to loosen the control of the PCO and PMO on communications across the federal government. But as Alex Marland observes, "The tendencies of coordinated politicization [through the PMO] will be in hibernation only as long as a prime minister and his (or her) entourage calculate that it in their political interest."[28]

Prime Ministerial Government

For decades various commentators on the Canadian political scene asked whether Canadian prime ministers were becoming more "presidential" in their stature and power. The question, however, was always based on the false premise that an American president is more powerful in relation to the country's legislation and his own party than is a Canadian prime minister. In fact, there have always been fewer checks on the behaviour of a Canadian prime minister than on an American president, and any occupant of the White House would envy the sort of constitutional latitude enjoyed by the leader of the Canadian government. Canadian commentators who purported to see creeping presidentialization occurring in Canada's system of government were, in fact, mistakenly attributing to the American head of state powers beyond those actually held by the US president, but which Canadian prime ministers have always had.

In recent years this ill-informed debate has come to a close. Indeed, it is now widely recognized that the Canadian prime minister has far more clout within the Canadian system of government than the president has in the American system and, moreover, that power has become increasingly centralized in the hands of the PM and those around him. These days, if one looks for counterweights to the PM's power they are more plausibly found in the courts, the media, and in some of the provincial capitals than in Parliament. This centralization of power has advanced to such a degree that some of Canada's most astute political commentators

have characterized Canada's system of government as *prime ministerial* rather than *parliamentary* government.[29] Donald Savoie and Jeffrey Simpson are among those who argue that not only has the influence of Parliament been effectively eclipsed by the growth of **prime ministerial government**, but cabinet, too, has been left on the margins of the policy-making process, "a kind of focus group for the prime minister," in the words of a recent Liberal cabinet minister,[30] or what Jeffrey Simpson calls a "mini-sounding board"[31] where decisions already approved by the PM and his advisers in key central agencies are rubber-stamped. This process continued and was even consolidated under Prime Minister Stephen Harper. Just months before his election in 2015, Justin Trudeau cited the concentration of executive power as a governance problem that needed to be addressed in Canada.[32]

The greater influence of the prime minister within the Canadian system of government than the president in the American system is due to structural differences between these two governmental systems. But the high degree of centralization of power that commentators such as Savoie and Simpson argue has occurred under recent prime ministers—a trend that Savoie and others argue actually began with the government of Pierre Trudeau and that is probably irreversible[33]—may be explained by a combination of personal style and the political incentives to choose more rather than less centralization. The individuals who occupy the role of prime minister all have their own preferences when it comes to decision-making. Some prefer a more participatory process, as was true of Lester Pearson (1963–8) and Pierre Trudeau (1968–79, 1980–4), at least during Trudeau's earlier years. Marc Lalonde, one of the most influential ministers during the Trudeau era, has described cabinet meetings under Trudeau as resembling university seminars during which the prime minister often remained silent for much of the time while the members of his government expressed their views. This is the decision-making style, as noted earlier, in which the prime minister has been depicted as "first among equals." The historical evidence from politicians' memoirs and journalistic accounts, however, suggests that the collegial style may have been less common

Governing Realities

BOX 9.2 Checks on Prime Ministerial Rule: One Insider's View

Ian Brodie was Prime Minister Harper's chief of staff for two and one-half years (2006–8). Prior to that he had been a professor of political science at the University of Western Ontario for six years before leaving academe to work for the Conservative Party in opposition. He is a thoughtful person whose 2018 book, *Government at the Centre*, weaves together an insider's perspective on government with a deep knowledge of the academic literature on what is almost universally believed to be an increasing concentration of power in and around the prime minister.

Brodie does not deny that this trend toward the concentration of power at the centre has taken place, going back to Pierre Trudeau's reforms of the PMO and of the process of cabinet decision-making. He argues, however, that this has been necessary in order to deal with the greater challenges of governance that modern prime ministers face. Moreover, and against the grain of the conventional wisdom on prime ministerial government, Brodie argues that this concentration is exaggerated. There exist, he argues, several checks on prime ministerial power within Canada's system of government that are overlooked or at least underestimated by those who argue that the prime minister has become a sort of "dictator." Among these constraints on prime ministerial power he mentions the following:

- *The government caucus.* "You cannot take on a chunk of caucus in a way that makes it sharply adversarial to the government's agenda without being very, very careful about it." Caucus meetings are closed affairs where no official record is kept of what is said. MPs, he argues, regularly feel emboldened to speak their mind about legislation and strategy and, contrary to popular belief, are not discouraged from doing so. No prime minister would permit legislation to be drafted and tabled in the House if it is too divisive in the government caucus.

- *Importance of the Finance perspective.* The view of the Department of Finance will always be represented at the cabinet table by the minister of Finance and when it comes to budget and fiscal matters generally, it is not simply one view among many. "Every prime minister should have a finance minister who'll say, hold on a minute, before I make this decision let's think this through," being willing to challenge the prime minister and the advice he may have received from other advisers in other central agencies. Brodie says that he observed this during his time as chief of staff.

- *Members of cabinet with exceptional standing in the party.* Although no member of cabinet will have influence close to that of the prime minister, the views of some of them simply can't be ignored. It often happens that some of those around the cabinet table have themselves been the party's leader at some point. Others may command respect at the table, in the party, and in the country for other reasons. Lesser suns are not simply eclipsed by the brightest sun in the solar system, that is, the prime minister.

- *Parliamentary procedure.* Brodie argues that various reforms to parliamentary procedure have actually increased the attention that private members' bills receive in the House and the likelihood that they may influence the government's legislative agenda. Moreover, he points to the opposition's successful efforts during the Harper years to prolong debate and slow down, if not stop, the government's efforts to move its legislation through Parliament.

You may hear more about all this in Colin Robertson's July 2018 interview with Ian Brodie: https://soundcloud.com/user-609485369/at-the-centre-of-government-a-discussion-with-ian-brodie. The quotations are from this interview.

than is sometimes believed. In an analysis of prime ministers' decision-making styles, Savoie points out that even Pierre Trudeau bypassed the formal process of cabinet decision-making in the case of all of the major policy initiatives taken during his last four years as PM. Likewise, Brian Mulroney and Jean Chrétien did the same when it came to some of the signature policies launched during their respective periods as prime minister.[34] This process of marginalizing cabinet, at least on certain issues, continued under Stephen Harper.[35] Justin Trudeau came to office expressing his commitment to a loosening of control from the centre and thus to a greater role in decision-making for cabinet ministers. But by the end of his first term it was not clear that prime ministerial domination of the policy process had declined very much from what it had been under his predecessors. A centralized decision-making style is a feature of contemporary Canadian government, where priorities are effectively set and decisions are made by the prime minister and a relatively small group of advisers, only some of whom may be cabinet ministers (see Box 9.2 for a dissenting opinion).

The Legislature

The legislature is a study in contrasts. Its physical setting is soberly impressive, yet the behaviour of its members, particularly during Question Period, is often thought to be unfit for the schoolyard. Its constitutional powers appear to be formidable, yet its actual influence on policy usually is much less than that of the cabinet and the bureaucracy. All major policies, including all laws, must be approved by the legislature, but the legislature's approval often seems a foregone conclusion and a mere formality. One of the two chambers of the legislature, the House of Commons, is democratically elected. The other, the Senate, is unelected and therefore not democratically accountable to Canadians (although senators are quick to deny this!) and is populated by persons who are unknown to the vast majority of Canadians.

The contradictions of the legislature have their source in the tension between traditional ideas about political democracy and the character of the modern state. Representation, accountability

to the people, and choice are the cornerstones of liberal democratic theory. An elected legislature that represents the population either on the basis of population or by region—or both—and party competition are the means by which these democratic goals are to be accomplished. But the modern state is also characterized by a vast bureaucratic apparatus that is not easily controlled by elected politicians. Moreover, while the prime minister's power has always been vastly greater than that of other members of Parliament, the concentration of power in and around the office of the prime minister appears to have reached unprecedented levels. As the scale and influence of the non-elected parts of the state have grown and prime ministerial government has been consolidated, the inadequacies of traditional democratic theory—centred on the role of the legislature—have become increasingly apparent.

If the legislature is less able to perform the functions associated with it in democratic theory, one solution may be to look elsewhere for representation and accountability. If power has drifted to non-elected officials, then perhaps ensuring that the bureaucracy is representative of the population may be a way to increase the likelihood that they will be democratically responsive. If the legislature is no longer able to control or effectively monitor the activities of the government, perhaps the answer lies in creating independent parliamentary officers. Many such officers have been empowered at both the federal and provincial levels, including, federally, the Office of the Auditor General, the Office of the Privacy Commissioner, the Commissioner of the Environment and Sustainable Development, and the Parliamentary Budget Officer. Critics charge that their proliferation—an estimated 80 such officers are employed at the federal, provincial, and territorial levels—is both a symptom of Parliament's decline and a contributing factor to the delegitimization of the legislature. "A veritable accountability industry," says David Pond, "is being created outside the walls of Parliament and the provincial legislatures."[36] But as long as the job of holding government accountable is getting done, does it matter if elected legislators are doing it? Some argue that there is no substitute for an elected legislature that is able to hold government accountable for its actions (see Box 9.3).

Representation in the elected House of Commons is roughly according to population—roughly, because as of 2015 an MP could represent as few as 26,728 constituents (Labrador) or as many as 128,357 (Niagara Falls). Each of the 338 members of the House of Commons is the sole representative for a constituency, also known as a riding or electoral district.

Senators are appointed by the government of the day as vacancies occur. Since 2016 the federal government has used a selection process that allows any Canadian citizen who meets the constitutional requirements for the position to apply for a Senate vacancy in his or her province. The Independent Advisory Board for Senate Appointments makes recommendations as to who should fill vacant seats, but the final determination remains in the hands of the government. Senators do not have set terms of office and may hold their seats until age 75. Representation in the Senate is on the basis of regions. Each of the four main regions (Ontario, Quebec, the

En route to taking office in 2006, Stephen Harper's Conservative government expressed the intent to introduce legislation on Senate reform. Their proposed overhauls of the Senate process included an eight-year limit on the term of Senate service and, eventually, the requirement that senators be elected to their seats rather than appointed. In an April 2014 ruling the Supreme Court of Canada determined that no significant reform of the Senate may take place without provincial consent.

four western provinces, and the Maritimes) has 24 seats. Newfoundland has six, and there is one from each of Yukon, the Northwest Territories, and Nunavut for a total of 105 seats. Eight temporary seats were added by the Mulroney government in 1990 to overcome Liberal opposition in the Senate to the Goods and Services Tax (GST), thus temporarily raising the total number of senators to 112.

In recent years there have been suggestions that senators be elected, that they serve limited terms, and some have proposed that a certain number of

Senate seats be reserved for women and Indigenous Canadians. Such changes seem unlikely. In a 2014 ruling the Supreme Court of Canada stated that any change to the basis of representation in the Senate or making its members subject to elections or term limits would require a constitutional amendment using the general formula for changing the Constitution. The Court also stated that the Senate could not be abolished without the consent of all provincial governments, and both the House of Commons and the Senate.[37]

Politics in Focus

BOX 9.3 Is Parliament Broken? Can It Be Fixed?

Michael Chong is a Conservative MP representing the constituency of Wellington–Halton Hills in Ontario. For several years he has been perhaps the most outspoken critic in the House of Commons of what he believes to be the dysfunctional features of Parliament that prevent it from doing its job probably and that, in consequence, have undermined Canadian democracy. In a 2017 book entitled Turning Parliament Inside Out: Practical Ideas for Reforming Canada's Democracy, *Chong argues that one of the things that needs to be fixed is the committee system.*

The committee system of the House of Commons is one area that could be reformed to rebalance power between party leaders and MPs. The committee system is at the heart of the day-to-day functioning of the Commons. Committees are made up of small groups of MPs (usually 10 members) and are created by the Commons, usually through standing orders. It's where much of MPs' work is done—where legislation is amended, and government spending and taxation are approved.

In theory, standing committees have immense power to hold the government to account. They're empowered to call witnesses, demand evidence and issue reports. In practice, they rarely exercise these rights. Why? Because party leaders exert substantial control over the chairs and membership of these committees.

In theory, parliamentary committees have immense power to hold the government to account. In practice, they rarely exercise these rights.

In a majority Parliament, for instance, at least six out of 10 members of a standing committee are appointed through the party whip by the prime minister. This means that the executive branch of government—the

Prime Minister's Office (PMO)—is effectively controlling a standing committee of the legislative branch. This is at complete odds with the fundamental role of a committee of the legislature, which is to hold the executive branch of government to account.

Committee reports are a good example of how the PMO exerts control over committees. Parliamentary secretaries—who work closely with the minister's office—sit on committees. When a draft report is being considered, the parliamentary secretary often sends the report to the minister's office. This means the minister's office is frequently participating in drafting the very reports that are supposed to hold the minister and department to account. It's like putting the fox in charge of the henhouse!

Committees rarely make amendments to improve government legislation. In any given year, amendments made to government bills by standing committees usually number in the single digits. In contrast, government bills in the British House of Commons are amended dozens—if not hundreds—of times in any given year.

A reform that would go a long way toward rebalancing power between party leaders and MPs would be to remove the power of party leaders—including the prime minister—to decide the membership of committees. Giving that power to MPs on a secret ballot vote at the beginning of a new Parliament would give committees much greater autonomy to hold the government to account.

Source: From Michael Chong, "Rebalancing Power in Ottawa: Committee Reform," in Michael Chong, Scott Simms, and Kennedy Stewart, *Turning Parliament Inside Out: Practical Ideas for Reforming Canada's Democracy* (Vancouver: Douglas & McIntyre, 2017).

In law, the powers of the House of Commons and Senate are roughly equal, and all bills must pass through identical stages in both bodies before becoming law (see the Appendix at the end of this chapter). But despite the similarity of their formal powers, the superiority of the House of Commons is

well established. For most of its history, the Senate generally deferred to the will of the Commons on all but relatively minor matters. This changed after the 1984 election of a Progressive Conservative majority in the House of Commons. On several occasions the Liberal-dominated Senate obstructed bills that had already been passed by the Commons, including the treaty approving the Canada–US Free Trade Agreement in 1988, triggering a federal election. When, two years later, the Senate balked at passage of the politically unpopular Goods and Services Tax, the government decided it had had enough. Using a largely unknown constitutional power it appointed eight new Conservative senators, thereby giving the Conservative Party a slender majority. Under the Chrétien government the partisan balance in the Senate shifted back to a Liberal majority. The squabbles that often occurred after 1984, when the House of Commons was controlled by one party and the Senate by another, became increasingly rare during the years 1993–2006 when the Liberals formed the government and re-established a Liberal majority in the Senate through the filling of vacancies.

This Liberal majority posed a problem for the minority Conservative government elected in 2006, blocking and delaying several pieces of legislation sent to it from the House of Commons. This changed when Prime Minister Harper filled 18 Senate vacancies in December 2008. Under Prime Minister Trudeau, as discussed earlier, new senators are appointed as independents.

The legislature performs a number of functions basic to political democracy. The most fundamental of these is the passage of laws by the people's elected representatives. Budget proposals and new policy initiatives must be placed before Parliament for its approval. The operation of party discipline ensures that bills tabled in the legislature are seldom modified in major ways during the law-passing process. This does not mean, however, that Parliament's approval of the government's legislative agenda is an empty formality. The rules under which the legislature operates ensure that the opposition parties have opportunities to debate and criticize the government's proposals. It should be said, however, that not everyone agrees.

What we might call parliamentary idealists argue that government is able to make and pass legislation without regard for the views of its party **caucus**. Savoie states that government party MPs "report that they are rarely, if ever, in a position to launch a new initiative, and worse, that they

are rarely effective in getting the government to change course. They also do not consider themselves to be an effective check on prime ministerial power."[38] In the words of one government party MP, "We simply respond to what Cabinet does, and there are limits to what you can do when you are always reacting."[39] But contrary to Savoie's conclusion, interviews conducted with MPs in 2010 by the Samara Centre for Democracy found that the chance to express one's point of view in the privacy of caucus was a source of satisfaction for many legislators. Indeed, of MPs' work in committees, caucus, Question Period and House duty during debates, caucus was rated highest by MPs in terms of their individual effectiveness. At the same time, however, many MPs acknowledged that they were frustrated by having to vote on the floor of the House as their party directed them, suggesting that caucus may be more about catharsis than influence.[40] It seems likely that most of the time, on most issues, the government pays more serious attention to the results of opinion polls and focus groups than to what it hears in caucus.

Although the legislature may often play second fiddle to more direct means used by government to take the public pulse on issues, it is far from being irrelevant in the policy-making process. Functions performed by the legislature include scrutiny of government performance, constituency representation, and the debate of public issues.

Oversight of Government Performance

Various regular opportunities exist for the legislature to prod, question, and criticize the government. These include the daily Question Period, the set-piece debates that follow the Speech from the Throne and the introduction of a new budget, and Opposition Days, when the opposition parties determine the topic of debate. Committee hearings and special parliamentary task forces also provide opportunities for legislative oversight of government actions and performance, although the subjects that these bodies deal with are mainly determined by the government. Party discipline is a key factor that limits the critical tendencies of parliamentary committees, particularly during periods of majority government.

For better or for worse, Question Period has become both the centrepiece of Parliament's day and the chief activity shaping the ideas that most Canadians have of what goes on in Parliament. The introduction of television cameras into the legislature in the late 1970s reinforced the stature of Question Period as the primary forum through which the opposition can scrutinize and criticize the government on matters big and small. This is the opposition parties' main chance to influence the issues that will be discussed in the media and the way the government will be portrayed by the press.

In fact, however, the dynamic of Question Period involves reciprocal influences between the media and opposition parties. It has often been said that this morning's *Globe and Mail* or *National Post* headline becomes this afternoon's leading volley in Question Period, but matters are not this simple. Journalists also react—although not always in the way that opposition parties may like—to the questions and lines of attack that opposition parties launch against the government. "[W]hile the stated purpose is to seek and give information," writes Andrea Ulrich, "the real objective [of Question Period], at least on the part of the opposition, is to point out many mistakes that the government is making, and call them to public account."[41] In this way it serves the interests of both the opposition parties, who wish to see the government embarrassed and its popular support drop, and the media, who know that controversy and the scent of wrongdoing attract more readers and viewers than do reports that all is well with the world.

Committees of the House of Commons, whose membership is generally limited to about 20 MPs, may appear to be a forum where the leash of party discipline can be loosened and backbench MPs may acquire some expertise in particular policy areas that will enable them to assess the merits of legislation in a more informed and less partisan manner. Students of American politics know that congressional committees are where the real action is in Congress, and that

what enters one end of the committee sausage-grinder may not bear much resemblance to what emerges from the other end, if it emerges at all. In Canada's Parliament, however, committees seldom modify in more than marginal ways what is placed before them and virtually never derail any bill the government has introduced in the House. Far from being a source of opportunity and satisfaction for MPs who wish to see themselves as being truly engaged in the law-making process, much evidence suggests that committees are a source of frustration for many MPs and that they do not provide a serious vehicle through which the legislature can scrutinize the activities of government and call it to account for its actions. In his study of MPs' behaviour and perceptions of their jobs, David Docherty states that "several rookie Liberals indicated that the failure of their own executive to treat committee work and reports seriously was the single most frustrating (and unexpected) aspect of their job as an MP."[42] Docherty found that frustration with House committees was not limited to government party members. Opposition MPs also expressed disappointment with the inability of committees to make more than a marginal and occasional difference. On the other hand, a 2010 study based on interviews with MPs found they were more likely to express satisfaction with their committee work, and to see it as constructive and relatively non-partisan, than with any other aspect of their job.[43] This said, most of the MPs interviewed about their experience on committees acknowledged that while the leash of party discipline was looser in committee, in large part because no one is watching except CPAC addicts,[44] the leash can and does shorten very quickly if the government senses that its MPs are straying from the path it wants them to take.

It may well be, as this 2010 study concludes, that committee work is not a source of frustration for all or even most MPs. It remains the case, however, that their work typically does not make much of a difference. "People will tell you," said one MP interviewed for the 2010 study, 'I've done great work on a committee.' But you really have to say, 'You did good work. You travelled. You studied this and that. But what did you accomplish? Show us where the legislation changed and what you did.'"[45] Despite

Listen to the "It's Not as Bad as You Think: Political Corruption in Canada" podcast, available at: www.oup.com/he/Brooks9e

some tinkering over the last couple of decades, the ostensible goal of which was to increase the independence of committees and thereby augment the influence of the legislature, the fact that party discipline operates in committees just as it does on the floor of the House of Commons undoes all of these reforms. Moreover, all but a small fraction of what committees do is reactive—responding to a bill tabled in Parliament by the government, examining spending proposals submitted by the government, or pursuing some investigative task assigned to a committee by the government. Within this straitjacket there can be little wiggle room for nonpartisan accounting of the government's record and proposals.

Senators argue that life is different in the red chamber. They point to the Senate's long string of committee and task force studies over the years on topics ranging from corporate concentration in Canada's media industries to the decriminalization of marijuana possession. Being appointed to serve until the age of 75, most of them argue, loosens the constraint of party discipline. This may appear to have been loosened further by the Trudeau government's practice of appointing senators as independents. Not having to worry about whether their party leader will sign their nomination papers at some future election and being unconcerned with how their actions might affect their prospect of being appointed someday to cabinet, senators can behave with far greater independence than their House of Commons colleagues.

This argument, while not totally false, is both naive and self-serving. It is naive in that it ignores the palpable reality that most senators have demonstrated pretty firm and unswerving loyalty to the party, and especially to the prime minister, that appointed them. This is not surprising when one looks at who becomes a senator and why. Until the reforms to the selection process instituted by Justin Trudeau, most were people who had served their party long and loyally. It would have been more than a bit unusual if they were suddenly, after appointment to the Senate, to change the patterns of loyalty that got them there in the first place.

That, Paul Thomas argues, was yesterday's Senate. Prime Minister Trudeau's decision to exclude Liberal senators from the party caucus and to change the selection process in ways that, ostensibly, would reduce the significance of partisanship have contributed to a reformed and better Senate, more capable of performing well and independently the legislative functions assigned to it by the Constitution. "[T]he Senate is becoming more of a political force to be reckoned with in the formulation, approval and evaluation of public policy," argues Thomas. "This is a positive development because a stronger Senate can act as a counterweight to power concentrated in the office of the prime minister, who is supported by loyal and disciplined partisan majorities in the House of Commons."[46] This conclusion may be called into question, however, given that Trudeau's independent appointees have been highly likely to support the government's legislation.

The legislature's oversight function also operates through the Office of the Auditor General (OAG). Created in 1878, the modern history of the office dates from 1977 when the Auditor General Act broadened its responsibilities from what were essentially auditing and accounting functions (attest and compliance audits) to include an evaluation of how well government programs and Crown corporations were being managed (value-for-money or performance audits).[47] This has proven to be a wide-ranging mandate. The Auditor General reports to the House of Commons and is authorized to issue up to three reports per year in addition to an annual report. The first annual reports of the Auditor General tended to focus rather narrowly on the question of whether money appropriated by Parliament was spent in authorized ways and followed required accountability guidelines. Since passage of the 1977 Act, the concept of "value for money" has been part of the Auditor General's terms of reference. In 1995 the Auditor General Act was changed again, creating the position of Commissioner of the Environment and Sustainable Development within the Office of the Auditor General, thereby broadening its mandate to include the environmental audit of government programs and institutions. The statute also allows the Auditor General wide discretion in the selection of

Listen to the "Canada's Senate" podcast, available at: www.oup .com/he/Brooks9e

particular aspects of government spending for special scrutiny.

The result of all this has been that the Office of the Auditor General is today much larger, with about 600 employees, than it was before value-for-money auditing became part of its role. Its annual reports and special studies often generate extensive and unfavourable media coverage of particular aspects of government performance. Sharon Sutherland, a long-time critic of the OAG, has argued that its more intrusive role usurps that of opposition parties and elected representatives when it comes to holding government accountable for spending and performance. It is hard to see, however, how MPs and opposition parties could carry out the sort of in-depth oversight of government financial activities that takes place through the OAG.[48]

Representation

Whatever its shortcomings, the House of Commons is an important point of contact between citizens and government. Symbolically, the elected House embodies the principle of government by popular consent. The partisan divisions within it, between government and opposition parties, have the additional effect of affirming for most citizens their belief in the competitive character of politics and that the different points of view that exist among Canadians are reflected in the different positions taken by parties in the House. At a practical level, citizens often turn to their elected representatives when they experience problems with bureaucracy or when they want to express their views on government policy.

Unlike the elected Commons, the Senate does not perform a significant representational role in Canadian politics. This is despite the fact that senators are appointed to represent the various provinces and regions of Canada. The unelected character of Canada's upper house and the blatantly partisan criteria that prime ministers have usually used in filling Senate vacancies, until the 2016 selection reforms, have undermined whatever legitimacy senators might otherwise have achieved as spokespersons for the regions. Provincial governments, regional spokespersons in the federal

cabinet, and regional blocs of MPs within the party caucuses are, in about that order of importance, vastly more significant in representing regional interests.

Debate

The image that most Canadians have of Parliament is of the heated exchanges that take place across the aisle that separates the government and opposition parties. Parliamentary procedure and even the physical layout of the legislature are based on the adversarial principle of "them versus us." This principle is most clearly seen in the daily Question Period and the debates following the Speech from the Throne and the introduction of a new budget. At its best, the thrust and riposte of partisan debate can provide a very public forum for the discussion of national issues, as well as highlight the policy differences between the parties. Unfortunately for the quality of political discourse in Canada, parliamentary debate is more often dragged down by the wooden reading of prepared remarks, heckling and personal invective, and occasional blatant abuses of either the government's majority or the opposition's opportunities to hold up the business of Parliament.

It is a mistake to imagine that the purpose of parliamentary debate is to allow for a searching discussion of issues in a spirit of open-mindedness. Generally, MPs' minds are made up when a measure is first tabled in Parliament. Or if their minds are not made up on a bill, they know that, in most cases, they will be under enormous pressure to vote as their party leadership directs. So if debate is really theatre, what is the point of the long hours spent criticizing and defending legislative proposals and the government's record, all at taxpayers' expense?

Legislative debate is important for two reasons. First, outcomes are not always predictable. Even when the government party holds a commanding majority in Parliament, or when the policy differences between government and opposition are not significant, the dynamic of debate on an issue is not entirely controllable by the government or by Parliament. Media coverage of the issue, reporting of public opinion polls, the interventions of organized interests, other governments, and even individuals who have credibility in the eyes of the media and the public all will have a bearing on the trajectory of parliamentary debate.

Parliamentary debate is also important because it reinforces the popular belief in the open and competitive qualities of Canadian democracy. "[T]he challenging of the 'noble lies' of the state," writes C.E.S. Franks, "through the institutionalization of doubt in question period and debate is one of the unusual and underappreciated virtues of the parliamentary system."[49] The stylized conflict between government and opposition parties, which is the essence of the British parliamentary system, emphasizes disagreements and differences. At the same time, adversarial politics obscures the fact that these partisan disagreements often take place within a fairly narrow band of consensus on basic values. The words and deeds of the opposition, when it holds power, have frequently borne a strong resemblance to the government that preceded it.

What Franks describes as an "underappreciated virtue" of the parliamentary system is, in fact, seen to be an indecorous shouting match by many, if not most, Canadians. They are more likely to view this give and take—Question Period at least, which is the only activity in Parliament that a significant share of the population has seen either in person or, more usually, on television—as dysfunctional rather than virtuous. It is clear, however, that the blame for this situation does not belong entirely to the parties and their MPs. "Partisan attacks and political jousting," observes Andrea Ulrich, "result in exciting exchanges that are deemed [by the media to be] newsworthy, and the public eagerly watches the battles, all the while complaining about the behaviour of those they elected for just those qualities that hold their attention."[50]

What Does an MP Do?

Many Canadians believe that their politicians are overpaid, underworked, and liable to line their own pockets at public expense. In recent years stories of "gold-clad" MPs' pensions and of senators guilty of ethically questionable billing practices have helped to fuel this widespread but generally unfair charge. Most backbench MPs work very long hours, whether in Ottawa or at home in their constituencies (see Box 9.4). The demands on their time ratchet upward in the case of members of the government and party leaders, all of whom are required to travel extensively in carrying out their jobs. For most MPs, the single largest block of their working day is devoted to taking care of constituency business. David Docherty reports that the MPs he surveyed from the thirty-fourth (1988–93) and thirty-fifth (1993–7) parliaments claimed to devote just over 40 per cent of their working time to constituency affairs. The second largest block of time was spent on legislative work, such as committee assignments and attending Question Period and debates. These activities ran a fairly distant second to constituency work. Although Docherty's survey of how backbench MPs spend their time has not been replicated, the MP exit interviews conducted by the Samara Centre for Democracy in 2017 suggest that not much has changed and that constituency service remains the foremost activity for most MPs.[51]

In performing their functions, all MPs are provided with a budget that enables them to hire staff in Ottawa and in their riding office. How they allocate these resources is up to them, but most MPs opt to have two staffers in Ottawa and two in the constituency office. MPs are also provided with public funds to maintain their constituency office and are allowed an unlimited regular mail budget and four mass mailings to constituents—known as "householders"—per year.[52] Although these resources are paltry compared to those at the disposal of US congressional representatives and senators, they are superior to those of legislators in the United Kingdom, Belgium, France, and many other democracies. And while they may be adequate to enable an MP to carry out his or her constituency duties, they are not sufficient to pay for high-powered policy analysts and other research staff.

Docherty found that MPs who were new to Parliament tended to spend more time on constituency work than those who had been in the legislature for a longer period of time. "[T]he longer members serve in office," he observes, "the less time they will devote to

Listen to the "Is Canada's Political System Broken?" podcast, available at: www.oup .com/he/Brooks9e

Governing Realities

BOX 9.4 One Veteran MP Explains How He Organizes His Time

Scott Reid was first elected to the House of Commons as a Conservative MP for Lanark–Frontenac–Kingston in 2000. His family owns Giant Tiger, a chain of over 200 stores across much of Canada. Reid was asked by a Toronto Star *journalist how he managed to balance his role as a member of the board of directors of this family business with his work as an MP. His answer included this insightful explanation of how many MPs spend their time and how, in his case and certainly that of many others, one becomes better organized over time.*

Parliament sits only 26 weeks a year, so any MP who is sufficiently organized has a larger amount of free time than would be true for most jobs. Many MPs devote the majority of this time to partisan work. (By "partisan work," I most emphatically do not mean parliamentary work, as most MPs who are not in Cabinet or Shadow Cabinet spend relatively little time during break weeks on Commons-related activity, unless they are involved in a Commons committee that is meeting during a break week. I am referring to work on behalf of, or for, the party itself, or in preparation for the next election—assisting with candidate nominations in other ridings, working on one's own riding database and mailing list, etc.)

Some of the typical MP's remaining time is spent on constituency-related activity, but the most genuinely meaningful constituency work consists of resolving government-relations issues regarding passports, pension-related issues, etc., and in my own case I find that this can be done either by my staff at my constituency office in my absence, or (in cases where my personal attention is required) can be done by means of a teleconference call just as well on weeks when the Commons is sitting, as on weeks when I'm back in the riding. On such a call, the constituent is typically at his or her home, my staffer is attending from the riding office, and I call in from my Parliament Hill office.

I have served for over seventeen years, and as time goes on, I have been able to find ways of reducing the amount of time it takes to complete the same task. For example: I host two Robbie Burns events each January. But the amount of time that is needed for set-up and takedown, and for finding a piper, providing food, etc. has been reduced to a fraction of what it was when I first started doing this. I estimate that good planning and carefully-maintained routines have reduced the time-commitment needed for routine/scheduled constituency tasks by about two-thirds, with no loss of output.

Most MPs spend somewhere between a day and a day and a half on the weekly round trip from Ottawa to their constituencies, on each of the 26 weeks that the Commons is sitting. Compared to the travel time that is eaten up each week by MPs travelling back and forth between (say) Labrador or rural Saskatchewan, the fifteen or twenty MPs who live within driving distance of Ottawa therefore are left with something between 25 and 35 extra days of available work-time per annum. I'm one of the lucky fifteen-to-twenty: My house in Perth is almost exactly a one-hour drive from Parliament Hill, when there's no traffic.

Source: Scott Reid's Blog, "On My Roles as MP and with Giant Tiger Stores Ltd," 23 Apr. 2018, http://scottreid.ca/on-my-roles-as-mp-and-with-giant-tiger-stores-ltd/.

constituency work."[53] This shift from constituency to policy-oriented work, however, does not mean that a veteran MP's constituents are less well served than those of an MP who is new to Parliament. Docherty found that the Ottawa staffs of veteran MPs tended to make up the difference, spending more of their time on constituency business as their MPs' focus shifted to policy concerns. "No matter what stage of their career," Docherty states, "members of parliament see helping individuals as their most crucial duty."[54] In this, MPs show themselves to be realistic about the limits on their ability to be lawmakers.

A Democratic Deficit?

Mention Canada's **democratic deficit** at any gathering of persons who have an above average interest in and knowledge of Canadian politics and the term is sure to be received with knowing nods. A quick Google search will turn up what seems to be an endless number of books, articles, conferences, op-ed pieces, blog entries, and other communications on this theme. (Even more will be found if you insert "American" or "European Union" along with "democratic deficit"!) While the term means somewhat different things to different people, it is usually used to signify a lack of accountability in government or, to put it differently, a disconnect between the preferences and interests of citizens and the decisions of those who govern them. In Canada, the conversation on what many believe to be a democratic deficit focuses on two main causes. One involves the system of government, which is said to be dysfunctional in various ways, with too much power concentrated in the hands of the prime minister and those around him or her. The other involves what are believed to be undemocratic consequences of the electoral system. This second issue is discussed in Chapter 11.

In considering whether there is a democratic deficit a baseline must first be established. A deficit compared to what? Is political power concentrated in fewer hands today than in the heyday of the so-called "mandarins," the cabal of senior public servants who effectively ran the federal government in the post-World War II era and whose ties to the Liberal Party, which formed the government most of the time, were very intimate? Perhaps we have more democratic and participatory expectations as a result of cultural changes that have swept across the Western world. Europeans have talked for many years about a democratic deficit in EU politics, so we are certainly not alone, nor are we the first to wring our hands about unresponsive political elites and broken institutions of accountability. There is little doubt that "democratic deficit" sometimes is merely a slogan when used by some critics who do not like the ideological coloration or policy direction of a particular government or the sort of outcomes produced by the electoral or legislative system. At the same time, the term performs the very useful function of causing us to think about how well our political institutions achieve the goals we associate with democracy. And if we find they do not provide the transparency, accountability,

and responsiveness to the popular will that we expect, then this indeed is a democratic deficit (see Box 9.5).

The Courts

Responsibility for Canada's judicial system is divided between Ottawa and the provinces. While the Constitution gives the federal government the exclusive right to make criminal law, it assigns responsibility for the administration of justice and for most law enforcement to the provinces. Consequently, all provinces have established their own systems of courts that interpret and apply both federal and provincial laws.

The Constitution also gives Ottawa the authority to create courts. This authority was used in 1875 to create the Supreme Court of Canada. Since 1949 the Supreme Court has been Canada's highest court of appeal. Ottawa again used this constitutional power in 1971 to create the Federal Court of Canada. It was assigned jurisdiction over civil claims involving the federal government, cases arising from the decisions of federally appointed administrative bodies like the Immigration Appeal Board, and matters relating to federal income tax, copyrights, and maritime law—all of which fall under the legislative authority of Ottawa. In 2003 the Federal Court of Canada was divided to create the Federal Court, with the jurisdictions assigned by the 1971 statute, and the Federal Court of Appeal, which hears appeals from the rulings of the Federal Court, the Tax Court, and some federal tribunals. The structure of Canada's court system is shown in Figure 9.3.

Courts apply and interpret the law. They perform this role in matters ranging from contested driving offences and squabbles over wills to disputes over the most fundamental principles of the Constitution. The decisions of judges often have profound implications for the rights and status of individuals and groups, for the balance of social and economic power, and for the federal division of powers. It is, therefore, crucial that we understand the political significance of the judicial process and the methods of interpretation typically used by the courts.

Governing Realities

BOX 9.5 Thomas Axworthy on Claims That Canada Has a Democratic Deficit

Tom Axworthy was a speechwriter and principal secretary in the PMO under Prime Minister Pierre Trudeau, with whom he later co-authored Towards a Just Society. *Axworthy is currently a Senior Fellow at the Munk School of Global Affairs. In the following passage, from a presentation he made at the House of Commons in 2016, Axworthy reminds us that in talking about a democratic deficit in Canada, some comparative perspective is useful.*

Canada is one of the world's most successful liberal democracies: there is no crisis in democratic practice or outcomes in this country. As this Committee undertakes its important work, the perspective should be how to improve even more an already well-functioning system whose merits are recognized internationally.

Every international comparison puts Canada in the top rank in governance, election outcomes and human development achievement. The World Bank, for example, sponsors a worldwide governance indicators project. In 2014, Canada had a 96 per cent rating in the category of voice and accountability, 91 per cent in political stability, 95 per cent in government effectiveness, 98 per cent in regulatory quality, 93 per cent in the rule of law, and 94 per cent in control of corruption. On electoral systems, the Electoral Integrity Project rated Canada in 2015 as "very high" at 75 per cent in electoral integrity overall, holding top place among those employing majoritarian

electoral rule. This combination of high achieving governance and political practice has certainly contributed to the most important success of all, the expansion of human development and choice. Here too, for many decades, Canada has been at the top of the list in the United Nations Human Development Index, ranked first in 1985, second in 1995, and in 2014 ranked 9th out of 183 countries, just behind the Nordic Nations.

Our success is due, in large part, because we are a parliamentary democracy. The Westminster system, when it works right (and in Canada it has mostly worked right), concentrates power in the executive so that things can get done while ensuring that those holding this power are accountable for its use. When Parliament is sitting, the government is accountable to the legislature on a daily basis and its record will eventually be scrutinized and judged by the people at election time. Parliament represents and speaks on behalf of all Canadians in making and questioning governments. David E. Smith rightly describes our preeminent institution as "The People's House of Commons."

Source: From the text of Axworthy's presentation before the House of Commons Special Committee on Electoral Reform, 23 Aug. 2016. The full text of his remarks is reproduced in the *Ottawa Citizen*, 14 Sept. 2016, https://ottawacitizen.com/opinion/columnists/axworthy-no-crisis-in-canadian-democracy-but-we-keep-improving-it-and-perhaps-still-can.

The independence of judges is the cornerstone of the Canadian judicial system. Judges are appointed by governments. But once appointed they hold office "during good behaviour,"[55] being required to retire at age 75. What constitutes a lapse from "good behaviour"? A criminal or a serious moral offence could provide grounds for removal, as could decisions of such incompetence that they undermine public respect for the law and the judiciary. This test of judicial misconduct was set down more clearly in the 1990 Nova Scotia Court of Appeal inquiry into the exoneration of Donald Marshall Jr following his having spent 11 years in

prison for a murder he did not commit. The test was this: "Is the conduct alleged so manifestly and profoundly destructive of the concept of impartiality, integrity and independence of the judicial role, that public confidence would be sufficiently undermined to render the judge incapable of executing judicial office?"[56] In such circumstances the appointing government may launch removal proceedings against a judge. In fact, this has seldom happened. Formal proceedings have rarely been initiated and have very seldom been prosecuted to their ultimate conclusion, i.e., the actual removal of a judge by resolution of Parliament or a provincial legislature. Indeed, no federal judge has ever been removed from office through this process. Judicial independence is also protected by the fact that judges' salaries and conditions of service are established by law. Consequently, governments cannot single out any individual judge for special reward or punishment.

To say that judges are "independent" is not the end of the story. They are independent of the government of the day and may not be given instructions or otherwise interfered with in carrying out their duties. As members of the societies in which they live, however, usually successful members of the middle and upper-middle classes, they cannot be neutral in the values they bring to their task. As is true of everyone else, they have acquired a world view, beliefs, values, and, being human beings, perhaps even prejudices of various sorts they may not be aware of. Thus, when one says that the judiciary is "independent" this should be understood as a description of its formal separation from the executive and legislative branches of the state. When it comes to the dominant value system of their society, judges are no more independent than are the members of any other part of the state elite. Leaving aside the socio-economically unrepresentative character of the legal profession and the effects of formal training in the law, in Canada, as in the vast majority of democracies, all judges are appointed by governments.[57] One would hardly expect these governments to appoint radical critics of society, even supposing that a significant number of such individuals existed within the more respected ranks of the legal profession from which judges are selected. Moreover, governments control promotion within the system of courts—who will be promoted from a district court to a superior court, and so on. This may also exert a chilling effect on unconventional judicial behaviour.

The socio-economic background of judges and the process by which they are selected have been argued by some to introduce certain biases into the judiciary. In recent years the legal profession from which judges are selected has become more representative than it was through most of Canada's history. The process of representation starts with who is admitted to law school. For a profession that prides itself on what it believes to be its sensitivity to issues of fairness and social justice, there is frustratingly little and at best only scattered information on this subject. Law schools and the legal profession have collected data on gender and racial representation among their student bodies and practitioners, and more recently on sexual orientation and persons with disabilities, but there is not much in the way of systematically collected data on the socio-economic background of those who get into law school, enter the legal profession, and subsequently become part of the pool from which judges are selected. It would be no more difficult, in most cases, to ascertain the socio-economic status of a law student's family than, say, his or her gender, ethnicity, or sexual orientation. The conventional wisdom is that these latter characteristics are likely to make a difference in the world view, values, beliefs, and, ultimately, behaviour of lawyers, some of whom will go on to become judges. Is there any reason to imagine that the socio-economic circumstances in which they were raised would have less of a formative impact?

Data from the United States confirm the dramatic class bias in the legal profession, particularly in the more prestigious and influential legal circles and among judges, a bias that begins with the selection process at law schools.[58] Most of the evidence for Canada, however, is hardly more than anecdotal. Of course, a class bias already exists in who is more likely to attend university. This bias becomes more pronounced in the case of who is likely to be accepted into and graduate from professional programs. There may be no reason to imagine that such bias is greater in the case of law schools than, say, MBA programs or medical schools. Nonetheless, life experiences and socio-economic background certainly have some influence on how one views the world and, in this case, interprets the law.

A study by sociologist Michael Ornstein found that the representation of visible minorities in the legal profession in Ontario increased steadily between 1981 and 2001. It was highest among younger members of the profession and increased from about 2 per cent of lawyers between the ages of 25 and 34 in 1981 to 17 per cent in 2001. For Canada as a whole, and across all age groups, it was about 14 per cent in 2001. The representation of non-white Canadians in the legal profession, Ornstein found, was significantly lower than in most other professions, including medicine, engineering, university professors, and business managers.[59] A study of the BC legal profession conducted in 2006 found broadly similar numbers to those reported by Ornstein.[60] The representation of minorities in the legal profession has been increasing gradually. Ornstein revisited the case of Ontario based on data collected in 2014. He found that the representation of Indigenous Canadians and members of ethnic or racial minorities was greater among younger members of the profession and that they were in fact somewhat over-represented, compared to the non-white and non-Indigenous share of Ontario's population, among lawyers under 35 years of age.[61]

Judges, of course, are selected from the ranks of the legal profession. Moreover, it is uncommon for a person to be made a judge before having acquired significant professional experience and having reached middle age. Thus it comes as no surprise that Canada's judicial elite lags behind the legal profession in terms of the representation of various minorities. A 2012 study by Ryerson University's Diversity Institute found that visible minority judges constituted under 3 per cent of all federally appointed judges.[62]

Women have much greater representation in the legal profession and on the courts than in the past. In 1971 they comprised only about 5 per cent of the legal profession. Today they constitute close to 40 per cent of all lawyers. As of 1 July 2018, 40 per cent of all federally appointed judges were female. Prior to 2016 there was no reliable demographic data on

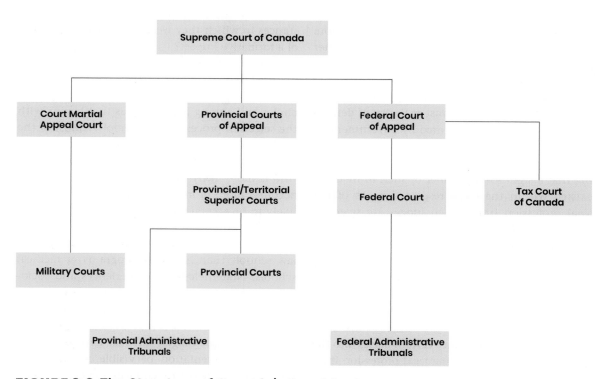

FIGURE 9.3 **The Structure of Canada's Court System**

Source: Canada's Court System, Figure: Outline of Canada's Court System, http://www.justice.gc.ca/eng/csj-sjc/ccs-ajc/02.html. Department of Justice Canada, 2005. Reproduced with the permission of the Department of Justice Canada, 2019.

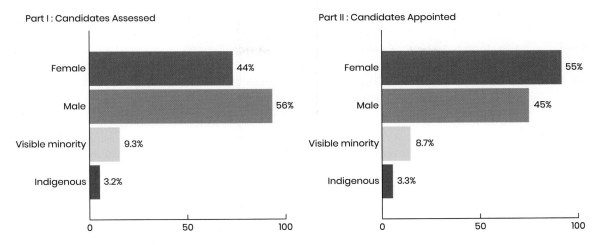

Part I : Candidates Assessed

Part II : Candidates Appointed

FIGURE 9.4 Federal Judicial Appointments, 2016–19

Note: Between 21 October 2016 and 27 October 2018, 1,070 candidate assessments were made. Some applicants were assessed for more than one appointment. A total of 153 appointments were made, 83 to females, 70 to males, 16 to members of visible minority groups, and 6 to Indigenous persons.

Source: Based on data from the Office of the Commissioner for Federal Judicial Affairs Canada, "Statistics Regarding Judicial Applicants and Appointees," www .fja-cmf.gc.ca.

judges appointed by Ottawa. Since then judicial applicants are invited to self-identify. Although we lack a pre-2016 baseline for comparison, it is clear from data collected on federal judicial appointments over the past few years that females and applicants from various minority groups are being appointed in greater numbers than in the past (see Figure 9.4). The main argument for the increased representation of women on the courts has been that they bring important perspectives on the law and on society that have been less likely to be embraced by male judges.[63] The same argument is made for the increased representation of some other under-represented groups, including visible minorities.

At the same time, it is simplistic and incorrect to assume any sort of automatic correspondence between a judge's ethnicity, gender, sexual orientation, or socio-economic background and the likelihood that he or she will decide cases in a particular way. The judicial profession in Canada—still mainly male, white, and from middle- and upper-class origins—is much more liberal today than it was 40 or 50 years ago. It may be, as Joel Bakan and some others argue, that more important than the demographic characteristics of the legal profession and the judges is the nature of the legal system within which they work. "The Charter's potentially radical and liberatory principles of equality, freedom, and democracy," argues Bakan, "are administered by a fundamentally conservative institution—the legal system—and operate in social conditions that routinely undermine their realization."[64] By his account, judges are for the most part incapable of escaping from certain conservative understandings of the Charter and of rights—particularly an unwillingness to recognize social rights—and from conservative legal conceptions that prevent them from playing a transformative role in Canadian society.

Of course, this just leads us to wonder what Canadians want or expect from judges! Those who argue that the courts should play a transformative role were deeply disappointed in September 2013 when the Ontario Superior Court refused to hear a case involving homelessness. Advocates for the homeless argued that sections 7 and 15 of the Charter should be interpreted as providing a right to housing and that the existence of homelessness involves a Charter violation as well as a failure on the part of Canadian governments to live up to commitments entered into under the

Governing Realities

BOX 9.6 Former Chief Justice McLachlin Defends the Court's Involvement with Questions of Social Policy

The fact that judges rule on social questions that affect large numbers of people does not, however, mean that judges are political. There is much confusion on this point in the popular press. Judges are said to be acting politically, to have descended (or perhaps ascended) into the political arena. Judges, on this view, are simply politicians who do not need to stand for election and can never be removed.

This misapprehension confuses outcome with process. Many judicial decisions on important social issues—say affirmative action, or abortion, or gay rights—will be political in the sense that they will satisfy some political factions at the expense of others. But the term "political" is used in the context to describe an outcome, not a process. While the outcomes of cases are inevitably political in some broad sense of the term, it is important—critical, even—that the process be impartial. It is inescapable that judges' decisions will have political ramifications. But it is essential that they not be partisan. In their final form, judgments on social policy questions are often not all that different from legislation. It is the process by which the judgments are arrived at that distinguishes them. Legislation is often the product of compromise or conflict between various political factions, each faction pushing its own agenda. The judicial arena does not, and should not, provide simply another forum for the same kind of contests. Judges must *maintain the appearance and reality of impartiality*. It is impartiality that distinguishes us from the other branches of government, and impartiality that gives us our legitimacy.

. . . [Our] changing society affects the work of judges. The nature of the questions they decide, and the public expectation that they will decide them fairly and well, place new demands on judges. It no longer suffices to be a competent legal scholar and a fair arbiter. To perform their modern role well, judges must be sensitive to a broad range of social concerns. They must possess a keen appreciation of the importance of individual and group interests and rights. And they must be in touch with the society in which they work, understanding its values and its tensions. The ivory tower no longer suffices as the residence of choice for judges.

Source: Excerpt from remarks of the Right Honourable Beverley McLachlin, PC, former Chief Justice of Canada, "The Role of Judges in Modern Society," 4th Worldwide Common Law Judiciary Conference, Vancouver, 5 May 2001, www.scc-csc.gc.ca/aboutcourt/judges/speeches/role-of-judges_e.html.

International Covenant on Economic, Social, and Cultural Rights (1976). Article 11 of that agreement recognizes "the right of everyone to an adequate standard of living for himself and his family, including adequate food, clothing and housing, and to the continuous improvement of living conditions." Bakan, Martha Jackman, and other critics claim that the courts in Canada are trapped in a conservative mindset and decision-making model that prevents them from being bolder in the interpretation of social rights.

Legal reasoning in Anglo-American judicial systems is based on the concept of *stare decisis*. This means that judges should be guided by decisions from previous cases where the circumstances and issues were similar, and also that lower courts are bound by the rulings of higher courts. Recent history has shown, however, that Canadian judges are quite prepared to depart from established precedents when they think the circumstances warrant this and, moreover, that they have sometimes shown a willingness to be ahead of public opinion on some issues. Particularly at the highest levels of the judicial system, judges are certainly quite aware of the socio-economic and political consequences of their decisions (see Box 9.6). Canadian courts were surely ahead of public opinion on same-sex marriage. The Charter has been a decisive factor in this matter of judges being more willing to depart from legal precedents. Already, in one of the earliest Charter decisions, *R. v. Big M Drug Mart Ltd.* (1985), the Supreme Court stated that the Charter "does not simply 'recognize and declare' existing rights as they were circumscribed by legislation current at the time of the Charter's entrenchment." The Charter has enabled Canadian judges to look at familiar issues through a different lens and arrive at very different rulings, thus weakening the conservative tug of *stare decisis*.

Summing Up

Canada has a parliamentary system of government that concentrates power in and around the prime minister. Although some believe this undermines Canadian democracy and the accountability of Parliament to the people, not everyone agrees. Many of the criticisms of the concentration of power in the executive and the declining influence of the legislature are premised on rather nostalgic and not particularly accurate notions of how Canadian government worked in the past. The idea that the prime minister was once first among equals in a cabinet that was a more collegial decision-making body does not describe the reality of the prime minister's clear dominance throughout most of Canada's political history. Nor is it true that there was once a golden age of Parliament when the House of Commons was a much more influential player in the law-making process than it has been in recent times.[65] If the Canadian system of government is broken, as its critics charge, it is not because it does not work the way it once did.

This does not mean that it could not be improved. Some of Canada's most prominent political figures from recent decades, including Bob Rae, Preston Manning, and Ed Broadbent, who typically disagree on much when it comes to politics, all agree that major reforms to Parliament are needed. They may be right. At the same time, however, one must always be wary of the "law of unintended consequences." Party discipline in the House of Commons is much reviled and most often pointed to as something that needs to be changed.

But what happens to accountability if, instead of being able to associate a law with a particular party or prime minister, citizens can no longer pinpoint with any certainty who is responsible? As Adam Przeworski writes in *Sustainable Democracy*, "Governments are accountable only when voters can clearly assign the responsibility for performance to competing teams of politicians, when the incumbents can be effectively punished for inadequate performance in office, and when voters are sufficiently well informed to accurately assess this performance."[66] Other reforms may have other consequences, some positive and expected, and others perhaps less so.

Appendix: How a Law Is Passed

The law takes various forms. A statute passed by the House of Commons and the Senate, and given royal assent by the governor general, is clearly a law. But decisions taken by cabinet that have not been approved in the legislature also have the force of law. These are called "Orders-in-Council." Thousands of them are issued each year, and they are published in the *Canada Gazette*. The decisions of agencies, boards, and commissions that receive their regulatory powers from a statute also have the force of law. Finally, there are the regulations and guidelines issued and enforced by the departmental bureaucracy in accordance with the discretionary powers delegated to them under a statute. These also have the force of law.

In a strictly numerical sense the statutes passed annually by Parliament represent only the tip of the iceberg of laws promulgated each year. Nevertheless, virtually all major policy decisions—including budget measures and the laws that assign discretionary power to the bureaucracy—come before the legislature. The only exception has been when the normal process of government was suspended by passage of the War Measures Act. This happened during World War I, again during World War II, and briefly in 1970 when Ottawa proclaimed the War Measures Act after two political kidnappings in Quebec by the Front de libération du Québec. The War Measures Act was replaced by the Emergencies Act in 1988.

During normal times the law-making process involves several stages and opportunities for debate and amendment. The steps from the introduction of a bill in Parliament to the final proclamation of a statute are set out in Figure 9.5.

There are two types of bills: private members' bills and government bills. Private members' bills originate from any individual MP, but unless they get the backing of government they have little chance of passing. Government bills dominate Parliament's legislative agenda. When major legislation is being proposed, a bill is sometimes preceded by a *white paper*. This is a report for

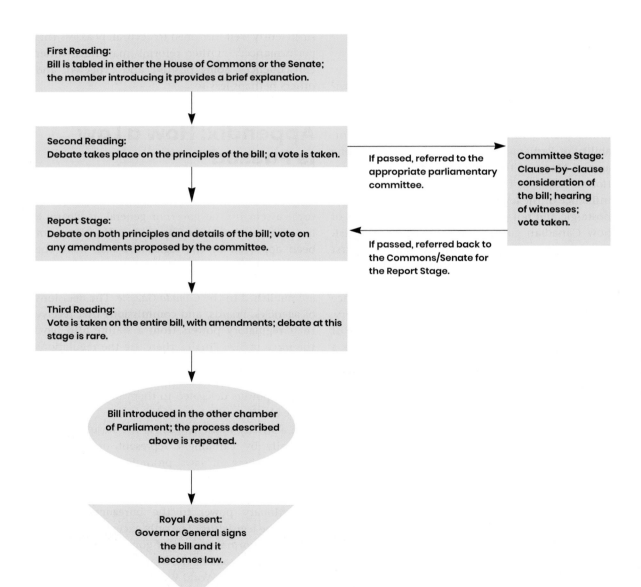

FIGURE 9.5 From Bill to Statute

discussion, based on research by the bureaucracy (and sometimes the legislature as well), and serves as a statement of the government's legislative intentions. Major legislation may also follow from the recommendations of a Royal Commission, a task force, or some other consultative body created by the government to study and make recommendations on an issue.

Once a bill has been drafted by government, it is introduced in the Senate, or more usually, in the House of Commons. Here, it is given *first reading*, which is just a formality and involves no debate. Then the bill goes to *second reading*, when the main principles of the bill are debated and a vote is taken. If the bill passes second reading it is sent to a smaller legislative committee, where the details of the bill are considered clause by clause and witnesses may be heard. At this committee stage, amendments can be made but the principle of the bill cannot be altered. The bill is then reported back to the House, where all aspects, including any amendments, are debated. At this *report stage* new amendments also can be introduced. If a bill passes this hurdle it then goes to *third reading* where a final vote is taken, sometimes after further debate. Once a bill has been passed in the House, it is then sent to the Senate where a virtually identical process takes place. If a bill was first introduced in the Senate, then it would now be sent to the House. Finally, a bill that has been passed in both the House and the Senate may be given royal assent and become law.

Starting Points for Research

Carleton University, MacOdrum Library, Canadian Government Policy Cycle: https://library.carleton.ca/research/subject-guides/canadian-government-policy-cycle-detailed-guide. A step-by-step guide to the policy-making process that includes a wealth of useful weblinks.

David Docherty, *Mr. Smith Goes to Ottawa: Life in the House of Commons* (Vancouver: University of British Columbia Press, 1997). This excellent analysis of legislative behaviour and influence in the House of Commons is based largely on surveys of MPs. It deserves an updated version.

Donald Savoie, *Governing from the Centre: The Concentration of Power in Canadian Politics* (Toronto: University of Toronto Press, 1999). Here Savoie makes the case that the concentration of power in and around the Prime Minister's Office had reached unprecedented and undemocratic levels. This "must read" for those interested in the history of and current inner workings of the machinery of government should be followed by Savoie's *Court Government and the Collapse of Accountability in Canada and the United Kingdom* (Toronto: University of Toronto Press, 2008) and, *Power: Where Is It?* (Montreal and Kingston: McGill-Queen's University Press, 2013).

Review Exercises

1. Who is the current chief of staff to the prime minister? Who is the current clerk of the Privy Council? What are their backgrounds (education, professional experience, partisan involvement, etc.). Find a story in the media that discusses the influence of one of these individuals.

2. Put together a list of the various governmental organizations (federal, provincial, municipal) you have been in contact with during your life and the reasons for the contact(s). Think hard—the list is probably longer than you first imagine.

3. Question Period is probably the activity of Parliament that most Canadians have heard

of and perhaps have seen on the news. You may view both the daily Question Period from Canada's House of Commons and the British Prime Minister's Question Time at the Cable Public Affairs Channel (www.cpac.ca/en/).

Watch one broadcast of each from the same week. How would you compare these two models for holding the government of the day accountable for its actions and policies?

Visitors take in the view at Banff National Park in Alberta in 2017, a year that saw record-high numbers of visitors due to Parks Canada's 2017 free entry program in celebration of the country's 150th birthday. Parks Canada, along with the Canadian Broadcasting Corporation (CBC), Canada Post Corporation, the Bank of Canada, Canada Revenue Agency, Export Development Canada, and a whole host of other government institutions, make up the federal bureaucracy and are responsible for carrying out the policies set by the government of Canada. (Lmspencer/Shutterstock)

10 The Administrative State

For policies to have an impact they must be implemented. This is the role of the bureaucracy. Implementation, however, is not an automatic process of converting laws into actions. Unelected officials often wield significant discretion in applying laws and administering programs. Moreover, their influence may be felt at numerous points in the decision-making process preceding the actual introduction of a bill in Parliament. This chapter examines the federal bureaucracy, focusing on the following topics:

- The development of the administrative state
- Professionalization of the public service in Canada
- The political rights of public servants
- Efficiency and accountability
- The structure and functions of the bureaucracy
- Globalization and the state
- Representative bureaucracy

During the first year after Confederation, the government of Canada spent about $14 million. Its revenues were about the same. It is uncertain how many employees worked for the federal government. Apparently no one thought it worthwhile to keep track of this information before 1900, when it was found that the Canadian government had 12,000 employees. The organization of the federal government was fairly simple in the years after Confederation, with 10 major departments and four main agencies by 1873.[1]

This uncomplicated structure did not last. By 1960 federal spending had reached $5.7 billion. The federal government consisted of 92 major departments and agencies employing about 200,000 persons. The need for an organization chart to help keep track of this growing complexity was keenly felt and, indeed, the Financial Administration Act had been passed in 1951, providing a legal framework to make sense of the variety of structures that had emerged in a mainly ad hoc and unco-ordinated manner over the years. By the 1960s, how to keep on top of the leviathan of modern government had become an important concern of those who studied Canadian government and **bureaucracy**. It has been so ever since.

Today, annual federal spending exceeds $360 billion. The list of federal departments and agencies runs into the hundreds.[2] Roughly 273,000 people (2018) work for these organizations, a total that does not include the Canadian military or the Royal Canadian Mounted Police. The size of government in Canada is even larger and its complexity much greater if one includes provincial, territorial, and local governments. Indeed, the activities of these other levels of government affect the lives of most Canadians in ways that may appear to be more direct and significant than those of the federal government. Hospitals, doctors' services, schools, rubbish collection and disposal, water treatment, public housing, police, roads, and urban mass transit: these are all primarily the responsibilities of provincial and local governments. Together, these governments outspend and out-tax the federal government.[3]

Statistics like these, however, tell only part of the story. When the American writer Henry David Thoreau visited Canada in 1850 he was struck by what he perceived to be the statist culture: "In Canada you are reminded of the government every day. It parades itself before you. It is not content to be the servant but will be the master."[4] For Thoreau, remnants of the British aristocratic system and of the French feudal system gave to Canada an Old World character where hierarchy, distinction, and deference were woven through the culture. Although the state was not large in terms of its resources, its influence was more pervasive and the awe—understood as a combination of deference and respect—that it elicited from citizens was greater than in the United States. So Thoreau believed from his travels through what is today Quebec.

A statist mentality may have existed in nineteenth-century Canada, although the testimony of Thoreau needs to be placed alongside that of others, such as fellow writer Susanna Moodie. She believed that the arrival of the "lower orders" in the British North American colonies caused them to abandon the proper deference they owed their social superiors and adopt an "I'm as good as you, Jack" mentality.[5] But whether Thoreau or Moodie comes closer to the mark in characterizing the mentality of the times, the state in Canada was puny. It employed comparatively few people, accounted for but a small share of the country's economy, and did many fewer things than it does today.

It was different from the contemporary state in another important way. Today we take for granted that most state officials will be bureaucrats who are hired and promoted according to job-relevant criteria and who keep their positions regardless of which party controls the government. In other words, we expect that **patronage**—the practice of making decisions about the distribution of public resources based on friendship, family, loyalty, or in exchange for benefits of various sorts—will be very limited and in some cases against the law. It may still be fine if the prime minister appoints a loyal friend and partisan ally to a position in the PMO, but we would find it unacceptable if he stuffed the bureaucracy, the courts, the higher rungs of the military, or the RCMP with such people. And, indeed, laws and staffing rules limit the possibility of such practices occurring. Nor would most of us consider appropriate the awarding of public contracts based on political favouritism. Patronage continues to exist, but the point is that in the nineteenth century such practices were both common and believed by many to be normal and acceptable. The gears of the state were lubricated with generous amounts of patronage to a degree and in circumstances that today would be considered unethical and sometimes even illegal.

Professionalization of the Public Service

The **merit principle**, whereby hiring and promotion decisions were expected to be based on such qualifications as relevant experience, academic degrees, professional credentials and certification, and other attributes deemed to be relevant to the competent performance of the job, was introduced by the Civil Service Amendment Act, 1908. Prior to this reform, the practice of patronage-based appointments was rampant, as was also true in most other democracies and certainly in the United States, where pressures for public service reform also were building. The Royal Commission to Enquire into and Report on the Operation of the Civil Service Act and Kindred Legislation stated that "patronage seems to run more or less through every department of the public service. It was the universal feeling among the officials who gave evidence before the Commissioners that this patronage evil was the curse of the public service."[6]

But the reforms instituted by the 1908 law were quite limited, extending the merit principle in hiring only to what was called the "inside service" in Ottawa but not to the thousands of federal civil service positions elsewhere in the country. This changed 10 years later when the Conservative government of Robert Borden passed the Civil Service Act, 1918, extending merit principle hiring and the authority of the non-partisan Civil Service Commission (today called the Public Service Commission of Canada) to federal positions outside of Ottawa.

The merit principle was a key part of a larger process of professionalization of the public service.

Another reform involved various prohibitions on the political activities of unelected state officials. The reasoning was quite simple. Bureaucrats should be able to serve whatever party formed the government, uninfluenced by their own political beliefs and partisan preferences. A politically neutral public service was considered essential to a modern, professional bureaucracy. This reasoning was premised on the **politics–administration dichotomy** that was an important aspect of progressive thought about the democratic state in the late nineteenth and early twentieth centuries. It held that only elected politicians should make choices between competing values and interests, choices that would be embodied in the laws. The proper function of non-elected state officials was to implement these choices without regard for their personal views and preferences. Even some of those who supported the politics–administration dichotomy worried about what would eventually be seen as the dehumanizing and even totalitarian implications of viewing state bureaucrats as, in Max Weber's words, "specialists without spirit, sensualists without heart."[7]

In any case, the 1908 and 1918 reforms placed strict limits on the rights of public servants to participate in politics beyond voting. They could not contribute money to a party or a candidate for public office and, although the law was not entirely clear on these matters, it appeared they could not put campaign signs on their lawns, make public speeches or publish articles in newspapers or elsewhere in which they expressed their political views, or even belong to a party and attend its meetings.

This would not change until 1967 when the Public Service Employment Act was passed. The Act specifically omitted attending political meetings and contributing money from the political activities that were off limits to public servants. It also gave to the Public Service Commission the authority to grant unpaid leaves of absence to public servants running for office. Increasingly, however, the inherent tension between the obligation of political neutrality imposed on public servants and their political rights as citizens was viewed as a problem, at least by those whose right to participate in the political process was restricted on account of their employment status. Their demands for the same rights enjoyed by other citizens were part of the broader movement towards the expansion and recognition of rights that produced human rights codes in the 1960s and 1970s and the Charter of Rights and Freedoms in 1982. Armed with the Charter, public servants have gone to court to challenge what they believed to be unconstitutional limitations on their political rights. Here is what the courts have said in three of the most important of these cases.

Fraser v. Public Service Staff Relations Board (1985)

Neil Fraser was a public servant with Revenue Canada's Kingston office. He was outspoken and even vitriolic in his criticism of the federal government's adoption of the metric system and also of the Charter of Rights and Freedoms. After repeated warnings and suspensions by his employer, Fraser was dismissed from his job. In challenging his dismissal, Fraser did not argue that his right to free speech under the Charter had been violated (the Charter was not part of the Constitution when his dismissal occurred). Instead, he argued that federal law concerning the dismissal of employees made a crucial distinction between job-related and non-job-related criticism and that a public servant ought to be as free as any private citizen to criticize policies unrelated to his or her job or department. The government responded that public criticism by an employee of any government policy may have the effect of undermining the actual and perceived neutrality and impartiality of the public service.

The Supreme Court agreed with Fraser's contention that public servants should be allowed non-job-related criticism of government policy. But it held that, in this case, his criticisms crossed the line and could, in fact, be considered job-related. Here is the key section of the Court's ruling:

> . . . As a general rule, federal public servants should be loyal to their employer, the Government of Canada. The loyalty owed is to the Government of Canada, not the political party in power at any one time. . . .
> In some circumstances a public servant may

actively and publicly express opposition to the policies of a government . . . if, for example the Government were engaged in illegal acts, or if its policies jeopardized the life, health or safety of the public servant or others, or if the public servant's criticisms had no impact on his or her ability to perform effectively the duties of a public servant or on the public perception of that ability. But, having stated these qualifications . . . it is my view that a public servant . . . must not engage, as the appellant did in the present case, in sustained and highly visible attacks on major Government policies.[8]

Osborne v. Canada (Treasury Board) (1991)

Bryan Osborne was a public servant working in the Actuarial Branch of the Department of Insurance within the Treasury Board. He was elected by his Liberal Party riding association to serve as a delegate at the party's 1984 leadership convention. Osborne resigned as a delegate after his employer warned him that he would face disciplinary action if he failed to do so. But subsequently, when a by-election was called in his riding, Osborne requested and received a leave of absence from his job to stand as a candidate for the Liberal Party nomination. He admitted that he did this to be free to attend the party's leadership convention, after which Osborne withdrew from the nomination race and requested that he be reinstated in his job. His political leave was terminated and Osborne did, in fact, return to his job.

Other public servants were also involved in this case, but the issue was the same: did s. 33(1) of the Public Service Employment Act, which prohibits public servants from engaging in work for or against a candidate, violate their Charter rights? Osborne and the other public servants in this case argued that their rights of free speech and freedom of association were infringed. In a 1991 judgment, the Supreme Court agreed. It ruled that these prohibitions were "over-inclusive and went beyond what is necessary to achieve the objective of an impartial and loyal civil service." The government's argument that these were reasonable limits on Charter rights was rejected. Only the requirement that a public servant must take an unpaid leave to stand as a candidate and the restrictions on the political activities of deputy ministers were upheld by the Court.[9]

Haydon v. Canada (2004)

Dr Margaret Haydon was a veterinarian with Health Canada. In 2001 she was given a 10-day suspension after having told a *Globe and Mail* reporter that a ban imposed by the Canadian government on imports of Brazilian beef was motivated more by political factors than genuine health concerns. Prior to this incident Dr Haydon had been publicly critical of government health policies on two occasions, one of which resulted in a warning from her employer.

This case involved issues similar to those in *Fraser*. In the 2004 *Haydon* ruling, the Federal Court of Canada reiterated what the Supreme Court had said in that earlier decision on the employee's duty of loyalty and the reasons for this duty. It then elaborated on the balance between a public servant's free speech rights and his or her duty of loyalty:

> The following factors are relevant in determining whether a public servant in speaking out has breached his loyalty duty: the employee's level within the hierarchy; nature and content of the expression; visibility of the expression; sensitivity of the issue; truth of the statement made; steps taken to determine the facts prior to speaking; efforts to raise concerns with the employer; extent of damage to employer's reputation and impact upon employer's ability to conduct business.
>
> Where disciplinary action is taken against a public servant, the employer must demonstrate that the comments were inappropriate and harmful. . . .
>
> The duty of loyalty constitutes a reasonable limit on freedom of expression. . . .[10]

If Dr Haydon had been engaged in what is called **whistleblowing**—bringing public attention to government actions or policies that she believed endangered public health or safety, based on her careful examination of the facts—the balance between her right to free speech and her duty of loyalty would have tipped in favour of the former. But that was not what she was doing, the Court decided. Another recent case of a public-sector worker being critical of the government of the day is described in Box 10.1.

Efficiency and Accountability

When the state was small and its functions many fewer than today, the need for expertise was felt less strongly. Some positions required special skills and training, such as government surveyors, statisticians with the Dominion Bureau of Statistics (rechristened Statistics Canada in 1971), and accountants working for the Treasury Board. But most positions in the bureaucracy did not require much, if anything, in the way of higher education, specialized credentials, and professional certification. The long struggle for adoption of the merit principle in public-sector hiring and promotion was largely a response to the obvious inefficiencies likely to result from staffing decisions based on friendship, family, and partisan connections. But it was also related to an important shift taking place by the late nineteenth century in ideas about the state, its proper functions, and its potential.

These ideas are sometimes referred to as the **positive state**: a state that is active in attempting to shape society and influence its direction. It was championed by liberal intellectuals such as John Dewey in the United States (*The Public and Its Problems*, 1927); socialist thinkers in the United Kingdom, most prominently the members of the Fabian Society; and, in Canada, by Progressive movement intellectuals such as Adam Shortt, a University of Chicago-educated economic historian at Queen's University and an original member of the Civil Service Commission. Shortt expressed the intellectual spirit of his times when he wrote, "One does not attempt fine work through the instrumentality of a mob. . . . It is through a select,

Governing Realities

BOX 10.1 When Public Servants Express Themselves via Social Media

In June 2015, shortly before the beginning of the federal election campaign, an Environment Canada scientist by the name of Tony Turner posted a music video at YouTube. Called "Harperman," the roughly five-minute song was composed by Turner, who was also the main performer. It is a satirical and highly critical condemnation of the record of the Conservative government of Stephen Harper. Halfway through the election campaign the video had over half a million views. Environment Canada suspended Turner from his job using GPS to track migratory birds, pending an investigation into whether he had violated the 2012 Values and Ethics Code governing the political activities of public servants. In the end the matter was moot. Turner was already scheduled to retire and did so a few months later, before his case was decided.

THE CANADIAN PRESS/Darryl Dyck

Former Environment Canada scientist Tony Turner holds a "Harperman" sign after performing his song at a Green Party campaign rally in Vancouver on 3 October 2015—the same week that his retirement from the civil service took effect.

active minority that the most effective and progressive ideas as to political and social welfare must be introduced."[11] The state, thinkers like Shortt believed, needed to be staffed by people with expert training to meet the challenges of a modern society in which policy problems were increasingly complex and not capable of being understood, let alone solved, by non-experts.

One of the first of such experts to make an important mark on the federal public service was Oscar Douglas Skelton. Like Shortt, he had been educated at the University of Chicago and taught at Queen's University. It is part of the lore of Canadian intellectual history that Skelton's *Socialism: A Critical Appraisal* (1911) received the backhanded

compliment of being referred to by Lenin as a sophisticated embodiment of intellectual power in the service of capitalism. Skelton's insistence that Canadian foreign policy should be determined independently of the British Empire, and that Canada's most important external relationship was with the United States, coincided with the views of Liberal Prime Minister Mackenzie King. In 1925 Skelton was appointed by King as under-secretary of state for External Affairs. Until his death in 1941, Skelton was beyond doubt the most influential figure in the determination of Canada's foreign policy, an influence acknowledged by King in several passages from his diaries. Indeed, J.L. Granatstein dates the beginning of the modern

Like many thousands of Canadian public servants, Turner used social media. Posting a politically sensitive music video at YouTube and seeing it go viral might seem to be rather different from posting a photo of oneself holding a "Down with Prime Minister X" sign on Instagram or "liking" a Facebook post that is highly critical of the government. In fact, however, the issue is the same: What ought to be the limits of a public servant's right to publicly criticize the government for whom he or she works?

The Public Service Alliance of Canada has advice for its members on this matter. "Online political expression," the PSAC notes, "does not benefit from any greater or any less protection than other forms of political expression." Well, this is almost accurate. The PSAC webpage on expressing political views via social media quickly adds that this might not be Charter-protected speech if it has been shared during working hours or using a government phone, laptop, or other device. It then goes on to make the following suggestions:

- Do not identify yourself as a government employee or include information or comments that might be interpreted that you are a government employee.

- Be careful not to criticize government policies that are directly related to your job or department.
- Consider your level of visibility and influence: "Federal public employees holding jobs with a higher level of responsibility, influence and visibility may be more easily perceived as being politically partisan and more limited in what they can say publicly."[12]

Public service union representatives, the PSAC document observes, when speaking on behalf of their union, have greater freedom to be critical of the government and its policies.

So, do you think the foot-tapping music video of Environment Canada scientist Tony Turner crossed the line of what ought to be allowed? Keep in mind that the Values and Ethics Code for the Public Sector says that one of the expected behaviours of public servants involves "Respecting the rule of law and carrying out their duties in accordance with legislation, policies and directives in a non-partisan and impartial manner" (1.1).[13]

Tony Turner's performance of "Harperman" may be viewed at https://www.nationalobserver.com/2017/02/14/video/harperman-protest-song.

civil service in Canada from Skelton's entry into the Ottawa bureaucracy. Skelton recruited into External Affairs highly educated individuals, many of whom had done post-graduate work at Oxford or at American universities. In addition, he was the director of research for the Royal Commission on Dominion–Provincial Relations (1937).

Another professor from Queen's, the economist W.C. Clark, was appointed in 1932 as deputy minister of Finance. Clark's role as one of the key architects of Keynesian economic policy after World War II is well known. He was at the centre of a group of Queen's economists who were prominent members of the bureaucratic elite through their positions in the Department of Finance and the Bank

of Canada. This group included W.A. Mackintosh and John Deutsch, both of whom served as deputy minister of Finance and ultimately became principal of Queen's. Indeed, Queen's developed a reputation as a recruiting ground for the senior levels of the bureaucracy.

The links between the federal bureaucracy and academe during this period when the administrative state was being consolidated have been examined by John Porter. He found that in 1953 just under a fifth of the bureaucratic elite (composed of the 243 senior officials of federal government departments, agencies, and Crown corporations) had taught in a university at some point, and an even greater proportion of the highest-ranking bureaucrats (nine out of 40 at the deputy minister level) were former university teachers.[14] The unrivalled dominance of the Department of Finance in economic policy and in the developing field of social policy meant that this group, and the economics profession generally, had a relationship to public policy and the state not enjoyed by other social scientists. This certainly was evident in the formation and activities of the Royal Commission on Canada's Economic Prospects (Gordon Commission, 1956). In the words of one commentator, "The Gordon Commission was like a vast wind tunnel with the door accidentally left open: it sucked up practically every available economist in the country."[15]

The special relationship of economics to public policy and the state already had begun to take shape in the 1930s. The recruitment of university-trained economists for the Department of Finance and the research department of the Bank of Canada, created in 1935, as well as for the economic studies commissioned for the Nova Scotia Royal Commission on the Economy (1934), the National Employment Commission (1936), and the Royal Commission on Dominion–Provincial Relations (1937–40), provided the institutional opportunities for the increasing integration of the economics profession into the state. Even before John Maynard Keynes's ideas on the manipulation of aggregate demand by government became the orthodox view among economists and policy-makers, providing what appeared to be an irrefutable intellectual foundation for the positive state, widespread skepticism clearly existed about what had been thought to be the self-correcting markets of classical economic theory. Likewise, governments were willing to rely on trained professionals for advice on how to influence macroeconomic activity.

World War II saw state planning on a level never previously experienced in Canada, with increasing recruitment of university economists into such government bodies as the Department of Finance and the Wartime Prices and Trade Board. They formed the core of what Mackenzie King referred to as the "intelligentsia," a group of experts for whom wartime planning provided opportunities to influence policy from within the state. Their influence and the special relationship of the economics profession

to public policy were consolidated by the federal government's formal acceptance of Keynesian economic policy in the White Paper on Employment and Income (1945) and in the governing Liberal Party's 1945 election platform.

These decades stretching from the 1925 appointment of Skelton at External Affairs to the 1950s saw the rise of what historian Doug Owram has called "the government generation."[16] Trained in the modern social sciences, often holding graduate degrees from American universities, they represented a new breed of senior bureaucrat for whom government was viewed as the necessary instrument for maintaining economic prosperity and solving social problems. They were, in an important sense, the architects of the positive state in Canada, a state characterized by professionalism and an increasingly influential role for the bureaucracy.

By the end of the 1950s some were of the opinion that the senior bureaucracy had become, in fact, too influential. The election of the Progressive Conservative Party in 1957 under John Diefenbaker, after 22 uninterrupted years of Liberal government, presented a challenge to the model of an impartial and politically neutral bureaucracy. Would senior bureaucrats, who had worked with Liberal politicians for almost a generation developing the modern Canadian state, be willing and able to transfer their loyalty to a new set of political masters and to whatever changes in policy they might insist upon? It is well known that Prime Minister Diefenbaker and some of his cabinet ministers mistrusted the bureaucracy, suspecting many senior officials of Liberal sympathies and of being subtly unco-operative with the Conservative government and its policies. In *Lament for a Nation*, the philosopher George Grant famously accused the senior Ottawa bureaucrats of being complicit with the Liberal Party and the representatives of American capital in a continentalist vision of the Canada–United States relationship that Diefenbaker rejected.

Ironically, soon after the 1963 defeat of Diefenbaker and the return to power of the Liberal Party, the power of the **"Ottawa mandarins"** whom Diefenbaker so mistrusted began to decline. The Canadian administrative state was entering a new phase in its development, characterized by dramatic growth in revenue, expenditure, personnel, and programs. Between 1965 and 1975, the number of federal public servants increased by 50 per cent, from 203,419 to 307,390.[17] The growth was greatest in Health and Welfare, National Revenue, and the Unemployment Insurance Commission, but also took place because of the creation of new departments, each with its own raft of programs to administer. These included Communications (1970), Consumer and Corporate Affairs (1968), the Environment (1972), Regional Economic Expansion (1970), and Science and Technology (1973). Federal revenue increased between 1965 and 1975 by almost 400 per cent, from $9.3 billion to $34.7 billion. Expenditures grew from $8.6 billion to $36.8 billion. Spending increased most rapidly on social services, including health, social welfare, and education. Much of this increase in social spending took the form of transfer payments to the provinces, whose expenditures were growing even more rapidly than Ottawa's. As the administrative state grew in size and complexity, the influence of the so-called mandarins declined. Influence within the state became more diffuse and, in a sense, impersonal. Of course, some officials would continue to be found at the top of the administrative food chain, including the deputy ministers of Finance and Justice, the governor of the Bank of Canada, and the chief clerk of the Privy Council. But the days when the bureaucratic power-brokers could be gathered around a medium-sized table in the dining room of the Château Laurier were definitely over.

The 1970s marked the beginning of what some social and political commentators, particularly on the left, began to call the **crisis of the state**. This referred to what appeared to be the inability or unwillingness of governments to finance the welfare state policies put in place over the preceding four decades. The Keynesian consensus—the belief that governments could and should manage their economies by using a repertoire of fiscal policy measures, notably taxation and government spending—was increasingly challenged in the economics and policy-making communities and was largely discredited in many Western democracies by the 1980s. The reason had to do largely with a rapid

and dramatic increase in accumulated public-sector debt. Federal deficits increased during the 1970s and 1980s, a trend that was not reversed until the late 1990s. Year after year of deficit spending, financed through borrowing, necessarily produced an increase in the stockpile of government debt. Public debt charges that amounted to $1.9 billion in 1970, or about 13 per cent of total federal expenditures, reached $30 billion, or 16 per cent of total spending, in 1980 and about $41 billion (27 per cent of total spending) in 1990, peaking at 30 per cent of total federal expenditure in 1997. (These figures compare to about 8 per cent of federal spending in 2017.)

The term "crisis" is often used too casually and for ideological purposes. Whether there was a crisis of the state during these decades depends on what one means by crisis. What is certain, however, is that the confidence associated with the Keynesian welfare state declined and government spending increasingly was seen to be a problem. But state spending in Canada as a share of GDP did not decline until the late 1990s (see Figure 10.1), nor was there any significant slashing of government programs and regulation during this same period. Healthy economic growth in Canada from 1993 to 2007 produced significant growth in government revenues. This, rather than spending cuts, was the key factor that transformed years of government deficits into surpluses starting in 1997, ending only in 2008 when the Canadian economy followed the American and other Western economies into recession.

The last few decades, perhaps even extending as far back as the late 1970s, might be characterized as an era of diminished expectations for the Canadian state. The idea of governments "fine-tuning" their economies through a judicious spending increase here or a timely tax measure there was widely accepted, as was the more general notion that the solution to economic, social, or cultural problems could be achieved through government intervention. According to Gallup polls, in the late 1970s only slightly more than a quarter of Canadians agreed that government wastes "a good deal" of tax money. Between 1984 and 1997 the percentage of Canadians who agreed that government wastes a good deal of money ranged from 46 to 80 per cent.[18] Faith in the positive state was in decline. The neo-liberal ideology of smaller government, less regulation, and a greater reliance on markets was ascendant. Not everyone shares in the diminished expectations for the state that have become more prevalent over the past few decades. The NDP, labour unions, the Council of Canadians, much of the social sciences and social services communities, a significant number of those in the media, the environmental movement, and many others remain optimistic, to varying degrees and depending on the circumstances, about the ability of the state to solve problems. Moreover, they see the state as a necessary instrument for the promotion of social justice, environmental protection and improvement, and economic prosperity, the benefits of which do not accrue mainly to a few. It is simply incorrect to argue that a consensus about an activist state has been replaced by a new popular consensus that a diminished state is preferable. The mood of lesser expectations for the state surely may have had the upper hand in recent decades, but it has been vigorously contested.

Finally, it is also not the case that the administrative state has been downsized significantly over this same period of time. The public sector's share of the Canadian labour force today is about as large as it was in 1980, with about one in four workers employed either directly or indirectly by the state.[19] Although some of Canada's most prominent public enterprises have been sold to private investors since the 1980s, including Petro-Canada, Air Canada, and Canadian National, the role of the federal and provincial governments in the Canadian economy, through direct ownership but more significantly through regulation, taxation, and purchasing remains very important. Human rights codes, pay equity rulings, and environmental laws have made the state more rather than less intrusive in some ways over the past couple of decades. So is the downsized neo-liberal state in Canada a myth or reality?

It may be a bit of both. Despite widespread public skepticism about bureaucracy and the effectiveness of government, most people continue to demand that government "do something" when a perceived problem arises. For example, when the Canadian economy slid into recession in late 2008, the reaction of most Canadians was not that the government should stand back and let market forces take their course. On the contrary, most expected the government to act—to spend money, pass laws, bail out industries, and protect jobs. Although there was no agreement about what industries should be helped and whose jobs should be protected, there appeared to be a widespread sense that government actions were needed. Since being elected in 2015 the Liberal government has been persistently upbeat about the role of government in solving problems. It has matched its rhetoric with action, increasing real per capita spending by the federal government to the highest level in Canadian history, higher than during World War II and slightly higher than during the recession of 2008–9.[20] Canadians and their leaders may not be as optimistic about the ability of the state to manage problems as they were when another Trudeau was prime minister. But it would be too much to say that they have given up hope on the positive state.

Globalization and the State

The administrative state arose over time in response to changes in the nature of society and the economy. It is unrealistic to assume that its particular form will remain fixed as conditions around it change. Foremost among these changes has been the process of globalization. It has affected the Canadian state in regard to its capacity, structure, and the idea of what the state can and ought to do.

State Fiscal Capacity

For the administrative state to carry out its many functions it must have the resources to do so. In turn, this requires an adequate stream of revenue to cover the cost of paying bureaucrats' salaries and benefits, building and maintaining roads, funding for schools and hospitals, paying those on state pensions and social assistance, and all the other expenditures of government. This is part of what is meant by state capacity. It has been affected by the unprecedented ease and speed of capital movements between countries, provinces and states, and even between cities, which is, of course, an important feature of globalization.

The consequences have been twofold. Governments have become more sensitive to the demands of businesses whose activities create jobs and thereby contribute to state revenues in various ways, from the payroll taxes (i.e., Employment Insurance and Canada Pension Plan premiums) paid by employers and employees to the sales taxes paid when workers and their families make purchases. They are also more sensitive to the expectations of investors, a category that often includes foreign governments and institutional investors such as large pension funds, who buy their bonds. The degree of this sensitivity should not be exaggerated. Governments in Canada and elsewhere obviously have not scrapped all of those laws and regulations that are unpopular with various parts of the business and investment community. The mobility of capital, while greater during the last few decades than at any other time in history, is limited by a number of factors. These include the economic costs associated with relocating production facilities or services. Such costs involve more than mothballing existing facilities and opening new ones. Even more significant, in some cases, may be the cultural friction that results when services, such as customer services in communications and banking, are moved to another country where labour may be cheap, but proficiency in the language of clients and understanding of the myriad cultural nuances that contribute to satisfactory service may be weaker than in the country where these services were originally based. Moreover, the state is not always as defenceless in the face of capital movements and investors' preferences as is often suggested. "There are many good reasons for doubting the theoretical and empirical basis of claims that states are being eclipsed by contemporary patterns of globalization," argue David Held and Anthony McGrew. "[A]ny assessment of the cumulative impacts of globalization," they write,

"must acknowledge their highly differentiated character since it is not experienced uniformly by all states."[21]

A second consequence of the unprecedented ease with which capital and jobs move around the globe is that, to maintain the state's fiscal capacity, governments have become less dependent on revenue generated by the direct taxation of businesses and more dependent on revenue from the taxation of individuals. Income taxes, sales taxes, payroll taxes, and user fees all have become more important as sources of state revenue. The personal income tax accounts for roughly half of all federal government revenue, up from about one-third of total revenue in the late 1960s. It is followed in importance as a source of federal government revenue by social security contributions (the CPP/QPP and EI) and consumption taxes. Corporate income taxes in 2017 accounted for about 14 per cent of total government revenues, but this can vary significantly from year to year. Since 1966 they have accounted for as little as about 6 per cent of total revenue to as much as 19 per cent. In some years consumption taxes, most of which are paid by individuals, account for a greater share of federal revenue than do corporate taxes (see Figure 10.1). At the provincial level, the personal income tax is by the far the major source of government revenue, typically two to three times more important than corporation taxes.

State Structure

It is often said that globalization and the neo-liberal policies associated with it have contributed to the downsizing of the state, but this is too simplistic, rather misleading, and in some cases just plain wrong. Certainly, the privatization of some services and the sale of some state enterprises to private investors have occurred in Canada, as in many other countries, as governments have searched for infusions of money or have sought to offload costs. And in some cases privatization very clearly has been motivated by ideology. The outsourcing of certain functions, for example, may be seen as a way of reducing the influence of public-sector unions, in addition to whatever cost savings might be expected. Deregulation of

A. Federal Government Revenues

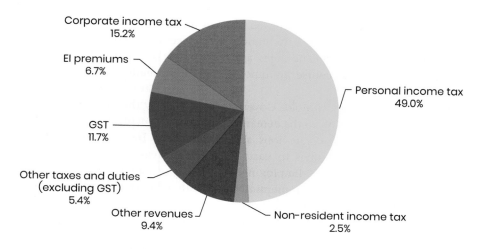

Corporate income tax
15.2%

EI premiums
6.7%

GST
11.7%

Other taxes and duties
(excluding GST)
5.4%

Other revenues
9.4%

Personal income tax
49.0%

Non-resident income tax
2.5%

B. Federal Government Expenditures

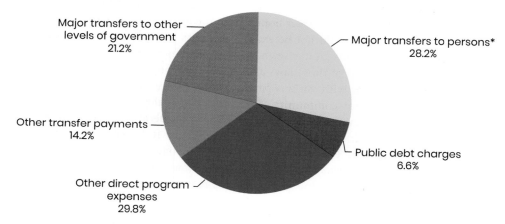

Major transfers to other
levels of government
21.2%

Other transfer payments
14.2%

Other direct program
expenses
29.8%

Major transfers to persons*
28.2%

Public debt charges
6.6%

FIGURE 10.1 Where Does the Money Come from and Where Does It Go?

Source: Department of Finance, Annual Financial Report of the Government of Canada, Fiscal Year 2017–2018.

certain economic activities is also pointed to as a consequence of globalization, as governments are forced to compete for increasingly mobile capital and thus feel compelled to lower the costs of doing business in order to retain or attract investment. Another consequence involves the reconfiguration of the bureaucracy, combining, creating, and repurposing some of its institutions in response to issues that have arisen or become more pressing as a result of globalization. All of these policy shifts involve changes to the structure of the state,

whether motivated by considerations of costs or ideology, or both.

The reality, as Held and McGrew remind us, is that globalization has affected the structure of the state in different ways in different societies. In the case of Canada, it cannot credibly be argued that the forces of globalization have enfeebled the state at any level of government. Expenditures by all governments in Canada amount to about 40 per cent of GDP. This is less than the 50 per cent of GDP accounted for by all government spending in the early

1990s, but it is about what it has been most years since 2000.[22] Public-sector employment, at all levels of government, accounted for about one-quarter of all employment in Canada in 1992 and accounts for roughly the same share of total employment today.[23] No complete picture exists of the scope of economic, environmental, social, and cultural regulation by governments in Canada. Nevertheless, there is absolutely no reason to imagine that it is less today than when "globalization" was still a relatively novel word in the 1980s.[24] At the same time, globalization has contributed to the state taking on new or expanded functions or legitimizing its actions based on ideas and institutions that have been generated by this process. Although we tend to associate globalization with economics, this is only part of what it involves. Fundamentally, globalization is about interdependence and the various ways in which the world has become a "smaller" place. One of these ways involves the development of an international architecture of policy-making and globalized networks of interests and ideas that influence domestic state officials and civil society. Human rights commissions and courts in Canada regularly refer to international agreements and developments concerning rights. Canadian state officials involved with matters of Arctic sovereignty and economic development participate in negotiations with other Arctic states, sometimes bilaterally and other times in multilateral forums. Energy and environment officials in Canada are very aware that they do not operate in isolation from the rest of the world in regard to oil sands development, climate change measures, species at risk, and so on. Officials in the Department of Defence and Canada's intelligence services are influenced by their participation in international missions, organizations, and policy communities. The same may be said of officials in health care, education, immigration, and other fields.

The Structure of Canadian Bureaucracy

The federal public sector employs roughly 530,000 people working in close to 400 different organizations. About half of them work directly for government departments and agencies. They are public servants, in the narrow legal sense of this term. Their employer is the Treasury Board and the organizations they work for fall directly under the authority of a cabinet minister. Close to 20 per cent are employed by federally owned Crown corporations and the remainder work in some capacity in the Canadian Forces, the RCMP, or some other federal agency. The organizations they work for receive all or part of their funding from the federal government and are subject to rules that it sets, but these organizations operate with some degree of autonomy.

Public-sector employment is even greater at the provincial, territorial, and local levels, at roughly 1 million employees. If hospitals and other health-care facilities, schools, and enterprises owned by these levels of government are included, the figure rises to over 3 million employees. A full account of the scope of public sector's importance for employment in Canada would also include non-profit and charitable organizations that depend on government funding for a significant part of their revenue. It has been estimated that about one-third of the revenues of the roughly 170,000 non-profit organizations in Canada comes from government sources. About two-thirds of these organizations carry out activities related to public policy. Although slightly more than half of all such organizations depend entirely on volunteers, this vast sector is estimated to employ close to 1 million persons.[25] Despite frequently heard claims that the welfare state has been replaced by a new reality of downsized government, the public sector remains quite extensive. That part of it often labelled the "bureaucracy" may be divided into three main components: the public service (chiefly departments); independent and semi-independent agencies and tribunals; and Crown corporations.

Public service. About half of the federal public sector falls under this category. It includes all statutory departments and other organizations whose members are appointed by the Public Service Commission (PSC) and are employees of the Treasury Board. This is the part of the bureaucracy most directly under the authority of cabinet.

Agencies and tribunals. These organizations perform a wide variety of regulatory, research, and advisory functions. Among the most widely known federal regulatory agencies are the Canadian Radio-television and Telecommunications Commission (CRTC, which regulates communications and broadcasting), the National Transportation Agency (air, water, and rail transportation), and the Canada Energy Regulator (energy when it crosses provincial and international boundaries). Many important areas of regulation, including trucking, public utilities within provincial boundaries, and most labour relations, are controlled by provincial governments.

These organizations have a greater degree of independence from government than those that fall under the public service. With few exceptions their members are not appointed by the PSC, nor are they employees of the Treasury Board. The precise degree of autonomy enjoyed by an agency or tribunal varies, but in some cases it is almost total.

Crown corporations. These organizations, in most cases, perform commercial functions and typically operate at "arm's length" from the government of the day. As of 2018 there were 43 such corporations. The largest by far in terms of employment is Canada Post, with about 60,000 employees. Crown corporations hire their own employees, determine their own internal administrative structures, and in many instances behave much like privately owned businesses. Over the last few decades some of the largest of these corporations, notably Atomic Energy of Canada Limited, Air Canada, Canadian National Railway, and Petro-Canada, have been privatized. Crown corporations are also quite numerous at the provincial level, with an estimated 180 such organizations.[26]

These three categories do not cover the entire federal bureaucracy. Some relatively small but important parts of that bureaucracy, including the Auditor General's Office (discussed in Chapter 9) and the Commissioner of Official Languages, are independent of cabinet, reporting directly to Parliament. The Royal Canadian Mounted Police also has a distinct legal status, as do the Canadian Forces.

One can identify several different functions performed by the organizations that comprise the Canadian administrative state. These include:

- the provision and administration of services to the public, often to narrow economic, social, or cultural clientele groups;
  - the provision of services to other parts of the bureaucracy;
  - the integration of policy in a particular field, or the generation of policy advice;
  - the adjudication of applications and/or the development and application of regulations (such as food, product, or hazardous waste safety standards, issuing of broadcast licences, licensing pilots and flight engineers, and literally hundreds upon hundreds of similar activities);
  - the disbursement of funds to groups or individuals, as with the grants to artists and cultural organizations administered by the Canada Council;
  - the production of a good or the operation of a service that is sold to buyers.

RCMP officers on duty at Parliament Hill. An agency of the Ministry of Public Safety Canada, the RCMP acts as Canada's national police service, while also providing provincial and municipal policing in three territories and eight provinces on a contract basis.

These functions are not mutually exclusive. A large and organizationally complex department such as Health Canada is involved in service delivery, mainly to First Nations and Inuit communities; the determination of food, drug, and other standards related to health; regulating certain consumer products; promoting healthy lifestyles and workplaces; registering and evaluating pesticides; scientific research; and the development of policy. Depending on the nature of the programs that a department administers, it may have extensive and regular contact with provincial bureaucracies. It is common for departments and agencies to organize public opinion research related to their activities, although the actual survey or focus group is likely to be carried out by a pre-authorized public opinion research firm. Almost all government departments, regardless of their primary orientation, have a policy analysis and development capacity.

Together, this vast administrative apparatus has responsibility for implementing public policy. At the most prosaic level—the level where virtually all of us have made personal contact with the state—officials deal with passport applications, meat inspections, taxation queries, Employment Insurance benefits, job seekers at Canada Employment centres, and a vast number of similarly routine administrative tasks. But at the top of the bureaucratic pyramid are women and men whose relationship to public policy is much more active. Senior officials within the departmental bureaucracy, particularly deputy ministers and assistant deputy ministers, interact frequently with cabinet ministers and senior officials in central agencies. They are called on to testify before committees of the legislature. These officials often deal directly with the representatives of organized interests. They are universally acknowledged to have influence in shaping public policy, although the extent of their influence is a matter of debate.

When the Canadian state was smaller, programs fewer, and the complexity of co-ordinating the federal government's activities less daunting, the influence of these senior bureaucrats was greater than appears to be the case today, notably during the post-World War II era of the "Ottawa mandarins." It was usual for these senior officials to serve as deputy ministers of particular departments for many years, enabling them to acquire unrivalled expertise in regard to the programs and activities they managed.

This era is long past. The turnover rate for deputy ministers is typically a couple of years. Since the 1980s the emphasis has been on senior officials as managers, whose management skills are transferable across policy fields. This may indeed be the proper approach in regard to management per se. At the same time, however, deputies who are valued and rewarded for their managerial skills over their expert grasp of the programs and activities of their department will probably have less policy influence. They certainly will have less time to make that influence felt before they are moved on to another senior bureaucratic position.[27] The phenomenon of very rapid turnover is also observed in the ranks of the roughly 400 assistant deputy ministers (ADMs) in the federal bureaucracy, the corps from which deputy ministers are recruited. A recent study by James Lahey and Mark Goldenberg concludes that "ADMs' jobs appear to have become 'smaller' . . . with ADMs having less scope and authority to lead their organization and deliver on key files and issues. . . . The trend is also to ADMs being more generalists, 'generic' managers rather than subject-matter experts. Decision-making is being pushed up and centralized, and knowledge pushed down."[28] By "pushed up and centralized" Lahey and Goldenberg don't mean that this policy influence has migrated into the hands of deputy ministers, where the turnover rate is about the same as for ADMs. Their argument is that this turnover and what they believe to be the devaluing of the policy role of ADMs contributes to the centralization of policy influence in and around the prime minister and the central agencies that support him.

The days when a mere handful of key deputy ministers could dominate the policy-making process are long gone. Nevertheless, there is little doubt that senior bureaucrats continue to matter in the policy-making process. Their influence rests on several factors that have not been swept away by the trend towards the centralization of power in Ottawa. They include the following:

- Departments are repositories for a vast amount of information about current and past programs and about the day-to-day details of their administration. Cabinet ministers continue to depend on the permanent bureaucracy for advice on some policies, at least some of time. Senior bureaucrats occupy strategic positions in the policy process because of their ability to shape the information and recommendations reaching the minister.

- The relationship of a department to the social or economic interests that benefit from the programs it administers is a source of departmental influence on policy. Departmental officials clearly are not indifferent in their sympathies towards conflicting societal interests. Moreover, the bureaucracy is an important target for professional lobbyists and interest group representatives who wish to influence policy.

- "Ministers," observes Donald Savoie, "do not manage."[29] Their deputy ministers perform this job. Given the competing pressures on a minister's time, the deputy minister inevitably assumes the job of senior manager of the department over which a cabinet minister nominally presides. In many instances the chief responsibility for policy direction also will be assumed by the deputy minister.

- Most laws contain provisions delegating to bureaucrats the authority to interpret the general terms of the law in its application to actual cases (see Box 10.2). This is also true of other statutory instruments with the force of law (for example, the thousands of Orders-in-Council that issue from cabinet each year). The task of implementation—applying the law to actual cases—is not a neutral one. In some cases this discretion is exercised at a low level in the bureaucratic hierarchy (for example, decisions by a border officer on whether a person re-entering Canada with certain goods, or goods of a certain value, should be required to pay duties).

To summarize, the bureaucracy enters the policy process both early and late. Bureaucrats are the people who actually administer the programs established by law. In doing so they regularly exercise considerable discretion, a fact that often leads special interests to focus at least part of their attention on the bureaucracy. Departmental officials are also involved in the early stages of the policy process because of the intimate knowledge they have of existing programs and the daily contact between bureaucrats and the groups directly affected by the programs they administer. Moreover, the annual expenditure budget, which provides a fairly reasonable indication of a government's policy priorities, is based largely on the information provided by departments. New legislation is usually influenced, to a greater or lesser degree, by the input of senior permanent officials. These officials are both managers and policy advisers, and at least some of them are part of the inner circle of policy-making that extends outward from cabinet. They may not be as close to the inner circle of power as was once the case, but they remain key players in the state elite.

Representative Bureaucracy

On top of all the other expectations held for bureaucracy in democratic societies, it is also expected to "represent" the population. This means that the composition of the bureaucracy should reflect in fair proportion certain demographic characteristics of society. Affirmative action programs for recruitment and promotion are the tools used in pursuit of this goal. The basic reasoning behind arguments for **representative bureaucracy** is twofold. It is expected to have greater popular legitimacy than one that does not reflect certain features of the nation's demography (e.g., people of all genders, ethnic groups, Indigenous peoples, disabled people). Second, advocates claim that its representative character will help ensure that the advice bureaucrats give to politicians and the services they provide to their clienteles are sensitive to the values and aspirations of the governed, including minority groups.[30]

As reasonable as this may sound, the idea and implementation of representative bureaucracy have always been somewhat problematic. Some

Media Spotlight

BOX 10.2 The Delegation of Discretion

The Broadcasting Act is the key law regulating television, radio, and telecommunications in Canada. Like many laws it delegates to non-elected officials the power to make rules that flesh out the very general terms of the statute they implement. For example, officials with the Canadian Broadcasting Corporation, a Crown corporation, and with the Canadian Radio-television and Telecommunications Commission, the regulatory agency that licenses broadcasters, must determine the meaning of the following vague objectives set down in the Broadcasting Act:

3. (1) It is hereby declared as the broadcasting policy for Canada that...
   (d) the Canadian broadcasting system should
   (i) serve to safeguard, enrich and strengthen the cultural, political, social and economic fabric of Canada,
   (ii) encourage the development of Canadian expression by providing a wide range of programming that reflects Canadian attitudes, opinions, ideas, values and artistic creativity, by displaying Canadian talent in entertainment programming and by offering information and analysis concerning Canada and other countries from a Canadian point of view,
   (iii) through its programming and the employment opportunities arising out of its operations, serve the needs and interests, and reflect the circumstances and aspirations, of Canadian men, women and children, including equal rights, the linguistic duality and multicultural and multiracial nature of Canadian society and the special place of aboriginal peoples within that society, and

   (iv) be readily adaptable to scientific and technological change; ...

And moreover,
   (l) the Canadian Broadcasting Corporation, as the national public broadcaster, should provide radio and television services incorporating a wide range of programming that informs, enlightens and entertains;
   (m) the programming provided by the Corporation should
   (i) be predominantly and distinctly Canadian,
   (ii) reflect Canada and its regions to national and regional audiences, while serving the special needs of those regions,
   (iii) actively contribute to the flow and exchange of cultural expression,
   (iv) be in English and in French, reflecting the different needs and circumstances of each official language community, including the particular needs and circumstances of English and French linguistic minorities,
   (v) strive to be of equivalent quality in English and in French,
   (vi) contribute to shared national consciousness and identity,
   (vii) be made available throughout Canada by the most appropriate and efficient means and as resources become available for the purpose, and
   (viii) reflect the multicultural and multiracial nature of Canada....

Source: Broadcasting Act, Chapter B-9.01, section 3 (1991).

of the questions that arise include the following. Which groups should be singled out for representation? What constitutes "fair proportion"? To what extent, if at all, are other values like efficient performance and equal rights for all compromised by such a policy? Can the idea of a representative bureaucracy be squared with that of a politically neutral one?

The roots of representative bureaucracy in Canada are found in the 1960s. The issue of national unity focused attention on the under-representation of francophones in the Canadian public service. This was identified by the Royal Commission on Bilingualism and Biculturalism (1963–9) as one of the factors contributing to the sense among many French Canadians they were not full and equal partners in Canadian government. Ottawa responded by passing the Official Languages Act (1969), one of whose stated goals was the equitable representation of francophones and anglophones in the Canadian public service. Implementing this goal required that the language requirements of every position in the federal bureaucracy be identified and that hiring and promotion decisions take these requirements into account. As we will see in Chapter 14, the result has been a significant increase in the federal bureaucracy and, at its uppermost ranks, in the representation of francophones.

At roughly the same time, the publication of sociologist John Porter's influential book *The Vertical Mosaic* (1965) drew attention to the fact that at the senior ranks of the federal bureaucracy only males of British, French, and Jewish ethnic ancestry were significantly represented. Those of British origin were clearly dominant. Women and visible minorities were almost completely absent from the senior levels of the public service.[31]

As the ethnic composition of Canadian society changed in the 1970s and 1980s, and as the discourse of collective rights and group identities achieved greater prominence, the policy of increasing the representation of French-speakers in the federal bureaucracy was joined by efforts to recruit and promote women, visible minorities, Indigenous peoples in Canada, and the disabled. The 1984 Report of the Royal Commission on Equality in Employment was followed by passage of the federal Employment Equity Act (1986). The Act's stated purpose is:

> to achieve equality in the workplace so that no person shall be denied employment opportunities or benefits for reasons unrelated to ability and, in the fulfillment of that goal, to correct the conditions of disadvantage in employment experienced by women, aboriginal peoples, persons with disabilities and members of visible minorities by giving effect to the principle that employment equity means more than treating persons in the same way but also requires special measures and the accommodation of differences.[32]

Since their beginnings in the 1980s these employment equity programs—the term "employment equity" was chosen instead of "affirmative action," but they mean the same thing—have relied mainly on a system of employment targets rather than on formally stated quotas for group representation. The results have been evident, as may be seen in Figures 10.2 and 10.3. As of 2016, women held slightly under half of all executive positions in the public service, visible minorities slightly under 10 per cent, and Indigenous Canadians just under 4 per cent. In the case of female senior public servants, their share of all executive positions is close to or above 50 per cent in most departments. Female representation is lowest in Finance and National Defence, at about 36 per cent in both departments. Visible minority representation is highest in Shared Services Canada (22 per cent), a relatively small department of about 6,000 employees that provides IT services to other parts of the federal government, and lowest in Statistics Canada (6 per cent) and the Department of Canadian Heritage (7 per cent). Indigenous Canadians account for close to 20 per cent of all executives in the ministries of Indigenous Services and Crown–Indigenous Relations and Northern Affairs, but they have much lower levels of representation in other parts of the federal bureaucracy.[33]

The line separating targets from quotas is always a matter of debate, as is the determination of what groups should be represented in what proportion. Canadian governments, both Liberal and Conservative, have been reluctant to use the language of quotas or to require that hard targets for representation be met by fixed dates (see Box 10.3). This is not true of some governments. In 2006 the Quebec government passed legislative quotas for gender representation on the boards of directors of its Crown corporations. Beginning with Norway in 2003, many European countries have imposed such quotas on either or both state-owned enterprises

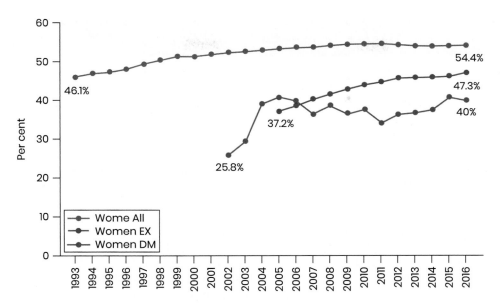

FIGURE 10.2 Women in the Public Service, 1993–2016

Source: Andrew Griffith, "Diversity in the Public Service's Executive Ranks," *Policy Options*, 16 Oct. 2017, Figure 1, https://policyoptions.irpp.org/magazines/october-2017/diversity-in-the-public-services-executive-ranks/.

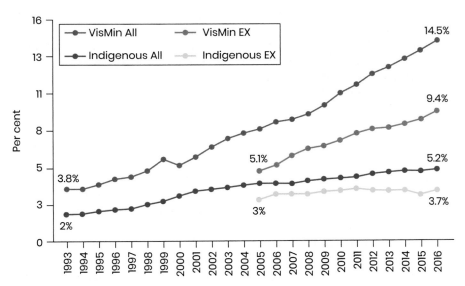

FIGURE 10.3 Visible Minorities and Indigenous People in the Public Service, 1993–2016

Source: Andrew Griffith, "Diversity in the Public Service's Executive Ranks," *Policy Options*, 16 Oct. 2017, Figure 2, https://policyoptions.irpp.org/magazines/october-2017/diversity-in-the-public-services-executive-ranks/.

and publicly traded corporations. Over the past several years a number of private members' bills have been introduced in the House of Commons, the goal of which would be to require such quotas for the boards of Canadian Crown corporations.[34] To this point none has passed. However, in 2018 Parliament passed Bill C-25, which amends the Canada Business Corporations Act to require

Governing Realities

BOX 10.3 Targets versus Quotas: What Works?

Since the 1986 passage of the federal Employment Equity Act, the federal government has avoided the language of quotas. Targets have been set from time to time for certain organizations and employment categories within the federal bureaucracy. Governments have tended, however, to frame their commitment to the equitable representation of specific segments of the population in more general language. Here is an example. It lays out the federal government's position on what are called Governor-in-Council (i.e., cabinet) appointments to federal boards, commissions, tribunals, agencies, and Crown corporations:

> We know that our country is stronger—and our government more effective—when decision-makers reflect Canada's diversity. Moving forward, the Government of Canada will use an appointment process that is transparent and merit-based, strives for gender parity, and ensures that Indigenous Canadians and minority groups are properly represented in positions of leadership. We will continue to search for Canadians who reflect the values that we all embrace: inclusion, honesty, fiscal prudence, and generosity of spirit. Together, we will build a government as diverse as Canada.

Not everyone agrees that this approach is adequate. Sheila Malcolmson, NDP member of Parliament for Nanaimo-Ladysmith (BC), believes that anything short of legislative quotas is not enough. During the debate on her private member's bill that would have imposed gender representation quotas on the boards of federal Crown corporations, she said, "When we legislate, we find women. When we do not legislate, we find excuses."[35]

On the other hand, one of Canada's foremost experts on employment equity in the federal government believes that the approach taken, which stops short of quotas, is working. Andrew Griffith writes:

> Overall, the historical and current data show that the transparency- and reporting-based approach of the *Employment Equity Act* has largely succeeded in improving representation of women, visible minorities and Indigenous people both at the executive level and among all employees in the public service. The gaps between executives and representation overall should continue to shrink, given the demographic profile of these groups.[36]

"prescribed corporations" to provide shareholders with information on diversity on the corporation's board and in the ranks of its senior management. The Act does not specify exactly what corporations would be covered, nor does it establish quotas or penalties for non-compliance.[37]

Summing Up

"The terms bureaucracy and democracy," observes B. Guy Peters, one of the world's leading authorities on bureaucracy, "are usually thought of, both in the academic and the popular literature, as antithetical approaches to providing governance

for a society."[38] Democracy has a positive resonance for most of us, whereas bureaucracy tends to evoke negative images and ideas of inefficiency, frustrating procedures and forms, and long waiting times for service. The reality, however, is that modern democracy is impossible without bureaucracy. Many of the negative characteristics that we tend to attribute to bureaucracy are linked to values that, on reflection, most of us believe are important. Implementing the laws in an impartial spirit and manner, following procedures intended to ensure that public money is spent as authorized, and operating with clear lines of authority and accountability are expectations that most of us hold for the bureaucracy. Some persons may judge that these expectations are not adequately met, or that they could be achieved with fewer public servants, less spending, and fewer regulations. The fact remains, however, as Peters argues, that bureaucracy is not in its nature antithetical to democratic governance.

Canada's federal bureaucracy is a large, complex, and specialized set of organizations whose principal role is to administer the policies determined by the government and enshrined in laws and other statutory instruments. In performing this role the bureaucracy is not a mere conveyor belt between politicians and citizens. It is common for laws to delegate significant discretion to bureaucrats in determining how the general provisions of the law will be applied. Moreover, senior bureaucrats often play an important role in shaping legislation, an influence that may be less today than at some points in the past, but that continues to exist.

Starting Points for Research

Blavatnik School of Government (Oxford University), *The International Civil Service Effectiveness (InCiSE) Index 2017*, https://www.bsg.ox.ac.uk/about/partnerships/international-civil-service-effectiveness-index. Canadians may be surprised, but should be pleased, to learn that their federal bureaucracy is rated the most effective in the world by this Oxford University-based analysis.

Christopher Dunn, ed., *The Handbook of Canadian Public Administration*, 3rd edn (Toronto: Oxford University Press, 2014). Virtually all key aspects of the structures and processes of Canadian public administration are covered in this fine collection, with contributions from some of the foremost students of Canadian bureaucracy and policy-making.

David Good, *The Politics of Public Money* **(Toronto: University of Toronto Press, 2007).** A worthy successor to the spenders and guardians analysis found in Donald Savoie's 1990 book, *The Politics of Public Spending in Canada.*

David Johnson, *Thinking Government: Public Sector Management in Canada,* **4th edn (Toronto: University of Toronto Press, 2016).** An excellent textbook on public administration in Canada.

Review Exercises

1. How does one go about becoming a federal government employee? What qualifications would you need to have to become a policy analyst with Crown–Indigenous Relations and Northern Affairs Canada, a foreign service officer with Global Affairs Canada, or an inspector with the Canadian Food Inspection Agency?

2. Most Canadians believe that public-sector organizations are less efficient than those in the private sector. How would you measure efficiency in private and public organizations? Put together a list of the criteria you would use and how straightforward or difficult each would be to measure. How have you defined "efficiency"? Should other qualities be taken into account in assessing the performance of public and private organizations? What might they be and can they be measured?

3. Do unelected officials have too much discretion? Can you think of instances where you have encountered public-sector bureaucrats whose decision(s) seemed to have been based on their personal judgment rather than simply and entirely on rules? Can anything be done about such cases? Should anything be done?

PART IV
Participation in Politics

Politics does not stop at the doors of Parliament. It spills out onto the streets and into community halls, online chat rooms, and corporate boardrooms, involving citizens, organized interests, and the media. What is sometimes referred to as *civil society* both acts on and in turn is acted on by the institutions of the state, making demands, organizing resistance, and providing support in various ways.

The participation of groups in civil society assumes many forms. Individual citizens play a role as voters and collectively through what is described as public opinion. Some of them are involved in more active ways, belonging to and working for political parties or participating in groups that attempt to shape the political conversation and government policy. Organized interests often attempt to influence the actions of government, through a range of techniques that include lobbying, legal action, and attempting to influence public opinion. The media's specialized function involves reporting and framing the political conversation. Most of what we know about the political world is mediated by those whose jobs involve selecting, framing, and interpreting information that provides the basis for our images and ideas of politics.

In the following three chapters we will examine some of the most important forms of participation in Canadian politics. The focus is on parties, elections, and voters, organized interests, and the media. In any democracy these elements of civil society must be largely independent of the state. Indeed, the extent to which they are able to act autonomously, setting their own agendas and behaving free of direct control or indirect manipulation by the state, is one of the tests of any democracy. At the same time, we need to be alert to the possibility that concentrated power in civil society can pose the same sort of danger to democracy that government by the few and mainly for the few can represent.

Jagmeet Singh and his mother, Harmeet Kaur (centre), celebrate the annoucement that Singh won the first ballot for leader of the NDP on 1 October 2017. Under his leadership the NDP won the fourth largest number of seats in the 2019 election, behind the Liberals, Conservatives, and the Bloc Québécois. (THE CANADIAN PRESS/Chris Young)

11 Parties and Elections

Political parties and elections are essential features of modern democracy. This chapter examines the characteristics and influence of these institutions in Canadian political life. The following topics are covered:

- The origins and evolution of Canada's party system
- Brokerage politics
- The role of minor parties
- From a two and one-half party system and back again?
- Party leadership selection
- The electoral system and its consequences
- Voting behaviour
- Party finances and special interests

Elections and the political parties that contest them represent the main contact points between most citizens and their political system. A majority of adult citizens vote at least some of the time, although perhaps not in every election and probably more often federally than in provincial and local elections. This may be, in fact, the extent of their participation in politics: short bursts of attention to candidates and their messages and occasional visits to the polls, interspersed between lengthier periods of inattention and political inactivity. Only about two-thirds of eligible voters actually cast their ballots in the last few federal elections, but even among those who did not vote we can probably assume that most were at least aware that an election was taking place.

Elections remind us that we live in a democracy in which those who wish to govern must win the support of the governed—or of some considerable number of the governed. Elections are the cornerstone of democratic governance, yet many believe they have become meaningless and even farcical affairs in which political parties and their candidates serve up sound bites instead of sound policy in campaigns orchestrated by the same people who put together marketing campaigns for cars and deodorants. These causes of cynicism have been around for many years. They have been joined more recently by fears that voters are being fed "fake news," a term that achieved considerable prominence in the 2016 American presidential election, and that some of this may be deliberately and maliciously spread by groups or foreign governments wanting to generate instability and doubt about the legitimacy of the political process or even to influence the outcome of an election. None of this is helped by the fact that political parties in Canada have for years ranked among the lowest of social institutions in public esteem. It would seem, therefore, that democracy's cornerstone suffers from some worrisome cracks.

Doubts about the democratic qualities of democracy's showpiece are not new. One of the oldest fears is that those with money are more likely than those without it to be able to influence voter behaviour. In the nineteenth century the influence of money often took such petty forms as candidates buying beer or whisky for voters, a practice encouraged by the fact that voters cast their ballots in public and thus the "buyer" could see whether he got what he expected for his money! But the role of money also assumed more dramatic forms, as when Hugh Allan essentially bankrolled the Conservative Party leading up to the 1874 federal election in exchange for a promise from John A. Macdonald that Allan would be made president of the railroad company chartered to build the Canadian Pacific Railway. Over a century ago Liberal cabinet minister Israël Tarte remarked that "Elections are not won with prayers," a fact of political life that has become even truer in an age where campaigning is largely through the electronic media and political ads are always the single largest expenditure for a national political party. But fact of life or not, if parties and votes can be purchased by those with deep pockets, this surely undermines the democratic credibility of the electoral process.

Money is not the only factor that stands accused of defiling democracy's temple. Political parties and candidates have often been criticized for avoiding important issues and framing the campaign conversation in ways that deflect attention from major divisions in society, oversimplifying the issues, or trivializing politics by substituting style and image for substance. The "dumbing down" of public life has been facilitated—some would argue necessitated—by the fact that modern elections are fought largely through the medium of television, a medium that by its very nature elevates images over ideas. The increasing importance of social media in election campaigns and in political life more generally has done nothing to reverse this trend. But the claims that parties and candidates avoid certain divisive issues and attempt to frame electoral discourse in ways that privilege certain interests while marginalizing others predate the rise of television campaigning and social media. The criticisms occasionally levelled at parties and elections in Canada may appear petty when viewed alongside the problems of one-party states and the practices of ballot fraud, voter intimidation, and bribery that are routine in many countries where elections are held. But Canadians are not used to comparing their democratic institutions and processes to those of

Venezuela, Zimbabwe, Russia, or Egypt. They place the bar higher than this and measure the performance of their political parties and electoral system against ideas of equality and participation that have evolved out of the country's liberal democratic tradition. Judged against these values, the Canadian experience is not perfect, although critics differ over the nature and extent of its shortcomings.

Parties: Definition and Functions

Political parties may be defined as organizations that offer slates of candidates to voters at election time. To this end they recruit and select party candidates, raise money to pay for their campaigns, develop policies that express the ideas and goals for which their candidates campaign, and attempt to persuade citizens to vote for their candidates. In a democracy parties are not created by the state, nor are they agents of the state. They are, in Eugene Forsey's words, "voluntary associations of people who hold broadly similar opinions on public questions."[1]

It is usual to give as one of the distinguishing characteristics of political parties their attempt to "elect governmental office-holders."[2] This can, however, be somewhat misleading. While most parties hope to elect candidates to office, and some even have a realistic prospect of electing enough candidates to form a government, other parties may contest elections chiefly to get their ideas onto the public stage, without any expectation of garnering more than a small fraction of the vote. This was surely true of the Marijuana Party, whose stated mission was the decriminalization of cannabis (achieved in October 2018), and has been of other single-issue or otherwise narrow-appeal parties such as the Animal Protection Party of Canada and the Libertarian Party of Canada.[3] John Meisel and Matthew Mendelsohn identify seven functions that political parties play in a democracy.[4]

1. *Integrating citizens into the political system.* Historically, parties have served as important linkages between citizens and the governmental system. Through voting for parties and

thinking about public affairs in terms of the policies and ideologies represented by parties, citizens develop attachments to the political system more generally. This connection, Meisel and Mendelsohn argue, has weakened as political parties have fallen in public esteem and have come to be perceived by many as simply another unresponsive and unaccountable institution in a political system characterized by alienating and underperforming institutions.

2. *Developing policy.* In many democracies different parties represent clear ideological and policy options. Moreover, party members and their deliberations are important sources of the policies that a party will advocate during election campaigns and seek to implement when in power. Canada's historically dominant Liberal and Conservative parties have seldom been dramatically different from one another in ideological terms, and even less in their behaviour when in power. They have occasionally stood for significantly different policies during election campaigns, as was true in 1988 when the Liberals opposed the Canada–United States Free Trade Agreement negotiated by the Conservative government. In 2008, 2015 and 2019 the Liberals stood for a carbon tax, a policy condemned in all three of these election campaigns by the Conservatives.

   Neither party, once in office, has felt tied to the policy platforms developed and voted on by the extra-parliamentary wing of the party. The New Democratic Party (NDP) has been, of all Canada's main national parties, the one characterized by the greatest involvement of the party's extra-parliamentary membership in policy development. Of course, if the NDP were to form a national government it might well distance itself from policy promises in ways similar to the Conservatives and Liberals when they have been in power. This certainly was the experience of the NDP when it was elected to govern in Ontario (1990–5) and instituted policies never contemplated by the party when it was in opposition. It was also true of the NDP government elected in Alberta in 2015, which quickly distanced itself from the party's criticisms of the oil sands and pipelines in the straitened economic circumstances that followed its election.

3. *Elite recruitment.* With rare exceptions, those elected to federal and provincial office in Canada are associated with a political party and run as the official candidates of their parties. In 2019, for example, only 4 per cent of all candidates ran as independents. Together they received roughly 73,000 of the 17,890,264 votes cast. One independent candidate, Jody Wilson-Raybould, alone accounted for about one-fifth of all votes going to independents.

Parties choose their candidates and their leaders, and in doing so they determine the pool of persons from whom elected public officials, including members of the government, will be drawn. In most democracies the bar to participation in the selection of party leaders is fairly low, requiring mainly the interest and personal motivation to join and be active in a political party. The fact of the matter, however, is that in virtually all democracies those with more formal education, higher incomes, and jobs that carry greater social status are more likely than their fellow citizens to participate in the selection of party candidates and leaders, and are also more likely to stand for and be chosen as party candidates.

4. *Organization of government.* Governing parties propose; opposition parties oppose. This somewhat oversimplified formula expresses an important fact about the role that parties play within the system of government. They provide a partisan structure to the process of law-making and the debate of public affairs. Under the British parliamentary system that exists in Canada, this partisan structure is by design an adversarial one. The principle of "us versus them" is reflected in the physical layout of the legislature, in which the government benches face those of the opposition parties (separated by a distance said to be that of two sword lengths!), and in the traditions and procedures observed in conducting the business of Parliament.

5. *Structuring the vote.* Just as parties lend structure to the activities of the legislature and allow for the identification of the government with a particular party (or coalition of parties in some democratic systems), parties also serve to structure the vote in elections. In Canada, and in many democracies, only a handful of political parties are serious contenders for citizens' votes, which simplifies enormously the information-gathering task facing voters. Instead of having to determine what every individual candidate stands for they can—and most people do—rely on party labels as a sort of shorthand for the ideas and policies that a candidate represents. Each party represents, in a sense, a particular selection from a limited menu. The parties will differ from one another in their voter appeal with different segments of the population, and most voters can be said to have most-favoured and least-favoured political parties. These partisan leanings, at the weak end, or loyalties and identifications, at the strong end, provide a degree of continuity in voting behaviour. This continuity, in some circumstances, can be shattered rather quickly. This happened in a dramatic fashion in the 1993 general election in Canada, and in the French presidential election of 2017.

6. *Organizing public opinion.* Parties are often characterized as right-wing or left-wing. They may be described as moderate or extremist. The labels "liberal," "conservative," and "socialist"—or some other descriptors—may be used to signify that they occupy particular places on the ideological map. Parties reflect, but may also help create or at least reinforce, divisions within society. They do so through the issues they identify as important, the way they frame these issues, and the policies they propose.

Canada's two historically dominant political parties have largely avoided outright ideological appeals in favour of a flexible centrist style of politics often labelled **brokerage politics**. They have not talked to voters using the language of class politics: rich vs poor, bosses vs workers, corporations vs unions, the 1 per cent vs the 99 per cent. Instead, they have attempted to accommodate the preferences of major interests, regions, and communities through a flexible policy style. Of course, politics has to be about something, and even the most centrist and waffling of parties cannot avoid taking positions on some divisive issues. Historically, language, religion, and region have been among the key issues distinguishing the Liberals from the Conservatives, the Liberals doing better among francophones, Catholics, and in the provinces east of Manitoba, and the Conservatives doing better among Protestants and western Canadians. These differences have helped to organize Canadian public opinion on religious (in the past), linguistic, and territorial lines. The NDP and its predecessor, the **Co-operative Commonwealth Federation** (CCF), have been the only significant parties presenting voters with a class-based definition of Canadian politics. In recent decades the ability of the historically dominant parties to organize public opinion in ways that preserved their dominance, by bridging major divisions in Canadian politics, was challenged by parties of protest. The Reform Party/Canadian Alliance emerged out of westerners' dissatisfaction with the older parties. Likewise the Bloc Québécois, which enjoyed strong support in Quebec from 1993 to 2008, and then again in 2019, emerged from the failure of brokerage politics to accommodate Quebec nationalism.

7. *Interest aggregation.* Organizations that represent those who believe that it is wrong for people to kill and consume animals, advocate

Len Norris/© Simon Fraser University

"Then it's settled. We model ourselves on Canada and use a four-party system."

There are advantages and disadvantages to Canada's multi-party approach to politics. One clear advantage is that it provides more opportunities for disparate viewpoints to be heard, as evidenced by issues brought forward by parties such as the Reform/Alliance, NDP, Bloc Québécois, and Green Party. Disadvantages of a multi-party state are discussed later in the chapter.

for wetlands preservation, and those that take the position that no immigrant to Canada should be considered illegal may have political influence. However, the narrowness of their respective agendas makes it highly unlikely that they will attract enough voters to win seats in the legislature. Parties, especially parties that hope to form a government, must aggregate different interests. This requires that they be willing to reach compromises on issues, bringing together under the party's tent a coalition of different interests and ideas sufficiently broad to win election.

The Origins and Evolution of Canada's Party System[5]

The Nature of Brokerage Politics

The origins of Canada's two historically dominant political parties—the Conservatives and the Liberals—can be traced back to the shifting coalitions and alignments in the United Province of Canada in the 1840s and 1850s. Although these groups were much more amorphous and unstable than modern political parties and would not really coalesce into cohesive organizations until the 1880s, they did represent distinct political tendencies. On the one hand was the governing coalition of Liberal-Conservatives (which would eventually drop the "Liberal" from its official name) under the leadership of John A. Macdonald in Canada West and his French-Canadian counterpart, George-Étienne Cartier, in Canada East. This disparate organization encompassed a number of distinct groups: moderate Reformers from what was to become Ontario, moderate Conservatives (the *bleus*) from Canada East (Quebec), the commercial and industrial interests of English-speaking Quebec, and the remnants of the old ruling oligarchies in Upper and Lower Canada, the Family Compact and the Château Clique. Many of these groups had potentially conflicting interests (Catholics and Protestants, French and English, urban and rural elements), but the coalition was held together

largely by the political dexterity of Macdonald and by the gradual development of a unifying vision, one based on the nation-building program eventually enshrined in the **National Policy** of 1878–9. The key elements of this program were the implementation of a protective tariff designed to promote the growth of manufacturing in Ontario and Quebec, the encouragement of western settlement to open up a market for the products of central Canadian industry and to protect this territory from American encroachment, and the creation of a transcontinental railroad to ship the manufactured goods of central Canada to the newly opened western territories.

On the other hand was an even looser opposition coalition, comprising the Clear Grits of Canada West and the *rouges* of Canada East. Both of these groups shared a common admiration for the republican and individualist ideas of the United States and both advocated free trade with the Americans. They also shared a deep hostility to the commercial and banking interests linked to Macdonald's governing party. But the two groups made for rather uneasy partners, since the Grits were outspokenly critical of the Roman Catholic Church. So were the *rouges*, for that matter (and their anti-clericalism placed serious obstacles in the path of electoral success in their home province of Quebec), but there was nonetheless considerable ethnic and religious tension between the two groups. It was only when Wilfrid Laurier assumed the leadership of the Liberal Party in 1887 that these diverse elements were moulded into a relatively cohesive political organization.

It would be a mistake to make too much of the differences in ideas and policies that separated the Liberals and Conservatives during the formative years of the Canadian party system (roughly 1880 to 1920). Admittedly, the Liberals were identified with free trade and provincial rights, and after 1885 (when Louis Riel was hanged for treason following the failed Northwest Rebellion) they appeared to be "more sensitive to the interests of French Canada" than the Tories.[6] They were also more sympathetic to the plight of the farmer than were the Conservatives. The latter, meanwhile, were generally thought of as the party of the British connection, the party of privilege—in the sense that its leading spokesmen claimed that all healthy and stable societies are ruled by a *natural* governing elite—the party of centralization and economic protection. But these ideological differences, far from constituting fundamental clashes of world outlooks on which the two sides sought to mobilize their supporters, were almost always subordinated to the central preoccupation of Canadian politics: *patronage*.

The scramble to control the distribution of government largesse was undoubtedly the dominant feature of Canadian politics during the 1860s and 1870s, when a number of provisions in our electoral law helped to force political life into that mould. In particular, the use of the open ballot, whereby voters simply declared their choice at the polls in the presence of a government official (and anybody else who happened to be in the room at the time!), provided numerous opportunities for bribery, coercion, and intimidation, and made it difficult for anybody whose livelihood depended on government contracts to vote against candidates supported by the ruling cabinet. Non-simultaneous or staggered elections permitted the government to call elections in safe ridings before having to work its way into more doubtful territory. The governing Conservatives stretched the voting period over three months in the 1872 election. This practice encouraged candidates in many ridings to be *ministerialists*, so called because their "politics were not to support a party but a ministry and any ministry would do."[7] This was the surest way to provide for a steady flow of government patronage into the successful candidate's **constituency**.

The elimination of the open ballot and staggered elections by the mid-1870s, along with the gradual standardization of electoral regulations across the different provinces, did not reduce the importance of patronage in federal politics—far from it. Despite the removal of some of the crasser forms of electoral corruption by the 1880s, the two federal parties still operated in a political environment characterized by the absence of civil service reform (the merit principle), a highly restricted franchise, and a weak working class (there were plenty of workers, but they tended to be unorganized and did not share a collective political identity). "[B]oth Macdonald's

Conservatives and Laurier's Liberals made extensive use of pork-barrel [politics], trying to provide something for every part of the country. . . . Distributive politics helped unite a far-flung federation, then as now prone to centrifugal tendencies."[8]

This is precisely the situation described by the French political sociologist André Siegfried based on his visits to Canada in 1898 and again in 1904. Siegfried complained that the preoccupation with questions of "material interest" and "public works" tended to "lower the general level of political life" in Canada. He also noted that Canadian politics was hardly lacking in substantive issues—rivalries between Catholics and Protestants, and between French- and English-speakers, for example—that could have been addressed by the two major parties, but that the party leaders "prefer that they should not be talked about. The subjects which remain available for discussion are not numerous. In addition, the parties borrow one another's policies periodically, displaying a coolness in this process that would disconcert us Europeans."[9]

Siegfried's comments on the nature of party competition in Canada are still remarkably relevant (see Box 11.1). If Siegfried were somehow transported to present-day Canada, he would probably conclude that there are some strong resemblances between the current party system and that described in his analysis of Canadian society and politics in 1906. The emphasis on accommodating the diverse interests—regional, linguistic, ethnic, class, religious—of the electorate through the prudent employment of "public works" and individual material incentives is still a prominent feature of federal and provincial politics. Elections are usually preceded by a barrage of new government programs and spending initiatives in various parts of the country—ill-disguised attempts by the party in power to purchase electoral support in key ridings. When one of the historically dominant parties replaces the other as the government, it is not uncommon that policies that were the target of heavy criticism and scorn continue in force, and that major campaign promises that were showcased in the campaign as key differences between the parties are abandoned.

The electoral opportunism exhibited over the years by both the Liberals and the Conservatives should not to be taken to mean that the two older parties have no principles or ideological commitments whatsoever. As was also the case when Siegfried was studying the Canadian party system, in more recent times Canada's oldest parties have represented somewhat distinct traditions, particularly on matters concerning federalism and Canada–US relations. In recent years the federal Liberal Party has been associated with a somewhat more centralist vision of federal–provincial relations and a brand of mild to occasionally hotter anti-Americanism, while the Conservatives have branded themselves as a more decentralist party and more sympathetic to Washington than their Liberal rivals. The two historically dominant parties have also taken significantly different positions on climate change and energy policy.

Despite these apparent differences in the policy orientations of the two older parties in recent times, Siegfried's central contention about the Canadian party system remains indisputable. The historically dominant parties have continued to be much more flexible, opportunistic, and wary of ideological appeals to the electorate than those in most European nations. The nature of Canada's electoral system and the norms that govern party competition in this country are such that the Liberals and Conservatives usually have been able to fight elections without having to worry too much about keeping their principles intact or consistent. Many observers of the Canadian party system have attached a specific label to this type of flexible, non-ideological party system: it is a *brokerage* party system. That is, the two older parties at the federal

Politics in Focus

BOX 11.1 An Early Illustration of the Brokerage Theory of Canadian Politics

The fact that in the Dominion parties exist apart from their programs, or even without a program at all, frequently deprives [election campaigns] of their true meaning. In the absence of ideas or doctrines to divide the voters, there remain only questions of material interest, collective or individual. Against their pressure the candidate cannot maintain his integrity, for he knows that his opponent will not show the same self-restraint. The result is that the same promises are made on both sides, following an absolutely identical conception of the meaning of power. Posed in this way, the issue of an election manifestly changes. Whoever may be the winner, everyone knows that the country will be administered in the same way, or almost the same. The only difference will be in the personnel of the government. This is the prevailing conception of politics—except when some great wave of opinion sweeps over the whole country, covering under its waters all the political pygmies....

The reason for this ... is easy to understand. Canada, we know, is a country of violent oppositions. English and French, Protestant and Catholic, are jealous of each other and fear each other. The lack of ideas, programs, convictions, is only apparent. Let a question of race or religion be raised, and you will immediately see most of the sordid preoccupations of patronage or connection disappear below the surface. The elections will become struggles of political principle, sincere and passionate. Now this is exactly what is feared by the prudent and far-sighted men who have been given the responsibility of maintaining the national equilibrium. Aware of the sharpness of certain rivalries, they know that if these are let loose without any counter-balance, the unity of the Dominion may be endangered. That is why they persistently apply themselves to prevent the formation of homogeneous parties, divided according to race, religion, or class— a French party, for instance, or a Catholic party, or a Labour party. The clarity of political life suffers from this, but perhaps the existence of the federation can be preserved only at this price.

Source: André Siegfried, *The Race Question in Canada* (Toronto: Macmillan, 1966: first published in 1906), 113.

level act as "brokers of ideas . . . middlemen who select from all the ideas pressing for recognition as public policy those they think can be shaped to have the widest appeal."[10] Each of the parties attempts to cobble together a winning coalition of voters at election time, tending to avoid polarizing messages in favour of a sort of pragmatic politics that emphasizes electability over ideological purity. Class identities and conflicts have been avoided by the historically dominant parties. Without such cues and with issues framed by the older parties in a language that did not recognize the relevance or often the existence of class divisions, Canadian voters grew used to thinking about politics in terms of regional and ethnolinguistic divisions, leadership and sound management of public affairs, Canada–US relations, and other non-class issues.

Brokerage theory, then, makes two fundamental claims about Canada's two historically dominant political parties: first, they lack cohesive and distinct ideological visions (especially those based on class interests and identity); second, the parties are flexible and opportunistic because this is the path to electoral victory. As Carty and Cross put it, "At the core of a brokerage party's approach to democratic politics is a fierce *electoral pragmatism*. These are organizations consumed with winning and holding office, and they combine an organizational ruthlessness marked by a propensity to abandon losing leaders, with an ideological catholicity that engenders great policy flexibility."[11]

An alternative perspective on brokerage parties and the relative weakness of class in Canadian politics in Canada is advanced by Janine Brodie and Jane Jenson in *Crisis, Challenge, and Change*.[12] They argue that brokerage theory tends to view political parties as more or less passive transmission belts for societal demands. In the vocabulary of empirical social science, brokerage theorists consider parties to be *dependent variables*: their behaviour is shaped by the divisions that exist in society—in Canada's case, the most important divisions being those of language, ethnicity, region, and religion. Brodie and Jenson call for a rather different view of parties, one that treats them simultaneously as *dependent* (influenced by society) and *independent* (actively shaping societal demands) variables. The most important

aspect of the independent, creative function of political parties in liberal democracies like Canada is their role in creating a *definition of politics*. "From a myriad of social tensions," they write, "the definition of politics identifies and selects those susceptible to 'political' solutions. Political parties, in other words, by defining the political, contribute to the organization and disorganization of groups in the electorate."[13] Since the decades immediately following Confederation, they argue, the Liberal and Conservative parties have studiously avoided appeals to class-based interests and the language of class conflict, thus contributing to the rather low profile and weak appeal that class politics has had over the course of Canadian history (see Box 11.2).

A rather different criticism of the brokerage theory of Canadian politics maintains that the historically dominant parties are today less likely to offer voters a sort of non-ideological choice between Tweedledee and Tweedledum than in the past. Christopher Cochrane points to several studies that show the existence of significant value differences between those who vote for the parties, differences that are even greater among activists for the respective parties, and content analyses of the parties' platforms that reveal, as he puts it, "systematic and enduring differences."[14] He does not conclude, however, that the brokerage model of Canadian political parties no longer applies. "It is a fundamental mistake," Cochrane argues, "to suppose that brokerage and ideology are inimical models of political operation. Office-seeking politicians need party activists to support them. Policy-seeking activists need their party's politicians in power. This quid pro quo between policy seekers and office seekers is what drives brokerage politics."[15]

The Role of Minor Parties in the Brokerage System

Only two parties have formed a government at the federal level in Canada, but several others have had significant support among Canadian voters, support that usually has been concentrated in a particular region of the country and sometimes in a single province. These are minor parties. Among the

Politics in Focus

BOX 11.2 Prime Minister Mackenzie King: The Master of Brokerage Politics

William Lyon Mackenzie King was Canada's longest-serving prime minister, holding office for just under 22 years (1921–6, 1926–30, and 1935–48). Probably more than any other person to hold this office, King was adept at managing those issues and divisions that might have undermined the Liberal Party's support across the country, particularly the division between English and French Canadians. His centrist, non-ideological style of politics infuriated those on the left, including one of Canada's foremost constitutionalists, poets, and a founder of the Co-operative Commonwealth Federation (the predecessor to the NDP), Francis Reginald Scott.

In the following poem, entitled "W.L.M.K.," Scott offers what might be described as a rather satirical elegy on Mackenzie King's prime ministerial style.

How shall we speak of Canada,
Mackenzie King dead?
The Mother's boy in the lonely room
With his dog, his medium and his ruins?[16]

He blunted us.

We had no shape
Because he never took sides,
And no sides
Because he never allowed them to take shape.

He skilfully avoided what was wrong
Without saying what was right,
And never let his on the one hand

Know what his on the other hand was doing.
The height of his ambition
Was to pile a Parliamentary Committee on a Royal Commission,
To have "conscription if necessary
But not necessarily conscription,"
To let Parliament decide—
Later.

Postpone, postpone, abstain.

Only one thread was certain:
After World War I
Business as usual,
After World War II
Orderly decontrol.
Always he led us back to where we were before.

He seemed to be in the centre
Because we had no centre,
No vision
To pierce the smoke-screen of his politics.

Truly he will be remembered
Wherever men honour ingenuity,
Ambiguity, inactivity, and political longevity.

Let us raise up a temple
To the cult of mediocrity,
Do nothing by halves
Which can be done by quarters.

Source: Francis Reginald Scott, "W.L.M.K." *The Eye of the Needle: Satire, Sorties, Sundries*. Montreal: Contact Press, 1957.

most prominent in terms of the support they have received and their influence on Canadian politics have been the Progressive Party, the Co-operative Commonwealth Federation, the Reform Party, the Bloc Québécois, and the Green Party. These parties should not be confused with fringe parties such as the Communist Party of Canada, the Libertarian Party of Canada, the Rhinoceros Party, the Animal Protection Party, and the Christian Heritage Party.

These fringe parties typically win under 1 per cent of the vote in the ridings where they run candidates and often receive only a few thousand votes nationally.

Minor parties in Canada may be thought of as the consequence of the inability of brokerage politics to provide an adequate voice and representation to certain segments of society. In fact, they sometimes have been associated with regional grievances.

Politics in Focus

BOX 11.3 Developing a Winning "Brand": Brokerage Politics Today

The Liberal Party of Canada has often been described as Canada's "government party" or "natural governing party." Such labels are based on the fact that for almost three-quarters of the twentieth century the Liberals held power federally. While both of Canada's historically dominant parties practised brokerage politics, the Liberal Party was more successful in bringing together a winning coalition of groups and interests than was the Conservative Party. In the following excerpt Alex Marland explains the secret of the Liberal's historical brand and what he argues is the party's more recent brand under Justin Trudeau.

The Liberal Party of Canada surely ranks among the most durable political brands in the world. More than any other Canadian party, it embodies the state, to the point of ownership and entitlement. Liberals believe that governing Canada is their purpose. Their leader is a brand phenomenon in his own right . . . .

Historically, the Liberal "master brand" (i.e., its core brand promise) has been as a defender of national unity. The party won elections by practising brokerage politics. Liberals placated regional divisions and stood for a unified Canada. Their leaders urged togetherness when others urged decentralization or separatism. It is no coincidence the Liberal Party became a shell of its former self in the four elections held from 2004 to 2011, a period when Quebec nationalism and regional tensions were declining. The main reason to vote Liberal—to save Canada from itself—eroded. A different strand of sunny ways was needed.

The Liberals' master brand is no longer about unifying Canadians amidst regional strife. Rather, the brand has pivoted to become synonymous with the Charter of Rights and Freedoms. Unity through diversity. This is a powerful space to occupy. Those who argue against

it will probably lose in courts of law and public opinion. Though, urbanites who preach the moral high ground risk stoking feelings of classism and elitism, setting the stage for populist revolt.

Liberals have been using Charter issues as a wedge for some time. In the 1990s and early 2000s, they ruthlessly exploited so-called bozo eruptions. Any socially disparaging remark made by a right-wing candidate or parliamentarian was cited as evidence that person's party harboured extremists. A 2004 internal Conservative Party memo, reproduced in *Brand Command* [an award-winning 2016 book by Alex Marland], features the following observation from Conservative political marketers: "With tight messaging we can win or neutralize the debate on specific social issues (which split the Liberals' base as well as ours), but we lose when the debate shifts to the emotive, patriotic symbolism of the Charter." This has been magnified under Justin Trudeau and with the spread of social media. The image that he and his handlers promote is of a leader of democracy, equality and human rights in a Canadian context. This means promoting multiculturalism, feminism, bilingualism, Indigenous rights and so on. All of this is grounded in Charter values and related legal/moral convictions.

Brands mean different things to different people, and image management has been going on for a long time. Unlocking a master brand is a useful tool for interpreting the behaviour of political elites and anticipating future policy directions. As I see it, the Charter of Rights and Freedoms anchors the Liberal brand and that of Prime Minister Trudeau.

Source: Alex Marland, "How the Liberals Became Masters of Their Brand," *Globe and Mail*, 16 May 2017, https://www.theglobeandmail.com/opinion/how-the-liberals-became-masters-of-their-brand/article34999255/, and Alex Marland, *Brand Command: Canadian Politics and Messaging in the Age of Message Control* (Vancouver: University of British Columbia Press, 2016), 390–1.

The Reform Party of Canada (1987, roots in Western Canada) and the Bloc Québécois (1990, with candidates only from Quebec) are examples of this, as are the Social Credit Party (1935, origins in western Canada) and the Bloc populaire canadien (1943,

all of its candidates except two ran in Quebec). The Progressive Party (1920) is often thought of as a party that arose out of agrarian discontent in western Canada, but it won about one-quarter of the popular vote and about a quarter of the seats in

Ontario in the 1921 federal election. Nevertheless, during its short history the Progressive Party's popularity was greatest in the Prairie provinces.

The NDP traces its origins to another party of protest, the Co-operative Commonwealth Federation. Unlike the minor parties mentioned above, however, the CCF cannot be described as a product of regional protest. The anger of farmers in western Canada over their diminishing influence in Canadian politics was a factor that contributed to the rise of the CCF—not to mention that early in the Great Depression the price of wheat fell below the price of the seed needed to grow it!—but there were more farmers in Ontario than in the West and they were angry too. Agrarian protest was joined by the voices of organized labour and those of mainly Ontario and Quebec intellectuals who believed that the Great Depression had demonstrated the failure of capitalism and that society and the economy needed to be reformed along socialist lines.

Walter Young, in his history of the national CCF, describes the contribution of third parties to the Canadian political system:

> By providing . . . the kind of ideological confrontation which is typically absent in contests between the two major parties, [minor parties] have served to stimulate the older parties and reactivate their previously dormant philosophies. . . . Two parties alone cannot successfully represent all the interests or act as a broker—honest or otherwise. Attempts to represent a national consensus have been usually based on the assessment of a few with limited access to the attitudes of the whole. The result has been that the national consensus has in fact been the view of the most dominant voices in the old parties. And these are the voices at the centre; historically, the voices of the elite or the establishment.[17]

Although only the Conservative and Liberal parties have formed the government in Ottawa, several other parties, from time to time and for shorter or longer periods, have played an important role on the federal scene. These minor parties occasionally have won enough seats to form the official opposition in Parliament and sometimes have held the balance of power during periods of minority government. They have also influenced the political conversation and, at times, have had an important impact on the policies of the governing party. In short, minor parties perform an important function in our brokerage party system: they provide a much-needed source of policy innovation, goading the major parties into acting on the concerns of regions, classes, or significant social groups they have traditionally ignored or underestimated.

From Party of Protest to the Mainstream: The Case of the Reform Party of Canada

Under the leadership of Preston Manning, the son of the former Social Credit premier of Alberta, Ernest Manning, the Reform Party was founded in late 1987. It was the latest in a string of western protest movements—its most successful predecessors having been the Progressives in the 1920s, Social Credit and the CCF in the 1930s and 1940s, and the Western Canada Concept in the early 1980s—that have tapped into the powerful feelings of economic and political alienation in the western provinces. These feelings originate in the firm conviction that the West is getting the short end of the stick, economically and politically. For most of Canada's history, many westerners believed that federal policies, reinforced by the practices of the banks and the railroads, enabled Ontario and Quebec to siphon off the resource wealth of the West to fuel growth and prosperity in the centre. The two major parties were seen as co-conspirators in this vicious circle of exploitation, since they were beholden to the powerful economic interests in the metropolitan areas and therefore compelled to enact policies that favoured those regions where the bulk of the seats were to be won in a federal election.

This sense of resentment towards Ottawa and the economic interests of central Canada was reignited during the 1970s and early 1980s when the Liberal government of Pierre Trudeau enacted policies seen by many westerners and their provincial governments as a blatant attempt to redistribute wealth from the natural resource economies of the West to the industrial economies of central Canada. These policies included limits placed on the price that Canadian producers, most of whom were in Alberta, could receive for oil sold on the Canadian market, the creation of state-owned Petro-Canada, and the National Energy Program, which limited the price that could be received in Canada for domestically produced oil and natural gas and also created significant incentives for Canadian ownership in the petroleum sector. Western resentment was evident at the polls. In the federal elections of 1974 the Liberal Party of Canada won only 13 of 68 seats west of Ontario, three of 77 in 1979, and two of 77 in 1980. It did not win any seats in Alberta during those three elections and only three in Saskatchewan.

This deep-seated suspicion among westerners of central Canada and national political institutions was briefly dispelled by the 1984 federal election in which the Progressive Conservative Party swept the country, particularly western Canada. The new prime minister, Brian Mulroney, was a bilingual Quebecer. When he proceeded to place several western Canadian MPs in key cabinet positions, voters who had long felt ignored and worse by Liberal governments believed their concerns would now get a positive response from Ottawa. Gradually, however, their guarded optimism gave way to a shattering disillusionment, as the Conservative government made a number of policy decisions that were viewed as detrimental to western interests. Without a doubt the most publicized instance of "biased" government decision-making was Ottawa's awarding of a multi-million dollar maintenance contract for the CF-18 fighter aircraft to a Quebec-based firm, despite the fact that Bristol Aerospace of Winnipeg had presented what federal officials acknowledged was a technically superior bid. "This enraged not only Manitobans, but most westerners, and the CF-18 decision quickly joined the National Energy Program as a symbol of regional resentment and injustice."[18] Many westerners drew the conclusion from this affair that no matter how many representatives they sent to the House of Commons, the system itself—especially the "national" parties—was biased against the West. A new voice, therefore,

that of a regionally based protest party like the Reform Party, was necessary to extract favourable policies from Ottawa.

Although the Reform Party began life as a strictly regional organization—its constitution originally included a prohibition on fielding candidates east of Manitoba—it quickly capitalized on the public's growing disenchantment with so-called "traditional" political parties to gain support in Ontario, the bastion of central Canadian power. The percentage of Canadians expressing "a great deal" or "quite a lot" of confidence in political parties had dropped from 30 per cent in 1979 to only 7 per cent in 1991.[19] Reform attacked existing political institutions as being unresponsive, unaccountable, and elitist, and attempted to portray itself as a populist movement rather than a political party. Rigid party discipline was singled out by both voters and the Reform Party as one of the biggest causes of citizen dissatisfaction with the political system. Under the Mulroney Conservatives, two Tory backbenchers who were publicly critical of the hugely unpopular Goods and Services Tax (GST) found themselves expelled from the party's **caucus**. Likewise, and despite Jean Chrétien's promise to relax party discipline, those Liberal MPs who opposed the government's 1995 gun control law were stripped of their parliamentary committee assignments. Such incidents reminded voters that under the traditional parties those they elect to Parliament are expected to vote as the party brass decides, even if this collides with the strongly held desires of their constituents.

Responding to the widely held demands among the electorate for greater accountability and a more democratic political structure, the Reform Party, rechristened the Canadian Alliance in 2000, followed in the path of its populist predecessors, the Progressives and Social Credit, calling for the implementation of a number of institutional reforms expected to increase citizens' control over their representatives. The party advocated greater use of referendums and citizen initiatives; the right of constituents to recall their MPs; and relaxation of party discipline, so that most votes in Parliament would be free votes. The Reform/Alliance ideology was both populist and conservative, and the party regularly found itself alone as the sole political party advocating radical change to the policy status quo. For example, during the 1993 election campaign it was the only party to advocate a major reduction in Canada's annual intake of immigrants during times when the economy was weak. It was also the only party to insist that deficit reduction be achieved mainly through spending cuts and that this should be Ottawa's top priority. Reform Party MPs were the main critics in Parliament of the 1995 gun control law requiring the registration of all firearms. The party also stood alone in its opposition to official multiculturalism and bilingualism, although it softened its stance over time.

Although the Conservatives, Liberals, and NDP all initially tried to ignore or downplay the significance of the Reform Party, by the summer of 1991—when the report of the Citizens' Forum on National Unity (the Spicer Commission) documented the deep dissatisfaction of many Canadians with the functioning of their traditional democratic institutions, especially the political parties—this protest movement was simply too powerful to be casually dismissed as a sort of political chinook. If the Conservatives and the New Democrats hoped to hold onto at least some of their traditional electoral strongholds in the West, they had to respond to the policy concerns raised by Preston Manning's organization, no matter how distasteful or "populist" they considered them to be.

This is exactly what happened during previous cycles of regional protest: the major parties were eventually compelled to head off the electoral challenge of an emergent protest movement (whether it was the Progressives, the CCF, or Social Credit) by endorsing policies that appealed to the new party's supporters. In the case of the Progressives, for instance, the party was opposed to the National Policy tariff (which kept the price of central Canada's manufactured goods relatively high and drove up the costs of farming) and to the discriminatory freight rates charged by the Canadian Pacific Railway (which made it cheaper to ship manufactured goods from central Canada to the West than to send grain eastward). After the Progressives' meteoric rise to prominence in the 1921 federal election, however, the protest they represented was gradually dissipated by the skilful manoeuvring

of Liberal Prime Minister Mackenzie King. King made relatively minor changes in the tariff and in freight rate policy and managed to mollify some of the Progressive leaders with offers of cabinet posts in his government. This was largely the fate of the Co-operative Commonwealth Federation as well: Mackenzie King sought to take the wind out of the socialist party's sails by implementing a number of social welfare policies that its supporters were advocating, including old-age pensions and unemployment insurance.

Today's Conservative Party of Canada is very much a direct descendant of the Reform Party. Gone is the angry edge of western alienation, expressed in Reform's original slogan, "The West wants in." But the populist, libertarian, and socially conservative elements that were all present in the Reform Party are still present and important parts of the Conservative Party message. Stephen Harper, Conservative prime minister from 2006 to 2015, was a founding member of the Reform Party. The current leader of the Conservative Party, Andrew Scheer, worked for Preston Manning when Manning unsuccessfully ran for election as the leader of the Canadian Alliance in 2000. Several of the most prominent members of the Conservative Party under Scheer were once members of the Reform Party or its successor, the Canadian Alliance. But more important than these personal connections to Reform is the fact that the orientation and values of today's Conservative Party bear much more resemblance to those of Reform than to the Progressive Conservative Party that fought unsuccessfully to maintain its role as Canada's national right-of-centre party before joining forces with the Alliance in 2003.[20]

From Two and One-Half Party System and Back Again?

Before the 1993 election it was common to speak of Canada's "two and one-half" party system. The Liberals and Progressive Conservatives were the parties with a realistic chance of forming a government, while the NDP was a stable minority party

KRIEGER 1997
The Province

Bob Krieger/© Simon Fraser University

Preston Manning, who founded and led the Reform Party of Canada from 1987 to 2000, helped to "fan the flames" on western regional and social conservative issues, forcing the country's dominant parties into ideological debates that would not have surfaced otherwise.

Neither the Conservatives (2 seats) nor the NDP (9 seats) elected enough MPs to qualify for official party status, which guarantees the opportunity to speak in the House during Question Period as well as automatic funding for research staff. On the other hand, the Reform Party jumped from one seat that had been won in a by-election to 52 seats. The Bloc Québécois (BQ), created in 1990 by the defections of several Conservative and Liberal MPs, went from seven seats to 54. Not since 1921, when the Progressives came second to the Liberals, had voters given the national party system such a jolt.

With the Conservatives and NDP reduced to near irrelevance in the Commons and two new opposition parties, each with strong regional support and neither signalling an interest in brokerage-style politics, it was natural that political analysts should ask if Canada's tradition of brokerage politics was finished and whether a realignment was taking place in the national party system. Realignment suggests a durable change, not one caused by transient and unusual factors. Several of the elements for such a durable restructuring of the vote and the party system appeared to exist. One of these involved the low esteem in which parties and politicians were—

on the federal scene, regularly winning 15–20 per cent of the popular vote and occasionally holding the balance of power during a period of **minority government**. The distinction commonly made between major and minor parties was rooted in the realities of electoral competition.

The old certainties were shattered by the 1993 election results. The Liberals won a solid majority, taking 177 of the 295 seats in the House of Commons and 41.3 per cent of the popular vote.

and continue to be—held by voters. In the words of the 1991 Royal Commission on Electoral Reform and Party Financing:

Canadians appear to distrust their political leaders, the political process and political institutions. Parties themselves may be contributing to the malaise of voters. . . . whatever the cause, there is little doubt that Canadian political parties are held in low public esteem, and that their standing has declined steadily over the past decade. They are under attack from citizens for failing to achieve a variety of goals deemed important by significant groups within society.[21]

The wave of cynicism building in the Canadian electorate weakened attachments to the traditional parties. This opened the door for newcomers on the party scene, the votes won by BQ and Reform candidates having gone mainly to Liberals and Conservatives before 1993.

A second element that seemed to presage a re-alignment of the party system involved what might be described as the shrinking centre in Canadian politics. The traditional dominance of the centrist Liberals and Progressive Conservatives depended on the existence of a broad popular consensus on the role of government and on the older parties' ability to keep political debate within the familiar confines of language, regionalism, leadership, and good government. This popular consensus had become frayed and the traditionally dominant parties' ability to keep political conflict within "safe" boundaries was diminished.

The political consensus that developed during the post-World War II era was based on the welfare state, an active economic management role for government, and official bilingualism. The Liberals and Conservatives, but particularly the Liberal Party in its role as the government for most of this era, were the architects of the policies that were the practical expressions of this consensus. On constitutional issues, too, the traditional parties were capable of broad agreement. This was evident in the support that all three parties gave to both the Meech Lake Accord and the Charlottetown Accord, a unanimity that certainly was not found in the Canadian population.

Popular consensus on the Keynesian welfare state and activist government was unravelling during the 1980s. Issues like deficit reduction, welfare reform, and lower taxes became the rallying points for dissent from the post-war consensus. Opposition to what was perceived to be state-sponsored plural-ism through official multiculturalism and to bi-lingualism provided another pole for this dissent.

In broadening its organization from the West to include Ontario and eastern Canada, the Reform Party was clearly attempting to provide a voice for this dissent that many voters believed was not being provided by the Progressive Conservative Party. Reform's second-place finish in Ontario in the 1993 federal election, capturing 20 per cent of the popular vote, cannot be explained in terms of "western alienation." These Ontario voters de-fected mainly from the Conservatives in search of a party that defined the issues in a way they be-lieved responded to the country's true problems. At the provincial level this dissent contributed to the election of the Conservatives under Ralph Klein in Alberta and Mike Harris in Ontario, prov-incial Progressive Conservative governments that were much closer to the outlook of the Reform Party than they were to the national Progressive Conservative Party under Jean Charest (1993–8) and Joe Clark (1998–2003).

Only the Liberal Party succeeded in practising the old brokerage-style politics. It emerged from the 1993 election as the only truly national party, electing members from every province and terri-tory and receiving no less than one-quarter of the votes cast in any province. The Liberals did only slightly less well in 1997, failing to elect a member only in Nova Scotia and Yukon. In the 2000 elec-tion Liberal support ranged from a low of 20.7 per cent of the popular vote in Saskatchewan to a high of 51.5 per cent in Ontario. The party won seats in every province and territory, no other party coming close to this accomplishment. The lesson some drew was that enough space no longer existed in the centre of the Canadian electorate to support two centrist brokerage parties. It became increas-ingly evident that the Progressive Conservative Party would have to reposition itself ideologically if it wanted to regain the votes that Reform/Canadian Alliance siphoned off in the 1993, 1997, and 2000 elections. It could not afford to remain a near-clone of the Liberal Party. The electoral success of un-apologetically right-wing Progressive Conservatives in Alberta and Ontario suggested that the future of the national party was in this direction.

Looking back on the years between the 1993 and 2008 elections, it is clear that they did not produce the degree or types of shifts in party support generally associated with a period of realignment. A **realignment election**, or series of elections, produces a durable change in the parties' bases of support. In Canada the 1896 election comes closest to deserving the realignment label. French-Canadian Catholics, a voting bloc that had leaned towards the Conservative Party in Canada's first several elections, shifted to the Liberals after the execution of the Métis leader Louis Riel and the selection of Quebec francophone Wilfrid Laurier as the Liberal leader. French-Canadian voters, most of whom are in Quebec, would be a mainstay of Liberal Party support in all but a couple of federal elections until the BQ's breakthrough in Quebec in 1993.[22] The 1993 election brought about a temporary realignment in Quebec that lasted until 2011, when support for the BQ collapsed. In the rest of Canada, the 2003 merger of the Canadian Alliance and the Progressive Conservative Party to form the Conservative Party of Canada appeared to re-establish business as usual. The two historically dominant parties competed to form a national government, with the NDP back in its familiar role as a third party capable of tipping the balance between the larger parties and exercising leverage over a minority government. It seemed as though the long familiar two and one-half party system had been re-established.

Business as usual ended, however, with the 2011 election. When the election was called on 26 March 2011, the conventional wisdom was that not very much was likely to change in the party standings. In the absence of a clear issue dividing the parties and galvanizing voters, what excitement existed as the campaign began was generated in large part by the prospect of yet another Conservative minority government. It was widely expected that if this were to happen, the opposition parties would take the first opportunity to defeat the Conservatives in the House and install a coalition government of the sort they had contemplated in 2008 and again in 2009.

And then the unexpected happened. The election of 2011 was a jolting reminder that campaigns matter. No one predicted at the outset that the once mighty Liberal Party, Canada's "natural governing party," as it came to be known in the latter half of the twentieth century, would fall to third place with the support of fewer than one out of five voters. Nor did anyone imagine that the NDP would vault into second place, winning more than twice as many seats as its previous election high of 43 in 1988 and doubling its share of the popular vote. These would have been surprises enough for one election. But perhaps the greatest surprise in this election full of startling results was the almost total collapse of the BQ in Quebec—a party that was comfortably in the lead in that province when the election was called—and the emergence of the NDP as Quebec's leading party. In its entire history the NDP, going back to its original incarnation as the CCF, had elected only two MPs from Quebec. On 2 May 2011, the party captured 59 of the province's 75 seats.

Explanations for these seismic changes in Canadian party politics focused on two major factors: leadership and what was believed to be Quebecers' fatigue with the sovereignists and their goal of Quebec independence. The NDP leader, Jack Layton, was said to have caught the imagination of Canadians, including Quebecers, appearing confident, compassionate, and articulate. Of course, some voters thought that he already showed these leadership qualities in 2004, 2006, and 2008. Layton's death in August of 2011 demonstrated the breadth and depth of the admiration that many Canadians, including those who did not share his social democratic ideology, felt for him. Not since the death of Pierre Trudeau in 2000 had the passing of a public figure provoked such an outpouring of grief and tributes.

Layton's rivals for the centre-left vote in the 2011 election, the Liberals' Michael Ignatieff and the BQ's Gilles Duceppe, failed to connect with many of their respective parties' usual supporters. The reasons were different in each case. Ignatieff proved unable to shake the narrative that the Conservatives had done so much to instill in the minds of Canadians from the time of his selection as Liberal leader in 2009. He seemed, according to the critics, aloof and uninspiring after his 35 years spent outside of Canada. In the case of Gilles Duceppe, it was not that his style or personal story—a story that Quebecers knew very well and seemed to approve of in the five previous elections—alienated voters. Rather, his message no longer seemed to resonate with *les québécois*. Ideologically, in terms of such

People gather at Toronto City Hall to leave messages and tributes to the late Jack Layton in August 2011. Layton's body lay in state at Parliament Hill and Gatineau, Quebec, as well as at Toronto City Hall, in the days before his state funeral, reflecting the wide impact of his legacy in Canada.

issues as taxation, social spending, the environment, and Canadian troops abroad, the BQ and the NDP were not very different. From its inception in the wake of the failed Meech Lake Accord, the BQ's competitive advantage was its special relationship to Quebec nationalism. That advantage no longer seemed to matter to voters in 2011.

Over the years Quebecers have shown themselves to be capable of dramatic change in how they cast their votes. In 1958 they abandoned the Liberal Party in droves for the Conservatives—a party that had done poorly in the province for several decades—only to return to the Liberals in the next election. With a Conservative victory imminent in 1984, Quebec voters again swung their allegiance from the Liberals to the Conservatives. But only nine years later the Conservatives could not elect a single member from Quebec and the BQ, which had existed for only a couple of years,

won most of the seats from the province and received close to half of the popular vote. Support for the BQ was widely seen as a means whereby nationalist Quebec voters could leverage their province's influence in the House of Commons without having to make the compromises with English-speaking Canada that were necessary in the Liberal and Conservative parties. These dramatic swings in Quebecers' party preferences have been interpreted by many as evidence of strategic voting in a province whose citizens recognize that it is *pas comme les autres*.[23]

The fact that four out of 10 Quebec voters cast a ballot for the NDP in 2011 was seen as being due, at least in part, to strategic voting. When the NDP edged closer to the Liberals in the polls and then appeared to be about level with them just after the midpoint of the campaign, media

Listen to "The 60/40 Country?" podcast, available at: www.oup .com/he/Brooks9e

speculation on the possibility of a coalition government led by the NDP became rampant. We cannot know for certain whether a significant number of voters who usually would have voted either Liberal or BQ decided to vote for the NDP for strategic reasons, thinking that Jack Layton's party might actually head a coalition government. We do know, however, that polls in Quebec showed Layton to be more popular than the other party leaders. If strategic reasoning and a bandwagon effect in Quebec were an important part of the mix of factors that contributed to the massive shift in Quebecers' party preferences in 2011, the gamble did not pay off. The Conservatives won a clear majority nationally and the possibility of an NDP-led coalition melted away along with the last snow in the province of Quebec.

The 2011 election appeared to be all about change and, indeed, the changes were significant. But buried underneath the focus on the NDP surge, the BQ collapse, and the Liberals' worst showing in the party's history were two important elements of continuity. First, issues appeared to take a back seat to the leaders and their perceived strengths and shortcomings. As we saw earlier in this chapter, this is something that André Siegfried remarked upon over 100 years ago: the tendency for Canadian elections to be contests between the parties' leaders rather than struggles between rival ideas and ideologies. This is only partly correct, however. It is not that ideas do not matter in Canadian elections, but rather that they become associated with and absorbed into images that voters have of the party leaders and, in the process, lose some of their independent force. The electoral conversation is not bereft of policy ideas and promises. But these are refracted through perceptions of the party leaders. Leadership becomes the pre-eminent issue and this necessarily focuses attention on what are believed to be the personal attributes of the men and women who lead the parties.

Second, the election results seemed to demonstrate that Canada is a 60/40 country. The Conservative Party, the only party with a centre-right platform, won with about 40 per cent of the popular vote. The four centre-left parties, the Liberals being the most centrist of this group, together accounted for about 60 per cent of the vote. This had been the pattern for the past three decades, with the exception of 1984 when the Conservative Party won 50 per cent of the popular

vote. Of course, one can quibble about whether the Liberal Party became a more right-leaning than left-leaning party during the mid- to late 1990s, as some believe, when Paul Martin was minister of Finance and debt reduction appeared to be the priority. But ideological characterizations are relative and the Liberal brand, as most commentators agree, has always been a bit to the left of the Conservative brand on the Canadian ideological spectrum. In the nine elections from 1988 to 2019 the percentage of the vote received by centre-right parties (a category that includes the Progressive Conservative Party, the Reform Party, the Canadian Alliance, the Conservative Party of Canada, and the People's Party of Canada) has ranged between 29.6 per cent (2004) and 43 per cent (1988), averaging about 36 per cent.

The election of 2011 and in particular the NDP's historic breakthrough in Quebec, dubbed the "Orange Crush," was interpreted by some as an indication that the Liberal and Conservative duopoly in federal politics was over. The strong performance of the NDP in the polls in the years leading up to the 2015 election—the NDP actually went into that election campaign in first place in the polls—reinforced the view that Canada now had a three-party system and that the NDP was finally a contender to form a national government.[24]

The "Orange Crush" of 2011 was followed by the "Orange Crash" in the 2015 election. The collapse of the NDP, which went into the election campaign as the official opposition and leading in the polls, was chiefly due to the erosion of its support in Quebec. The party dropped from 59 to 16 seats in Quebec. In the rest of Canada the NDP's losses were considerably less, falling from 44 seats outside Quebec in the 2011 election to 28 in 2015, almost all of this decline accounted for by a swing in the centre-left vote to the Liberals in Atlantic Canada and Ontario. The Liberal Party won 39.5 per cent of the popular vote and 184 of the seats in the expanded 338-seat House of Commons. As may be seen in Table 11.1, the Liberals were massively over-rewarded by Canada's single-member/simple plurality electoral system in Atlantic Canada and were also over-rewarded in Quebec, Ontario, Manitoba, and British Columbia. We will have more to say on the subject of the electoral system and its consequences later in this chapter.

The results of the 2015 election were described by the *New York Times* as a "stunning rout" for the Liberals, and an "epic victory" for the Liberal Party by *Maclean's*. In fact, however, in some respects it was a return to business as usual in Canadian party politics. The victorious Liberal Party won a majority of seats on the strength of just under 40 per cent of the popular vote, as the Conservative Party had done in 2011. Indeed, 38–43 per cent of the popular vote has been enough for a party to form a majority government on eight occasions since Canada went from a two-party system to a two and one-half party system in 1935.[25] The NDP returned to third-party status and won just under 20 per cent of the popular vote, numbers that have been pretty

typical of its performance in federal elections for most of the past 50 years. The Liberals were once again the most successful party in Quebec, a status that the party has enjoyed in the vast majority of elections since 1896. The Conservative Party's greatest strength was in western Canada, where it won 54 of its 99 seats, although its support in Manitoba and British Columbia was somewhat weaker than had been the case in the last several elections.

The election of 2019 may be summed up in the French saying, "Plus ça change, plus c'est la même chose." The most striking result of the election was the evidence of a strong regional divide in the Canadian electorate, a divide that has been evident in most elections since the late 1950s. The victorious Liberal

WARREN TODA/EPA-EFE/Shutterstock

Prime Minister and Liberal Party leader Justin Trudeau at a campaign stop in Whitby, Ontario, before the October 2019 federal election. This election saw Trudeau's Liberals win 157 seats and lose 20. With 33 per cent of the popular vote, the Liberals fell short of the threshold typically required for a majority government.

Party, which formed a minority government, dominated in Atlantic Canada and in Ontario, and edged out the BQ for the largest share of the popular vote and number of seats in Quebec. The Conservatives were the most popular party in the Prairie provinces, the Liberals failing to win a single seat in Alberta and Saskatchewan. British Columbia was the most competitive of the provinces, but here too the Liberals lost ground and the Conservatives gained seats. The election seemed to confirm an old adage of Canadian politics: Elections are won in Ontario and majority government status is won in Quebec. The Liberals were denied that majority government status by the resurgence of support for the BQ. For its part, the NDP's share of the national popular vote dropped by several percentage points, it fell to only one seat in Quebec, and it finished in fourth place in number of seats, behind the BQ (see Table 11.1).

TABLE 11.1 Percentage of Vote and Seats Won by Each Party, Nationally and by Province/Territory, 2015 and 2019

A. Percentage of Vote and Candidates Elected by Party and Province/Territory, 2015

	Bloc Québécois	Conservative	Green	Liberal	NDP	Others	Total, Province/ Territory
Newfoundland and Labrador		10.30% 0	1.10% 0	64.50% 7	21.10% 0	3.9% 0	7
Prince Edward Island	—	19.3% 0	6% 0	58.3% 4	16% 0	0.3% 0	4
Nova Scotia	—	17.9% 0	3.4% 0	62% 11	16.3% 0	0.3% 0	11
New Brunswick	—	25.4% 12	4.7% 0	51.6% 10	18.4% 0	0.1% 0	10
Quebec	19.4% 10	16.7% 12	2.8% 0	35.7% 40	25.4% 16	0.6% 0	78
Ontario	—	35.1% 33	2.8% 0	44.8% 80	16.6% 8	0.5% 0	121
Manitoba	—	37.4% 5	3.2% 0	44.7% 7	13.6% 2	1.1% 0	14
Saskatchewan	—	48.5% 10	2.1% 0	23.9% 1	25.1% 3	0.4% 0	14
Alberta	—	59.6% 29	2.5% 0	24.5% 4	11.6% 1	1.6% 0	34
British Columbia	—	29.9% 10	8.2% 1	35.1% 17	26% 14	0.7% 0	42
Northwest Territories	—	18.3% 0	2.8% 0	48.3% 1	30.5% 0	—	1
Nunavut	—	24.8% 0	1.5% 0	47.1% 1	26.6% 0	—	1
Yukon	—	24.3% 0	2.8% 0	53.7% 1	19.4% 0	—	1
Canada	4.7% 10	31.9% 99	3.4% 1	39.5% 184	19.7% 44	0.8% 0	338

B. Percentage of Vote and Candidates Elected by Party and Province/Territory, 2019

	Bloc Québécois	Conservative	Green	Liberal	NDP	Others	Total, Province/ Territory
Newfoundland and Labrador		28%	3.10%	44.70%	23.90%	0.3%	
		0	0	6	1	0	7
Prince Edward Island	—	27.4%	20.9%	43.6%	7.6%	0.5%	
		0	0	4	0	0	4
Nova Scotia	—	25.6%	11%	41.4%	19%	3.1%	
		1	0	10	0	0	11
New Brunswick	—	32.8%	17%	37.6%	9.4%	3.2%	
		3	1	6	0	0	10
Quebec	32.5%	16%	4.5%	34.2%	10.7%	1.7%	
	32	10	0	35	1	0	78
Ontario	—	33.2%	6.2%	41.4%	16.8%	2.4%	
		36	0	79	6	0	121
Manitoba	—	45.8%	5%	26.2%	20.6%	2.4%	
		7	0	4	3	0	14
Saskatchewan	—	64.3%	2.5%	11.6%	19.5%	2.2%	
		14	0	0	3	0	14
Alberta	—	69.2%	2.8%	13.7%	11.5%	2.7%	
		33	0	4	1	0	34
British Columbia	—	34%	12.4%	26.1%	24.4%	3.2%	
		17	2	11	11	0	42
Northwest Territories	—	25.8%	10.6%	40%	21.8%	1.8%	
		0	0	1	0	0	1
Nunavut	—	25.8%	2.1%	31%	41.2%	2.1%	
		0	0	0	1	0	1
Yukon	—	33.1%	10.3%	33.4%	21.8%	1.4%	
		0	0	1	0	0	1
Canada	7.7%	34.4%	6.5%	33.1%	15.9%	20%	
	32	121	3	157	24	1	338

Source: Elections Canada

Selecting Party Leaders in Canada

When Wilfrid Laurier was chosen as the first French-Canadian leader of the Liberal Party in 1887, about 80 men did the choosing. They were the Liberal MPs in Canada's Sixth Parliament. Laurier's candidacy was promoted by Edward Blake, then leader of the party, after Blake's poor showing in the 1887 general election. Some prominent members of the Liberal Party opposed Laurier as leader, but in the end he had no serious opposition for the post. The rules followed in this leadership selection process were not written down in any formal document. It was simply understood that, following the British parliamentary tradition, it was the prerogative of caucus to choose who among its members would be the party leader.

When the Conservative Party of Canada chose Andrew Scheer as its new leader on 27 May 2017, about 141,000 party members cast ballots. Some did so in person at the Toronto Congress Centre, where the party's leadership convention was held, others at polling stations across the country, and about one-third through mail-in ballots. Party members voted using a preferential ballot that allowed them to indicate up to 10 candidates (there were in fact 13), rank-ordered from one to 10. The candidate who had the most support through the first 12 rounds of voting, Maxime Bernier, lost to Andrew Scheer in the 13th round, 51 per cent to 49 per cent.

With some minor variations, this has become the model for how Canadian political parties choose their leaders. At the national level it began when the Bloc Québécois used the one-member, one-vote (OMOV) method of choosing its leader in the 1997 election won by Gilles Duceppe. This model was also used by the Progressive Conservative Party in 1998 when it chose Joe Clark as its leader. Prior to these leadership elections, all of the main parties used a convention model to choose their leaders. This began with the Liberal leadership convention of 1919, when over 900 party delegates assembled in Ottawa and chose Mackenzie King as the party's leader on the fourth ballot. The Conservatives abandoned the caucus selection model in 1927, when R.B. Bennett was elected party leader on the second ballot by the more than 1,500 delegates at the party's convention in Winnipeg.

The convention model occasionally produced moments of drama. Convention speeches by the candidates and the dynamics on the convention floor, as when a candidate withdrew or was dropped from the election because of having received the fewest votes in a round of voting, and then expressed his or her support for another candidate, provided some of these moments. The dynamic on the convention floor sometimes produced unexpected results. Most of the time, however, the candidate with the most votes on the first ballot emerged as party leader. Of the 26 leadership elections held by the Liberal, Conservative, and New Democratic parties using the convention model, 16 required more than one ballot to choose the new leader and in 13 of these cases the victor was the candidate who led on the first ballot. The only exceptions were the Progressive Conservative Party conventions of 1976 (Joe Clark was third on the first ballot and won on

the fourth) and 1983 (Brian Mulroney was second on the first ballot and won on the fourth) and the Liberal convention of 2006 (Stéphane Dion was third on the first ballot and won on the fourth).

Speculation about money sometimes added to the drama of leadership contests and also raised questions about their democratic character. Until 2004 there were no legislated limits on how much money donors could contribute to candidates or how much could be spent, nor was there a requirement that the names of donors be revealed. The parties were responsible for setting their own rules. The amounts spent by some candidates in the Conservative leadership races of 1983 and 1993, and in the Liberal races of 1984 and 1993,[26] increased pressure to bring the parties' leadership election rules under some of the same legal requirements that had already existed since the 1970s in the case of contributions to parties and their candidates for office.

The three models for selecting party leaders—caucus, delegate-convention, and OMOV—are summarized in Table 11.2. They differ most obviously in terms of the size and nature of the *selectorate*, that portion of the electorate that has a voice in the selection of a party leader. The parliamentary caucus and delegate-convention or party congress selection models may appear to belong to yesterday, to times and societies less committed to democratic norms of participation and inclusiveness. In fact, however, a 2009 study by Ofer Kenig found that only about half of the 50 political parties that he examined in 17 democracies used some variation of the OMOV model. Just under one-fifth of them still used the parliamentary caucus model for selecting leaders.[27] Nevertheless, the last few decades have seen a movement across the democratic world towards the broadening of the selectorate used to choose party leaders.

Whether the OMOV model produces better results than the caucus or convention models depends on what one means by "better." The argument for OMOV is that it democratizes the leadership selection process, broadening the scope of participation and thereby reducing the influence of elites within the party. Combined with limitations that all of the parties place on leadership campaign spending and the contribution limits and reporting requirements that have existed under Canadian law since

TABLE 11.2 Three Models of Leadership Selection

Model 1	Model 2	Model 3
Parliamentary Caucus	Party Activists (narrow)	Party Activists (broad)
Few and closed ——————————————————————————— Many and open		
Participants		
Elected members of the party (i.e., MPs)	Party members elected by members of their riding associations to serve as delegates at the leadership convention, plus ex officio delegates*	Party members
Procedures		
Selection takes place behind closed doors, often without competition between rival candidates	Selection takes place at a party leadership convention, often after several months of campaigning	Selection takes place through votes cast by party members: some voting may take place at a fixed convention site but most votes are cast by party members who are elsewhere
Examples		
Liberal Party: Mackenzie, 1873; Blake, 1880; Laurier, 1887; Ignatieff, 2008	King, 1919; St Laurent, 1948; Pearson, 1958; Trudeau, 1968; Turner, 1984; Chrétien, 1990; Martin, 2003; Dion, 2006	Justin Trudeau, 2013
Conservative Party: Macdonald, 1867; Abbott, 1891; Thompson, 1892; Bowell, 1894; Tupper, 1896; Borden, 1901; Meighen, 1920; Gutherie, 1926; Meighen, 1941	Bennett, 1927; Manion, 1938; Bracken, 1942; Drew, 1948; Diefenbaker, 1956; Stanfield, 1967; Clark, 1976; Mulroney, 1983; Campbell, 1993; Charest, 1995	Clark, 1998; Harper, 2004; Scheer, 2017
CCF-NDP:	xWoodsworth, 1933; Caldwell, 1942; Argue, 1960;** Douglas, 1961; Lewis, 1971; Broadbent, 1975; McLaughlin, 1989; McDonough, 1995; McDonough, 2001	Layton, 2003; Mulcair, 2012; Singh, 2017
Bloc Québécois: Bouchard, 1990	Bouchard, 1991; Blanchet, 2019***	Duceppe, 1997; Paillé, 2011; Beaulieu, 2014; Ouellet, 2017

*An ex officio delegate is one whose formal position entitles him or her to a vote in the choice of party leader. Elected MPs and party office-holders are examples.
**The three national CCF leaders, Woodsworth, Caldwell, and Argue, were in fact selected by the CCF's caucus and the decisions were subsequently ratified at party conventions where the choice of new leader was unchallenged. So while this process was not the caucus model in the strict sense, it was not much of a departure from that elitist method of selecting the leader.
***Blanchet's candidacy was uncontested and he was acclaimed by the BQ organization as the party's leader without a vote of the membership.

2004, this is expected to make leadership races more open, less about who has the most dollars and more about who has the most supporters within the rank and file of the party. It is hard to argue against such aims. At the same time, however, it is not yet clear that these reforms to the leadership selection process produce leaders who are more likely to be successful at winning elections and holding together the different elements that exist within any political party (see Box 11.4).

Politics in Focus

BOX 11.4 Democratizing Leader Selection: What Could Possibly Go Wrong?

Doug Ford was elected leader of Canada's largest provincial conservative party last weekend with little support from the caucus he will soon lead in an election or, for that matter, from much of the Ontario Tory establishment.

A mobilized so-called Ford Nation and an assist from the social conservative wing of the party helped the former Toronto mayoral candidate secure the leadership.

The grassroots path—for lack of a better word—to political leadership has become a well-trodden one in Canada.

...Last fall Jagmeet Singh, who has yet to serve a single day in the House of Commons, easily beat frontline MPs to become Thomas Mulcair's successor.

Singh might have won the NDP leadership without the help of scores of fellow members of the Sikh community but probably not on the first ballot.

Almost a year ago, a coalition of Quebec dairy farmers determined to punish Conservative front-runner Maxime Bernier for his opposition to Canada's supply management system helped tilt the balance in favour of rival Andrew Scheer.

At the time of Justin Trudeau's 2013 leadership bid, his political rock-star status and the impressive social-media following that attended it made his ascension to the top virtually unstoppable. Like Singh, he might have had a harder run for his money under a system that was not based on winning a membership drive.

For most of Canada's history, the leadership selection process was essentially the purview of a mix of committed volunteers, the apparatchiks who organized campaigns and ran party backrooms and past and present members of a political organization's elected wing.

But over the past two decades, Canada's mainstream parties all adopted some form of one-member-one-vote leadership formula.

The decision to open the process to thousands of members was supposed to breathe new life into party politics.

It may be achieving the opposite.

That is not to say that the previous system was infallible.

To wit, the last main federal leader to be dispensed from fighting for the job in an open contest as the result of a caucus and party brass consensus was Michael Ignatieff.

He subsequently earned his place in the history books for leading the federal Liberal party to the only third-place finish in its history.

Membership-wide votes have dramatically reduced the influence of the party's elected and non-elected insiders and the self-serving backroom deals that sometimes attended their leadership choices.

But the need to secure as many boots on the ground as possible has also translated into a bias toward populist candidates and/or platforms that can be more reflective of the political flavour of the day than of a party's core identity.

By encouraging alliances of convenience, the system has also rendered parties more vulnerable to single-interest groups.

In some instances, those groups will mobilize only long enough to achieve their preferred leadership outcome, leaving more committed party members to pick up the post-leadership pieces.

...[T]here will be no going back to the days when caucus members and other party insiders had a definitive or even a meaningful say on who would be best to lead them.

But a party can only rent its soul to the latest leadership comer so many times before it loses that soul.

The Electoral System and Its Consequences

The evening of his election victory on 19 October 2015, Prime Minister-elect Justin Trudeau repeated a promise that he had made on several occasions before and during the campaign. It wasn't about taxes, health care, or climate change and a carbon tax. It was about the electoral system. Trudeau stated categorically that 2015 would be the last federal election fought under Canada's first-past-the-post electoral system.

A little more than a year after his government was sworn in, the promise had been put on hold and it was clear that the next election would indeed be fought under the old familiar rules. Circumstances change and the point is not to criticize Trudeau or any other prime minister for changing his or her mind on a campaign promise. More significant is the fact that Trudeau felt the need to mention this particular promise and place it at the top of his to-do list. Given that polls have shown that a majority of Canadians appear to believe that the prime minister is directly elected by Canadians—this is not the case—it would be rather surprising to find that their knowledge of how the electoral system works is particularly great or that their passion to reform it very keen. So why mention electoral reform as a leading priority for the new government?

Part of the answer may well be Prime Minister Trudeau's often expressed preference for a system of preferential voting. But another part probably has to do with the previous 10 years of Conservative government. The Conservative Party formed minority governments after the elections of 2006 and 2008 with 36.3 per cent and 37.6 per cent, respectively, of the popular vote, and then formed a majority government in 2011 with 39.6 per cent of the vote. The Liberal Party and the NDP split most of the rest of the vote, neither being strong enough alone to defeat the Conservatives. The situation actually led some of the most respected Liberal and NDP elders, including Lloyd Axworthy, Ed Broadbent, and even former Prime Minister Jean Chrétien, to talk about whether a unite-the-left strategy of some sort might be needed to defeat the Conservatives.

Electoral reform would eliminate the need for such a strategy.

Canada's electoral system is often referred to as a first-past-the-post or single-member, simple plurality system. It is based on the **single-member constituency**: one person is elected to represent the citizens of a particular electoral district, also called a constituency or riding. The candidate who receives the most votes in a constituency election becomes the member of Parliament (or provincial legislator) for that constituency. This is called a **plurality electoral system**. A majority of votes is not necessary to be elected and, given the fragmentation of votes between the three main parties, is the exception rather than the rule. A political party's representation in the House of Commons will depend, therefore, on how well its candidates fare in the 338 constituency races that take place across Canada on election day.

This electoral system does not reward parties in proportion to their share of the popular vote. The Liberal Party, whose candidates garnered 33 per cent of the popular vote in the 2019 election, won 46 per cent of all seats in the House of Commons. Conservative candidates received a total of 34.4 percent of the national popular vote, which translated into only 36 per cent of the seats in the House. The Green Party's 6.5 per cent of the popular vote produced three MPs representing just under 1 per cent of all seats in the House of Commons. These are just some of the ways in which the representation in the House of Commons after the 2019 election did not mirror the popular vote.

The advocates of the single-member, simple plurality electoral system point to its ability to produce majority governments as being one of the system's chief virtues. It manages, they claim, to transform something less than a majority of votes for a party into a majority of seats, thereby delivering stable majority government. In fact, however, the system's performance on this count has been rather mediocre. Ten of the 21 general elections from 1957 to 2019 produced minority governments. Moreover, the premise of this argued virtue, i.e., that majority government is preferable to minority government, deserves some careful thought. In what way or ways is it preferable? Is it preferable because Canadians won't have to go to the polls as often as they would with minority governments that might last only a year or two? Would it really be so onerous for Canadians to have the opportunity to vote more often federally than once every four years when the only decision they have to make once in the voting booth is which circle to mark their X? Perhaps even more importantly, is there any proof that majority governments deliver better governance and produce better legislation than minority governments? One of the very few people to examine this question in an empirical manner concludes that there may be good reasons to believe that minority governments perform better than majority governments.[28]

The chief alternative to the single-member, plurality electoral system is some form of **proportional representation** (PR). Under a PR system, the number of members elected by each party about coincides with its share of the popular vote. This sounds eminently fair, but PR has its critics. Detractors criticize it on three main counts. First, they claim it promotes a splintering of the party system, encouraging the creation of minor parties that represent very narrow interests and undermining the development of broad-based national parties capable of bridging sectional rivalries and the differences between special interests. Second, proportional representation is said to produce unstable government. The unlikelihood that any party will have a majority of seats and, therefore, the need to cobble together and maintain a coalition government may result in more frequent elections. And even between elections, the inter-party deals necessary to maintain a coalition government may paralyze cabinet decision-making or produce other forms of instability (although it has to be said that some empirical studies have arrived at the opposite conclusion). [29]

A third standard criticism of PR systems is that they encourage ideological polarity and enable extremist parties to achieve representation in the legislature. There is no doubt that countries having proportional electoral systems do tend to have more political parties represented in their legislatures than those with plurality systems, and the ideological distance between the extreme ends of the party spectrum will inevitably be greater than that

separating Canada's major parties, or Democrats and Republicans in the United States (another plurality electoral system). In fact, however, the ideological distance between those parties in proportional systems that are likely to be the main partners in any coalition government tends to be no greater than between, say, the Liberal Party and the NDP in Canada. Moreover, not everyone would agree that more, rather than less, ideological dispersion between parties represented in the legislature is a bad thing. One might argue that it improves voters' ability to distinguish between parties on the basis of the values and policies they represent. The prospect that extremist parties will infiltrate the legislature through a proportional system is also less worrisome than is claimed by detractors. Both theory and experience suggest that the closer a party gets to membership in a governing coalition, the more moderate its behaviour will be. Nevertheless, the fear that proportional representation might open the door for extremist parties to win seats in Parliament was one of the principal reasons that Prime Minister Trudeau gave when he changed his mind about electoral reform.[30]

The first-past-the-post electoral system in Canada is not without its own detractors. In a classic analysis that still repays reading, Alan Cairns identifies several consequences for Canada's party system and national unity that flow from the single-member, simple plurality system.[31]

- It tends to produce more seats than votes for the strongest major party and for minor parties whose support is regionally concentrated.
- It gives the impression that some parties have little or no support in certain regions, when in fact their candidates may regularly account for 15–30 per cent of the popular vote.
- The parliamentary composition of a party will be less representative of the different regions of the country than is that party's electoral support.
- Minor parties whose appeal is to interests that are distributed widely across the country will receive a smaller percentage of seats than votes.

Cairns concludes that the overall impact of Canada's electoral system has been negative. The system, he argues, has exacerbated regional and ethnolinguistic divisions in Canadian political life by under-representing the Conservative Party in Quebec for most of the last century and, for most of that time, giving the impression that the Liberal Party was the only national party with support in French Canada.

Cairns's article on the electoral system's effects was written in the late 1960s. If it were written today it would also mention, among other consequences, the gross under-representation of the Liberals in western Canada over the last few decades, despite their receiving between one-quarter and one-third of western votes in most elections,

the fact that the Conservatives and NDP together received about 40 per cent of the vote in Atlantic Canada in the 2015 election but the Liberal Party won all 32 seats, and that with close to 50 per cent of the popular vote across the GTA in 2015 the Liberals won all but three of the region's 50 seats. The 2019 election produced similar distortions. As William Irvine observes, "the electoral system confers a spurious image of unanimity on provinces. By magnifying the success of the provincial vote leader, the electoral system ensures that party caucuses will over-represent any party's 'best' province."[32] Along with the distortions that Canada's electoral system produces, another argument for reform is that the present system leaves many voters feeling disempowered and contributes to low

THE CANADIAN PRSS/Chad Hipolito

British Columbia NDP Premier John Horgan and provincial Green Party leader Andrew Weaver at a rally in support of proportional representation in Victoria, BC. Despite vocal support for electoral reform during the 2015 federal election, a majority of British Columbia voters rejected proportional representation during a 2018 referendum. Proportional representation was also voted down in a 2019 referendum in PEI, leaving the future of electoral reform in Canada uncertain.

levels of voter turnout. Critics also charge that this sense of being disempowered may lead to "strategic voting," whereby a voter in a particular riding will cast his or her ballot not for the party or candidate of choice but for the party or candidate with the greatest likelihood of defeating the projected front-runner in that riding. Such a phenomenon might be a reasonably compelling argument for reform of the electoral system, but little evidence beyond the anecdotal suggests that it exists. Those who study voting behaviour have been unable to find strong evidence that any significant number of Canadians vote strategically.[33] On the contrary, there appear to be many cases where labour and other groups have advocated such voting, without any indication that this has had the desired effect. There is stronger evidence that voter disillusionment with the choices on offer and apathy may cause some to stay home on election day.

Historically, the party that has stood to gain most from the replacement of Canada's electoral system by some form of proportional representation has been the CCF-NDP. It received a smaller percentage of total seats in the Commons than its share of the national vote in every general election until 2011 and then returned to the historical pattern in 2015 and 2019. The Green Party has also been strongly supportive of PR, although it has to be said that the party's popular vote often has been lower than the usual thresholds that exist for party representation in countries that have PR systems. The likely consequences of PR and of a preferential voting system are considered in Box 11.5.

Voting Behaviour

Few generalizations regarding Canadians' voting behaviour withstand the test of time. Regionally, the Conservative Party began its long association with western voters in 1957 with the election of the Diefenbaker government. Conservative candidates outpolled Liberals and the party elected more MPs from the four westernmost provinces in most elections after 1957. This tendency was accentuated after the 1972 election. The Liberal Party's fortunes in the West sank dramatically under the leadership of Pierre Trudeau and the region became thought of as mainly Conservative and NDP turf. The Reform

Party, we have seen, was for a time the vehicle for this anti-Liberal resentment after many western voters became disappointed with the behaviour in office of the Conservative government of Brian Mulroney. A pox on both your houses, westerners seemed to say.

Quebec was an electoral stronghold for the Liberal Party over most of the last century. But this association was weakened with the emergence of the Bloc Québécois. The BQ outpolled the Liberals in six of the seven general elections between 1993 and 2011. The Liberal Party's support in Quebec reached its lowest level ever in the 2011 election, but has bounced back, although not to the historically high levels enjoyed during most of the twentieth century, in the 2015 and 2019 elections.

Studies of voter choice in Canada, the United States, and other Western democracies suggest that the decision to vote for a particular party or candidate associated with a party is the result of a complex set of interrelated factors. These factors, and the causal relationships between them, may be seen in Figure 11.1. This is a revised version of Cameron Anderson and Laura Stephenson's funnel of causality model. It traces the path leading from socio-demographic characteristics of voters through their partisan identification and ideological leaning, which in turn affect the information universe that shapes how they view candidates, issues, and parties at a particular point in time (most crucially during an election campaign), leading ultimately to voter choice.

Partisan identification was long believed to be a key factor influencing voter choice. At the same time, the share of the electorate claiming to identify with a particular party has been lower in Canada than in many other democracies, including the United States, and has declined over the last few decades.[34] Dramatic shifts in voter support for particular parties—major cases in point include the collapse of the Progressive Conservative Party vote and the sudden emergence of large numbers of voters supporting the Reform Party and the BQ in 1993, the more gradual but very significant drop in the Liberal Party's share of the popular vote in the 2008 and 2011 elections, and the dramatic spike in support for the NDP in

Politics in Focus

BOX 11.5 Who's for What Sort of Electoral Reform?

All of the main political parties in Canada recognize that Canadians want to retain an electoral system that enables them to elect their local MP. Canada has always had such a system and the idea of moving to what is called a *list proportional representation* system is unappealing to many voters. Under such a system multiple candidates are elected to represent large geographic regions. These could be as large as provinces, but they might be drawn on other lines. In any case they would be much larger than current ridings. The most common variant of this model involves voters casting a single vote for their preferred party instead of voting for a particular candidate of that party. If that party wins 30 per cent of the vote in the geographic region for which there are, say, 10 representatives, then three of them will be from that party. Norway, Denmark, and Spain are among the countries that have such a system.

The New Democrats have long favoured a variation of this system known as *mixed-member proportional* (MMP). Under MMP voters cast a ballot both for a local candidate and for their preferred party. MPs would still be elected to represent ridings. At the same time, however, each party's share of the provincial popular vote would be used to adjust party representation in the legislature, making it proportional to each party's share of the preferred party vote in a province. These province-wide MPs would be those on each party's provincial list who receive the most votes.

Although some in the Liberal Party are happy with the existing first-past-the-post electoral system, many would prefer a system known as *preferential voting*. Under this system, also known as instant run-off voting, voters are able to rank candidates. If no candidate gets a majority of first-ranked ballots, the candidate with the fewest first-rank votes is dropped and his or her votes are distributed to voters' second-choice candidates. This process continues until one candidate has a majority.

The existing first-past-the-post system is preferred by the Conservative Party. Its reasons for supporting the status quo and the other parties' reasons for preferring reform may be based on various considerations. Éric Grenier, one of Canada's foremost elections analysts, examined the impact that the MMP and preferential voting systems would have had on the 2015 election results. Of course, if the election had been conducted under one of these other electoral systems, the parties and candidates might have campaigned differently and voters' thinking about their choices might also have been altered. Nevertheless, assuming that the only thing that changed was the electoral system and the way that it processes votes into representation, Grenier's calculations of the results of the 2015 election, had it been determined by preferential or proportional methods, are shown in Table 11.3.[35]

TABLE 11.3 Hypothetical Outcomes of the 2015 Federal Election under Proportional and Preferential Voting Systems

	Election	Proportional	Preferential
Liberal	184	134	224
Conservative	99	109	61
NDP	44	67	50
Bloc	10	16	2
Green	1	12	1

Source: Éric Grenier, "Change to preferential ballot would benefit Liberals," CBC, November 26, 2015

Quebec in 2011 and the collapse of that support in 2019—alert us to the fact that party identification is easily abandoned by many voters. It continues, however, to be a significant predictor of how one is likely to vote.

One is not born, of course, with a party identification, any more than one is born with an ideological disposition or any other political value, belief, or world view. The factors influencing the likelihood of acquiring a particular partisan identification or

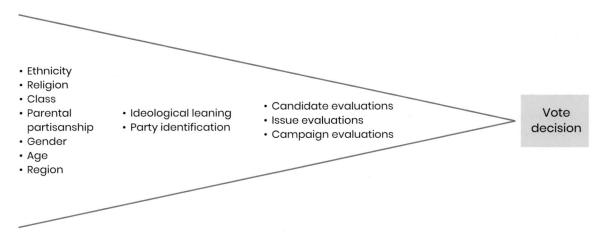

FIGURE 11.1 The Funnel of Causality Model of Voter Choice

Source: Adapted from Cameron D. Anderson and Laura B. Stephenson, eds, *Voting Behaviour in Canada* (Vancouver: University of British Columbia Press, 2010), 4, Figure 1.1.

ideological leaning that may be associated with voter choice have been widely studied in Canada since the first Canadian Election Study carried out in 1965. Some of the main socio-demographic factors thought to influence partisan identification and, ultimately, voting behaviour are indicated in the left-hand column of Figure 11.1.

Partisan identification influences voters' perceptions of issues. Based on the 2004 and 2006 Canadian election surveys, Blais and his colleagues conclude that, "There is strong support . . . for the view that party identification critically affects political judgments. To be sure, information does play a role. . . . But partisanship remains a crucial factor and its impact is not conditional on general level of political information."[36] Identifying with a political party operates as a filter that may influence a voter's perceptions of issues, candidates, and party leaders.

In regard to social class, differences between voters for the Liberal and Conservative parties have never been very great and certainly have been less important than regional and ethnolinguistic differences. The NDP's formal affiliation to organized labour might have been expected to reflect a preference among working-class Canadians for that party. But as we have seen, class identity has never been particularly strong for most Canadians. A perusal of publications at the website of the Canadian Election Study, based on federal elections from

1988 through 2011, turns up no articles directly related to the impact of class on voting behaviour and only a few that touch on the effects of class in any significant manner. This reflects the reality of the comparative insignificance of class as a factor influencing voter behaviour in federal elections. The main qualification to this general rule involves the fact that NDP support generally is stronger among voters who belong to unions than it is among most other segments of the electorate. Class appears to be a stronger predictor of voter choice if it is measured subjectively, according to how individual voters perceive their class membership and ideological leanings. But, as Elisabeth Gidengil observes, "there is only a loose connection in Canada between objective class position and class ideology."[37] The reasons for the weak impact of class position on partisan identification and voting continue to be debated.

Whereas the influence of class on voting is weak, that of religion continues to be significant. As mentioned earlier, the overwhelming support given by Catholics to the Liberal Party was a major factor contributing to that party's electoral success in the twentieth century. Support for the Liberals collapsed across the board in 2011, but even before that election the Catholic pillar of Liberal Party support was weakening. Data from the 2008 Canadian Election Study show that about 42 per cent of

Catholics outside of Quebec claim to have voted for Liberal candidates, compared to 36 per cent for the Conservatives and 21 per cent for the NDP. The declining significance of Catholic religious affiliation for voter choice outside of Quebec is corroborated by Sarah Wilkins-Laflamme, based on her study of the 2011 federal election.[38]

If instead of denominational affiliation we look at religiosity, measured by the percentage of respondents who agree with the statement, "Religion is very important in my life," we find a strong correlation among voters outside of Quebec. In 2008, 54 per cent of these respondents claimed to have voted for the Conservative Party, compared to 28 per cent who voted Liberal and about 18 per cent for the NDP. Wilkins-Laflamme notes that, "in 2011 in the ROC, those who thought that religion was very important in their lives were an estimated 14 per cent more likely to vote Conservative and 18 per cent less likely to vote NDP than those who thought that it was not at all important."[39] A similar relationship between religiosity and voter preference in the 2011 election was observed in Quebec, with those who said that religion is very important in their lives being 16 per cent more likely to vote Conservative and 21 per cent less likely to vote for the NDP compared to respondents who said that religion was not at all important in their lives.[40]

The impact of ethnicity on partisanship and voting behaviour has operated mainly through the fact that those of French ancestry, and particularly those whose mother tongue is French, have been very likely to support the Liberal Party. This relationship has not been particularly strong since the election of 1993. Most Canadians of French ancestry and about 90 per cent of Canadian francophones reside in Quebec. In only one federal election between 1993 and 2011 did the Liberal Party receive more votes in Quebec than any other political party. The BQ was more popular with French-speaking voters in Quebec in several elections, as was the NDP in the 2011 election. Outside of Quebec, the correlation between French ancestry and language and voting for the Liberal Party appears to remain strong. Once such factors as education, income, and occupation are controlled for, other ethnic identities appear to be rather weak as

predictors of either voter choice or whether one is likely to vote.[41]

On the other hand, a gender gap between male and female voting patterns has been observed in both Canadian and American elections. In American presidential elections (the pattern is less clear in congressional and state elections), the Democratic Party's candidate has received more votes from women than has the Republican candidate in every election since 1992. The explanation usually advanced is that female and male voters tend to differ to some degree in the importance they assign to certain issues and their preferences on these issues. The values more likely to be found among women than men result in female voters being more likely than males to vote for parties of the left. This is also true in Canada.[42] The Conservative Party receives a larger share of its popular vote from men than from women. The NDP, on the other hand, has received a larger share of its vote from women than from men, at least in recent elections. The combined share of the female popular vote received by the Liberal Party and the NDP is always somewhat greater than their combined share of the male popular vote. The picture is complicated somewhat by the existence of what Wilson and Lusztig call a "marriage gap." Married voters, including women, are more likely than unmarried voters to prefer an ideologically conservative party.[43]

Immigration has been an important component of Canadian population growth and, therefore, a significant proportion of the Canadian electorate consists of people born outside the country, which has attracted the attention of those who study voting behaviour. Data from the Canadian election studies, going back to the 1960s, show that the Liberal Party has been the most popular party among voters born outside of Canada. The Liberals have received a larger share of the votes of the foreign-born than of those born in Canada, while the reverse has been true for the Conservative Party (and its predecessors, the Progressive Conservative Party, the Reform Party, and the Canadian Alliance Party). In the case of the NDP, the difference between foreign- and Canadian-born voters has tended to be small. The difference, however, has been quite significant in the case of the BQ, with foreign-born voters being much less likely than Canadian-born voters to support this party.

Recent elections suggest this picture of strong immigrant support for the Liberal Party may be changing. In the 2008 election the Conservatives did almost as well as the Liberals among voters born outside of Canada and in 2011 non-Canadian born voters were somewhat more likely to vote for the Conservative Party than for the Liberals. This Conservative advantage disappeared in 2015. Looked at somewhat differently, in 2004 the Liberals held all 18 of the majority-immigrant constituencies in the GTA. In 2011 they were reduced to five of these ridings. The Conservatives won 10 of these seats and the NDP won three.[44] In 2015 and 2019 the Liberals won all of them again, but they also won all but a few of the GTA ridings where those born outside of Canada were a minority. Without reading too much into these recent fluctuations, it is probably fair to say that what was over many election cycles a Liberal hammerlock on majority-immigrant constituencies no longer exists.

Over the years, few socio-demographic factors have been as strongly correlated with voting behaviour as the region where voters live. The likelihood that a voter will support the Conservative Party is much greater if that voter lives in one of the four western provinces than in Ontario, and is especially strong if that voter lives in Alberta. This is true after controlling for such variables as income, education, and gender. Some argue that the independent effect of region on voting operates through the existence of different regional political cultures. But as we saw in Chapter 5, there is no agreement among Canadian political scientists that, with the exception of Quebec, these interprovincial differences are particularly significant and the weight of the evidence suggests that they are not very great. There is, however, a consensus that region provides a context for voting and for the evaluation of the parties, their leaders, and the issues. In other words, the issues that matter to voters and how these issues tend to be framed by the media, opinion leaders, and politicians in their region will influence voting behaviour. This may be reinforced by the manner in which the parties and their leaders campaign in particular provinces, if they campaign there at all![45]

Political Participation

The 2015 election reversed a trend that began after the 1988 election. Over several election cycles the percentage of Canadians eligible to vote and who bothered to cast a ballot had been in decline. In the elections of 2000 to 2011 Canadians were less likely to vote than at almost any time since Confederation. Indeed, Americans, ridiculed by Canadians and democratic populations throughout the world for having low rates of voter participation, had rates about as high as in Canada in their 2004 election and then higher than Canada in 2008. Canadians have not been alone in staying away from the ballot box. Voter turnout has been slipping in Western democracies generally, a trend that has generated a good deal of hand-wringing about the health of democracies and various explanations for this decline in participation.

In Canada, at least, the trend was at least temporarily halted by the 2015 and 2019 elections. Voter turnout in these elections was up significantly from the 2011 election and was, in fact, higher than at any time since 1993. Whether this represents the beginning of a reversal in a decades-old trend of declining voter turnout, only time will tell. Much of the decline over the past couple of decades has been due to lower rates of voting among younger voters, particularly those under the age of 30, compared to the rates for this age cohort in previous generations.[46] In 2015, younger voters (between 18 and 34 years of age) still voted at lower rates than any other age cohort, but the increase in the participation rate of younger voters between the 2011 and 2015 elections was much greater than for other age cohorts.[47]

Notwithstanding the uptick in voting among younger citizens in 2015, two facts are clear, in Canada and elsewhere. Younger citizens are considerably less likely to vote than their older compatriots. Second, they vote at a lower rate than people their age did in the past. "We know that age is the best predictor of voting," write André Blais and his colleagues on the Canadian Election Study team; "the older one is, the more likely one is to vote. The challenge is to unravel the meaning of that relationship, to ascertain whether this reflects a life cycle effect . . . a generation effect . . . or both."[48] The life cycle effect refers to the fact that people become more likely to vote as they grow older, a phenomenon generally attributed to changes in their life circumstances (entering a permanent relationship, having children, buying a home, establishing roots in a community) that cause them to feel more invested in their community and to better recognize the relevance of government decisions to their own lives. The generation effect refers to the possibility that the members of a particular generation may be less likely than those of preceding ones to vote. This could be caused by various factors, such as a society-wide increase in cynicism about politics or a drop in those non-age factors known to be linked to the likelihood of voting, including years of formal education and political interest and knowledge.

Based on voter surveys between 1968 and 2000, Blais and his colleagues arrive at a number of conclusions with regard to declining voter turnout:

- There are important life cycle effects. For example, a person who is 30 is about 8–11 percentage points more likely to vote than someone 20 years old. The likelihood of voting increases by about 15 percentage points from age 20 to age 50.[49] This gap did not shrink in 2015, notwithstanding the increase in the turnout rate among younger voters.
- There is a clear generational effect. Comparing voters in the same age cohort but belonging to different generations (for example, a 25-year-old baby boomer surveyed for the 1974 election study and a 25-year-old surveyed for the 2000 study), the generation effect on declining voter turnout is at least as significant as life cycle effects: "[A]ge being held constant, the propensity to vote decreases by more than 20 points from the oldest to the most recent cohort."[50]
- Blais and his colleagues note that "younger generations view the act of voting differently" from previous generations.[51] They are less likely to see it as important and less likely to view it as a civic duty.
- The generational difference is not found among the university-educated. Controlling

for age, voters with a university degree who are post-baby boomers are as likely to vote as their boomer predecessors. But among those in other educational cohorts there is a sizable generational gap in the likelihood of voting.

Of course, all of this just poses a question—two questions, really. Why are the members of more recent generations less likely to be interested in politics and less likely to believe that they have a moral responsibility to vote? Second, does declining turnout matter?

The answer to the first question is unlikely to involve a single factor; two rather different clusters of causes have been identified by researchers. One involves a lower level of deference towards authority and established institutions among post-baby boomers and a greater tendency to embrace values and beliefs associated with what has been called postmaterialism (see Chapter 2). The weaker belief that voting is a civic duty is said to reflect the less deferential character of the more recent generation of voters. This explanation does not help to understand, however, why university-educated members of recent generations vote at about the same rate as earlier generations of voters with similar levels of education.

A second cluster of causes focuses on what are argued to be the failings of parties and politicians. Those who have entered the electorate during the last couple of decades are more likely than those who entered earlier to feel alienated from conventional politics, including parties and elections, and cynical about politicians and their craft. Such alienation and cynicism have been produced, at least in part, by a failure of parties and politicians to convince these newer members of the electorate that what they do is relevant to the lives of citizens or that any meaningful change can be effected by participating in the electoral process. This explanation focuses less on the generational characteristics of young voters than on the shortcomings of the political system they encounter when they enter the electorate. But if parties and politicians are doing a poorer job than in the past in connecting with voters, we still need to explain why younger voters more than older ones react by disengaging from traditional political processes. A possible answer is provided by Henry Milner and others.[52] Milner argues that political literacy and interest among younger voters is lower than used to be the case. They are less likely to read newspapers, follow politics in the media, or be able to correctly identify political figures, institutions, and events than members of previous generations. They have less interest and less knowledge about politics, contributing to a reduced propensity to vote. Milner and most other commentators believe that the quality of democracy will suffer as more of society's members choose to abstain from voting.

But will society really suffer and are the non-voters truly abstaining from political participation? It is understandable that parties and voting are seen by most of us to be the essential linchpins in the relationship between the population and government. The struggle for universal voting rights was long and arduous and its achievement was not so very long ago. Quebec was the last province to grant women the right to vote in 1940 and Indigenous Canadians, if they maintained their status under the Indian Act, did not have the right to vote until 1960. That the self-disenfranchisement of millions of citizens who choose seldom or never to vote might be treated with indifference is shocking to many.

But as important as voting is, it is not the only form of political engagement. The 2013 General Social Survey, carried out by Statistics Canada,[53] asked respondents whether they had engaged in any of the following political activities during the previous year:

- signing a petition;
- searching for political information;
- attending a public meeting;
- boycotting/choosing a product for ethical reasons;
- contacting a newspaper or politician;
- participating in a demonstration or march;
- volunteering for a political party.

The bad news is that almost half of all Canadians say they do not participate in any of these non-voting activities. Moreover, there were declines in the rate of participation in all of these activities between 2003 and 2013, with the exception of boycotting or choosing a particular product for ethical reasons. At the same time, however, the percentage of Canadians who said that they had looked for information on a political issue over the previous 12 months increased from 26 to 40 per cent between 2003 and 2013. This apparent increase in at least one measure of political interest seems not to have translated into increased participation. The good news is that this Statistics Canada survey found that younger Canadians are actually more likely than their older compatriots to participate in some political activities. Those between the ages of 15 and 34 are much more likely than older cohorts of Canadians to have searched for information on a political issue, to have expressed views on a political or social issue on an Internet forum or news website, and to have participated in a demonstration or protest march. They are somewhat more likely to have signed a petition. And they are about as likely as older Canadians to have boycotted or chosen a product for ethical reasons and much more likely than those over 65 years of age to have done this.[54]

It appears, then, that although younger Canadians are much less likely to vote than their older fellow citizens, they are as likely to participate in politics in other ways. Is boycotting or choosing a product on ethical grounds or signing a petition a less significant political act than voting in an election? Reasonable people will disagree on this matter. But perhaps we should at least be open to the possibility that declining voter turnout, particularly among the young, is not necessarily evidence that they are disengaged politically or that the health of democracy is imperilled by this decline. "Much conventional wisdom to the contrary," writes Brenda O'Neill, "young Canadians do not reveal lower levels of engagement in formal politics than other Canadians because of increased political cynicism or unhappiness with the political system."[55]

Traditional thinking and models of civic participation have no place for tweeting, Facebooking, and other recent and widespread forms of social networking. These are forms of engagement that do not rely on parties or politicians and that may be dismissed as less demanding and less valid than voting, joining a party, attending a political meeting, and similar traditional forms of political participation. It is not obvious, however, that they are less valid or important as expressions of democratic engagement.

Party Finances and Special Interests

Throughout most of their history, the Liberal and Conservative parties relied heavily on corporate contributors to finance their activities. The NDP, by contrast, depended mainly on contributions from individuals and on the financial support of affiliated trade unions. Corporate donations to the national NDP were minuscule.

It is difficult to attach precise numbers to party finances before 1974, for the simple reason that parties were not legally required to disclose their sources of revenue. A pioneering study done by Khayyam Paltiel for the federally appointed Committee on Election Expenses (1966) estimated that, before the 1974 reforms, the older parties were dependent on business contributions for between 75 and 90 per cent of their incomes,[56] a figure that did not even include the value of services in kind that they received from businesses, particularly from advertising and polling firms during election campaigns.[57] Not only did the Liberals and Conservatives rely on business for all but a small share of their revenue, but most of this corporate money was collected from big businesses in Toronto and Montreal.[58] Other experts on party finances have confirmed this historical pattern of dependence on big financial and industrial capital.[59]

Passage of the **Election Expenses Act in 1974** marked a watershed in Canadian party finance. The Act included spending limits for individual candidates and political parties during election campaigns and a requirement that parties and candidates disclose the name of any contributor donating at least $100. A system of public subsidies was introduced, whereby candidates would be reimbursed for half of their expenses if they stayed within the spending limit set by law and if they received at least 15 per cent of the popular vote.[60] The idea behind this particular reform was to weaken

parties' financial dependence on special interests. The Income Tax Act was changed to permit the deduction of political contributions. Changes to the Broadcasting Act also were passed, requiring radio and television stations to make advertising time during election campaigns available to the parties represented in the House of Commons.[61]

Tax credits for political contributions and public disclosure requirements for candidates and political parties were intended to reduce the role of money in party politics and elections. The Income Tax Act allows individuals to deduct from their taxable income a percentage of their donation to a registered political party or candidate, up to a maximum tax credit of $650. As of 2020, the maximum amount an individual may donate to a political party or candidate is $1,625. The maximum tax credit of $650 is reached once a donor has given $1,125 in total contributions during a single taxation year. With regard to disclosure, parties and candidates are required to provide the chief electoral officer with a list of all donors who have contributed at least $20 or more in money or services in kind, as well as an itemized account of their expenditures. Before the 2004 revisions to the Canada Elections Act, parties were not required to disclose how much they spent on important activities such as fundraising and polling between elections, although such evidence as existed suggested that these were very expensive functions. Since 2004, the law requires much more transparency in the parties' reporting of their annual and election campaign expenditures.

Perhaps the most striking consequence of the 1974 reforms was the dramatic increase in the importance of donations by individuals. These contributions were always the mainstay of NDP finances. Spurred by the tax credit for political donations and the older parties' adoption of sophisticated direct-mail techniques of fundraising, first developed in the United States,[62] contributions by individuals became a major source of income for all three political parties. In fact, the value of contributions from individuals exceeded business contributions to both the Conservative and Liberal parties in many of the years after the tax credit came into effect. In the case of the NDP and its candidates, they had always depended on union contributions and donations from individuals. Although the Liberal and Conservative parties' financial dependence on business appeared to have been diluted under the post-1974 model for party and election financing, corporate donations continued to be a tremendously important. Until the 2004 reforms, this corporate money typically accounted for close to half of total contributions during election years and roughly 40–50 per cent between elections. Moreover, very large corporate contributions represented a sizable share of the older parties' total revenues. If we define a large corporate donation as being at least $10,000, we find that these contributions accounted for about 15 to 30 per cent of total contributions for both the Liberal and Progressive Conservative parties over the 30-year period from the introduction of the 1974 Canada Elections Act to its overhaul in 2004. In 2003, the last year under which the old party financing rules applied, the 10 largest contributions to each of the Liberal, Conservative (the finances of the Progressive Conservative and Canadian Alliance parties were merged towards the end of 2003), and New Democratic parties accounted for 16 per cent, 16 per cent, and 39 per cent of total party revenues, respectively. All of the leading 10 contributions to the Liberal and Conservative parties were from corporate donors and all 10 of the NDP's biggest donors were unions.

The most important consequence of special-interest contributions to parties and individual politicians was almost certainly the access it bought to policy-makers. Although cases of influence-peddling came to light from time to time, it was usually erroneous to think of political contributions as payments offered in the expectation of receiving some particular favour. There were, no doubt, instances where firms that relied on government contracts for some part of their revenue, or that hoped to receive government business in the future, found it prudent to donate money to parties or candidates. But for most corporate contributors, and certainly for large donors like the banks and those leading industrial firms that were perennial contributors to the two older parties, there was no expectation of a specific quid pro quo.

So why did they bother? It was long understood that donations helped buy access. In the words of Dalton Camp, a long-time Conservative strategist and media commentator, "Toronto money merely maintains access to the parties, keeping open essential lines of communication, corporate hotlines, so to speak, to the right ears at appropriate times."[63] In many cases the sheer size and importance of a corporation was sufficient, however, to ensure a hearing when the corporation's owners or managers felt its interests were at stake. In any given year under the 1974–2003 model of party and election finance, about half of the largest 100 industrial firms in Canada did not contribute anything to either of the two older parties. It would be ridiculous to conclude that their lack of generosity cut them off from direct access to political decision-makers. All things being equal, however, contributions probably opened the door a bit wider.

In 2004 corporate contributions to parties and candidates, including candidates for the leadership of political parties, were strictly limited and then banned altogether in 2006. So, too, were contributions from unions and private associations. Contributions from non-Canadians had already been unlawful. Contributions from individual Canadians were still allowed, but the annual limit was $5,000 and then lowered to $1,100 in 2007. Starting in 2004 the parties were provided with public subsidies based on how many votes they had received in the previous election. This began at $1.75 per vote, indexed to inflation. The subsidy reached $2.00 per vote in 2011 before being phased out in 2015. While they existed, these public subsidies became the main source of revenue for most of the main federal parties, although to a lesser degree for the Conservative Party. The Conservatives proved to be better able to raise private money from individual donors than the Liberals, NDP, and Bloc Québécois.

The argument for the public subsidy model, which is common in much of Western Europe, is that it reduces the dependence of the parties and their candidates on special-interest donations and therefore makes it less likely that policy will be sold to the highest bidder. Those who oppose the subsidy regime argue that citizens should not be required to finance the activities of parties and candidates, including parties and candidates they may not support, and that if parties truly represent the views and interests of a significant number of people then they should be able to get at least some of those people to finance the party in which they believe. Opponents also argue that a system that bases subsidies on how parties have done in the previous election supports the status quo, providing existing parties with a financial advantage over new parties trying to get their message out to voters.

Public subsidies have been eliminated since 2015, with the exception of the reimbursement for candidate expenses provision of the law that goes back to 1974. But controversy over how to finance parties and candidates and over the role of money in politics more generally has not disappeared. The link between contributions and access to influential decision-makers continues to arise from time to time in the case of **paid access opportunities**. These are fundraising events such as dinners and cocktail parties where, for an admission price that may range up to the annual legal limit on an individual's donation to a party or candidate, invited guests receive the opportunity to rub shoulders and exchange views with key party members and perhaps even with the party leader. Money obviously acts as a filter in determining who is likely to participate in such events, as does the invitation list. Since the 1980s the Liberal and Conservative parties have had special clubs for their largest contributors. The cost of membership is limited to the legal limit on the annual amount that a person may contribute to a political party. These special donor clubs are now less exclusive than they were prior to the 2004 party finance reforms, when the price of membership was several thousand dollars.

In the eyes of some, paid access opportunities such as these, regardless of whether the price of admission is high or very high, raise an ethical question: at what point does the ability to pay for special access to political decision-makers subvert the democratic process by favouring those with the money to make their views known directly? Defenders argue that parties need funds to carry out their activities and that, even with a tax credit

for political contributions, only a small portion of all Canadian taxpayers contribute money directly to parties or candidates. With the elimination of public subsidies for parties the money to pay for advertising, polling, the campaign bus, hall rentals, and so on needs to come from somewhere. One might argue that donating money is a form of political engagement and expression not unlike devoting time. Some people have more time than money and may prefer to knock on doors, make phone calls, or in other ways contribute their time in the hope of electing a candidate or party. Others may have more money than time and prefer to make a donation.

The reforms to Canada's party finance laws that date from 2004 place no restrictions on spending by political parties, groups, or individuals during periods other than election and leadership campaigns. As a result, considerable money is spent on fundraising, polling, consultants, and pre-campaign advertising before an election is called. Some argue that pre-campaign spending, intended to shape the public's image of a leader or party or to frame issues in particular ways, undermines the intent of the 2004 reforms. Others maintain that the ability to spend money in order to craft a political message and communicate it to citizens is a basic democratic right that is already unjustifiably limited by these reforms. As we saw in Chapter 7, the majority on the Supreme Court took the view in *Harper v. Canada* (2004) that unequal spending power during an election campaign undermines the equality of citizens and skews the political conversation towards the interests and values of those with deep pockets. Although their logic would seem to apply between elections too, it is difficult to imagine that restrictions on political communications spending between election campaigns would be upheld as a reasonable limit on the Charter's guarantees of free speech and freedom of the media. In any case, it would be virtually impossible, short of imposing Chinese-style Internet censorship, to enforce such restrictions.

In recognition of the fact that a good deal of election-related advertising by political parties and other groups wanting to influence an election outcome was taking place before the several

Governing Realities

BOX 11.6 How Much Influence Does $1,525 Buy?

On 2 October 2014, 25 people had lunch with President Barack Obama at the Chicago home of investment banker Meredith Bluhm-Wolf. Each of them paid $50,000 to attend. It was a fundraiser intended to support the re-election campaign of Illinois's Democratic Governor Pat Quinn. The president was the draw at a number of similar events that fall, leading up to the 2014 elections. In this he was simply doing what many presidents before him and since his time in office have done, although it must be said that Obama was busier and better at the presidential fundraising function than most. In the seven months leading up to the 2014 congressional elections he attended 30 functions similar to the one at Bluhm-Wolf's Chicago mansion, raising an estimated US$40 million for the Democratic Party's candidates.

A year after being sworn in as prime minister, Justin Trudeau found himself in the crosshairs of media and opposition party criticism for fundraising activities that were somewhat similar to those of Obama, except that the price tag for admission was rather more affordable. The Liberal Party held roughly 100 fundraisers in 2016. When the prime minister was in attendance, the admission price—assuming that you received an invitation—was usually the maximum annual donation permitted to a Canadian political party, $1,525. Some events where Finance Minister Bill Morneau was the headliner cost less, at between $1,000 and $1,500. An event attended by Minister of Infrastructure and Communities Amarjeet Sohi required a donation of $500.

Donations of at least $1,525 per year were rewarded with membership in the Liberal Party's Laurier Club. But if a donor also managed to persuade at least 10 other persons to donate the maximum amount allowed in a year—a process that in the United States is referred to as bundling contributions—then he or she would become a member of the party's Leader's Circle. A party fundraising document said this about membership in the Leader's Circle: "Leader's Circle members can look forward to a variety of recognition opportunities including an annual dinner with the Leader and invitations to events and discussions with leaders within the Party. Top Leader's Circle members will be recognized within the program and the Party."

Many Canadians appear to have been appalled by these revelations. Critics portrayed these activities as "cash for access" and "buying influence." But how much influence did $1,525 buy? And if you were one of hundreds people who exchanged a few words and had a selfie taken with Justin Trudeau at one of these events, how likely is it that this contribution alone would have made a difference in your or your organization's influence on the Liberal government?

Unless Canadians want to go back to the public subsidy model of financing parties and their activities, the money needed for campaigning and all that parties do between elections has to come from somewhere. A spokesperson for the Liberal Party defended the elite admission events by saying, "federal political donations are governed by some of the most strict political financing rules in Canada and all of North America—and rightly so." He was right.

Sources: Justin Sink, "Reporters Kept Out as Obama Attends $50,000 per Plate Fundraiser," *The Hill*, 2 Oct. 2014, http://thehill.com/homenews/administration/219582-reporters-kept-out-as-obama-attends-50k-per-plate-fundraiser; Justin Ling, "The Liberal Party Has Scheduled More Than 100 Cash-For-Access Events in 2016 Alone," Vice, 28 Oct. 2016, https://www.vice.com/en_ca/article/9b8jba/the-trudeau-government-scheduled-more-than-100-cash-for-access-events-in-2016-alone.

weeks of a formal election campaign, the Liberal government introduced Bill C-76 creating spending rules for a "pre-election period"—i.e., the several weeks before the formal commencement of the election campaign. The Elections Modernization Act, which received royal assent in December 2018, limits what is called third-party spending to about $1 million during the pre-writ campaign period and to $511,700 during the formal campaign, at which time a group's spending in any particular constituency is limited to $4,386.[64] It also limits the amounts that registered political parties may spend during the roughly two-month pre-writ period to about $2 million. (In 2019, this pre-writ period began on 30 June, which led some deep-pocketed groups to flood the airwaves with partisan advertising during telecasts of the Toronto Raptors run to the NBA championship during May and June.) The Act also includes provisions having to do with political spending by foreign entities and requirements regarding the registration of online campaign content. Taken together, these reforms represent an attempt to catch up with the new realities of campaigning and political communications more generally.

Summing Up

For most Canadians, as for the citizens of all democratic societies, elections and political parties occupy a special place when it comes to their expectations for democracy. A 2012 survey found that on an open-ended question asking respondents to describe in their own words what democracy meant to them, more people indicated freedom to vote and participate in politics than gave any other response.[65] Elections may not be a sufficient condition to certify a political system as being genuinely democratic, but it is certainly a necessary condition. These elections are contested by political parties. Although they are held in low esteem by Canadians, parties perform important functions in organizing political life and enabling citizens to hold government accountable at election time.

Canada's national party system has been dominated since Confederation by two political parties. Only the Liberals and Conservatives have formed the government in Ottawa, although some other parties, notably the NDP, have been quite influential at various moments in Canadian history. The historically dominant parties have occupied much of the same ideological space and have competed with each other for the votes of many of the same groups during elections. Nevertheless, in every election since 1935, when the NDP's predecessor, the CCF, emerged onto the national scene, other parties have together managed to win anywhere from 12 to 43 per cent of the popular vote, averaging about 25 per cent in general elections. Minor parties, therefore, are an important component of Canada's party system.

For many years Canada's single-member, simple plurality electoral system has generated criticism, particularly from the political left. When the Liberal Party was elected in 2015 it appeared that the moment for reform of the system had arrived. For various reasons the Trudeau government backed away from its promise to replace the existing system. The consequences of reform would ripple through the entire system of governance, probably in ways that many citizens do not anticipate. It is doubtful that Canadians have heard the last of this issue.

Starting Points for Research

Cameron D. Anderson and Laura B. Stephenson, eds, *Voting Behaviour in Canada* (Vancouver: University of British Columbia Press, 2010). This book brings together contributions from several of Canada's leading experts on voting.

Cable Public Affairs Channel (CPAC), "The Campaigns," http://www.cpac.ca/en/programs/the-campaigns/. CPAC documentaries chronicling some of the most important federal elections of the twentieth century.

Canadian Election Study, ces-eec.org/pagesE/home.html. A large number of publications based on the most recent and past election studies may be found at this website.

Richard Johnston, *The Canadian Party System: An Analytic History* (Vancouver: University of British Columbia Press, 2017). One of Canada's keenest students of parties and voting provides a persuasive interpretation of elections over the course of Canada's history.

Mebs Kanji, Antoine Bilodeau, and Thomas J. Scotto, eds, *The Canadian Election Studies: Assessing Four Decades of Influence* (Vancouver: University of British Columbia Press, 2012). This volume includes contributions from researchers who have been involved in Canadian election studies over the years and provides fascinating perspectives on how the understanding of voter choice has evolved over the past four decades.

Review Exercises

1. Using data available at the website of the Chief Electoral Officer of Canada (www.elections.ca), determine the following:
   (a) the number of seats each party would have received in the last general election under a straight proportional representation system;
   (b) the number of votes and percentage of the vote received by each candidate in your constituency during the last federal election; and
   (c) the money spent by both the party that won the last election, compared to the amount spent by the party that came in second in number of seats, and by the winning candidate in your constituency, compared to the candidate who finished in second place.

2. How do Canadian political parties select their local candidates? For information on this, visit the websites of a couple of the national political parties. Click on the party's constitution, looking for the rules on candidate selection.

3. Studies of Canadian voting behaviour have examined a large number of factors believed to influence voter choice. How would you rank the influence of the following factors on your personal decision about which party and candidate to vote for in a federal election?
   • party leader
   • local candidate
   • particular campaign issue or issues
   • what the party stands for
   • the views of persons whose judgment I respect.

Now think about the sources of your information and views about parties, leaders, local candidates, and issues. What are they? Do you think that some might be more reliable than others? Explain why.

Every interest imaginable is represented by groups who work to influence various levels of government as a way to achieve their goals. In February 2019, former justice minister Jody Wilson-Raybould appeared at the House of Commons Justice Committee to testify that she had been pressured to grant a deferred prosecution agreement (DPA) to Montreal-based engineering and construction firm SNC Lavalin. A report released by the ethics commissioner in August 2019 documented SNC Lavalin's lobbying of senior members of parliament to create a DPA regime that would help it avoid a criminal trial. (THE CANADIAN PRESS/Sean Kilpatrick)

12 Interest Groups

Politics does not stop between election campaigns. Much of the effort to influence the actions of government is channelled through interest groups. This chapter examines their characteristics and the role they play in Canadian politics. Topics include the following:

- How many groups, representing what interests?
- The bias of the interest group system
- Perspectives on interest groups
- Factors in interest group success
- Strategies for influence
- Lobbying and lobbyists

Elections are democracy's showpiece. Important as they are, however, the influence of elections on what governments do is usually rather blunt and indirect. Policies are more likely to be determined by the actions and demands of organized groups than by the latest election results. Indeed, it may often seem that special interests dominate the policy-making process in democracies. Their attempts to influence government are unremitting. The resources they marshal often are impressive. And their access to policy-makers is, in the case of some organized interests, privileged. Compared to this, the role of elections and the influence of voters may appear feeble.

Interest groups or *pressure groups*—the terms can be used interchangeably—have been defined as "private associations . . . [that] promote their interests by attempting to influence government rather than by nominating candidates and seeking responsibility for the management of government."[1] They arise from a very basic fact of social life, the reality of diversity in the interests and values of human beings. This diversity, in turn, gives rise to what James Madison called **political factions**: groups of citizens whose goals and behaviour are contrary to those of other groups or to the interests of the community as a whole.[2] If these factions, or special interests as we are apt to call them today, appear to overshadow the public interest in democracies, there is a simple explanation. The tug of one's personal interests—as an automotive worker, business owner, teacher, farmer, or student—tend to be felt more keenly than the rather nebulous concept of the public interest. Arguments that appeal to such general interests as consumer benefits or economic efficiency are unlikely to convince the farmer whose income is protected by a supply management policy. But material interests are not the only basis for factionalism in politics. Group characteristics such as ethnicity, language, religion, and gender, or the sharing of similar values, may also provide the basis for the political organization of interests.

Economically based or not, interest groups are distinguished by the fact that they seek to promote goals not shared by all members of society. This leads critics to refer to such groups as *special interests* and their activities, particularly those that are described as *lobbying*, as contrary to the public interest. Although we may all agree that something warrants the label "the public interest," it is almost certain that if we randomly choose 10 persons and ask each to explain in 100 words or fewer what it entails, we will get more than one answer. In a diverse and free society, people and the organizations they belong to will see the world and understand the public interest in different ways. In a democracy, those that will be most successful in influencing government policy will also be most successful in persuading the public and lawmakers that their interests and ideas align with the greater good and with values shared by most citizens. Whether or not this is the case may be another matter and, where this alignment is dubious, there may be reason to ask serious questions about the democratic nature of such a political system.

Charting the Territory

The world of interest groups is both vast and characterized by enormous variety. Although no unified reliable list of interest groups exists for Canada or any other democracy, some idea of the sheer number of groups may be had from the directory *Associations Canada*.[3] Its 2018 edition lists 19,681 organizations, not all of which would meet the criterion of attempting to influence government action. Many groups focus exclusively on non-political activities such as providing services and information to their members, but several thousand perform political functions on a regular or occasional basis.

Almost every imaginable interest is represented. There are several hundred women's associations across Canada, close to 1,000 environmental groups, over 2,000 business associations, perhaps 500 organizations representing agricultural interests, about 200 that focus on Indigenous issues[4]—the range of organized interests and the sheer number of groups within each general category of interests are enormous. Impressive as these figures may seem, they do not provide a complete map of Canada's associational system. They do not, for example, include those transitory groups that emerge briefly around a single issue and then disappear from the scene. Nor do they include international organizations that may attempt to influence the actions of Canadian governments. However we draw its boundaries, the universe of organized interests is vast.

While it is impossible to say exactly how many of these associations qualify as interest groups, no doubt a large number of them are politically active. One way to get a sense of this activity is to look at the list of groups that make representations to a legislative body or a government-sponsored commission considering some issue. For example, roughly 1,000 groups made representations and submitted briefs to the Royal Commission on Aboriginal Peoples during its six months of public hearings (1993). The Commission on the Future of Health Care in Canada received submissions from 429 groups and associations during the public consultation phase of its work (2001). Just under 100 groups submitted briefs and in many cases testified before the House's Standing Committee on Justice and Human Rights when it considered Bill C-14 on physician-assisted death (2016). Roughly the same number made submissions to the House of Commons Standing Committee on Health when it considered Bill C-45

on the decriminalization of cannabis (2017). Even issues that might appear to be rather mundane and rather narrow in scope will often generate considerable interest group activity. In 2017 the House Standing Committee on Fisheries and Oceans reviewed changes made in 2012 to the Fisheries Act. The Committee received briefs from about 150 groups, including those representing Indigenous, mining, energy, fishing, and environmental interests, as well as from several provincial and territorial governments. Twenty-nine of them appeared as witnesses during the committee's hearings.

The Bias of the Interest Group System

> The notion that the pressure system is automatically representative of the whole community is a myth. . . . The system is skewed, loaded and unbalanced in favor of a fraction of a minority.[5]

Obviously, some interest groups are more influential than others. Determining why some groups are more influential and the circumstances, resources, strategies, and tactics that contribute to interest group influence have long interested students of politics and policy. Many have concluded, as E.E. Schattschneider argued many years ago, that the interest group system is biased "in favor of a fraction of a minority." Are they right?

Schattschneider argues that the interest group system—he calls it the pressure system—has a business and upper-class bias. Writing about American politics in the early 1960s, he observed that business associations comprised the single largest group of organized interests in American society; they were far more likely than other interests to lobby government and they tended to spend much more money on attempting to influence policy-makers than did other interest groups. Moreover, Schattschneider cited impressive evidence demonstrating that "even non-business organizations reflect an upper-class tendency."[6] Persons with higher than average incomes and/or years of formal education are more

Activists gather at an event organized by the Euthanasia Prevention Coalition to rally against Bill C-14, which would allow for medically assisted death. The bill, which met with vocal lobbying on both sides, was eventually passed and received royal assent in 2016.

likely to belong to organized groups than those lower down the socio-economic ladder. He explains the business and upper-class bias of interest group politics as being a product both of superior resources and of the relatively limited size and exclusive character of these special interests. "Special-interest organizations," he argues, "are most easily formed when they deal with small numbers of individuals [or corporations] who are acutely aware of their exclusive interests."[7] A similar observation would be made two years later by Mancur Olson in his classic study of group behaviour and influence, *The Logic of Collective Action: Public Goods and the Theory of Groups*.[8] This awareness of special interests that are vital to one's material well-being or the well-being of one's organization is characteristic of trade associations with a relatively small number of members, such as the Canadian Association of Petroleum Producers, the Canadian Bankers' Association, or even a more broadly based business organization like the Business Council of Canada (until 2016 known as the Canadian Council of Chief Executives). It is far from being the only factor that explains a group's influence, but it can be an important one.

Most social scientists and political journalists agree with Schattschneider. As Éric Monpetit writes in a survey of interest groups in Canada, "The idea of an unequal distribution of power among interest groups remains largely uncontested today."[9] Charles Lindblom argues that business occupies a "privileged position" in the politics of capitalist societies. In his book *Politics and Markets*,[10] Lindblom attributes this pre-eminence to business's superior financial resources and lobbying organization, greater access than other groups to government officials, and, most importantly, propagandistic activities that—directly through political advertising and indirectly through commercial advertising—reinforce the ideological dominance of business values in society.

One of the key factors most often cited by those who argue that business interests are politically more influential than other organized groups is the **mobility of capital**. Investors enjoy a wide although not absolute freedom to shift their capital between sectors of the economy and from one national economy to another. The epitome of this mobility is found in the transnational corporation—an enterprise whose activities span a number of national economies and whose international character often is used as a lever in dealing with the government of a particular country. In addition to being territorially mobile, investment capital also has the capacity to expand and contract in response to investors' perceptions of the political-economic climate for business. Governments cannot force business and private investors to invest, and what punitive measures they might use to prevent businesses from sitting on earnings—high tax rates on savings or dividends, for example—could easily backfire. Governments in all capitalist societies are concerned with levels of business confidence and are reluctant to take actions that carry a high risk of causing a cutback in investment. The consequences of such a cutback are felt politically by governments. Weak economic activity tends to translate into popular dissatisfaction and a loss of political support.

The mobility of capital gives rise, in turn, to concern with *business confidence*. Politicians need to care about business confidence because of the very real possibility that they will not be re-elected if business's unwillingness to invest causes unemployment and falling incomes. But another factor that gives pause even to governments that can count on strong popular backing is the state's financial dependence on business. A decline in the levels of investment or profit soon will be felt as a drop in government revenues from the taxation of corporate and employment income, payroll taxes, and the taxation of consumption. The problem of falling revenues is almost certain to be compounded by an increase in state expenditures on social programs whose costs are sensitive to changes in the level of economic activity. Borrowing on the public credit is only a temporary solution to this dilemma, and experience has shown this to be both costly and subject to the limits of international investor confidence (see Box 12.1).

Neither Lindblom nor anyone else would argue that business interests "win" all of the time, or even that powerful business groups cannot experience major defeats. Instead, they maintain that

Politics in Focus

BOX 12.1 The Limits on Reform in Capitalist Democracies: The Case of Alberta under the NDP

In 2015, after 44 consecutive years during which the right-of-centre Progressive Conservative Party formed the government, the NDP came to power with a clear majority in the provincial legislature. The party and its leader, Rachel Notley, were widely seen as being unsympathetic to many of the business interests that have long been vital to the Alberta economy, particularly the petrochemical sector. The NDP came to power just as the world price for oil was in freefall, dropping from a high of US$91 in the summer of 2014 to about US$35 in early 2016, just a half year after the NDP government assumed office. Alberta's heavy crude oil, which requires more processing than the light crude whose price is the one quoted in reports of the international price of oil, was worth even less than the world price.

The impact on Alberta's government revenues was devastating. Revenue from non-renewable resources, almost all of which was from the petroleum sector, dropped from about $9 billion in 2014–15 to under $3 billion in 2015–16. It increased slightly to about $3.5 billion the following year and then to about $4.5 billion in 2017–18, as the international price for oil edged upward. This was, of course, only half the revenue that the Alberta government had received from this sector before the NDP came to power. The Notley government reacted with various tax increases, including increases in the corporate income tax and on higher income earners. But even as the price of oil recovered somewhat from its 2015 low point, it became clear that an equally significant challenge to the Alberta economy and provincial revenues existed: the opposition of various groups, including some provincial governments and the national NDP, to pipelines needed to move Alberta's oil to markets.

Consequently, a premier who had often been present at anti-pipeline rallies when her party was in opposition, and who had called for greater oversight of the petroleum sector and higher royalties on oil, found herself defending the Kinder Morgan pipeline expansion that would move more Alberta oil to the Pacific coast. In the words of one Alberta anti-pipeline and pro-sustainable energy activist, "There isn't an alternative that stands and speaks for us and what we believe in. That is something that is so isolating and difficult to navigate."[11]

The disappointment of Premier Notley's erstwhile allies and supporters became even greater when, on 30 August 2018, she announced that Alberta would be pulling out of the national climate plan that requires provinces to impose a minimum tax on carbon production. Alberta's own provincial carbon tax, however, would remain in place. Her decision was in reaction to a Federal Court ruling that struck down Ottawa's approval of the Kinder Morgan pipeline expansion. As the *Financial Post* put it, "The Trans Mountain pipeline has dominated Alberta politics in the last year and it, along with everything it represents—including Alberta's carbon tax—is expected to overshadow all other issues in the spring [2019] election. The pipeline is also a financial lifeline for Notley's government, which has been running multibillion-dollar deficits while avoiding introducing a sales tax or making significant cuts to the budget."[12]

The NDP under Rachel Notley is not the first left-of-centre political party to come to power only to discover that economic circumstances, investor reaction, and the realities of provincial government finances impose serious limits on what it is able to do in government. A rather similar scenario played out in Ontario during the NDP government of Bob Rae (1990–5). The facts of having to make policy choices in a capitalist economy in which many of the factors affecting provincial government finances and, ultimately, the governing party's chances for re-election can be very constraining. And, as might have been predicted, Notley's NDP government fell in the 2019 election to the right-wing United Conservatives led by Jason Kenney, just as the Bob Rae government in Ontario was toppled decades earlier by Mike Harris's Progressive Conservatives.

systemic characteristics of capitalist societies tend to favour business interests over others. This is one of the few propositions about politics that manages to cut across the ideological spectrum, generating agreement on the left and right alike (if rather more heavily from the left). There are, however, dissenters.

Those who teach or write for a business school audience, for example, are more likely to view business interests as being simply one set of interests in a sea of competing interest groups making claims on government. Business historian Michael Bliss argues that whatever privileged access business people may have enjoyed in the corridors of political power and whatever superiority business interests may have had in relation to rival claims on government had largely disappeared by the 1980s. "Groups with powerful vested interests," he writes, "including trade unions, civil servants, tenured academics, and courtesanal cultural producers, perpetuated a hostility toward business enterprise rooted in their own fear of competition on open markets."[13]

Bliss's skepticism on the matter of business enjoying a privileged position in Canada's interest group system was expressed after two decades of increasing government regulation and a series of major policy setbacks experienced by certain industries. Geoffrey Hale, the author of the standard textbook on business–government relations in Canada, does not go as far in writing off business power. "The extent of business influence varies widely," he explains, ". . . depending on the relative influence of other stakeholders and the capacity of political or bureaucratic decision-makers to control the policy process and to mobilize public opinion in favour of their initiatives."[14]

In his rebuttal to Lindblom's "privileged position" thesis, David Vogel argues that, on balance, "business is more affected by broad political and economic trends than it is able to affect them."[15] Although Vogel focuses on the United States, he develops a more general argument about the political power of business interests in capitalist democracies. Popular opinion and the sophistication of interest group organization are, he maintains, the keys to understanding the political successes and

failures of business and other interest groups. Vogel argues that business's ability to influence public policy is greatest when the public is worried about the long-term strength of the economy and weakest when the economy's ability to produce jobs and to increase incomes is taken for granted.

The political organization of business interests is the second key to understanding the ebb and flow of business influence. In his earlier writing on this subject, Vogel maintained that the victories of environmental, consumer, and other public interest groups in the 1960s and 1970s were largely due to their ability to read the Washington map and work the levers of congressional and media politics. Business interests, by comparison, were poorly organized and amateurish. They reacted by investing in political organization through lobbying, issue advertising, support for think-tanks sympathetic to business points of view, and political donations to candidates and parties. But despite the greater organizational sophistication and political influence that business interests achieved, divisions within the business community served to check its influence on public policy.

In a subsequent study of business influence in the United States, the United Kingdom, Germany, and Japan, Vogel concluded that "most of the factors that affect the relative political strength of business are beyond the control of business."[16] Business's resources, organization, and personal connections to policy-makers are less important in determining whether business interests win or lose on a particular issue, he argued, than are the nature of the opposition it faces and the openness of the political system to non-business interests. In *The Conspicuous Corporation*, Neil Mitchell makes a broadly similar argument. He agrees that business generally enjoys a privileged position in the politics of capitalist democracies, but that its influence can be seriously impaired if its actions and positions come to be seen as violating important community standards and values, thus weakening public confidence in business or in a particular industry and undermining the legitimacy of business's demands.[17]

So are business interests perched securely atop the interest group system in capitalist societies, or do business groups have to slug it out in the political trenches just like other groups and with no more likelihood of victory? Perhaps neither position is correct. This, at any rate, is the rather agnostic conclusion suggested by much of the work on Canadian interest groups.

This approach is sometimes referred to as *neo-institutionalism. It* is based on a simple observable fact: policy-making generally involves the participation of a relatively limited set of state and societal actors, a **policy community** centred around a sub-government, i.e., that set of state institutions and interest groups usually involved in making and implementing policy in some field. We will have more to say about the approach later in the chapter. For now, the point is simply that groups representing business interests may or may not be members of a sub-government or policy community. Whether they are and how influential they may be depends on the policy field in question and on the particular configuration of interests active in the policy community. Moreover, neo-institutionalists tend to emphasize the capacity of state actors to act independently of the pressures and demands placed on them by societal interests. This capacity will vary across policy sectors. But the bottom line of the neo-institutionalist approach is that state actors in some policy communities may be quite capable of resisting pressures coming from highly organized, well-heeled business interests—or from any societal interests, for that matter.[18]

Analytical Perspectives on Interest Groups

Pluralism

Pluralism or group theory may be defined as an explanation of politics that sees organized interests as the central fact of political life. It is a societal explanation of politics in that it locates the main causes of government action in the efforts and activities of voluntary associations—trade associations, labour unions, churches, PTAs, etc.—outside the state. When it turns its attention to the role and character of the state in democratic societies, pluralist theory draws two main conclusions. First,

the state itself is viewed as a sort of group interest or, more precisely, as an assortment of different interests associated with various components of the state. Second, despite the possibility that the state may have interests of its own, its chief political function is to ratify the balance of group interests in society and to enforce the policies that embody this balance of power. A classic formulation of this theoretical premise is provided by Earl Latham, one of the founders of this approach: "The legislature referees the group struggle, ratifies the victories of the successful coalition, and records the terms of the surrenders, compromises, and conquests in the form of statutes."[19]

The purest embodiment of group theory is found in the work of Arthur Bentley. Society, Bentley argues, can be understood only in terms of the groups that comprise it. He views government as simply a process of "groups pressing one another, forming one another, and pushing out new groups and group representatives (the organs or agencies of government) to mediate the adjustments."[20] This is an extremely reductionist approach. Pluralists after Bentley, including David Truman, Robert Dahl, and John Kenneth Galbraith,[21] were certainly aware of the danger of trying to squeeze too much explanation out of a single cause. But they remained faithful to two basic elements of pluralist theory, one empirical and the other normative. The empirical element is the claim that politics is a competitive process where power is widely distributed, there is no single ruling elite or dominant class, and the interaction of organized interests outside the state is the chief driver behind the actions of government. The normative element suggests that the outcome of this competitive struggle among groups represents the public interest and, indeed, that this is the only reasonable way of understanding the public interest in a democracy.

Pluralism begat *neo-pluralism*. The neo-pluralist assault took issue with both the empirical and normative claims of group theory. Writers like E.E. Schattschneider, Theodore Lowi, and Charles Lindblom had little difficulty in showing that the interest group system was much less open and competitive than the earlier pluralists had argued. Regarding pluralism's normative features, Lowi took aim at its equation of the public interest with the outcome of struggles between special interests. He argued that the special interest state—what Lowi called interest group liberalism—actually trivializes the public interest and ends up undermining it by pretending that it is no more than the latest set of deals struck between the powerful through the intermediary offices of government.[22]

As if these indictments were not enough, pluralism also stands accused of misunderstanding the true character of political power. By focusing on group competition, their critics argue, pluralists are inclined to see political life as relatively open and competitive because they focus on struggles between groups and the choices made by governments. But as Bachrach and Baratz argue, "power may be, and often is, exercised by confining the scope of decision-making to relatively 'safe' issues."[23] Non-decision-making—the ability to keep issues unformulated and off the public agenda—is a form of power. Having to defend your position against others is an indication of weakness. This insight is part of the neo-pluralist model of interest groups.

Class Analysis

Viewed through the prism of class analysis, interest groups do not disappear, but their edges become blurred and they take a back seat to the class interests these groups are argued to represent. Some of the major works of contemporary Marxist scholarship do not even mention such terms as "interest group," "pressure group," or "social group."[24] In Canada the class analysis approach is sometimes referred to as the political economy tradition.[25] The principal Canadian scholarly journal for work in the Canadian political economy tradition describes its role this way: "Established in 1979, *Studies in Political Economy* has . . . become a major forum for people who identify with the struggles to overcome exploitation, exclusion and oppression in Canada and abroad. . . . [The journal] welcomes contributions in every field of political economy and within all the traditions of socialist scholarship."[26] This acknowledged left-wing ideological orientation is characteristic of the class analysis perspective on interest groups.

This is not to say that the reality and significance of organized interests in politics are either denied or ignored by class analysis. But as Miriam Smith says of this approach, "The pattern of group formation is affected by economic and social inequality, which create systemic obstacles for marginalized groups in the political system. . . . [T]he main cleavages in society are based not on multiple group memberships but on economic divisions rooted in the capitalist economic system."[27] In other words, group interests exist and the members of groups will often mobilize for economic and political purposes. From the perspective of class analysis, however, interest groups are not the basic units of society and political life. Classes are. Thus, organized groups are seen as the bearers of more fundamental interests and ideologies, namely those of classes and their factions. This enables one to acknowledge the uniqueness of individual groups and associations while focusing on larger collective interests represented by individual groups. An association like the Business Council of Canada, which represents 150 of the largest private-sector corporations, would be seen as a representative of "monopoly capital." The Canadian Manufacturers & Exporters, although it represents over 3,000 corporations spanning virtually all manufacturing industries and ranging in size from thousands of employees to a handful, is viewed as an organizational voice for the manufacturing faction of the capitalist class. In fact, some class analyses characterize this organization as an instrument of the oligopolistic, American-oriented faction of the capitalist class. Labour unions, from the class analysis perspective, are viewed as representative of subordinate class interests and ideologies, as are groups representing women, Indigenous peoples, and ethnic and racial minorities.

"[T]he policy process," observes Peter John, "far from being a rational weighing up of alternatives, is driven by powerful socio-economic forces that set the agenda, structure decision-makers' choices, constrain implementation, and ensure that the interests of the most powerful (or of the system as a whole) determine the outputs and the outcomes of the political system."[28] Viewed through this lens, corporations and their associations, environmental groups, labour unions, groups representing

Indigenous Canadians, and other interest groups are properly understood in their relationship to broader forces of class struggle. Failure to view them in this context results in a misunderstanding of how political struggle really operates and what is at stake.

Neo-Institutionalism

Neo-institutionalism is a perspective on policy-making that emphasizes the impact of structures and rules, formal and informal, on political outcomes. "[T]he preferences and rules of policy actors," argue William D. Coleman and Grace Skogstad, "are shaped fundamentally by their structural position. Institutions are conceived as structuring political reality and as defining the terms and nature of political discourse."[29] What does this mean and how does it help us understand the behaviour and influence of interest groups?

First, what has been called neo-institutionalism or the new institutionalism is not so much a model of politics and policy-making as a theoretical premise shared by an otherwise diverse group of disciplines and perspectives. The premise, quite simply, is that institutions—their structural characteristics, formal rules, and informal norms—play a central role in shaping the actions of individuals and the organizations to which they belong. The neo-institutionalist perspective on interest groups has its roots in economics, organization theory, and a reaction against what, until the 1970s, was a tendency among most political scientists to locate the major influences on public policy in society rather than the state.

Economics

Rational choice theory forms the bedrock of modern economics. Beginning in the 1950s and 1960s, economists began to systematically apply the concepts of individual (limited) rationality and market behaviour to the study of elections, political parties, interest groups, bureaucracy, and other political phenomena.[30] The economic theory of politics developed from this work emphasizes the role played by rules, formal and informal, in shaping individual choices and policy outcomes. Viewed from this perspective, "institutions are bundles of rules that make collective action possible."[31]

Organization Theory

Appropriately enough, organization theory has been an important source of inspiration and ideas for the neo-institutionalist approach. One of the first political scientists to apply the behavioural insights of organization theory to Canadian politics was Alan Cairns. His 1977 presidential address to the Canadian Political Science Association relied heavily on organization theory. He argued that Canadian federalism is influenced mainly by state actors, the "needs" of the organizations they belong to, and the constitutional rules within which they operate.[32] James March, Herbert Simon, and Johan Olsen are among the organization theorists frequently cited by neo-institutionalists.[33] The spirit of the organizational perspective is captured in Charles Perrow's declaration that "The formal structure of the organization is the single most important key to its functioning."[34]

State- and Society-Centred Analysis

The rising popularity of neo-institutional analysis can be attributed in part to a reaction against explanations of politics and policy-making that emphasized the role of such societal factors as interest groups, voters, political culture, and social classes. This reaction produced an enormous outpouring of work on the autonomy, or relative autonomy, of the state, i.e., the ability of state actors to act on their own preferences and to actively shape societal demands and interest configurations rather than simply responding to and mediating societal interests. Neo-institutionalism, which focuses on the structural characteristics of and relationships between political actors, has been inspired by this same reaction. This is not to say that neo-institutionalism is a state-centred explanation of politics. But in ascribing a key role to institutions—structures and rules—it inevitably takes seriously the structural characteristics of the state.

Neo-institutionalism deals intensively with what might be called the interior lives of interest groups: the factors responsible for their creation, maintenance, and capacity for concerted political action.

James Q. Wilson identifies four categories of incentives that underlie the interior dynamics of interest groups:[35]

- *material incentives*—tangible rewards that include money and other material benefits that clearly have a monetary value;
- *specific solidarity incentives*—intangible rewards like honours, official deference, and recognition that are scarce, i.e., they have value precisely because some people are excluded from their enjoyment;
- *collective solidarity incentives*—intangible rewards created by the act of associating together in an organized group and enjoyed by all members of the group, such as a collective sense of group esteem or affirmation;
- *purposive incentives*—"intangible rewards that derive from the sense of satisfaction of having contributed to the attainment of a worthwhile cause."

Neo-institutionalism tends to agnosticism when it comes to the old debate on whether societal or state forces are more important determinants of political outcomes. Such concepts as *policy communities*—the constellation of actors in a particular policy field—or **policy networks**[36]—the nature of the relationships between the key actors in a policy community—are the building blocks of the neo-institutional approach. Embedded in them is the irrefutable claim that "the state" is in fact a fragmented structure when it comes to actual policy-making. So, too, is society. The active and influential interests on the issue of international trade or securities market regulation, for example, are very different from those that are part of the official-language policy community. What Coleman and Skogstad describe as the "diversity in arrangements between civil society and the state"[37] inspires this spirit of openness on the state-versus-society debate. The reality is that the relative strength of state and societal actors and the characteristics of policy networks vary between policy communities in the same society and, moreover, the line between state and society often is not very distinct. Paul Pross's visual depiction of what a

policy community looks like conveys a good sense of the complexity and potential for fluidity in the relations between interest groups and the state (see Figure 12.1).[38]

A group's capacity for influence within a policy community will depend on its internal characteristics and its external relationships to the larger political system and the state. Philippe Schmitter and Wolfgang Streeck call these the logics of membership and influence, respectively.[39] We have already mentioned some of the factors that may be relevant to understanding a group's interior life. On the logic of influence, Coleman and Skogstad argue that the key determinant of a group's influence is "the structure of the state itself at the sectoral level,"[40] i.e., within a particular policy community. Perhaps. But *macro*-political factors like political culture, the dominant ideology, and the state system's more general characteristics also are important to understanding the political influence of organized interests. Policy communities are perhaps best viewed as solar systems that are themselves influenced by the gravitational tug of cultural and institutional forces emanating from the centre of the larger galaxy in which they move. The diversity of state–society relations between policy communities can be reconciled with larger generalizations about the interest group system, including the widely but not universally accepted claim that business interests occupy a privileged position within this system.

The Ingredients of Interest Group Success

There is no magic recipe for group influence. Successful strategies and appropriate targets depend on the issue, the resources and actions of other groups, the state of public opinion, and the characteristics of the political system. But although there is no single formula for influence, it is possible to generalize about the factors associated with powerful interest groups. As we will see, these factors are more likely to characterize business groups and their dealings with government than any other set of societal interests.

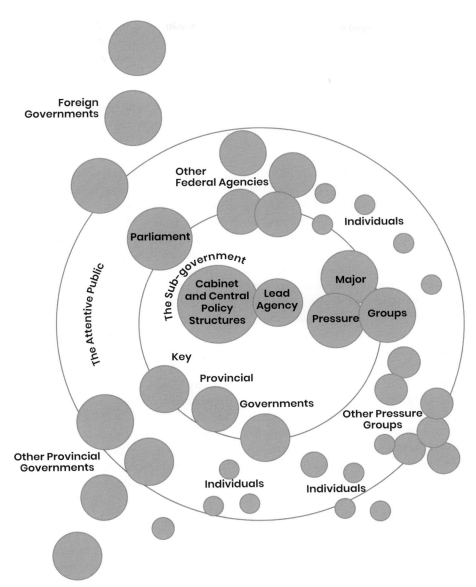

FIGURE 12.1 Policy Community "Bubble Diagram"

Organization

It may seem a trite observation, but organized interests are usually more influential than unorganized ones and are always better equipped to apply sustained pressure on policy-makers. A lone person who writes a letter to the prime minister demanding that the government act in a particular way is

unlikely to have much impact, even if that person is someone of national stature. If that person is supported by tens of thousands of people writing to the prime minister and taking to the streets in front of television and cellphone cameras that bring their demonstrations to the screens viewed by millions of others, they are more likely to get the prime minister's attention. Their impact will be even greater if their demand is channelled through an organization or organizations that can credibly claim to speak on behalf of these thousands of like-minded people, especially if the organizations are skilled at media and government relations. The unco-ordinated efforts of individuals and the fury of a spontaneous protest can have an impact on policy-makers. But this impact is unlikely to be sustained without organization.

Paul Pross, one of Canada's most distinguished experts on interest groups, points to the character of modern government and the policy-making process in explaining why organization is crucial. Modern government, he observes, is a sprawling, highly bureaucratized affair in which the power to influence policy is widely diffused. When government was smaller, the policies and programs affecting societal interests were fewer, and power was concentrated in the hands of a small group of senior bureaucratic officials and cabinet. Groups did not require sophisticated organizational structures to manage their dealings with government. This was the era of the "Ottawa mandarins," the tightly knit group of deputy ministers who dominated the policy process.[41] Pathways to influence were relatively uncomplicated. A conversation with the minister or deputy minister in the restaurant of the Château Laurier or at the Five Lakes Fishing Club, an hour's drive from Parliament in Quebec, was the preferred method of communicating a group's views. Access at this rarefied level, however, was restricted to members of the corporate elite and those representing their interests.

This era began to pass into history during the 1960s. The more complex interventionist state that emerged was not as amenable to the informal, discreet style of influence that powerful economic interests had grown used to during the 1940s and 1950s. As the scope of state intervention widened and its regulation of economic and social matters deepened, it became increasingly necessary that groups have the ongoing capacity to monitor government and deal with it at those levels where power resided. Inevitably, a large, intrusive state means that power is more widely diffused throughout the administrative apparatus of government. It resides in officials who draw up regulatory guidelines and

who interpret and administer technical matters delegated to them under the authority of vaguely worded statutes, and in those who provide advice on programs and policies to the prime minister and cabinet.

To deal with the reality of the modern administrative state, groups need to organize. And organize they have. A veritable explosion of associations representing business interests, environmental concerns, women, ethnic groups, official-language minorities, Indigenous peoples, and other interests has taken place during the last several decades. Although most of this expansion in the interest group system has been due to the efforts of those who saw the need and advantage of organization in dealing with government and in order to influence policy and public opinion, some of it has been invited and even orchestrated by the state. The active role of government in promoting the creation of associations that would in turn represent and articulate the interests of their group interests is well documented. It is a phenomenon that appears to have begun in World War I, when the federal Department of Trade and Commerce encouraged the creation of trade associations to represent corporations in the same industry.[42] During the 1960s and 1970s, the Department of Secretary of State was instrumental in the creation and proliferation of a large number of organizations representing women, ethnic groups, and official-language minorities, particularly through the provision of core funding to finance the activities of these groups.[43] If the motivation of the governments and state agencies that encouraged the creation of interest groups or that funded their activities once they were up and running was not self-serving, the consequences sometimes were. They were helping to organize the interests that depended on their programs and budgets and thereby created constituencies whose support could be useful to the bureaucracy in protecting its policy and budgetary turf.[44]

This practice of state funding for organized groups has continued in recent times. For example, Canadian Parents for French, a group active in promoting French-language schools in English-speaking Canada, receives a large part of its budget from the Official Languages Support Programs

Branch of the Department of Canadian Heritage. The Multiculturalism Program administered by the Department of Canadian Heritage involves a wide array of ethnic, racial, religious, and cultural organizations in Canada, many of which have lobbied government officials or attempted to influence public opinion on matters of concern to them. Many Indigenous and human rights groups receive a significant part of their funding from the Canadian government. The Court Challenges Program, which began in 1978 but was suspended under the Conservative government in 2006, and then revived under the Liberal government in 2016, has provided funding to organizations representing "members of historically disadvantaged groups" or official-language minorities. The Women's Legal Education and Action Fund (LEAF), a regular and prominent intervenor in Charter cases involving alleged sexual discrimination, often received funding under this program, usually between $35,000 and $50,000 per case.[45] LEAF, Planned Parenthood, Equal Voice, and a number of other women's groups receive significant funding through Status of Women Canada. A number of studies have shown that Ottawa's financial assistance to various groups to support litigation under the Charter has been an important factor in their ability to use the courts to influence equality and language rights.[46]

Sophisticated organization has become a *sine qua non* for sustained group influence. Paul Pross uses the term **institutional groups** to describe those interests that possess the highest level of organization. These groups have the following characteristics:

- organizational continuity and cohesion;
- extensive knowledge of those sectors of government that affect their clients and easy communications with those sectors;
- stable memberships;
- concrete and immediate objectives;
- overall goals of more importance than any particular objective.[47]

While many different types of groups can claim to have these characteristics, business associations are more likely to conform to Pross's criteria for institutionalized groups than those representing other interests. Indeed, associations like the Business Council of Canada, Canadian Manufacturers & Exporters, the Canadian Chamber of Commerce, the Conseil du Patronat du Québec, the Canadian Federation of Agriculture, the Canadian Federation of Independent Business, as well as many of the major trade associations in Canada, are among the most organizationally sophisticated interest groups in this country.

Resources

Money is no guarantee of interest group success—but it usually doesn't hurt. It is no accident that the most organizationally sophisticated groups, which enjoy regularized access to policy-makers and have the best track records of success in protecting and promoting the interests they represent, tend also to be well-heeled. Money is necessary to pay for the services that are vital to interest group success. A permanent staff costs money—a good deal of money if it includes lawyers, economists, accountants, researchers, public relations and media specialists, and others whose services are needed to monitor the government scene and communicate both with the group's membership and with policy-makers. The services of public relations firms, polling companies, and professional lobbyists are costly and certainly beyond the reach of many interest groups.

Interest groups representing business tend to have more affluent and stable financial footings than other groups. Their closest rivals are major labour associations; some occupational groups, such as physicians, dentists, lawyers, university professors, and teachers; and some agricultural producer groups. The budgets and personnel of some non-economic groups may also appear to be considerable. For example, in 2017 Ecojustice, one of the foremost environmental groups in Canada, had a budget of about $6.4 million and a staff of 73 distributed across five regional offices. Inuit Tapiriit Kanatami, representing Canada's Inuit population, had a 2018 budget of $9.6 million and a staff of 36. These budgets are small, however, alongside those of such groups as the Canadian

Bankers' Association, the Canadian Federation of Independent Business, and the Canadian Medical Association, all of which have annual spending budgets in excess of $25 million. The size of an association's staff is not always a reliable indicator of its probable influence with decision-makers—for example, the Business Council of Canada has a full-time staff of only 15—but these more affluent interest groups tend also to have larger staffs with more specialized personnel. The Canadian Medical Association, for example, employs over 200 persons, the Canadian Bankers' Association about 60, and the Canadian Association of Petroleum Producers about 80. Moreover, there are three important differences between the monetary resources of the major business interest groups and those of other organized interests.

First, the members of some business interest groups do not rely on their collective associations for political influence to the extent that the members of other interest groups do. Large corporations usually have their own public affairs/government relations departments that, among other functions, manage the organization's lobbying and advocacy activities. Moreover, large corporations will often act on their own in employing the services of a professional lobbying firm or other service that is expected to help them influence policymakers. Indeed, the clientele lists of such firms as Hill+Knowlton Strategies, Earnscliffe Strategy Group, and the Capital Hill Group read like a "Who's Who" of the Canadian corporate elite (with many non-Canadian corporate clients too).

The second important difference in the monetary resources of business and non-business associations relates to stability. Simply put, business groups rest on more secure financial footings. They are less subject to the vicissitudes of economic recession and because they do not depend on government or charitable foundation funding they are not exposed to the vagaries of cutbacks and budgetary shuffles. Many other groups cannot make this claim. The effects of economic downturn can be quite dramatic, as was seen during the 2008 recession. A 2009 survey by the Ontario Trillium Foundation reported that about two-thirds of non-profit groups, including social, cultural, and environmental organizations, said their funding had decreased compared to the previous year.[48] Ecojustice experienced a decline of about one-third in its foundation grants in 2009, from $1.25 million to $779,627, a story that could be told by social advocacy and environmental groups across the country. In addition, changes in the party in power can also affect the bottom lines of interest groups that depend on government funding for a significant part of their finances. Some women's, environmental, and other advocacy groups complained that they experienced funding cuts under the Conservative government between 2006 and 2015, arguing that this was due to the government's hostility towards their ideas and advocacy activities. Some of this support was restored after the Liberal Party was elected in 2015. The point is simply that dependency on charitable donations, foundation grants, or government funding makes a group's finances more vulnerable than dependence on required contributions from its members.

A third difference involves the ability of business and non-business groups to raise money to deal with a "crisis" issue. The issue of free trade in the federal election campaign of 1988 is perhaps the classic case in point. Although hard numbers do not exist, no one seriously denies that business associations in favour of the Canada–US Free Trade Agreement outspent their opponents by a wide margin in an attempt to influence public opinion on the deal and thereby ensure the election of the Conservatives, the only party that supported the FTA. When a Conservative victory seemed in doubt, the Alliance for Trade and Job Opportunities, an ad hoc association of 112 corporations, financed a media blitz during the last three weeks of the 1988 campaign. More recently, groups (and the governments of Alberta and Canada!) spent millions of dollars on both sides of the Canada–US border during the decade preceding the 2017 approval by President Donald Trump of the Keystone XL pipeline that runs between northern Alberta and the Gulf of Mexico. Anti-pipeline groups also spent millions of dollars. Based on the best guesstimates that can be arrived at from figures provided by Open Secrets and the Center for Public Integrity in the United

Protesters in Toronto march in November 2016 against the Dakota Access Pipeline in solidarity with water protectors at Standing Rock, North Dakota. Despite widespread protest against the pipeline in Canada and the United States, President Donald Trump signed orders to move forward with both the Dakota Access and Keystone XL pipelines shortly after taking office. Based on data from the United States, anti-pipeline protesters were unable to match the funds available to pro-pipeline groups and corporations.

States, and rather fragmentary data reported in the media on advocacy spending in Canada, pro-pipeline groups and the governments aligned with them outspent environmental and Indigenous rights groups by a large margin.

But it's not always a matter of who has the deepest pockets, and in any case it is usually difficult to say with any certainty what influence was had by a particular lobbying or public opinion. During the late 1990s the Canadian corporate elite and its lead association, the Business Council of Canada, lobbied hard for the Multilateral Agreement on Investment (MAI). The MAI was a proposed treaty among the wealthy industrialized countries that would have imposed serious restrictions on

governments' ability to discriminate against foreign investors, for example, through requirements that they source materials locally or meet other conditions for investing in a nation's economy. In the end, opposition to the MAI from labour unions and anti-globalization groups in Canada and abroad led the governments who were championing the MAI to abandon their efforts. The superior resources of the corporate backers of the MAI were not enough to win this particular battle. Likewise, it was not the millions spent on lobbying lawmakers and attempting to influence American public opinion that secured approval of the Keystone XL pipeline. President Obama rejected it, notwithstanding majority support in Congress. It took another

American president, Donald Trump, to approve the pipeline, a decision he doubtless would have made even without all this spending by pro-pipeline groups and governments.

Money is not the only useful resource in promoting an interest group's objectives. John Kingdon identifies several other resources that enable a group to influence what gets on (or stays off) the policy agenda and the alternatives considered by policy-makers. These include electoral influence, the capacity to affect the economy negatively, and group cohesion.[49]

Electoral Influence

The perceived ability to swing a significant bloc of votes is an important group resource. While all interest group leaders claim to speak on behalf of the group's membership, politicians know that the claim is more credible in some cases than in others. The sheer size of a group's membership can be an important resource, as can the status or wealth of its members and their geographic distribution. The distribution factor can cut two ways. In political systems like Canada's, characterized by the election of a single member from each constituency, the concentration of a group's members in a particular region, other things being equal, will increase the political influence of that group. An example of this would be the dairy industry in Quebec. As of 2018, about half of all Canadian dairy farms, roughly 40 per cent of dairy farm revenue, half of Canadian cheese production, and, by the dairy industry's reckoning, close to 80,000 direct and indirect jobs in the Quebec economy depended on this industry. Not surprisingly, Les Producteurs de lait du Québec has long been considered one of the most influential interest groups in that province. Candidates and parties are likely to see the advantage of proposing policies that are attractive to such a regionally concentrated interest, whose votes are crucial in order to win seats in that region. On the other hand, geographic dispersion of a group's membership may also be advantageous, even under an electoral system like Canada's. A group's claim to speak on behalf of members who are found across the country, and who can be mobilized to vote in a particular

way, can be an impressive electoral resource. It is, for example, an argument regularly used by the Canadian Federation of Independent Business, which has about 109,000 members across Canada.

Capacity to Inflict Damage on the Economy

The ability to "down tools," close businesses, scale back investment plans, refuse to purchase government bonds, or in some other way inflict harm on the economy or public finances (or both!) can be a powerful group resource. It is a resource possessed mainly by business groups. Unions and such other occupational groups as physicians or agricultural producers have a more difficult time using their economic clout, which may be considerable, to influence policy-makers. There are two reasons for this. First, when a group such as nurses, teachers, postal workers, truckers, or airline employees attempts to tie up the economy or some important public service by withholding their labour, the linkage between the behaviour of such a group and the social or economic consequences of their actions is extremely visible. Regardless of the factors that led to their action, the general public is likely to perceive the situation as one where the *special* interests of such a group stand in sharp contrast to the *public* interest. A union or other occupational group that attempts to use the threat of economic or social chaos to back up its demands should not count on favourable public opinion. On the contrary, public support for or indifference towards a group's demands is likely to change to hostility in such circumstances. In the case of unions, they suffer from the additional disadvantage of being held in rather low esteem by Canadians. Surveys regularly show that public confidence in labour unions is lower than for most other major social institutions.[50]

A second reason why business interests are better able than other economic interest groups to successfully use the threat of economic damage in pursuing their objectives has to do with culture. In a capitalist society like ours, the fundamental values that underpin the strength of business interests—the belief in private property, the importance of profits, and faith in markets as the best mechanism for generating and distributing wealth—lend legitimacy to the general interests of business. Particular industries or corporations may be perceived as being greedy or socially irresponsible, but the values generally associated with a capitalist economy enjoy widespread support. When workers lay down their tools to apply pressure in support of their demands there is a good chance their action will be interpreted as selfish and socially irresponsible. But if a business refuses to invest in new plant and machinery, lays off workers, or relocates, the reactions of policy-makers and the public are likely

to be quite different. Most of us accept that business is about making a profit. The damage that a failure of business confidence may do to an economy may be regrettable, but business people are less likely to be accused of being irresponsible because they are seen to be acting in accordance with the rules of a system that most of us accept.

Group Cohesion

"United we stand, divided we fall" has always been an accepted rule of interest group influence. Other things being equal, an association's hand will be strengthened if it is able to convince policy-makers

THE CANADIAN PRESS/Fred Chartrand

Carolyn Bennett (right), minister of Crown–Indigenous Relations, and Francyne Joe (centre), president of the Native Women's Association of Canada, look on as Lorraine Whitman, president of the Nova Scotia Native Women's Association, signs an accord to allow the NWAC to participate in public policy decisions related to Indigenous health, housing, and education within Canada and internationally.

that it speaks with a single voice and genuinely represents the views of its membership. This is not always easy. We have already noted that both labour and business interests are highly fragmented in Canada and are represented by a large number of associations, not one of which can credibly claim to speak on behalf of all labour or business interests.

The same is true for many other collective interests in Canadian society. Hundreds of organizations represent different groups of agricultural and food producers. Indigenous Canadians are represented by many associations, the largest of which is the Assembly of First Nations (AFN). The AFN's ability to speak on behalf of all Indigenous groups is limited, however, by the fact that it does not speak for Métis and non-status Indians (who are represented, respectively, by the Métis National Council and the Congress of Aboriginal Peoples) or for the Inuit (represented by Inuit Tapiriit Kanatami). Moreover, the Native Women's Association of Canada (NWAC), another of the five National Indigenous organizations recognized by the Canadian government, describes itself as the national voice for Indigenous women and does not take direction from any of these other Indigenous organizations. There are dozens of politically significant environmental groups in Canada, but no one of them is so predominant that it can credibly claim to speak for the environmental movement.

Group cohesion typically becomes less problematic as the number of members represented by an organization grows fewer and the similarity between members increases. But what is gained in cohesion may, of course, be lost as a result of the perception that an association represents a narrow special interest. As well, it is easier to present a united front when an association is speaking on behalf of just one group. Alliances with associations representing other group interests, however, may be politically useful. The downside, again, is the problem of reconciling group differences to achieve such a common front.

A rather different problem of cohesion involves the relationship between a group's leaders and its membership. Evidence of a gap between the goals of leaders and those they purport to represent will undermine an association's credibility in the eyes of policy-makers. A variation of this problem exists when an interest group claims to speak on behalf of a largely unorganized collectivity, or where there are good reasons for doubting that the group actually expresses the views of those it claims to represent. Labour unions' claims to speak on behalf of Canadian workers are weakened, in the eyes of some, because they represent less than one-third of the labour force. The legitimacy of the AFN as the voice of status Indians in treaty negotiations with Ottawa has been challenged in recent times by influential Indigenous groups that prefer to speak on their own behalf. "Whatever meetings and decisions are made at that meeting at AFN (in Whitehorse), for the record . . . [the AFN] do not speak on behalf of Onion Lake Cree Nation people, period," said Chief Wallace Fox, referring to the matter of treaty negotiations. "Our people speak for themselves."[51] This matter of when the AFN may be said to speak on behalf of its member First Nations was a major issue at the 2018 convention that re-elected Perry Bellegarde as its National Chief (see Chapter 16).

Clearly, then, the dynamics of group cohesion tend to favour certain types of interests more than others. As is also true of the other group resources we have examined, the winners are mainly business interest groups. To understand why this is the case, consider two widely accepted propositions about interest group cohesion.[52] First, as the number of members in an organization increases, the likelihood that some individuals will believe they can reap the benefits of the organization's actions without having to contribute to it also increases. This is called the **free-rider problem**. Other things being equal, smaller groups are less likely to have members who behave as free-riders and are more cohesive than larger ones. Second, groups able to offer exclusive benefits to their members, i.e., benefits only available to members of the organization, will be more cohesive and more capable of concerted political pressure than those that rely on collective benefits, i.e., benefits that will accrue to society as a whole. A corollary of this second proposition is that organizations relying on material incentives to attract and retain members, and that therefore can motivate members with the prospect of shared material benefits, will be more cohesive than groups that rely on non-material incentives.[53]

When we examine the actual interest group system, we find that business groups tend to have smaller memberships. Indeed, some are quite small, particularly those that represent companies in oligopolistic industries. For example, the Canadian Vehicle Manufacturers' Association represents only three companies, the Forest Products Association of Canada has only 15 members, and the Canadian Bankers Association has 69 member organizations. Even an industry association with a larger membership such as the Canadian Association of Petroleum Producers, which has about 90 producer members and roughly 150 members in supplier and other allied industries, is more cohesive in terms of member interests than most non-business groups. Some business associations, such as Chambers of Commerce, the Canadian Federation of Independent Business, and Canadian Manufacturers & Exporters, have very large memberships. But these organizations represent more general interests of the business community, while the more specific interests of corporations are represented through trade associations that have smaller memberships.

Business groups are not the only ones to rely on exclusive benefits and material incentives to attract, maintain, and motivate members. Labour unions, agricultural producer groups, and professional associations do as well. But one needs to remember that cohesion is only one group resource. Farmers' groups or labour unions may be as cohesive as business associations but still inferior to business in terms of the other resources at their disposal.

Safety in the Shadows

Placard-carrying animal rights activists, a blue-suited spokesperson for an organization presenting a brief to a parliamentary committee, a prime-time television ad that advocates a particular policy, or a social media campaign aimed at mobilizing public opinion on an issue are all highly visible manifestations of interest groups in action. They are not, however, necessarily the most effective pathways of group influence. Often it is what is not obvious

and out in the open—the absence of visible signs of groups exerting themselves to influence policy—that tells us most about the strength of organized interests. In the jungle that is the interest group system, there may be safety in the shadows.

The status, privileges, or interests of some groups are not matters of public debate, and this tells us something about the power of these groups. As E.E. Schattschneider writes, "The very expression 'pressure politics' invites us to misconceive the role of special-interest groups in politics."[54] "Private conflicts," he argues, "are taken into the public arena precisely because someone wants to make certain that the power ratio among the private interests most immediately involved shall not prevail."[55] On reflection, the point is obvious and yet profoundly important. Society's most powerful interests would prefer to avoid the public arena where they have to justify themselves and respond to those who advocate changes that would affect their interests. They are safer in the shadows. But when the light of public debate is shone on them they become prey to attacks from other groups and they lose their security. Conflict, Schattschneider notes, always includes an element of unpredictability. Consequently, even private interests with impressive group resources may suffer losses in their status and privileges, depending on what alliances form against them, the direction of public opinion, and the behaviour of political parties. Indeed, when previously unquestioned interests have reached the public agenda and are recognized as group interests, this may register a loss of influence on the part of such a group.

When the security of the shadows is lost, the relative safety of a fairly closed policy community may be a decent substitute. In the United States, the concept of an iron triangle has been used to describe the relatively closed system of relations between an interest group and the administrative agencies and congressional committees with which it routinely deals. Most commentators agree that the "iron triangles" that may once have characterized policy-making in the United States have become less rigid and fewer over the last few decades.[56] Moreover, because one of the corners in these triangular relationships involved Congress and its powerful committees, the "iron triangle" concept never travelled very well beyond the United States. The terms "sub-governments," "policy communities," and "policy networks" are now more commonly used, including in the United States, to describe the reality of relatively exclusive constellations of state and societal actors who dominate routine policy-making in a particular field. Indeed, the ability to maintain the routine nature of policy-making is vital to preserving the privileged status of the dominant actors in a policy community.

Strategies for Influence

Three basic strategies are open to interest groups. One is to target policy-makers directly, through personal meetings with officials, briefs, and exchanges of information. This is the *lobbying option*. Another strategy is to target *public opinion* in the expectation that policy-makers will respond to indications of considerable popular support for a group's position. The media play a crucial role here, because they are the channel by which a group's message will be communicated to the wider public. A variation of the public opinion option involves alliance-building. By building visible bridges with other groups on some issue, a group may hope to persuade policy-makers that its position has broad support. A third strategy involves *judicial action*. This confrontational strategy involves a very public challenge and an outcome likely to leave one side a winner and the other a loser. For some groups it tends to be an option of last resort, used after other strategies have failed. But for other groups, such as the Women's Legal Education and Action Fund (LEAF), Equality for Gays and Lesbians Everywhere (EGALE), Ecojustice, and the Canadian Civil Liberties Association, litigation is a basic weapon in their arsenal of pressure tactics.

These strategies are not mutually exclusive. A group may use more than one of them at once or switch from one strategy to another. Nor can one draw firm conclusions about the relative effectiveness of different influence strategies. Much depends on the nature of the issue and the character of the policy community within which a group's actions reverberate. Despite the contingent quality

of group influence, a few generalizations are possible. They include the following:

- Everyone recognizes that one of the keys to influence is being involved early in the policy-making process, when ideas are just being considered and legislation has not yet been drafted. Lobbying is the generally preferred strategy at this stage of the policy process. Confrontation and visibility are relatively low, and the importance of thorough preparation and credible technical information is high.
- Groups that are well-established members of a policy community, routinely consulted by government officials, will tend to prefer a lobbying strategy. More public and confrontational strategies involve the risk of bringing unpredictable elements into the policy-making process and will be used only as measures of last resort.
- Groups not well established within a policy community are more likely to rely on confrontation, media campaigns, and other public strategies to get policy-makers to pay attention and respond to the interests they represent.
- Where a group's interests are significantly affected by regulation, lobbying strategies that rely on research and technical information supplied to the bureaucratic officials doing the regulating will be most successful.
- The era of vested interests relying on lobbying strategies has passed. Lobbying remains a very important influence strategy, but even groups enjoying regular high-level access to policy-makers now often find that lobbying is not enough.
- A successful influence strategy is usually quite expensive. This is true whether one is talking about lobbying (which often involves hiring a professional government relations firm), aiming to influence public opinion (which may involve the use of paid advertisements and the services of public relations and polling experts), or going to court. Business groups tend to be better able to pay for these expensive strategies than other groups.

Just what *is* the price of influence? It varies, but a legal challenge that makes its way to the Supreme Court can certainly cost millions of dollars in legal bills. If much of the legal work has been contributed on a pro bono basis, as has often been true of sexual equality, same-sex discrimination, and environmental cases, the costs may be considerably less. Large business corporations and industry associations have the financial means to go to court in defence of their interests. For other groups, it is often necessary for a litigation-oriented advocacy group such as Ecojustice or LEAF to take on the burden of their representation. Environmental and other so-called public interest groups that do not rely entirely on pro bono law services are understandably wary of bringing legal actions in cases they are not confident of winning and where the defendant might be awarded costs.[57] Legal costs in a case that reaches a provincial appeals court or the Supreme Court of Canada may easily reach hundreds of thousands or even over a million dollars.[58]

A campaign directed at influencing public opinion can also be costly. We have already mentioned the multi-million dollar campaign waged by the pro-FTA Canadian Alliance for Trade and Job Opportunities—probably over $2 million spent even before the final blitz during the 1988 federal election campaign. Although this case is three decades old and the amount of money may sound rather paltry by today's standards, its importance lies in the fact that it became the catalyst for reform of the law on spending by organizations or individuals other than political parties and candidates during election campaigns. Group spending between election campaigns continues to be considerable. In 2012 Enbridge announced it would spend millions of dollars on an ad campaign in support of its Northern Gateway pipeline project (a proposal that would be rejected several years later).[59] This level of spending by a single organization with the aim of moving the needle of public opinion on a divisive policy issue may sound shockingly high. In fact, however, it is dwarfed by what governments sometimes spend to influence public opinion. On the pipeline issue alone, tens of millions of dollars were spent by the Alberta and federal governments on advertising in Canada and the United States between 2008 and 2018, in support of various pipeline projects. Environmental groups and their allies may also spend large sums of money on advertising. But as is true of other non-governmental organizations (NGOs) that spend on advocacy campaigns, it is usually difficult to know how much has been spent and where the money came from. Most of this spending does not take place during official election campaigns, so it is not covered by legal limits and disclosure requirements relating to third-party advertising.

Not only is it usually difficult to know how much was spent by whom on a particular policy advocacy campaign, it is equally difficult to determine with any degree of certainty whether this spending made a difference. There is no empirical evidence to support the claim that pro-free trade business groups "bought" a Conservative victory in the 1988 election. Nor can it be said with any certainty that advertising spending by anti-pipeline groups was responsible for the demise of Enbridge's Northern Gateway proposal in 2016 or the TransCanada Energy East pipeline proposal in 2017. In these and most other cases where groups employ advocacy advertising in the hope of influencing public opinion on an issue, a mix of factors and interest group strategies and tactics are at play. Isolating the independent impact of advocacy advertising is difficult and, according to some, virtually impossible. Based on a survey of 34 studies that examined the impact of environmental advocacy campaigns, a team of researchers concluded:

> the scientific evidence is fairly weak for any claims about the effectiveness of advocacy campaigns. . . . We found no studies that rigorously or experimentally measured the impact of environmental campaigns. Much of the literature we reviewed used perception-based measurements (such as asking people if they thought the campaigns were effective), did not consider counterfactual scenarios (what would have happened if the campaign hadn't occurred), and were based on case reports that did not use controls or take into account confounding variables.[60]

These very same conclusions are reached by those who study the impact of advertising more generally.

Less costly than advertising—and potentially at least as or even more effective—is what might be described as insurgent advocacy tactics. These involve boycotts of a product, an organization, or even of a country, or disruptive and/or sensational measures intended to attract attention to an issue and advance a particular narrative with the aim of influencing either government policy or the behaviour of the targeted organization, industry or other object of such actions. Arguably the first such use of insurgency tactics on a wide scale began in 1977 with the boycott of Nestlé by a large number of human rights, international development, and other groups. The boycott was in response to the company's marketing of infant milk formula in developing countries. In more recent years such campaigns have become quite frequent. "Boycotts are shockingly common," says Maurice Schweitzer. "One group or another has boycotted almost every major company at some point, whether it's Walmart for its development procedures or union policies, Procter & Gamble for the treatment of animals, Nike for employment practices or Kentucky Fried Chicken for the treatment of chickens." The literature on their impact suggests, however, that they are often unsuccessful in achieving their goals. As is also true of advocacy advertising campaigns, a mix of factors determines the effectiveness of a boycott that may be organized by a particular group or coalition of groups.[61] Boycotts in Canada have achieved mixed and uncertain results. In 2010 the US-based NGO Corporate Ethics International and ForestEthics (now called Stand.earth) called for a boycott of products sourced from petroleum from the Alberta oil sands as well as a boycott of Alberta as a tourist destination. It is not clear that the boycott had the impact expected by the groups that organized it, although it did generate media coverage (see Box 12.2).

There is no doubt that strategies aimed at influencing public opinion have become increasingly important to interest groups and to the broader social movements to which they may be allied. In fact, in discussing advocacy advertising and what we have called insurgency tactics used by some groups, we have only scratched the surface of these strategies (see Box 12.3).[62] Important as they are, however, well-established interest groups, and in particular those that represent business interests, tend to prefer strategies that target policy-makers directly. These are lobbying strategies.

Lobbying may be defined as any form of direct or indirect communication with government that is designed to influence public policy. Although the term continues to conjure up rather dated images of smoke-filled rooms, "old boy networks," and sleazy deal-making, this is a somewhat unfair caricature of lobbying on two counts. First, lobbying is a basic democratic right. When a group of citizens organizes to demand a traffic light at a dangerous neighbourhood corner and meets with their local city councillor to express their concerns, this is lobbying. When the president of a powerful business association arranges a lunch rendezvous with an official in the Prime Minister's Office (PMO) with whom she went to law school, this, too, is lobbying. Although lobbying is often associated in the minds of the public and journalists with privileged access and even corruption, it is not an activity limited to organizations representing the powerful or that is inherently undemocratic. Nevertheless, the perception of lobbying and lobbyists as being corrupt and a blight on democracy persists. A 2014 poll conducted for Ryerson University found that only 9 per cent of respondents trusted lobbyists to behave ethically in fulfilling their duties (politicians came in at 13 per cent; at the other end of the spectrum, doctors were trusted by 78 per cent and judges by 65 per cent).[63]

The "sleaze" caricature of lobbying conveys a rather inaccurate and certainly outdated impression by associating it with practices that constitute only a small part of what lobbyists actually do. Direct meetings with influential public officials are certainly an important aspect of lobbying. Likewise, there is no shortage of evidence that ethically dubious relations occasionally exist between lobbyists and policy-makers (see Box 12.4). But lobbying involves a much wider set of activities than simply buttonholing cabinet ministers or their senior officials. Most professional lobbyists, whether they work for a company or interest group, or for

Media Spotlight

BOX 12.2 Do Boycotts Work? The Case of ForestEthics versus the Alberta Oil Sands

Whole Foods and home furnishings retailer Bed Bath & Beyond Inc. have signed onto a campaign by environmental group, ForestEthics, in which they commit to reduce their reliance on fuel that is produced from Alberta's oil sands bitumen.

ForestEthics expects to sign up other Fortune 500 companies, and says it is currently negotiating with 30 companies, as it looks to increase public pressure on Canada to impose dramatic emission reductions on the oil sector.

"The goal here is to demonstrate to Alberta and to the oil patch that this problem isn't going away. In fact, it's going to get a lot worse," ForestEthics executive director Todd Paglia said in an interview.

But industry experts say that it is extremely difficult for consumers to know the crude source of the diesel that fuels their trucks because refiners mix their feedstocks and swap product with competitors for efficiency reasons.

It's difficult to see the boycott as much more than a publicity stunt, said Alan Knight, a U.K.-based sustainable development consultant who worked with Virgin Airlines when it considered the possibility of refusing to use oil-sands-derived jet fuel.

Mr. Knight determined that not only was it impossible, it was the wrong thing to do for the environment.

He recommends that companies like Whole Foods work to improve oil sands' environmental performance by prodding the industry to accelerate investment in clean new technology, and by refusing to buy from those oil companies that are laggards among their peers.

"Boycotting is a lot easier. It's a lot cheaper and you get really good PR," Mr. Knight said. "But you won't solve the problem. You'll bury the problem and hide it and probably make it worse."

Still, Whole Foods switched its Indiana distribution centre from Marathon Oil Co. to CountryMark, a farmer-owned co-operative that produces its own conventional crude and processes it at a small refinery in Mount Vernon, Ind.

Whole Foods senior vice-president Michael Besancon insists the company is working with its suppliers to ensure they can provide fuel that is not derived from Alberta bitumen, and has been assured that they can.

Source: Shawn McCarthy and Nathan Vanderklippe, "Boycott of Oil Sands Fuel Called 'Greenwashing,'" *Globe and Mail*, updated 29 Nov. 2016, https://www.theglobeandmail.com/report-on-business/industry-news/energy-and-resources/boycott-of-oil-sands-fuel-called-greenwashing/article4306385/.

a government relations firm that sells its lobbying expertise to clients, spend the better part of their time collecting and communicating information on behalf of the interests they represent. They monitor the political scene as it affects their client's interests. An effective lobbyist does not simply react, but instead is like an early warning system, providing information about policy when it is still in its formative stages and tracking public opinion on the issues vital to a client's interests. Lobbyists provide information about how and where to access the policy-making system and strategies for influencing policies or winning contracts. They may also provide advice and professional assistance in putting together briefs, press releases, speeches, and other communications, as well as public relations services such as identifying and targeting those segments of public opinion that influence policy-makers on some issue (see Box 12.5). Helping to build strategic coalitions with other groups is another function that lobbyists may perform.

Most interest groups lobby government on their own. But for those who can afford it, the services of a professional lobbying firm may also be purchased. There are many such businesses, some of which, including the Capital Hill Group, Sussex Strategy Group, Earnscliffe, Hill + Knowlton Strategies, have as their clients the most important corporations and associations in the country. These businesses employ dozens of professional staff and have

Politics in Focus

BOX 12.3 Think-Tanks and Interest Group Influence

A think-tank is an organization that carries out research on some matter of public importance and seeks to communicate its findings and recommendations for government policy to a wider audience that may range from citizens to policy-makers at the highest levels. Its goals tend to be broader and its influence strategies rather different from those of interest groups. Think-tanks are in the business of influencing the climate of ideas within which policy choices are discussed, as well as the particular options considered in dealing with an issue. Some of them are not anchored to an ideological agenda and seldom, if ever, advocate a particular policy option. But others resemble broad-based interest groups such as the Canadian Labour Congress and the Canadian Chamber of Commerce in that they have a clear ideological orientation—for example, market-oriented in the case of the Fraser Institute and the Frontier Centre for Public Policy, or left-of-centre and anti-globalization in the case of the Centre for Social Justice and the Canadian Centre for Policy Alternatives—and attempt to nudge public policy in a specific direction.

Many of the world's most prominent think-tanks, particularly in the United States where most such organizations are found, were created by donors in the expectation that they would work to influence the policy conversation in ways favourable to their benefactors. In Canada, the Fraser Institute was created in 1974 at a time when, in the organization's own words, "the intellectual consensus was that government action was the best means of meeting the economic and social aspirations of Canadians." The Institute was originally funded by corporate donations, and from its inception has had a strong business presence on its board of directors.

The Canadian Centre for Policy Alternatives was founded in 1980. It was the idea of several university professors, mainly at Carleton University, including former Carleton University president Michael Oliver, who became the CCPA's first president. Over its roughly 30-year history it has been best known for its Alternative Federal Budget. In fact, however, the annual number of the CCPA's publications is quite large and the range of policy issues they cover is vast. The Centre's original funding came from trade unions and individuals.

These research and advocacy organizations, one on the right and the other on the left of Canada's political spectrum, are among the most prominent think-tanks in Canada. Their work is often cited and their experts are frequently interviewed in the media. Other think-tanks also contribute to the political and policy conversation in Canada, including some, such as the Pembina Institute and the Atlantic Institute for Market Studies, with clear ideological orientations and others, such as the C.D. Howe Institute and the Macdonald-Laurier Institute, whose orientation is more centrist.

annual billings in the tens of millions of dollars. Others are much smaller operations, employing a handful of persons. In addition, many law firms and accounting companies, including such prominent ones as Osler, Hoskin & Harcourt LLP, Fraser Milner Casgrain LLP (since 2013, Dentons), MacMillan LLP, and Stikeman Elliot LLP, do lobbying work. The line between legal representation and lobbying is often non-existent, a fact attested to by the presence of many law firms on the public registry of lobbyists.

Since 1989, those who are paid to lobby federal public office-holders have been required to register with a federal agency. The Lobbying Act provides for three categories of lobbyists:

- *Consultant lobbyists* are those who, for a fee, work for various clients. As of September 2018, there were 976 such individuals registered as active consultant lobbyists, an increase of about 12 per cent over the previous 10 years.

- *Corporate in-house lobbyists* are those who work for a single corporation and who lobby federal officials as a significant part of their duties. As of September 2018, there were

Governing Realities

BOX 12.4 The Potential Influence of Foreign Money, Hospitality, and Lobbying

In June of 2010 the director of the Canadian Security Intelligence Service, Richard Fadden, testified before a parliamentary committee. What he said came as a shock to many Canadians. Their public officials, he said, were being targeted by foreign nationals who hoped to buy political goodwill and policy influence in Canada. One of the main ways this is done is through foreign corporations, governments, or associations funded by foreign governments paying for trips to visit their country.

Canadian politicians at all levels of government frequently take such trips, often described as "fact-finding missions." The stated goal may be to nurture contacts and identify business possibilities—a reason often given by municipal politicians who travel abroad—or to learn more about a policy issue that relates to one's committee responsibilities or other policy interests. The hospitality is often lavish and spouses are frequently invited. According to House of Commons Ethics Commissioner Mario Dion, 73 of the 338 MPs took trips to foreign destinations or, in a handful of cases, trips within Canada in 2017. These trips were paid for in whole or in part by groups with clear ties to foreign governments. Trips paid for by the Taipei Economic and Cultural Office in Canada and the Centre for Israel and Jewish Affairs were the most popular.

Such trips are not the equivalent of bribes. There is seldom an expectation of a specific quid pro quo. But the foreign government or organization footing the bill does so in the expectation that, at a minimum, it is investing in goodwill that may ultimately translate into influence in Canadian political decision-making.

Foreign influence may operate in other ways. Although it is against the law for political parties and candidates to accept contributions from foreign nationals, there is no law against foreign corporations, NGOs, other organizations, or individuals contributing money to Canadian organizations, including advocacy groups and think-tanks, that are engaged in trying to influence public opinion and government policy. Nor is it illegal for foreign organizations to lobby Canadian public officials either directly or by employing the services of a government consulting firm. According to the database maintained by the Office of the Commissioner of Lobbying, such US-based firms as Amazon, Google, and Microsoft have been among the busiest lobbyists in their respective individual registrations (i.e., a specific meeting or other communication with a government official on a particular matter).

Should there be limits on foreign lobbying and other spending intended to influence government policy in Canada? Before you answer this question keep in mind that Canadian organizations, including corporations, and both the federal and provincial governments spend money with the same aims in countries throughout the world. Indeed, in today's globalized world the nationality of a business, NGO, or other organization may not be clear. There is, in fact, quite a literature on how to determine the national identity of a corporation and whether it is even possible in many cases. The same may be said of environmental groups like the Sierra Club and Greenpeace, and of human rights NGOs such as Amnesty International and Human Rights Watch. They have offices and activities throughout the world, including in Canada, and the revenues that enable them to do what they do come from contributions from many countries. Even if you feel uneasy about foreign influences on public opinion and government policy in Canada, would it be possible to regulate them?

1,945 individuals registered as in-house corporate lobbyists, an increase of about 11 per cent over the previous 10 years.

- *Organization in-house lobbyists* are the senior paid officers and other employees of organizations—business, labour, environmental, charitable, etc.—whose activities would include lobbying federal officials. As of September 2018, there were 2,286 in-house organization lobbyists registered with the Lobbyists Registration Branch of Industry Canada, about the same number as 10 years earlier.

The majority of active consultant and in-house organization lobbyists represent corporations and business associations (as do the in-house corporate lobbyists). The clientele lists of Canada's leading

BOX 12.5 A Revolving Door?

For those familiar with Canadian politics, a casual perusal of the names of executives, principals, and senior consultants with Canada's leading government relations firms inspires a sensation of déjà vu. Some of these people were, in previous lives, politicians, senior bureaucrats, leading political party officials, or high-level advisers to prime ministers and cabinet members. Often they have worn more than one of these hats before entering the world of government consulting. Those who study politics have long referred to this as "the revolving door," a term that originated in the United States. The Washington-based public interest group, Open Secrets, describes the phenomenon this way:

> [There is] a door—a revolving door that shuffles former federal employees into jobs as lobbyists, consultants and strategists just as the door pulls former hired guns into government careers. While officials in the executive branch, Congress and senior congressional staffers spin in and out of the private and public sectors, so too does privilege, power, access and, of course, money.

This door has also existed in Canada, with former bureaucrats and elected officials becoming consultants and industry representatives, although movement from the lobbying world into the public sector has been rare. But in both countries, and in other democracies, part of what lobbyists market to clients is the expectation of access to influential public officials. This expectation is more likely to exist and to be realized when the lobbyist comes from a background where he or she has been part of the government sector and acquired personal contacts and knowledge that may open doors for one's clients. But when does access based on personal connections, reputation, or past experience become influence-peddling? Influence peddling is a criminal offence under s. 121(1)(d) of the *Criminal Code*.

Since the passage of the Federal Accountability Act in 2008, some former government officials, elected or unelected, are prohibited from lobbying government officials for a period of five years after leaving the public sector. These officials are referred to in the Act as "designated public office holders," and include ministers and ministerial staff as well as bureaucrats down to and including the level of assistant deputy minister. But matters are not as simple as they may seem. These former public officials are permitted to lobby on behalf of their new employer or clients as long as this does not "*constitute a significant part of the individual's work on its behalf*" (Lobbying Act, Section 10.11 [1][c]). Moreover, the limits on a former politician, senior staff member, or high-ranking bureaucrat providing "strategic advice" to clients or to colleagues that may indeed contribute to more successful lobbying of government officials appear to be flexible.

The rules may be flexible, but a 2018 Supreme Court decision demonstrated that this flexibility has limits. The case involved Bruce Carson, a former PMO adviser under Prime Minister Stephen Harper. Carson was found guilty of influence-peddling, having demanded a benefit for his then girlfriend from his client, a water filtration system company, in exchange for the contracts that he promised to arrange. Commenting on this decision, the law firm McCarthy Tétrault, which lobbies on behalf of clients in addition to its other services, observed: "After *Carson*, it is more important than ever for those who engage in federal or provincial lobbying to refrain from suggesting that they have any particular sway with the government or its officials. Rather, lobbyists should focus their pitches on their skills as communicators."[64]

government relations firms include major players in the Canadian and international corporate world. Earnscliffe Strategy Group, for example, boasts that it represents such clients as Microsoft, DeBeers, Novartis Pharmaceutical, Chevron, General Motors Canada, and McDonald's Canada (www.earnscliffe .ca/clients.php).

As the scope and process of governance have changed, so, too, has the character of lobbying. What was once a rather shadowy activity undertaken by well-connected individuals, who often worked for major law firms that relatively few Canadians had heard of, became increasingly complicated and characterized by a broader range of influence strategies and tools. The old model of lobbying—personal communications on a specific matter to a cabinet minister or high-ranking bureaucrat on behalf of a client—morphed into an activity more akin to Sherpas guiding their climbers towards a destination. Personal contacts with key policy-makers continue to be a large part of what lobbying firms sell, but this is reinforced by extensive knowledge and intensive analysis of the policy matters of concern to clients. Under the leadership of Allan Gregg during the 1980s (Gregg is now a principal with Earnscliffe), Decima Research played an important role in this transformation. It offered clients analysis of the public opinion environment in which their activities were situated and that affected the achievement of their goals. The *Decima Quarterly* provided clients with confidential and up-to-date information on public opinion. When Hill + Knowlton, already a world leader in the lobbying industry, acquired Decima the fusion of public opinion expertise, marketing skills, policy analysis, and personal access to government officials was achieved. A sort of one-stop-shopping model for public affairs advice and strategic communication became the new standard and has continued to this day. As social media have become increasingly important, major government consulting firms have added web designers and marketers to their staffs. Their role is to "dissect the wealth of demographic data gathered and made available to advertisers by digital platforms like Facebook, compare it to vulnerable ridings across the country and go to work; using targeted ads, they send tailored pitches to voters they think they can enlist to their client's cause, and begin to build a bloc of supporters."[65]

Most of the activities engaged in by the consultant lobbyists who work for Canada's major government relations firms involve economic affairs. The Lobbyists Registration Act requires that lobbyists identify the general subject matter of their activities as well as the government departments and agencies that they contact on behalf of those they represent. From the beginning of the registration system, "industry," "international trade," and "taxation and finance" have been at or near the top of the list of the most frequent subjects on which lobbyists have plied their trade. "Environment" has moved steadily up the list, reflecting the increasing importance of environmental laws and regulations for corporations and business associations. Matters relating to health policy and Indigenous affairs also have been among the most frequent subjects of lobbying in recent years.

Lobbyists are required to indicate the government institutions they contact or expect to contact and, since 2006, the particular public officials they lobby. The Department of Finance, Innovation, Science and Economic Development Canada (formerly the Department of Industry) and Global Affairs Canada (formerly Foreign Affairs and International Trade), as well as the Privy Council Office (PCO) and the PMO, are perennially among the most targeted institutions. MPs and senators, who were seldom targeted by lobbyists a couple of decades ago, have become among the most frequently contacted of public officials. Indeed, among those institutions most frequently targeted by lobbyists in recent years, the increase in lobbying activity between 2006 and 2018 has been greatest in the case of the PMO and the House of Commons, each of which saw an increase of about 300 per cent in active lobbying registrations, and the Senate, where active registrations increased by over 3,000 per cent (60 to 2,088) during this period (see Box 12.6).[66]

Summing Up

Interest groups and their activities occupy an ambivalent place in Canada and other democracies. On the one hand, the fact of individuals or

Governing Realities

BOX 12.6 The Senate and the Law of Unexpected Consequences

Sometimes the wheel does come full circle, or at least it seems to. In a 1978 book entitled *The Senate: A Lobby from Within*, Colin Campbell made the argument that the business backgrounds and sympathies of many Canadian senators ensured that the corporate community had ready and influential allies inside the Senate, and in particular on its Banking, Trade and Commerce Committee. Contrary to the widely held view that the Senate was a mere chamber for "sober second thought," occasionally tinkering with bills sent from the House of Commons but not doing much more than this, Campbell demonstrated that business-friendly senators had used delay and amendments to secure legislative outcomes preferred by big business and the financial sector. These senators, Campbell argued, were effectively lobbyists on behalf of these corporate interests.

Over the years the Senate's role as a lobby from within diminished. Senators, from time to time and controversially, would flex their constitutional muscles. But the words "lobbying" and "Senate" were rarely, if ever, heard in the same sentence. Once Canada's Lobbying Act was amended in 1996, requiring lobbyists to indicate the target of their communications, what everyone already knew became measureable. Among the institutions of the federal government, the Senate was very far down the list of lobbying targets. Some years there were only a handful of lobbyist communications with senators.

This has changed dramatically. In 2006, when the Conservatives took over from the Liberals as the government, the number of active lobbyist registrations concerning the Senate was 60. In 2018 it was 2,088. Lobbyists are now paying serious attention to the Senate.

What has caused this change is the basis for selecting senators and Justin Trudeau's 2014 decision, going back to when he was in opposition, to expel all Liberal senators from the party's caucus. This was followed, once the Liberals were in power after the 2015 election, by the decision to appoint all new senators as Independents (although whether they decided to remain as Independents has been up to them). Moreover, starting in 2016 the long-standing system of mainly partisan appointment to the Senate was replaced by a merit-based selection process (although the prime minister continues to have the final word). The weakening of party discipline in the Senate and the fact that many senators seem to have taken this independence seriously have encouraged lobbyists to spend more time and resources attempting to convince senators of the merits of their clients' particular cases. When many fewer independents were in the Senate and partisan affiliation determined all but a small proportion of senators' votes, this would have been seen as a waste of time.

It is doubtful that anyone expected, much less hoped, that increased attention from lobbyists would result from the Liberal government's reforms to the Senate. In politics, however, as in other realms of life, the law of unintended consequences may apply. The Senate is far from having the importance of the PMO, the PCO, or the Department of Finance in the eyes of most lobbyists. But as in the days when it was a "lobby from within," it once again matters.

the organizations to which they belong acting in unison to advance ideas or interests that they have in common would appear to be entirely legitimate. At the same time, however, because these ideas or interests are those of only a part of society, we may suspect those who advocate them of being self-interested and motivated by a desire to advance their particular interests at the expense of the public interest. Moreover, while some interest groups operate in plain view most or all of the time, others prefer influence strategies that operate behind the scenes. And then there is the issue of money. We know that some groups have financial resources far superior to what others are able to muster, and these resources, available or not, may be needed to hire lobbyists, pay for advertising campaigns, support the activities of sympathetic think-tanks, finance legal challenges, and in other ways advocate for and defend their special interests.

In response to these concerns, federal and provincial laws have been passed in Canada with the aim of making more transparent those aspects of interest group activities that involve the lobbying of public officials. There are, however, no limits on how much any group may spend on lobbying, advertising, or other activities that aim to promote the goals of their members. The fact that groups have unequal financial resources that may be deployed in the attempt to influence public opinion and public policy may cause some unease. This inequality, however, is inevitable, as is the fact that, in a free society, individuals and groups will pursue their selfish ends and their particular visions of the public interest. To paraphrase James Madison in *The Federalist Papers* No. 10, the solution in a democratic society is not to eliminate the causes that contribute to interest group formation and the inequalities that exist between groups, but to control the negative effects that may sometimes arise from these facts of democratic life. Transparency and a vigilant media are foremost among these controls.

Starting Points for Research

Geoffrey Hale, *Uneasy Partnership: The Politics of Business and Government*, 2nd edn (Toronto: University of Toronto Press, 2018). This leading textbook on business–government relations in Canada provides a solid introduction to the factors that contribute to and limit the political influence of business interests.

***The Hill Times*, https://www.hilltimes.com/.** Daily insider coverage of federal politics, including lots of analysis of interest groups, lobbyists, and the issues on which they are active. You need to subscribe in order to have access, but your university may have an institutional subscription. See also *The Lobby Monitor*, published by The Hill Times Publishing group: http://www.lobbymonitor.ca/about.

Miriam Smith, *Collective Actors in Canadian Political Life* (Toronto: University of Toronto Press, 2018). A well-structured analysis of interest groups and the ways in which they attempt to influence politics and policy.

Review Exercises

1. Go to the issues page at the website of the Canadian Taxpayers Federation (www.taxpayer.com/campaign-and-issues/). Click on "Campaigns and Issues." Identify three petition issues and the arguments made by the Federation. Would you think of signing them? Why or why not?

2. How many organized groups do you belong to or have you belonged to or contributed to in some way? Make a list. Which of these do you think attempt to influence public opinion or policy? If you are having trouble coming up with a list, just think about jobs that you may have had (were they unionized?), churches, clubs, or associations that you may have belonged to, causes to which you might have donated money, petitions (online or traditional) you may have signed, etc.

3. Make a list of the various political activities engaged in by interest groups. Which activities do you consider to be strongly democratic, somewhat democratic, and undemocratic? Explain your reasons.

4. A Member of Parliament—we'll call her "X"—has been active on environmental issues in the House of Commons for 16 years. She has

earned the respect of MPs from all parties in the House and is widely considered to be one of the country's foremost experts on biodiversity and species protection. "X" decides that she will not run for re-election. She is offered a position as the CEO of the David Suzuki Foundation. In this role she will be expected to communicate with some of the elected and non-elected public officials with whom she worked for the previous 16 years. But Canada's Lobbying Act establishes a five-year "cooling off" period during which former politicians like "X" cannot lobby on matters they were involved in while holding office. Does this strike you as right in the case of "X"? Explain.

Media personnel wait for caucus meetings to break in the rotunda at Parliament Hill. Media scrums are held daily in the hallway outside of the House of Commons, where journalists can obtain unprepared (and potentially controversial) comments from politicians. (THE CANADIAN PRESS/Adrian Wyld)

13   The Media

Media impact on modern political life is profound. In this chapter the following aspects of media influence on politics are examined:

- Shaping the political agenda
- What are Canadians watching and listening to?
- Gatekeepers, then and now
- Media bias: nature, sources, and consequences
- Two media worlds: one French, one English
- The media and democracy

Few readers of this book will have met the prime minister of Canada. Even fewer will have met the president of the United States. However, virtually all readers will have ideas about these two leaders and many will have strongly held views on their character, abilities, and performance, despite never having exchanged a word with them. What most of us know and believe about presidents and prime ministers, the facts upon which we form our ideas and judgments concerning them, is based on third-hand information, at best. The same may be said, of course, about how we acquire our knowledge and beliefs about most of the world outside of our own neighbourhoods. We rely on the edited images and information offered on the screens of our tablets, smartphones, computers, and televisions, over the radio waves, and via other media in our information-saturated societies. Indeed, some people even rely on newspapers, magazines, and books!

The fact that our ideas are based largely on third-hand information means that we should pay careful attention to the character of the "hands" that communicate this information. Think for a moment about the typical political story that you might find at a news organization's website or watch on the evening television news. It may involve about 30–90 seconds of images of the prime minister, other cabinet ministers, and opposition leaders and critics, probably in the House of Commons during Question Period or in the foyer near the entrance to the Commons, where journalists and cameras await their daily feeding by politicians exiting Question Period. The story may include brief segments featuring politicians, experts, and interest group spokespersons commenting on the prime minister's remarks. Some portion of the story will consist of the reporter's narration of what is happening and what it means. The news clip has involved a large number of choices by those who assign stories to be covered and those who edit and package the story. This is why the information is described as third-hand. The viewer is not personally a witness to the action or occurrence covered in the story. The reporter's account of what happened is shaped by the decisions of others who have been involved in packaging the story for the television news. Consequently, what the viewer ultimately sees has been influenced by a number of people whose choices contribute to what we call "the news."

Most citizens have always depended on the media for many of their ideas and information about the world they live in. What is more recent is our awareness of the possibilities for selection, distortion, and manipulation in the process of reporting the news and, for that matter, the representation of any aspect of reality. Long-standing fears that media might have a partisan or ideological bias, or

Louis.Roth/Shutterstock

Protesters at the January 2018 Women's March in Toronto decried the proliferation of "fake news" and false claims coming out of the Trump White House. While the Internet has become a key organizing tool for activists across the political spectrum, governments across the world struggle to contend with how social media can be used to influence voters.

that propaganda might subvert democratic politics by depriving citizens of independent sources of information and varied perspectives on their societies, have been joined in recent years by worries that the biases of the media are more deeply rooted and insidious than ever before. The "seductions of language," says media theorist Neil Postman, are trivial compared to the seductions and manipulative powers of the image-based media.[1]

Indeed, all of these fears, as serious as they are, seem to belong to a more innocent time now that we are mired in an era characterized by what has come to be called *fake news*. Selected as the 2017 "word of the year" by Collins Dictionary and popularized by American President Donald Trump as meaning any media report that casts him or his actions in a less than favourable light, it is defined by Collins as "false, often sensational, information disseminated under the guise of news reporting." This phenomenon is not new. What is new, however, is the scale of this activity, the unprecedented difficulty in determining fake from authentic news reporting, and the widespread and deliberate use of fake news for purposes ranging from influencing an election campaign to destabilizing a political system. Also new is the technology through which deliberately false stories are spread. This technology, and in particular social media, appear to make the truth more difficult to discern (see Box 13.1).

The ability of those in the media to report on public affairs as they see fit—within the limits of defamation law and recognizing that the public disclosure of some government information could be prejudicial to legitimate national security or policy-making interests that state officials are expected to protect—is crucial to democracy. If broadcasters, Internet sites, social media, or print outlets can be shut down, censored, or punished because public officials do not like the information they convey, the free discussion of public issues is diminished and democracy suffers. Likewise, when governments get into the business of broadcasting, publishing, and advertising, fears are often expressed that public dollars may be spent on partisan and propagandistic purposes. This, too, may threaten democracy.

Nevertheless, all countries regulate the media system in some ways and to some degree. Historically, this has been particularly true of broadcasting, where the airwaves have been defined as public property throughout the world and where technological reasons existed for restricting the number of broadcasters to protect the quality of the television or radio signals reaching consumers. This traditional argument for regulation has been rendered irrelevant by technologies that rely on cable or satellite transmission and the digitization of data, producing an explosion in the quantity of information and messages that can be sent and received at any time. And this has meant, for better and worse, that "those in the media" now includes practically everyone with an Internet connection or cell phone. The proliferation of websites and blogs on the Internet and the explosion of social media have produced a globalized media universe in which more information and a more diverse range of perspectives are available to more people than at any time in human history. In addition, this flood of information has meant that state regulation of information has become increasingly difficult.

State regulation of the media is not, in the eyes of some critics, the only or even the main threat to freedom of the press and the health of democracy. A more serious threat than state control and censorship, they argue, is the economic censorship and biases that may result when too few owners control too many media organs that account for too great a share of the market. Moreover, they point to the dependence of most mass media organs on advertising as a key factor that may operate to filter out certain forms of controversial, critical, and non-mainstream coverage of political, economic, and social affairs. Whether censorship results from governmental *diktat* or from the working of capitalist markets, they insist, it is censorship just the same.

The relationship of the media to politics is a subject that generates enormous controversy. Before we attempt to make sense of this relationship, let us begin by examining the mass media's role in social learning and the chief characteristics of Canada's media system.

Media Spotlight

BOX 13.1 The Bad News about the Online Spread of True and False Stories

A team of researchers at the Massachusetts Institute of Technology examined 126,000 news stories, some true and some false, tweeted between 2006 and 2017 by 3 million people more than 4.5 million times. In determining whether a story was true the research team relied on six independent fact-checking organizations. These organizations were in agreement over 95 per cent of the time on whether a story was true or false. The researchers then identified what they called a "rumor cascade" related to a particular story. Such a cascade, they write, "begins on Twitter when a user makes an assertion about a topic in a tweet, which could include written text, photos, or links to articles online. Others then propagate the rumor by retweeting it."

What they found was discouraging, to say the least. Here are some excerpts from their article in the 9 March 2018 issue of Science.

It took the truth about six times as long as falsehood to reach 1,500 people and 20 times as long as falsehood to reach a cascade depth* of 10. As the truth never diffused beyond a depth of 10, we saw that falsehood reached a depth of 19 nearly 10 times faster than the truth reached a depth of 10. Falsehood also diffused significantly more broadly and was retweeted by more unique users than the truth at every cascade depth....

False political news traveled deeper and more broadly, reached more people, and was more viral than any other category of false information. False political news also diffused deeper more quickly and reached more than 20,000 people nearly three times faster than all other types of false news reached 10,000 people. Although the other categories of false news reached about the same number of unique users at depths between 1 and 10, false political news routinely reached the most unique users at depths greater than 10. Although all other categories of false news traveled slightly more broadly at shallower depths, false political news traveled more broadly at greater depths,

indicating that more-popular false political news items exhibited broader and more-accelerated diffusion dynamics. Analysis of all news categories showed that news about politics, urban legends, and science spread to the most people, whereas news about politics and urban legends spread the fastest and were the most viral in terms of their structural virality.

False news can drive the misallocation of resources during terror attacks and natural disasters, the misalignment of business investments, and misinformed elections. Unfortunately, although the amount of false news online is clearly increasing, the scientific understanding of how and why false news spreads is currently based on ad hoc rather than large-scale systematic analyses. Our analysis of all the verified true and false rumors that spread on Twitter confirms that false news spreads more pervasively than the truth online. It also overturns conventional wisdom about how false news spreads.... The greater likelihood of people to retweet falsity more than the truth is what drives the spread of false news, despite network and individual factors that favor the truth. Furthermore, although recent testimony before congressional committees on misinformation in the United States has focused on the role of bots in spreading false news, we conclude that human behavior contributes more to the differential spread of falsity and truth than automated robots do. This implies that misinformation-containment policies should also emphasize behavioral interventions, like labeling and incentives to dissuade the spread of misinformation, rather than focusing exclusively on curtailing bots. Understanding how false news spreads is the first step toward containing it.

*A cascade is defined by the MIT researchers as "a rumor-spreading pattern that exhibits an unbroken retweet chain with a common, singular origin. For example, an individual could start a rumor cascade by tweeting a story or claim with an assertion in it, and another individual could independently start a second cascade of the same rumor (pertaining to the same story or claim) that is completely independent of the first, except that it pertains to the same story or claim."

Source: Soroush Vosoughi, Deb Roy, and Sinan Aral, "The Spread of True and False News Online," *Science* 359, no. 6380 (9 Mar. 2018): 1146–51.

"The Pictures in Our Heads"

The media are creators and purveyors of images and information. As such, they play a role in social learning—the process of acquiring knowledge, values, and beliefs about the world and ourselves. This is a role the media share with other agents of social learning: the family, schools, peer groups, and various formal and informal organizations to which one belongs.

While the family and other agents of social learning all contribute to what Walter Lippmann called "the pictures in our heads," none of them rival the media in their impact on the ideas and information we have about political life. Lippmann wrote, "The only feeling that anyone can have about an event that he does not experience is the feeling aroused by his mental image of that event."[2] The contours of modern political discourse are largely determined by the mass media as they process and report on "reality." Moreover, when it comes to matters remote from one's personal experience and daily life—political turmoil in the countries of the Middle East, the latest battle in the United States Congress, or news from Parliament Hill in Ottawa—the media provide the main source of images and information about the events, issues, and personalities involved. Politicians and generals realize the media's importance, which is why one of the first steps taken in any serious *coup d'état* is to seize control of broadcasting and either shut down or muzzle any newspapers, websites, and other media outlets not sympathetic to the new regime.

It has often been remarked that the media do not determine *what we think* so much as *what we think about*. Of course, their ability to do so is neither complete nor unrivalled. Other agents of social learning also influence what we think about and what we believe. Unlike these other agents of social learning, however, the special role of the media is the communication of information about the world around us. Indeed, in eighteenth-century Britain the term *fourth estate* was added to the traditional three—the nobility, the clergy, and the common people—to signify the power of the press. British essayist Thomas Carlyle quotes Edmund Burke as having said, "Whoever can speak, speaking now to the whole nation, becomes a power, a branch of government, with inalienable weight in lawmaking, in all acts of authority."[3]

Such power implies an enormous responsibility. A "free press" has been viewed as a necessary ingredient of democratic politics since the American Revolution. The reasoning is that all other groups and individuals—political parties, candidates for public office, corporations, interest group representatives, and so on—are self-interested. They cannot

John Larter/Artizans

In this political cartoon, is the artist arguing that the media can be distracted from the central issues of a cause by celebrity activists, or about the implicit hypocrisy of using fossil fuels to come to Alberta to protest the exploitation of the oil sands? Or both? Do you follow celebrities on Twitter or other social media, and have they influenced your thinking on an issue?

be counted on to give an objective assessment of their goals and actions. Too often their interests will be best served through concealment, deception, and manipulation—by **propaganda** that espouses a particular ideology or policy through the public dissemination of selected information and/ or misinformation. Only the media, so the argument goes, have an interest in presenting the facts. They may perform this function imperfectly, and particular media organs may have political biases that reflect the views of their owners, the values of their editors, producers, and journalists, or the prejudices of their readership/viewership. But competition ensures that all significant points of view reach the public.

Is this an accurate picture of the media's role in political democracies? How well do the media cover all significant points of view? Who determines "the facts," or are they self-evident? Regardless of what the intentions of those in the media might be, what are the actual consequences for politics of the stories they choose to cover and how they frame these stories? Let us start by examining media consumption in Canada.

What Are Canadians Watching and Listening To?

Canadians are avid consumers of media, most of it viewed on screens. In 2018 Canadians over the age of 18 years spent an average of just over nine hours per day watching, listening, and reading various media. About half of this time was spent online. Watching television was the second most popular medium (34 per cent), at an average of three hours per day, followed by an average of a bit more than an hour listening to radio (14 per cent) and about 10–15 minutes (2 per cent) reading print media. Americans and Britons consume more media, but among major Western democracies only Britons spend more time online than Canadians.[4]

For most Canadians, a relatively small portion of the time they spend watching, reading, and listening to media is devoted to public affairs. We know from television rating services that news broadcasts and other programs that focus on public affairs account for only a handful of the most-viewed programs each week. This is true in both the English- and French-language television markets.[5] The main source of information on television viewing habits in Canada reports that, in recent years, only about 17 per cent of television viewing time is devoted to news and documentary programming.[6] When most people turn to the media, most of the time, it is to be entertained or diverted, to communicate with others, or to be informed about matters that are not about politics, or at least not in a direct or obvious sense.[7]

Increasingly, Canadians consume media online, using their phones, laptops, and other devices that enable them to connect with the Internet. This is true whether they are seeking information on a product or service, watching video, listening to music, or following the news and politics. A 2017 study by the Policy Forum reported that Facebook had an estimated 17 million active users in Canada *every day*. By comparison, the news sites of the CBC and Radio-Canada, the most visited news sites in Canada, had about 15 million visitors *per month*.[8] Traditional media—print newspapers and magazines, and television and radio broadcasters—have lost enormous ground in terms of market shares and revenues to online distributors of news and public affairs coverage.

The decline of print media, particularly newspapers but also magazines, is well known but not always well understood. Many fewer Canadians read a daily newspaper today than a generation ago and dramatically fewer than two generations ago. In 1975 about 80 per cent of Canadian households subscribed to a newspaper. This fell to about half of all households in 1995 and to about one-fifth in 2014 and has continued to fall rapidly. The decline in Canada's magazine industry also has been dramatic. The principal cause for the decline of these print media is well known. Their economic model, based largely on advertising revenues, began to collapse in the 1990s with the rise of online competition. As advertising migrated to online sites, newspapers and magazines attempted to reinvent themselves with digital editions, hoping to recapture some of the subscription and advertising revenue they had lost. Some have done better than others, but the industry as a whole has declined rather dramatically, in Canada as in most countries. To illustrate this, Canadian newspaper industry advertising revenues dropped by about 50 per cent between 2003 and 2015, and by about 55 per cent in the UK and 60 per cent in the US. The decline was less dramatic in France and Germany but still significant, at about 25 and 30 per cent, respectively.

Not only has advertising migrated online, it has gone disproportionately to a handful of information organizations, mainly Google and Facebook. By one estimate, as of 2016 digital news carried by these two organizations accounted for over 80 per cent of the value of all online ads in the Canadian online news market. The consequences for traditional print news organizations has been the elimination of many journalistic positions and pressures to cover news and public affairs—to say nothing of the other subjects they cover—with fewer resources. Traditional television broadcasters have experienced similar challenges from online rivals, notably YouTube but also specialized cable providers. The results, says John Cruickshank, former publisher of the *Toronto Star* and one-time head of CBC News, are significant transformations in what is covered and how issues are framed:

> Because feature writing, beat reporting and investigations are now rarer, the news agenda today is more highly skewed to crime, natural disasters and institutional stories driven by press releases and press conferences. The daily picture of our local and national life provided by Canada's news media is already less complete, less nuanced, less authentic, more sensational, more staged and more negative. As the business crisis worsens, the news media's representation of Canada becomes less reflective of our collective reality.[9]

This pessimistic assessment is not shared by everyone. One might argue that what Cruikshank and others who echo his concerns are lamenting is in fact the decline of a media model that privileged their authority as journalists and the role of the organizations they worked for as gatekeepers of the news (see Box 13.2). The phenomenon of citizen journalism, whereby persons who are not paid professional journalists and who do not work for news organizations generate and circulate stories, images, and analyses challenges this authority. Indeed, in a 2009 Supreme Court of Canada ruling on defamation in news reporting, the Court seemed to acknowledge that the days were past when journalists had a special claim to credibility in reporting the news: "[T]he traditional media are rapidly being complemented by new ways of communicating on matters of public interest, many of them online, which do not involve journalists. These new disseminators of news and information should, absent good reasons for exclusion, be subject to the same laws as established media outlets."[10] The eyewitness videos and images that citizens record and disseminate of natural disasters, crime scenes, demonstrations, personal encounters, and confrontations that are newsworthy, and of other events that in times past would have been covered, if at all, only by traditional journalists, have become commonplace in news reporting. "It's a normalised part of the news cycle now," writes Einar Thorsen, author of several studies on citizen journalism. "We expect eyewitness footage during any terrorist attack or disaster."[11]

It is clear that Canadians, and indeed to varying degrees national populations throughout the developed and developing world, rely increasingly on media platforms other than traditional print and broadcasting for information and understanding of news and public affairs. A 2018 Pew Research Center survey found that 42 per cent of Canadians said they went to such social media sites as Facebook, Twitter, or Instagram at least once per day for news and 27 per cent said they went to such sites for news several times per day. Canadians between the ages of 18 and 29 were over twice as likely as older Canadians to rely on social media for news, a pattern found to varying degrees in virtually all developed and developing countries.[12] These numbers do not mean that Canadians, including younger members of the population, are not also reading newspapers and magazines, either in their hard copy or digital versions, going to the websites

Media Spotlight

BOX 13.2 Is Media Decline Old News?

Advertising revenue migrating to new media. Journalists losing their jobs in droves. Less coverage of local news. It all adds up to a decline in the quality of news and public affairs coverage and, consequently, a weakening of the information life blood on which democracy depends.

This probably sounds like a rather familiar narrative. But the year is 1954. Those lamenting the changes taking place at what must have seemed a dizzying speed were in the newspaper industry. The threat, as they saw it, came from broadcasting, especially television. The decline of print journalism would end up being gradual by today's standards. But within a decade more people relied mainly on television for national and international news than relied on newspapers.

In a 1954 speech to the National Editorial Association in the United States, the publisher of the *Tulsa Tribune* described the plight of small and medium-sized daily papers such as his. The *Tribune* had about 500 employees and required 18,000 tons of newsprint and several delivery trucks to distribute its paper each day. "At the same time in television," he said, "we see a literal newcomer deliver a picture with voice accompaniment to the same area, with thirty-three employees." Politicians and other public figures were quick to recognize the ascendance of broadcasting. David Davies writes:

> President Dwight D. Eisenhower noted in 1955 that television was becoming more important than newspapers in fostering understanding of public issues. Broadcasting, Eisenhower said, could engage and involve viewers to a degree that cold print never could. "In many ways therefore the effect of [the television] industry in swaying public opinion, and I think, particularly about

of broadcasters, and in other ways going directly to the sources of the news content that makes its way onto social media. But virtually every study concludes that they do so with decreasing frequency.

What is not well understood about the decline of traditional media is that they have provided—and at this writing still provide—most of the news and public affairs content that appears online at such news aggregators as Facebook and Google and that is tweeted and retweeted via Twitter. On any typical day virtually all of the stories under the categories of headlines, national news, world news, and business will be drawn from newspapers or television and radio broadcasters. The category of technology news is one where the overwhelming dominance of content from traditional media is somewhat less. Without traditional media the news aggregators that Canadians and many other national populations have come to depend on would not have content or, more precisely, they would have to rely on content that viewers and readers might find to be less reliable. "[W]here will Apple, Google and Facebook get their news?" asks Canadian media expert Ken Goldstein. He acknowledges that "there are numerous online-only [news] start-ups, often specialized in nature, but few, if any, provide the kind of journalistic scope of our current local daily newspapers or local broadcast television."[13]

Gatekeepers: Then and Now

It is often said that the media perform a gatekeeping function. This may be defined as "the process by which the billions of messages that are available in the world get cut down and transformed into the hundreds of messages that reach a given person on a given day."[14] This understanding of gatekeeping as a process, argues Stuart Soroka, alerts us to the "strong possibility that there will be *systematic* differences between news content burning questions of the moment, may be even greater than the press.[15]

The analogy between the transition that already was taking place in the 1950s and that which has been unfolding since the beginning of the digital revolution in information technology is imperfect. Nevertheless, it should prompt us to ask whether the hand-wringing about the demise of print media and traditional broadcasting is influenced at least in part by the vested interests that have done well under a model that finds itself unable to compete for advertising dollars with online news aggregators like Facebook, Google, and the *Huffington Post*, and by a sort of nostalgia for the "good old days" when a handful of television broadcasters, along with a small number of major newspapers, operated as gatekeepers when it came to the news that citizens received at their door and on their television screens.

There are, of course, genuine concerns about the online media model. The content has to come from somewhere, and it remains the case that for coverage of news and public affairs, that "somewhere" continues to be mainly the traditional media. So-called "fake news" is much more of a problem than it was when the print journalism/broadcasting model was relied on by the vast majority of people for their news about everything from their neighbourhood to the other side of the world. The privacy concerns that have arisen, particularly in connection with social media, simply did not exist when people relied on newspapers and broadcasting for the news. And whether citizen journalism and other non-traditional methods of collecting, interpreting, and communicating news about politics and society will be able to provide citizens with what they need to make informed decisions continues to be a matter of heated debate.

and the real world." He identifies three principal sources of such differences:

- *Organization-level factors*. These include those characteristics of the news organization in which one works such as costs, deadlines, and the process by which stories are assigned and edited.
- *Story-level factors*. Among these are the location of the story (is it minutes away, on the other side of the world, or somewhere in between, and does the news organization have personnel and technical facilities where the story is?), and visual aspects of the story (is it complicated or unfamiliar for audiences and, if so, can it be framed in a way that minimizes ambiguity and whatever else might be confusing for viewers?).
- *Extra-organizational or professional factors*. This last possible source of difference between how stories are told and the reality of whatever is being explained involves ideas about

what is newsworthy, as well as the norms and values of those who make decisions about what to report, how prominently to cover it, and how to tell the story (personal interest; local, national, or international importance; social, political, or other significance).[16]

The choices made by media gatekeepers are not random. Several factors influence how reality is represented and how politics and public affairs are reported by the media. To switch metaphors, these factors may be understood as a series of filters that are more likely to let through certain information and images than others. These filters operate at the level of selection—what is covered and how prominently—and also at the level of representation, communicating the meaning of the story. Much of the work on the media's gatekeeping function has focused on the question of whether what Soroka calls the "systematic differences between news content and the real world" involves a persistent and significant ideological bias. Many scholars have argued that, on the whole, information and images that threaten the standing and interests of dominant social and economic groups are less likely to make it through these media filters than those that are fairly orthodox and non-menacing. Many others have made the opposite claim, arguing that the media tend to have a liberal bias against capitalism and large corporations, traditional religion and the values associated with it, and conservative political parties and policies.[17]

The decline of traditional media and, therefore, of their role as gatekeepers is a process that has been underway for many years. For example, at the end of 2018 there were only three Canadian newspaper journalists who covered American politics and Canada–US relations from Washington, DC, and about twice that number affiliated with major Canadian television broadcasters. Altogether their number was roughly the size of the BBC's United States and Canada bureau (none of whose correspondents is stationed in Canada), this may seem rather astounding in view of the size and importance, particularly for Canada, of the economic relationship between the two countries, to say nothing about the cultural, environmental, and security aspects of this relationship. Moreover, and perhaps not surprisingly, Canadians are more likely than any national population to be interested in American news, 28 per cent saying that they follow American news very closely (2018).[18] This level of popular interest is not reflected in the resources devoted to the subject on site by Canadian media outlets.

But perhaps this no longer matters. Does a journalist, producer, or editor have to be physically present in a place in order to cover it adequately and in a manner that is pertinent for his or her national audience? In September 2018 the US-based journalism organization, Politico, launched a daily newsletter on Canada–US affairs targeted at "professionals with a stake in the Canada–U.S. relationship and the integrated border economy." At the time of this launch Politico's website had about 25 million visitors per month, including about half a million from Canada. The Canada–US newsletter's editor, formerly a journalist with *Maclean's*, explained why this new service would provide superior coverage compared to that provided by the small number of journalists working for traditional Canadian media in Washington: "We

have 250 reporters at Politico, so we are drawing on this incredible resource that we have and we are picking and choosing the stories that we think matter to Canada. . . . We can go deep on the Congress—that's not something the Canadian correspondents usually do, because they are not well sourced on the Hill. That's something that we have in spades at Politico."[19]

The conversation on the decline of traditional media includes fears that coverage of local affairs will decline as the number of small and medium-sized community newspapers continues to shrink and as local news broadcasts disappear. There is little doubt that both of these trends have been underway for years. In a 2018 study by the Public Policy Forum, 20 Canadian newspaper markets across all regions of the country were examined to determine what changes had occurred in the quantity and quality of local news and civic affairs in particular. The researchers found that "the number of English-language newspaper articles published in the communities we examined decreased by almost half between 2008 and 2017, while the number of articles specifically reporting on civic affairs declined by more than a third." They also found that within the dwindling coverage of civic affairs, the number of articles that identified opposing views, provided historical context, included statistics or polling data, or that offered illustrative examples also declined, although not dramatically. The study concludes that "the information that reporter-based news organizations provide to inform democratic choice, hold officials to account, and allow communities to know themselves better is in sharp decline."[20]

The plight of traditional print journalism, and in particular the decline of local newspapers, has produced two very different responses. Those in the industry or sympathetic to it have called for government intervention. The creation of a journalism fund that would support individual print journalists was proposed by the industry's association, News Media Canada. The Public Policy Forum proposed the creation of a media fund that would subsidize newspapers through a tax on foreign media companies selling online subscriptions in Canada. The House of Commons Standing Committee on Canadian Heritage proposed tax credits for newspapers investing in their digital editions. In 2017 the Liberal government seemed open to providing more money to newspapers and Canadian magazines through the Canadian Periodical Fund, which has provided grants to Canadian print media since 2009. *Maclean's*, for example, received about $1.5 million in the fiscal year 2017–18, and *Chatelaine*'s English and French editions received about $1.2 million and $570,000, respectively, that same year. In short, taxpayer subsidies for Canadian-owned print media and the abolishment of advertising tax breaks for non-Canadian online companies such as Google and Facebook were among the preferred options of those who believed that the proper response to the challenge posed by newer media is government intervention (see Box 13.3).

Writing in 2018, when there was much anticipation that the Liberal government might well adopt some of the protectionist measures mentioned above, economist William Watson acknowledged the important role played by those who report and interpret the news: "I can't imagine a world without my daily fix of news and opinion," Watson said, adding, "I assume there are lots of people out there like me, and so tend to think that in some way or other our demand for these things will end up being satisfied, albeit in formats and through delivery mechanisms we can't yet anticipate and which, in fact, may only become evident once newspapers have suffered whatever their ultimate fate is to be."[21] The Trudeau government did not agree. In its Economic Statement of 21 November 2018, one year before the expected date of the next federal election, it announced subsidies of roughly $600 million over five years for Canada's media sector, including newspapers, magazines, and local news outlets.

In point of fact, Canadians have long subsidized their media system. Most of the time this has been to ensure that the amount of **Canadian content** in that system would be greater than in the absence of such support or in order to protect Canadian-owned media outlets from American competition. As John Aird famously remarked at the birth of the country's broadcasting system, in Canada it is a choice between the state or the United States. Since the 1930s Canadian governments have done quite a lot with taxpayer dollars to promote the production and diffusion of Canadian content in the country's broadcasting system. Protectionist measures for Canadian print media through lower postal rates for Canadian magazines and banning taxes on the Canadian editions of American-based magazines began in the 1960s. Despite such policies, the overwhelming majority of magazine sales in Canada were of American magazines whose prices were higher than they would otherwise have been because of these protectionist measures. So, too, in the case of broadcasting. Much more Canadian content was produced and broadcast than would have been the case in the absence of the CBC/Radio-Canada and licensing requirements on all broadcasters. But viewer preferences, at least in English-speaking Canada, have always been for American programming.

The nationalist concern that there be Canadian content in the country's media system has been joined by the newer fear that the demise of traditional media will jeopardize the information life blood on which democracy relies. Most Canadians don't share this concern. A 2017 Abacus poll found that 86 per cent of respondents believed that if their local newspaper went out of business they would still get the news they needed. The poll also found that 56 per cent of Canadians disagreed that "the federal government has a responsibility to do something to make sure there are strong local media serving communities across Canada."[22]

Media Bias?

Those who report the news are often accused by conservatives and business people of having liberal-left and anti-business biases. They are more likely, it is argued, to favour stories and groups that challenge established authority. The CBC in general and some of its programs in particular have occasionally been accused of ideological bias against conservatism, big business, and globalization. Similar charges have been heard in the United States, where Republicans, conservatives, some religious groups, and business interests have often accused the major networks, and journalists generally, of having liberal biases.

The evidence for this claim is mixed. Studies done in the United States a generation ago found that workers in the media typically gave more liberal responses to such statements as "Government should substantially reduce the income gap between rich and poor." The researchers concluded that "leading

Media Spotlight

BOX 13.3 "Gatekeepers in a World in Which There May Be No Gates"

For more than 50 years the Canadian Radio-television and Telecommunications Commission (CRTC) has imposed Canadian content requirements on radio and television broadcasters as part of the conditions under which they are licensed to send their signals through the airwaves or via cable. These content requirements are generated by a concern that, without them, Canadian stories, news and public affairs, music, and so on would find it difficult to compete against foreign—read American—offerings. The content rules established and enforced by the CRTC involve a point system whereby Canadian-ness is determined by whether a Canadian wrote the music, performed in the song, starred in the television program, directed the film, produced the series, etc., or if it was recorded or filmed in Canada. This has led some critics to claim that the Canadian content rules have always been chiefly about generating and protecting jobs and business activity in Canada's television, radio, and film industries and not mainly about Canadian content per se.

YouTube, Netflix, Spotify, and all the other media that rely on the Internet represent a full-frontal challenge to the traditional regulatory model. In 2013, the CRTC's vice-chairman, Peter Menzies, expressed the view that Canada's broadcast regulators "can no longer define ourselves as gatekeepers in a world in which there may be no gates." Instead, he argued, regulation needs to "act as an enabler of Canadian expression, rather than as a protector."[23]

In a 2018 report entitled "Harnessing Change," the CRTC indicated that the future should look much like the past. It called for the taxation and regulation of all Internet communication in Canada, regardless of where it originates. Peter Menzies, who had left the CRTC, described

the report's vision this way: "[E]very podcast and audio-video news report from anywhere should be subject to the scrutiny of steely-eyed Ottawa-Gatineau bureaucrats as they lure the world once beyond the regulator's grasp into 'the system.' And to ensure change is not just harnessed but milked for the care and feeding of Cancon creators, those same bureaucrats insist that a tax be levied on the country's Internet Service Providers and paid by—you got it—everyone in the country with an internet subscription."[24]

In 2017 the Canadian government came to an agreement with Netflix whereby that company agreed to invest $500 million over five years producing Canadian content. Canadian subscribers will pay for this in increased Netflix subscription costs. Steven Globerman, for many decades one of Canada's most astute analysts of media, suggests that Netflix's willingness to invest in Canadian content may have been motivated by a desire to avoid the tax-and-regulate model that the CRTC proposed in 2018.[25]

Regulating Internet communications is not a dilemma faced exclusively by Canadian policy-makers. The European Union, the United States, and other jurisdictions throughout the world are struggling to come to grips with how to regulate what has become, for an increasing number of people, the principal medium through which they divert and inform themselves and communicate with others. But unlike most of these other jurisdictions, where the chief concerns involve whether service providers should be able to charge more for faster access and issues of privacy and personal data protection, Canada's telecommunications regulators remain fixated on continuing the policy of protecting the producers of Canadian culture. Should they be?

journalists seem to inhabit a symbolic universe which is quite different from that of businessmen, with implications for the manner in which they report the news to the general public."[26] Several more recent American studies have confirmed

that those in the media, particularly the electronic media, tend to be much more liberal than members of the general population. For example, since 1971 the School of Journalism at Indiana State University has surveyed journalists on a number of matters, including their party identification. Those identifying with the Democratic Party have always outnumbered those identifying with the Republican Party by a significant margin. The School's latest survey, carried out in 2013, found that American journalists were four times more likely to say they were Democrats than Republicans.[27]

The few empirical studies of journalistic bias that have been undertaken in Canada appear to find that, as in the United States, those in the Canadian media tend to be more liberal than the general population and that the ideological proclivities of journalists affect the way news stories are reported. These are the main conclusions of what is probably the most systematic study of Canadian journalists' values and beliefs to date, based on a survey by Barry Cooper and Lydia Miljan of 270 electronic and print journalists and a sample of the general public (804 respondents).[28] They argue that English-Canadian journalists differ from their audiences and readerships in several ways:

- Journalists are less religious than the public, 57 per cent saying that they did not espouse a particular religious faith and 32 per cent saying that they definitely believed in God compared to 39 per cent (no religious affiliation) and 56 per cent (definitely believe in God) for the university-educated public.
- Although the ideas of private-sector journalists on the desirability of capitalism, free markets, and private property are broadly the same as those of the general public, the views of the public-sector CBC journalists are significantly to the left.
- The public is more conservative on social issues than are those in the media. For example, journalists are more likely than the general public to believe that abortion should be considered a moral and legal right and a much greater share of the public than journalists believes that gay and lesbian issues receive too much media attention.
- Journalists are considerably more likely than the general public to vote for the NDP, the highest level of NDP support by far being among CBC radio journalists.

Miljan and Cooper's conclusions are broadly similar to those reached by Marsha Barber and Ann Rauhala in their study of Canadian television news directors. In particular, Barber and Rauhala found that news directors were less religious than the general public and somewhat more left-leaning in their party preferences (in particular among those who worked for the CBC).[29] Both the Miljan/Cooper and Barber/Rauhala surveys were carried out almost two decades ago. Unfortunately, no similar survey allowing us to compare the politically relevant attitudes and behaviours of those in the media to the general population has been undertaken since then.

Studies of media bias in election coverage have arrived at mixed conclusions, some of them concluding that there was clear evidence of bias against the major right-of-centre party[30] and others finding no clear evidence of media bias towards or against any of the main parties.[31] A 2015 analysis of Twitter behaviour among members of the parliamentary press corps in Ottawa found that journalists covering national politics tended to skew towards the Liberal Party over the Conservative Party, notwithstanding that the Conservatives formed the government at the time. Much of this lean towards the Twitter accounts of Liberal MPs was due to the Twitter preferences of CBC journalists.[32] At the same time, however, when Indigenous protests associated with the Idle No More movement dominated the Canadian media landscape in early 2013, many opinion leaders in the Indigenous community and critics on the left charged that the Canadian media, including major newspapers and broadcasters and several of the country's most prominent journalists, were guilty of conservative, anti-Indigenous biases. Clearly, not everyone agrees with the claim that the sympathies of Canada's media system are on the left.

A rather different set of questions about the beliefs and attitudes of journalists was put to a sample of 352 Canadian journalists in 2016 by a team of researchers from the University of Ottawa and Ryerson University.[33] Respondents were asked about various journalistic roles and how important they felt each was. The vast majority of journalists agreed that classically objective roles—"report things as they are"; "educate the audience"; "tell stories about the world"; "be a detached observer"; "provide information people need to make political decisions"—were extremely or very important. At the same time, a significant share of journalists agreed that "promote tolerance and cultural diversity" (61 per cent), "motivate people to participate in political activity" (36 per cent), and "advocate for social change" (36 per cent) were significant journalistic roles. Although this does not tell us anything directly about the ideological leanings of the journalists who responded to these questions, it does suggest that a significant percentage of those in the profession do not see themselves as passive gatekeepers.

The Ottawa/Ryerson survey also asked journalists how much trust they had in various institutions. Levels of trust in the police, the military, and religious leaders were significantly lower than were those of the Canadian population as a whole. About one-quarter of the journalists surveyed expressed a great deal or complete trust in the military and the police, and only about 12 per cent expressed these levels of trust in religious leaders. Surveys taken at roughly the same time (2016) showed levels of trust in the military that were about three times greater among members of the general public, more than twice as great when it came to the police, and several times greater in the case of religious leaders. Again, it may not be safe to conclude from this that those in the media tend to be more left-leaning than the general public. It is, however, safe to conclude that they are more skeptical about most institutions and those who run them.[34]

Two Solitudes?

Canada's media system has never been an important factor contributing to the political unity of the country. The reason has to do with language. From the earliest days of print journalism to the present, English- and French-speaking Canadians have read different newspapers and magazines, listened to and watched different radio and television programs, and often have preferred different films. These differences continue to be reflected in their online media consumption. None of this would matter, or perhaps not so much, if the content of what they read, watch, and listen to is broadly the same. But it is not.

Canada is not unique in this respect. Belgium has long had two media silos, one French and the other Flemish, with relatively little crossover between these language communities in terms of their media consumption habits. Spain is another case where citizens are divided by their media system, Catalans having an overwhelming preference for broadcasting and print media in their own language. In the case of both Belgium and Spain, this media divide between linguistic communities is not without political consequences. The Flemish media in Belgium and the Catalan media in Spain have contributed significantly to the sense of national identity in their respective ethnolinguistic communities and to the political strength of separatist movements in each country.

Even in countries where the vast majority of people read, watch, and listen to media in the same language, the media system's influence on politics may be divisive. In recent times the best-known example of this has been the United States. The increasing polarization of American politics since the 1990s has been reflected, but also fuelled to some degree, by a media system that has become increasingly divided along ideological lines,[35] to the point where many in the left-leaning media, with some justification, have regularly referred to the Fox cable news network as Trump TV. Recent research shows that ideological polarization in the news media is also quite high in several European democracies, although in no case does it appear to be as great as in the United States.[36] It is generally and rather uncritically believed that social media are a major factor contributing to this polarization, facilitating the clustering of individuals in echo chambers where they are exposed to information and images that confirm their political predispositions and insulate them from other views. According to some recent research, this view is not supported by the facts (see Box 13.4).

The degree of ideological dispersion between major sources of news and public affairs coverage in Canada is considerably less than in the United States. The divisive effects of the Canadian media system are produced not so much by ideology as by the fact that the two main language communities are exposed to significantly different content. This contributes to what the philosopher Charles Taylor has called the "misrecognition" of each community

Media Spotlight

BOX 13.4 Don't Blame Political Polarization on Social Media

The argument against echo chambers is well documented: helped by social media algorithms, we are increasingly choosing to interact in safe spaces, with people who think and act like us—effectively preaching our opinions to the converted. As a result, this behaviour is distorting our world view and, in the process, our ability to compromise, which in turn stimulates political polarization. However, new Oxford University research suggests that social media and the Internet are not the root of today's fragmented society, and echo chambers may not be the threat they are perceived to be. In fact, most people use multiple media outlets and social media platforms, meaning that only a small proportion of the population, at most, is influenced by echo chambers.

Using a random sample of adult Internet users in the UK, researchers at the Oxford Internet Institute and the University of Ottawa examined people's media choices, and how much they influenced their interaction with echo chambers, against six key variables: gender, income, ethnicity, age, breadth of media use, and political interest. The findings reveal that rather than encouraging the use and development of echo chambers, the breadth of media available actually makes it easier for people to avoid them.

Dr Grant Blank, co-author and research fellow at the Oxford Internet Institute, said:

Whatever the causes of political polarisation today, it is not social media or the internet. If anything, most people use the internet to broaden their media horizons. We found evidence that people actively look to confirm the information that they read online, in a multitude of ways. They mainly do this by using a search engine to find offline media and validate political information. In the process they often encounter opinions that differ from their own and as a result whether they stumbled across the content passively or use their own initiative to search for answers while double checking their "facts," some changed their own opinion on certain issues.

Dr Elizabeth Dubois, co-author and assistant professor at the University of Ottawa, said: "Our results show that most people are not in a political echo chamber. The people at risk are those who depend on only a single medium for political news and who are not politically interested: about 8 per cent of the population. However, because of their lack of political engagement, their opinions are less formative and their influence on others is likely to be comparatively small."

Source: "Social Media and Internet Not Cause of Political Polarization, New Research Suggests," 22 Feb. 2018, https://phys.org/news/2018-02-social-media-internet-political-polarization.html#jCp.

---

by the other. It involves a failure to understand the identity, perspectives, concerns, and aspirations of the other. This failure, Taylor argues, may have serious consequences for relations between groups and for politics: "[A] person or group of people can suffer real damage, real distortion, if the people or society around them mirror back to them a confining or demeaning or contemptible picture of themselves. Nonrecognition or misrecognition can inflict harm, can be a form of oppression, imprisoning someone in a false, distorted, and reduced mode of being."[37]

Taylor's argument that oppression and a "reduced mode of being" may result from improper recognition

may seem a bit extreme. Nevertheless, the idea that misrecognition can get in the way of one group understanding another, as has so often been true of French–English relations over the span of Canadian history, is indisputable. This failure of mutual understanding may be attributed to various causes, but among them surely must be included the rift between the media systems of French- and English-speaking Canada. A study of news content on the French and English television networks of the CBC in the 1970s found that the overlap in terms of stories covered was often below 20 per cent. The study's author, Arthur Siegel, observed, "The pattern of content tends to reinforce value differences along linguistic lines. . . . In this sense, the news content patterns can be seen as not contributing in any significant way to a shared sense of Canadian identity."[38] But even when the same stories have been covered, the interpretations often have been very different depending on the linguistic audience. David Taras is among those who found that news coverage of the Meech Lake and Charlottetown accords on constitutional reform, leading up to the referendum of 1992, was sharply different on the two sides of the language divide.[39] Those who follow political news in both French- and English-speaking Canada know that this pattern of significantly different content and interpretation has continued down to the present day. The translation of English-language

news programming into French, and vice versa, has been proposed by some as a bridge to overcome the problem of misrecognition.[40] This already occurs to a significant extent on the Cable Public Affairs Channel (CPAC), but the audience for this channel is very small.

If the news and public affairs worlds of French- and English-speaking Canada are quite different, what these two communities watch for entertainment and diversion is no less so. In a typical week all of the most viewed entertainment programs in the English-language market and, indeed, usually at least nine of the 10 most viewed programs of any sort will be American. All of the most viewed programs in the French market are likely to be programs created in French in Quebec. Many of the

While he may be less familiar to English Canadians, Guy A. Lepage (centre), host of *Tout le monde en parle*, is a household name in Quebec. Lepage is pictured here with Guillaume Lesperance and Jacques Primeau at the 27th annual Les Gemeaux awards gala in Montreal, where their show won a viewer's choice award.

THE CANADIAN PRESS IMAGES/Graham Hughes

Media Spotlight

BOX 13.5 *Tout le monde en parle* (in Quebec, at least)

This Sunday night at around 8 p.m., it's a safe bet that hundreds of thousands of Quebecers, perhaps a million or more, will turn on their TVs or pop open a browser window to watch two former comedians share a bottle of wine with entertainers, athletes, politicians, citizen activists, and the occasional hypnotist. The resulting conversations will light up francophone Twitter and become fodder for Monday-morning water-cooler conversations across Quebec. Journalists for major morning papers and websites will analyze the show as if it were a leaders' debate.

The talk show in question, *Tout le monde en parle* (Everyone's Talking about It), has no real equivalent in English Canada. Influential columnist Patrick Lagacé has called it "Quebec's TV confessional." Public figures submit to a long line of questioning from former comedian Guy A. Lepage and his sidekick Dany Turcotte, the *fou du roi* (court jester). The Radio-Canada show's mix of wide-ranging interviews, spontaneous debates, off-colour humour, quirky rituals (Turcotte gives each guest a personalized one-liner written on a card at the end of their appearance), and five-hour recording sessions with strategically placed alcohol makes it unique.

"We have nothing like it in English Canada, and it can make or break a politician," says Brad Lavigne, a former NDP strategist who was with the party when Jack Layton made a much-hyped appearance on the show in 2011. "It had a tremendous impact on our [party's] campaign."

"The [guest list] balances people who have been in the news in the past week and people who are less high-profile," says Université de Montréal political communication professor Frédéric Bastien. "Most of the [guests] are from art and culture, but there's usually at least one public affairs item, with a politician, an academic, or a journalist who has broken an important story."

Tout le monde en parle ... was originally adapted from a concept that had been successful in France. Its first season was in 2004, and its renewal for a fifteenth season was announced on air on 11 March. "After 14 seasons, it's still drawing about a million people [each week]," says Bastien. "Considering the fragmented media landscape we have, that's exceptional. It's a huge opportunity if you're a politician or a spokesperson for a cause."

Source: Ruby Irene Pratkar, "The Most Important TV Show in Quebec Has No Equivalent in English Canada," *Canadaland*, 22 Mar. 2018, http://www.canadalandshow.com/tout-le-monde-en-parle-the-most-important-tv-show-in-quebec/.

most popular television programs in the French-language market are virtually unknown in English-speaking Canada (see Box 13.5). Reinforced by the very different teaching of history, culture, and social studies in Quebec compared to the predominantly English-speaking provinces, the different viewing preferences of English- and French-speaking Canadians amplify the distance between the two solitudes. These differences make it less likely that members of these two language communities will share the same stories, myths, and cultural symbols. It would probably be too strong to say that this contributes to national disunity, although this claim has sometimes been made.

The Media and Democracy

If a nation expects to be ignorant and free, it expects what never was and never will be. . . . The people cannot be safe without information. Where the press is free, and every man able to read, all is safe.[41]

In Canada, as in many countries throughout the world, concerns are frequently expressed that the media do not provide citizens with the information they need in order to understand public affairs and make informed choices. Fears that "fake news" may be mistaken for real news—that is, news that is factually accurate and verifiable—is only the tip of this iceberg of doubt about the quality of what the media offers. Job losses among traditional journalists, particularly in the newspaper and local television and radio broadcasting sectors, have contributed to worries that the quality of news and public affairs coverage will suffer, or that it has already suffered and will continue to decline. The rise of citizen journalism, celebrated by some as a more democratic, responsive, and civically engaged genre of reporting, is lamented by others. Morley Safer, a Canadian-born journalist who spent most of his career working for *60 Minutes*, CBS's iconic public affairs program, expressed the view of many traditional journalists in saying, "I would trust citizen journalism as much as I would trust citizen surgery. . . . The blogosphere is no alternative, crammed as it is with ravings and manipulations of every nut with a keyboard."[42] Social media is derided and mistrusted by many, at the same time as Canadians and other national populations increasingly rely on them, and Internet news aggregators have been accused of undermining the business model on which serious journalism has been based.

At the same time, however, Canadians continue to express considerable confidence in their media system, or at least in parts of it. According to a 2018 IPSOS survey, about two-thirds of Canadians said they had a great deal (11 per cent) or a fair amount (54 per cent) of trust and confidence in traditional news media. That survey also found that Canadians still appear to believe in the watchdog role of the media, being about four times more likely to say that if a senior government official says that a news report is not accurate, they are more likely to believe the news report.[43] About six out of 10 Canadians have a positive opinion of journalists (19 per cent very and 44 per cent somewhat positive).[44] These levels of trust appear to be much higher than in Britain, where a 2017 IPSOS-Mori poll found that only one in four respondents believed that journalists could generally be trusted to tell the truth,[45] or in the United States, where a Gallup poll in that same year found that only about one in three said they had a great deal or a fair amount of trust in traditional media to report the news fully, accurately, and fairly.[46]

Canadians, however, are somewhat more doubtful when it comes to the veracity of online media, notwithstanding that for many years they have been turning in droves to online sources of news. The 2019 Edelman Report on Canada found that about seven in 10 respondents expressed fear that disinformation and fake news could be used as a weapon of propaganda. That same survey found that while 71 per cent of Canadians expressed confidence in traditional media, confidence fell to 49 per cent in the case of online-only media and 31 per cent in the case of social media.[47] This mistrust and the concerns that are so frequently heard about social media make it easy to overlook the fact that criticisms of the media's relationship to democracy are as old as the dawn of independent newspapers in the late eighteenth century. In Canada, independent newspapers—papers that were not mere information extensions of colonial governments—emerged in the first decades of the nineteenth century. These earliest papers were closely tied to particular political parties and interests and would not have come close to meeting contemporary standards of journalistic objectivity that cause so many persons today to lament media bias and "fake news." It would not be until the twentieth century that print media, when commercial advertising became the major source of newspaper revenue, would be loosened from the ties of partisanship to and influence by the state.[48]

Concern with partisan biases would be replaced in the late twentieth century by worries that too few owners controlled too much of the newspaper industry. The 1970 Special Senate Committee on Mass Media was categorical in its condemnation of concentrated media ownership: "this country should no longer tolerate a situation where the public interest in so vital a field as information [is] dependent on the greed or goodwill of an extremely privileged group of businessmen."[49] The *Report* added that "*all transactions that increase concentration of ownership in the mass media are undesirable and contrary to the public interest—unless shown to be otherwise*".[50] A decade later, the federal government launched the Royal Commission on Newspapers to investigate what many believed was a worsening situation in the newspaper industry. Its *Report* was no more optimistic than that of the Senate in 1970. "[I]ndustrial conglomerates produce poor newspapers,"[51] the Royal Commission concluded, referring to what had been an ongoing process not only of increasingly concentrated ownership but of the acquisition of newspapers by conglomerates with investments in other industries. "In a country that has allowed so many newspapers to be owned by a few conglomerates, freedom of the press means, in itself, only that enormous influence without responsibility is conferred on a handful of people. For the heads of such organizations to justify their position by appealing to the principle of freedom of the press is offensive to intellectual honesty."[52] As critics pointed out, however, the Commission failed to provide any hard evidence that the quality of news and public affairs coverage in chain newspapers and those owned by conglomerates was inferior to that in the single-owner newspaper that appeared to be its perhaps nostalgic model for how news ought to be reported.

Television broadcasting, which by the 1970s had become the dominant medium relied on by Canadians for their information and images of the country and the world, also was accused of contributing to the decline of the information life blood on which democracy relies. These criticisms took a number of forms, most of which were not peculiar to Canada. Privately owned television, whose profitability depended on being able to sell advertising time, was (and continues to be) roundly criticized for devoting fewer resources to the serious coverage of news and public affairs and, when these matters were covered, doing so in a shallow and often sensationalized manner, relying on celebrity reporters and news anchors and formats that came to be called "infotainment." Another charge was that concentrated ownership in the broadcasting industry and cross-media ownership reduced the number of voices in the marketplace of ideas about public affairs. A third claim was that the corporations that dominated the broadcasting industry imposed a sort of soft censorship on how the news and politics would be framed not by directly intervening in the selection of stories and how they would be told, but

indirectly through the selection of executives whose chief concern would be their corporate bottom line.

A fourth criticism shifted the focus away from the owners of television broadcasters and their industry's model to the intersection of technology and human nature. Aldous Huxley, the author of *Brave New World*, was one of the first to suggest that the rationalist faith in the importance of a free press for democracy, as well as in the capacity of educated, informed citizens to distinguish between facts and falsehoods, was founded on wishful thinking. Huxley wrote, "In regard to propaganda the early advocates of universal literacy and a free press envisaged only two possibilities: the propaganda might be true, or it might be false. They did not foresee what in fact has happened, above all in our Western capitalist democracies—the development of a vast mass communications industry, concerned in the main neither with the true nor the false, but with the unreal, the more or less totally irrelevant. In a word, they failed to take into account man's almost infinite appetite for distractions."[53] (See Box 13.6.)

No one seriously disagrees with Thomas Jefferson's observation, quoted at the beginning of this section, that the quality of democracy depends on citizens having access to reliable information. In recent years many have questioned whether the media can be counted on to perform this vital role. However, questions about how well the media report news and public affairs are not new. Moreover, the belief that the media are letting Canadians down, a belief embodied in such recent influential critiques as the Policy Forum's 2017 report *The Shattered Mirror* is not unchallenged. Citizen journalism and a media system that is more open, less hierarchical, and in which traditional media elites and organizations are less dominant are heralded by some as positives for democracy. "[S]ocial media make it easier for interests to organise," writes *The Economist*, "they give voice and power to people who have neither."[54] There is abundant evidence of this, from the Idle No More movement in Canada to the Arab Spring in North Africa and the Middle East and the Black Lives Matter movement in the United States and Canada.

This democratization of the media system is not without problems, and they are not only or even

Media Spotlight

BOX 13.6 Media Theorists on How Image-Based Media May Affect the Presentation of Reality

The well known phrase, "A picture is worth a thousand words," expresses an important truth about human beings. The visual is predominant among our senses. As no end of studies have shown, we are more likely to believe what we see with our eyes than what we read on a page or hear from another person, even someone whose authority we generally would respect. The Canadian communications theorist, Marshall McLuhan, famously said that the medium is the message. When film and television became the dominant media in the developed world in the mid-twentieth century and soon after across virtually the entire world, an important change took place. Images, especially moving images, became the principal data that most of us rely on to understand our world. According to one of McLuhan's former students, media theorist Neil Postman, writing in 1985, this transformation has had important implications for how news and public affairs are reported and what they mean for viewers.

> Entertainment is the supra-ideology of all discourse on television. No matter what is depicted or from what point of view, the overarching presumption is that it is there for our amusement and pleasure. That is why even on news shows which provide us daily with fragments of tragedy and barbarism, we are urged by the newscasters to "join them tomorrow." What for? One would think that several minutes of murder and mayhem would suffice as material for a month of sleepless nights. We accept the newscasters' invitation because we know that the "news" is not to be taken seriously, that it is all in fun, so to say. Everything about a news show tells us this—the good looks and amiability of the cast, their pleasant banter, the exciting music that opens and closes the show, the vivid film footage, the attractive commercials—all these and more suggest that what we have just seen is no cause for weeping. A news show, to put it plainly, is a format for entertainment, not for education, reflection or catharsis. And we must not judge too harshly those who have framed it in this way. They are not assembling the news to be read, or broadcasting it to be heard. *They are televising the news to be seen. They must follow where their medium leads.* There is no conspiracy here, no lack of intelligence, only a straightforward recognition that "good television" has little to do with what is "good" about exposition or other forms of verbal communication but everything to do with what the pictorial images look like.[55]

One might respond, that was then. We now live in the online age of the Internet. But as Iranian-Canadian writer Hossein Derakhshan argues:

> Two decades after the web posed an unexpectedly serious challenge to television in the 1990s, we can now comfortably say television has won. It has conquered the internet, the media, and thereby the world. Not just as a medium, but as a discourse which has deeply affected our understanding of ourselves and the world. Its linear, centralized, emotion-driven, and photography-centered form has prevailed over the decentralized, text-based, and reason-driven form of the World Wide Web, which was itself inspired by books and newspapers.[56]

Huxley, Postman, and Derakhshan may be correct in their belief that the possibility of rational discourse on which informed democratic choices rests has become ever more elusive as television and now the Internet have come to dominate the media. Or they may be curmudgeonly nostalgists, longing for a print world of rationality that never really existed. What do you think?

chiefly the ones often mentioned, such as the decline of print journalism and local news coverage. The main problem may not be that the traditional gatekeepers are less important than in the past, but that the new ones, Facebook, Google, and the other online media platforms to which people now turn for information, come with their own sets of problems. Data privacy concerns and what may be the unprecedented possibilities for the dissemination of disinformation are among these.

At the same time, citizens cannot avoid shouldering some of the responsibility for whatever information deficit they experience and ill-founded views they hold. For all the problems surrounding the quality of what may be found via the Internet, there is also no doubt that it has put within the reach of almost everyone an unprecedentedly vast range of information and points of view. Increasingly, some of the highest-quality sources of news and public affairs—the *Globe and Mail*, *Maclean's*, the *New York Times*, the *Washington Post*, *The Economist*, *The Atlantic*, *Le Monde*, and many others—have established paywalls requiring readers to purchase a subscription for access to all or some of their content. This model will doubtless continue; indeed, it has to if these sorts of media outlets are to survive. But Canadians, and the same is true for most other national populations, seem to expect that online news and public affairs information should be provided free of charge. A 2018 survey found that only about one in 10 Canadians claimed to pay for an online news source.[57] For now, at least, there is still an abundance of choice when it comes to sources of news, information, and commentary for which one does not have to pay. This, some say, is the problem. Too much choice adds to the difficulty of distinguishing quality coverage and analysis from that which is simply shoddy or, worse, deliberately misleading.

The future of the media and its relationship to democracy is difficult to predict. A 2017 Pew Research Center survey of over 1,000 technology experts, academics, digital communications practitioners, and futurists found that they were just about evenly split on the question of whether "the information environment will be IMPROVED by changes that reduce the spread of lies and other misinformation online." Stay tuned, as they say on television.

Summing Up

The media play a vitally important role in Canadian politics. Unlike governments, political parties, interest groups, corporations, labour unions, and other organized interests, we traditionally have expected that the views expressed by those in the media will be less biased by self-interest or ideology. Journalists and others in the media argue that their special role in society and in the political system is based on accuracy in reporting, fairness, and impartiality in the treatment of individuals and organizations, and on independence from those who might like their story told in a particular way. On this last point, the ethics guidelines of the Canadian Association of Journalists states, "We serve democracy and the public interest by reporting the truth. This sometimes conflicts with various public and private interests, including those of sources, governments, advertisers and, on occasion, with our duty and obligation to an employer."[58] These and other principles are part of the journalist's creed, in Canada and in other democracies. Skepticism about how well the media system delivers on these promises has probably never been greater.

Most of this skepticism is associated with social media and fears that some of what is presented as factual coverage of the news and public affairs is false. Despite Canadians' concerns, their media consumption habits have migrated away from traditional media to online sources of the news, including social media platforms. Much of what they find there is content that was created by newspapers, magazines, and broadcasters—the traditional media whose advertising revenue base has been seriously eroded by the ascendance of the Internet and, in particular, by online giants Facebook and Google. The era when a relatively small number of major newspapers and broadcasters served as media gatekeepers, defining the news agenda, framing the stories, and guiding their audiences' attention in particular directions—if not towards specific conclusions—is over. Some of these legacy media continue to play a major role in Canadian public life. But they now compete in a much more crowded and chaotic media universe whose future state is a matter of conjecture.

Starting Points for Research

Canada, House of Commons Standing Committee on Access to Information, Privacy and Ethics, *Democracy Under Threat: Risks and Solutions in the Era of Disinformation and Data Monopoly* (Dec. 2018), http://www.ourcommons.ca/Content/Committee/421/ETHI/Reports/RP10242267/ethirp17/ethirp17-e.pdf. Focusing on social media, this committee report concludes that "changes to Canada's legislative and regulatory landscape are needed in order to neutralize the threat that disinformation and misinformation campaigns pose to the country's democratic process."

Alex Marland, *Brand Command: Canadian Politics and Democracy in the Age of Message Control* (Vancouver: University of British Columbia Press, 2016). A fascinating analysis of how governments use the same branding principles and techniques as private corporations, and do so in a centralized manner that, Marland argues, undermines public involvement in policy development.

Eli Pariser, "Beware Online Filter Bubbles," TED Talk, 2 May 2011, https://www.youtube.com/watch?v=B8ofWFx525s. Social and political implications of the online media we have come to depend on.

Public Policy Forum, *The Shattered Mirror: News, Democracy and Trust in the Digital Age* (Ottawa, 2017). The media should contribute to the health of democracy, not undermine it. Starting from this premise, this Ottawa-based think-tank offers a rather dismal assessment of the consequences of recent changes in the media system. The study may be found at https://shatteredmirror.ca/wp-content/uploads/theShatteredMirror.pdf.

David Taras, *Digital Mosaic: Media, Power, and Identity in Canada* (Toronto: University of Toronto Press, 2015). One of Canada's foremost students of media and politics argues that newer digital media are failing to perform the national unity functions that were performed by traditional media.

Review Exercises

1. How many of the following terms are familiar to you?
   - astroturfing
   - filter bubble
   - confirmation bias
   - bots
   - trolls
   - disinformation
   - propaganda
   - hoax
   - post-truth
   - clickbait
   - echo chamber

2. Examine the "Ethics Guidelines" of the Canadian Association of Journalists, last revised in June 2011: http://caj.ca/content.php?page=ethics-guidelines. Do you think Canadian journalists, editors, and producers follow these principles? What about others in the media—e.g., owners, social media platforms, bloggers—who make decisions about what is presented and how? Can you think of a case where they may not have behaved as the guidelines indicate they should?

3. Visit the websites of *The Guardian* (www.guardianunlimited.co.uk), National Public Radio (www.npr.org), the British Broadcasting Corporation's World Service (www.bbc.co.uk), *The Rebel* (https://www.therebel.media/), (www.ipolitics.ca), (www.adbusters.org), and (www.motherjones.com). Have you ever used any of these websites? Do you think many Canadians are aware of them? Do you think they provide perspectives or coverage of national or world affairs that is different from what is offered by the media outlets relied on by most people?

PART V
Contemporary Issues in Canadian Political Life

The complex interplay of ideas, institutions, and processes is best understood through the examination of particular issues that roil the political waters. For example, the long-standing conflict between French and English Canadians, a conflict historically rooted in language, ethnicity, values, and an imbalance in power, has been played out within the framework of particular institutions and managed through certain processes that have evolved over the more than 250 years that French- and English-speakers have lived under the same political roof in what today is Canada. These institutions and processes have affected the relationship between the two communities, at the same time as the values and demographic characteristics and circumstances of these communities have also shaped the laws, constitutional changes, and processes that influence their relations. Case studies of particular issues enable us to untangle the complex web of cause and effect that exists between ideas, institutions, and processes in the real world of politics.

The next four chapters will focus on several important issues in Canadian politics, all of which are crucial to an understanding of the Canadian political condition. The first involves language politics and Quebec, home to about nine out of 10 French-speaking Canadians. This is the oldest continuing—or visible—conflict in Canadian politics. The second issue involves women and politics, including the developments that have taken place in laws, attitudes, and social conditions pertaining to women and their participation in politics. The third issue, which in many ways is just as old as the French–English conflict, although it was pushed below the surface of Canadian politics for most of the time Canada has been a country, involves Indigenous Canadians and their relationship to other citizens and governments in Canada. The final chapter examines Canada's relations with the rest of the world, with a particular emphasis on Canada–US relations. Together, the study of these issues helps us to understand the Canadian political condition as it has evolved over time and as it exists today.

The main stage of the St. Jean Baptiste celebrations in Laval, Quebec. St Jean Baptiste Day (24 June) is a statutory holiday in Quebec. Originally a religious festival, 24 June has become more politicized (and sometimes violent) in the years since the Quiet Revolution, as the religious symbolism of the day was occasionally accompanied by demonstrations for Quebec separatism. (THE CANADIAN PRESS/Mario Beauregard)

14 Language Politics

Conflict over language has always been a central feature of Canadian politics. This chapter explains why language and the status of Quebec are such prominent issues in Canada. It also examines the chief aspects of federal and Quebec language policies. Topics include the following:

- The demographics of language politics
- The shift from French-Canadian nationalism to Quebec nationalism
- The Quiet Revolution and its legacy
- Language policy in Quebec
- Federal language policy
- Is separatism yesterday's issue?
- Appendix: Proposals for a distinct society clause

For over half a century Quebec has had a political party, the Parti Québécois, whose fundamental principle is the independence of Quebec. Since its first victory in Quebec's 1976 election, the PQ has won five of the last 12 provincial elections. Another separatist party, the Bloc Québécois, emerged onto the federal scene in 1990, becoming the official opposition in the House of Commons after the 1993 election. The BQ was the most successful federal party in Quebec from 1993 until the 2011 election. Public opinion polls taken since the creation of the PQ show that support for Quebec independence is never lower than about 20 to 25 per cent of the population, where it stands today.[1] Most of the time over the last several decades support for independence has been closer to 40 per cent. Two referendums have been held on the question.

Well before the possibility of Quebec separating from Canada arose, tensions, misunderstandings, and occasional ill will existed between French- and English-speaking Canadians. Indeed, conflict between the two communities goes back to the British military conquest of New France, when French-speaking Catholic colonists suddenly found themselves ruled by a minority who did not share their language or their religion. After the 1837 rebellions in Upper and Lower Canada, the British authorities sent the Earl of Durham to the Canadian colonies to report on the causes of political unrest. Lord Durham's report is best remembered for his observation that he found "two nations warring in the bosom of a single state." French and English Canadians would find themselves on opposing sides of many issues in the decades that followed Confederation, including Canada's participation in the Boer War, World War I, conscription for military service in World Wars I and II, and French-language educational rights in Ontario and Manitoba, to mention only some of the conflicts that divided them. *The Two Solitudes*,[2] the title of Hugh MacLennan's 1945 classic novel of two families, one French and one English, became shorthand for the distance separating Canada's two ethnolinguistic communities.

At the same time, the story of relations between French and English Canada, and between predominantly French-speaking Quebec and the rest of Canada, has not been one of unmitigated and continuous conflict. French and English Canadians have often voted for the same leaders, liking such politicians as Wilfrid Laurier, Mackenzie King, Louis St-Laurent, Pierre Trudeau, Brian Mulroney, Jean Chrétien, and Justin Trudeau, albeit to varying degrees (and all except King from Quebec). They have celebrated many of the same successes, particularly when it comes to international hockey and the Winter Olympics (sports seems to be a great if transient unifier in many divided societies). And it cannot go unremarked that they are still living under the same Constitution and sending politicians to the same Parliament more than 150 years after Confederation. Few political systems can boast such longevity. But the conflicts remain important, and no account of Canadian politics, past and present, is complete without an understanding of the language issue and Quebec nationalism.

The Demographics of Language Politics

When New France was formally placed under British control in 1763, francophones outnumbered anglophones by about eight to one in the territory that would become Canada. Forty years later, the two groups were of roughly equal size. From the late 1700s through the mid-1800s the English language gained ground on the French because of the wave of immigrants from the United States and then the British Isles, so that by the 1871 census—Canada's first—Canadians of French origin comprised about one-third of the population.[3] The exceptionally high birth rate among French-Canadian women enabled francophones to hold their own until the end of the 1950s against an English-speaking population that was buoyed by immigration. Regardless of their ancestry and native language, immigrants overwhelmingly adopted English as their new language. Since then, birth rates have dropped precipitously in Quebec, where about 90 per cent of Canadian francophones reside, and the French-speaking share of Canada's population has nudged down to its present all-time low of just over 21 per cent (see Figure 14.1).

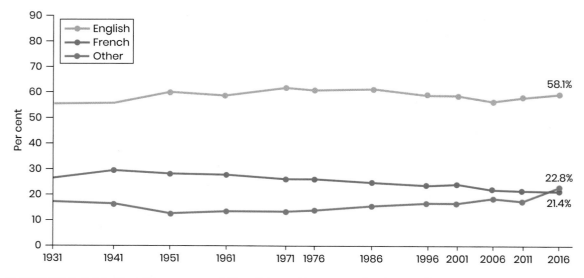

FIGURE 14.1 Mother Tongues of the Canadian Population, 1931–2016

Sources: Compiled from F.H. Leacy, ed., *Historical Statistics of Canada*, 2nd edn, Series A185–237 (Ottawa: Minister of Supply and Services Canada, 1983); *Canada Year Book* (1990), 2–25; Statistics Canada, *2016 Census of Population*, www.statcan.ca/.

The end of *la revanche des berceaux*—the high birth rate that for close to a century enabled French Canada to maintain its numerical strength against English Canada—coupled with the fact that the vast majority of immigrants have chosen English as their adopted language, produced a decline in the francophone share of the Canadian population by the early 1960s. More worrisome from the standpoint of Quebec governments was demographers' prediction of a dramatic fall in the francophone share of that province's population, particularly in Montreal where most new immigrants chose to establish themselves. Montreal was expected to be about equally divided between anglophones and francophones by the early twenty-first century.[4] The possibility that francophones would become a minority in Quebec was often raised by Quebec nationalists, although serious demographers like Jacques Henripin argued that this possibility was quite remote.[5] Nevertheless, this decline provided the impetus for provincial language laws intended to stem this tide.

The key factor in shifting the linguistic balance of Quebec, it should be emphasized, was immigration. Given that the province's anglophones were no more fecund than francophones, the language choices of *allophones*—Canadian demographers'

term for those whose native language is neither English nor French, or an Indigenous language—would be crucial in shaping the linguistic landscape of Quebec. Immigration became the sole contributor to provincial population growth by the 1960s, when the provincial fertility rate fell below the replacement level (i.e., the average number of births per female needed to offset the mortality rate).

With the exception of the relatively few immigrants whose native tongue was French, all other groups overwhelmingly adopted English for themselves and their children. As of the 1961 census, 46 per cent of foreign-born residents of Quebec spoke only English, another 25 per cent spoke English and French, and only 17 per cent spoke only French. Despite provincial language laws that require immigrants to send their children to French schools, make French the sole official language for provincial public services, and promote the use of French in the Quebec economy, evidence indicates that many allophones still opt for English. Figure 14.2 shows that the percentage of Quebecers claiming French as their mother tongue is almost identical to the percentage who speak mainly French in the home. But the percentage speaking English in the home is greater than that which claims English as

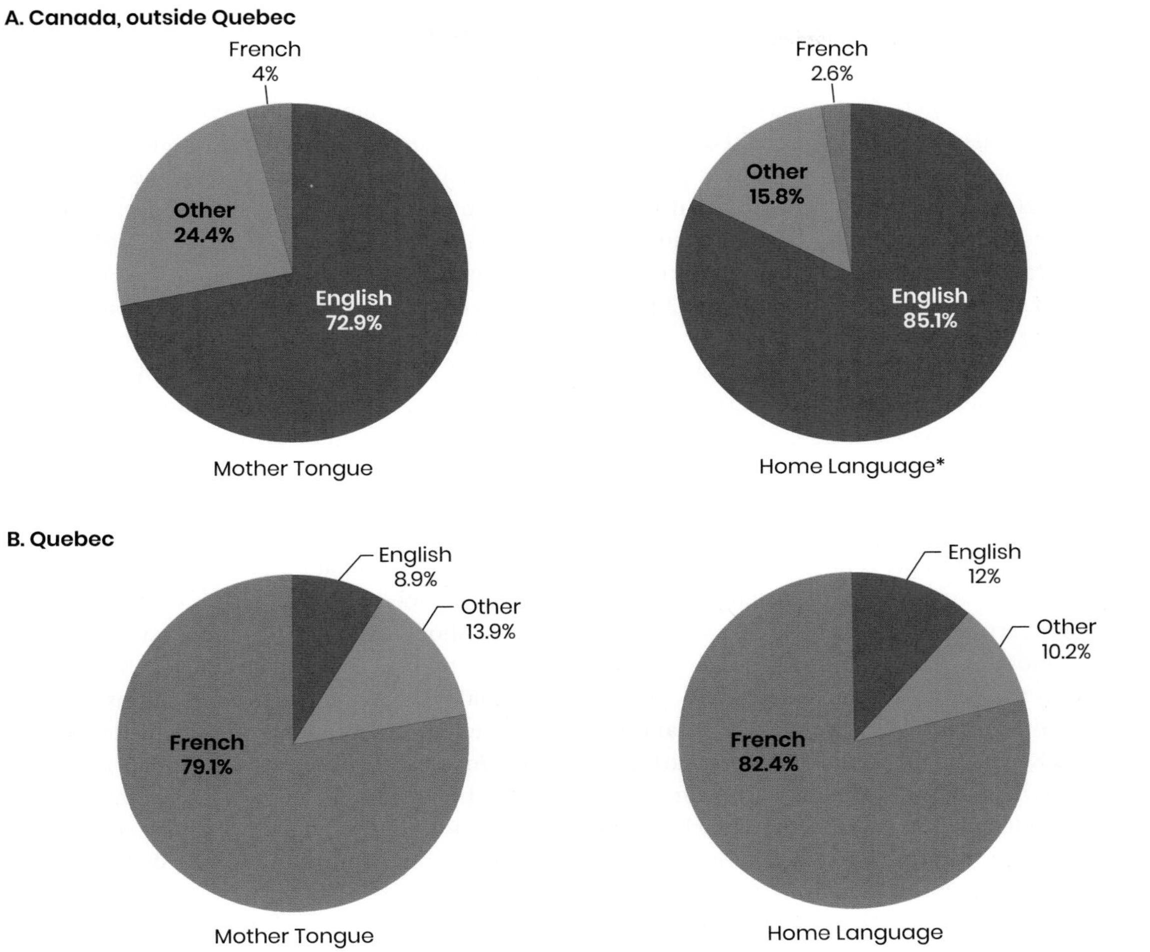

A. Canada, outside Quebec

B. Quebec

FIGURE 14.2 Mother Tongue and Language Spoken at Home, 2016

*Percentages may not total 100 because those answering English and French, English or French and a non-official language, or English and French and a non-official language are not included.

Source: Statistics Canada, *Census of Canada*, 2016.

its mother tongue. The gains made by the English-speaking community can only be explained by the linguistic choices of those whose mother tongue is neither French nor English. New Quebecers have continued to find English an attractive choice, although less often than before the existing provincial language laws were put into place.

Inside Quebec, the current demographic picture includes the following characteristics.

- French is spoken at home by 79 per cent of the population (2016 census).

- Contrary to projections made in the 1960s and early 1970s, Quebec has not become much less francophone. The 79 per cent of the population speaking French at home compares to 80 per cent in 1901 and 81 per cent in 1961.

- Most of the province's population increase is due to immigration and consequently the linguistic choices made by newcomers to Quebec are crucial to the language balance in the province. According to the 2016 census, about 30 per cent of allophones say they speak French as their main home language compared to 22 per cent who speak English at home most of the time.[6]

- Quebec's share of Canada's total population has fallen over the last several decades, from 28 per cent in 1971 to about 23 per cent in 2016. As a result of the decennial readjustments in the distribution of seats in the House of Commons, the province's share of all seats has fallen from 28 to 23 per cent over that same period.

Outside Quebec the language picture looks very different. With the exceptions of New Brunswick (231,110 or 31.4 per cent of the population) and Ontario (490,720 or 3.7 per cent of the population), the francophone populations of the other provinces are tiny. Roughly 3 per cent of Canadians outside of Quebec report French as their first language. The percentages vary between the provinces and territories, but in most cases native French-speakers comprise between about 1 and 3 per cent of the population. In certain provinces and in all but a handful of Canada's major metropolitan areas outside Quebec, some of the non-official-language communities are considerably larger than the French-speaking minority. For example, in Vancouver the number of people who speak French at home, mainly or along with another language, is just over 5,000. Those who speak Cantonese or Mandarin at home number about 124,000. There are about as many people who speak Spanish at home in Vancouver as speak French. In Toronto, those who speak mainly French or French along with another language are outnumbered by several language communities. In all provinces except Quebec, the French-language community continuously loses some of its members to the English majority. Outside Quebec, 65.6 per cent of people whose mother tongue is French speak another language at home. In all but a tiny fraction of cases that language is English. Only in Quebec, where the number of people who speak only or mainly French at home is about equal to the number of those for whom French is their mother tongue, and to a somewhat lesser degree in New Brunswick, is the rate of French-language retention high. By contrast, the rate of language retention

among native English-speakers is high everywhere in Canada.[7]

This is not a recent development. In *Languages in Conflict*, first published in 1967, Richard Joy carefully documented the trend towards the assimilation of francophones outside Quebec. Joy was the first to make what today seems an obvious point, namely, that the rate of language transfer is greatest among the younger generations. For example, using data from the 1961 census he found that the transfer rate from French to English in the four western provinces was 25 per cent among those aged 45–54, but was 60 per cent for those aged 5–14 and 67 per cent among infants aged 0–4.[8] Only in what Joy called the **bilingual belt**, a narrow region running from Moncton, New Brunswick, in the east, to Sault Ste Marie, Ontario, in the west, was the rate of assimilation among all generations significantly lower. The reason, of course, was the ability to shop, work, go to church, and do the other things that keep a language alive. Outside the bilingual belt, this supportive milieu was seldom encountered. The francophone population in every province except Quebec and New Brunswick was older than in Canada as a whole, confirming Joy's prediction that the failure to retain young francophones would contribute to the steady erosion of the community's base.

A 2017 Statistics Canada analysis confirms that the situation of francophone minority populations outside Quebec continues to be precarious. What the study refers to as the "incomplete transmission of French from parents to children,"[9] a process that has been going on for several decades, has produced a situation where francophone minority populations are older than the rest of the provincial populations in majority anglophone Canada. The study projects that by 2036 the relative size of francophone communities in all of the predominantly English-speaking provinces, whether measured by mother tongue or language spoken at home, will be smaller than today. The territories may see slight growth in the share of the francophone minority population.[10]

This picture of the future of francophone minority communities outside Quebec may strike some as unrealistically gloomy. Some are quick to point out

THE CANADIAN PRESS/Patrick Doyle

Franco-Ontarians gather at the Human Rights Monument in Ottawa to protest cuts to French services by the Ontario government. These cuts were experienced as part of a historical pattern in which francophones living outside of Quebec must struggle to have their rights recognized by provincial governments that may be unaware of or insensitive to the particular concerns of their communities.

that bilingualism outside of Quebec has been increasing in recent years. In fact, it is today highest among the young, the very group that Joy argued was most likely to transfer to the dominant language group. Indeed, the rate of bilingualism in the Canadian population outside Quebec has been on the rise for several decades. The rapid expansion of French immersion schools since the 1980s, particularly in Ontario, which accounts for over half of all immersion students in Canada, is responsible for most of this increase.

As shown in Table 14.1, the level of bilingualism in Canada has increased over the past several decades, although this growth has levelled off in recent years (see Figure 14.3). It would be a mistake, however,

to conclude from this that the prospects for living in French outside of Quebec have improved. The census question that measures bilingualism ("Can you carry on a conversation in the other official language?") does not provide a measure of languages in use. The fact that increasing numbers of those whose mother tongue is English or some other language other than French claim to be functionally fluent in French does not mean that French will be used more often in the home, the workplace, at the pub, shopping, and wherever else communication takes place. Indeed, a good deal of evidence suggests that more than four decades of French immersion education[11] have produced a wave of **receptive bilinguals**—people who are capable of responding to French

TABLE 14.1 Bilingualism in Canada, 1961, 2001, 2016			
	1961 %	2001 %	2016 %
Canada	12.2	17.7	17.9
Newfoundland and Labrador	1.2	4.1	5.0
Prince Edward Island	7.6	12.0	12.6
Nova Scotia	6.1	10.1	10.5
New Brunswick	19.0	34.2	33.9
Quebec	25.5	40.8	44.5
Ontario	7.9	11.7	11.2
Manitoba	7.4	9.3	8.6
Saskatchewan	4.5	5.1	4.7
Alberta	4.3	6.9	6.6
British Columbia	3.5	7.0	6.8
Yukon	5.6	10.2	13.8
Northwest Territories*	7.0	6.5	10.3
Nunavut	—	3.8	4.3
Canada excluding Quebec	6.9	10.3	9.8

*In 1961 Nunavut was part of the Northwest Territories.

Sources: Jean-François Lepage and Jean-Pierre Corbeil, "The Evolution of English–French Bilingualism in Canada from 1961 to 2011," Statistics Canada (May 2013), www.statcan.gc.ca/pub/75-006-x/2013001/article/11795-eng.pdf; Statistics Canada, "English–French Bilingualism Reaches New Heights," 2 Aug. 2017, Table 1. https://www12.statcan.gc.ca/census-recensement/2016/as-sa/98-200-x/2016009/98-200-x2016009-eng.cfm.

communications but do not themselves initiate conversations in French, consume French-language media, or seek out opportunities to live in their acquired second language. A recent study by Statistics Canada notes that bilingualism peaks during school years among anglophones but then drops off over the years as a result of lack of continued exposure to French. In Quebec, however, both francophones and anglophones are more likely to remain bilingual over their life cycle due to greater second-language exposure in that province than elsewhere in Canada.[12] None of this is an argument against bilingual education anywhere in Canada. But claims that four decades of immersion education in Canada have contributed significantly to the greater use of French in the workplace, the home, and public spaces outside Quebec should be viewed with a certain amount of caution and even skepticism.

Moreover, despite more than 40 years of immersion education in Canada, the rate of functional bilingualism is still relatively low outside of Quebec, at 9.8 per cent in 2016.[13] Almost 60 per cent of all bilingual Canadians reside in Quebec, where the rate of bilingualism is four times greater than in Ontario and four and one-half times greater than the level in Canada outside Quebec. The increase in the level of bilingualism in Quebec since the 1960s has been greater than in the rest of Canada. This is simply to say that Canadian bilingualism is to a considerable degree a predominantly Quebec phenomenon. In fact, the most recent census found that the level of bilingualism among anglophones outside Quebec has declined in recent years.

The bottom line is that the social and economic milieu outside Quebec has not become more supportive for francophones. While provincial government services for the francophone communities of Ontario have improved since the mid-1980s and those in New Brunswick are quite good, few people outside the "bilingual belt" can manage to shop, work, and do the other daily social activities in French that help keep a language alive. Even francophone schools in predominantly English-speaking communities experience the pressures of language erosion. René Lévesque, the founder of the Parti Québécois, once characterized francophones outside Quebec as "dead ducks." This may be somewhat overstated. Species at risk might be closer to the truth.

The Trajectory of Nationalism

French-Canadian nationalism, Pierre Trudeau writes, was originally a system of self-defence. This was certainly true. Conquered by arms, the French-speaking people of New France found themselves

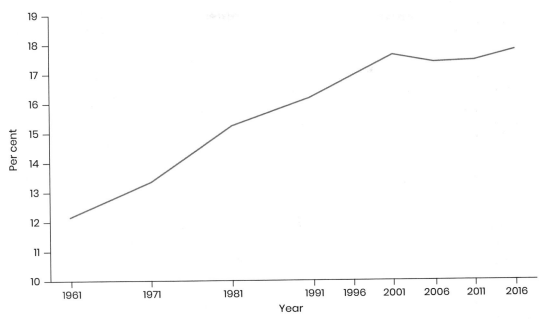

FIGURE 14.3 English–French Bilingualism in Canada, 1961–2016

Source: Statistics Canada, "English–French Bilingualism Reaches New Heights," 31 Aug. 2017, https://www12.statcan.gc.ca/census-recensement/2016/as-sa/
98-200-x/2016009/98-200-x2016009-eng.cfm.

subordinated to an anglophone minority about one-eighth their size. English was the language of the new political and commercial elites. The **Conquest of 1759** left French a second-class language within Quebec, with francophones largely excluded from the colony's structures of power.

Why did francophones not succumb to assimilationist pressures, as they did in Louisiana after it, too, passed from French control? The answer is complex, but three chief factors can be identified. One involved the policies of the British colonial authorities in New France. By the terms of the Quebec Act, 1774, they granted formal protection to the status of the Roman Catholic religion and the *code civil*, the basis of civil law in New France.[14] Faced with rebellion in the Thirteen Colonies, which two years later successfully declared their independence from Britain, this recognition for the rights of the French-Canadian population may have been motivated chiefly by the desire to ensure the allegiance of the clerical and civil leaders of that population. Regardless, it involved official recognition of the rights of the francophone Catholic majority and

reinforced the leadership role of that community's clerical elite.

A second factor that explains the different fates of the French language and culture in Louisiana compared to Quebec was demography. French-speakers in the south of the United States were very quickly swamped by a rapidly growing anglophone population. But as we observed earlier in this chapter, although immigration from the United States and then the British Isles tipped the linguistic balance in Canada towards English by the early nineteenth century, the high fertility rate among French Canadians enabled them to hold their ground at about one-third of Canada's population between Confederation and the 1950s.

The defensive posture that Pierre Trudeau argues was characteristic of French-Canadian nationalism is the third factor that explains the ability of French Canada to resist the pressures of assimilation. Under the guidance of a clerical elite whose leading social role was strengthened when anglophones occupied the political and commercial elites of the colony, French Canada met the challenge of

English domination by remaining loyal to traditional values and institutions. The nationalist ideology that developed in French Canada after the Conquest is summed up in a famous passage from *Maria Chapdelaine*, the classic novel of traditional French Canada:

> Round about us strangers have come, whom we are wont to call barbarians; they have seized almost all the power; they have acquired almost all the money, but in the country of Quebec nothing has changed. . . . [W]e have held our own, so that, it may be, after several centuries more, the world will turn to us and say: these people are of a race that knows not how to perish . . . . In the country of Quebec, nothing shall die, and nothing shall be changed.[15]

Traditional French-Canadian nationalism was guided by the idea of **la survivance**—survival, against the pressures of a dominant culture that was anglicizing, Protestant, materialistic, liberal democratic, and business-oriented. In other words, this dominant anglophone culture was all the things that French Canada, according to the spokespersons for this ideology, was not and should not become. The main ideas expressed in the writings and public pronouncements of the exponents of the traditional nationalism may be summarized as follows:

- French Canada comprised a distinct nation, whose chief characteristics were the Catholic religion and the French language. Preservation of the French language and the Catholic religion were considered inseparable, as the title of Henri Bourassa's book *La langue, guardienne de la foi*[16] explicitly declared. "The preservation of language," Bourassa wrote, "is absolutely necessary for the preservation of a race, its spirit, character and temperament."[17]
- French Canada had a mission, a special vocation as a people. This mission was to remain faithful to its roots, and to resist the lure of materialistic, English, Protestant pressures. The democratic belief in the separation of

church and state was seen to be a lamentable heresy spawned by the French Revolution, the American Constitution, and liberalism generally.
- The character of the French-Canadian people was most secure in the province of Quebec, but French Canada was not restricted to the boundaries of that province. In other words, French Canada was defined by socio-cultural characteristics, not by the territory of Quebec.

While these were the chief characteristics of the nationalist ideology that became dominant in French Canada during the nineteenth century, a dominance that it maintained until the middle of the twentieth century, there were voices of dissent. In fact, sociologist Marcel Rioux argues that the idea of the French-Canadian nation was first developed by the secular elites of Quebec who espoused liberal and often aggressively anti-clerical views.[18] Political scientist Denis Monière concurs, noting that the authority of the Church was much weaker before and in the decades immediately following the Conquest than is usually believed (especially by English-Canadian historians).[19] He maintains that the "victory" of the conservative traditional nationalism became assured only after the defeat of Louis-Joseph Papineau's liberal forces in the Lower Canada Rebellion of 1837. Even after the ideological dominance of the Church and the voices of traditional nationalism were firmly established, however, liberal voices of dissent were occasionally heard.[20]

The traditional nationalism came under mounting pressure during the middle of the twentieth century. Its chief tenets were increasingly at odds with the economic and social reality of Quebec. The emigration of an estimated 900,000 French-speaking Quebecers to the northeastern and midwestern regions of the United States from about the mid-1800s to the Great Depression demonstrated more clearly than anything else the weakness of the traditional nationalism's hymn to the pastoral vocation of French Canadians. There simply was not enough arable land to support the rural parish lifestyle that the ideologues of the traditional nationalism clung to so tenaciously. The urban population of Quebec surpassed the rural population in the 1921 census (56 per cent to 44 per cent). Between 1926 and 1950 the number of people employed in Quebec's manufacturing sector increased by about 220 per cent, slightly higher than the rate of increase for Canada as a whole (210 per cent), but significantly higher than the rate for the rest of the country if Ontario—where most new investment in manufacturing was located—is omitted from the picture.[21] By mid-century manufacturing workers outnumbered farm workers in Quebec by a large margin.[22] In short, by the early to mid-twentieth century the "typical" Québécois lived in a city or town, worked in a factory, store, or office, and had family members who had left the province in search of employment opportunities. It was no longer the rural, agrarian society idealized by the traditional nationalism.

Quebec was following the path of modernization. The urbanization and industrialization that this involved also produced a political side effect of enormous importance. This was the increasing realization that francophones, despite accounting for about four-fifths of the Quebec population, were largely excluded from the centres of economic decision-making and controlled relatively little of the province's wealth. "Is there any inherent or unavoidable reason why," asked Abbé Lionel Groulx in 1934, "with 2,500,000 French Canadians in Quebec, all big business, all high finance, all the public utilities, all our water rights, forests and mines, should belong to a minority of 300,000?"[23] Although the question was not new—Édouard Montpetit, Errol Bouchette, Étienne Parent, and others had raised basically the same issue in arguing that educated francophones needed to rid themselves of their apparent distaste for careers in industry and finance—it was being asked with increasing frequency between the 1930s and the 1950s.[24]

These decades saw the emergence of the first serious challenge to the conservative ideology since the crushed rebellion of 1837. It brought together a diverse group of university professors and students, journalists, union activists, liberal politicians, and even some elements within the Catholic Church (particularly Action catholique). They were united by their opposition to the so-called **unholy alliance** of the Catholic Church, anglophone capital, and the Union Nationale party of Maurice Duplessis—and, of course, to the conservative nationalism that seemed unconcerned with French Canadians' marginal economic status. Marcel Rioux calls this anti-establishment challenge the ideology of contestation and recoupment.[25] It contested the traditional elites' monopoly over power in the province and what was argued to be their backward characterization of French-Canadian society and culture. Its goal was to recoup lost ground, to bring Quebec's society, economy, and government up to date, a goal that became known in Quebec as **rattrapage** (catching up).

The nerve centre of this challenge to the conservative establishment and ideology included the Faculty of Social Sciences at Laval University; the intellectual revue *Cité libre*, founded by such figures as Pierre Trudeau and Gérard Pelletier; and the provincial Liberal Party. As the political party attempting to defeat Duplessis, it was natural that the Quebec Liberal Party would attract the energies of those who saw the Union Nationale under *le Chef*, as Duplessis was routinely referred to, as one of the principal obstacles to reform.

The traditional ideology and the interests it defended were doomed by their failure to adapt to a changing environment. As Marcel Rioux observes, "the ideology and old power structure in Quebec were becoming anachronistic in the face of the demographic, economic, and social changes that Quebec was experiencing."[26] They managed to hold on until the 1960s largely because of the tight web of patronage politics that Maurice Duplessis used to keep the ideologically conservative Union Nationale in power for most of the period from 1936 until his death in 1959.

The Quiet Revolution and Its Legacy

The first several years of the 1960s are justly considered a turning point in the history of Quebec. Duplessis's death in 1959 and the election of the provincial Liberals under Jean Lesage in 1960 opened the way for the political reforms and social changes referred to as the **Quiet Revolution**. At the heart of these reforms lay an increased role for the Quebec state. It replaced the authority of the Catholic Church in the areas of social services and education, and also acquired a vastly broader range of economic functions. The provincial state was seen as the *moteur principal* of Quebec's attempt to modernize social and political institutions that were ill-suited to the urbanized, industrialized society that Quebec had become. The state, traditionally viewed as a second-class institution in a province where most social services were controlled by the Church and where government was associated with crass patronage, became the focus of nationalist energies.

The nationalism that emerged in the crucible of the Quiet Revolution marked a sharp break with the past. The traditional nationalism had emphasized preservation of the *patrimoine*—the language, the faith, the mores of a community whose roots went back to New France. Although some of its chief spokespersons, such as Abbé Lionel Groulx, associated this community with the region of the St Lawrence River and even with the vision of a Laurentian state whose territory would include what is today the southern region of the province, the essential elements of the traditional nationalism were not defined by either the territory or the powers of the Quebec state.

Rioux has characterized the traditional nationalism as an ideology of conservation. Its goals were the preservation of the traditional values and social

Boris Spremo/GetStock.com

A man paints a fleur-de-lys—a symbol of Quebec—on a building under the words "We know what we want" at the time of the 1980 referendum, which sought a mandate for the provincial government to negotiate with the rest of Canada a new status for Quebecers. The new nationalism that arose during the Quiet Revolution was—and still is—felt keenly by supporters of a sovereign Quebec.

structures of French Canada, including the leading role played by the Church in articulating these values and controlling these structures (i.e., the schools, hospitals, labour unions, etc.). The modern welfare state necessarily threatens the dominant social role of the Church and was generally rejected by spokespersons for the traditional nationalism. Although they insisted on constitutional protections for the province's exclusive right to make education policy and put limits on Ottawa's ability to interfere with social affairs in the province, they did not expect that the Quebec state would be particularly active in these fields. The traditional nationalism attached no particular value to the Quebec state, except insofar as its powers could be used to ward off federal intrusions that challenged the status of conservative values and the power of the traditional elites—the clergy, anglophone business leaders, and provincial politicians.

Nationalism is always based on some concept of the nation: who belongs to it and who does not. The traditional nationalism did not identify *la nation canadienne-française* with *la société française du Québec*. The boundaries of *la nation* extended beyond Quebec to embrace French Canadians throughout Canada. There were two reasons for this. First, Catholicism and the role of the Church were important elements of the traditional nationalism. Obviously, neither of these stopped at the Quebec border. Second, the anti-statist quality of the traditional nationalism prevented it from associating the French-Canadian nation with the Quebec state.

History had shown that assimilationist pressures and unsympathetic governments faced francophones outside of Quebec. Nevertheless, to identify the nation with the Quebec state would have challenged the dominant social role of the Church. The survival of the nation did not depend, according to the traditional nationalism, on the activities of the Quebec state. Instead, it depended primarily on those institutions that were crucial to the continuation from generation to generation of the French language and the Catholic religion—family, school, and parish. Family and parish obviously fell outside the state's authority. And although the schools were under the constitutional jurisdiction

of the provincial state, their control was mainly left in the hands of the Church. This did not change until the early 1960s.

The central elements of the traditional nationalism were located outside of the state. This would not be true of the new nationalism that both spurred and was influenced by the Quiet Revolution. Instead of defining *la nation* in terms of language and religion, the ascendant nationalism of the 1960s developed an understanding of Quebec's history, its economy, and its social structure that was based on language and dependency. The dependency perspective portrayed Quebec as a society whose evolution had been shaped and distorted by the economic and political domination of English Canadians.

This secularized version of French-Canadian history, and more particularly of francophone Quebec, cast an entirely different light on the future of the Quebec nation and its relationship to English Canada. If the problem was that the Québécois were dominated economically and politically, then the solution required that they take control of their economic and political destiny. To do so, they would have to use the Quebec state. All of the major reforms of the Quiet Revolution—the establishment of a provincial ministry of education, the nationalization of privately owned hydroelectric companies to create a vastly expanded Hydro-Québec, the creation of such state-owned enterprises as la Caisse de dépôt et placement and la Société générale de financement, and passage of the Quebec Pension Plan—involved using the Quebec state in a newly assertive way.

The replacement of the traditional nationalism by the state-centred nationalism of the Quiet Revolution was not as abrupt as history might suggest, nor did this new nationalism go unchallenged. The traditional social order and its values had been crumbling at the edges for at least a couple of decades before Duplessis's death finally provided the opportunity for opposition groups to gain power. Once the doors were opened to reform, it quickly became apparent that the anti-Duplessis forces shared little more than a common antipathy towards the old order. They were divided on at least three main levels.

First, there was a split between the federalists and those who advocated either special status or independence for Quebec. The federalists included such prominent figures as Pierre Elliott Trudeau, Jean Marchand, and Gérard Pelletier, all of whom entered federal politics through the Liberal Party in 1965. Leadership of the Quebec autonomy side would fall on René Lévesque, formerly a popular television journalist who had masterminded the nationalization of the hydroelectric industry as a minister in the Lesage government and who became the first leader of the Parti Québécois in 1968.

The second division concerned the size and functions of the Quebec state. Even within the reformist Liberal government of Jean Lesage, sharp differences existed over such major policies as the nationalization of the hydroelectricity industry and the role of the province's investment agency, la Caisse de dépôt et placement. Agreement that the provincial state should play a larger role in Quebec society was not matched by consensus on what that role should be.

Finally, Quebec separatists were divided on ideological lines. Those who came to form the leadership of the *indépendantiste* Parti Québécois, including René Lévesque, Jacques Parizeau, and Claude Morin, were ideologically liberal. But there were others, within the PQ and in other pro-independence organizations, for whom Quebec independence was inseparably linked to the overthrow of what they argued was a repressive capitalist state. PQ members Pierre Bourgault and Robert Burns, for example, wanted the end of *la domination anglaise* of the Quebec economy but also a radical redistribution of economic power between classes in the province. Although the electoral strength of these left-wing groups never amounted to much, they managed to have a significant impact on political discourse in Quebec, particularly through the province's universities and labour unions and in the extra-parliamentary wing of the PQ.

In view of these divisions, two developments justify the claim that a state-centred nationalism emerged out of the Quiet Revolution. First, the identification of French Canada with the territory of Quebec was a view shared by most nationalists. Indeed, the entry of Trudeau and his fellow federalists into national politics was chiefly a reaction to this Quebec-oriented nationalism. The provincial Liberals' 1962 campaign slogan, **maîtres chez nous**—masters in our own house—captured a nationalist consensus that since then has been an accepted tenet of Quebec politics. Second, key institutional reforms of the Quiet Revolution, including the Caisse de dépôt et placement, Hydro-Québec, and the jurisdictional terrain that the Quebec government wrested from Ottawa in the areas of social policy, immigration, and taxation, have left an important mark on Quebec nationalism. They constitute the key institutions and policies of the provincial state upon which the aspirations summed up in the phrase *maîtres chez nous* depend.

The Unilingual Approach of Quebec

The origins of present-day language policy in Canada lie in developments in Quebec during the 1960s. The ideology of *rattrapage* and the identification of French Canada with Quebec had important consequences for language policy in that province. As the instrument for economic and social development, the Quebec state assumed functions previously administered by the Church authorities and also expanded the scope of its economic activities. In doing so it provided career opportunities for the growing number of educated francophones graduating from the province's universities. Access to high-paying managerial and technical jobs in the private sector, however, remained blocked by anglophone domination of the Quebec economy. The relative exclusion of francophones from management positions in larger businesses and the concentration of francophone businesses in the *petites et moyennes enterprises* sector of the economy had long been known.[27] This situation ran directly counter to the expectations of the Quiet Revolution and became an important political issue when the capacity of the public sector to absorb the increasing ranks of highly educated francophones became strained.

Demographic trends comprised an additional factor that shaped provincial language policy in Quebec. Immigrants to the province overwhelmingly adopted the English language. This fact, combined with a dramatic reduction in the birth rate among francophones, lent credibility to a scenario where francophones might eventually become a minority within Quebec. Along with evidence of the exclusion of francophones from much of the province's economic structure, these trends formed the basis for the policy recommendations of the Quebec Royal Commission of Inquiry on the Position of the French Language and on Language Rights in Quebec (the Gendron Commission, 1972). The Commission recommended that the provincial government take legislative action to promote the use of French in business and in the schools. These recommendations were translated into law under the Quebec Liberal government that introduced the Official Language Act[28] and in the Charte de la langue française[29]—or **Bill 101** as it was more commonly known outside Quebec—passed under the subsequent Parti Québécois government.

The principal features of Bill 101—principles that continue to guide language policy in Quebec—include the following.

1. French is established as the sole official language in Quebec, subject to the bilingual requirements imposed on Quebec courts and the province's legislature by s. 133 of the Constitution Act, 1867. In the public services, including the working language of provincial and municipal institutions and of public utilities, as well as the language of communication between these organizations and Quebec citizens, French is the only official language. Certain recognized bodies and institutions, including school boards, municipalities, and hospitals, where those served are mainly non-francophones, may be allowed to provide services in English, but these organizations must also "ensure that their services to the public are available in the official language."[30]

2. Through the requirement that businesses with 50 or more employees receive a *francisation* certificate as a condition of doing business in the province, the Quebec government seeks to increase the use of French as a working language of business in the province. The Charter of the French Language does not establish linguistic quotas for corporations. Instead, it leaves the conditions of certification a matter for individual negotiations between a firm and the Office de la langue française. Despite some initial resistance from the anglophone business community, symbolized by the immediate move of Sun Life's head office from Montreal to Toronto in 1977, this section of Quebec's language law has generally been accepted by employers. More controversial have been the provisions requiring that public signs and advertisements be in French only. A 1988 decision of the Supreme Court ruled that this ban violated the freedom of expression guaranteed in the Charter of Rights and Freedoms.[31] The signage provisions of Quebec's language law were modified in 1989 through Bill 178, which required that exterior commercial signs be in French only, but allowed bilingual interior signs so long as the French language was more prominently displayed. These provisions were amended again in 1993 through Bill 86, which states that the rules governing when signs must be unilingual French and when other languages are allowed shall be established by government regulations—a more flexible approach than enshrining the rules in the statute.[32]

3. The provisions of Bill 101 that initially excited the most controversy were those restricting access to English-language schools in Quebec. Under this law, children could enrol in an English school if one of the following conditions was met: their parents had been educated in English in Quebec; they had a sibling already going to an English school; their parents were educated in English outside of Quebec but were living in the province when the law was passed (1977); they were already enrolled in an English school when the law came into effect. The intent, obviously, was to reverse the overwhelming preference of immigrants for the English language, a preference that demographers predicted would eventually change the linguistic balance in the province, and even more dramatically in Montreal, which

attracted the vast majority of immigrants. In one of the first Supreme Court decisions on the Charter of Rights and Freedoms, the Court held that the requirement that at least one of a child's parents must have been educated in English in Quebec violated section 23 of the Charter, a section that clearly had been drafted with Bill 101 in mind. The practical importance of this ruling is small, given the low level of migration to Quebec from other Canadian provinces. More significant is the fact that the Supreme Court was unwilling to accept the Quebec government's argument that the demographic threat to the position of the French language justified this restriction on language rights under the "reasonable limits" section of the Charter. In 1993 the education provisions of Bill 101 were brought into conformity with s. 23 of the Charter.[33]

Despite some setbacks in the courts, the principles on which Quebec's language policy rests have remained substantially unchanged since the passage of Bill 101. Controversy over the application of the Charter of the French Language erupts from time to time, often over the alleged non-compliance of small businesses with regulations made under the law. The dramatic decline in the English-language school system—the number of students enrolled in these schools has dropped by about 150,000 since the 1970s—is another factor that upsets the province's English-language minority. This decline is, of course, a measure of the success of the Charter of the French Language. Indeed, the province's language policy has achieved its two main objectives, namely, increasing the use of the French language in the Quebec economy and slowing, although not reversing, the decline in the francophone share of the provincial population.

The Bilingual Approach of Ottawa

A very different approach to language policy—one based on a conception of French and English Canada that cuts across provincial borders—has been pursued by successive federal governments since the 1960s. Responding to the new assertive

nationalism of the Quiet Revolution, the signs of which ranged from Quebec's demands for greater taxation powers and less interference by Ottawa in areas of provincial constitutional responsibility to bombs placed in mailboxes and at public monuments, the Liberal government of Lester Pearson established the **Royal Commission on Bilingualism and Biculturalism**. As Eric Waddell writes, "The federal government was facing a legitimacy crisis in the 1960s and 1970s and had the immediate task of proposing a Canadian alternative to Quebec nationalism."[34] The B&B Commission was a first step towards the adoption by Ottawa of a policy of official bilingualism. This policy was to some degree intended to defuse the *indépendantiste* sentiment building in Quebec, especially among young francophones, by opening Ottawa as a field of career opportunities to rival the growing Quebec public service.

The alternative Ottawa offered, and that was expressed in the federalist philosophy of Pierre Trudeau, was of a Canada in which language rights would be guaranteed to the individual and protected by national institutions. In practical terms this meant changing the overwhelmingly anglophone character of the federal state so that francophones would not have grounds to view it as an "alien" level of government from which they were largely excluded. These changes have been carried out on two main fronts.

First, what Raymond Breton refers to as the "Canadian symbolic order" has been transformed since the 1960s.[35] Through a new flag, the proclamation of "O Canada" as the official national anthem, new designs for stamps and currency, and the neutralizing of language in the names of some federal institutions, documents, and celebrations (for example, Trans-Canada Airlines became Air Canada, the BNA Act is now officially titled the Constitution Act, 1867, and what was once officially known as Dominion Day is now called Canada Day), a deliberate attempt has been made to create symbols that do not evoke Canada's colonial past and British domination.

Second, the passage of the Official Languages Act (1969) gave statutory expression to the policy of bilingualism that had been set in motion under

Lester Pearson. This Act established the Office of the Commissioner of Official Languages as a "watchdog" agency to monitor the three main components of language equality set forth in the Act: (1) the public's right to be served by the federal government in the official language of their choice; (2) the equitable representation of francophones and anglophones in the federal public service; and (3) the ability of public servants of both language groups to work in the language of their choice. The situation that the Official Languages Act was intended to redress was one where francophone representation in the federal state was less than their share of the national population. Francophone under-representation was greatest in managerial, scientific, and technical job categories (see Figure 14.4). Moreover, the language of the public service—the language that officials worked in and, in most parts of the country, the language in which citizens could realistically be expected to be served—was English. In view of these circumstances, Ottawa's claim to "represent" the interests of francophones lacked credibility.

Among the main actions taken to increase the bilingual character of the federal bureaucracy have been language training for public servants, the designation of an increasing share of positions as bilingual, and the creation of the National Capital Region as the office blocks of the federal state spread across the Ottawa River into Hull (now Gatineau), Quebec, during the 1970s. Language training for public servants has been perhaps the most controversial of these measures. In his annual report for 1984 the Commissioner of Official Languages, D'Iberville Fortier, noted that a relatively small proportion of public servants in positions designated bilingual appeared to have acquired their second-language skills as a result of taxpayer-funded language training. This led Fortier to question the extent to which language training was capable of making public servants effectively bilingual, particularly anglophones who were the main consumers of federal language courses.[36] Fortier's successors occasionally have expressed similar reservations, and over the last few decades the focus has shifted away from training current public servants in the other official language to recruiting people who already have the language skills needed for particular positions. Nevertheless, providing language training for public servants who wish to upgrade their proficiency in the other official language, which usually means anglophones learning or improving their proficiency in French, continues to take place. Roughly 40 years after the beginning of taxpayer-funded language training for federal public servants, a recent study commissioned by the Privy Council Office made this rather shocking observation: "There is currently very limited data related to the costs and effectiveness of language training or investment in tools to support bilingualism in the workplace."[37]

In view of the fact that two of the original objectives of the Official Languages Act have been to increase the number of francophones recruited into the public service and to improve francophones' opportunities for upward mobility within it, the designation of positions according to their linguistic requirements probably has been the most significant feature of Ottawa's language policy. Today, slightly under half of positions in the federal public service are designated either bilingual or French essential, about two-thirds of these at a superior proficiency level. Roughly two-thirds of federal public service positions in the National Capital Region (Ottawa–Gatineau) require a knowledge of both official languages. For positions outside of Canada, working in embassies, consulates, and other federal agencies abroad, the requirement is close to 100 per cent. Evidence on recruitment to the federal public service and upward mobility within it demonstrate that the linguistic designation of positions has worked to the advantage of francophones. In recent years close to one-third of new appointments to the federal public service have gone to those who claim French as their mother tongue, a level significantly higher than the approximately 21 per cent of the Canadian population comprised of native French speakers. A clear majority of appointments to bilingual positions are filled by francophones. This is true for both new appointments to the public service and for reappointments within the federal bureaucracy, about 70 per cent of each going to francophones.

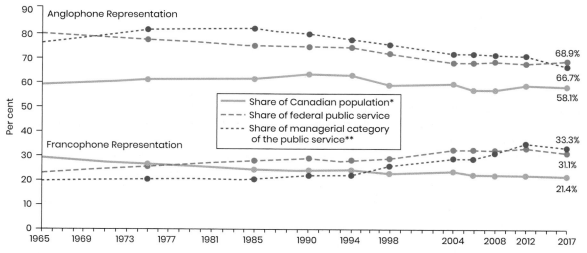

FIGURE 14.4 Anglophone and Francophone Representation in the Federal Public Service as a Whole, in the Management Category of the Public Service, and in the Canadian Population, 1965–2017

*Data for the representation of French- and English-language groups in the Canadian population are taken from the censuses for various years. The question refers to mother tongue, and therefore the figures do not add up to 100 per cent because some persons have a mother tongue other than English or French.

**The 1965 survey used to determine the language of those in the management category asked respondents to indicate their mother tongue; 5.2 per cent indicated a language other than English or French.

Sources: Compiled from figures provided in various annual reports of the Commissioner of Official Languages, the *Canada Year Book*, the *Report of the Royal Commission on Bilingualism and Biculturalism*, volume 3A (Ottawa: Queen's Printer, 1969), 215, table 50 and Treasury Board of Canada Secretariat, Annual Report on Official Languages. http://www.tbs-sct.gc.ca/reports-rapports/ol-lo/11-12/arol-ralo/arol-ralo06-eng.asp#sec6

Nevertheless, and as Commissioners of Official Languages have regularly observed, increased representation of francophones should not be taken as an indication that French and English are approaching greater equality as *languages of work* in the federal state. Outside of federal departments and agencies located in Quebec, the language of work remains predominantly English. The 2017 Privy Council study on official languages in the federal workplace made these observations:

English is the dominant language for most daily activities and Francophone employees do not consistently feel that they can work in the language of their choice. . . . [M]ost written materials are prepared in English and most meetings are conducted in English, particularly for the core items of discussion. . . . [I]n order to be understood on important issues, Francophone employees feel they must work in English. This is eroding our

capacity to write good briefing materials in French, and creates an environment where it is difficult for staff to maintain their bilingual competencies due to a lack of ongoing and sustained experience using both official languages.[38]

The tables are turned in Quebec, where anglophone federal employees often find that their ability to work in English is limited.[39]

The policy of designating federal public service positions by their linguistic requirements and increasing the number of positions requiring proficiency in both official languages has certainly increased the bilingual character of Canada's public service as a whole. At the same time, however, most of this bilingualism has been concentrated in the federal bureaucracies of the National Capital Region (68 per cent bilingual), Quebec (67 per cent), and New Brunswick (54 per cent). In the rest of Canada the percentage of federal public servants

Politics in Focus

BOX 14.1 Another Model for Language Rights: The Case of Belgium

Canada and Belgium have often been compared in regard to language politics. Both countries have two main linguistic communities, English and French in Canada and French and Flemish in Belgium. In each country these languages have official and equal status under the constitution (German is also an official language in Belgium, but the German-speaking minority is less than 1 per cent of the population). Both countries have a history of unequal and sometimes tense relations between their major language communities, English being the dominant community in Canada and the French dominating in Belgium, despite being outnumbered by the Flemish, until the late 1960s. Finally, both countries have federal constitutions and they both have separatist movements.

Given these similarities, comparison comes naturally. But Belgium has adopted a model of language rights quite different from Canada's. The Canadian model, we know, is based on the premise that every citizen, anglophone or francophone, has certain language rights that must be recognized anywhere in Canada and that French and English have equal constitutional status in national affairs across the country. The Belgian model is based on the idea that one's language rights depend on where a person lives. This is a *territorial* model of language rights, unlike the Canadian *personal* model.

Here is how the Belgian model works. In Flanders, the Flemish-speaking northern region of the country, public education, government services, election ballots, and signage on roads, at train stations, and for buses are in Flemish only. In Wallonia, the southern French-speaking region, French is the only official language. Brussels, the national capital, is officially bilingual, although French speakers outnumber Flemish speakers by a very wide margin. Citizens vote in national, regional, and local elections, as in Canada. But unlike Canada, there are no national political parties in Belgium. There is a Flemish socialist party and a French one, a Flemish Green party and a French one, and so on. Consequently, the party system cannot be counted on to help bridge the gap between the linguistic communities and their respective regions.

Over the years many Quebec nationalists have pointed to Belgium as a model to be emulated. But Canadian and Quebec federalists from Pierre Trudeau to the present day have always argued that the territorial model, instead of providing a better recipe for coexistence between the linguistic communities, would lead to fewer points of contact and space for understanding between Canada's "two solitudes" and ultimately to separation.

The federalists may be right. Although *indépendantisme* is far from dead in Quebec, a certain modus vivendi seems to have existed in Canada since the 1995 referendum. In Belgium, on the other hand, conflict over language rights in the linguistically mixed periphery of Brussels is a continuous fact of political life. In 2010, 2014, and again in 2019 the avowedly separatist Flemish Nationalist Party won more seats in the Belgian legislature than any other party. It seems that the territorial model of language rights used in Belgium is not a surefire way of avoiding conflict between linguistic communities.

Belgians have sometimes looked to Canada for lessons in how to make language relations work, and Canadians have returned the gaze. But it is clear that there is no one-size-fits-all formula for peace between language communities. The particulars of a country's history and demography are crucial determinants of whether a certain language rights model will satisfy a country's linguistic communities. They may often prefer an occasionally uneasy cohabitation to divorce.

who are required to be bilingual is quite low. It is 11 per cent in Ontario outside of the National Capital Region and under 5 per cent in most other provinces.[40] The linguistic polarization of the federal public service on regional lines has been lamented by some Commissioners of Official Languages. It is, however, a not very surprising consequence of the rather small size of francophone minorities in all provinces except Ontario and New Brunswick.

Ottawa's language policy acquired two additional thrusts in the 1970s. The first of these has involved financial assistance to organizations and individuals seeking to defend or expand the rights of official-language minorities and to local francophone cultural organizations outside of Quebec. Most significant in terms of results has been financial support for court challenges to provincial laws respecting language rights. These challenges have included Supreme Court decisions in 1979 and 1985 that established the official status of French in the province of Manitoba,[41] successful challenges to the restrictions on education and public signs and advertising contained in Quebec's Bill 101,[42] and protections for official-language minority educational rights under s. 23 of the Charter.[43] Until 1985, language rights cases were the only ones supported by Ottawa under its Court Challenges Program. Funding for the program was temporarily discontinued in 2006 and then restored in 2008, but only for language rights cases. After the election of the Liberal government in 2015 the Court Challenges Program (CCP) was reinvented. It is funded by the Canadian government but operates through the University of Ottawa. In addition to language rights under the Constitution, the CCP's mandate includes equality rights cases.

A second thrust of federal policy to promote bilingualism in Canadian society has been through financial assistance for second-language instruction and minority-language schools controlled by the provinces, including French immersion schools and support for summer immersion programs. The immersion phenomenon has seen the proliferation of French immersion schools in cities throughout English Canada. In 2016, about 430,000 students were enrolled in French immersion elementary and secondary schools outside Quebec,[44] compared to roughly 75,000 in 1980. More than half of all French immersion schools and about half of all immersion students in Canada are in Ontario.

The popularity of French immersion education has grown steadily over the last few decades, fuelled by non-francophone parents' perception that bilingualism will give their children an edge in the future competition for good jobs. This perception of greater opportunities for bilinguals, at least in the private sector, remains to be substantiated. The 2013 annual report of the Commissioner of Official Languages quoted approvingly from a

Maclean's article in which the author states that bilingual graduates are in greater demand than ever before and that, on average, they make more money than unilingual graduates. The fact that they make higher incomes may, of course, simply confirm the self-selection class bias that has always influenced who goes to a French immersion school.[45] A recent study of French immersion in British Columbia concludes that "French immersion programmes operate as a 'cream-skimming' phenomenon . . . [that] allows white, middle class parents to access markers of higher social status and prestige."[46]

As for the claim that bilingual graduates are in great demand, the 2013 *Maclean's* article relied on Language Commissioner Graham Fraser's statement that "the federal government is Canada's largest employer, and it needs bilingual employees." No evidence was provided to show that, with the exception of those aiming to work for the federal government or in the province of Quebec, bilingual graduates are likely to use both languages at work in the private sector. In fact, data from the 2016 census show that about 2 per cent of those who work outside of Quebec claim to use French only, mainly, or equally with another language at work. This figure includes public-sector workers, including those who work for the federal government. About 97 per cent of workers outside of Quebec claim to work in English only (90.1 per cent), mainly (5.4 per cent), or equally with another language (1.6 per cent).[47] In fact, no reliable evidence shows that, outside of the federal public sector, any significant number of immersion graduates use their acquired French in the Canadian workplace. None of this is an argument against immersion education and other public investments in the promotion of bilingualism. It is simply a caution against uncritical acceptance of some of the inflated claims made for such programs.

Is Separatism Yesterday's Issue?

The signs were everywhere. It may have begun with the federal election of 2011, when the Bloc Québécois fell to four seats in the House of Commons and 23.4 per cent of the vote in Quebec from the 49 seats

THE CANADIAN PRESS/Graham Hughes

A Parti Québécois supporter watches the results of the October 2018 Quebec general election. With its worst showing in at least 45 years, the PQ lost its official party status during the election, raising questions of whether the party could survive.

and 38.1 per cent it had won in 2008. A few years later the separatist Parti Québécois went from forming the government in Quebec as recently as 2014 to crushing defeats in the 2014 and 2018 elections. In the 2018 provincial election the PQ won only 17 per cent of the popular vote, its weakest showing since 1970, the first election contested by the PQ. In 2016, a widely reported—and in English-speaking Canada, much celebrated—poll found that 82 per cent of Quebec respondents agreed with the statement, "Ultimately, Quebec should stay in Canada." This included 73 per cent of francophones who said that Quebec should stay in Canada and 64 per cent who agreed that "the issue of Quebec sovereignty is settled, and Quebec will remain in Canada."[48] Two years later an Ipsos poll found that only 25 per cent of Quebecers said they would vote for independence, versus 55 per cent who said they would vote to remain in Canada. Things continued to get worse

for the separatist cause when, in May 2018, seven of the 10 Bloc Québécois MPs resigned from the party to form their own party, Québec Debout. The reason for their departure was the uncompromising stand on Quebec independence taken by the BQ's leader, Martine Ouellet, who resigned a month later after more than two-thirds of party members rejected her leadership. Just over 50 years since the creation of the Parti Québécois, it seemed that the separatist movement had run its course.

In view of these developments, it was hardly surprising that the death of the separatism movement has been widely proclaimed. This conclusion may prove to be correct. But as has so often happened in matters of French–English relations in Canada, it is influenced to some degree by wishful projection on the part of those who want to see Quebec remain in Canada and by ignorance of or indifference to some important continuing sources of tension within the province. Foremost among these tensions is the language situation in Montreal. As Quebec author Karel Maynard puts it, "Montreal is on the highway to anglicisation."[49]

Montreal, in particular the Island of Montreal in the centre of the city, has become significantly more English-speaking over the past couple of decades. Between 2006 and 2016 the percentage of Montrealers who mainly speak French at home has remained stable at about 66 per cent across the Greater Montreal Area. In the workplace, however, French appears to be losing some ground. The predominant use (only or mainly) of French fell from 72.2 per cent in 2006 to 69.6 per cent in 2016. However, the predominant use of English also declined over this period, from 19.1 per cent to 17.9 per cent. Across the province, the percentage

Photo by John Londono

The band Les Cowboys Fringants enjoys wild popularity in Quebec and is an important part of the Québécois néo-trad genre (modernized Quebec folk music with a rock sound). While Les Cowboys have garnered a following in France and French-speaking Belgium and Switzerland, they remain relatively unknown to anglophones in the rest of Canada. Is such a cultural factor an indicator of Quebec's distinct nature or does it have little political relevance?

of Quebec workers who say they use English and French equally at work increased from 4.6 to 7.2 per cent over this 10-year period, most of the increase taking place in Montreal. For those who believe that increased bilingualism ought to be the goal, this is good news. For those who believe that anything that erodes the dominant status of French in Montreal and in the province is a setback, this is a worrisome trend.

A 2017 Statistics Canada study projects that on the Island of Montreal the percentage of the population with French as their mother tongue will drop from just under 50 per cent in 2011 to about 40 per cent in 2036, and the percentage speaking mainly French at home will slip from about 54 per cent to just under 50 per cent over this same period.[50] For the Greater Montreal Area, the decline is expected to be on the same scale, French as mother tongue dropping from 80 per cent to about 67 per cent and as home language from 83 per cent to about 72 per cent. Across the province, and taking into account uncertainty as to the levels of immigration to Quebec over the next couple of decades, the percentage of the population with French as their mother tongue is expected to drop from about 79 per cent in 2011 to about 70 per cent in 2036. French–English bilingualism, already much higher in Quebec than in other provinces, is expected to increase from 43 per cent of the population in 2011 to about 52 per cent in 2036. Again, if one believes that increasing knowledge and use of the two official languages is the goal, these projections are cause for celebration. If, however, the predominance of French is the standard against which these trends should be measured, then the projections are cause for alarm.

Most English-speaking Canadians have not heard these alarm bells, or if they have they wonder what the fuss is about. What they do not understand is that the nationalism that has been built in Quebec since the Quiet Revolution, and that is embodied in Bill 101, is not about ensuring that the French language and the Quebec culture can exist side by side, on a basis of equality, with English and other cultures. This formula, embraced so enthusiastically in predominantly English-speaking Canada, is seen by Quebecers who believe the independence option should not be taken off the table as leading inevitably to a

The Social Fabric

BOX 14.2 Does Bilingualism Threaten Quebec's Identity?

Montreal journalist, writer, and professor, Mathieu Bock-Côté, is a leading figure among the younger generation of separatist intellectuals in Quebec. He argues that bilingualism is a form of surrender—surrender of the identité québécoise in the name of cultural accommodation, equality of the two official languages of Canada, and the widespread belief that cultural globalization cannot and should not be resisted. Here is what he believes needs to be done to preserve the French language and the distinctive identity of Quebec.

Immigration levels should of course be reduced to suit our integration capabilities. We should put an end to the systematic but unacknowledged bilingualism of the Quebec state that allows newcomers to interact with the public authorities without having to speak French. The rights of the historical English minority, which are indisputable, must not be used to restore by indirect means state bilingualism. In a normal world, Bill 101 should also be enforced at the post-secondary level, which, alas, no major political leader wants at this time. And we will not be able to avoid a real francisation of the world of work. Quebecers themselves, in their daily lives, should resist the anglicisation that surrounds them and that is sold to them in the name of globalization and openness to others.

In regard to the anglicisation of Montreal, Bock-Côté believes the situation is dire:

Montreal is above all a city where it is no longer necessary to speak French to function on a daily basis. This is passed off as an effect of globalization without ever asking whether the state exists for a reason. This is what happens when we declare, a bit stupidly, that politics no longer counts in the lives of peoples. One can live very well in Montreal without ever coming into contact with Quebec culture. It's a bit as if we were optional in our own place—and soon we'll be told that we are too many.

Sources: Mathieu Bock-Côté, "Le français en danger ou l'illusoire sécurité linguistique," *Le Journal de Montréal*, 28 Jan. 2017; Mathieu Bock-Côté, "À Montréal, les Québécois francophones, sont-ils de trop?" *Le Journal de Montréal*, 4 Jan. 2016. Author's translations.

decline in the relative status and importance of French in the province (see Box 14.2).

It may well be that the sovereignist project in Quebec, nurtured and led for decades by the generation that entered adulthood during the Quiet Revolution and the heady years of Quebec nationalism that followed the election of the PQ in 1976, is winding down. A 2017 Léger poll found that support for Quebec independence was opposed by 77 per cent of Quebecers between the ages of 18 and 24. Such numbers do not augur well for the future of the separatist movement in Quebec.

Waning enthusiasm for Quebec independence should not be interpreted, however, as a sign that tensions over language and culture have disappeared. They continue to surface from time to time, sometimes in ways that, to some, may seem rather trivial. One such instance involved the 2017 controversy over the Quebec National Assembly's unanimously passed resolution to encourage store and restaurant employees to greet customers with "Bonjour" instead of the common "Bonjour/Hi" greeting. The renaissance of the Bloc Québécois in the 2019 election, winning about one-third of the popular vote and almost as many seats as the Liberal Party, was interpreted by some as a sign that predictions of separatism's demise are premature. What is clear is that the gap between the two solitudes remains (see Box 14.3).

Summing Up

The fact of having two main language communities has cut deep grooves across Canada's political history. It has influenced how political issues are framed, how the parties campaign and who they select as leaders, the manner in which the Canadian state represents itself abroad, the nature

The Social Fabric

BOX 14.3 Still Two Solitudes in Montreal?

Dan Bilefsky is a Canada correspondent for the New York Times. *A native Montrealer, Bilefsky has lived and worked as a reporter in Brussels, London, Paris, and other parts of Europe and recently returned to live in Montreal after 28 years abroad. Here are some of his reflections on the current state of his hometown.*

Snaking through the heart of Montreal is St. Laurent Boulevard, a long and storied street peppered with Jewish delis, Portuguese chicken rotisserie joints and former brothels reincarnated as luxury condominiums. Historically, Francophones lived to the east of St. Laurent while Anglophones lived to the west.

Today, gaggles of French, English, Chinese and Indian students sit hunched over computers at cafes, chatting on Facebook or writing on Twitter.

But—a Berlin Wall of the mind lingers.

While the younger generation of Anglophone residents will confidently pronounce "St.-Laurent," some of their parents stubbornly cling to "St. Lawrence."

While Anglos read *The Montreal Gazette* or turn to the CBC for their news, Francophones read *La Presse* or *Le Devoir* or watch TVA. Utter the name Xavier Dolan or Marie Mai, a wildly popular Quebec singer, to an Anglophone Montrealer, and you risk being greeted by a blank stare.

"It is taboo to talk about the two solitudes, because we are supposed to pretend that we all get along when we are, in many ways, still separate," said Heather O'Neill, a Montreal-based Anglophone novelist, who has daringly explored the city's decadent underworld from the perspective of French Québécois characters.

. . . In December [2017], provincial legislators unanimously passed a resolution calling for shopkeepers to stop saying "Bonjour-hi" when they greet customers and to say simply "Bonjour" instead.

Meanwhile, Valérie Plante, the outward-looking mayor of Montreal, was recently criticized for releasing highlights of the city's budget in English.

. . . A few streets farther east on Avenue du Mont-Royal, Marie Bouchard, a 23-year-old political science student at Université de Montréal, was munching on a sandwich at a cafe.

She said her favorite television show was the British science fiction series "Black Mirror," while she loved French Québécois pop music and adored her large group of Anglo friends.

"I love French, it's my language," she said, quickly adding, "But if I only spoke French, it would limit my horizons."

Source: Dan Bilefsky, "In Montreal, a Berlin Wall of the Mind?" *New York Times*, 5 Mar. 2018, https://www.nytimes.com/2018/03/05/world/canada/montreal-french-english-divide.html.

of Canadian federalism, and many other aspects of Canadian political life. Language became an existential issue for Canada during the Quiet Revolution of the 1960s. Today, after two referendums on Quebec independence, the sovereignty movement in Quebec appears to be on the defensive and in retreat. This does not mean, however, that whatever modus vivendi has been arrived at is based on a consensus among francophone and non-francophone Quebecers about the sort of society they would like their province to be.

Controversy over language rights has not been limited to Quebec. Indeed, the federal and Quebec governments have pursued quite different tracks when it comes to Canada's two official languages. Ottawa's policy has been and continues to be based on the idea that language rights are personal and portable: they belong to the individual as a member of the English- or French-speaking community and these rights are not relinquished when one moves from one region of the country to another. Quebec's language policy is based on a territorial model. Its basic premise is that within the jurisdictional boundaries of the province, certain rules apply when it comes to the language in the workplace, schools, provincial and municipal services, and the *visage linguistique* of Quebec. The predominant status of the French language is recognized by provincial law.

The 2019 federal election, which saw resurgent support in Quebec for the Bloc Québécois, should give pause to those who were inclined to dismiss separatism as yesterday's issue. While it is true that the BQ elected in 2019 was less aggressive in its advocacy of independence than the party was in its early years under Gilles Duceppe's leadership, it is not difficult to imagine circumstances that could rekindle that earlier fire.

Appendix: Proposals for a Distinct Society Clause

The demand for constitutional recognition of Quebec as a **distinct society** has been an important item on the agenda of Quebec's political elite since the late 1980s. It was reiterated in the Quebec Liberal government's 2017 statement on constitutional policy, *Quebecers: Our Way of Being Canadian* (pages 45–7, 95–8). Here are six proposals and resolutions from over the years that recognize Quebec's distinctiveness.

Version I: Meech Lake Accord (1987)

(Died when the Meech Lake Accord proposals expired on 23 June 1990.)

1. The Constitution Act, 1867, is amended by adding thereto, immediately after Section 1 thereof, the following section:
2. (1) The Constitution of Canada shall be interpreted in a manner consistent with: (a) The recognition that the existence of French-speaking Canadians, centred in Quebec but also present elsewhere in Canada, and English-speaking Canadians, concentrated outside Quebec but also present in Quebec, constitutes a fundamental characteristic of Canada; and, (b) The recognition that Quebec constitutes within Canada a distinct society;

(2) The role of the Parliament of Canada and the provincial legislatures to preserve the fundamental characteristic of Canada referred to in paragraph (1)(a) is affirmed;

(3) The role of the Legislature and Government of Quebec to preserve and promote the distinct identity of Quebec referred to in paragraph (1)(b) is affirmed;

(4) Nothing in this section derogates from the powers, rights or privileges of Parliament or the Government of Canada, or of the legislatures or governments of the provinces, including any powers, rights or privileges relating to language.

Version II: Charlottetown Accord (1992)

(Rejected by a majority of Canadians in the 1992 referendum.)

The Constitution Act, 1867 is amended by adding thereto, immediately after Section 1 thereof, the following section:

2. (1) The Constitution of Canada, including the Canadian Charter of Rights and Freedoms, shall be interpreted in a manner consistent with the following fundamental characteristics:

   . . .

   (c) Quebec constitutes within Canada a distinct society, which includes a French-speaking majority, a unique culture and a civil law tradition;

   . . .

(2) The role of the legislature and Government of Quebec to preserve and promote the distinct society of Quebec is affirmed.

Version III: Motion Passed by Parliament (1995)

THAT

Whereas the people of Quebec have expressed the desire for recognition of Quebec's distinct society;

(1) the House recognize that Quebec is a distinct society within Canada;

(2) the House recognize that Quebec's distinct society includes its French-speaking majority, unique culture and civil law tradition;

(3) the House undertake to be guided by this reality;

(4) the House encourage all components of the legislative and executive branches of government to take note of this recognition and be guided in their conduct accordingly.

Version IV: The Calgary Declaration (1997)

(Adopted by all provincial governments except that of Quebec.)

In Canada's federal system, where respect for diversity and equality underlines unity, the unique character of Quebec society, including its French-speaking majority, its culture and its tradition of civil law, is fundamental to the wellbeing of Canada. Consequently, the legislature and the Government of Quebec have a role to protect and develop the unique character of Quebec society within Canada.

Version V: An Act Respecting the Fundamental Rights and Prerogatives of the Quebec People and the Quebec State (2000)

(This was the Quebec legislature's response to the Clarity Act passed by Parliament in 2000. All parties in Quebec's National Assembly agreed that the Québécois constitute a nation with a right to self-determination and, moreover, that only the citizens and legislature of Quebec have a legitimate voice in the determination of whether the province will become an independent state.)

[T]he Québec people, in the majority French-speaking, possesses specific characteristics and a deep-rooted historical continuity in a territory over which it exercises its rights through a modern national state, having a government, a national assembly and impartial and independent courts of justice.

Version VI: The 2006 House of Commons Resolution

(Passed by a vote of 266 for, to 16 against.)

That this House recognize that the Québécois form a nation within a united Canada.

Starting Points for Research

Michael D. Behiels and Matthew Hayday, eds, *Contemporary Quebec: Selected Readings and Commentaries* **(Montreal and Kingston: McGill-Queen's University Press, 2011).** Although this very fine collection is already becoming rather dated, it remains the best English-language reader on Quebec politics and society.

Ramsay Cook, ed., *French Canadian Nationalism: An Anthology* **(Toronto: Macmillan, 1969).** This volume contains a wide selection of writings from French-Canadian nationalists and about French-Canadian and Quebec nationalists, from the mid-nineteenth century to the Quiet Revolution. An indispensable historical resource.

Chantal Hébert, *The Morning After: The 1995 Quebec Referendum and the Day That Almost Was* **(Toronto: Knopf, 2014).** A journalist well known as a regular commentator on English-language television, Hébert reflects on the near breakup of Canada in 1995 and the consequences that might have followed had a majority of Quebecers voted yes.

Vigile Québec. https://vigile.quebec/. This Quebec news aggregator is the best single location for articles in the Quebec media. Most are in French.

Review Exercises

1. If you are bilingual, this exercise is for you. Watch the video clip entitled "Frenglish: Bilingual Montrealers," at www.youtube.com/watch?v=-yYPD6JJtDM. Based on what you now know about Quebec after having read Chapter 14, what is your reaction to journalist Ann Marie Withenshaw's views on bilingualism in Quebec and Canada? Do you think that what she says mainly supports those who worry about the anglicization of Montreal or those who believe that bilingualism is the glue that holds Canada together?

2. How bilingual is your community? Make an inventory of the indications that French (or English, if you are in Quebec) language rights are protected and the French language promoted. It should include such items as the following:

   A. Schools
      - French schools
      - Immersion schools
   B. Media
      - Newspapers and other print media (traditional and digital versions)
      - Radio (locally produced?)
      - Television (locally produced?)
   C. Signage (stores, traffic signs, billboards, product labels, etc.)
   D. Churches and community centres
   E. Clubs, bars, restaurants, etc.
   F. Employment
      - Teaching jobs in French (or English in Quebec); businesses that require French-speaking employees; government agencies that hire French-speaking workers
   G. Public services
      - Do you have the option of communicating with officials of government agencies in both French and English? Which levels of government?

3. What would be the consequences of Quebec independence for official bilingualism in the rest of Canada? Move past the immediate emotion and backlash to consider what possible consequences separation might have for schools, political parties, government services, business, and the Constitution.

Srosh Hassan, a delegate from Sherwood Park–Fort Saskatchewan, delivers a passionate speech against Islamophobia in Canada at the 2019 Daughters of the Vote (DOV) event at Parliament Hill, in which 338 delegates of the DOV replaced their Member of Parliament in the House of Commons to represent their community for a day. During this event, dozens of delegates turned their backs during Trudeau's speech to protest the expulsion of Jody Wilson-Raybould and Jane Philpott from the Liberal caucus. Roughly the same number simply walked out during Conservative leader Andrew Scheer's speech. (THE CANADIAN PRESS/Sean Kilpatrick)

15 Women and Politics

In 1928 the Supreme Court of Canada, in the *Persons* case, addressed the question of whether women had the status of persons under certain laws, including those determining who could be a judge. The Supreme Court said they were not. Common sense and justice prevailed in 1929, however, when the ruling was reversed by the Judicial Committee of the Privy Council, at the time the highest appellate court for Canada. Today, four of the nine justices of the Supreme Court are women. Gender equality was a major issue in Canadian politics from the 1970s to the 1990s. Although the issue may not appear to be as controversial today, this is because of legislative and court victories, the increased representation of women in politics and in other fields, and important changes in public opinion. Topics in this chapter include the following:

- The social construction of gender differences
- First-wave feminism: industrialization and democratization
- Second-wave feminism: equality beyond citizenship rights
- Third-wave feminism: diversity, multiple identities, and choice
- Women in Canadian public life
- How does Canada compare to other countries?

The Social Construction of Gender Differences

Men and women are biologically different. Although obvious, the social implications of this have been the subject of enormous controversy. Until the 1960s and 1970s, there was widespread agreement that the biological attributes of the sexes played a major role in the determination of their respective personality traits, intellectual aptitudes, general abilities, and social roles. Males were considered to be more aggressive, rational, analytical, adventurous, and active than females—and more fitted to leadership roles. Females were generally believed to be more nurturing, emotional, intuitive, cautious, and passive. Nature, not nurture, was considered to be the primary reason for the behavioural and attitudinal differences between males and females and for the social superiority of men over women. This was not only the conventional wisdom, believed and expressed by average men and women. It was also widely subscribed to by health-care professionals, including psychologists.[1]

This view was even shared by the first wave of the women's movement. Beginning in the late 1800s, the objectives of this movement focused on extending voting rights to women and on legal and social reforms geared towards the protection of the family and traditional values. The arguments used to support these demands emphasized fairness and morality. Extending voting rights to women and eliminating some of the grosser forms of legal discrimination against them—such as the common law's ambiguity about whether a woman was a person in law, or the law's failure to ensure a woman's right to property acquired during the course of married life—were matters of fundamental justice based on the equal humanity of the sexes. This argument, however, did not challenge the conventional wisdom on the biological determination of gender differences.

Suffragists often allied themselves with organizations promoting such causes as temperance, educational reform, child labour laws, and public service reform (to eliminate corruption). These causes were central to the character of the early women's movement. Groups like the Woman's Christian Temperance Union (WCTU), the National Council of Women of Canada (NCWC), and the Women's Institutes comprised the movement's organizational hub. These organizations supported female suffrage on the grounds that women voters would inject a morally uplifting element into the grubby business of politics. It was in a woman's nature, they argued, to care more about life and the conditions that nurtured it. Extending full democratic rights to women would immediately elevate the prominence of those issues that most concerned the women's movement, including mothers' pensions, minimum wage laws for women, better industrial health and safety standards, prison and family law reform, and more public spending on education. Women were the morally superior sex, and their participation in politics would make the world a better, more civilized place.

These arguments formed the basis of the first wave of the feminist movement, often referred to as *social feminism or **maternal feminism***. Far from challenging the notion that different **gender roles** are the inevitable product of biology, maternal feminists accepted this assumption wholeheartedly. But they turned it from an argument against political rights for women into the basis of their case for political equality. Some of the leaders of the feminist movement, such as Nellie McClung, in fact used both contemporary-sounding and maternal feminism arguments in demanding the vote and social reforms.[2] The mainstream of this first wave of the women's movement, however, was dominated by the more moderate arguments of social feminism and by traditional family and Christian values. Indeed, looking back on women's struggle to achieve political rights, the wonder is that female suffrage was resisted so vigorously and for so long. Although it challenged men's monopoly on public life, the early women's movement did not threaten the social and economic pillars of male dominance.

But the second wave of feminism did. Simone de Beauvoir's declaration that "One is not born, but rather becomes, a woman"[3] suggests that gender role differences are not inherent. They are socially constructed—passed on and relearned from generation to generation. This is the basic premise of the second wave of the women's movement.

Library and Archives Canada

Agnes Macphail was elected to the House of Commons for the riding of Grey Southeast (Ontario) in the 1921 federal election, making her the first female MP in Canada. Throughout her political career, Macphail advocated for rural issues, penal reform, and seniors' and workers' rights. Macphail founded the Elizabeth Fry Society of Canada to advocate for women and girls in the criminal justice system, and was the first woman delegate to the League of Nations in Geneva, Switzerland.

This premise has generated an enormous body of research, much of it in the fields of neuropsychology and social psychology (see Box 15.1). It also continues to fuel political and policy debates that arise around specific issues such as the continuing under-representation of females in the fields of science, technology, engineering, and mathematics (STEM), the causes of pay differentials between males and females, whether male and female politicians tend to have different representational and decision-making styles, and so on.

The idea that male/female differences are socially constructed is not a recent invention. In the late nineteenth century the British philosopher, John Stuart Mill, commented on the hypocrisy of society's attitudes towards women. Stripped of its moral pretensions, this attitude, Mill argued, could be summarized as follows: "It is necessary to society that women should marry and produce children. They will not do so unless they are compelled. Therefore it is necessary to compel them."[4] Mill was not suggesting that women did not have biological impulses or nurturing tendencies that, perhaps in most cases, would cause them to assume a disproportionate share of child-rearing and household tasks. His argument was simply that the weight of the law and social convention left them with no choice.

Mill's explanation had two parts. He argued that the subservient condition of a married woman—her lack of rights, standing, and personhood in relation to a husband whom the law and society treated as her master—would not be voluntarily chosen by many women, and certainly not by women capable of doing something else. But at the same time, this form of legalized "slavery" or "impressment"—the analogies are Mill's—provided men with a free source of domestic labour. Rather than pay women the "honest value of their labour,"[5] male-dominated society chose to institutionalize this sexual exploitation, at the same time claiming that woman's condition was naturally and even divinely ordained.

According to Mill, men wanted to deny women equal recognition and fair compensation for their domestic labour, simply because most men preferred the status and privileges of master, even if their mastery was limited to the confines of their home. This, argued Mill, was an egotism that inflicted costs on society. By depriving women of opportunities outside of marriage and the home, male-dominated society deprived itself of the talents, intelligence, and contributions of half the population.

Mill's arguments on the social construction of gender differences and the subordination of women were in the tradition of liberal utilitarianism. A rather different angle on women, the family, and power was provided at about the same time by Karl Marx's collaborator, Friedrich Engels.[6]

Engels sought to show that the subservience of women to men within the family and, by extension, in society is based on economic foundations. He argued that the free domestic labour provided by women subsidized capitalist production by reducing the wages that employers had to pay to attract the services of male employers. The male breadwinner/ female homemaker family served the interests of the capitalist class because it ensured the reproduction of the working class at low cost. Marxists ever since have pointed out that the values associated with the traditional family also perform an ideological function, helping to ensure the acceptance by subordinate classes and by women of a social system that ensures their subordination. The state actively promoted the sexual exploitation of women within the family through laws restricting the legal and property rights and opportunities of females.

Within the institution of marriage, Engels contended, the relationship between man and woman was analogous to that between the bourgeoisie and the proletariat in society. The property relations that provided the basis for inequalities in power between social classes were mirrored in the relations between husband and wife. It followed from this, he argued, that the emancipation of women required their full integration into society and the economy in order to eliminate their dependence on male wage earners. Women cannot be dependent and equal at the same time, an argument that became an important part of second-wave feminism.

Both Mill and Engels argued that dominant ideas about differences between men and women were ideational creations that protected and perpetuated the dominant status of males and, in the case of Engels, that also subsidized capitalist exploitation of the working class. Neither of them, however, seriously challenged the notion that biological differences between the sexes were at the root of many of the social inequalities between the sexes. They were not alone. No less a scholar than the anthropologist Margaret Mead found herself on both sides of this question, arguing for the overwhelming importance of social learning earlier in her career and then for what she came to believe was the decisive importance

of females' mothering instinct in her later writings.[7] Today, the dominant view among Western political scientists, sociologists, and social psychologists is that socialization into a set of gender expectations matters more than whatever biologically inherent differences may exist between males and females. There is, however, considerably less agreement on this point among neuropsychologists and others who study the brain, as evident in Box 15.1.

First-Wave Feminism

Feminist writings and occasional incidents of women mobilizing around particular events or issues before the nineteenth century were quite rare. The democratic impulses released by the overthrow of absolute monarchy in Britain (1688) and by the American (1776) and French revolutions (1789) generated some agitation for equality of political rights, but their consequences in regard to social change were negligible. One early feminist, Olympe de Gouges in France, argued in *Declaration of the Rights of Woman and the Female Citizen* (1791) that patriarchy was the source of society's ills. Her challenge to the patriarchal assumptions that prevailed at the time earned de Gouges the equality of the guillotine during the 1793 Reign of Terror.[8] Although married women did have the right to vote in some societies, they were expected to follow the lead of their husbands—particularly during an era before the secret ballot. In matters of law and property, a woman was subsumed under the person of her father and, after marriage, her husband. This state of affairs had been the focus of calls for reform by late eighteenth-century feminists such as de Gouges and England's Mary Wollstonecraft.

The origins of the women's movement as social action, as opposed to the ideas of a handful of visionary women like de Gouges and Wollstonecraft, usually are located in the mid-nineteenth century. As Sheila Rowbotham writes, "Feminism came, like socialism, out of the tangled, confused response of men and women to capitalism."[9] The progress of capitalism produced both affluence and misery. As more and more people crowded into the cities whose growth was spawned by factory production, a new set of social problems arose. Working-class

The Social Fabric

BOX 15.1 Nature, Nurture, and Politics

The scientific literature on behavioural differences between males and females and their causes is vast. The official position of the American Psychological Association is that gender similarities far outweigh gender differences and that most of the behavioural differences that may be observed are due to socialization (nurture), not biology (nature). "[M]en and women," the APA states, "are basically alike in terms of personality, cognitive ability and leadership."[10] The Association supports the gender similarities hypothesis, advanced by psychologist Janet Shibley Hyde[11] and others, which maintains that male/female differences in cognitive abilities, verbal and non-verbal communication, aggression, leadership, self-esteem, moral reasoning, and motor behaviours tend to be quite small and not rooted in biology. A recent study of males and females in STEM fields concludes that "women's interests in more people-oriented, and less things-oriented work environments was a key factor that influenced their career choice in STEM fields."[12] These differences in interests, the researchers note, may well be due to social learning.

Just as the nurture thesis has many advocates, so too does the nature thesis. Psychologist Diane Halpern's work on cognitive differences between males and females, many of which appear in early infancy, is frequently referred to on the nature side of this debate.[13] It is also supported by much, but by no means all,

research in neuroscience, a field in which sex influences on behaviour, aptitudes, and abilities were, until recently, generally dismissed or ignored. Neuroscientist Larry Cahill remarks that, "Due to a deeply ingrained, implicit (but false) assumption that 'equal' means 'the same,' most neuroscientists *knew*, and even feared that establishing that males and females are not the same in some aspect of brain function meant establishing that they were not equal."[14]

The nature versus nurture debate on male/female behavioural, cognitive, and other differences that might be perceived to matter for educational choices, career aptitudes, etc. is a classic example of a false dichotomy. As Diane Halpern writes, "The role of culture is not zero. The role of biology is not zero." She adds, "[E]veryone can improve in any cognitive area—that is the reason for education—and rapid changes in the proportion of men and women in some fields show that huge changes can occur across populations by changing educational opportunities and social expectations."[15]

Wisdom like this does not stop those with pre-existing political agendas from cherry-picking the research on male/female differences that they believe supports their case, nor from ignoring the nuance and sophistication that characterizes much of the work that has been done by serious scientists on these issues.

women, girls, and children were employed in many industries. In fact, their cheap labour provided the basis for the profitability of such industries as textiles, clothing, footwear, and cigar-making. As historian Terry Copp observes of working-class Montreal in the early twentieth century:

> Large numbers of working class women were "emancipated" from the bondage of unpaid labour at home long before their middle class

counterparts won entry into male-dominated high income occupations. There was no need to struggle against an exclusionist policy, since employers were only too happy to provide opportunities for women in the factories, shops, and garment lofts of the city.[16]

Hard numbers on female participation in the workforce do not exist before twentieth-century census-takers began to keep track of such things.

It has been estimated, however, that women comprised about 20 per cent of the labour force in Montreal during the 1890s. There is no reason to think that the percentage was lower in other cities in which textile mills and footwear and clothing factories were major employers. The low wages put downward pressure on the wages of all unskilled working people.

Working conditions in most manufacturing establishments were hard, to say the least. There were no laws regulating the hours of work, minimum wages, or safety and sanitation in the workplace. A disabling injury on the job usually meant personal financial disaster. While both men and women suffered under these conditions, the exposure of women—usually single—to the harsh environment of the factory and sweatshop was considered more serious because of the era's views on femininity. A woman's natural place was considered to be the home, and her participation in the wage economy was believed, by conservatives and social reformers alike, to be "one of the sad novelties of the modern world . . . a true social heresy."[17]

Early industrialization took its toll on women in other ways as well. The brutal grind and crushing squalor that characterized the lives of many working people could be numbed through drink. And in an era before heavy "sin taxes," beer and spirits were very cheap. Alcohol abuse, although by no means restricted to the working class, was one of the side effects of the long hours of work, inadequate wages, and sordid workplace conditions characteristic of workers' lives. It not only contributed to the ruin of individuals, but to the suffering of their families. Poor sanitation, overcrowding in improperly ventilated housing, and improper diet combined to produce low life expectancy—average life expectancy was about 45–50 years in the last decades of the nineteenth century and tuberculosis was a major killer among the urban working class—and high infant mortality.

The harshness of early industrialization was experienced by both men and women. Its manifestations—child labour, poverty, alcohol abuse—became central issues in the early women's movement because of their perceived impact on the family and on prevailing standards of decency. The Woman's Christian Temperance Union, the Young Women's Christian Association, and the Women's Institutes that sprang up in cities across Canada starting in the late nineteenth century were keenly aware of the clash between the material conditions of working-class women and prevailing notions of femininity and family. The social reforms they urged on government were intended to protect women and the family from what they saw as the corrosive influences of industrial life.

Early feminism, however, was not merely a response to the contradictions that industrialization created for women. The achievement of democracy was also full of contradictions. If democracy was a system of government based on the will of the people, and that recognized the equal humanity and dignity of human beings, half of the population could not be denied the rights and status enjoyed by the other half.

As John Stuart Mill observed in his essay *On the Subjection of Women*, arguments against the political and legal equality of the sexes took several forms. The principal arguments, and Mill's refutations (*in italic*), included the following:

- Unlike the slavery of one race by another, or the subordination of a defeated nation by its military conqueror, the subjection of women to men is natural. *When hasn't the subordination of one category of the human race by another been labelled "natural" by members of the dominant group? What is said to be natural turns out to be, on closer examination, merely customary and convenient for those who enslave others.*

- Unlike other forms of domination, the rule of men over women is accepted voluntarily by the female population. *This is not true. Some women do not accept the subordinate lot of their sex. And if a majority appear to acquiesce in their second-class status, this should surprise no one. From their earliest years women are trained in the habits of submission and learn what male-dominated society expects of them.*

- Granting equal rights to women will not promote the interests of society. *What this means, in fact, is that equality will not promote the interests of male society. It is a mere argument of convenience and self-interest.*

- What good could possibly come from extending full political and legal rights to women? *Leaving aside the good that this would produce for women—for their character, dignity, and material conditions—all society would benefit from a situation where the competition for any particular vocation is determined by interest and capabilities. Society loses when any group is barred from contributing its talents to humanity. Finally, equality for women would improve the character of men, who would no longer enjoy the sense of being superior to one-half of the human race because of an accident of birth, rather than to any merit or earned distinction on their part.*

Despite Mill's compelling arguments for equality, men who would have been shocked at the imputation that they were anything but democratic continued to ignore and resist demands that women be treated as full citizens. The arguments used to deny political rights for women were intellectually flabby and often amounted to nothing more than "nice women do not want the vote" or "my wife doesn't want the vote."[18] But the logic of democratic rights is universal, and the exclusion of the female half of the population from the enjoyment of these rights was one of the major contradictions of most democracies until well into the twentieth century.

The early women's movement in Canada, as in Great Britain and the United States, focused mainly on three sets of issues: political rights, legal rights, and social reform. Anti-militarism was a fourth, but somewhat less prominent, issue on the political agenda of feminists. The social feminism mainstream of the movement was concerned chiefly with what it perceived as threats to the security of women and the family and to the traditional values associated with them. The demands made by organizations like the WCTU and YWCA and by prominent feminists like Nellie McClung were based solidly on the middle-class morality of the times.

In fact, many of the leading individuals in the first wave of feminism were women of strong religious conviction and even fervour. As well, some of the key organizations in the suffrage and social feminism movements, such as the WCTU, the Imperial Order of the Daughters of the Empire, and the National Council of Women of Canada, had either direct links or an affinity of views with some of the Protestant churches. Early feminism had strong ties to the social gospel movement of the period between the 1890s and the 1930s, a movement that "attempt[ed] to apply Christianity to the collective ills of an industrializing society."[19] Those in the social gospel movement, in common with the early feminist leaders, believed that a New Jerusalem could be created on earth through social reforms. Their Christianity had a worldly aspect insofar as it focused on changing conditions in the here and now. But their vision of reform was inspired by traditional Christian ideals.[20]

The mainstream organizations of the women's movement were politically moderate in terms of their goals and their strategies for attaining them. Indeed, it would be fair to say that their goals were fundamentally conservative, aimed at protecting women and the family from the corrosive influences of the industrial age. Political rights for women were expected to make the political parties and government more sensitive to issues of concern to women, such as working conditions for females, child labour, alcohol abuse, and pensions for widowed mothers. Legal rights enabling a married woman to own property in her own name or protecting her from disinheritance in the event of her husband's death were demanded in order to provide more economic security for women and their dependent children. Such social reforms as the prohibition of alcohol sales, family allowances, more humane conditions in women's prisons, and labour legislation dealing with women and children were expected to produce a more civilized, compassionate society. Finally, peace issues within the women's movement were tied directly to the image of woman as the giver and nurturer of life, to what were believed to be the maternal instincts of women.

The political tactics employed by mainstream women's groups hardly ever strayed beyond the familiar bounds of accepted practice. Unlike their sisters in Great Britain and the United States, Canadian **suffragists** did not resort to such confrontational methods as chaining themselves to the fences surrounding Parliament, physically resisting the police, or hunger strikes. Instead, they relied on petitions to government and efforts to persuade public opinion.

After about 40 years of campaigning, the first success came in Manitoba in 1916. The other three western provinces and Ontario followed suit within about a year. In the Maritimes, where the suffrage movement was comparatively weak, the achievement of political rights for women was preceded by much less agitation than in the West. Nova Scotia (1918), New Brunswick (1919), PEI (1922), and Newfoundland (1925) extended political rights to women, although in the case of New Brunswick, women were granted only voting rights. They could not hold provincial public office until 1934. Quebec was the straggler among Canada's provinces. Opposition from the Catholic Church blocked political rights for women until 1940.

Nationally, women became citizens between 1917 and 1919. The Wartime Elections Act of 1917 extended federal voting rights to the relatively small number of women serving in the military and to the much larger pool of females whose male relatives were in military service. This was broadened in 1918 to include all women aged 21 years and over. The right to hold office in the House of Commons followed a year later, although women appeared to be barred from entry into the non-elected Senate and from holding other appointive public offices, such as judgeships, by virtue of not qualifying as "persons," as this term was understood in law.

Absurd though it may seem, the personhood of women was considered to be dubious in the years following their enfranchisement.[21] Two prime ministers rejected calls for the appointment of a woman to the Senate on the grounds that women, not being persons as understood in law, were not eligible. The right of females to sit as judges was challenged in the handful of cases where they were appointed to the bench. After a couple of provincial rulings in their favour, the question was placed before the Supreme Court of Canada in 1927. Feminists were shocked when the Court ruled that the legal meaning of "persons" excluded females.

Library and Archives Canada/C-008408

Cairine Wilson became Canada's first woman senator after her appointment by Prime Minister William Lyon Mackenzie King in February 1930, four months after the 1929 ruling in the case initiated by the Famous Five declared women persons under the law, thereby making them eligible to sit in the Senate. She served until her death in 1962.

This decision was reversed on appeal by the Judicial Committee of the Privy Council. Its ruling was blunt: "The exclusion of women from all public offices is a relic of days more barbarous than ours . . . and to ask why the word [person] should include females, the obvious answer is, why should it not?"[22] Voting rights for women and formal access to the male world of politics and the professions did not change the fact that society still viewed a woman's place as being in the home. Social feminists never really challenged this belief.

Political rights for women might have provided the basis for the reforms envisaged by early feminists if two conditions had existed: (1) a sufficient number of voters were prepared to cast their ballots for candidates and parties who supported the reforms advocated by the women's movement; and (2) a political vehicle existed to articulate the movement's agenda and provide a feminist alternative in electoral politics. Indeed, it appears to have been the belief of many in the women's suffrage movement that the major political parties either would crumble when a flood of independent candidates was elected or would tremble submissively before the demands of reform-minded female voters. But in fact the parties continued to set the agenda of electoral politics along the familiar lines that had long served them so well. That the parties felt no need to respond to the agenda of the women's movement or to recruit more women as candidates showed how slight was the impact of feminism on public consciousness.

The major parties' indifference to the demands of the women's movement was matched by the movement's distrust of the party system. Early feminists were reluctant to rely on the established political parties as vehicles for reform. There were two main reasons for this. One involved the attitude of those who controlled the parties. It was not simply that the Liberal and Conservative parties showed little enthusiasm for the goals of the women's movement, including political rights for women; they were often dismissive and even hostile towards women's concerns and those expressing them. So after achieving the same formal political rights as men, women found that little of substance had changed. They were marginalized within parties dominated by men who, in the words of Canada's first female MP, Agnes Macphail, "Want to Hog Everything."[23] This was not surprising. The parties reflected the dominant beliefs of the time, beliefs that made women in public life—or in any of what were traditionally male preserves—appear an oddity. Even the more egalitarian of Canada's male politicians were not immune from sexism when it came to women in politics. J.S. Woodsworth, at the time a Labour MP from Winnipeg, probably summed up male politicians' grudging acceptance of women in *their* game when he said, "I still don't think a woman has any place in politics."[24]

A second reason why early feminists were reluctant to work within the framework of the party system was that their movement, like the farmers' movement of the same era, was issue-based. The organizations that formed the core of the movement took hard, uncompromising positions on issues like prohibition, political rights for women, and social reform. Political parties, the two major ones at least, were based on principles that rejected the issue-based approach. One of these principles was partisan loyalty, the chief manifestation of which was the sheep-like obedience of elected members to the policy positions established by their party's leaders. Feminists wanted to be able to take positions based on their perception of what was in the interests of women without having to compromise the movement's goals. This concept of direct representation was shared by the farmers' movement of the time but was discouraged by the partisan norms of British parliamentary government.

The anti-party inclinations of feminists were reinforced by the parties' tendency to avoid if possible, and fudge, if avoidance was not possible, issue stances that might alienate important groups of voters. This has been called "brokerage politics" (see Chapter 11). It is an approach that had no appeal to single-issue groups like prohibitionists and suffragists, or to the reform-minded women's movement more generally.

Working outside the established party system and the legislature, in an era when the media were less effective channels for political influence than they are today, carried heavy costs. A legislator who sits as an independent is marginalized in British parliamentary government, not sharing in the opportunities for participation available to the members of political parties. Moreover, the organizational and financial resources of the parties are important advantages that their candidates have over independents. It very quickly became apparent that non-partyism favoured by leaders of the early feminist movement faced insurmountable obstacles.

It is usual to treat the period from suffrage to the new feminism that gained momentum in the 1960s as one long hiatus in the women's movement.[25] A small number of women did run for public office, and an even smaller number won election. Of those elected or appointed to public office, some achieved national prominence. Among them were Ottawa mayor Charlotte Whitton, five-term MP and two-term Ontario MPP Agnes Macphail, British Columbia judges Emily Murphy and Helen Gregory MacGill, and Conservative cabinet minister Ellen Louise Fairclough. But the distinction of being the first woman to enter what had been an exclusive preserve of men, or to achieve recognition for one's talents and capabilities, had little impact on the political and social status of women more generally. The breakthroughs and accomplishments of a few stood in sharp contrast to the unchanged status of the many. Societal attitudes about what were believed to be the appropriate roles of men and women remained largely unchanged.

This raises the question of why social attitudes about gender roles were slow in changing. It is a complex issue that cannot be reduced to a single explanation. Nevertheless, an important part of the explanation involved limits on the ability of women to exert some greater degree of control over their reproductive role. Fairly reliable contraceptive devices became widely available and used during the 1950s (mainly condoms and diaphragms) and the 1960s (the birth control pill). It was no coincidence that women began to have fewer children. Smaller families and the ability to be sexually active without fear of becoming pregnant provided the opportunity for women to stay in school longer or participate in the workforce for more years of their reproductive lives. Choice in the realm of reproduction was a crucial material condition for **women's liberation** in other aspects of life.

Second-Wave Feminism

Simone de Beauvoir's aphorism, "One is not born, but rather becomes, a woman," was the intellectual premise for the second wave of the feminist movement. Some of the ideas she introduced in *The Second Sex* (originally published in French in 1949) were elaborated and applied to circumstances more familiar to North Americans by such leaders of the movement as Betty Friedan and Gloria Steinem in the 1960s. Women had become increasingly restive with their traditional role. "[C]hained to these [domestic] pursuits," wrote Betty Friedan, "she is

stunted at a lower level of living, blocked from the realization of her higher human needs." Friedan called this "the problem that has no name."[26] Although difficult to label and express in a culture that told women they should feel fulfilled in the home, the problem amounted to this: "I want something more than my husband and my children and my home."[27] A paying job and greater participation in the world outside of the home were often seen to be that "something more."

As it happened, however, the world of work outside the home did not recognize the equality of men and women. Expansion of the service economy in the decades after World War II produced an increase in the demand for clerical, secretarial, retail sales, cashier/teller, and food service workers. All of these occupations were dominated by females and tended to be lower paid than predominantly male jobs requiring similar levels of education and responsibility. Underpaid "female" occupations remained underpaid because of conventional beliefs that undervalued the work performed by women, seeing it as temporary or merely a supplement to the main (male) breadwinner's income. Not surprisingly, the world of work and the norms that determined why some jobs were seen as female and other as male, and that influenced compensation levels, became a central part of modern feminism's reform agenda.

The exploitation of female workers had been an important concern of social feminists, but they never questioned the belief that a married woman's proper place was in the home and that marriage was the most desirable estate for a woman. By the 1960s, the material basis of these conventional views had become shaky. Female participation in the workforce doubled from about 20 to 40 per cent between 1950 and 1970.[28] The economic forces that caused a growing number of married women to seek wage employment, combined with the psychological impetus for women to seek fulfillment beyond their homemaker role, changed the nature of women's involvement in the economy. The reality of their segregation into low-pay, low-prestige occupations[29] became less and less palatable to women as their participation in the wage economy increased.

By the early sixties voices of discontent were being increasingly heard. Women were challenging the deep-seated beliefs and social structures that limited their participation in the male-dominated world. The "problem that has no name" became known as **sexism**. This word is not found in dictionaries before the 1970s, a fact that reflected the unconscious acceptance by most people of gender role differences as natural and even desirable. "Sexism" was coined in the 1960s as a label for behaviour that treated males and females unequally. The critique developed by such second-wave feminists as Betty Friedan in *The Feminine Mystique* (1963) and Germaine Greer in *The Female Eunuch* (1970) went far beyond matters of political and legal rights and social reform, the chief concerns of earlier feminists. Instead, they exposed the social, cultural, and economic roots of inequality. Friedan's approach was typical in its range. She traced the causes of female subordination to the family, the social sciences (particularly psychology, sociology, and anthropology), education, advertising and the media, mass consumption capitalism, and sexual mores.

Anti-establishment ideas always face an uphill struggle and rarely triumph by their intellectual weight alone. The feminist critiques of Beauvoir, Friedan, Steinem, and others were given traction by the material conditions and social climate of the 1960s. As an increasing proportion of women worked outside the home, including roughly 30 per cent of married women by 1970, and as more women continued their education after high school (university attendance in the 18–24 age cohort among women increased from about 5 to 10 per cent between 1965 and 1975, compared to an increase from about 12 to 15 per cent among men),[30] sexual double standards were increasingly apparent. Articles on the dilemmas facing the "new woman," telling her how to juggle family, romance, and job, became standard fare in popular women's magazines like *Chatelaine* and *Redbook*. The argument of second-wave feminism that **the personal is political**, and that the fight for gender equality had to be waged in the workplace, the media, the schools, and over women's bodies, struck a responsive chord with many.

What the lived experience of women confirmed, the social climate of the 1960s encouraged. This was the era of the civil rights movement in the United States, mounting opposition to American military involvement in Vietnam, the Paris riots of 1968, and anti-establishment political causes generally. Attacks on the "establishment" and on traditional values and institutions were common. Student radicalism, protest marches, sit-ins, and occasional violence were the visible signs of a reaction against the status quo. Although the feminist movement did not spearhead the protest movements of the 1960s, it profited from the tendency of these movements to question established power relations.

The protest politics of the 1960s affected the women's movement in a second, more enduring way as well. Civil rights advocates in the United States argued that **affirmative action** programs were necessary to provide real equality of opportunity for blacks. Quotas and preferential hiring policies for targeted minorities were justified, they reasoned, because these groups were the victims of systemic discrimination that ensured that few of them would acquire the formal qualifications—degrees, professional school admission scores, job-relevant experience—needed to compete with the members of more advantaged groups. The arguments and demands made by the North American women's movement in the 1960s and 1970s bore a strong resemblance to those that emerged during the struggle to advance the rights of African Americans.

As was true of the civil rights movement of this era more generally, change did not happen overnight. "There are fifty-six whooping cranes in Canada and one female federal politician."[31] So began a 1971 article by Barbara Frum in *Chatelaine*. Half a century after winning the same political rights as men, the inroads made by women in Canada's political parties were pitifully small. Their participation was still channelled mainly into the activities of women's auxiliaries, whose role was to provide support services for their respective political parties. Although vital to the parties, these activities—social, administrative, fundraising, and campaigning—had low prestige and were remote from their policy- and strategy-oriented structures and roles. Separate women's associations were singled out in the 1970 report of the Royal Commission on the Status of Women as a serious barrier to the full participation of women in party politics. The Commission recommended that they be abolished.

Support-oriented women's associations within the parties mirrored the sexual division of labour that modern feminism condemned. Their elimination at the national and provincial levels in all of the major parties dates from the 1970s. The traditional women's associations were replaced by new women's groups dedicated to increasing women's representation and policy influence within the parties. As Sylvia Bashevkin notes, this transition was not frictionless and greater female influence within the parties, including the nomination of more female candidates, was slow to come.[32] The two historically dominant parties, in particular, were disinclined to alienate those voters and organized interests that objected to such elements of the feminist agenda as the elimination of legal restrictions on abortion, pay equity and affirmative action in hiring, and a national program of publicly subsidized daycare. Consequently, the women's movement sought influence by other means.

One of these means was through the courts. Litigation in support of sexual equality claims has a long history in Canada, going back to the turn of the century when women challenged barriers to their entry into certain professions. But with the notable exception of the 1929 **Persons case**, in which the JCPC overruled Canadian courts in determining that women were persons in law, most of the pre-Charter litigation on sexual equality resulted in defeats for women's claims.[33] Given this dismal track record in the courts, plus the high cost of litigation—several of the pre-Charter cases reached the Supreme Court only because certain lawyers were willing to freely donate their time—it comes as no surprise that this strategy was seldom chosen by women.

The Charter was expected to change all this. Indeed, women's groups fought hard and successfully for the inclusion of section 28 of the Charter, which states that "the rights and freedoms referred to in [the Charter] are guaranteed equally to male and female persons." Their efforts had already ensured that the equality section of the Charter (s. 15) proscribed discrimination based on sex. With sections 15 and 28 in hand, it appeared likely that women's groups would turn to the courts as never before.

They did, but with mixed results. In the first four years after the equality section came into effect (1985–9), 44 cases of sexual discrimination under section 15 were decided by the courts. Most of these cases were instigated by or on behalf of men. In only nine cases were equality claims made by women. Despite victories in some of these cases, feminist legal scholars quickly became dubious about the usefulness of section 15. Michael Mandel uses the term "equality with a vengeance" to describe what he argues was the early tendency of courts, and of governments responding to court decisions, to interpret the Charter's equality provisions in ways that sometimes backfired against women.[34]

Feminists argued that the sexual equality guarantees of the Charter could be undermined by two aspects of judicial interpretation. One was the courts' unwillingness to elevate equality rights over other rights and freedoms guaranteed in the Charter. For example, in *Casagrande v. Hinton Roman Catholic Separate School District* (1987),[35] a Catholic school board's decision to fire an unmarried pregnant teacher was upheld on the grounds that section 15 equality rights did not take precedence over the rights of "denominational, separate or dissentient schools" that are also guaranteed by the Constitution. Second, and even more serious according to feminists, was the fear that judges would interpret equality in terms of **formal equality** rather than **substantive equality**, being satisfied that no discrimination has occurred if laws treat identically persons who are similarly situated. This is an "equality before the law" approach that, according to feminists, fails to understand the real mechanisms, rooted in history, culture, and institutions, through which discrimination occurs. **Systemic discrimination**—the inequality created and maintained through social practices and beliefs—cannot be overcome if, in interpreting the law, judges are blind to the sex or other group characteristic(s) of a section 15 claimant. Substantive equality, they argue, requires that judges determine whether a claimant belongs to a disadvantaged group and, second, "whether the impugned law, policy or practice is operating to the detriment of [that disadvantaged group]."[36]

In fact, however, this fear proved unfounded. In *Law Society of British Columbia v. Andrews and*

Kinersley (1989),[37] which dealt with a resident non-citizen having been rejected for admission to the British Columbia bar because of BC statutory law, Canada's highest court very decisively embraced the concept of substantive equality in interpreting section 15 of the Charter. Although this case did not directly relate to the rights holders enumerated in s. 15, a number of these groups, including LEAF, were granted intervenor status.[38] The Supreme Court argued that the Charter's equality section prohibits laws that have had a discriminatory impact on the members of some group or groups. The decisions written by Justices Wilson and McIntyre both cited approvingly an American Supreme Court precedent that identified "discrete and insular minorities" as groups requiring the protection of constitutional equality guarantees. In fact, the formal equality test so maligned by feminist legal scholars was explicitly rejected by all of the Supreme Court justices. Since then, the substantive equality test has been routinely used by the courts in applying s. 15 of the Charter.

Before the equality rights section of the Charter took effect, making legal strategies for reform more promising than they had been previously, women's groups had relied on other, usually less effective means. They ranged from grassroots organizing to deal with emergencies (e.g., a rash of sexual assaults in a neighbourhood) or chronic local problems (e.g., inadequate public transportation or pollution) to

Louis.Roth/Shutterstock

The first annual Women's March in Toronto, held in solidarity with the Women's March on Washington following the inauguration of Donald Trump in January 2017. Like Take Back the Night rallies or the more recent #MeToo protests, this form of activism can be a powerful way to draw attention to the women's movement.

representations made through official channels, lobbying campaigns directed at decision-makers and potential supporters, and media strategies.[39] Lacking the financial resources and the personal access to decision-makers possessed by many business and professional interest groups, the women's movement made extensive use of all of these political action strategies.

Jacquetta Newman and Linda White distinguish between what they call *insider* and *outsider* influence strategies that have been used by women's groups.[40] Using the court system has been perhaps the most effective of the insider strategies. But lobbying, presentations to royal commissions, task forces, and other government inquiries, pressure applied within political parties, and media strategies have also been part of the repertoire of strategies used to influence the political conversation and policies. These are insider strategies insofar as they operate within the familiar confines of politics and are focused on influencing state action.

Outsider strategies involve mobilization outside the state that is not focused directly on influencing the actions of government officials. Examples include women-centred services such as rape crisis centres and hotlines, shelters for abused women, and various other women's and family services not directly linked to the state. In most instances, however, the state is an important—sometimes the most important—source of funding for such organizations. This dependence can create tensions in the relationship between the state and the women's organizations that turn to it for money, creating an ever-present possibility that these organizations may be co-opted and their activities influenced by government agencies that provide some portion of their finances. Activism, including take-back-the-night marches and more recently the #MeToo marches and other events, and protests and mobilization on university campuses, in front of legislatures, or elsewhere, is another feature of outsider strategies. The effectiveness of such action varies, as Cheryl Collier has shown in a study of the impact of women's movement activism on childcare and anti-violence policies.[41]

While it is not possible to say just how effective each of these political strategies has been—indeed, their effectiveness is highly contingent, depending on the particular issue and circumstances—there is little doubt that the legal strategy has produced important results. This would not have been the case without the Charter's equality guarantees and the decision by the Supreme Court of Canada, very quickly after the Charter's passage, to interpret s. 15 in a manner that, in Kathleen Mahoney's words, "favours context rather than detached objectivity." Reflecting on the Charter's impact for women's rights during this era, Mahoney writes:

> The Supreme Court of Canada has demonstrated . . . that gender equality in the Canadian context is result-oriented. Rights and duties are being allocated equitably, not simply on the basis of abstract, doctrinally stagnant principles of formal equality which thwart rather than achieve substantive equality. . . . [W]hat is critically important is that women can now address, in constitutional terms, the deepest roots of social inequality of the sexes. Issues such as reproductive control and sexual violence can now be considered as sex equality issues and laws dealing with them subjected to constitutional scrutiny.[42]

Third-Wave Feminism

For both first- and second-wave feminism, it is possible to point to a fairly coherent set of theoretical premises and issues that defined each of these stages in the history of the movement. In the case of first-wave feminism, and admittedly with a good deal of simplification, it is the idea that women should have the same political and legal rights as men and that the state should legislate in ways so as to protect women and the family. For second-wave feminism the core premise was that ideas about femininity and masculinity—and thus the roles and behaviours thought appropriate to the sexes—are socially constructed and need to be challenged if women are to achieve more than the equality of the ballot box. Change requires that the state legislate in ways aimed at dismantling forms of discrimination regarding labour markets and the workplace, women's reproductive rights, sexual violence, and women's participation as decision-makers in political, economic, and social institutions. It also requires cultural change and a rethinking of norms about male and female roles.

The defining features of third-wave feminism are somewhat more difficult to encapsulate. Indeed, an enormous literature has emerged over the past couple of decades that seeks to answer the question, "What is third-wave feminism?" This points to what is, in fact, an important and characteristic aspect of developments in feminism over the past generation. As R. Claire Snyder writes, "third-wavers embrace a multiplicity of identities, accept the messiness of lived contradiction, and eschew a unifying agenda; these hallmarks make third-wave feminism difficult to define."[43] Rebecca Walker, one of the founders of third-wave feminism, puts it this way:

> For many of us it seems that to be a feminist in the way that we have seen or understood feminism is to conform to an identity and way of living that doesn't allow for individuality, complexity, or less than perfect personal histories. We fear that the identity will dictate and regulate our lives, instantaneously pitting us against someone, forcing us to choose inflexible and unchanging sides, female against male, black against white, oppressed against oppressor, good against bad. This way of ordering the world is especially difficult for a generation that has grown up transgender, bisexual, interracial, and knowing and loving people who are racist, sexist, and otherwise afflicted.[44]

The idea that second-wave feminism involved an identity that, in Walker's words, did not allow for individuality and complexity in one's personal narrative is certainly an important aspect of third-wave feminism. Indeed, third-wave feminism is in many ways defined by its rejection of what it perceives, fairly or not, to be the white, middle-class character of the previous generation of feminism and what is seen by third-wavers to have been the insistence of the second wave on the primacy of one's gender identity. As Leslie Heywood writes, third-wave feminism "has never had a monolithically identifiable, single-issue agenda that distinguishes it from other movements for social justice. One of its main emphases, in

fact, has been on feminism and gender activism as only one part of a much larger agenda for environmental, economic, and social justice, and one of its main arguments is that it is counterproductive to isolate gender as a single variable."[45] Commenting on what appears to be the rejection by the third wave of the overarching category of women and of the focus of second-wave feminism on patriarchy, Snyder observes: "Third-wave feminists rightly reject the universalist claim that all women share a set of common experiences, but they do not discard the concept of experience altogether."[46] The core premise of the second wave that the personal is political also informs third-wave feminism, Snyder argues, through the emphasis that the latter places on personal experiences as a way of understanding larger truths about how the world, including discrimination, marginalization, and oppression, operates.

An important feature of third-wave feminism is the concept of intersectionality. This involves the personal experience of intersecting identities—being both female and black, for example—and the multiple oppressions associated with these identities. Black feminists in the United States were already writing about this experience as early as the late 1960s. "[I]ntersectionality emerged," writes Jasbir Puar, "from the struggles of second wave feminism as a crucial black feminist intervention challenging the hegemonic rubrics of race, class, and gender within predominantly white feminist frames."[47] For Kimberlé Crenshaw, who coined the term "intersectionality" in 1989,[48] and others who pioneered this work at the intersection of feminist and black studies, the primacy of the double oppression of race and sex was assumed. At the same time, however, the reality of other forms of marginalization and oppression were acknowledged and would become increasingly important in third-wave feminism. The intersectionality perspective was a direct challenge to what was seen as the fundamentally white and middle-class character of the second wave.

This clash between older and newer feminist perspectives was experienced in the early 1990s by the National Action Committee on the Status of Women (NAC). NAC's authority to speak on behalf of Canadian women was generally accepted by Ottawa and many provincial governments across English-speaking Canada in the 1980s. Its demise was due to a number of factors, but one of them was whether it was inclusive enough. In 1992, NAC's departing president, Judy Rebick, declared, "[our organization], which has been dominated by white middle class women, must transform almost everything we do to respond to the needs of doubly oppressed women."[49] After Rebick's departure, NAC's orientation very definitely shifted towards an emphasis on the special problems of racial and ethnic minorities and poor women from such groups. This redefinition of the feminist project and the sometimes rancorous divisions among feminists made it easier for governments to question whether NAC truly represented the concerns and values of a majority of Canadian women. By 2004, what had once been Canada's most prominent organizational voice for feminist concerns no longer had enough money to staff a permanent office and answer its phones.[50]

The decline of NAC is sometimes seen as indicative of a more widespread decline in the organizational power of women. Indeed, one of the features distinguishing second- and third-wave feminism is the latter's emphasis on individual empowerment and on personally claiming the gains of the second wave rather than continuing what some third-wavers have argued is the self-defeating narrative of "victimhood."[51] Nonetheless, consolidating and extending the achievements of the second wave remains the task of a number of vibrant women's organizations, including, to name but a few, LEAF, la Fédération des Femmes du Québec, and the National Association of Women and the Law. But even more significantly, women's issues and representation have been institutionalized through labour unions, professional associations, and departments and agencies of the state at all levels. Although some will disagree, it may simply be that a national umbrella organization like NAC was necessary at one time but is no longer. Many of the battles it fought and that provided its raison d'être have been won or have seen significant progress. Moreover, the organizational voice of women is today far more pervasive and entrenched in institutions across Canadian society than was true only a generation ago.

The idea that the battles fought by feminists of the baby boomer generation no longer matter for millennials and those born after them, or at least not to the same degree, is another feature of third-wave feminism. This putative generational gap was highlighted during the 2016 Democratic Party primary election campaign in the United States when surveys showed that younger educated women preferred the candidacy of Bernie Sanders while older cohorts of women supported Hillary Clinton. Leaders of an older generation of feminists were highly critical of younger women who failed to support a female candidate for their party's presidential nomination. "There's a special place in hell for women who don't help each other," declared Madeleine Albright, secretary of state during the Bill Clinton presidency. Feminist icon Gloria Steinem suggested that younger women were supporting Sanders instead of Hillary Clinton because they saw this as a better way to meet young men. The reaction from younger women, including voices in the third-wave feminist movement, was understandably furious. Jill Filipovic spoke for many younger feminists in explaining why Clinton's gender was not enough:

> Her own wealth and race . . . undermine her appeal: Just as Americans are increasingly nonwhite, so too are feminists; just as being gay, lesbian, bisexual or transgender is increasingly normalized, so too are LGBT folks more visible and vocal in feminist activism. For young women, feminism today must take into account all of these constituencies and elevate the voices of the most marginalized. For all the challenges she's faced because of her gender, Clinton is not entirely representative of a broad movement in which many women find their particular experiences shaped by their gender *and* their race *and* their class, or some other combination.[52]

Some survey data suggest an age gap exists among women when it comes to some issues related to gender equality. A 2017 Nielsen international survey found that female millennials were twice as likely as baby boomers to strongly agree that "I am paid fairly for the work I do" and "Men and women are treated equally in society." That same survey, however, found little generational difference among women in their beliefs about whether men were more likely to be preferred for senior-level roles in corporations as well as a high level of agreement among females of all ages that women have to work harder than men to prove themselves as leaders.[53] Moreover, a widely reported survey of American women carried out in 2018 found that the differences between females above and below the age of 35 on issues related to sexual harassment in the workplace were for the most part very small, the single largest difference involving whether it is acceptable for a man to lose his job as a result of an allegation of sexual misconduct in the absence of concrete evidence (48 per cent of women under 35 saying no, compared to 65 per cent of those over 35).[54] Other surveys carried out in the UK and the United States seem to indicate fairly significant generational differences among women when it comes to behaviour in the workplace, but also more generally in regard to appropriate behaviour between men and women.[55]

The survey data allow for cherry-picking in support of whatever side one leans towards on this question of a generational divide among women on issues related to gender roles and equality. Nevertheless, the idea that such a gap exists is widely accepted. An important aspect of this gap is said to involve ideas about sexual behaviour and the line separating what is and is not acceptable. Snyder writes, "In contrast to their perception of their mothers' feminism, third-wavers feel entitled to interact with men as equals, claim sexual pleasure as they desire it (heterosexual or otherwise), and actively play with femininity. Girl power, or girlie culture, is a central—yet contested—strand within the third wave. Its proponents argue that our desires aren't simply booby traps set by the

Stephanie Kenner/Shutterstock

Activists attend the 2017 Slut Walk in Detroit, Michigan. Slut Walks, which originated in Toronto after a police officer advised women that they should "avoid dressing like sluts" to protect themselves from sexual assault, have become an international movement to combat slut-shaming and raise awareness about the importance of consent—two issues that have become defining features of the modern feminist movement.

Media Spotlight

BOX 15.2 Feminist Icon or Fallen Hero?

Margaret Atwood is one of Canada's leading cultural figures. She has also been one of the country's most prominent feminists since the 1969 publication of her novel, *The Edible Woman*. More recently she has been celebrated for the award-winning HBO series, "The Handmaid's Tale," based on her 1985 novel by the same name. Her career and life as a writer, social activist, and feminist are nothing short of remarkable.

But as Atwood discovered in 2017, none of her accomplishments insulate her from charges that she is a "bad feminist." The immediate cause of the barrage of criticisms she received from many feminists was her defence of Steven Galloway, an English professor and fiction writer suspended by the University of British Columbia following anonymous charges that he was guilty of having sexually assaulted female students and at least one colleague. Atwood and many others in the Canadian literature establishment argued that Galloway should have a right to due process and transparency in the face of these charges. She compared the secrecy and apparent presumption of guilt that characterized Galloway's suspension by UBC to the Salem witchcraft trials, "in which a person was guilty because accused, since the rules of evidence were such that you could not be found innocent."[56]

This issue of the rights of victims (usually women) in matters involving allegations of sexual assault or misconduct versus those of the accused (usually men) was already very much part of the conversation. It was a prominent issue on American university campuses, where a flurry of lawsuits were launched by male students who had been dismissed from their schools because of sexual assault allegations. The #MeToo movement gained momentum in 2017 after revelations concerning Hollywood mogul Harvey Weinstein, followed by accusations against hundreds of other high-profile men, raising the prominence of the issue of sexual violence and harassment and contributing to an increased willingness on the part of women to come forward with their stories.

At the same time, the #MeToo movement generated a backlash. A poll commissioned by *The Economist* in the United States in November 2017 found that equal percentages of men and women, 44 per cent, agreed that "sexual assaults that go unreported or unpunished" and "false accusations of sexual assault" are equally problematic.[57] No similar survey was conducted in Canada, so it is not clear whether the findings would have been different from what they were in the United States. What was clear on both sides of the border, however, was that much of the conversation on the #MeToo movement had become about whether accusers should automatically be believed and, indeed, whether they should have to identify themselves. Research certainly shows that sexual assault is under-reported and that an important part of the reason for this is that those who experience it fear that they will not be believed. On the other side is the value that our culture and legal system assigns to due process and the rights of the accused.

This is the vice in which Margaret Atwood found herself squeezed. To her critics, she replied that it is certainly true that "too frequently, women and other sexual-abuse complainants couldn't get a fair hearing through institutions," and that the legal system was seen as one of the institutions that failed women. But, Atwood argued, trial by social media and disregard for due process and transparency were not the answer to its limitations. Her critics did not agree.

---

patriarchy."[58] This strand of third-wave feminism is represented in the writings of such prominent figures as Naomi Wolf and in zines that older feminists sometimes admit to finding disconcerting, such as *Bitch* and *Bust*.[59]

Evidence of a generational divide among women in regard to issues relating to gender roles and equality is also found among those who are actively engaged in the feminist movement. Based on a survey of self-identified feminists in French- and English-speaking Canada, Brenda O'Neill sought to test the proposition that the "context in place when an individual joins a social movement defines a political generation."[60] She found that those who became activists in the feminist movement before 1989 are more likely than younger recruits to the movement to attach high importance to workplace equality, child care, housing, and women's treatment by the judicial system. All of these are issues where women have made substantial gains over the past generation, a fact that might explain why younger feminists find them to be less compelling. On the other hand, Indigenous women's equality, sexual freedom, and sexual orientation issues were more likely to be considered very important by younger feminists than by those who entered the movement before 1989. Pornography was another issue that distinguished older from younger activists, the latter being somewhat less likely to say that it is a very important issue. These differences are of the sort that one would expect from the literature on the ways in which younger women part company from those who came into adulthood during the era of second-wave feminism. At the same time, however, O'Neill cautions against emphasizing differences. The data, she writes, "also reveal evidence of strong continuity. Canadian feminists are of one mind in the importance assigned to a range of issues and in their commitment to advocacy work and engagement with women's groups and organizations despite increasing diversity among its members and significant changes over time in the social and political contexts in which it is located."[61]

The Under-Representation of Women in Canadian Public Life

Women constitute just over 50 per cent of the Canadian population and a slightly larger percentage of the electorate. Despite this and notwithstanding significant gains made over the past couple of decades in the number of women elected to public office, their representation in politics continues to be far below their share of the population. As of 2019, women comprised almost one in four parliamentarians, federal and provincial. Just over one-third of all candidates in the 2019 federal election, running for the five parties represented in the House of Commons, were women (Figure 15.1). Only one of the national party leaders, Elizabeth May of the Green Party, was female. About one-quarter of municipal councillors across Canada were female. At the same time, however, only one of 10 provincial premiers was a woman (although there had been five women premiers in 2013).

The percentage of women in Canada's House of Commons was below 10 per cent until the 1988 election, when 39 female MPs, representing 13 per cent of the seats in the Commons, were elected. As may be seen in Figure 15.2, the number of female MPs has increased steadily since then, to 98 in the 2019 election. The representation of women in the Canadian Senate has increased even more rapidly, from about 10 per cent in 1980 to just over 40 per cent today. The fact that, with very rare exceptions, those who become MPs must first be selected by their parties to run for office and then must win election, whereas senators are chosen by the government of the day when vacancies occur, explains the greater percentage of females in the Senate than in the House.

Female representation among unelected public officials, including judges and high-level bureaucrats, is greater than for politicians. As is also true for elected politicians, most of this increased representation has occurred over the past generation. Before the 1982 appointment of Justice Bertha Wilson (1982–91), no woman had ever been a member of the Supreme Court of Canada. Since then Claire L'Heureux-Dubé (1987–2002), Beverley McLachlin (1989–2017), Louise Arbour (1999–2004), Marie Deschamps (2002–12), Rosalie Silberman Abella (2004–), Louise Charron (2004–11), Andromache Karakatsanis (2011–), Suzanne Côté (2014–), and Sheilah L. Martin (2017–) have been appointed to the Supreme Court. Currently, four of the nine Supreme Court justices and about 41 per cent of all federally appointed judges (492 of 1,193 as of 2019) are women. Significant inroads also have been cut into the senior ranks of the bureaucracy. Women account for about half of senior executive personnel in the federal public service and about 40 per cent of all deputy ministers.

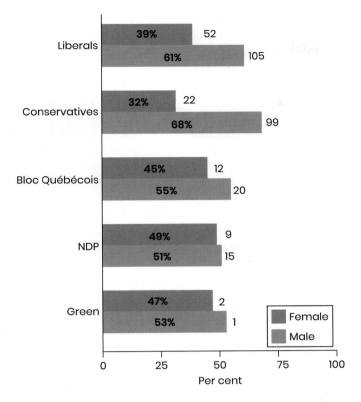

FIGURE 15.1 Gender of Candidates for the Five Main Parties in the 2019 Election

Note: The number of male and female candidates for each party who were elected is shown to the right of each bar. These totals include only the candidates of these five registered parties in the 2019 election.

Source: Based on data provided in the Report of the Chief Electoral Officer of Canada, 43rd General Election (2019).

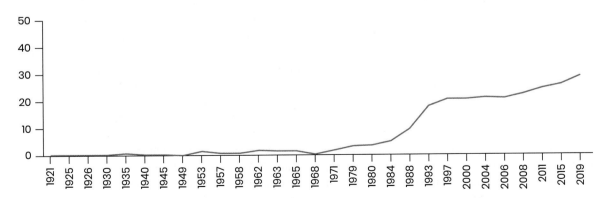

FIGURE 15.2 Percentage of Women in the House of Commons, 1921–2019

It is no longer uncommon for women to be appointed to the boards of directors of Crown corporations and to hold leading management roles in these companies. As of 2016, about one-third of the senior officers of federal Crown corporations, tribunals, boards, and agencies were female and about 40 per cent of those on their boards of directors were female.

The gains made by women over the past few decades are significant and undeniable. At the same time, the gap between the participation of males and females in Canadian public life is wide. Why this is the case and why it may matter are questions that continue to be asked.

At a superficial level, the explanation for women's under-representation in public life once appeared to be straightforward: they tended to be less interested in and less knowledgeable about politics and government than were men. Countless studies in Canada, the United States, and the UK have documented the existence of a gender gap in political knowledge, from which it has been inferred that females tend to be less interested in politics than men.[62] Nevertheless, female participation levels have long been about the same as men's for political activities like voting and campaigning. They have, however, been much lower for more demanding activities, such as holding office in a political party and running for office. **"The higher, the fewer"** is how Sylvia Bashevkin describes this political participation gap between males and females.[63] This gap has narrowed over time, but it continues to exist.

Pippa Norris and Joni Lovenduski developed a model focusing on the demand and supply of party candidates and how this is affected by gender (see Figure 15.3).[64] It plots the various steps on the ladder of recruitment from the citizenry, where females make up slightly more than half the population, to the levels of party candidates, elected officials, and members of government. While there are certainly barriers to the movement of women up this ladder at various stages, they are fewer than in the past and those relating to interest in and knowledge of politics appear towards the bottom of this model, reducing the numbers of females who are party members and aspirants for public office from what they might otherwise be.

If interest, which is closely related to knowledge of politics, is one of the key determinants of participation at levels above voting, including aspiring to become a candidate for public office, what explains lower levels of interest among women? The answer lies in social learning. Traditionally,

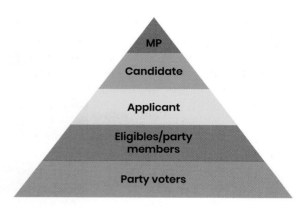

FIGURE 15.3 Demand and Supply Factors Affecting the Recruitment of Party Candidates

Source: Joni Lovenduski, "The Supply and Demand Model of Candidate Selection: Some Reflections," *Government and Opposition* 51, 3 (July 2016): 521.

females learned from the world around them that politics was a predominantly male occupation. The signals were unmistakable. The prime minister or president was a man. So, too, were all but a handful of cabinet ministers and elected representatives. More subtle than the evident maleness of the political profession, but probably more important in discouraging most females from seeing themselves in political roles beyond those of voter, was the sheer weight of social customs and expectations, communicated in the family, in school, in churches, and through the media. Leadership and an active involvement in the world beyond the family and neighbourhood were associated with masculinity. If females were not actively discouraged from developing an interest in politics, they generally were not encouraged to apply their energies and time to such matters.

The influence of social learning was reinforced by the sexual division of labour in society, particularly in the family but also, and relatedly, in the workplace. Women were likely to bear a disproportionate share of household and child-rearing responsibilities. In times before the possibility that men or women could elect to take parental leave, let alone paid parental leave, they were also much more likely than men to take time out of their careers to raise children. (This is one of the factors that historically and currently has contributed to the income gap between men and women working in the same professions.) The sexual division of labour within the household, therefore, has worked to reduce women's opportunities to achieve the sorts of experience and professional status that often provide the basis for recruitment into parties and other political organizations. If, however, a woman has the motivation and the status achievements to break into public life, there is still a good chance that the competing pressures of household responsibilities may limit either the scope of her aspirations or her ability to achieve them. Recent data from Statistics Canada indicate that while the gap between males and females in the time spent on domestic and child-rearing responsibilities has narrowed considerably from what it was a generation ago, it remains the case that on average women still spend about 50 per cent more time each day on these responsibilities than do men.[65]

The domestic division of labour is less unequal than in past generations, particularly among younger families, and the participation of women in the workforce is much greater than in the past, including in higher-paying and higher-status professions. Nevertheless, gender differences continue to place limits on women's opportunities for political participation that men are less likely to experience. "[G]ender expectations create beliefs that can directly discourage women from seeing themselves as feasible candidates," writes Brenda O'Neill. "[A]lthough perhaps less explicitly than in the past, a political candidate who is the mother of small children is still likely to raise more eyebrows among the public and some party members, than one who is the father of small children. Many women have internalized these expectations and norms, and as such, they are brought to bear on their willingness to stand for office."[66]

Other factors are important too, affecting both the demand and supply sides when it comes to female involvement and success in party politics. Among them, researchers have pointed to what some have argued is an unsupportive media climate that undermines the candidacies of some

female candidates,[67] the over-representation of rural Canada, where women are less likely to be candidates and less likely to win seats in the federal and provincial legislatures,[68] and the impact of the electoral system and the parties' candidate selection processes.[69]

Canada in the Global Context

On several indices measuring gender equality and the condition of women in countries across the world, Canada generally falls within the top 10. The United Nations Gender Equality Index is one of the best known of these international rankings. It is a composite measure that includes several indicators relating to health, empowerment (political and economic), and labour market inequalities. In 2017 Canada ranked sixth in the world, behind Norway, Sweden, Switzerland, the United States, and France. The World Economic Forum index ranked Canada 16th in that same year, using various measures of economic participation and opportunity, education, health, and political participation. This index, however, measures only the gap between men and women and thus such countries as Rwanda, Nicaragua, the Philippines, and Namibia ranked higher than Canada and many other developed countries where the life prospects and conditions of women are typically much better, yet where the male-to-female gap is greater. The Georgetown Institute for Women, Peace and Security also compiles an annual index, which measures inclusion, justice, and security. In 2018 it ranked Canada seventh among the 153 countries included in its study. Finally, U.S. News & World Report issues an annual ranking of the best countries in the world in which to live. It includes a separate ranking of countries where females experience the best lives, based on responses from women in the countries included in the survey. In 2018 Canada ranked third in the world out of the 80 countries included in the study, surpassed only by Sweden and Denmark.[70]

A 2017 international survey by Ipsos Public Affairs[71] found that Canadian women are more likely than their counterparts in any other affluent democracy to believe that they are treated equally with men. Only 22 per cent disagreed with the statement, "In my country, I have full equality with men and the freedom to reach my full dreams and aspirations," compared to 26 per cent in Sweden, 30 per cent in the United Kingdom, 36 per cent in Germany, and 37 per cent in the United States. In response to the statement that "Men are more capable of doing things in society such as working, earning money, being educated and teaching than women," only 11 per cent of Canadians, males and females, agreed, and only about one in 10 Canadians agreed that "Women should not aspire to do anything outside of the household and should produce children and tend to their family." There was no difference between the answers that males and females gave to these questions. Canada's support for gender equality was just slightly behind Spain on the first of these questions and tied with Spain and the UK on the second.

When it comes to beliefs about gender equality in the workplace, Canada ranks near the top among affluent democracies. A 2016 international survey by Randstad,[72] a Dutch human resource consulting firm, reported the following findings:

- In most developed economies, upward of 80 per cent of employees believe that men and women are treated equally at their workplace and over 70 per cent agree that women and men are treated equally in hiring and promotion. The percentages of Canadians who agree are among the highest of all countries surveyed.

- Just under two-thirds of Canadian employees say that if a female and a male have equivalent qualifications for a job, the male will be hired. The percentage who believe that males will be favoured is greater in most countries and is as high as almost four out of five respondents in such countries as Italy, France, and Spain.

- Six in 10 Canadian employees say they prefer to have a male as their direct manager, including majorities among both men and women. This is lower than in most countries.

- Canadians are more likely than employees in almost all other countries surveyed to say

that where they work, men and women in similar positions are rewarded equally (86 per cent) compared to an average of 79 per cent for all the national populations in the survey).

The rather positive picture that emerges from the above data may appear to be at odds with recent surveys showing that about half of Canadian women claim to have experienced some form of sexual harassment in the workplace.[73] They may also appear to run counter to regular media reports on the fact that men employed full-time continue to earn, on average, more than women who hold the same jobs. This wage gap has narrowed over the years, but it continues to exist. In addition, women are far less well represented in positions of influence in the business world than in politics and government where, we have seen, they continue to be under-represented in relation to their share of the population.

The difference between the average annual earnings of males and females is a component of most international indices on gender inequality and is probably the single most cited statistic in the conversation on this subject. As of 2017, the average weekly income of Canadian women was about 77 per cent of that earned by males. If one compares only men and women holding full-time jobs, women made about 87 cents for every dollar earned by men. Highly educated women did somewhat better. Those with degrees above the bachelor's level earned slightly more than 90 cents for every dollar earned by men with this level of education. These figures represent a significant narrowing of the gender income gap over the past several decades (see Figure 15.4).[74]

The causes for the persistent gender gap in pay are well known by serious students of labour markets, at the same time as they are often ignored, misrepresented, or even dismissed in media reports on the subject. Statistics Canada analyst Melissa Moyser identifies them in her 2017 study[75] of the gender pay gap in Canada:

- Women tend to have fewer hours of paid work per week than men and are more likely than

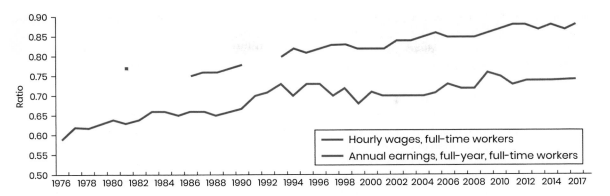

FIGURE 15.4 Gender Pay Ratio in Canada, 1976–2017

Source: Adapted from data at Statistics Canada, https://www150.statcan.gc.ca/n1/pub/89-503-x/2015001/article/14694/c-g/c-g017-eng.htm, with updates from additional data reported by Statistics Canada.

men to work part-time. The reason women most often given for this involves caring for children. "Women have retained 'ultimate' responsibility for childrearing and household operation," writes Moyser, "in accordance with traditional gender roles, even as they have assumed earning responsibilities."

- Women are more likely than men to interrupt their careers and for longer durations than is typical for men, mainly for reasons due to greater responsibility for children, including maternity and parental leave, and caring for other family members.

- Although much less dramatically than even a generation ago, women are over-represented in lower-paying occupations and under-represented in high-paying ones.

- Differences continue to exist in the relative value attached to female-dominated and male-dominated jobs. Even when the required years of formal education and skill level may be the same, female-dominated occupations tend to be compensated at lower wage rates than male-dominated occupations.

Education makes a significant difference when it comes to the gender pay gap. Thus, the fact that the last few decades have seen Canadian women catch up to and surpass the average educational attainments of men has been a major contributing factor to a narrowing of the pay gap. In 2015 the average hourly pay of women with some high school or who graduated from high school was about 80 per cent of that earned by males with the same level of education. For women with a bachelor's degree it was 88 per cent and for women with even higher educational qualifications it was 90 per cent. Part of the remaining difference may be attributed to the different occupational fields in which males and females tend to predominate. But much of it may be due to what is sometimes called the "motherhood penalty." In 2015, mothers with at least one child under the age of 18 earned about 85 cents for every dollar earned by fathers. Women without children earned about 90 cents for every dollar earned by men without children. Even in those countries such as Sweden and Denmark that have the most generous state-paid child-care services and maternity and paternity leaves, this gap associated with motherhood persists.[76] The solution, according to some, is simple. Make fathers take paternity leave (see Box 15.3).

Another measure of economic inequality between men and women involves their representation in the business elite. As of 2018, only one of the CEOs of the 100 leading businesses listed on the composite Standard & Poors/Toronto Stock Exchange composite index was a woman, Nancy Southern, the head of Calgary-based Canadian Utilities.[77] The picture looks somewhat better if one looks at the 540 executive officers (CEOs, CFOs,

The Social Fabric

BOX 15.3 How to Close the Gender Pay Gap? Make Dads Stay Home

Boston-based people analytics firm Humanyze is among the first not only to give men and women equal lengths of paid parental leave but to insist that men take it. The firm instituted the policy in 2016 because most men don't take leave even when it's offered, for fear that it will derail their careers. That message—that having a baby will kill your career—isn't lost on women who do take leaves.

"Bias plays such a clear role, we decided we are going to say, 'It's not an option. You [men] have to take the time off,'" Humanyze co-founder Ben Waber told me. After all, if men and women have to take equal leaves, there's no excuse to penalize either one....

More than a third of American firms offer at least some paid maternity leave, and an increasing number of them are extending such benefits to new dads as well. But paternity leave is useless if men don't take it. A 2018 Deloitte survey of more than 1,000 men found that a third worried that taking a leave would hurt their careers, and more than half feared it would signal that they weren't serious about their jobs. A 2017 Pew survey found that the median paternity leave was just one week. New moms, meanwhile, typically take whatever time they can get.

That's why the "mandatory" piece for men is key. Most organizations that offer voluntary leave have a "use it or lose it" approach, which, it turns out, actually hurts women, since they are more likely than men to use it. In Denmark, for example, a generous leave policy offers families 52 weeks of paid time off to be split between both parents. Yet in practice, women end up taking 92.8 per cent of the total time, according to the OECD. These women find it almost impossible to climb back on the career track afterward. As a result, even two decades after the birth of their first child, they face a 20 per cent gender wage gap, a 2018 National Bureau of Economic Research working paper concluded....

[The economic costs of child-bearing and child-rearing] fall especially heavily on women, who often have to take a leave for medical reasons, who spend more time than men on child care, and who suffer an economic hit when they have children. Michelle Budig, a sociology professor at the University of Massachusetts, Amherst, found in a 30-year longitudinal study of 12,686 people that women's earnings decrease 4 per cent after the birth of each child—a "motherhood penalty"—while new dads receive more than a 6 per cent bump, known as a "fatherhood bonus," largely reflecting employer biases.

This might be a solution in the case of middle-class professionals, who have high levels of education and good income growth prospects. It is much less relevant to the circumstances of single mothers and less educated Canadian women. The average income for single mothers (about 80 per cent of single parents are female) is about half what it is for couples with children.[78] Where there is no spouse who can be required to take child-care leave, the fact that this might be mandatory for males in couples that have children is moot.

Source: Joanne Lipman, "Want Equality? Make New Dads Stay Home," *Wall Street Journal*, 28 Sept. 2018, https://www.wsj.com/articles/want-equality-make-new-dads-stay-home-1538151219.

etc.) at Canada's 100 largest private-sector corporations. As of 2018, 9.4 per cent were women, about double the percentage of 4.6 in 2006.[79] It is difficult to compare these data to that which is available from other countries. Nevertheless, an idea of how Canada performs on gender equality at the top of the corporate ladder compared to other wealthy democracies is provided by the fact that as of 2017, about 8 per cent of the CEOs (not including CFOs or any other C-level executives) of the top 100 companies in the United States, 6 per cent of the top 100 in the UK, 1 per cent of the leading 80 in Germany, and 2 per cent of the largest 120 in France were women.[80] The boards of directors of companies listed on national stock exchanges provide a reliable measure of differences between countries in the representation of women at this level of corporate decision-making. Here, Canada's performance is mediocre at best. As of 2016, just under 20 per cent of such seats were held by females. This compared to 41 per cent in Norway, 36 per cent in Sweden, 37 per cent in France, 30 per cent in Italy, 28 per cent in the Netherlands, 27 per cent in Belgium and also in Germany, and 27 per cent in the UK. The percentage for Canada was marginally greater than in the United States.[81] Several of the European countries mentioned above have legislatively mandated quotas for female representation on the boards of publicly traded corporations, a measure that has been discussed in Canada for many years.

The roots of economic differences between men and women in Canada and other developed societies lie in culture and social institutions. Although attitudes regarding appropriate roles and behaviour for males and females have changed significantly over the last two generations, the scale and nature of these changes have not been enough to erase the differences that persist. Among these is the greater time that women typically devote to child care and household activities in all of these societies. Among OECD countries, only in Sweden, Norway, and Denmark is the female-to-male ratio of time spent per day on unpaid work—a reasonable surrogate measure of these activities—lower than in Canada.[82] In regard to the gender distribution of users of publicly paid parental leave and associated parental leave benefits, Canada ranks in the middle of those OECD countries for which information is reported. About 10 per cent of all users are male, compared to roughly 40 per cent in Sweden, Norway, and Iceland.

In 2012 an article written by Anne-Marie Slaughter, a former director of policy planning for the US Department of State during the Obama presidency, before that the dean of Princeton's Woodrow Wilson School of Public and International Affairs, and currently the CEO of the think-tank New America—in short, a person of no mean accomplishments—created a major stir on the subject of whether and how the economic gap discussed above could be closed. Her answer is often mischaracterized as "no." In fact, what Slaughter argued was far more nuanced than this. "If women are ever to achieve real equality as leaders," she wrote, "then we have to stop accepting male behavior and male choices as the default and the ideal. We must insist on changing social policies and bending career tracks to accommodate *our* choices, too."[83] By "our" choices Slaughter was referring to the sorts of preferences that she believed women, more than men, were likely to have regarding the family/work balance. Slaughter makes the case for changes in our cultural norms and public policies that would allow women to sequence their careers differently and in ways that would eliminate the motherhood penalty. Harvard economist Claudia Goldin, in her 2014 presidential address to the American Economic Association, agreed. Goldin's argument about what needs to change is found in Box 15.4

Summing Up

The women's movement in Canada has evolved through the same stages that have characterized the movement across the Western world. The first wave focused on achieving voting and other citizenship rights for women, as well as legislative reforms that would make the status and conditions of women and their children more secure. For the most part it did not challenge most of society's most deeply entrenched ideas about appropriate roles for and differences between males and females. The second wave did. Its key intellectual premise, "One is not born, but rather becomes, a woman," provided the basis for a much more sweeping agenda of reform that included cultural norms, ideas about the family, what counts as sexual violence, reproductive rights, increased participation of women in politics, and gender equality in the workplace. The third wave of the women's movement has been to some significant degree a reaction against what some have seen to be the failure of second-wave feminism to accommodate the diversity and multiple identities that exist among women, and the sense that the issues of second-wave feminists are less relevant today than in the past. This latter view is only possible because of the undeniable achievements of the second wave of the movement.

The Social Fabric

BOX 15.4 An Economist Offers a Labour Market Solution to the Gender Gap

Quotas for women on corporate boards of directors is not the solution. Nor is increasing the percentage of females in STEM *fields or more generous state funding for child care and parental leave. The solution lies elsewhere, argues Claudia Goldin. And it is probably more difficult to achieve than any of these other reforms.*

. . . A gender gap in earnings exists today that greatly expands with age, to some point, and differs significantly by occupation. The gap is much lower than it had once been and the decline has been largely due to an increase in the productive human capital of women relative to men. Education at all levels increased for women relative to men and the fields that women pursue in college and beyond shifted to the more remunerative and career-oriented ones. Job experience of women also expanded with increased labor force participation. The portion of the difference in earnings by gender that was once due to differences in productive characteristics has largely been eliminated. What, then, is the cause of the remaining pay gap? Quite simply the gap exists because hours of work in many occupations are worth more when given at particular moments and when the hours are more continuous. That is, in many occupations earnings have a nonlinear relationship with respect to hours. A flexible schedule often comes at a high price, particularly in the corporate, financial, and legal worlds. (pp. 1116–17)

The solution [to the gender gap] does not (necessarily) have to involve government intervention. It does not have to improve women's bargaining skills and desire to compete. And it does not necessarily have to make men more responsible in the home (although that wouldn't hurt). But it must involve alterations in the labor market, in particular changing how jobs are structured and remunerated to enhance temporal flexibility. The gender gap in pay would be considerably reduced and might even vanish if firms did not have an incentive to disproportionately reward individuals who worked long hours and who worked particular hours. Such change has already occurred in various sectors, but not in enough. (p. 1092)

Source: Claudia Goldin, "A Grand Gender Convergence: Its Last Chapter," *American Economic Review* 104, 4 (2014): 1091–1119, http://dx.doi.org/10.1257/aer.104.4.1091.

Among these achievements has been much greater representation of women in Canadian public life than even a generation ago. There are many more female MPs and elected officials at all levels of government than was the case 20–30 years ago, more female judges and senior bureaucrats, and several of the provinces have had female premiers. To this point, however, only three women have been chosen to lead any of the three main federal political parties—the NDP's Audrey McLaughlin (1989–95) and Alexa McDonough (1995–2002), and the Conservative Party's Kim Campbell (1993)—none of whom have led their party to election victory. When it comes to the economy, women have made substantial gains in terms of their representation in fields that were once dominated by men, and the pay gap between male and female workers has also narrowed over time. At the same time, however, women continue to be scarce in the corporate elite.

Compared to other affluent democracies, the status of women in Canada is, on most dimensions, better than in most. As is true of other forms of inequality, however, the persistence of disparities that are rooted in unfairness and discrimination is inconsistent with democratic ideals. Spokespersons for Indigenous Canadians, the poor, and racial minorities are among those who argue that marginalized groups of women have not shared in the gains made by their middle-class and white Canadian sisters.[84]

Starting Points for Research

Sylvia Bashevkin, *Women, Power, Politics: The Hidden Story of Canada's Unfinished Democracy* (Toronto: Oxford University Press, 2009). Written by one of Canada's foremost feminist scholars, this book argues that women's progress in Canadian politics has stalled in recent years.

Jacquetta Newman and Linda White, *Women, Politics, and Public Policy: The Political Struggles of Canadian Women*, 2nd edn (Toronto: Oxford University Press, 2012). This edited volume provides a feminist analysis of the history of the women's movement in Canada and the gender dimensions of public policy.

Statistics Canada, *Women in Canada: A Gender-Based Statistical Report, 2017* (30 July). This is the seventh edition of a report that Statistics Canada has produced periodically since the 1980s. Contains a wealth of statistical information tracking the changing conditions of Canadian women over time.

Linda Trimble, Jane Arscott, and Manon Tremblay, eds, *Stalled: The Representation of Women in Canadian Governments* (Vancouver: University of British Columbia Press, 2013). Covering every province, the territories, and the federal and municipal levels of government, this collection provides an unmatched survey of female representation in Canadian politics.

Review Exercises

1. How many women hold public office in your community? Make a list of elected office-holders on your local city, town, or township council, your mayor, your MP, and your provincial representative. Don't forget judges, if there are courts in your community, and also senior administrators with your local government. What about university and community college presidents, the CEOs of hospitals, and the heads of public utilities? You can find all this information by going to websites and with a little bit of resourcefulness.

2. Prime Minister Justin Trudeau has often referred to himself and his government as feminist. Some critics aren't so sure. There is an abundance of commentary on this topic that you will find by Googling "Trudeau government feminist." What does the prime minister mean when he talks about his government being feminist? Do you believe that his government has made progress towards its goal of greater gender equality at home and abroad? What criticisms have been made of the prime minister's approach and achievements?

3. Some European countries have passed laws requiring that a minimum percentage of the directors of publicly traded companies be female. This is a policy supported by some groups in Canada and the United States. Based on the information from Catalyst (https://www.catalyst.org/gender-diversity-boards-canada-recommendations-accelerating-progress), explain in 300–500 words what if any differences you believe would result from state-mandated gender quotas.

Chief Commissioner Marion Buller speaks at the National Inquiry into Missing and Murdered Indigenous Women and Girls in Whitehorse, Yukon. Launched by the federal government in December 2015, the Inquiry investigated the disproportionately high rates of violence against Indigenous women and girls across Canada and submitted a final report on 3 June 2019. (THE CANADIAN PRESS/Jonathan Hayward)

16 Indigenous Politics

For most of Canada's history Indigenous Canadians and the conditions of their lives and communities were relegated to the dim corners of public life. Politicians and most Canadians paid them little attention. This has changed. Indigenous groups have become much more sophisticated in their political strategies and tactics, and the issues that concern them, from landownership to abuse and discrimination, have become important parts of the political conversation in Canada. In this chapter we will examine the following topics:

- The demographic picture
- The language of Indigenous politics
- The reserve system
- Assimilation, integration, self-determination
- The White Paper of 1969
- The Royal Commission on Aboriginal Peoples
- The Truth and Reconciliation Commission
- Organizing for political influence
- Sovereignty, landownership, and Indigenous rights
- The institutionalization of Indigenous affairs
- The politics of protest

The Canadian Museum of History sits on the edge of the Ottawa River in Gatineau, Quebec, across from the Parliament buildings. Its sinuous curves and striking vistas are the creation of Douglas Cardinal, a Métis and one of Canada's foremost architects. Visitors to the museum start their tour in the Grand Hall, where several totem poles tower over them in an atmosphere of quiet grandeur.

The incorporation and celebration of Indigenous symbols and culture in the official life of Canada sits uneasily alongside the bleak reality that characterizes the lives of many Indigenous Canadians. This reality was highlighted yet again in the United Nations Human Rights Council's 2018 review of Canada.[1] Its report cited several aspects of government policy and of the conditions experienced by Indigenous peoples that, in its view, constituted human rights violations. Among these were: the endangerment of Indigenous languages; a failure to provide meaningful consultation with Indigenous communities regarding development on lands they claim by historic right of occupancy and about environmentally destructive practices on such lands; and a general legacy of trauma rooted in the colonial relationship between the government of Canada and Indigenous peoples, in particular, the experiences of so many Indigenous Canadians in the Indian residential school system that existed for much of Canada's history. Two years earlier the world's attention had been drawn to Canada by yet another wave of suicides among First Nations people at the Cree communities in Cross Lake, Manitoba,[2] and Attawapiskat, Ontario.[3]

This contrast is jarring. Non-Indigenous Canadians are often puzzled by circumstances like those that led to multiple suicides at Cross Lake and Attawapiskat, and to suicide rates among Indigenous people that are several times higher than the rate for the general population. After all, government expenditures per Indigenous person in Canada are estimated to be roughly twice the average for non-Indigenous persons.[4] Non-Indigenous Canadians also are sometimes perplexed by news

Sergei Bachlakov/Shutterstock

The Idle No More movement, a grassroots movement founded in 2012 by four women from Saskatchewan, has become the largest Indigenous mass movement in Canadian history, prompting solidarity protests worldwide. As this chapter will discuss, this movement is a continuation of centuries of activism by Indigenous peoples within Canada against the colonial state.

stories showing the continuing tensions that occasionally have produced confrontations between Indigenous communities and their neighbours or the state authorities. Why, they wonder, after years of treaties, legislation, government programs, inquiries, restitution, and financial settlements does so much remain unresolved in relations between Indigenous peoples and the rest of the country?

Indigenous Demography: Who and How Many?

Indigenous Canadians are those who can trace their ancestry before the arrival and permanent settlement of Europeans in what would become Canada. The actual size of this population has been a matter of disagreement among demographers and historians over the years.[5] There is also some controversy over whether some of the increase that has taken place in the Indigenous population over the past couple of decades may be due to factors other than

natural increase.[6] Using a definition of "Aboriginal" that comprises those persons who report identification with at least one Indigenous group—North American Indian, Métis, and Inuit are the official categories used by Statistics Canada—the following numbers are reported in the 2016 census.

- 2,204,695 people, or about 6.2 per cent of the national population, gave as their ethnic origins North American Indian, Métis, Inuit, or a combination of one of these with some other ethnic origin.
- 1,673,780 people, representing 4.9 per cent of the Canadian population, reported identifying with an Indigenous group. This was up significantly from 3.3 per cent in the 2001 census.
- 744,855, or 2.2 per cent of the population, are status Indians, i.e., those to whom the Indian Act applies. Just under half of these persons live on reserves.

The regional distribution of those who identify themselves as Indigenous is shown in Figure 16.1.

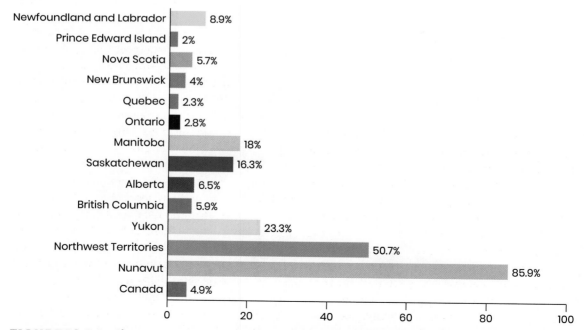

FIGURE 16.1 Indigenous Identity Population as Percentage of Total Population, Provinces and Territories, 2016

Source: Statistics Canada, Aboriginal Identity Population, 2016 Census, https://www12.statcan.gc.ca/census-recensement/2016/dp-pd/hlt-fst/abo-aut/Table .cfm?Lang=Eng&S=99&O=A&RPP=25.

As we saw in Chapter 3, the social and economic conditions of Indigenous Canadians tend to be considerably less favourable than those of the general population. Those who claim Indigenous identity are twice as likely as other Canadians to be unemployed and status Indians living on reserves are four times more likely to be unemployed. On average, those of Indigenous identity earn about three-quarters of what other Canadians earn. Government transfer payments make up about one-fifth of Indigenous income, compared to about one-tenth of income for non-Indigenous Canadians. The likelihood of falling below the Statistics Canada low-income line is twice as great for the non-reserve Indigenous identity population as for the non-Indigenous population, and is considerably higher than this for those living on reserves. About three out of 10 Indigenous people within Canada have not completed high school, a figure that rises to almost half for those who live on reserves, compared to about 12 per cent for the non-Indigenous population. Non-Indigenous Canadians are almost three times more likely than Indigenous people to have graduated from university.[7]

Labels and Their Significance: The Language of Indigenous Politics

The words used to describe those who trace their ancestry back to the period before the arrival of Europeans in North America provide a useful starting point for understanding the politics associated with the status of Indigenous peoples. For most of Canada's history these individuals and their communities were acknowledged in only a marginal way in the official life of the country and were barely visible in mainstream interpretations of Canadian history and society. The terms "Indians," "Métis," and "Eskimos" were used to describe various segments of the Indigenous population. The legal meanings and implications of these terms were sometimes contested in the courts, as in the case of the 1939 Supreme Court ruling that the people known as Eskimos did not fall under the meaning of "Indians" as set down in the Indian Act of 1876. On the whole, however, there was little controversy over the terms used to characterize the Indigenous population of Canada and virtually no sense that the words applied to these communities made a significant difference.

This began to change by the 1960s. Labels that previously had been considered appropriate and unobjectionable, and the concepts and assumptions associated with them, were increasingly brought into question. These challenges resulted from an important change that was underway in Western thought. *Communitarianism*—the belief that communities and communal identities are essential to individual dignity and the maintenance of truly democratic societies—was gaining ground among intellectuals. At the street level this belief was embodied in those elements of the black civil rights movement that called for greater awareness of black identity as something separate and apart from that of American society's white majority. There were echoes of this in the Quebec nationalism of that era, from Pierre Vallières's polemic *Les Nègres blancs d'Amérique* to René Lévesque's insistence that Quebecers needed their own independent state in order to form a free and democratic society.

These years saw the emergence of black, ethnic, and women's studies at universities across North America, a development that would gain momentum in the 1970s. The intellectual premises underlying these programs proved to be far-reaching in their practical implications. One of these premises was that the members of groups, and in particular minority groups that experienced a history of oppression, achieved dignity through their identity with the group and the recognition of that identity by society and the state. A related premise was that treating persons identically, without regard for their group membership and the historical conditions experienced by members of their group, did not produce genuine equality. On the contrary, equality required that these group identities and historical differences be recognized and taken into account by the law. Virtually all calls for greater group self-awareness and demands for official recognition of this collective identity were linked to an analysis and historical narrative of discrimination, exploitation, and unjust treatment—in brief, inequality—in relations between the group in question and the state. Much of the intellectual impetus for this new analysis came from the writings of such colonial and post-colonial authors as Edward Said and Frantz Fanon as the European imperial colonies in Africa, the Middle East, and Asia disintegrated in the two decades following World War II.

This was a full-frontal challenge to what had been thought of as progressive liberal thinking in the decades after World War II. Liberal opinion leaders during this era trained their sights on the eradication of poverty, socio-economic inequality, and discrimination, but believed that achieving these goals involved the full and equal integration of all people, as individuals, into society and the dismantlement of laws, norms, and practices that treated people differently on the basis of skin colour, ethnicity, or religion. The idea that the path to progress could only be found in official recognition and institutionalization of difference represented a radical change in thinking.

In the case of Indigenous peoples in Canada, the first step involved rejection of the language of integration and liberal notions of equality that prevailed in the mid-twentieth century. Whatever the motives behind integrationist proposals, their consequences were said to be assimilation and even cultural genocide. The term "Indian" was not immediately rejected by Indigenous leaders, despite the historical fact of this being an obvious misnomer applied by the early European explorers to those who lived in the lands that they mistakenly assumed to be the Far East. Indeed, the label "Indian" continues to be regularly used in Canada by those who are status Indians, and in the United States the terms "Indian" and "Indian country" are often used by Indigenous people without a sense that they carry stigma or some negative connotation. By the late 1970s and certainly by the 1980s, "Indian" had lost favour to preference for "Native," "Aboriginal," and "First Nations," a shift that was both intellectual and political. Intellectually, the change in language reflected a reappropriation of the identities and histories of those to whom the descriptions applied. Whereas the word "Indian" inevitably carried historical baggage of conquest, displacement,

and subordination, in addition to the fundamental fact of having one's identity named by others, these more recent terms did not. Politically, the terms "**First Nations**" and "First Nations peoples" carried connotations of communal status and rights as well as prior claims. The language of nationalism and the claims of nations—particularly nations that had been colonized by foreign powers—were familiar and powerful in the post-World War II era. The dismantlement of the colonial empires of the European powers and the 1960 United Nations Declaration on the Granting of Independence to Colonial Countries and Peoples both reflected and reinforced nationalist claims and the idea that, in the words of the UN Declaration, "All peoples have the right to self-determination."

Quebec nationalist intellectuals were enthusiastic supporters of this doctrine of national self-determination. They argued that the Québécois constituted a nation or people within any reasonable meaning of these terms and, moreover, that the Quebec nation had experienced "alien subjugation, domination and exploitation [constituting] a denial of fundamental human rights," in contravention of the 1960 UN Declaration. If such claims could be made on behalf of the Quebec nation or people, then surely they applied in the case of Indigenous Canadians. This, at any rate, was the reasoning of many Indigenous leaders and intellectuals sympathetic to their demands. Indeed, it is difficult to argue that Indigenous peoples are somehow less deserving of nation status than the Québécois. They certainly can make a more compelling case for having experienced "alien subjugation" and "domination" within the plain meaning of these words in the UN Declaration.

The question of whether Indigenous peoples are nations is not one on which everyone agrees. But the same may be said of the question of whether there is such a thing as the Québécois nation and, if so, what constitutional and other implications ought to follow. More important than the judgments of philosophers and other scholars, however, is whether the language used to describe Indigenous communities has practical consequences. There can be no doubt that the widespread acceptance of the terms "First Nations," "First Nations peoples," "original peoples," and "Indigenous peoples" has had important consequences through the greater perceived legitimacy that such terms confer on a group's claims.

Grown accustomed to hearing some Indigenous groups in Canada referred to by public officials, journalists, and academics as First Nations, many Canadians probably assume that there is some obvious inevitability to this description. But there is not. In fact, the terms "First Nations" and "Indigenous" are seldom used in the United States, where "Native American" and "Indians" are commonly used to designate the members of these groups. In Australia the words "Native" and "Aboriginal," used as nouns, are widely considered to be offensive and derogatory. Even "Aborigines" is rejected by many on the grounds that it has inevitable associations with colonialism. "Indigenous Australians," for the last couple of decades, has been the generally accepted description for those whose ancestry in Australia predates the arrival of European settlers. The word "aboriginality"—or, more commonly today, "Indigeneity"—is used internationally to refer to the quality or state of being aboriginal or of aboriginal descent and essentially has the same meaning as "nativeness."[8]

The term "Eskimo"—a Native American word that, by popular account, meant "eaters of raw meat," although some linguists believe that it comes from an Ojibwa word meaning "to net snowshoes" or "snowshoe netter"—was long used to refer to the Indigenous people who inhabit the Arctic coasts of Canada, Alaska, Russia, and Greenland. It has been pushed aside in Canada, replaced by the word **Inuit**. But the Indigenous peoples of Alaska and Russia prefer to be called Yupik or Eskimo, and those of Greenland refer to themselves as Greenlanders or Kalaallit, again demonstrating that there is no inevitability to the terms used in the conversation on Indigenous politics.

Relations between Indigenous communities and the Canadian state were long about treaty obligations and reserves, at least for those groups under treaty. Those who had never signed treaties with the British or Canadian government, such as the Inuit of the Far North and the Innu of Labrador, were often ignored. The language of treaty obligations

continues to be important and reserves still exist, but several other terms and the issues associated with them have become part of the policy conversation. These include "sovereignty," "self-government," "self-determination," and "nation-to-nation." These additions to the vocabulary of Indigenous politics in Canada reflect the enormous change that has taken place over the last four decades in the scope and nature of Indigenous demands.

The importance of language was demonstrated in the reaction of many Indigenous groups to the Conservative government's 2012 decision to rename the Department of Indian Affairs and Northern Development, the Department of *Aboriginal* Affairs and Northern Development. The government explained that this change was intended to be more inclusive, the word "Aboriginal" embracing not just Indians but all the other Indigenous groups that fall within the meaning of this word. Moreover, "aboriginal" is used in s. 35 of the Constitution Act, 1982, where it is stated that the term applies to the Indian, Inuit, and Métis people of Canada. These explanations did not convince some in Canada's Indigenous communities, particularly groups representing status and non-status Indians. The word "Aboriginal," declared the Chiefs of Ontario, "fails to acknowledge the distinct cultures, histories, and rights of First Nations, Inuit, and Métis Peoples." They went on to say that "'Aboriginal' is dismissive of the sacred relationship and obligations which were clearly established in the Treaties between First Nations and the Crown. Using the term 'Aboriginal' reveals indifference towards First Nations' right to self-determination."[9] The Trudeau government's 2015 decision to rename the department as Indigenous and Northern Affairs Canada was greeted by most as a more inclusive label for the department.[10] While the meanings of "Indigenous" and "Aboriginal" are more or less identical, Indigenous has become more widely used since the United Nations' 2007 Declaration on the Rights of Indigenous Peoples and is currently the preferred term used by many advocacy groups and academics.

The terms and labels used in the conversation on Indigenous peoples in Canada matter symbolically and conceptually (see Box 16.1). They shape our thinking about those to whom they apply, their histories, their relationship to the state and to the rest of Canadian society, and about the justice of their arguments and claims. But they also matter legally. This may be seen in the case of the word "Indian." While it has become unfashionable in Canada to use this word when speaking of the descendants of those who occupied North America before the arrival of Europeans, there are very practical reasons for not banning the word "Indian" from a discussion of government policies towards some Indigenous peoples. Under Canada's Indian Act, which has been on the statute books since 1876, a person who qualifies as an Indian or status Indian under the law has certain entitlements that do not apply to non-Indians. Moreover, those Indian bands that live on land referred to in law as Indian **reserves** are subject to special legal provisions concerning such matters as individual landownership and transfer, a prohibition against

The Social Fabric

BOX 16.1 Coming to Terms: Indian, Inuit, Métis

For those who are not familiar with Indigenous affairs, the distinctions between the various groups that make up Canada's Indigenous population may be unclear. The following short definitions are provided by Indigenous Foundations, a website developed by First Nations and Indigenous Studies at the University of British Columbia.

Aboriginal

The term "Aboriginal" refers to the first inhabitants of Canada, and includes First Nations, Inuit, and Métis peoples. This term came into popular usage in Canadian contexts after 1982, when Section 35 of the Canadian Constitution defined the term as such.... This term is not commonly used in the United States.

First Nations

"First Nation" is a term used to describe Aboriginal peoples of Canada who are ethnically neither Métis nor Inuit. This term came into common usage in the 1970s and '80s and generally replaced the term "Indian," although unlike "Indian," the term "First Nation" does not have a legal definition.

Inuit

This term refers to specific groups of people generally living in the Far North who are not considered "Indians" under Canadian law.

Métis

The term "*Métis*" refers to a collective of cultures and ethnic identities that resulted from unions between Aboriginal and European people in what is now Canada. This term has general and specific uses, and the differences between them are often contentious. It is sometimes used as a general term to refer to people of mixed ancestry, whereas in a legal context, "Métis" refers to descendants of specific historic communities.

Indian

The term "Indian" refers to the legal identity of a First Nations person who is registered under the Indian Act. The term "Indian" should be used only when referring to a First Nations person with status under the *Indian Act*, and only within its legal context.... In the United States, however, the term "American Indian" and "Native Indian" are both in current and common usage.

Indigenous

"Indigenous" is a term used to encompass a variety of Aboriginal groups. It is most frequently used in an international, transnational, or global context. This term came into wide usage during the 1970s when Aboriginal groups organized transnationally and pushed for greater presence in the United Nations (UN). This is the term most commonly accepted and used in Canada today.

Source: Adapted from Indigenous Foundations, https://indigenous foundations.arts.ubc.ca/terminology/.

mortgages on reserve land, and numerous restrictions on permissible economic activities. Until the Indian Act and the legal status of "Indian" are abolished, any analysis of Indigenous persons who belong to such communities and to whom such policies apply cannot avoid using these terms. Indeed, as of this writing (2019), the Department of Indian Affairs and Northern Development and the position of minister of Indian Affairs, neither of which has been used publicly by Canadian governments since 2012, continue to exist in law.

Under Canadian law, an Indian or status Indian is anyone who has been registered or is entitled to be registered under the Indian Act, including those who belong to communities covered by treaties. The Indian Act of 1876 stipulated that an Indian was any male person of Indian blood who belonged to a band recognized by the federal government, and any child of such a person or a woman married to such a person. Thus, a woman could acquire Indian status as a result of marriage. This was, however, a one-way street. An Indian woman who married a non-Indian lost her legal status as an Indian and the entitlements associated with that status.

This changed in 1985 with Bill C-31. In response to pressure from First Nations women, from Canada's obligations under the United Nations International Covenant on Civil and Political Rights, and, most importantly, from the sexual equality provisions of the Charter of Rights and Freedoms (sections 15 and 28), the federal government eliminated this obviously discriminatory section of the Indian Act. Bill C-31 provided women who lost their Indian status as a result of marrying a non-Indian, and any children of such unions, with the right to apply for Indian status. The law also eliminated the possibility of males or females acquiring Indian status as a result of marriage.

Under the Indian Act the federal government sets the rules that determine who is an "Indian," but First Nations bands—the communities linked to particular reserves—determine within certain limits set by the law who is entitled to be a band member and therefore live on their reserve. Their right to determine who may be a member of the band has been seen as an important aspect of Indigenous self-government. There have been cases where rules regarding band membership and who has the right to live on a reserve—the so-called "marry out, get out" rules long enforced by some bands—have been met with charges of discrimination. From the perspectives of the bands, however, their reluctance to admit new members or to threaten those who marry someone from outside the band with expulsion from the reserve has often been justified on cultural and economic grounds. A 2018 ruling by the Quebec Superior Court held that the "marry out, get out" rule enforced by the Mohawk Council of Kahnawake violated the Charter. "We maintain the position," responded Grand Chief Joseph North, "that matters that are so integral to our identity have no business in outside courts."[11]

Canadian law also recognizes the Métis and Inuit as two other categories of the Aboriginal peoples of Canada. Although the Constitution Act, 1867 speaks only of "Indians, and Lands reserved for Indians" (s. 91[24]), a 1939 decision of the Supreme Court of Canada pronounced the Inuit to be Indians within the meaning of the Constitution,[12] which meant that the federal government had a paternalistic responsibility for the welfare of these people. They were excluded, however, from the provisions of the Indian Act. **Métis**, a term originally understood to be limited to the mixed-blood descendants of unions between Indian women and Scots or French-speaking traders and settlers in the Red River region of Manitoba, may also be considered Indians under the law if they are the descendants of Métis who were part of Indian communities that fell under treaties. Descendants of Métis who received scrip (certificates that could be used to purchase land) or lands from the federal government were excluded from the provisions of the Indian Act. Nevertheless, Métis are considered to be Aboriginal people within the meaning of the Constitution, and so Ottawa has the authority to pass laws concerning the members of this group. The Inuit and Métis are grouped with the Indian people of Canada by section 35 of the Constitution Act, 1982, which recognizes and affirms the "existing aboriginal and treaty rights of the aboriginal peoples of Canada."

Today, for a combination of political, legal, economic, and historical reasons, some people of mixed Indigenous and European ancestry, such as the Labrador Métis Nation (now called the NunatuKavut Community Council), have appropriated the term "Métis," even though their origins are not related to the early western fur trade and their lifestyle, arguably, is not so different from that of many non-Indigenous people.[13] Between 1996 and 2006 the number of persons self-identifying as Métis doubled to about 388,465. The number increased by roughly another 50 per cent between 2006 and 2016, to 587,545 or 1.7 per cent of the Canadian population. A 2016 decision of the Supreme Court of Canada ruled that Métis persons, as well as non-status Indians (those who are not on the Indian registry, estimated to number about 230,000 as of the 2016 census), must be treated the same as status Indians under Canadian law.[14] This does not mean that those determined to be Métis have Indian status under the Indian Act or that they have a right to reserves. It does appear to mean, however, that Ottawa has jurisdiction over the Métis and non-status Indians and the same responsibilities towards them as is the case for status Indians and the Inuit. In addition to being the latest wrinkle in the long and complicated story of what "Indian-ness" means under the law, this court ruling appeared to open the door to these groups being able to claim health and education benefits that Ottawa provides to status Indians, and possibly an exemption from certain forms of taxation. It is also expected to provide incentives for individuals to discover and claim what may well be their Métis ancestry, thus contributing to continuing growth in the size of Canada's Métis population.[15] There is considerable controversy among stakeholder groups and experts about who is entitled to Métis status, as this is understood in law.[16]

The Reserve System

Some have called Indian reserves Canada's own system of apartheid. Indeed, a South African delegation came to Canada early in the twentieth century to study the pass system then used on Canadian reserves. Under this system, which persisted on some reserves in the Prairie provinces into the 1940s, status Indians were not allowed to leave their home reserve without the written permission of the Indian

agent appointed by Ottawa.[17] Indeed, in some respects the apartheid label continues to seem apt. Average life expectancy and incomes of those who live on reserves are significantly lower than the Canadian norms. Rates of suicide, alcoholism, violent death, unemployment, crowded housing conditions, and infant mortality are all higher than the Canadian average, in some cases dramatically higher. Moreover, although being of First Nations descent is not a necessary condition for residence on a reserve, the reserve system was created to provide small, fixed homelands for Indians—mostly in remote areas at or beyond the agricultural fringe—and the vast majority of those residing on reserves today are status Indians. This combination of enormous disparity between life on reserves compared to the mainstream of society and the racial basis for the physical segregation of Indians does sound a lot like apartheid. Non-Indigenous Canadians who have seen first-hand the squalor and obvious destitution that characterize many of this country's reserves often wonder how such a system has been allowed to survive in a country that prides itself on being a compassionate democracy and an affluent society.

But when the Liberal government's 1969 White Paper proposed the abolition of reserves along with all the other legal structures that have treated Indians differently from other Canadians, the leadership of Canada's First Nations communities responded with a vehement "No." They rejected these reforms at the same time as they, and virtually everyone else, acknowledged that the reserves involved a system of paternalistic control by Ottawa over the lives of First Nations peoples. This paternalistic, racially based system, whose origins in Canada appear to go back to New France, continues today, as does resistance to its abolition. If the system is truly as ill-conceived and broken as its many critics have charged, why is it not rejected outright by the very people who are subject to it?

The answer is complex. To understand how a racially based system of segregation manages to survive in a liberal democratic society one must examine the origins and operation of the reserve system in Canada. We also need to consider the goals of today's First Nations leaders, many of whom are opposed to the dismantling of this system.

The Indian Act of 1876 defines reserves in the following way:

> The term "reserve" means any tract or tracts of land set apart by treaty or otherwise for the use or benefit of or granted to a particular band of Indians, of which the legal title is in the Crown, but which is unsurrendered, and includes all the trees, wood, timber, soil, stone, minerals, metals, or other valuables thereon or therein.

At the heart of this definition, and central to the quandary of the reserve system, is the guardianship relationship established between the federal government and those living on reserves. The legal ownership of reserve land belongs to the Crown, but the land and all the resources appertaining to it must be managed for the "use or benefit" of the people residing there. In practice this has meant that virtually no legal or commercial transaction of consequence could be undertaken by those living on a reserve without the permission of the federal Department of Indian Affairs, although in recent years these restrictions have been eased somewhat.[18] This is what critics are referring to when they speak of the Indian Act's paternalism. For example:

- Band members may not sell any part of the reserve.
- The federal government retains the ultimate authority to grant timber-cutting licences and to establish their terms.
- Reserve land may not be used as security for loans.

There are over 2,300 Indian reserves in Canada (a 2011 Statistics Canada report placed the number at closer to 3,100), about two-thirds of them—and of a considerably smaller size—in British Columbia. Together they comprise about 28,000 square kilometres, an area roughly half the size of Nova Scotia.[19] About three-quarters of all reserves are uninhabited. Many bands have leased their reserve land to non-Indians for purposes that include resource exploitation, rights of way, farming, and recreational uses. Reserve populations vary from a handful of persons to just under 13,000 (the Six Nations of the Grand River reserve in southern Ontario), and most inhabited reserves have populations of fewer than 1,000 people. Roughly 330,000 First Nations people live on reserves. It is impossible to arrive at a more precise number because census enumerations of the population have not been permitted on many reserves over the last couple of decades, including the Six Nations reserve mentioned above (which has a total membership, including those residing off-reserve, of more than 27,000) and some of the other larger reserves. Although there are reserves in all regions of the country, most reserves and the vast majority of those living on them are located in rural and remote areas and often cannot be reached by road. This has important social and economic consequences. Job opportunities are fewer, those residing on reserves are generally required to leave home to acquire secondary and post-secondary education, and physical isolation impedes the integration of reserve populations into the rest of society. This last effect is not considered to be a bad thing by many in First Nations communities. As Harvey McCue and Zach Parrott explain:

> To many Registered Indians whether on or off reserve residents, reserves represent the last tangible evidence that they are the original people of Canada. Reserves nurture a sense of history and culture where Indigenous languages, spiritual beliefs and values are shared. Although conditions of extreme poverty, poor health, insufficient housing, and impoverished social and health services still exist in many reserves, the reserve and the traditional values, and the kinship affiliation it nurtures contribute to their members' sense of identity and sense of self. For many Registered Indians and those without legal status, the reserve is a physical and spiritual home, despite the privations that may exist therein.[20]

This explanation of the role that reserves can play in the retention of Indigenous culture is echoed by Cole Harris: "Native lives were still being lived. There were still joys as well as sorrows in Native households. There were still Native people taking charge of their own lives and getting along in the different world that had overtaken them. . . . Their identities were still Native."[21]

The pressures on Indigenous people within Canada to assimilate to the dominant culture are weaker on reserves and in Nunavut, where most of the population is Inuit. But for most Indigenous people the retention of their culture is a challenge, to say the least. This may be seen in the case of Indigenous languages, the loss of one's mother tongue being an obvious and important aspect of assimilation. Only three of Canada's roughly 70 Indigenous languages—Cree (96,575), Inuktitut (39,770), and Ojibway (28,130)—continue to be spoken by significant numbers of people within these communities. About two-thirds of those for whom Cree is their mother tongue say that this is the language they speak most often at home. For those whose mother tongue is Inuktitut, the figure is 84 per cent, and for Ojibway speakers it is about 44 per cent.[22] Recognizing the importance of their language to how they understand themselves and the world, some Indigenous groups are making impressive attempts at language learning and retention within their communities.[23] Indeed, rates of language retention among many Indigenous language groups, including the three largest, have increased over the past decade. Overall, however, rates of language retention are low, except among the Inuit. Close to two-thirds of Inuit in Canada claim to be able to speak Inuktitut. Among status Indians, about one in five say they are able to speak an Indigenous language. The rate is about three times greater (45 per cent) among those who live on reserves.

Assimilation, Integration, Self–Determination: The Evolution of Indigenous Policy in Canada

Although some of the major components of present-day Indigenous policy have their roots in Canada's early history, the principles underlying federal policy have undergone important

transformations. Under French colonial rule there was no official recognition of any Indigenous title to, or other proprietary interest in, the lands that these peoples had long occupied and used before European settlement. France laid claim to territory in the New World by right of discovery and conquest. As G.F.G. Stanley writes:

> The French settler occupied his lands in Canada without any thought of compensating the native. There were no formal surrenders from the Indians, no negotiations, and no treaties such as marked the Indian policy of the British period. . . . Whatever rights the Indians acquired flowed not from a theoretical aboriginal title but from clemency of the crown or the charity of individuals.[24]

Conversion of the Native population to Christianity was a central objective of French colonial policy, implemented through the missionary work of the Jesuits and the Recollets. While clearly based on the premise that Indigenous people were uncivilized, economically backward, and morally inferior to Europeans, French policy did not consider the Indigenous population to be subhuman and beyond redemption. On the contrary, the 1627 Charter of the Company of One Hundred Associates declared that a converted Indigenous person had the status and rights of a naturalized French citizen. Assimilation and non-recognition of any Indigenous proprietary interest in the lands claimed by France were, therefore, the two key principles underlying policy in New France.

With the transfer of French territories in Canada to the British, the foundation was laid for Indigenous policies that would span the next two centuries. The **Royal Proclamation of 1763** and the treaties entered into between the colonial authorities and what that document referred to as "Nations or Tribes of Indians" very clearly were based on the assumption that Indigenous peoples had fallen under the protective stewardship of the British state. A proprietary Indigenous interest in the land was acknowledged, but within the broader context of British sovereignty and the colonial authorities' expectations that European settlement would continue to expand onto land traditionally occupied by the First Inhabitants. Moreover, as both the Royal Proclamation and early dealings between the British and these Indigenous communities show, the British believed they were required to compensate the Indigenous population for land that was formally alienated through treaties and purchase agreements. This was an important departure from colonial policy under the French regime.

Efforts at assimilation were much less rigorous under the British than under the French. There is some truth in Francis Parkman's observation that "Spanish civilization crushed the Indian; English civilization scorned and neglected him; French civilization embraced and cherished him."[25] The British colonial authorities were much less concerned with the state of Indigenous persons' souls than with ensuring that these communities did not impede the growth and development of the colonies. To this end the policy of reserving certain lands for occupation and use by Indians was practised by the British. This policy of establishing Indian reserves was continued after Confederation.

Under the British North America Act (now called the Constitution Act, 1867), Ottawa was assigned exclusive legislative authority over Indian affairs. Within a decade of Confederation the federal government passed the Indian Act, a sweeping piece of legislation that consolidated the dependency relationship that already had been developing between First Nations and the state. Under the Act, Indians living on reserves were placed under the almost total control of the superintendent-general of Indian Affairs, whose god-like powers would be exercised by federal bureaucrats in Ottawa and by officials in the field referred to as Indian agents. Little of importance could be done by status Indians without the authorization of the Indian agent. All money paid by the federal government to members of a reserve or generated from economic activities on reserve lands was controlled by the federal authorities. To give an idea of how this system operated, if a licence to cut timber on reserve land was issued to a company, that licence could be granted by Ottawa only upon the recommendation of the Indian agent in whose territory the reserve was located, after which payments from the timber

company would be received by the federal authorities in trust for the residents of the reserve. The Indian Act made it impossible for those living on reserves to assume responsibility and control over their social and economic development.

The extremely limited powers of self-government assigned by the Act to reserve bands (powers that were always subject to approval by Ottawa) were to be exercised through band councils and chiefs elected for three-year terms (see sections 61–63 of the Act). This method for selecting chiefs reflects the assimilationist thinking of the time, whereby democratic practices of European origin were expected to replace Indigenous traditions of governance that involved traditional and inherited leadership. The goal of assimilation is even more apparent in those sections of the Indian Act dealing with citizenship and voting. The Act laid out a procedure whereby an Indian could request to become a full and equal Canadian citizen. While enfranchisement was automatic for Indigenous persons who acquired a certain social rank, including those with university degrees, lawyers, ordained ministers, and physicians, there was no automatic right to Canadian citizenship for status Indians before 1960, when an amendment to the Act extended Canadian citizenship and the right to vote to all Indigenous people.

Until well into the latter half of the twentieth century it was widely assumed that Indigenous peoples would gradually abandon their languages, customs, and lifestyles and be absorbed into Euro-Canadian society. Speaking in 1950, Minister of Indian Affairs Walter Harris expressed this view. "The ultimate goal of our Indian policy," he said, "is the integration of the Indians into the general life and economy of the country. It is recognized, however, that during a temporary transition period special treatment and legislation are necessary."[26] Integration progressed slowly, however, despite various prohibitions and inducements intended to eradicate what were considered to be backward practices and to reward bands that behaved in what were deemed to be suitable ways. The 1884 ban on the potlatch ceremony (repeated and clarified in 1895) and on religious ceremonies that involved dances (e.g., the sun dance or thirst dance) exemplifies the sanctions used to stamp out Indigenous traditions. The prohibition on using Indigenous languages in the residential schools operated under the authority of the federal government was another method of assimilating Indigenous people into the mainstream of Canadian society. The Indian Advancement Act, also passed in 1884, whereby much more extensive powers could be delegated to a band by Ottawa, was an example of the carrot approach to encouraging compliant Indigenous leadership and advancing the goal of integration. The extension of voting rights in 1960 brought their political status closer to that of other Canadians, but their legal and social status, and their civil rights, remained quite distinct. Moreover, instead of disappearing from the scene as the early architects of Canada's Indigenous policy doubtless hoped and expected, reserves continued to exist as islands of shame within an affluent and democratic society.

The government of Pierre Trudeau set out to change this. Within a year of taking office

Trudeau's minister of Indian Affairs, Jean Chrétien, introduced the 1969 **White Paper—the Statement of the Government of Canada on Indian Policy**. In a patronizing tone (see Box 16.2), it proposed the total dismantling of the Indian Affairs bureaucracy, an end to the reserve system, the abolition of different status for Indians under the law, and the transfer of responsibility for the education, health care, and social needs of Indigenous citizens to the provinces, which provide these services for all other citizens. In short, it proposed an end to the nation-to-nation treaty relationship between First Nations and the Crown and an abrogation by the government of its responsibilities as set forth in the numerous treaties.

The background to these dramatic proposals involved an elevated awareness of social inequality and discrimination during the 1960s. The civil rights movement in the United States and the student activism that arose during those years took aim at the exclusion of minority groups from the

Politics in Focus

BOX 16.2 The Integrationist Philosophy of the 1969 White Paper

To be an Indian is to be a man, with all a man's needs and abilities. To be an Indian is also to be different. It is to speak different languages, draw different pictures, tell different tales and to rely on a set of values developed in a different world.

Canada is richer for its Indian component, although there have been times when diversity seemed of little value to many Canadians.

But to be a Canadian Indian today is to be someone different in another way. It is to be someone apart— apart in law, apart in the provision of government services and, too often, apart in social contacts.

To be an Indian is to lack power—the power to act as owner of your lands, the power to spend your own money and, too often, the power to change your own condition.

Not always, but too often, to be an Indian is to be without—without a job, a good house, or running water;

without knowledge, training or technical skill and, above all, without those feelings of dignity and self-confidence that a man must have if he is to walk with his head held high.

All these conditions of the Indians are the product of history and have nothing to do with their abilities and capacities. Indian relations with other Canadians began with special treatment by government and society, and special treatment has been the rule since Europeans first settled in Canada. Special treatment has made of the Indians a community disadvantaged and apart.

Obviously, the course of history must be changed.

To be an Indian must be to be free—free to develop Indian cultures in an environment of legal, social and economic equality with other Canadians.

Source: *White Paper on Indian Policy*, 1969: http://epe.lac-bac .gc.ca/100/200/301/inac-ainc/indian_policy-e/cp1969_e.pdf.

rights and opportunities available to the majority. The creation of the American Indian Movement in 1968 raised awareness of the conditions and demands of Indigenous groups on both sides of the border.[27] The remedy that many mainstream social activists and civil libertarians proposed was integration, whereby barriers to the full economic, social, and political participation of historically disadvantaged minorities would be abolished. Integration was, in fact, the banner under which the civil rights movement marched in the 1950s and 1960s. It was not believed to be synonymous with assimilation, much less with "cultural genocide" and "extermination" that some critics have since equated with the liberal integrationist vision.

The reaction to the 1969 White Paper from Canada's Indigenous leadership was swift and overwhelmingly negative. "Now, at a time when our fellow Canadians consider the promise of the Just Society, once more the Indians of Canada are betrayed by a programme which offers nothing better than cultural genocide" was the verdict of Chief Harold Cardinal of the National Indian Brotherhood. "For the Indian to survive," he said, "the government [says] he must become a good little brown white man."[28]

While much in the White Paper proved to be controversial, nothing galvanized Indigenous opposition more than its proposals concerning treaty obligations and land claims. The government acknowledged that the lawful obligations of the Canadian government must be respected. However, it went on to argue that a "plain reading of the words used in the treaties reveals the limited and minimal promises which were included in them" and that they should not be expected to define in perpetuity the relationship between First Nations and the government of Canada. Moreover, the very concept of a treaty between one part of society and the government of all the people was morally and philosophically repugnant to Pierre Trudeau and the vision of inclusive integration laid out in the White Paper.

This vision and the premises on which it was based survive today as a minority point of view among Canada's political and intellectual elites. They have been refuted by numerous court decisions on treaty rights and Indigenous land claims. Indeed, the trajectory of government policy since the ill-fated 1969

White Paper has been in the direction of recognizing, in the law and in the Constitution, the separate and distinct status of Indigenous communities within Canadian society. Self-government, a concept almost unheard of a couple of generations ago—or, at least, rarely mentioned by Canada's political leaders or in the media—is endorsed by all of the major organizations representing Indigenous peoples and is accepted as both fair and desirable by many Canadians, although most have little idea of what it might involve in practice.

Stumbling towards Living Together and Apart: Commissions and Inquiries

Royal commissions, parliamentary investigations, national inquiries, and special reports have been a time-tested way for governments in Canada to address, resolve, or delay action on intractable public policy issues. Nowhere has this been more the case than in regard to issues involving Canada's Indigenous peoples, as evidenced by the following major inquiries appointed by the federal government over the past half-century:

- Hawthorn Report, 1966–7. A team of scholars led by anthropologist Harry B. Hawthorn produced the two-volume *Survey of the Contemporary Indians of Canada* that examined the economic, political, and educational situation of Canada's First Nations, concluding that assimilation was not desirable and that Indigenous peoples, in the words of political scientist Alan Cairns, should be understood and treated as "citizens plus," i.e., Canadian citizens with additional treaty rights and benefits. Ironically, the Liberal government response was the 1969 White Paper.
- Berger Inquiry, 1974–7. Justice Thomas Berger of the BC Supreme Court, who formerly had argued before the Supreme Court of Canada as counsel for the Nisga'a in the landmark *Calder* case (discussed below), was appointed to head the Mackenzie Valley Pipeline

Inquiry. This inquiry, which delayed construction of a natural gas pipeline, set a new standard for all future inquiries by travelling to remote Indigenous communities for testimony, and in the process captured wide media attention and the public imagination in southern Canada. Berger's two-volume report, *Northern Frontier, Northern Homeland*, became a best-seller in Canada.

- Penner Report, 1983. The report of the Special Parliamentary Committee on Indian Self-Government, under MP Keith Penner, picked up on the "citizens plus" theme of the Hawthorn Report and urged government to facilitate Indigenous self-government on Indigenous lands. The Committee's recommendations were ignored when the Mulroney Conservatives—more concerned with resolving constitutional problems related to Quebec—won election the following year.

- Royal Commission on Aboriginal Peoples (RCAP), 1991–6. The 440 recommendations of the massive five-volume RCAP *Report* drew on the work of earlier inquiries and added some new ingredients to the recipe for accommodation, including a separate Indigenous House of Parliament. Some recommendations have been enacted; many others have not.

Media Spotlight

BOX 16.3 The Lasting Legacy of Assimilation

Ottawa's 2008 apology to the victims of the residential schools and the roughly $5 billion in reparations that had been paid by the federal government by the end of 2018 did not cover all of those who were victimized during the decades when assimilation was the guiding principle of Indigenous policy. The article below describes the case of several Inuit who were selected for what the architects of this particular program doubtless would have described as a beneficial experience.

Inuit who as children were taken south as part of Ottawa's so-called "Eskimo experiment" are suing the federal government, demanding compensation and an apology.

Seven Inuit children were used as "guinea pigs" in the 1950s and 1960s when the government brought them from the Arctic to live with families from Alberta to Nova Scotia.

There they attended southern schools, without a chance to speak Inuktitut, learn traditional practices and eat country food.

"If you just said to the government 'You used us as an experiment, I think you should pay us for that,'" said Peter Ittinuar, who lived with a family in suburban Ottawa. "'You used us unwittingly, you didn't ask our parents, you just took us and in official documents you employed us as experimentees to determine how policy would be written about educating Inuit kids in Canada.'"

Statements of claim filed in the Nunavut Court of Justice allege Canada denied the seven former students the right to communicate with their famil[ies] for long periods.

The court documents allege the seven Inuit were forbidden from practicing their culture, and were "taught that their native language, cultural practices, customs and spiritual beliefs were inferior, wrong, sinful and shameful."

That led to "a loss of cultural identity and sense of belonging within their own community and within Canadian culture," and "a loss of Inuit skills that are necessary to traditional living in the North."

One of the plaintiffs, Zebedee Nungak, described in a 2000 article in *Inuktitut Magazine* his life in suburban Ottawa as growing up alongside "textbook Dicks, Janes and Sallys" while taking part in judo and swimming, playing in rock bands and going to the cottage on summer weekends.

"Here we were, literate Eskimos, able to read and write English, and relate to the works of Shakespeare, yet no longer able to cut snow blocks with a pana

- Truth and Reconciliation Commission of Canada (TRC), 2008–15. The 94 "Calls to Action" of the TRC, which investigated the history and individual and cultural consequences of the Indian residential schools in Canada, focus on the need to know about and remember past injustices and emphasize a way forward in reconciliation for all peoples in Canada, with emphasis on child welfare, education, health, and the justice system.
- National Inquiry into Missing and Murdered Indigenous Women and Girls (MMIWG), 2015–19. The MMIWG inquiry, which reported

in June 2019, became a political football from the outset, with Stephen Harper's Conservative government resisting calls for an inquiry, claiming this was a criminal issue, not a sociological one, and Justin Trudeau and the Liberals insisting that such an inquiry was needed. Once in power, Trudeau soon established the investigation. The inquiry's conclusion—that the astounding number of missing and murdered Indigenous women and girls over the past decades represented a clear case of genocide against Canada's First Peoples—promised to keep that football bouncing.

(snow knife)," Nungak wrote. "Well versed in calculus, we didn't know how to remove the sungaq (bile sac) from a seal's liver."

Nungak wrote this "cultural starvation" crippled his "sense of identity."

"These scars are hidden from the eye, but cut deep into our souls."

The seven plaintiffs are seeking a total of $350,000 each in damages. More importantly, Ittinuar said, they're looking for an apology, much like former residential school students, who received cash payouts and, last month, an apology from the federal government.

"I think we deserve no less," Ittinuar said.

The "Eskimo experiment" was, in fact, the tip of the iceberg of a practice of removing Indigenous children from their families and communities and placing them with non-Indigenous families. Known as the "Sixties Scoop," a term coined by Patrick Johnston in his 1983 report Native Children and the Child Welfare System, from roughly 1960 until the beginning of the 1980s, thousands of Indigenous children, perhaps as many as 20,000, were removed from their families and communities by child welfare workers and placed with non-Indigenous foster

or adoptive families. Whereas the Eskimo experiment was a deliberate policy, the Sixties Scoop was not a specific policy of any particular government, but rather a practice that reflected widespread assumptions at the time about what was in the best interests of Indigenous children. It was part of the assimilationist mindset that also produced the residential schools policy.

In a 2017 class action decision, Brown v. Canada, the Ontario Superior Court ruled in favour of the Indigenous plaintiffs who claimed loss and suffering as a result of this practice. The judge's ruling stated that "the uncontroverted evidence of the plaintiffs' experts is that the loss of their Aboriginal identity left the children fundamentally disoriented, with a reduced ability to lead healthy and fulfilling lives. The loss of Aboriginal identity resulted in psychiatric disorders, substance abuse, unemployment, violence and numerous suicides." The Court awarded damages of $800 million. On the other hand, those few Inuit who were taken from their homeland for the Eskimo experiment still awaited resolution of their case.

Source: Chris Windeyer, "'Eskimo Experiment' Claimants Seek Cash, Apology," *Nunatsiaq News*, 4 July 2008.

Of all of these investigations, the mandate of the **Royal Commission on Aboriginal Peoples** was the most expansive and its *Report*, at more than 3,300 pages, spread across multiple policy areas. The vision it set forth for Indigenous Canadians emphasized self-government and self-determination. The Commission, formed in the wake of the 1990 "Indian summer" of protest centred on the Oka Crisis, started from the premise that Indigenous Canadians constitute First Peoples whose sovereignty should be respected by the government of Canada. Its *Report* called for the creation of an Indigenous third order of government whose existence would be based on the acknowledgement by Ottawa and the provinces that the inherent right to self-government is a treaty right guaranteed by the Constitution of Canada. A form of dual citizenship for Indigenous Canadians, who would be both Canadian citizens and citizens of their Indigenous communities, was proposed by the Commission. The philosophical premises and policy proposals of the Royal Commission could hardly have been further from those of the 1969 White Paper. Among the most prominent of the Commission's 440 recommendations were the following:

- The government should issue an official admission of the wrongs done to Indigenous people.
- The inherent right of Indigenous self-government should be recognized by all governments as a right that exists under the Constitution.
- Indigenous persons should hold dual citizenship, as Canadians and as citizens of Indigenous communities. The *Report* proposed, instead of the hundreds of Indian reserves and bands and over 1,000 Indigenous communities in the country, that about 60–80 self-governing groups be created through the political merger of these communities.
- An Indigenous parliament should be established with an advisory role concerning all legislation affecting Indigenous persons.
- The government should negotiate with Métis representatives on self-government and the allocation to the Métis people of an adequate land base.
- Indigenous representatives should be participants in all future talks on constitutional

reform, with a veto over any changes that affect Indigenous rights.
- Much more money should be spent on Indigenous programs.

Running through all of the RCAP *Report* was a simple and fundamental premise: the original sovereignty of Indigenous peoples and their ownership of the land to which they lay historical claim must be acknowledged and their continuing right to a land base and self-government must be embedded in the Constitution. Moreover, the survival and development of Indigenous cultures, the *Report* argued, can only be achieved through policies that recognize these pre-settler peoples as distinct communities with special rights and powers. The problem with federal policies for over a century is not, according to this view, that they have treated Indigenous peoples differently from other Canadians. It is that these policies have not provided the Indigenous population with either the decision-making autonomy or financial resources to take control over their lives and escape the cycle of dependency that the Indian Act and the reserve system have perpetuated.

Some of the Commission's recommendations have been acted on. Steps towards various forms of self-government for many Indigenous communities—though not a one-size-fits-all model enshrined in the Constitution—were already underway before the RCAP made its recommendations. The creation of Nunavut in 1999, with its own legislative assembly and premier and a population that is about 85 per cent Inuit, represents a form of "public" self-government under which the Indigenous population effectively exercises powers similar to those of provinces. Many other and more limited forms of self-government have been negotiated since the RCAP made its recommendations.[29] Reparations have been paid to thousands of First Nations persons who experienced mistreatment and abuse in the residential schools that operated from the late nineteenth century until 1996 when the last residential school, in Saskatchewan, was closed. Some others, however, have fallen through the bureaucratic cracks (Box 16.3). In June 2008 Prime Minister Stephen Harper issued a formal apology to the victims of these schools on behalf of the

Canadian government. A decade later, in a speech in the House of Commons, Prime Minister Justin Trudeau promised that the government would introduce legislation for relations between the federal government and Indigenous peoples that would involve a "new recognition and implementation of Indigenous rights framework that will include new ways to recognize and implement Indigenous rights" (also see Box 16.4). The legislation was not tabled in Parliament before the 2019 election. As has been true of previous governments, both Liberal and Conservative, the Trudeau government's proposals did not embrace the concept of divided sovereignty that was at the heart of the RCAP's approach to Indigenous reform. The notion of self-government that the RCAP had advocated was premised on the idea that Indigenous sovereignty must exist alongside and be in no way inferior to the sovereignty that Ottawa and the provinces enjoy under the Constitution.

Organizing for Political Influence

Between 1867 and 2015, 39 Indigenous Canadians were elected to the House of Commons, about two-thirds of them since the 1988 election. That represents slightly more than half of 1 per cent of all MPs elected since Confederation. The picture is

Politics in Focus

BOX 16.4 The Vision of the Truth and Reconciliation Commission

As part of the Indian Residential Schools Settlement Agreement of 2008, the federal government created the Truth and Reconciliation Commission. Among other activities, its mandate included documenting residential school experiences and their impacts on Indigenous peoples, promoting awareness and education among Canadians of the residential school system and its impacts, and creating "as complete an historical record as possible of the IRS system and legacy." The Commission's 2015 report offered a vision for future relations between Indigenous peoples and the Canadian state that was also expressed in the 1996 Report of the RCAP.

In Canada, law must cease to be a tool for the dispossession and dismantling of Aboriginal societies. It must dramatically change if it is going to have any legitimacy within First Nations, Inuit, and Métis communities. Until Canadian law becomes an instrument supporting Aboriginal peoples' empowerment, many Aboriginal people will continue to regard it as a morally and politically malignant force. A commitment to truth and reconciliation demands that Canada's legal system be transformed. It must ensure that Aboriginal peoples have greater ownership of, participation in, and access to its central driving forces. Canada's Constitution must become truly a constitution for all of Canada. Aboriginal peoples need to become the law's architects and interpreters where it applies to their collective rights and interests. Aboriginal peoples need to have more formal influence on national legal matters to advance and realize their diverse goals. At the same time, First Nations, Inuit, and Métis peoples need greater control of their own regulatory laws and dispute-resolution mechanisms. Aboriginal peoples must be recognized as possessing the responsibility, authority, and capability to address their disagreements by making laws within their communities. This is necessary to facilitating truth and reconciliation within Aboriginal societies. Law is necessary to protect communities and individuals from the harmful actions of others. When such harm occurs within Aboriginal communities, Indigenous law is needed to censure and correct citizens when they depart from what the community defines as being acceptable. Any failure to recognize First Nations, Inuit, and Métis law would be a failure to affirm that Aboriginal peoples, like all other peoples, need the power of law to effectively deal with the challenges they face.

Source: Truth and Reconciliation Commission of Canada, *Honouring the Truth, Reconciling for the Future: Summary of the Final Report of the Truth and Reconciliation Commission of Canada*, 2015, p. 205, http://www.myrobust.com/websites/trcinstitution/File/Reports/Executive_Summary_English_Web.pdf.

THE CANADIAN PRESS/Ben Nelms

Incumbent candidate Perry Bellegarde was re-elected as national chief of the Assembly of First Nations in July 2018. Bellegarde was elected on the second round of voting, as the presence of Carolyn Bennett, the minister of Crown–Indigenous Relations, raised concerns of federal interference in the election result.

about the same in the Senate, where 17 Indigenous members have sat, or about 1.5 per cent of all senators over the course of Canadian history. Only a handful of Indigenous parliamentarians have been members of cabinet, including two in the Conservative government that took office in 2011 and two in the Liberal government formed after the 2015 election. The Charlottetown Accord on constitutional reform would have guaranteed an unspecified number of Indigenous members of the Senate, somewhat along the lines of the representation guaranteed since 1867 to the Maori minority in New Zealand's Parliament. Of course, the Charlottetown Accord was rejected by the Canadian people—and by a large majority of Indigenous people—in a 1992 referendum, and the parliamentary path to Indigenous influence remains weak.

Parliament, however, is only one of the venues where Indigenous issues are debated and decisions are taken. The mere fact that Indigenous Canadians have had little direct representation in Parliament is not conclusive evidence of anything. Influence may be exercised in other ways and through other forums. This has certainly been the case for

Canada's Indigenous peoples, whose ability to affect policy has depended far more on their use of the courts, on public opinion, and on what might be called the institutionalization of Indigenous rights, representation, and issues in the structures of the state.

The reaction to the federal government's 1969 White Paper marked the real beginning of the politicization of the Indigenous movement in Canada, although earlier efforts had been made by Indigenous leaders to create pan-Canadian and provincial Indian organizations to lobby for their rights (see Box 16.5). Before the dramatic mobilization of opposition to the White Paper, Canada's Indigenous communities were represented by a small number of ineffective organizations that had difficulty co-operating with one another and in managing their internal divisions. In fact, the federal government, through the control that Indian agents exercised over spending by Indigenous communities, had long discouraged the political organization of Indigenous peoples beyond the band or tribal level. Nevertheless, some efforts at broader political organization were made throughout the twentieth century, leading to the formation of the Assembly of First Nations in 1982.

Sovereignty, Landownership, and Indigenous Rights: The Battle in the Courts

It has always been our belief that when God created this whole world he gave pieces of land to all races of people throughout this world, the Chinese people, Germans and you name them, including Indians. So at one time our land was this whole continent right from the tip of South America to the North

Pole. . . . It has always been our belief that God gave us the land . . . and we say that no one can take our title away except He who gave it to us to begin with.[30]

Disputes over land—who owns it, who has the right to live on it, to benefit from it, and to make laws that apply to those within the boundaries of a particular territory—are among the most intractable. Only recently have more than a small minority of non-Indigenous Canadians come to realize that the crux of Indigenous demands involves land. Phrases like "self-government for Canada's Indigenous peoples" have inoffensive and even positive associations for many Canadians until they are linked to exclusive Indigenous ownership of land and political sovereignty over territory that the majority of Canadians assume to be part of Canada. The words of James Gosnell, quoted above, have been repeated in one form or another by numerous Indigenous leaders, from Louis Riel to many of the current generation. Their message is simple: the land belonged to us, much of it was never lawfully surrendered by us, and much of what was surrendered under the terms of treaties was little more than a swindle of major proportions.

Ownership and control over lands to which Indigenous peoples claim a historic right are argued to be necessary for the survival of Indigenous culture. In highlighting what are said to be the chief differences between Indigenous and European-based cultures, nothing is invoked more often than how these respective cultures view the land and their relationship to it. Clearly, the land was crucial to the traditional lifestyles of Indigenous peoples. For this reason such matters as Indigenous hunting and fishing rights were recognized in the treaties entered into between Indigenous peoples and the governments of European settlers. However, these rights were often restricted or ignored by federal and provincial governments and private citizens.

More controversial and hugely significant in terms of financial implications are Indigenous claims to control mineral or other resources, the exploitation of which, according to some critics, has little or no relationship to traditional Indigenous cultures and their protection. This is a very complicated issue that the courts have dealt with since the 1997 *Delgamuukw* decision, where Chief Justice Antonio Lamer wrote that Aboriginal title does not include uses that are "irreconcilable with the nature of the occupation of that land and the relationship that the particular group has had with the land which together have given rise to aboriginal title in the first place."[31] For example, if land is claimed on the grounds that it was a traditional hunting ground, it could not be used in a manner that would destroy its value for this use. But in that same ruling Chief Justice Lamer also said the following: "[A]boriginal title also encompasses mineral rights, and lands held pursuant to aboriginal title should be capable of exploitation in the same way, which is certainly not a traditional use for those lands."[32] The Supreme Court's 2014 ruling in *Tsilhqot'in Nation v. British Columbia* provides the clearest statement yet of the meaning of Aboriginal title and has a great deal of relevance for mineral exploitation, pipelines, electrical transmission corridors, and other infrastructure. These cases are discussed in greater detail below.

Landownership is one thing. Sovereignty is another. The fact that a person or group of persons owns a particular parcel of land, regardless of its size and other characteristics, does not exempt them from the obligation to obey the law of the sovereign country within which their land is located. But most leaders within Canada's Indigenous communities deny the sovereignty of the Canadian state over them and their land. At the Special Chiefs Assembly of the Assembly of First Nations in May 2018, the following resolution was adopted: "The federal and provincial governments must recognize and respect First Nations sovereignty and jurisdiction over their reserves and traditional territories."[33]

The exact meaning of sovereignty and jurisdiction are not agreed upon and have often meant different things to the Canadian political authorities, including the courts, than they mean to Indigenous peoples. While virtually all spokespersons for Indigenous groups express support for the principles of **Indigenous self-government**, most advocate some form of self-determination that would be realized within the context of the Canadian state.

Governing Realities

BOX 16.5 Major Organizations Representing Indigenous Canadians

1870–1938 *Grand General Indian Council of Ontario.* Created by missionaries' efforts to organize the Ojibwa tribes, the Council was conciliatory in its dealings with the Indian Affairs bureaucracy.

1915–27 *Allied Tribes of British Columbia.* An organization of BC bands, one of whose chiefs had travelled to England in 1906 to petition King Edward VII concerning a land claim, the Allied Tribes took up this cause and others, petitioning the Canadian government and Prime Minister Laurier and Britain's Judicial Committee of the Privy Council in the hope of gaining Indigenous rights and more and larger reserves. They did not succeed.

1918 *League of Indians.* Spearheaded by Frederick Ogilvie Loft, a Mohawk veteran of World War I, this was the first real attempt to establish a national political organization representing Indigenous Canadians. Loft's efforts were actively opposed by the Department of Indian Affairs, which had him under police surveillance, and after some initial organizing success in western Canada the League had failed by the early 1940s.

1945 *North American Indian Brotherhood.* Created by Andrew Paull, a BC Indigenous leader, the Brotherhood advocated the extension of voting rights to Indigenous people without the loss of their status rights under the Indian Act (something Fred Loft had sought), an end to intoxication offences under the Indian Act, and better income support programs for Indigenous persons. It never achieved national support among Indigenous communities and was disbanded by the early 1950s.

1961–8 *National Indian Advisory Council (NIAC).* This was a classic example of the state creating an interest group in the expectation of being able to channel and to some degree control the demands it made. Although the stated goal of the Council was to promote "unity among all First Nations people," it soon fell apart because of statutory differences between the three groups that it brought together: status Indians, non-status Indians, and Métis. The Council did not purport to represent the Inuit.

1968–82 *National Indian Brotherhood (NIB).* The breakup of the NIAC was followed by the creation of the National Indian Brotherhood, representing status Indians, and the Congress of Aboriginal Peoples, which represented non-status Indians and the Métis. Despite the fact that it did not speak for all Indigenous Canadians, the NIB was the first national Indigenous organization to achieve high public visibility and to be recognized by the Canadian state as the principal voice on Indian affairs. But the NIB had problems of internal cohesion, as was apparent when the organization split over the Canadian government's 1980 proposal to patriate the Constitution.

1968 *Congress of Aboriginal Peoples (CAP).* The 1968 breakup of the NIAC led to the formation of the Canadian Métis Society, which a year later was renamed the Native Council of Canada (NCC). The NCC brought

The nature of such an arrangement, however, is the subject of much dispute.

The issues of sovereignty and landownership are obviously intertwined. These matters have been contested and determined largely through the courts, often based on the interpretation of treaties. Indeed, it is usual for those who make the case for Indigenous sovereignty to begin with the Royal Proclamation of 1763. The Proclamation dealt with the North American territories that were formally surrendered by France to England under the terms of the Treaty of Paris. It included detailed provisions regarding relations between the British and the Indigenous inhabitants of these territories (see Box 16.6).

Indigenous leaders generally view the Royal Proclamation as an affirmation of their existing right to the lands they occupied. Georges

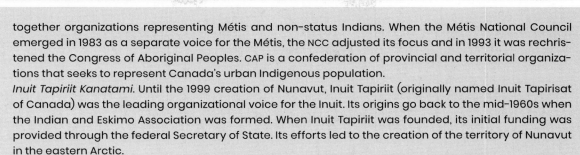

together organizations representing Métis and non-status Indians. When the Métis National Council emerged in 1983 as a separate voice for the Métis, the NCC adjusted its focus and in 1993 it was rechristened the Congress of Aboriginal Peoples. CAP is a confederation of provincial and territorial organizations that seeks to represent Canada's urban Indigenous population.

1971   *Inuit Tapiriit Kanatami.* Until the 1999 creation of Nunavut, Inuit Tapiriit (originally named Inuit Tapirisat of Canada) was the leading organizational voice for the Inuit. Its origins go back to the mid-1960s when the Indian and Eskimo Association was formed. When Inuit Tapiriit was founded, its initial funding was provided through the federal Secretary of State. Its efforts led to the creation of the territory of Nunavut in the eastern Arctic.

1974   *Native Women's Association of Canada (NWAC).* This organization, which speaks nationally for 13 regional Indigenous women's groups, has as its mandate the promotion and enhancement of the political, economic, social, and cultural well-being of First Nations and Métis women. The NWAC has been an important voice in seeking respect for Indigenous communities, families, and women.

1982   *Assembly of First Nations (AFN).* Since its creation the AFN has been the country's foremost interlocutor with government on Indigenous issues. In addition to being regularly consulted by government officials, the AFN has often been an intervener in court cases involving Indigenous rights.

1983   *Métis National Council (MNC).* Dissatisfied with being represented by the Congress of Aboriginal Peoples, the MNC was created to provide a more focused voice for Canada's Métis population. It is an umbrella organization that brings together the provincial Métis associations of British Columbia, Alberta, Saskatchewan, Manitoba, and Ontario.

2013/2015   *Treaty Alliance Against Tar Sands Expansion.* Created in July 2013 by a group of about 85 chiefs and band councillors who met at Onion Lake, Saskatchewan, the National Treaty Alliance challenged the view that the AFN should take the lead in treaty negotiations with the federal government. The organization's ambitious challenge to the AFN was soon abandoned and replaced by a focus on Indigenous opposition to pipelines. In 2015 the Treaty Alliance Against Tar Sands Expansion was formed, composed of about 150 Indigenous groups in Canada and the United States.

In addition, many provincial organizations represent Indigenous communities.

Source: Based on information provided in *The Canadian Encyclopedia* (https://www.thecanadianencyclopedia.ca/en/) and the websites of the Assembly of First Nations (www.afn.ca); the Native Women's Association of Canada (www.nwac.ca); Métis Nation (www.metisnation.ca); and Inuit Tapariit Kanatami (www.itk.ca).

Erasmus, a former national chief of the Assembly of First Nations (1985–91) and co-chair of the Royal Commission on Aboriginal Peoples, argues that "by virtue of that Proclamation, it can be said that First Nations became protected states of the British, while being recognized as sovereign nations competent to maintain the relations of peace and war and capable of governing themselves under this protection."[34] Regarding the treaties subsequently entered into between Indigenous communities and the British and then Canadian authorities, Erasmus writes, "First Nations did not perceive the treaties as being a surrender of authority."[35]

In fact, it is not entirely clear that the Royal Proclamation of 1763—which was formally incorporated into the Canadian Constitution through section 25 of the Charter of Rights and Freedoms—recognizes unqualified Indigenous sovereignty.

Governing Realities

BOX 16.6 From the Royal Proclamation of 1763

And whereas it is just and reasonable, and essential to our Interest, and the security of our Colonies, that the several Nations or Tribes of Indians with whom We are connected, and who live under our protection, should not be molested or disturbed in the Possession of such Parts of Our Dominions and Territories as, not having been ceded to or purchased by Us, are reserved to them or any of them, as their Hunting Grounds—We do therefore, with the Advice of our Privy Council, declare it to be our Royal Will and Pleasure, that no Governor or Commander in Chief in any of our Colonies of Quebec, East Florida, or West Florida, do presume, upon any Pretence whatever, to grant Warrants of Survey, or pass any Patents for Lands beyond the Bounds of their respective Governments, as described in their Commissions; as also that no Governor or Commander in Chief in any of our other Colonies or Plantations in America do presume for the present, and until our further Pleasure be Known, to grant Warrants of Survey, or pass Patents for any Lands beyond the Heads or Sources of any of the Rivers which fall into the Atlantic Ocean from the West and North West, or upon any Lands whatever, which, not having been ceded to or purchased by Us as aforesaid, are reserved to the said Indians, or any of them.

And We do further declare it to be Our Royal Will and Pleasure, for the present as aforesaid, to reserve under our Sovereignty, Protection, and Dominion, for the use of the said Indians, all the Lands and Territories not included within the Limits of Our Said Three New Governments, or within the Limits of the Territory granted to the Hudson's Bay Company, as also all the Lands and Territories lying to the Westward of the Sources of the Rivers which fall into the Sea from the West and North West as aforesaid;

And We do hereby strictly forbid, on Pain of our Displeasure, all our loving Subjects from making any Purchases or Settlements whatever, or taking Possession of any of the Lands above reserved, without our especial leave and Licence for the Purpose first obtained.

And, We do further strictly enjoin and require all Persons whatever who have either wilfully or inadvertently seated themselves upon any lands within the Countries above described, or upon any other Lands which, not having been ceded to or purchased by Us, are still reserved to the said Indians as aforesaid, forthwith to remove themselves from such Settlements.

And Whereas Great Frauds and Abuses have been committed in purchasing Lands of the Indians, to the Great Prejudice of our Interests, and to the Great Dissatisfaction of the said Indians; In order, therefore, to prevent such Irregularities for the future, and to the End that the Indians may be convinced of our justice and determined Resolution to remove all reasonable Cause of Discontent, We do, with the Advice of our Privy Council strictly enjoin and require, that no private Person do presume to make any Purchase from the said Indians of any Lands reserved to the said Indians, within those parts of our Colonies where, We have thought proper to allow Settlement; but that, if at any Time any of the said Indians should be inclined to dispose of the said Lands, the same shall be Purchased only for Us, in our Name, at some public Meeting or Assembly of the said Indians, to be held for the Purpose by the Governor or Commander in Chief of our Colony respectively within which they shall lie; and in case they shall lie within the limits of any Proprietary Government, they shall be purchased only for the Use and in the name of such Proprietaries, conformable to such Directions and Instructions as We or they shall think proper to give for the Purpose. . . .

What is clear, however, is that the Proclamation speaks of the "Sovereignty, Protection, and Dominion" of the Crown in relation to the "several Nations or tribes of Indians . . . who live under our protection." That the Royal Proclamation recognizes Indigenous rights is indisputable.

But perhaps there is, at a minimum, an implicit recognition of Indigenous sovereignty in the Proclamation. This argument is made by those who characterize the Indigenous–Crown relationship as a nation-to-nation arrangement, a characterization that seems to receive some support from the Proclamation's use of the words "the several Nations or Tribes of Indians," and also from the fact that the Proclamation states clearly that certain lands are reserved for the use of Indians and may not be purchased by private individuals or organizations, but only by the Crown. This restriction on the alienation of what the Proclamation refers to as "Lands of the Indians" might be interpreted as an acknowledgement of Indigenous sovereignty. At the very least it seems to establish the right of Indigenous peoples to compensation for land transferred by them to the Crown.

The courts have played a key role in determining the thorny questions raised by the words of the Royal Proclamation. This began in a major way with the 1973 Supreme Court ruling in *Calder et al. v. Attorney General of British Columbia*. At issue were the related issues of who owns the land, in what circumstances ownership may be said to have been transferred to the Canadian state, and whether Indigenous peoples have sovereign authority over lands that they claim by ancestral and historical right and that have not been formally ceded under a treaty. Although a divided Court did not rule in favour of the Nisga'a, six of the seven judges recognized the concept of Aboriginal title. The view expressed by Justice Emmett Hall in the Nisga'a case would eventually become the prevailing view in Canadian jurisprudence:

> This aboriginal title does not depend on treaty, executive order or legislative enactment but flows from the fact that the owners of the interest have from time immemorial occupied the areas in question and have established a pre-existing right of possession. In the absence of an [explicit] indication that the sovereign intends to extinguish that right the aboriginal title continues.[36]

The issue of Indigenous title has been addressed in a number of cases since *Calder*. In *Hamlet of Baker Lake et al. v. Minister of Indian Affairs* (1980), the Federal Court of Canada appeared to accept the spirit and reasoning of the minority in *Calder*, arguing that "The law of Canada recognizes the existence of an aboriginal title independent of the Royal Proclamation

of 1763 or any other prerogative Act or legislation. It arises at common law." While acknowledging, as has every other court decision on the issue, that the Crown exercises sovereign authority over Indigenous lands, the *Baker Lake* ruling repeated the view that Indigenous title continued to exist until explicitly extinguished by legislation passed by Parliament.

A decade later, in *Regina v. Sparrow* (1990), the Supreme Court of Canada again addressed the issue of Indigenous rights, including property rights. This decision continued the line of reasoning found in the *Calder* dissent and the *Baker Lake* ruling, holding that Indigenous rights are pre-existing rights that are not created by government legislation and that such rights continue to exist until such time as they are explicitly extinguished. "Historical policy on the part of the Crown," said the Court, "can neither extinguish the existing aboriginal right without clear intention nor, in itself, delineate that right. The nature of government regulations cannot be determinative of the content and scope of an existing aboriginal right. Government policy can, however, regulate the exercise of that right but such regulation must be in keeping with s. 35(1) [of the Constitution Act, 1982]."[37]

Calder, *Baker Lake*, and *Sparrow* were, in a sense, preliminaries to the main event that took place in the courts from 1987 to 1997. In *Delgamuukw v. British Columbia* the issue of Indigenous title was addressed head on. A group of Gitksan and Wet'suwet'en chiefs argued that they owned an area in British Columbia roughly the size of the province of Nova Scotia. In their Statement of Claim they asked the Court to make three specific findings:

- The Gitksan and Wet'suwet'en owned the territory in question.
- They had the right to establish their own laws for this territory, and these laws would supersede those of the province.
- They were entitled to compensation for all the resources exploited and removed from the territory since 1858.

The stakes could hardly have been greater, nor the issues of Indigenous title and the inherent right to self-government more squarely put.

In 1997 the Supreme Court of Canada ruled unanimously that the Gitksan and Wet'suwet'en are the owners of the land to which they claim a historic right of occupancy and use. Where title to land has not been extinguished by the terms of a treaty—this includes most of British Columbia as well as parts of Atlantic Canada—Indigenous communities able to prove that they historically occupied and used the land continue to have property rights. At a minimum the *Delgamuukw* decision established that Indigenous communities like the Gitksan and Wet'suwet'en have a right to compensation for land determined to be theirs by historical right. The ruling strengthened the hand of Indigenous groups who previously entered negotiations with governments armed with a rather nebulous concept of Indigenous title, but who now could say they have a constitutionally protected right of ownership that can only be extinguished through the terms of a treaty with the Crown. Landownership issues aside, the Supreme Court's 1997 decision did not establish a constitutional right to self-government for Indigenous communities. It did, however, establish that the oral historical accounts of an Indigenous people are admissible in court as proof of land occupancy and use, something the lower courts previously had refused to accept.

An even more momentous decision was delivered by the Supreme Court in 2014. In *Tsilhqot'in Nation v. British Columbia* the meaning of Indigenous title to lands was established with unprecedented clarity. The case arose out of a legal challenge by Chief Roger William of the Xeni Gwet'in First Nation on behalf of the Tsilhqot'in, a group of six Athabaskan-speaking communities in central BC. The argument was that the government of British Columbia, without consultation or compensation, had illegally granted logging rights on territory historically occupied and owned by the Tsilhqot'in. The Court found that the plaintiffs had legal title to an area of about 1,700 square kilometres in the interior of British Columbia, which their ancestors had occupied before the arrival of Europeans, despite the assertion of sovereignty over this territory by the British Crown and then by the governments of Canada and British Columbia. A test for determining whether an Indigenous group has

title to a particular territory was established and the rights and limitations associated with that title were clarified. The Court's ruling established the principle that the Crown is obliged to consult with Indigenous groups determined to have ownership rights over land before approving any development, such as a logging contract, pipeline, or mining activity.

This decision was greeted as a major victory for Indigenous groups. In particular, the Court declared that "governments and others seeking to use the land must obtain the consent of the Aboriginal title holders."[38] Moreover, the Court said, this requirement to consult and seek consent exists even if Aboriginal title has not been definitively established. Knowledge that there is a potential Indigenous claim of ownership over territory where some development is contemplated is sufficient to establish this obligation to consult.

Governments and corporations took some solace from the fact that the *Tsilhqot'in* decision referred approvingly to what had been said in *Delgamuukw* regarding incursions on Aboriginal title. In that earlier ruling Chief Justice Lamer wrote:

> In my opinion the development of agriculture, forestry, mining, and hydroelectric power, the general economic development of the interior of British Columbia, protection of the environment or endangered species, the building of infrastructure and the settlement of foreign populations to support those aims, are the kinds of objectives that are consistent with this purpose and, in principle, can justify the infringement of Aboriginal title.[39]

Thus, according to the *Delgamuukw* decision, the Crown may act without the consent of the Indigenous owners of land only if it has discharged its obligation to consult, its actions serve a "compelling and substantial objective" of the sorts listed above, and these actions do not "substantially deprive future generations [of Indigenous title holders] of the benefit of the land."[40]

In other words, there exists in law a duty to consult with Indigenous groups whose lands are affected by economic development, but there is no absolute Indigenous right of veto over such developments. This was confirmed by the 2017 ruling in the case of *Ktunaxa Nation v. British Columbia*, where the Court stated that "Section 35 [of the Constitution Act] guarantees a process, not a particular result. There is no guarantee that, in the end, the specific accommodation sought will be warranted or possible. Section 35 does not give unsatisfied claimants a veto. Where adequate consultation has occurred, a development may proceed without consent."[41]

The essential character of treaties between Indigenous peoples and the Crown is another important matter that has arisen in the courts. Some argue that treaties and other agreements between Indigenous peoples and the Crown are tantamount to international treaties. If this is so, then it would seem to follow that these Indigenous peoples have been recognized as sovereign nations capable of entering into agreements with other nations on a basis of legal equality. The Supreme Court of Canada, on a number of occasions, has expressly rejected this view of treaties.

Despite the courts' lack of sympathy for the interpretation of treaties as international agreements, Indigenous spokespersons and some governments have insisted that treaties be viewed in this light. Speaking of those Indigenous peoples who agreed to treaties with European powers, Georges Erasmus and Joe Sanders state, "The way [our people] dealt with the Europeans is ample proof of their capacity to enter into relations with foreign powers."[42] On the same subject they write:

> Our people understood what the non-native people were after when they came amongst our people and wanted to treaty with them, because they had done that many times amongst themselves. They recognized that a nation-to-nation agreement, defining

the specific terms of peaceful coexistence, was being arranged.[43]

Not only are treaties agreements between sovereign nations, according to this view, they are emphatically not real estate transactions comparable to, say, the US purchase of Alaska from Russia. This point is crucial because the position taken by the courts and most governments in Canada has been that any Indigenous right to ownership of the land covered by the terms of a treaty is *extinguished* by such an agreement. The nation-to-nation view of treaties denies that any extinguishment occurred, on the grounds that this was not how treaties were understood by the Indigenous peoples who agreed to them. That non-Indigenous persons understood these agreements differently, Indigenous leaders argue, does not mean that their view, rather than that of Indigenous peoples, should be considered the correct one (see Box 16.7). Indeed, in some instances Indigenous leaders only reluctantly agreed to put their marks on the treaties because of famine among their peoples and what appeared to be

Kevin Van Paassen/*The Globe and Mail*

Protest is not the only way in which groups and individuals can exercise their political agency in the real world. Here, Hayden King, who is Pottawatomi and Ojibwe from Beausoleil First Nation on Gchimnissing in Huronia, Ontario, takes part in a teach-in in Toronto in 2013 on the Indian Act, the 1969 White Paper, and government policies on Indigenous rights.

Politics in Focus

BOX 16.7 Two Very Different Perspectives on Historic Treaties

Historic treaties—notably the 11 numbered treaties dating from 1871 to 1921—are those that were agreed mainly in the late nineteenth and early twentieth centuries and include provisions regarding land. They cover most or all of the Prairie provinces and Ontario. Those signed in the Maritimes in the eighteenth century were what are known as peace and friendship treaties and do not have specific provisions regarding land. Quebec, most of British Columbia, and the territories were not covered by historic treaties.

What are called modern treaties and self-government agreements have been entered into since the 1970s. There are 26 of them, covering most of the territories, northern Quebec, the northeast coast of Labrador, and parts of British Columbia and Manitoba.[44]

The following brief excerpts, from the late sociologist Menno Boldt and from former Ontario NDP Premier Bob Rae, explain the different perspectives of the Indigenous peoples who agreed to the treaties and the representatives of the Crown, who initiated what many people today consider land-grab agreements.

The chiefs who marked the treaties profoundly believed themselves to be entrusted by the Creator with the protection of their tribal cultures— the Creator's blueprint for their survival and well-being. When they participated in the treaty-making process they did so from a conviction that they were honouring this sacred trust. In their minds, the treaty was an instrument for fulfilling this sacred obligation to the Creator, to their ancestors, and to generations yet to come. Another implicit understanding of the chiefs who marked the treaties was that they were autonomous peoples, and that the treaties affirmed the continuity of their autonomy. They marked the treaties in the spirit of coexistence, mutual obligation, sharing, and benefit, and as an agreement between themselves and the newcomers not to interfere in each other's way of life. They assumed the treaties would enshrine this intent and spirit as a permanent and living legacy. Thus, as a frame of reference for justice, the treaties provide a paradigm of high idealism.

—Menno Boldt, *Surviving as Indians, The Challenge of Self-Government*[45]

From the perspective of the government of Canada and of provinces, what the treaties said was this: First Nations give up all claim to the land, surrender absolutely any claim to the land, in exchange for which they would get, depending on the treaty, either 4 dollars or 5 dollars a year, the right to continue to live on a reserve, the right to continue to hunt on traditional territory and some sense that they were being protected by the crown.

—Bob Rae, "The Gap between Historic Treaty Peoples and Everyone Else"[46]

inevitable settler encroachments on their lands, and arguably they were misled by treaty negotiators for the Crown, who saw the treaties more as once-and-for-all-time land surrenders rather than as perpetual agreements for sharing and peaceful coexistence.

On a number of occasions courts have interpreted historic treaties as contractual agreements. They certainly resemble contracts in that they typically include a rather detailed enumeration of mutually binding obligations. The courts have recognized, however, that historic treaties constitute a rather unique sort of contractual agreement. This may be seen in the judges' tendency to interpret any ambiguous terms of treaties in favour of Indigenous rights. As the British Columbia Supreme Court said in *Regina v. Cooper* (1969), "The document embodying this larcenous arrangement must have been drawn by or on behalf of the Hudson's Bay Company and so any ambiguity must be construed in favour of the exploited Chiefs."[47] The Supreme Court of Canada repeated and expanded on this rule of treaty interpretation in a 1983 decision. The Court declared that "Indian treaties must be construed, not according to the technical meaning of their words, but in a sense in which they would naturally be understood by the Indians."[48]

The question of how treaties negotiated centuries ago should be interpreted today does not provide easy answers. After all, the treaties were negotiated in very different circumstances, by parties of very unequal power and resources who spoke different languages and operated from very different cultural premises, and they were written in the language of only one of the parties. In *R. v. Marshall* (1999), a case involving the claimed right of a Mi'kmaq, Donald Marshall Jr, to fish in contravention of federal fishery regulations, the Supreme Court said that "extrinsic evidence of the historical and cultural context of a treaty may be received even if the treaty document purports to contain all of the terms and even absent any ambiguity on the face of the treaty." The majority added that "where a treaty was concluded orally and afterwards written up by representatives of the Crown"—a practice that was common—"it would be unconscionable for the Crown to ignore the oral terms while relying on the written ones."[49]

The issue of title to lands and the conditions necessary to satisfy such title to ownership was revisited in *R. v. Marshall* (2005). In this case, Stephen Marshall (not related to Donald Marshall Jr) and 34 other Mi'kmaq were charged with cutting timber on Crown lands without a licence to do so. They argued that they held title to the land and therefore did not require authorization to log it and sell the timber. They also argued that commercial logging represented a natural evolution in the trading activities that their forebears engaged in at the time (1760–1) the treaties in question were entered into.

The Supreme Court rejected both claims. While acknowledging, per the *Delgamuukw* decision, that both European common law and Indigenous perspectives must be considered in assessing a claim of title and that "evidence of oral history is admissible, provided it meets the requisite standards of usefulness and reasonable reliability," the majority found that the Mi'kmaq claim to having exercised exclusive occupation of the land in question before the arrival of Europeans was unsubstantiated.

On the separate issue of whether modern commercial logging represents a logical evolution of the trading practices the Mi'kmaq engaged in over 200 years ago, the Supreme Court acknowledged that "ancestral trading activities are not frozen in time." But these treaty-guaranteed trading rights did not, it decided, extend to commercial logging. This was not surprising in view of what the Court had said on this question in previous cases. "[T]reaty rights are limited to securing 'necessaries' (which should be construed in the modern context as equivalent to a moderate livelihood), and do not extend to the open-ended accumulation of wealth."[50]

The Institutionalization of Indigenous Affairs

Treaties and the federal bureaucracy that has existed since before the 1876 passage of the Indian Act ensured that Indigenous affairs were embedded in the activities of the Canadian state. Government transfers to First Nations communities under the terms of treaties, which were administered through the Indian agents, and transfers to individual Indigenous persons through welfare spending (Indigenous Canadians living off-reserve are about three times more likely than other Canadians to receive social assistance) created a web of financial dependency on the state that continues to exist. Historically, the institutionalization of Indigenous affairs into the structure and activities of the Canadian state has also involved the creation and perpetuation of dependency relations. This continues to be the case, despite some important reforms whose ostensible goal is to break this cycle of dependence.

Sally Weaver has examined Ottawa's funding of the National Indian Brotherhood after the failure of the 1969 White Paper and the institutionalization (unsuccessful, as it turned out) of relations between the federal government and the NIB through procedures of joint consultation and decision-making.[51] A former Liberal minister of Indian Affairs, Hugh Faulkner, has argued that the motive behind his government's deliberate policy of funding selected interest groups, including Indigenous organizations, was progressive and intended to strengthen the political voice of such groups.[52] Others have been more skeptical. Noel Starblanket, a former president of the National Indian Brotherhood, accused Ottawa of using money as part of a divide-and-conquer strategy for dealing with Indigenous groups.[53] Roger Gibbins and Rick Ponting agree that the potential for the co-optation and control of Indigenous organizations certainly existed as Ottawa became increasingly involved in the funding of these groups. "[T]he provision of money is deemed to carry the right to specify how, for what, and by whom it will be spent," they write. "Other rights deemed to accompany the provision of money are the right to demand proof that the funds have been spent in accordance with the stipulations just cited, and the right to withdraw or terminate the funds."[54] Gibbins and Ponting provide examples of money having been used as a lever to control the behaviour of Indigenous groups.

When do state funding and other forms of privileged recognition, by design or simply by consequence, divide Indigenous groups and perhaps weaken the influence of those whose demands the government finds to be least acceptable? In recent years this issue has continued to generate much controversy. In January 2013 the AFN and the federal government agreed to work towards negotiations on treaty obligations. Many of the tribal groups represented by the AFN objected to this approach, claiming that the AFN had no authority to negotiate treaty matters on their behalf. The issue came to a head in July 2013 when some provincial chiefs attended the National Treaty Gathering at Onion Lake, Saskatchewan, instead of the annual meeting of the AFN held at the same time in Whitehorse, Yukon. "These are people in the same house who have different views on what the future looks like," said Indigenous policy expert Ken Coates.[55] Coates is doubtless correct, but the fact that they inhabit the same house does not mean that their differences are insignificant.

This was apparent leading up to and at the 2018 General Assembly of the AFN, held in Vancouver during July of that year. The AFN's National Chief, Perry Bellegarde, was re-elected to a second four-year term. Some of those who challenged his leadership accused him and the AFN of having been co-opted by the federal government through money and recognition. Derek Nepinak, former Grand Chief of the Assembly of Manitoba Chiefs, noted that it is not just the AFN that is almost entirely reliant on government funding. Other political organizations representing Indigenous peoples find themselves in the same situation. "These are sponsored agencies of the federal government," he argued. "The money comes from the top down not the bottom up. . . . [I]f we were funding it from the bottom up we would see where the priorities are because [First Nations will] put their money where the priorities are."[56] Indigenous activist and writer, Robert Jajo, expresses a similar criticism of dependence on the Canadian state, particularly in the case of the AFN:

> The Trudeau government's decision to treat the AFN as the sole legitimate representative of First Nations people is undemocratic and risky. Contrary to what many non-Native people may think, the AFN isn't the "Parliament of First Nations People"; at best, it's the "Association of Canadian Municipalities" of First Nations people. It's a body elected solely by chiefs (some of whom may have never been elected themselves). Far from being a representative body, during the Idle No More protests, the AFN found itself in conflict with the "Native Street."[57]

The leading organizational voices for Indigenous Canadians continue to depend on public funding provided mainly through the budget of the ministry now called Crown–Indigenous Relations and Northern Affairs Canada (CIRNAC). There is not much evidence to suggest, however, that this dependence has muzzled these groups. Indeed, over the last couple of decades the criticisms from various leaders of the Assembly of First Nations and other groups have frequently been scathing. These attacks have often been made at international forums, ensuring that the shame factor would be magnified. Moreover, money spent by some Indigenous groups on legal proceedings against the Canadian state, on retaining the services of some of Canada's most high-powered lobbying firms, and on advertising campaigns to influence public opinion in order to change government policy has come, at least in part, from state funding.

The institutionalization of Indigenous affairs and identity within the Canadian state has also occurred through broadcasting. The early beginnings go back to 1960 when the CBC Northern Service broadcast the first Indigenous-language program from its Montreal studios. This was followed by some Indigenous programming through the CBC Northern Television Service, established in 1972, and by $40 million earmarked for Indigenous-language television and radio programming in the Far North for the period 1983–7. Many other radio and television broadcasting initiatives were launched between 1960 and the mid-1990s, but the consensus is that the major impact of broadcasting to the North, where most viewers and listeners were Indigenous Canadians, was to "accelerate the process of cultural and language loss, particularly among the young."[58]

The last few decades have seen greater state involvement in support of Indigenous broadcasting. An official policy of support for Indigenous-language broadcasting was declared in public notices issued by the CRTC in 1985 and 1990, and in revisions to the Broadcasting Act passed in 1991. No major steps in this direction were taken, however, until the *Report* of the RCAP strongly emphasized the importance of such services to the cultural survival of Indigenous communities. Telefilm Canada began to fund Indigenous-language television productions in 1996. Since then, most of this funding has gone to documentary programs, although support for Indigenous feature films has increased in recent years. The Aboriginal Peoples Television Network, carried by all cable and satellite television providers in Canada, began operation in 1999. Most of its employees are Indigenous and close to 30 per cent of its programming is in Indigenous languages. The fact that the CRTC requires cable and satellite television providers to carry APTN provides the network with a secure financial basis from subscriber revenues

($0.31 per subscriber each month as of 2016). The Nunavut Film Development Corporation is another source of money for Indigenous television productions, as are grants from the Northern Aboriginal Broadcasting program in the Department of Canadian Heritage. Ottawa also provides funding for television and radio broadcasters that serve the Arctic, including CBC North, and for Indigenous-language broadcasting in southern regions of Canada. The amount of Indigenous-language programming broadcast by these networks and local stations varies considerably, most offering only a few hours per day.

A third way in which Indigenous concerns and issues have been institutionalized through the Canadian state involves employment. Indigenous representation in the federal public service, negligible for most of Canada's history, today is about proportional to the size of the Indigenous identity population of the country. As of 2016, Indigenous people comprised about 5.2 per cent of the federal public service, slightly above what was estimated to be their availability in the work force, and 3.7 per cent of all those in the executive category of the bureaucracy, somewhat less than their labour market availability. The largest employer of Indigenous people in the federal government is the now bifurcated Indigenous Affairs ministry, consisting of CIRNAC and Indigenous Services Canada, where close to one-third of employees self-identify as Indigenous. About one in five executives in these departments is Indigenous. Since 1994 Indigenous Affairs, through its various name changes, has had an official target of 50 per cent Indigenous employment. About one-quarter of federal bureaucrats in the combined territories of Yukon, the Northwest Territories, and Nunavut self-identify as Indigenous and about 40 per cent of all Indigenous federal employees work in the North or in the provinces west of Ontario.

The Politics of Protest

More than 20 years after the two-month stand-off between the Mohawk of Oka, Quebec, and the Canadian military, Indigenous protest again dominated the national news with the rise of the Idle

No More movement in 2012. The specific catalyst for the movement was legislation introduced by the federal Conservative government that many in both Indigenous communities and the environmental movement believed would undermine protections for waterways passing through Indigenous lands. In a very real sense, however, Idle No More emerged out of an accumulation of resentments and frustrations over several issues of concern to Indigenous peoples, as well as a sense that the Assembly of First Nations and other Indigenous organizations recognized formally as interlocutors by Ottawa for purposes of consultation were not sufficiently aggressive or effective in presenting and protecting Indigenous demands. Idle No More "seems to be a rejection of aboriginal leadership, a rejection of local chiefs and chiefs on the national stage," wrote Daniel Salée, adding, "People seem to feel as though their leaders aren't working in their best interest or that they simply aren't getting the job done."[59]

From mid-December 2012 into the first half of January 2013, protests and flash mobs appeared at shopping malls and on street corners, the train line between Toronto and Montreal was blockaded, protests shut down several border crossings between Canada and the United States, and demonstrations were held at many locations, including on Parliament Hill. Solidarity demonstrations took place in the United States and in some other countries. A hunger strike at Victoria Island in the Ottawa River near Parliament Hill by Chief Theresa Spence of the Attawapiskat First Nation embodied the Idle No More movement's strategy of relying on unconventional methods to raise awareness of the positions it represented.

Protests by Indigenous peoples have a long history in Canada.[60] As is also true of protests by organized labour, environmentalists, feminists, anti-globalization activists, and other movements, they are seen as ways of bringing public attention to an issue and to a group's demands. Indeed, attracting media coverage to a situation, an unjust condition, or a law is vital to acts of protest. Without this attention there would be no political reason to protest (although there might be moral, solidarity, and other reasons important to members of a movement). For example, when Indigenous protesters occupied the North Thompson River Provincial Park near Clearwater, BC, in July of 2018, the goal was not to inconvenience campers and not even principally to repossess land that the Secwepemc First Nation claimed was theirs by ancestral right. The primary purpose was to bring attention to their opposition to the Trans Mountain pipeline expansion that had been approved by the Trudeau government. Public protest is often resorted to by groups that believe the other channels of political influence—including parties and elections, lobbying, and the courts—are unavailable to them or that they provide results that are too little and too slow.

In this, Indigenous groups have often been successful (see Box 16.8). Public opinion has sometimes been quite supportive of their protests, even when these have involved illegal activities such as blockades, ignoring court orders, or violence. This was true during the early stages of the 78-day standoff at Oka, where public opinion polls showed considerable support among Canadians for what was seen as the justice of the Mohawk cause. But public opinion is not always sympathetic to Indigenous protests, as it was not in the case of the Idle No More movement.[61] What can be said with greater certainty is that such protests have generally helped generate greater public awareness of the grievances of Indigenous peoples at the same time as they have probably contributed to the polarizing of opinion on these issues and on the status of Indigenous peoples within Canada.

The divisions in Canadian public opinion were highlighted by the results of a 2018 Angus Reid survey.[62] As shown in Figure 16.2, Canadians are divided on such issues as whether Indigenous peoples should have a different status from other Canadians, on the consequences of residential schools, and on whether Indigenous Canadians should become more integrated into the broader Canadian society or remain apart. The survey found that those least sympathetic to the view that Indigenous peoples should be treated differently from other Canadians and that they continue to suffer from past injustices tend to be older, wealthier, and more likely to be male than the general population, and are found in greater numbers in the western provinces of Alberta, Saskatchewan,

Kanienkehaka (Mohawk) activists watch coverage of the Oka Crisis from behind the barricades in the summer of 1990. Media coverage of the crisis sparked solidarity movements in Indigenous communities across Canada and helped to grow awareness of Indigenous grievances among non-Indigenous Canadians.

and Manitoba. Those most sympathetic to these views of Indigenous peoples tend to be university-educated and younger, and are disproportionately from Ontario and Quebec.

Summing Up

Hidden from view and ignored by governments for most of Canada's history, Indigenous peoples and the issues of special concern to them have come to occupy an important place in the Canadian political conversation. Royal commissions and inquiries, protests, court rulings, and an increased awareness among Canadians of the human rights implications of the historical treatment and current conditions experienced by many in Canada's Indigenous

communities have raised the profile of these issues. While most Canadians acknowledge the injustices done to Indigenous peoples in the past, they are divided about whether they are treated fairly today and on the question of what the future relationship between the Canadian state and Indigenous communities should be.

The assimilationist premises that guided Indigenous policy have long since been abandoned. They have been replaced by a general acceptance that the way forward needs to involve various forms of self-government for Indigenous peoples, and indeed, considerable progress has been made in this regard over the past couple of decades. But as Ken Coates writes, "Canada's real problem is that there is no consensus on how to achieve meaningful

Media Spotlight

BOX 16.8 Paddling onto the Front Pages

Before Idle No More, there was the journey of the Odeyak. It was 25 years ago today [22 April 2015], on Earth Day, that 60 Cree and Inuit people from northern Quebec paddled a hybrid canoe called the Odeyak along the Hudson River into Manhattan to protest a hydroelectric dam project in Quebec.

The voyage of the Odeyak brought international attention to their protest of the dam. The project was denounced by the *New York Times* and *Time* magazine among other media outlets that picked up their story.

The development of the Great Whale hydroelectric dam was supposed to start in March of 1989. It was the second phase of the James Bay project.

Matthew Mukash was among the paddlers, and he said arriving in New York after a six week journey was very emotional.

"The Odeyak was put onto a stage at Times Square and it became the centre of attention for the media.

And our leadership was given the opportunity to speak before a crowd of about 10,000 people at Times Square, so that part was very emotional for all of us," Mukash tells *As It Happens* host, Carol Off.

"Of course it was a big undertaking because here you had a deal that was signed by the State of New York and Quebec that was about $17 billion that you wanted to kill. The strategy was to kill the market for electricity in the United States because that's where Hydro-Québec wanted to sell the power," says Mukash.

New York eventually pulled out of their contract with Quebec, and the dam was later cancelled by the province....

Source: CBC, "Commemorating 25th Anniversary of Historic Odeyak Voyage," 22 Apr. 2015,: https://www.cbc.ca/radio/asithappens/as-it-happens-wednesday-edition-1.3044034/commemorating-25th-anniversary-of-historic-odeyak-voyage-1.3044498.

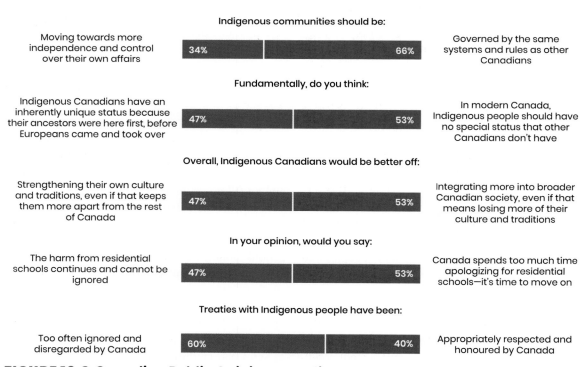

FIGURE 16.2 Canadian Public Opinion on Indigenous Issues, 2018

Source: Angus Reid Institute, "Truths of Reconciliation: Canadians Are Deeply Divided on How Best to Address Indigenous Issues," 7 June 2018, http://angusreid.org/indigenous-canada/.

change. . . . [T]here is substantial unevenness in the capacity of aboriginal communities to undertake reforms and large disagreements over priorities."[63] The often heard solution, "spend more money," may indeed be what is needed in the case of some communities. However, money alone may not address the needs and conditions of other Indigenous peoples. Just as policy-makers are divided over what the way forward should look like, leaders, scholars, and activists in Indigenous communities do not see matters in the same way or speak with a single voice. All of this ensures that disagreements over how to close the gap between the social, economic, and health conditions of Indigenous peoples and the rest of Canadian society will continue well into the future.

Starting Points for Research

Martin J. Cannon and Lina Sunseri, eds, *Racism, Colonialism, and Indigeneity in Canada: A Reader*, 2nd edn (Toronto: Oxford University Press, 2018). Collection of readings written primarily by Indigenous scholars, examining how the convergence of racism and colonialism has shaped the lives of Indigenous people.

CBC *Ideas*, "All Our Relations: Finding the Path Forward," https://www.cbc.ca/radio/ideas/the-2018-cbc-massey-lectures-all-our-relations-1.4763007. These five talks by Tanya Talaga, Indigenous author of the prize-winning book *Seven Fallen Feathers: Racism, Death and Hard Truths in a Northern City*, were given as the 2018 Massey Lectures. The talks are also available in a book by the same title, published by the House of Anansi Press.

Olive Patricia Dickason, with David T. McNab, *Canada's First Nations: A History of Founding Peoples from Earliest Times*, 4th edn (Toronto: Oxford University Press, 2009). The authors draw on research in political science, anthropology, archaeology, biology, and sociology in this history spanning the first peopling of the Americas to contemporary land claim settlements and conflicts.

James S. Frideres, *First Nations in the Twenty-First Century*, 2nd edn (Toronto: Oxford University Press, 2016). Frideres, an Indigenous sociologist and one of Canada's leading scholars on Indigenous peoples and ethnicity, examines the various aspects of government–First Nations relations within a framework of epistemology, Indigenous languages, and the trauma caused by residential schools.

Gabrielle Slowey, "Confederation Comes at a Cost: Indigenous Peoples and the Ongoing Reality of Colonialism in Canada," http://active history.ca/2016/07/19457/. This 2016 essay by the director of the Robarts Centre for Canadian Studies at York University is one that many students will find thought-provoking. It references such important contemporary Indigenous scholars as Glenn Coulthard and Kiera Ladner.

Review Exercises

1. How do the status and conditions of Indigenous people in Canada compare to those of their counterparts in the United States or Australia? You may find it useful to consult the data in United Nations, Department of Economic and Social Affairs, *State of the World's Indigenous*

Peoples, at: https://www.un.org/development/desa/indigenouspeoples/publications/state-of-the-worlds-indigenous-peoples.html. At three volumes it is a lot of reading! You may want to focus on health (vol. 2) or education (vol. 3).

2. Should the Charter of Rights and Freedoms apply to all Indigenous communities in all respects and at all times? Or should Indigenous rights and the concept of self-government be construed so that they take precedence over the Charter in some circumstances? Formulate an argument on one side of this issue.

3. In 2017 the first Indigenous Peoples Courts began to operate. What are they, how do they function, and what has been the assessment of them so far?

Thousands of people gather outside the United States Embassy in Ottawa on 30 January 2017 to protest the announcement of President Donald Trump's "Muslim Ban," an executive order that suspended travel into the United States from countries deemed a security risk. In a decade that has seen the rise of xenophobic political groups in many countries, Canada's willingness to accept refugees is seen by many as one of its most important strengths in a global context.
(THE CANADIAN PRESS/Fred Chartrand)

17 Canada in the World

Canadian politics has always unfolded against a backdrop of issues that transcend national boundaries, and this is especially true today. In this chapter we examine Canada's place in the world, focusing on the possibilities and limits available to Canadian policy-makers as they navigate a turbulent and fast-changing international scene. Topics include the following:

- How Canadians view their place in the world
- How the world sees Canada
- Globalization and its consequences for Canada
- Canada's relations with the United States
- Engagement in the world: Canada in comparative perspective

"The twentieth century will belong to Canada." This was the bold prediction of Sir Wilfrid Laurier, prime minister of Canada from 1896 to 1911. Laurier's forecast of greatness for Canada was made against the backdrop of the enormous growth that had occurred in the United States over the previous century, when Canada's southern neighbour went from being a cluster of states hugging the Atlantic seaboard to a continent-wide power with the world's largest economy. In the heady years of the early 1900s, as the nation-building strategy launched by Sir John A. Macdonald in 1879 appeared to be fulfilling its promise and about 200,000–400,000 immigrants arrived in Canada each year, Laurier's prediction that Canada was destined for greatness probably struck many as more than the usual political rhetoric.[1]

Over 100 years later it is clear that the twentieth century did not "belong" to Canada. The friends and foes of the United States would probably agree that it was the American century, during which the economic, cultural, and military dominance of the US was such that, in the eyes of many, comparisons to previous empires understated the sheer scale of America's global influence. In more recent years that dominance may well have declined, due largely to the rise of China.[2] Accounting for only about 2 per cent of global economic output and less than one-half of 1 per cent of the world's population, with a military that is barely a blip on the global radar screen, Canada is never thought of as one of the heavyweights of geopolitics.

Nevertheless, some Canadians believe their country has achieved the greatness predicted by Laurier, though in a form that Canada's first French-Canadian prime minister did not imagine. "For generations," says philosopher Mark Kingwell, "we have been busy creating, in [the shadow of the United States], a model of citizenship that is inclusive, diverse, open-ended and transnational. It is dedicated to far-reaching social justice and the rule of international law. And we're successfully exporting it around the world . . . ."[3] Canada is, according to many of its opinion leaders, the cosmopolitan, multicultural, equality-oriented, internationalist face of the future. John Ralston Saul, one of Canada's most prominent public intellectuals, argues that "Canada is above all an idea of what a country could be, a place of the imagination . . . it is very much its own invention."[4] Canada is, he has argued, a successful model of accommodation and flexible ways of thinking about citizenship. Michael Adams, the president of the polling firm Environics, has argued in several books and countless op-eds that Canada is a post-national example for the world. "Canadians' *lack* of nationalism," he writes, "is, in many ways, a distinguishing feature of the country."[5] The Canadian model, as it has come to be thought of by such public intellectuals as Kingwell, Saul, and Adams, is the real achievement of the last century and the one that is most likely to shape the direction of history in the twenty-first century.

Perhaps so, although Canadians might be surprised to learn that when the world's thoughts turn to the future of democracy, the evolving world order, or the trajectory of world history, few people other than Canadians mention this country as charting the course. A survey of books written in recent years by leading Western intellectuals on democracy—excluding those written by Canadians—turns up very few references to Canada and certainly no sense that the rest of the world is watching, much less emulating, whatever the Canadian model might involve. Indeed, we are used to hearing that Canada is loved and admired by the rest of the world—Canada regularly is ranked first or close to the top in international assessments of best countries to live in the world[6] and is as likely as almost any other country to be viewed as having a positive influence in the world[7]—and that we are often looked to for wise counsel and assistance on troublesome issues far from our shores. It may, therefore, come as something of a surprise to learn that not only our American neighbours, but other national populations as well, appear to know hardly anything about us. A recent book on Canadian studies abroad concludes that although there is considerable goodwill towards Canada throughout much of the world, knowledge of the country and its history among foreign populations and even their opinion-leaders seldom goes beyond the usual tropes and stereotypes that often frustrate Canadians when they are held by Americans.[8]

Politics in Focus

BOX 17.1 We're Not Always the Most Popular Kid in the Class

"Stop swooning over Justin Trudeau. The man is a disaster for the planet."[9] So read a 2017 headline from the prestigious London-based paper, *The Guardian*. Calling Canada one of the "worst students in the class," a Brussels newspaper headline from 2018 read, "The policies of Canada, Russia, China and Saudi Arabia could lead to an increase of 5 degrees Celsius in the world's temperature."[10] In a 2018 article, the Paris-based *Le Monde* lamented, "Despite opposition from environmental protection groups and from British Columbia, the Canadian government decides to triple the capacity of the Trans Mountain pipeline crossing the Rockies."[11] A couple of years earlier, China's foreign minister gave an angry response to a Canadian journalist's questions about human rights: "I have to say that your question is full of prejudice against China and arrogance . . . I don't know where that comes from. This is totally unacceptable."[12] His criticism of the question was amplified in the Chinese media in a manner that was interpreted as being a broader criticism of the Trudeau government for raising the issue in talks with China.

Prime Minister Trudeau is not the first leader to be in power when Canada has come in for criticism from the foreign media. In 1994 Canada's accumulated debt and succession of budget deficits led the *Wall Street Journal* to declare Canada "an honorary member of the Third World,"[13] a sentiment that was widely shared across the countries of the G7. From the 1970s, leading to the European Community's first ban on seal skins in 1983, to the European Union's 2015 ban on all seal products, Canada has regularly been in the crosshairs of European and other foreign media, NGOs, and politicians on the issue of the seal hunt. Alberta's oil sands have generated international criticism under Liberal and Conservative prime ministers. The conditions of Indigenous people in Canada and Canadian government policy towards them, past and present, have been the subject of a number of damning UN reports since 2004.

Canada is, on the whole, liked and admired, if not particularly well known by the world. Canadians should not imagine, however, that this affection exempts their country from occasional criticism.

It may also come as a surprise to Canadians to learn that when their country emerges onto the world's radar screen, it is not always in a positive way (see Box 17.1).

In a public lecture at Carleton University in 2003,[14] former Liberal Party leader Michael Ignatieff challenged his fellow Canadians to think about the ideas that most Canadians hold about their country and its role in the world. "Are we what we seem to be?" he asked. "Are the images that we have of ourselves true in the world?" These images, argued Ignatieff, include the following main elements:

- We are a peace-loving people.
- We are respected, listened to, and admired abroad.

- We stand for multilateralism and reliance on the United Nations and its agencies to solve global conflicts.
- We "hit above our weight" in international affairs.[15]

It is fair to say that Canadians continue to view their country's place in the world in the ways that Ignatieff described, and that they believe this image is reflected back by the world's mirror. A 2018 survey by Abacus Data asked Canadians how they think the world views their country.[16] Overwhelmingly, they agreed that the world sees Canada as tolerant (93 per cent), diplomatic (93 per cent), ethical (88 per cent), and a model to emulate (79 per cent). An Environics survey carried out that same year found that when respondents were asked to name Canada's most positive contribution to the world (Figure 17.1), the leading mentions were multiculturalism/accepting refugees (25 per cent), peacekeeping (19 per cent), and role model for the world (9 per cent).[17] About one in five said they didn't know. Roughly seven out of 10 respondents in the Environics survey said that Canada had a lot or some influence in the world and six out of 10 said that Canada's influence had increased over the past 20 years. In response to a differently worded question, respondents to the Abacus survey were not as certain that Canada has influence on the global stage, 55 per cent saying that Canada is seen as a follower by the rest of the world and 45 per cent saying that Canada is ignored.

In the language of international relations, Canadians are idealists who believe in the effectiveness of soft power. In this they are in accord with the majority of Canadian scholars who study international relations and Canadian foreign policy.[18] *Idealism* and *realism* are the two major theoretical frameworks used to explain why things happen the way they do in geopolitics and how countries and other international actors may best exercise influence. Realism sees the world as a tameable but largely ungovernable space in which the self-interests of

state and non-state actors compete and where violent conflict and war are inevitable. Realists stress the importance of what is often called **hard power**, including military capacity and economic sanctions, as means for the protection of national security and the advancement of national interests abroad. The idealist framework—sometimes called the liberal or constructivist model—is much less pessimistic about the prospects for the eradication of conflict and the achievement of peace that does not depend on a balance of military might. Idealists are much more likely than realists to emphasize what they believe to be the potential for diplomacy, multilateral co-operation, and structures of international governance to control and resolve international conflict and protect the security of nations. They stress the importance of what is often called **soft power**, influence that relies on the attractiveness of a nation's values, processes, and structures for representation, negotiation, and co-operation, and a leadership style that relies on example, persuasion, and engagement instead of threats and isolation. Realists are more skeptical of these tools and structures and more likely to place their faith in the nation-state, more limited strategic alliances, and the retention of hard-power capabilities as the best means for protecting and advancing a country's interests.

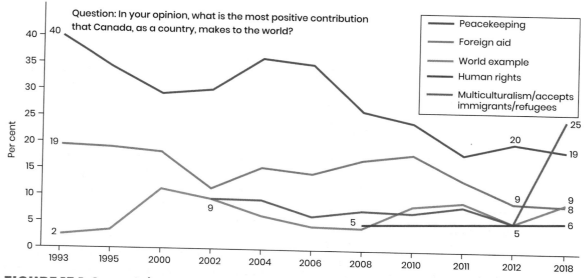

FIGURE 17.1 Canada's Most Positive Contribution to the World, 1993–2018

Source: Environics Institute, *Focus Canada 2012*, 48; Environics Institute, *Canada's World Survey 2018: Final Report*, 33.

The realism versus idealism debate is important for an understanding of analyses and assessments of Canada's role in the world. So, too, is the *nationalism* versus *continentalism* debate. This debate goes back to the end of World War II when the United States emerged as the world's foremost economic power. It was also one of two military superpowers, the other being the Soviet Union. During the nearly half-century known as the Cold War, which ended with the fall of the Berlin Wall in 1989 and the breakup of the Soviet Union in 1991, the United States was the acknowledged leader among Western capitalist nations. American dominance operated through its leadership in NATO and other regional military alliances, and its unrivalled economic power. No country felt the gravitational pull of American military and economic power more than Canada, its next-door neighbour. Between the end of World War II and the mid-1970s, economic and military integration between these two countries reached levels that generated a nationalist backlash in Canada. Nationalists argued that the advocates and architects of integration were complicit in a continentalist agenda of American domination of Canada. Canadian political sovereignty, cultural distinctiveness, and economic independence were all undermined, they argued, by this drift into a tighter American embrace.

Canadians pride themselves on the Maple Leaf being a "passport of goodwill"—that is, a symbol representing characteristics such as tolerance, compassion, prosperity, and politeness, making Canadians the envy of and welcome all around the world. Just how accurate is that self-perception?

These two debates, realism versus idealism and nationalism versus continentalism, overlap. Moreover, they are as relevant today as at any time in the past. Realists are likely to lean towards a continentalist understanding of how best to protect and promote Canada's economic and security interests. Idealists are more likely to be nationalists and therefore wary of Canada being tied too closely to the United States. On such issues as energy policy, missile defence, border security, and trade, realists are more likely to take positions sympathetic to maintaining or even deepening Canada–US integration. Idealists tend to believe that this integration has already gone too far and that a policy of building counterweights to American influence and strengthening international institutions is in Canada's best interests.

Listen to the "Security and Sovereignty: Perspectives on the World's Longest Undefended Border" podcast, available at: www.oup.com/he/Brooks9e

Globalization and Its Consequences for Canada

When the definitive history of the era from the 1970s to the first decade of the twenty-first century is written it will surely best be characterized by the word *globalization*. The 1970s saw the rising economic power of Japan and Germany, as well as the new wealth and influence of the Middle East's oil-rich states. The so-called Asian Tigers, the countries of Hong Kong, Singapore, South Korea, and Taiwan, exploded onto the world scene in the 1980s, with investment and growth rates far outstripping most of the world's economies. From the end of the 1990s into the early twenty-first century the dramatic rise of the BRIC countries—Brazil, Russia, India, and especially China—dramatically altered the international economic landscape. Hardly a corner of the globe escaped the consequences. For some countries, including Canada, the impact of the intensification of relations—particularly but not exclusively economic relations—with the rest of the world has been enormously significant.

Some historical perspective is necessary. Canada's economic condition, in fact, has always depended on markets outside its borders (see Appendix at the end

perc ds/iStockphoto

of this chapter). Already in 1925, exports accounted for about one-quarter of Canadian GDP. By 2000 this had reached a highpoint of about 40 per cent.[19] This dependence on trade goes back several centuries. From the arrival more than 500 years ago of European fishermen who trolled the cod-rich waters off the coast of Newfoundland until the middle of the twentieth century, the economic prosperity of the northern reaches of North America depended on the exploitation and export of a succession of natural resources—fish, fur, timber, and wheat—to markets abroad, and on the import of people, capital, and finished goods. From the time Europeans began to be seriously interested in what would become Canada by sending ships, settlers, and goods, the Canadian economy was integrated into greater patterns of trade and shaped by forces far from its shores.

Eventually, however, a hope and even an expectation developed that Canada would shake off this dependence and become the master of its economic destiny. One sees this already in Sir John A. Macdonald's ambitious National Policy of 1879, the first and only coherent and explicit economic development strategy that Canada had known before the decision to embrace free trade with the United States in the late 1980s. One sees it also in Sir Wilfrid Laurier's optimistic prediction that the twentieth century would belong to Canada. And one sees it in the rise of economic nationalism in Canada, particularly from the 1950s to the early 1980s, the path of which was marked by a series of policies and institutions designed to limit American influence in the economy and promote Canadian investment and ownership.

Some of these nationalistic hopes still survive, although they now appear increasingly atavistic in a world characterized by unprecedented levels of economic interdependence and global communication. Moreover, Canadians believe the clock cannot be turned back to the time before a policy of free trade with the United States was embraced through the **Canada–US Free Trade Agreement** (FTA, 1989), the **North American Free Trade Agreement** (NAFTA, 1994), and the **Canada–United States–Mexico Agreement** (CUSMA). CUSMA was intended to replace NAFTA and was signed by the countries' leaders in late 2018 and ratified about a year later. For many years a large majority of Canadians have expressed

their support for free trade with the United States, as well as for free trade in general.[20] Today, the serious debate is not about whether the forces of globalization can be rolled back, but how and in what instances they can and should be controlled. In Canada the question of globalization is inseparable from that of the country's relationship to the United States. Globalization has meant an intensification in economic and other ties to what is still the world's largest economy and whose dollar continues to serve as the reserve currency of the world. At the same time, however, it has also involved a larger and more complicated relationship with China and greater exposure to developments throughout the world.

Understanding Globalization

In some ways, globalization may appear to be a very old phenomenon.[21] The Spice Road that snaked from the ports of the eastern Mediterranean across the Middle East and Asia to China 2,000 years ago was an early precursor of the massive flow of goods and services that today knits together all corners of the globe. A characteristic of today's globalized world that usually is thought to distinguish it from international trade in earlier times is the unprecedented volume and speed of the economic exchanges in the contemporary global economy. The World Bank estimates that the percentage of global GDP generated by trade more than doubled between 1960 and 2016, from about 24 per cent to roughly 56 per cent.[22] The value of foreign direct investment worldwide has also more than doubled over this same period, reaching just under $2 trillion in 2017.[23] The Zurich-based Swiss Federal Institute of Technology produces an index of globalization for all of the world's countries. It is a highly sophisticated measure that includes economic, social, and political components. Based on data for 2015, Canada ranked fourteenth in the world in overall level of globalization: Belgium, the Netherlands, Sweden, and Switzerland topped the list. Among G7 countries, France, Germany, and the UK were ranked somewhat ahead of Canada.[24]

Since the end of World War II, policy-makers in Canada and across the developed world have generally favoured a more open trading environment. Although protectionism has gained some political popularity in recent years, in the United States in particular, there can be no doubt that barriers to the circulation of goods, services, and investment have declined over the last several decades. This has taken place through bilateral and regional trade agreements, as well as more comprehensive trade liberalization that took place under the aegis of the General Agreement on Tariffs and Trade (1948–94), leading to the 1995 creation of the more formalized and institutionalized trade regime overseen by the World Trade Organization (WTO). National subsidies and protectionism in various guises are still practised to varying degrees by all governments, but the overall trajectory of trade policy in Canada, as elsewhere, has been in the direction of more open markets.

The fact that free or at least freer trade has become the fashionable norm among the developed countries does not mean that doubt has been silenced or dissent squelched. The 1999 Seattle meeting of the WTO, the 2001 Organization of American States (OAS) Summit of the Americas in Quebec City, the G8 meetings in Genoa in 2001 and in Rostock, Germany, in 2007, the 2010 and 2017 G20 meetings in Toronto and Hamburg, respectively, were all accompanied by violent clashes between anti-globalization protesters and police. What were often dismissed as rather marginal if vocal protests from the radical left and anarchist groups moved towards

the mainstream with the 2016 presidential election in the United States. Both Donald Trump and Senator Bernie Sanders, an unsuccessful contender for the Democratic Party's nomination, were highly critical of globalization, striking a responsive chord with many workers in the middle and lower middle class. That same year a majority of British voters opted to leave the European Union, with support for Brexit being strongest in those parts of the UK where manufacturing had suffered most. Across Europe populist parties campaigned on anti-globalization platforms. "The main thing at stake in this election," declared Front National leader Marine Le Pen during France's 2017 presidential election campaign, "is the rampant globalisation that is endangering our civilisation."[25] Anti-globalization, which had always been an important theme of the political left, had become an issue on the political right. Some prestigious economists, including Nobel Prize winner Joseph Stiglitz and former chief economist at the World Bank and Treasury secretary under Barack Obama, Larry Summers, expressed their deep concerns that globalization had led to too much inequality.

In Canada the critics of globalization include many—very likely most—of those who teach in the social sciences, a significant part of the country's media elite, much of the leadership of the labour

AP Photo/Christophe Ena; Ewa Draze/Shutterstock

Police stand guard along a three-metre-high security fence circling the meeting site for G20 Summit leaders in Toronto in June 2010 (left). Seven years later, a similar scene plays out in Hamburg ahead of the 2017 G20 summit (right). Anti-globalization views have become more mainstream and the continuation of these protests demonstrates that large numbers of people still feel that more must be done to address the inequality that may be exacerbated by a global economy.

movement, the NDP, many religious and social justice organizations, environmental groups, and nationalist groups like the Council of Canadians. Their criticisms of globalization receive considerable coverage, from the small screen to the classroom. Indeed, the critique of globalization is probably better known to most Canadians and, for that matter, citizens in other wealthy countries than is its defence. Nevertheless, surveys regularly show that most Canadians are supportive of free trade and the two historically dominant political parties, the Liberals and Conservatives, represent this sentiment (see Box 17.2).

But globalization is not simply about economics and trade. It also involves the unprecedented movement of people between countries of the world, exchange in cultural values, the more rapid and widespread diffusion of diseases across the world, new security concerns that reach across borders, the introduction of animal and plant species, as well as bacteria and viruses, in parts of the world that did not previously know them, and the emergence of the virtual global village made possible by modern telecommunications technology. As in the case of trade, all of these flows have increased in volume, reach, and, in many instances, in their consequences for the people and natural environments affected by them. What we today call **"globalization"** may be defined as the historically unprecedented speed and scope of exchanges between different societies and regions of the world. Its consequences continue to be the subject of enormous debate.

The Social Fabric

BOX 17.2 Has Globalization Created Inequality in Canada?

Anyone who is reading this book—and just about everyone else, for that matter—has heard claims that globalization has led to a growing gap between the rich and the poor, to the shrinking of the middle class, and to increased poverty. Leaving aside whether they are true in China, India, South Korea, Germany, and other countries throughout the world, are they true in Canada?

First of all, the distribution of income in Canada is not significantly more unequal today than it was 40 years ago, at least if one compares the share of national income received by those in the top quintile of all families to that received by those in the bottom quintile. There are, granted, various ways of measuring the distribution of income. By some of these measures it appears that income inequality has increased over time. For example, if we focus on the share of income and wealth accounted for by the very highest income earners—say, the top 1 to 5 per cent of all earners—there is no doubt that this fraction of the population accounts for a greater share of all income and wealth than was true even a generation ago. Other measures, however, tell a different story. And in any case, the causal link between globalization and developments in the distribution of income is not as clear as many contend. Income inequality may change or remain the same in response to numerous factors, including government policies, shifting demographic patterns, economic restructuring caused by factors other than globalization, and so on. Globalization may be part of an explanation, but ideology more than analysis often elevates it to the status of the primary cause of income inequality. "In effect, [Canada] has become engaged in a vigorous struggle to define or 'frame' the new inequality and the social stresses it brings in its wake."[26]

The same caveats apply when we talk about the impact that globalization may have had on the size of the middle class and the extent and nature of poverty in Canada. As we saw in Chapter 3, the share of the Canadian population living in poverty, as this

Canada's Relations with the United States

Canada's economy has always depended on trade, today as much as at any point in its history. Some developed economies, including those of Italy, the UK, and France, are about as dependent on foreign trade as Canada, and some, including Germany and the Netherlands, depend on trade for an even larger share of their GDP than does the Canadian economy. But none of these other economies is as dependent on trade with a single trading partner as Canada is with the United States. In recent years between 20 and 25 per cent of Canadian GDP has been generated by exports to the United States, a share that has been as high as 35 per cent (2000). The historical evolution of Canadian trade may be seen in Figure 17.2.

Globalized production, sourcing, and investment have forced us to rethink what were, until fairly recently, firmly established ideas about what is Canadian. The case of the automotive industry is merely one example—though a particularly important one in terms of its employment and income implications—of the globalized economic realities that characterize much of the Canadian economy. Products exported from companies operating in Canada routinely include foreign content, and imported products will often include content produced in Canada. Moreover, most of Canada's provincial economies, including all of the largest ones, do more

is conventionally defined, has actually fallen over the past few decades. And despite the widely held belief that the middle class is smaller than in the past, some experts dispute this claim. Indeed, a 2014 study that uses the data compiled over three decades by the Luxembourg Income Study concludes that the size of the middle class in Canada is about the same as in Finland and greater than in Germany, and that it has not changed in recent years.[27] Among affluent democracies, it is mainly in the United States where the size of the middle class appears to have diminished significantly. Even in the United States, it is not possible to say that this squeezing of the middle class has been due principally or even largely to globalization, notwithstanding that this is a popular explanation among some on both the right and the left.

What about poverty? The argument is often made that globalization has increased the ranks of the marginalized, producing more who are unable to afford a decent standard of living. There are at least two problems with this claim. The first is the familiar one of wrongly attributed causality. As discussed in Chapter 3, poverty may be the result of a number of factors that have little or nothing to do with economic globalization. The other problem involves the very claim that poverty has increased. The truth of this claim is at the very least open to dispute. Using Statistics Canada's definition of what constitutes a low income, a smaller share of the population falls below what is often called the "poverty line" at present than was the case 40 years ago. Although poverty is an undeniable problem in a rich country like Canada, it requires a rather imaginative and contestable definition to conclude that the scale of poverty has increased.

There is no doubt that some Canadians, communities, and industries have lost as a result of globalization. At the same time some have done better, and not just those on the top rung of the income ladder and transnational corporations whose bottom lines have been improved by outsourcing. Globalization is a complex phenomenon that should not be reduced to political slogans and unsubstantiated claims.

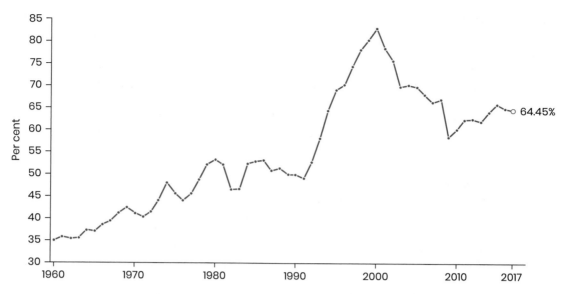

FIGURE 17.2 Exports of Goods and Services and Total Trade as Percentage of GDP, 1961–2017

Source: Data from the World Bank, https://data.worldbank.org/.

business with economies outside of Canada than with all of the other provinces combined. Thus, not only is the old idea of a made-in-Canada product cast in doubt, but the very notion of a Canadian economy seems a bit outdated given the reality of this country's enormous dependence on international trade.

The numbers speak for themselves. The total value of Canada–US trade in merchandise, services, and investment makes this the second largest bilateral trading relationship in the world, after that between China and the United States. Over 70 per cent of Canadian exports of goods and services go to the United States. In 2017 the value of these exports was almost 18 times greater than the value of the second largest destination for Canadian exports, China, and almost 13 times greater than the value of all Canadian exports to the European Union (including the UK). To put this a bit differently, Canada, mainly Ontario, exports more to the state of Michigan than it does to the entire EU, and more to the state of California than to all of China.[28]

A somewhat lower share of Canada's substantial import trade comes from the United States, at slightly more than 50 per cent of total imports of goods and services. This is down from about three-quarters of total imports around 1999–2001,

a decline due largely to the increased importance of imports from China and a drop in cross-border automotive vehicle and parts trade. Nevertheless, the value of imports from the United States is still about four times greater than those from China, the second leading source of imports. Canada has been the major export market for American goods for over half a century and as of 2017 was the leading export market for 35 of the 50 US state economies.

The United States has long been the largest source of foreign direct investment (FDI) in Canada, surpassing Britain to become the single largest foreign investor in Canada by the early 1920s.[29] The high-water mark for American ownership in the Canadian economy was in the 1970s when roughly 70 per cent of all non-financial assets were controlled by US corporations and investors. Currently the United States accounts for slightly more than half of the value of all FDI in Canada. For its part, Canada is the second largest source of FDI in the American economy, with a total value of US$500 billion in 2017 or 13 per cent of all FDI after the UK's 15 per cent. The United States is the location for about half of all Canadian FDI. This bilateral trade and investment relationship has a long history. In recent decades, however, the Canadian and American economies have achieved unprecedented levels of integration. The real value of trade between the Canadian and American economies has more than tripled since the Canada–US Free Trade Agreement took effect in 1989, increasing gradually at first and then more dramatically after NAFTA came into effect in 1994.[30] This economic relationship is very important for the United States, but is vital for Canada. Revealingly, when the Canadian media were full of stories about the renegotiation of NAFTA in 2017 and 2018, Canada was seldom mentioned, or only in passing, in the American media. South of the border the attention was almost all on Mexico, the other partner in NAFTA, with whom the value of US trade was less than trade with Canada. According to some accounts, Canada's minister of Global Affairs, Chrystia Freeland, spent most of her working hours on the Canada–US trade issue during this period.[31] It is certain that her counterpart, the American secretary of state, spent no more than a fraction of his time on US–Canada trade, delegating this function to American Trade Representative Robert Lighthizer. Canada–US trade disputes that lead the national news north of the border are lucky if they receive a mention in the American media, particularly outside border states that might be more immediately affected. The trading relationship is not only huge; it is hugely asymmetrical, affecting Canada's vital interests far more than it does those of the United States.[32]

Nevertheless, it would be an overstatement to say that Canada has no leverage in this relationship. Canada is the major source of foreign imports for 35 of the 50 American states, the destination for over half the value of all US automotive exports, and for many years has been the single largest foreign supplier of energy to the United States. The Canadian economy is very important, and even strategically important, to the United States. But the influence this might otherwise give Canadian negotiators in trade disputes with Washington is diluted by Canada's far greater across-the-board dependence on the American economy. To give but two examples, an end to petroleum exports from Alberta to the United States would bring Alberta's economy to its knees, producing an immediate drop of about one-quarter of the province's GDP, and would produce an immediate drop of about 4 per cent

in Canada's GDP. But although the value of oil imports from Canada exceed those of Saudi Arabia, Venezuela, and Mexico combined, an end to oil imported from Canada would represent only a drop of about 8 per cent in the total supply of petroleum consumed in the United States.[33] Likewise, if the American border were to be closed to automotive vehicles and parts from Canada this would represent an immediate loss of about 10 per cent of Ontario's GDP. State economies like those of Michigan and Ohio would experience serious losses from the end of automotive trade with Canada, but the impact on the overall American economy would amount to less than 1 per cent of American GDP.

This enormous imbalance in the Canada–US trade relationship was one of the chief arguments put forward in the 1980s by the Canadian advocates of free trade. The federal government's official policy of reducing Canada's reliance on trade and investment with the United States—a policy called the Third Option, adopted in 1972—had proven about as effective as a statute repealing the law of gravity. A decade later, Canada was even more dependent on the American economy as a destination for exports and a source of imports. Canada's major manufacturers, but also important exporters of natural resources such as wood products, oil and gas, and hydroelectricity, recognized that their growth prospects depended on access to the American market. The Canadian Manufacturers' Association,[34] which began life a century earlier calling for protectionist tariffs, became a convert to and a politically weighty advocate of a Canada–US free trade agreement. A growing wave of protectionist sentiment in the American Congress during the 1980s seemed to lend urgency to Canadian free traders' case, helped by the pro-free trade recommendations of the 1981–5 Royal Commission on the Economic Union and Development Prospects for Canada. Canada's best economic hope, big business and the country's leading economic experts agreed, was in tighter formal economic integration with the United States. Even among many of those who were dubious about some of the economic claims made for free trade, the political argument that this would help shield Canadian industries from Congress's protectionist moods was persuasive.

The Canada–US Free Trade Agreement took effect on 1 January 1989. It was followed in 1994 by the **North American Free Trade Agreement**, bringing Canada, the United States, and Mexico together into a free trade zone that encompassed most industries and forms of investment. Both agreements created an architecture of dispute settlement rules, agencies, and monitoring requirements, which did not take the politics out of trade disputes but provided administrative forums and procedures for their resolution. After more than two decades of experience with the trading regime created by NAFTA, the treaty was reopened after the 2016 election of American President Donald Trump. The agreement reached by the three countries in 2018 retained most of what has been in NAFTA. The major change, from the standpoint of Canada's trading relationship with the United States, involved greater access to the Canadian market for American agricultural producers in all of Canada's supply management sectors (dairy, poultry, and eggs). Otherwise, the Canada–United States–Mexico Agreement (CUSMA; called USMCA in the United States, T-MEC in Mexico) left intact most of the rules relating to trade between Canada and the United States that were already in NAFTA. Notwithstanding the barrage of fulminations that President Trump directed at Canada before and during the renegotiation of NAFTA, studies over the years have shown a deep reservoir of goodwill towards Canada in Congress and in the United States population.[35] The challenge is not so much reversing ideas that Americans and their policy-makers have about Canada and US–Canada relations as getting them to pay attention when it

AP Photo/Andrew Harnik

Global Affairs Minister Chrystia Freeland speaks to the media after arriving in Washington on 28 August 2018, shortly after President Trump announced a free trade agreement with Mexico that would have excluded Canada. Although Canada was eventually included in the updated agreement, Freeland continued to press Washington to lift tariffs on Canadian steel and aluminum before ratification of the treaty.

matters. As Allan Gotlieb, Canada's ambassador to the United States from 1981 to 1989, has observed, a major part of Canada's problem in its trade relations with the United States has always been getting the attention of those who matter in Washington.[36] He argues, however, that the answer may not lie in government-financed media blitzes or lobbying efforts, such as the roughly 200 visits to Washington in 2018 by members of the Liberal government during the negotiations that culminated in CUSMA. "Like it or not," Gotlieb says, "in the US political system a foreign country is just another special interest. And not a very special one at that. It lacks the clout of a domestic special interest because it cannot contribute to political campaigns or deliver votes." This was certainly evident when years of lobbying and millions of dollars spent on advertising by the Alberta and Canadian governments were unsuccessful in persuading the Obama administration to approve the Keystone XL pipeline. These efforts came to nought until a president sympathetic to the pipeline was elected in 2016.

Integration and Independence: Finding the Right Balance

Former Canadian Prime Minister and Nobel Peace Prize winner Lester B. Pearson was one of the chief architects of Canadian foreign policy in the post-World War II era. In his memoirs Pearson wrote that American dominance in the world and Canada's particular **dependence** on the United States were among the key hard realities confronting Canadian policy-makers.[37] These realities, Pearson observed, "brought us anxiety as well as assurance."

This continues to be the Canadian condition when it comes to the possibilities open to this country in world affairs. The asymmetrical economic relationship between Canada and the United States, overlain by structures of policy integration that have operated through the three comprehensive trade agreements signed between 1989 and 2019 and, before them, through sectoral treaties including the Auto Pact and the Canada–US Defence Production Sharing Agreement, leaves Canada with

little room to throw its weight around in conflicts with its American neighbour. As discussed above, Canada's economic prosperity continues to depend greatly on trade with the United States. The policy implications of this dependence can hardly be overstated.

For several decades the response of successive Canadian governments—the Progressive Conservative government of Brian Mulroney (1984–93) excluded—has been to search for and support counterweights to American dominance. Chief among these have been the United Nations and multilateral institutions more generally. **Multilateralism** involves the resolution of international differences and conflicts through structures and processes that represent many states and give all of them a voice, though not necessarily an equal voice, in decision-making. The United Nations has been the most prominent structure for multilateralism in the post-World War II era. There are, however, many other international organizations to which Canada belongs, including the North Atlantic Treaty Organization (NATO), the World Bank, the Organisation for Economic Co-operation and Development (OECD), the World Trade Organization (WTO), the Organization of American States (OAS), the Commonwealth, and la Francophonie.

Some of these multilateral organizations are dominated by the United States and therefore can hardly be said to serve as counterweights to its might. NATO, for example, has almost never blocked the will or modified the military objectives of American administrations. The 2003 refusal of several of its members to guarantee the alliance's support for Turkey in the event of an attack by Iraq was the chief exception to this rule. Influence in the International Monetary Fund's decision-making is weighted, based on the size of member-state contributions, and the United States is its major contributor. Multilateralism does not, therefore, necessarily dilute American influence. It can, in fact, magnify this influence by providing greater political legitimacy to American goals through their association with other countries and structures of multilateral decision-making. On the whole, however, multilateralism clearly holds out the possibility of allowing for the representation of interests and

The Canadian Press/Andrew Vaughan

United Nations Secretary-General Kofi Annan praises Canada's support for the United Nations to Prime Minister Jean Chrétien in September 2003. Earlier that year, Chrétien announced that Canada would not commit troops to the Iraq War effort without the support of the United Nations, marking the first time that Canada did not participate in a war effort in which both British and American troops were involved. Canada's lack of participation came as a surprise to its longstanding allies, but helped to establish its independence in international affairs.

points of view that might dilute the dominance of the United States.

"One of the great foreign policy challenges facing Canada," observes Michael Ignatieff, "is staying independent in an age of [American] empire."[38] This is a large part of the explanation for multilateralism's attractiveness in the eyes of many Canadians and those who govern them. Multilateralism, when it is not a convenient cover for the ambitions and interests of a single member state, implies that states are willing to accept some limitations on their national sovereignty. Canada's governing elites and opinion leaders, like their counterparts in Europe, "have a vision of a multilateral world in which . . . sovereignty is not unconditional, but limited and bound by human rights agreements, or multilateral engagements which limit and constrain the sovereignty of states in the name of collective

social goods."[39] It would be an overstatement to say that all Canadians accept this multilateral vision of the world, but recent history suggests it has broad popular support. The problem for Canada—a problem also experienced by many other allies of the United States, though less acutely—is that multilateralism has not been embraced as enthusiastically by its major trading partner and has sometimes produced outcomes setting Canada at odds with the United States.

There are, as there have long been, limits to how far and in what circumstances Canadian foreign policy can depart from that of the United States. In the case of Canada's refusal in 2003 to support the war on Iraq, this did not damage the security interests and military goals of the United States. The fact that the United Kingdom, Spain, over a dozen other European governments, Japan, Australia, and an assortment of other countries lent their support to this military action made the absence of Canadian support virtually unnoticed in the United States. Indeed, it was only noticed when some American media outlets reported the booing of the American national anthem at a hockey game in Montreal! The Liberal government's 2004 decision to reject participation in an American-led missile defence system—a system agreed to by governments in Britain, Australia, Japan, Germany, Italy, Israel, the Czech Republic, Denmark, Netherlands, Spain, Turkey, and Romania—did not produce any noticeable costs in the Canada–US relationship. In the case of American efforts to combat terrorism, which have been a major feature of US policy since the terrorist attacks of 11 September 2001, the space available for Canada to ignore American preferences has been considerably less. This is because the policy actions taken by the American government have involved border security, air travel, and immigration, matters that directly affect Canada. With close to $2 billion per day in trade crossing the border between

The Social Fabric

BOX 17.3 Potholes in a Normally Smooth Road

Even before his election in 2016, there were warning signs that a Trump presidency could mean a rocky road for Canada–US relations. As a candidate for the presidency, Donald Trump had called NAFTA "the single worst deal ever approved." As president he was quick to insist that it be renegotiated. Trump's 2018 visit to Canada for a G7 summit held in Quebec saw him leave early, tweeting that Prime Minister Trudeau was "weak" and "dishonest." At about the same time his administration imposed tariffs on steel and aluminum imports from Canada and some other countries, with the American chief trade negotiator referring to Canadian steel imports as "a national security threat."

It looked as though Canada–US relations had hit a low point. Whether this was true, it was certainly the case that the tone and optics of the relationship had acquired an unusually hostile character, essentially from the American side. It is not clear, however, that the reality of a relationship based on hundreds of state-to-state agreements covering trade, investment, security, culture, the environment, and other matters, and a dense network of relations and institutions that knit together civil society on both sides of the border—to say nothing of the thousands of Canadians and Americans living, working, and going to school in the other country or crossing the border every day for work or pleasure—was seriously damaged by a barrage of intemperate tweets and the fact that the two national leaders clearly did not like each other.

In fact, Canada–US relations have gone through some difficult times in the past. The refusal of Prime Minister John Diefenbaker to accept American nuclear weapons on Bomarc missiles as part of Canada's obligations under NORAD and NATO, and his failure to immediately agree to President Kennedy's request that the Canadian military be put on war alert during the Cuban Missile Crisis, ultimately contributed to Diefenbaker's loss in the 1963 federal election. When Prime Minister Pearson gave a speech in Philadelphia in 1965 critical of US policy in Vietnam, he was summoned to meet the following day with President Lyndon Johnson, who reportedly grabbed Pearson by the lapels and accused him of "pissing on my rug." And the prime ministership of Pierre Trudeau was characterized by several instances of nationalist and even anti-American policies and postures embodied in Trudeau's musings that Canada might withdraw from NATO, restrictions on foreign investment in Canada, warm relations with Cuba, the National Energy Program, and East–West relations and arms control, all of which resulted in frictions in Canada's relationship with the United States.

The period 2003-2005 saw several major policy disagreements between Canada and the United States, over the American-led invasion of Iraq, Canada's refusal (eventually reversed) to join in a North American missile defence program, the treatment of Canadian citizen Maher Arar during his detention by the United States on suspicion of terrorism, and what the United States—not for the first or last time—argued was Canada's failure to spend enough on defence. The years during which Stephen Harper was prime minister are usually thought to have been relatively free from major conflicts between Canada and the United States. In fact, however, the disagreement between Ottawa and the Obama administration over the Keystone XL pipeline and climate change was a major rift between the two governments.

All of these instances of acrimony between the governments of Canada and the United States were significant and well publicized—in Canada at least. But then, as now, such disagreements need to be weighed against the far greater number of matters where, on a daily basis, Canada–US relations are mainly smooth and co-operative. But don't expect to read a story at your favourite news app about pre-clearance agreements at border points, the bilateral electric grid strategy, or any of the other important but unglamorous forms of co-operation across the world's longest international border.

the two countries, and given the enormous number of jobs and investments in Canada that depend on the smooth flow of goods and people across this border, the Canadian government has had little choice but to co-ordinate its policies with those of the American government. This co-ordination, however, has stopped short of Canadian acceptance of the idea of a common security perimeter around Canada and the United States, a concept that would require that Canadian immigration policy be brought into line with American policy.

Listen to the "Does the Special Relationship Still Exist?" podcast, available at: www.oup .com/he/Brooks9e

Canadians have often felt a certain degree of unease in the face of their country's obvious and extensive dependence on the United States. They have been aware that the relationship between the two countries is not one of equals and that Canada will usually, but not always, have less leverage than its superpower neighbour.[40] "Close, but not too close" captures the ambivalence that many Canadians feel when they contemplate a relationship that has known moments of friction (see Box 17.3). These moments have been vastly overshadowed by a dense and complex web of co-operation and shared values and interests that ensure, in President John F. Kennedy's words, that "what unites us is far greater than what divides us."[41]

Engagement in the World: Canada in Comparative Perspective

Earlier in this chapter we saw that Canadians believe, correctly as it happens, that the world thinks well of their country and its influence globally. This goodwill towards Canada, however, is not based on very much knowledge of Canada's actual engagement in the world, including the ways in which the country and its government contribute to the security, environmental health, and well-being of the world and its less favoured regions and populations. How does Canada stack up in these respects against other wealthy democracies?

The record is mixed and probably not quite as good as one might expect based on Canada's perennially high ranking in international surveys that measure countries' global reputations. The Center for Global Development, a Washington-based think-tank, produces an annual Commitment to Development Index. It is a composite measure of what it describes as "dedication to policies that benefit people living in poorer regions."[42] This annual assessment includes Canada and 26 other wealthy democracies.

Overall, Canada placed 17 out of 27 countries in the Center's 2018 assessment. This overall score reflected the combined results of how well each country did on seven separate measures, each of which, in turn, was typically composed of at least two or three indicators. Here are the results for Canada.

- *Aid.* This is assessed based on the quantity of aid, measured by state aid as a percentage of GDP, but also on an evaluation of the quality and effectiveness of that aid. Canada ranked 8th.
- *Finance.* Investment in less developed countries, most of it through corporations and other private entities, and the transparency of and activities supported by that investment make up this measure. Canada did well, placing 6th among the 27 countries included in the assessment.
- *Technology.* This measure has two components. The first involves a measurement of innovation and investment in R&D. The second involves the degree to which a country makes this innovative technology available to the world, including to poorer countries. Canada placed 15th.
- *Environment.* This is a three-part measure that assesses countries' policies on global climate, sustainable fisheries, and biodiversity and ecosystems. The Center's reasoning is that all of these matters affect poorer regions of the world and their populations more than wealthier countries, at the same time as a disproportionate share of the responsibility for climate change, unsustainable fishing practices, and threats to biodiversity and ecosystems can be laid at the doorstep of the

latter. Canada placed 23rd of 27 countries in the Center's 2018 assessment.

- *Trade.* What is true of the environment, reasons the Center, is also true of trade. The policies and actions of richer countries can have significant consequences for poorer regions of the world. Subsidizing domestic agricultural producers, for example, may have the effect of depriving producers in poorer countries from the opportunity to compete in that market. Canada ranked 17th.
- *Security.* This is a three-part measure that includes a country's "contributions to peacekeeping, both financially and with personnel, arms exports to poor and/or undemocratic countries, and participation in security regimes." Many Canadians will probably be shocked and disappointed to learn that Canada came in 23rd.
- *Migration.* This measure has several components, including "countries' efforts in participating in international migration conventions, migration integration policies, and their receptiveness to asylum-seekers, refugees, foreign students, and migrants." It turns out to be Canada's greatest strength within the overall Commitment to Development Index. Canada ranked 6th.

As is true of any and all measures of countries' performance and their rankings related to a particular behaviour, impact, or value, one might take issue with the methodology used in arriving at these results. This in no way discredits them. It simply means that it is entirely reasonable to look carefully at how a concept has been operationalized and the procedures used in arriving at performance scores. Moreover, results vary somewhat from year to year. In the case of the Commitment to Development Index, Canada has slipped a bit in recent years, from 11th place overall in 2012, to 13th in 2014, 12th in 2016, and then 17th in 2018.

Accepting people from other countries—the migration component of the Commitment to Development Index—is something that Canadians are very likely to think of in relation to their country's role in the world. This self-image became even more prominent when, during the years 2015–17, enormous numbers of asylum-seekers fled Syria, but also Iraq and Afghanistan, placing far greater strains on such countries as Turkey and Lebanon than on wealthy democracies such as Canada. Germany had roughly 1.3 million asylum-seekers during this period, France about 250,000, Italy about 330,000, and Sweden, with a population less than one-third of Canada's, about 200,000. Canada had just over 90,000 asylum claims during this period. In the decade prior to the spike in asylum claims generated mainly by the civil war in Syria, asylum-seekers in Canada averaged about 20,000 per year, a level that was not exceptional in either absolute or per capita terms compared to other G7 countries.[43]

As we saw in Chapter 4, for the past several decades the main sources of immigration to Canada have been countries of the developing world. Whether one considers this a positive contribution to the welfare of poorer regions of the world is moot. Most of these persons enter under the immigration points system that rewards education and marketable skills, thus depriving their home countries of the talents of many of their best and brightest. Canada is also among the world's most open countries towards foreign students wishing to study in the country, a large percentage of whom come from less developed countries. As of 2017, about a half-million foreign students were studying in Canada. China (28 per cent) and India (25 per cent) were the two main countries of origin for these students. Developing countries accounted for over 80 per cent of all foreign students. Just over half of international students surveyed in 2017 said they planned to apply for permanent residence in Canada.[44]

Canadian students also go abroad in search of educational and cultural study opportunities, although the percentage remains quite low. A 2014 survey for the Association of Universities and Colleges of Canada found that about 3 per cent of Canadian respondents had studied abroad.[45] This is about the figure reported by many Canadian universities as of 2019, despite universities' recent efforts to encourage students to participate in a study abroad experience. Developed countries are by far the most popular destinations for those in study abroad programs, France, the United States, the UK, Germany, and Australia being perennial favourites. Among less developed countries, China has attracted about 3 per cent of Canadians in study abroad programs.[46] It is important to keep in mind that these numbers do not include Canadians who decide to do a degree at an institution in another country. Most of these Canadian students, about 27,000 as of 2017, register in programs in the United States.[47] Many if not most of these students plan to pursue their careers in the United States.

The movement of people—entering a country for an extended period of time or going to live abroad for study, work, or other reasons—is generally believed to contribute to the understanding of other societies and cultures. It is an aspect of soft power, as this was defined earlier in the chapter. Indeed, one of the world's most successful soft-power programs,

the United States Fulbright Program, named after Senator J. William Fulbright and in continuous operation since 1948, has always been based on the premise that enabling foreigners to study, teach, and carry out research in one's country, and sending that country's students, teachers, and researchers abroad, provides an important basis for mutual understanding and peace between nations. The Canadian government formally embraced such an approach in the 1970s, only to abandon it in 2012 (see Box 17.4).

The security component of the Commitment to Development Index includes, as one of its measures, a country's financial and personnel commitment to peacekeeping. It does not include the deployment of troops and other military forces for such reasons as combatting terrorism or military engagement against the forces of another state or non-state actor. Putting aside the issue of what forms of military engagement support development and which do not,

The Social Fabric

BOX 17.4 The Rise and Fall of Canadian Studies Abroad as a Tool of Foreign Policy

The value of promoting a country's image in the world has long been recognized. Some countries, including the United States through the Fulbright Program, France through Alliance Française, the UK through the British Council, and in more recent times, and on a large scale, China, through its funding of chairs in Chinese studies at universities in the United States, the UK, and elsewhere, recognize the importance of this soft-power tool for projecting an image abroad. Much of this effort is focused on media, academic, and cultural elites whose work may influence the ideas of their compatriots, including policy-makers.

Canada did very little in this respect before the 1970s. In 1974 Ottawa launched a program with the goal to promote Canadian studies at universities in other countries. This initiative, which would eventually be called the Understanding Canada Program, provided funding for

Canadian studies activities in more than three dozen countries across the world and funding for professors and researchers from abroad to visit Canada. The program never cost more than about $5 million dollars in a year and, based on the money spent by those who received small grants and spent time in Canada, it produced a return on investment many times greater than the annual expenditure. The program was terminated in 2012 by a Conservative government and has not been reinstated under the Liberals.

[D]oes it matter whether Canada's stories are known and whether people in other countries are motivated to tell them? One at least has to concede the possibility that the loss to the rest of the world would not be so great.... There is no doubt, however, that the loss to Canada would be considerable. Cumulatively, these stories about Canada's people, values, history, it is clear that all forms of Canada's military footprint in the world are smaller today than in the past.

To begin with peacekeeping, former Canadian senator and general, Roméo Dallaire, who led the UN peacekeeping mission in Rwanda in 1993–4, argues that the term is something of a misnomer because the reality of this activity has changed significantly over time. "I use the term conflict resolution," says Dallaire. "We're into assisting nations [to] resolve a conflict that is in their territory."[48] What originally involved the interposition of troops after a ceasefire, usually under UN auspices, has for many years become a more dangerous enterprise. As Michael Ignatieff described it in a 2016 interview, peacekeeping today "is combat-capable troops with the capacity to repel fire and defend civilian populations. . . . If we make a commitment to protect civilians we have to have the combat capability to do so otherwise we shouldn't go."[49] It is highly probable that this realization has contributed to the sharp decline over the past couple of decades in the number of troops that Canada has committed to peacekeeping missions. Although the number of peacekeepers in the world deployed under various UN missions has never been higher—103,000 across 14 operations in 2018—Canada's contribution has never been lower. It has dropped from about 3,000 at any point in time between the 1960s and 1980s to three or four dozen today, depending on whether administrative staff are defined as peacekeepers.

Peacekeeping is a form of hard power, notwithstanding that most Canadians probably think of it as something more akin to soft-power diplomacy carried out by soldiers. Hard-power images relating to wars and battles are not absent from Canadians' thoughts about their country's role on the global stage. They tend, however, to involve military actions that happened long ago. The Somme,

role on the world stage, and achievements constitute Canada's cultural capital. Unlike GDP or technology patents per capita, defence spending, or the number of embassies and consulates a country has throughout the world, there is no metric that allows one to say definitively, "Here is the value of our cultural capital." But as the British Council observes in its 2017 report, *The Art of Soft Power*, cultural capital is "based on the attractive qualities—the ideas and values, together with the behaviour, credibility and moral authority—of the agent. In this way, questions such as how [a] society is organized, its fundamental value system, and the (foreign and domestic) policies its government pursues, all affect [its] capacity to generate Soft Power."

Countries that have robust hard-power capacities may decide that these are sufficient in order to get others to listen, although their leaders may know and take seriously Machiavelli's dictum that it is better to be loved than to be feared. For countries like Canada, however, which are not able (or even inclined) to rely on military might, economic muscle, and sanctions of various sorts to achieve their foreign policy objectives, getting others to listen may depend on their country's image. Building and maintaining a positive image is not something that can simply be assumed. In their small way, the thousands of researchers, teachers, and students in countries throughout the world who have studied Canada contribute to this image and thus to Canada's cultural capital abroad.

Source: Adapted from Stephen Brooks, "Uncertain Embrace: The Rise and Fall of Canadian Studies Abroad as a Tool of Foreign Policy," in Stephen Brooks, ed., *Promoting Canadian Studies Abroad: Soft Power & Cultural Diplomacy* (London: Palgrave Macmillan, 2019), 31.

THE CANADIAN PRESS/Andrew Vaughan

Members of the Maritime Libyan Association chat with then Defence Minister Peter MacKay at the return of HMCS *Charlottetown* in Halifax, following its five-month deployment to Libya in 2011 as part of a NATO-led operation.

Vimy Ridge, and Passchendaele from World War I, and Dieppe, D-Day, and the Battle of Normandy from World War II live on through classroom teaching about Canadian history, public monuments and museums, occasional stories in the media, and annual Remembrance Day ceremonies. Most of Canada's more recent engagements in military action have been through its membership in the North Atlantic Treaty Organization (NATO). These engagements include the 1991 Gulf War, the 1999 campaign in Serbia and Kosovo, the War in Afghanistan (Canadian involvement was from 2001 to 2014, although at this writing there are still about 16,000 NATO troops in that country, 15,000 of them American), a 2011 mission against Libya, and the US-led coalition against the Islamic State in Iraq and Syria, which became a NATO mission in 2017.

All of these military interventions, with the exception of the bombing campaign against Serbia in 1999, were sanctioned by the UN Security Council.

The current reality of Canada's military is quite different from what it was a half-century ago. Of course, the same may be said for many wealthy democracies, most of which are Canada's NATO allies. Defence spending in Canada has fallen from about 3 per cent of GDP under Lester Pearson in 1964 to a bit more than 1 per cent in 2019. As a share of all federal program spending, it has fallen from about 12 per cent to roughly 7 per cent over the period from 1986 to 2019. This process of decline has taken place under both Liberal and Conservative governments. Among the 28 member states of NATO, only five (the US, the UK, Greece, Estonia, and Poland) meet the target of 2 per cent of GDP defence spending, Canada's level of spending being about average. About half of NATO member states reach or exceed the target of 20 per cent of all military spending devoted to equipment. Canada falls right about in the middle of countries on this measure.[50]

Although some lament Canada's shrinking military and the apparently smaller role that it plays in a world—the mission in Afghanistan being the major exception in recent times—it may be that contemporary geopolitics and Canada's own national security challenges do not warrant a more robust and engaged military. One of the functions associated with the Canadian military in recent times has been the defence of Canada's claims to territory and waters in the Arctic. The reality, however, is that Canada cannot defend these claims through the use of military force. Canadian claims of sovereignty are either questioned or outright rejected by such countries as Russia, China, the United States, Norway, and Denmark. The idea that, if push came to shove, Canadian forces would fire on or otherwise interfere with Russian, American, or Chinese ships in order to enforce Canadian claims to sovereignty is fanciful at best. Other domestic functions, including surveillance and monitoring of coastlines, search-and-rescue missions, and assistance in cases of flood, fires, and other natural disasters (or helping to remove the snow, as famously happened in Toronto, in 1999), are not ones that require a large and robust military.

If Canada were to invest more in its military, perhaps reaching NATO's 2 per cent of GDP target, it is not clear that this would make any difference geopolitically. Canada has the 14th largest defence budget in the world, but this represents just under 0.03 per cent of the combined budgets of the two largest spenders, the United States and China, and under 0.02 per cent of the combined budgets of the leading 10 spenders on defence. In a speech to the House of Commons in 2017, Foreign Affairs Minister Chrystia Freeland explained that it was important to spend more on Canada's defence, because "to rely solely on the US security umbrella would make us a client state."[51] But realistically, is there any way for Canada not to be a client state of its southern neighbour? Canada has been a client state for decades, even if some have failed to recognize this, without this status preventing Canada from taking an independent line from the United States on many issues.

Summing Up

Few matters of consequence in Canadian public life are not affected by forces outside the country's borders. The actions of other governments and international institutions, the requirements of treaties and other agreements to which Canada is a party, and the behaviour of corporations, investors, and NGOs are among the influences that shape in ways large and small the issues that face Canadians, how those issues are understood, and what options are considered by or even available to their governments. Globalization has ushered in what Thomas Friedman calls "the age of accelerations,"[52] in which all countries, even the most powerful, are exposed to these forces.

In recent years a wave of anti-globalization sentiment has gained strength in the United States and some of the wealthy democracies of Europe. Canadians appear not to have been carried along by this wave. A 2017 survey on public attitudes towards trade and globalization found strong support for both trade and globalization and, moreover, found that this support had increased significantly from levels in 2001.[53] This may reflect a belief that these forces have benefited Canada, or a resignation that they are irresistible. Or perhaps public support for trade and globalization reflects a bit of both. In any event, Canadians appear to be open to the world and they see themselves as being admired and influential on the global stage.

Canada's relationship with the United States continues to overshadow all other aspects of the country's foreign policy. No affluent democracy depends as much on trade with a single national economy as Canada does on trade with the United States. Other matters, including security, law enforcement, the environment, culture, and energy, are powerfully affected by the fact that Canada and the United States share the world's longest international border. This bilateral relationship has always been an unequal one, leading Canadian policy-makers to search for counterweights to the influence of the United States. The search for a balance between what history and current circumstances suggest is the inevitability of American influence, and Canada's ability to chart a path that reflects the country's distinctive values and interests, is a hallmark of Canadian foreign policy.

Appendix: Timeline of Canada in the World

Late 1400s–early 1500s   Fishing by Basque, English, Portuguese, French, and Spanish ships on the Grand Banks off the east coast of Newfoundland, and whaling, especially by the Basques, off the Labrador coast and in the Strait of Belle Isle, the first economic exploitation of Canadian resources by Europeans.

Late 1500s   Trade in beaver pelts and other furs begins, providing the basis for the eventual extension of trading routes from Quebec all the way to the north of Saskatchewan and Alberta.

1603–8   Samuel de Champlain makes two visits to Canada, establishing the city of Quebec in 1608 on his second voyage; European colonization of Canada begins.

1759–63   The war between Britain and France spills over into a rivalry in the New World, British troops defeating French forces at Quebec in 1759. The formal transfer of New France to Britain takes place in 1763 under the Treaty of Paris.

Early 1800s   Canada becomes a major supplier of white pine for British ships.

1812–14   The War of 1812 between Britain and the United States produces many battles on Canadian territory and the shared waters of the Great Lakes.

1820s   In an effort to dilute the influence of American-born residents of Canada the colonial authorities encourage immigration from the British Isles. The arrival of tens of thousands of immigrants from Ireland during the Potato Famine of the 1840s marks the significant beginning of ethnic pluralism that went beyond the French and English ethnic communities.

1854   The first Reciprocity Treaty with the United States is signed, abrogated by the US government in 1865.

1867   The creation of Canada as a sovereign state—in most respects, but with some important limitations—is prompted by fears that the United States might have designs on parts of British North America and by Britain's unwillingness to continue to pay for the defence of Canadian territory.

1870–1   The vast territories controlled by the Hudson's Bay Company are transferred by Britain to Canada in 1870 and British Columbia becomes the fifth province in 1871, after which Canada stretches from the Atlantic to the Pacific oceans.

1879   The National Policy is adopted by the Conservative government. It includes a sharp increase in tariffs on manufactured goods, a policy intended to protect fledgling Canadian producers from American competition but which also has the effect of encouraging US-based companies to set up operations in Canada, leading to very high levels of foreign ownership and lower levels of productivity in Canadian industry as a result of foreign-owned corporations that produce only for the small Canadian market.

1899–1902   The Boer War: The Canadian government sends troops to South Africa in support of Britain. English Canada is strongly supportive but French Canada is staunchly opposed.

1903   Resolution of the Alaskan Boundary Dispute: the lone British commissioner on a six-person joint commission sides with the three American commissioners, giving to the United States a long strip of coastal land that Canadian authorities claimed ought to be part of British Columbia.

1909   The International Boundary Waters Treaty between the United States and Canada takes effect, creating the International Joint Commission, with equal representation from both countries (see 2009, below).

1911   The Canadian general election is fought largely on the issue of reciprocity in trade with the United States. The pro-reciprocity government of Wilfrid Laurier is defeated.

1914–18   World War I: Canada is a junior partner in the alliance against Germany, Canadian troops falling under the command of British officers. Over 63,000 Canadian soldiers died in the war.

1919   Canada becomes a founding member of the League of Nations.

1920   Canada passes from the economic orbit of Great Britain into that of the United States: American investment now officially exceeds the value of British investment.

1921   Canadian Prime Minister Mackenzie King sees multilateralism as a way to assert Canada's independence from Great Britain in international affairs.

1931 Under the Statute of Westminster, Canada acquires the authority to negotiate and sign foreign treaties in its own right, a power that Great Britain had exercised on Canada's behalf.

1939–45 Canada participates in World War II, but no longer as a subordinate of Great Britain. Canada emerges from the war as one of the world's leading economies. About 47,000 Canadian soldiers died in the war.

1945 Canada becomes a founding member of the United Nations. The UN and multilateralism generally are seen as counterweights to the influence of the United States on Canadian foreign policy.

1947 Canada is a founding member of the General Agreement on Tariffs and Trade (GATT) and the North Atlantic Treaty Organization (NATO).

1950–3 Canada participates in the Korean War under the umbrella of a UN Security Council resolution. The official figure is that 516 Canadian soldiers died in this conflict.

1956 Suez crisis: Canada sides with the United States against the Franco–British invasion of Egypt, and Canadian Foreign Minister Lester Pearson, who brokers a settlement to end the crisis, is awarded the Nobel Peace Prize.

1957 The North American Air Defense Command (NORAD) is created, a partnership of Canada and the United States against the possibility of a Soviet missile attack. Early warning radar stations are established on Canadian territory: the Pinetree Line across southern Canada in 1954, and the Mid-Canada Line, at the 55th parallel, and the Distant Early Warning (DEW) Line, along the 70th parallel, in 1957.

1962 The Kennedy administration's request that the Canadian government permit nuclear warheads on missiles located on Canadian territory, which the American administration argued was required by Canada's obligations under NORAD and NATO, is refused by the Diefenbaker government, creating a major rift in Canada–US relations. The Liberal government elected in 1963 complies with the request.

1960s Under Lester Pearson, the Canadian government becomes critical of US involvement in the Vietnam War, although Canadian companies continue to profit from the production of defence-related exports used in that war. Under Quebec Premier Daniel Johnson, that province becomes more assertive in its demands for representation and an independent voice abroad. Canadian dependence on the United States becomes a prominent political issue as the level of American ownership in key resource and manufacturing sectors of the Canadian economy reaches unprecedented levels.

1972 The Liberal government of Pierre Trudeau announces the "Third Option" policy of diversifying Canadian trade and thus reducing Canada's economic dependence on the United States. By the end of the decade the percentage of total export and import trade tied to the American economy is at an all-time high.

1976 The G7, the annual meeting of the leaders of the world's seven largest capitalist democracies, is created when Canada joins the G6 countries of Britain, France, Italy, Japan, the United States, and West Germany.

1985 The Macdonald Royal Commission on the Economic Union and Development Prospects for Canada, created by the Trudeau government in 1982, makes free trade with the United States its major recommendation. The Conservative government of Brian Mulroney approaches the Reagan administration in 1985 to open free trade talks.

1989 The Canada–US Free Trade Agreement takes effect.

1994 The North American Free Trade Agreement (NAFTA) among Canada, Mexico, and the United States takes effect.

1997 Canada signs the Kyoto Accord, later ratified in 2002. A decade after signing, Canada's CO_2 emissions exceed the targets agreed to in the accord by about 25 per cent.

2000 Over 80 per cent of Canada's imports and exports are tied to the United States and about one-third of Canada's GDP depends on trade with the United States.

2001 After the terrorist attacks on New York City and Washington, DC, of 11 September 2001, movement across the Canada–US border becomes a major issue in the bilateral relations between these two countries. As a member of NATO, Canada supports the American-led invasion of Afghanistan to replace the Taliban regime. Eventually, Canada becomes a major contributor of combat forces in Afghanistan.

2003 The Liberal government of Jean Chrétien decides not to join the Anglo-American alliance that invades Iraq to overthrow the Saddam Hussein regime. Massive opposition to the war in Quebec, and within the Liberal Party's Quebec caucus, is an important factor in the government's decision to withhold any significant support.

Early 2000s   Canada's claim to full sovereignty in the waters of the High Arctic is not accepted by other nations with a direct Arctic presence, including the United States, Russia, Denmark, and Norway. As the possibility of a shipping passage through the Arctic increases and the prospects for natural resource exploitation in the High Arctic also become greater, the issue of Arctic sovereignty assumes greater urgency.

2005   Canada, Mexico, and the United States agree to the Security and Prosperity Partnership, an agreement that appears to pave the way towards greater policy co-ordination among the three countries. The first formal summit of the SPP is held in Montebello, Quebec, in 2007.

2008   Canada has roughly 2,500 troops stationed in Afghanistan and plays a major combat role within the NATO mission fighting the resurgent Taliban. Canadian public opinion remains divided on Canada's involvement as the number of Canadians killed in combat and on patrols exceeds 100.

2009   The 100th anniversary of the Boundary Waters Treaty between Canada and the United States, creating the IJC. Despite some high expectations associated with the IJC when it was created, most policy experts agree that the complex and important web of transboundary environmental governance between the countries now operates largely through agreements and networks of sub-national governments.

   Barack Obama assumes the presidency of the United States and Prime Minister Harper's office announces that the president's first official visit outside the US will be to Canada. Canadians have high expectations for the new president and his foreign policies.

2010   In March the Conservative government announces that Canadian troops in Afghanistan will be withdrawn in 2011, in compliance with a motion passed in the House of Commons in 2008; 157 Canadian troops and four civilians were killed during the course of this NATO mission.

2010   Canada's bid for a two-year non-permanent seat on the UN Security Council fails.

2013   Canada and the European Union conclude a free trade agreement. FTAs had already been negotiated over the previous few years with Panama, Jordan, Peru, and Colombia, and negotiations were ongoing with South Korea, India, Japan, and other countries.

2013   Nine hundred Canadian soldiers leave for Afghanistan as part of Operation Attention. Their mission is to train Afghan soldiers and police officers.

2014   Canada joins in the Western sanctions directed against Russia for its annexation of Crimea and support for the pro-Russian separatists in eastern Ukraine. Financial support is provided for various forms of training related to governance and civil society in Ukraine, as well as military transportation of non-combat supplies.

2016   Canada and 11 other Pacific Rim countries sign the Trans-Pacific Partnership Trading Agreement. The United States withdraws from the agreement in 2017 immediately after President Trump takes office. The remaining countries negotiate a new agreement, the Comprehensive and Progressive Agreement for Trans-Pacific Partnership, which comes into effect at the end of 2018.

   Canada accepts almost 50,000 refugees, mainly from Syria, the greatest number since the influx of Vietnamese refugees in 1980.

2018   After sometimes acrimonious negotiations, Canada, the United States, and Mexico agree on a new trade agreement to replace NAFTA, the Canada–United States–Mexico Agreement (CUSMA), which is signed by leaders of the three countries in November and ratified in December 2019.

2019   The number of Canadian peacekeepers on active duty falls below 100, the lowest level since UN peacekeeping began in 1956.

   In response to an extradition request from the United States, Canadian authorities detain Chinese tech-giant Huawei's chief financial officer, Meng Wanzhou, in December 2018. Over the subsequent months Canadians in China are arrested and charged with offences and China bans imports of Canadian canola, claiming that it fails to meet health standards.

Starting Points for Research

Brian Bow, *The Politics of Linkage: Power, Interdependence, and Ideas in Canada–US Relations* **(Vancouver: University of British Columbia Press, 2009).** Bow examines four cases of conflict (nuclear weapons, 1959–63; Canadian claims to sovereignty in Arctic waters, 1969–71; the National Energy Program, 1980–3; invasion of Iraq, 2002–4) between the Canadian and American governments and explains why Canada did not experience hard-power punishment despite its refusal to go along with American government preferences.

Canadian Global Affairs Institute, University of Calgary, https://www.cgai.ca/. Excellent coverage and analysis of global issues and Canadian foreign policy.

David Carment and Christopher Sands, eds., *Canada–US Relations: Sovereignty or Shared Institutions?* **(London: Palgrave Macmillan 2019).** This is the 32nd edition of the popular annual survey of major issues in Canadian foreign policy.

Michael Hawes and Christopher Kirkey, eds., *Canadian Foreign Policy in a Unipolar World* **(Toronto: Oxford University Press, 2017).** An excellent collection that includes chapters by many of Canada's foremost students of foreign policy.

Stephen Randall and John Herd Thompson, *Canada and the United States: Ambivalent Allies,* **4th edn (Montreal and Kingston: McGill-Queen's University Press, 2008).** Quite simply the best history of the Canada–US relationship.

Review Exercises

1. Canada participates in a large number of international organizations. For each of the following organizations explain what it does, the nature of Canada's participation, and the leading issues faced by the organization in recent years.

   • Organization of American States
   • North Atlantic Treaty Organization
   • World Trade Organization
   • International Criminal Court

2. How dependent is your community on international trade? To find out, identify the five or six leading employers in your area. You can do this by contacting your local Chamber of Commerce or the economic development office of city hall. Contact these companies (it may be that you can find this information online but, if not, give them a call) and ask for information about how much of their goods or services they export, to what countries, and how many people they employ. What other aspects of globalization can be observed in your community?

3. The transition from the Conservative government of Stephen Harper to the Liberal government of Justin Trudeau was expected to result in major changes in Canadian foreign policy. Has this been the case? Explain the factors that have contributed to change or continuity in Canadian foreign policy between these two governments.

Glossary

Aboriginal and treaty rights Rights dating to 1763 Royal Proclamation and to the numerous treaties signed by Indigenous groups and colonial and federal Canadian governments. Section 35 of the Constitution Act, 1982, refers to the "existing aboriginal and treaty rights of the aboriginal peoples of Canada," and defines "aboriginal peoples" to include "the Indian, Inuit and Métis peoples of Canada." In recent years "Indigenous" has come to be used more often than "Aboriginal" by spokespersons for Indigenous groups and by government officials.

Affirmative action Measures intended to increase the representation of a targeted group or groups beyond what it would be without special intervention. These measures may include hiring and promotion practices, school admission policies, selection rules for committees, and so on.

Authority A form of power based on the recognition by the person or persons obeying a command or rule that the person or organization issuing the command or rule has a legitimate right to do so and should be obeyed.

Bilingual belt A term coined by Richard Joy in *Languages in Conflict* referring to the narrow region running from Moncton, New Brunswick, in the east to Sault Ste Marie, Ontario, in the west, in which is found the vast majority of Canada's francophone population and where the rate of francophone assimilation is lower than elsewhere in Canada.

Bill 101 Quebec's Charte de la langue française, the first piece of legislation passed by Quebec's National Assembly in 1977, soon after the Parti Québécois came to power. It made French the sole official language in Quebec for purposes of provincial public administration, restricted access to English-language schools, and imposed French-language requirements on business in Quebec. Despite some setbacks in the courts over the years, Quebec's language policy continues to be based on the principles set forth in Bill 101.

Block funding Ottawa's financial contribution to a provincially administered program or policy field that is not geared to the level of provincial spending. The Federal–Provincial Fiscal Arrangements Act of 1977 began this practice of replacing the *shared-cost program* model with block funding. The Canada Health Transfer and Canada Social Transfer are the major block funding transfers from Ottawa to the provinces.

Brokerage politics Style of politics that stresses the ability of parties to accommodate diverse interests, a feat that requires flexibility in policy positions and ideological stance. Brokerage politics is often characterized as non-ideological, which is somewhat misleading because the claim of brokerage-style parties to be non-ideological simply means that they represent the dominant ideology accepted uncritically by most members of society. The Liberal and Conservative parties have been the main practitioners of brokerage politics on Canada's national stage, the Liberal Party being the more successful of the two over the last century.

Bureaucracy All of the unelected officials of the public service whose employment is within the central administration of a government and who may wield power on behalf of that government.

Calgary Declaration A statement agreed to in 1997 by all of the provincial premiers except Quebec's Lucien Bouchard. It stopped short of endorsing the recognition of Quebec as a distinct society, instead referring to the "unique character of Quebec society."

Canada–United States–Mexico Agreement (CUSMA) Trade agreement signed by the leaders of Canada, the United States, and Mexico in 2018 and ratified in December 2019. CUSMA retains most of the features and terms of NAFTA, differing mainly in terms of some concessions insisted on by the US government concerning quotas on automotive imports and somewhat greater access for American producers to supply management sectors of Canadian agriculture such as dairy.

Canada–US Free Trade Agreement (FTA) A wide-ranging trade agreement between Canada and the United States that took effect in January 1989. The FTA reversed the historical pattern of Canadian protectionism enshrined in the National Policy of 1878–9 but that had been steadily eroded after World War II. The FTA created an architecture of dispute settlement rules, agencies, and monitoring requirements. It was succeeded by the North American Free Trade Agreement (1994) and the Canada–United States–Mexico Agreement (2020).

Canadian Bill of Rights Federal legislation of 1960 that includes many of the same rights and freedoms guaranteed by the Charter. However, the Bill of Rights is a statute and has never had the status of constitutional law.

Canadian content Media content that is demonstrably Canadian according to various criteria related to writers and composers, performers (musicians, actors, etc.), producers, and place of production. Regulations developed and enforced by the Canadian Radio-television and Telecommunications Commission require television and radio broadcasters and cable companies to ensure that a specified share of their programming satisfies the criteria of Canadian content.

Caucus The elected members of a particular political party in the legislature, and also any group of elected representatives, defined by geography, gender, or ethnicity, who regularly meet to discuss and strategize in regard to current issues and policies. When Parliament is sitting, each party's caucus usually will meet at least once per week.

Central agencies Parts of the bureaucracy whose main or only purpose is to support the decision-making activities of cabinet. The four organizations usually considered to have central agency status are the Privy Council Office, the Prime Minister's Office, the Department of Finance, and the Treasury Board Secretariat.

Cité libre The intellectual review founded in the 1950s by such prominent Quebecers as Pierre Trudeau and Gérard Pelletier, which was one of the key centres for opposition to the so-called *unholy alliance* of the Church, anglophone capital, and the Union Nationale under Maurice Duplessis.

Clarity Act A federal law passed in 2000 that empowers Parliament to review any future referendum question on Quebec independence to determine whether it is unambiguously worded. This, according to a 1998 Supreme Court ruling, is one of the requirements that a question must satisfy if the outcome of a referendum is to be considered constitutional.

Class analysis A perspective on politics that insists on the overriding importance of social classes based on their relationship to the means of producing and distributing wealth.

Coercion A form of power based on the use or threat of force (e.g., fines, imprisonment).

Common law In Anglo-American legal systems such as Canada's, the component of the law based on the decisions of courts. Like statute law, passed by legislatures, common-law rules are enforceable in the courts.

Communitarianism Those belief systems, like socialism, based on the premise that real human freedom and dignity are only possible in the context of communal relations that allow for the public recognition of group identities and that are based on equal respect for these different group identities.

Conquest of 1759 The military victory of the British forces led by Wolfe over Montcalm in what was New France, but which subsequently became British territory under the Treaty of Paris of 1763. The Conquest has always been a symbol in French Canada, particularly in Quebec, of subjugation to the English community and the loss of communal autonomy.

Conservatism Historically, an ideology based on the importance of tradition that accepted human inequality and the organization of society into hierarchically arranged groups as part of the natural order of things. Today, conservatism in Canada and the United States is associated with the defence of private property rights and free trade, individualism, opposition to the welfare state, and, in the case of social conservatives, emphasis on the traditional family, religion, and what are sometimes referred to as "traditional values."

Constituencies Geographically defined districts represented by members of Parliament; also known as ridings. At present there are 338 constituencies, the populations of which range from a low of about 30,000 to a high of roughly 130,000 constituents.

Constitution The fundamental law of a political system. In Canada it includes written components—chiefly the Constitution Acts—and unwritten conventions that are more or less established, such as the understanding that the calling of an election is the prime minister's prerogative.

Constitutional conventions Practices that emerge over time and are generally accepted as binding rules of the political system, such as the convention that the leader of the political party with the most seats in the House of Commons after an election shall be called upon to try to form a government with majority support in the House. Unlike the written Constitution, conventions are not enforceable in the courts.

Constitutional supremacy Section 52(1) of the Constitution Act, 1982 declares that "The Constitution of Canada is the supreme law of Canada, and any law that is inconsistent with the provisions of the Constitution is, to the extent of the inconsistency, of no force or effect." This means that the laws of all governments and their agencies must conform to the Constitution. Before the Constitution Act, 1982 came into force, Parliament and provincial legislatures were supreme so long as each acted within its own sphere of legislative competence. This was known as parliamentary supremacy.

Co-operative Commonwealth Federation (CCF) Predecessor to the New Democratic Party, created in 1932 as an alliance of three main elements: disgruntled farmers, chiefly from western Canada, central Canadian intellectuals, and labour activists. The party first ran candidates in the 1935 federal election. Its founding policy document, the Regina Manifesto, called for extensive state planning and control of the economy, a steeply progressive income tax, and the creation of a welfare state.

Corporate elite Those who control the dominant corporations and investment firms in an economy. John Porter defined the term in *The Vertical Mosaic* (1965) to include the directors of Canada's dominant corporations, a usage that was followed by Wallace Clement and William Carroll in their later studies of this elite. All of these researchers concluded that the Canadian corporate elite is a largely self-perpetuating group whose exclusive social backgrounds and activities set them apart from the general population.

Crisis of the state The apparent inability or unwillingness of governments, beginning in the 1970s, to finance the welfare state policies put in place over the preceding four decades.

Cross-border regions (CBRS) Distinct groupings of neighbouring and nearby Canadian provinces and American states whose economic, cultural, and institutional linkages create commonalities between the members of these binational groupings and set each such region apart from other regions.

Cultural hegemony Originally a Marxist concept involving the claim that the values and beliefs of the dominant class are accepted as normal and inevitable by society as a whole, despite the fact that they are contrary to the true interests of subordinate classes. Feminism and theories of racial domination have also used the concept of cultural hegemony.

Democracy A political system based on the formal equality of all citizens, in which there is a realistic possibility that voters can replace the government, and in which certain basic rights and freedoms are protected.

Democratic deficit A term signifying the gap that critics argue exists between the principles and aspirations embodied in Canada's democratic political culture—including accountability, participation, and openness—and the actual practices and institutions of governance.

Dependence The limitations on a country's autonomy that may arise from its economic, cultural, or military ties to another country or countries. During the 1960s and 1970s it was popular on the left of Canadian politics to characterize Canada as a dependent satellite within the orbit of the United States. The ties between these two countries have not weakened since then, but it is now more common to view Canada's dependent condition within the broader framework of economic and cultural globalization.

Distinct society The Meech Lake Accord of 1987 proposed the amendment of the Constitution to recognize Quebec as a distinct society unlike other provincial societies. In both the Meech Lake and Charlottetown (1992) Accords the distinct society clause was explicitly linked to the fact that Quebec is the only province in which a majority of the population is francophone and would have required the Quebec government to protect and promote the French language. In 1995 Parliament passed a resolution recognizing Quebec as a distinct society. It does not, however, have the force of constitutional law.

Election Expenses Act Before 1974 party and candidate spending on election campaign activities was essentially unregulated and there were no legal requirements that revenues and expenditures be publicly disclosed. Beginning in 1974, the Election Expenses Act has place spending limits on registered political parties and their candidates during election campaigns, allows for the reimbursement of part of the expenses of candidates who receive at least 10 per cent of the vote, and requires the public disclosure of all but very small contributions to parties and candidates. Since 2004 the Act bans contributions from corporations, labour unions, and associations.

"End of ideology" A thesis advanced by American sociologist Daniel Bell in the 1960s, which argued that traditional right/left ideological thinking had become irrelevant and outmoded as a consequence of a developing consensus on the desirability of the welfare state, government regulation of business, and political pluralism.

Entitlements What might be called social rights of citizenship, such as public education, pensions, welfare, and various forms of assistance for those in need. It is a concept associated with the welfare state and a redistributive ethic in public life.

Equalization Transfers made by Ottawa to provincial governments whose per capita tax revenues (according to a complex formula negotiated between Ottawa and the provinces) fall below the average of the two most affluent provinces. Equalization is the third largest federal transfer to the provinces, after the Canada Health Transfer and the Canada Social Transfer.

Estimates Sometimes referred to as the expenditure budget. Every year towards the end of February the government will table its spending estimates for the forthcoming fiscal year (1 April to 31 March) in the House of Commons.

Executive federalism A term sometimes used to describe the relations between the prime minister and premiers and cabinet ministers of the two levels of government. The negotiations between them and the agreements they reach have often been undertaken with minimal, if any, input from their legislatures or the public.

False consciousness A Marxist concept describing the inability of subordinate social classes to see where their real interests lie and their acceptance of cultural values and beliefs that justify their exploitation by the dominant class. See *cultural hegemony*.

Feminism A framework for interpreting and explaining politics and society that sees gender as the fundamental basis of conflict in society and associates politics, in all its forms, with the systemic domination of males over females.

First Nations A term commonly used in Canada to refer to Indigenous communities descended from those who inhabited North America before the arrival of Europeans. It does not include the Inuit or the Métis.

Fiscal gap A term used to describe two aspects of imbalance in public intergovernmental finance in Canada. It has been used since the 1930s to refer to the shortfall between the spending requirements of provincial governments and their revenues, while the federal government had revenues sufficient to pay for its program requirements and to transfer revenue to the provinces. The other meaning ascribed to this term involves the gap that exists between what citizens and corporations in the wealthier provinces, particularly Alberta and Ontario, contribute to the federal government in various forms of taxation and what they and their provincial governments receive back in federal program spending and transfers. As of 2016, the fiscal imbalance for Ontario was estimated by the Mowat Centre to be $13 billion.

Formal equality One of two different standards, the other being *substantive equality*, that may be applied by the courts to the Charter's equality guarantees. The formal equality standard requires that all individuals be treated the same under the law, regardless of the fact that the life circumstances of members of different groups may be significantly different and may affect the likelihood of their achieving constitutional guarantees of equality.

Fragment theory Theory developed by American historian Louis Hartz that maintains that the ideological development of New World societies such as Canada, settled by European colonization, was strongly determined by the social characteristics and cultural values of their early immigrants. It has been applied to Canada by such scholars as Gad Horowitz and Kenneth D. McRae.

Free-rider problem The likelihood that some members in an organization will believe that they can reap the benefits of the organization's actions without having to contribute to it financially.

Gender roles One of the fundamental premises of much of contemporary feminism, that male and female genders are socially constructed. As Simone de Beauvoir put it, "One is not born, but rather becomes, a woman." This premise provides the intellectual basis for attacks on many of the traditional roles and expectations associated with males and females. A debate continues between those who argue that gender roles are fundamentally socially constructed and those who maintain that biological differences between the sexes provide the basis for many of the important differences in male and female behaviour, aptitudes, and preferences.

Globalization The increasing interdependence of states, economies, and societies throughout the world, a phenomenon characterized by, among other things, dramatically higher levels of international trade and capital mobility than in the past, the increased mobility and migration of peoples, cultural convergence in terms of consumer tastes between societies, particularly in the developed countries of the world, and the emergence of international institutions for the development and enforcement of economic and human rights standards.

Government The elected individuals and party controlling the state at a particular point in time.

Hard power Geopolitical view of realist scholars and policymakers that the threat (and use) of military might and economic sanctions are the best means for the protection of national security and the advancement of national interests abroad.

Human rights All the basic rights and freedoms of citizens. Also called "civil liberties" or "civil rights," these include political rights, democratic rights, legal rights, economic rights, and equality rights. Other human rights can include language rights, social entitlements, and environmental rights.

Ideology A set of interrelated beliefs about how society is organized and how it ought to function.

Indigenous self-government A concept premised on the idea that Indigenous communities should be viewed as possessing at least some of the attributes of sovereign peoples and that, therefore, they have a right to be self-governing. Various models and degrees of self-government have been implemented over the last several of decades, one of the most ambitious being the territory of Nunavut.

Influence A form of power that depends on the ability of a person or group of persons to persuade others that it is reasonable and/or in their self-interest to behave in a particular way (e.g., to vote for a particular candidate or party).

Institutional groups Interest groups characterized by a high degree of organizational sophistication, the distinguishing features of which include organizational continuity, stable membership, extensive knowledge of sectors of government that affect their members and easy access to public officials in these sectors, concrete and immediate objectives, and overall organizational goals that are more important than any specific objective.

Interculturalism A Quebec variant of *multiculturalism*. As explained by Quebec's Consultation Commission on Accommodation Practices Related to Cultural Differences (the Bouchard-Taylor Commission, 2008), interculturalism involves a policy of reconciliation and mutual adaptation on the part of both the dominant majority and minorities: both sides must be prepared to make cultural concessions. This is rather different from the more pluralistic concept of multiculturalism, which does not assume a majority group as part of the equation or an explicit need for minority group adaptations to majority norms and values.

Inuit Indigenous people who comprise the vast majority of those living in the Canadian Arctic, including in Nunavut, Nunavik (Arctic Quebec), Nunatsiavut (northern Labrador), and the Inuvialuit Settlement Region in the western Arctic (Northwest Territories). The forebears of Inuit migrated from northeast Asia to North America thousands of years later than most other Indigenous peoples migrated to the Americas.

Judicial independence The principle according to which judges should be free from any and all interference in their decision-making. It is particularly important that they be free from interference by the government to ensure that the courts are seen to be independent and non-partisan. One of the key protections for judicial independence is the fact that once judges are appointed they cannot be removed from office before retirement age, usually 75, except for serious cause (such as criminal behaviour or serious incompetence).

Judicial restraint The practice of judges deferring to the will of elected governments when laws and state actions are challenged as being unconstitutional. Before the Charter was passed in 1982, it was extremely rare for Canadian courts to declare duly passed laws unconstitutional, unless they were *ultra vires*.

Legitimacy The acceptance by most people that the rules and institutions comprising the state are fair and should be obeyed. It is closely related to the concept of consent in democracies.

LGBTQ+ An abbreviation that stands for Lesbian, Gay, Bisexual, Transgender, Queer (or Questioning). The "+" signifies other sexual identities that are included under the rubric of Queer.

Liberalism Historically, an individualistic ideology associated with freedom of religious choice and practice, free enterprise and free trade, and freedom of expression and association in politics. During the latter half of the twentieth century in Canada and the United States, liberalism came to be associated with support for the welfare state, the protection of minority rights, and the regulation of business.

Libertarianism The belief that individuals should be allowed the largest possible margin of freedom in all realms of life, including those that involve moral choices. Although they are often thought of as ideologically conservative, libertarians are more likely to align themselves with people and groups thought of as left-leaning on lifestyle and morality issues.

Lobbying Any form of direct or indirect communication with public officials that is intended to influence public policy. Although often associated in the public mind with unfair privilege and corruption, lobbying is not limited to organizations representing the powerful and is not inherently undemocratic.

Loyalism The value system associated with the Loyalists, those who opposed the American Revolution and who migrated north to the British colonies after the defeat of the British in the American War of Independence. Their ideological beliefs have been the subject of much debate, but there is a consensus that they brought to Canada a loyalty to the British Crown and a rejection of the developing American identity.

Maîtres chez nous The Quebec Liberal Party's 1962 election campaign slogan, meaning "masters in our own house." It captured the new spirit of Quebec nationalism that emerged during the period of the Quiet Revolution.

Marxism A framework for interpreting and explaining politics and society that sees class divisions as the fundamental basis of conflict in society and associates politics with a pervasive pattern of domination by those who own and control the means of creating and distributing wealth over those who do not; named after nineteenth-century political theorist Karl Marx.

Materialism Ideological view that stresses economic security, material well-being, and acquisition; consequently, from a materialist perspective, incomes and employment are of greater concern than human rights or the environment, for example.

Maternal feminism Also called social feminism, the approach taken by the early women's movement from the late 1800s to the early twentieth century. Maternal feminism accepted the assumption that the biological differences between men and women provided the basis for their different social roles, women being by nature more caring about life and the conditions that nurture it. Maternal feminists fought for legal and political reforms, such as temperance and child labour laws, they expected would improve the conditions of women and their families.

Merit principle Historically, the practice of making hiring and promotion decisions based on such qualifications as relevant experience, academic degrees, professional credentials and certification, and other attributes deemed to be relevant to the competent performance of the job. This policy was first adopted by the federal government with the passage of the Civil Service Amendment Act, 1908. Since the late twentieth century the concept of merit has been redefined by some to include representational concerns.

Métis Originally, the mixed-blood descendants of unions between Indian women and Scots or French-speaking traders and settlers in the Red River region of Manitoba; more recently, the term has been applied to and appropriated by other groups in Canada of mixed Indigenous and European ancestry.

Ministerial responsibility The obligation of a cabinet minister to explain and defend in the legislature—and, ultimately, to be responsible for—the policies and actions of his or her department.

Minority government A situation where no single political party controls a majority of seats in the House of Commons. In such circumstances the party with the largest number of seats will require the support of at least some members of one or more other parties in order to win votes in the House of Commons and govern. Majority government, when one party controls a majority of the seats in the House, has been more common in Canada, although the elections of 2004, 2006, 2008, and 2019, produced minority governments.

Mobility of capital Producers and investors enjoy a wide, but not absolute, freedom to shift their operations or investments between sectors of the economy and from one national economy to another. This mobility of capital is a major reason why governments must be concerned with business confidence and will often be reluctant to take measures that, while politically popular, may offend important business interests.

Multiculturalism A value system based on the premise that ethnic and cultural identities and traditions are important to human happiness and dignity and that public policy ought to recognize, support, and promote the retention of these identities and traditions. In Canada an official policy of multiculturalism has existed since 1971. The Charter of Rights and Freedoms acknowledges the "multicultural heritage of Canadians" and the Multiculturalism Act, 1988 commits the Canadian government to a policy of promoting multiculturalism. This is done largely through the Department of Canadian Heritage.

Multilateralism An approach to the resolution of problems that relies on collective decision-making through international organizations such as the UN, the International Criminal Court, NATO, and the WTO. It is based on an assumption that member states should be willing to give up some national sovereignty and accept the decisions of multilateral organizations to which they belong.

Nation A group of people who share a sense of being a community based on religion, language, ethnicity, a shared history, or some combination of these.

National Energy Program (NEP) Nationalist economic policy introduced in 1981 that limited the price that could be charged in Canada for oil and gas from Canadian sources and provided preferential tax treatment for Canadian-owned companies investing in the petroleum sector. It was viewed by Alberta as a thinly disguised subsidy that their province—Canada's leading petroleum producer—was made to pay to the petroleum-consuming populations and industries of central Canada. The NEP was opposed by multinational petroleum companies and the American government as discriminating against foreign investors.

National Policy (1878–9) The Conservative Party's election platform in 1878, this nation-building strategy began to be implemented in 1879. Its three components included a significant increase in protective tariffs to promote manufacturing in Ontario and Quebec, construction of a transcontinental railroad, and encouragement of western settlement to expand the market for the manufactured products of central Canada and to protect this territory from American encroachment.

National standards Rules established by the federal government that apply to areas of provincial jurisdiction, particularly health care and social assistance. For example, the Canada Health Act, 1985 prohibits extra-billing by doctors and imposes financial penalties on provinces that allow the practice. The enforcement of national standards depends primarily on the fact that Ottawa transfers money to the provinces to help pay for certain social programs.

Neo-institutionalism A perspective on policy-making that emphasizes the impact of formal and informal structures and rules on political outcomes. The roots of this perspective lie in economics, organization theory, and a reaction to society-centred approaches to understanding politics and policy.

North American Free Trade Agreement (NAFTA) A treaty signed by Canada, Mexico, and the United States that took effect in 1994, under which most duties on goods and services traded between these economies were eliminated and the treatment of each country's investors was, with some limited exceptions, the same as that of domestic investors. Most of the provisions of NAFTA are continued under the *Canada–United States–Mexico Agreement* (2020).

"Notwithstanding" clause Section 33 of the Charter of Rights and Freedoms, which states that either Parliament or a provincial legislature may expressly declare that a law shall operate even if it contravenes the fundamental freedoms (s. 2), legal rights (ss. 7–14), or equality rights (s. 15) in the Charter. This clause has been invoked rarely, most controversially by the Quebec government in 1989 and again in 2019.

***Oakes* test** Established by the Supreme Court of Canada, this is a test that the courts apply in determining whether a law or government action that contravenes a right or freedom guaranteed by the Charter is nevertheless constitutional under the "reasonable limits" section of the Charter (s. 1). To be considered "reasonable," a limitation must be based on an important public policy goal and must be proportionate to the importance of this goal.

Operationalize To define a concept in terms of the method or methods used to measure it. For example, democracy might be defined as a political system in which all adults have the legal right to vote and more than one political party competes to form the government. Both of these criteria can be measured.

Ottawa mandarins Term applied to the coterie of top officials, particularly deputy ministers and the governor of the Bank of Canada, who dominated federal policy-making during the period of the 1940s to the 1960s. "Mandarins" were high officials in the ancient Chinese empire.

Outsourcing The contracting out of parts of a production process to manufacturers in other countries or regions.

Paid access opportunities Fundraising events such as dinners and cocktail parties where, for an admission price, invited guests have the opportunity to rub shoulders and exchange views with key party members and perhaps even with the party leader.

Parliamentary supremacy A constitutional view that Parliament's authority is superior to that of all other institutions of government. In other words, the courts will not second-guess the right of the legislature to pass any law, on any subject, as long as it does not involve a matter that, under the Constitution, is properly legislated on by another level of government. Parliamentary supremacy was effectively replaced by *constitutional supremacy* as a result of the Constitution Act, 1982.

Party discipline The practice of MPs belonging to the same party voting as a unified bloc in the way directed by their leader. This practice is based on a combination of reasons, the foremost being the understanding that the government is required to resign if it loses an important vote in the House of Commons. The prime minister and other party leaders control various levers that can be used to maintain party discipline, including expulsion of a member from party caucus, withholding promotion or other rewards from an MP, or refusing to allow him or her to run as the party's candidate in the next election.

Path dependency models Models of analysis, such fragment theory, that aim to show the determinative nature of prior events and decisions on current events and decisions.

Patronage The awarding of favours, such as contracts, jobs, or public spending in a community, in exchange for political support. This was the central preoccupation of Canadian politics during the first several decades after Confederation. It continues to be an important practice in Canada and other democracies, although when the exchange of support for government largesse is too obvious or the scale too great this is likely to be viewed by many as corruption.

"Peace, order, and good government of Canada" (POGG) The preamble to section 91 of the Constitution Act, 1867 includes this phrase, which has been interpreted by some as a general grant of legislative power to the federal government. Over time, however, court rulings reduced POGG to an emergency power that can only provide the constitutional basis for federal actions in special circumstances. In a 1977 decision, the Supreme Court indicated that it would not be quick to question Parliament's judgment that special circumstances exist that warrant legislation under the authority of POGG.

(The) personal is political The slogan of the second-wave feminist movement that emerged in the 1960s, expressing the feminist view that the roots of gender inequality are found in structured male–female relations throughout society and that therefore the achievement of equality for women requires that attitudes and practices in the home, school, workplace, media, and elsewhere must be changed.

***Persons* case (1929)** Decision of the Judicial Committee of the Privy Council that overturned a Supreme Court of Canada ruling that women were not considered persons for purposes of holding certain public offices.

Pluralism An explanation of politics that sees organized interests as the central fact of political life and explains politics chiefly in terms of the activities of groups.

Plurality electoral system An electoral system in which the candidate with the most votes is elected by a simple plurality; in multi-party states such as Canada, those who are elected usually have not received a majority of the votes.

Policy community The constellation of state and societal actors active in a particular policy field.

Policy network The nature of relations among the actors in a *policy community*.

Political factions Groups of citizens whose goals and behaviour are contrary to those of other groups or to the interests of the community as a whole.

Political identities A sense of belonging to a community that is defined by its language, ethnic origins, religion, regional location, gender, or some other social or cultural characteristics. Identities become political when those who share them make demands on the state or when the state recognizes a group identity as a reason for treating a group's members in a special way.

Politics The activity by which rival claims are settled by public authorities. See also Box 1.1.

Politics–administration dichotomy Advocated by progressive reformers beginning in the late nineteenth century, a concept involving an ideal of governance whereby only elected politicians should make choices between competing values and interests, choices that would be embodied in the laws. The proper function of non-elected state officials is to implement these choices without regard for their personal views and preferences.

Populism A vision of politics based on the premise that the general population should have as many opportunities as possible to participate directly in political decision-making and that those elected to govern ought to view themselves as delegates of the people and therefore are obliged to reflect their preferences; thus, a political stance upholding and appealing to "the common people" as opposed to any of various political, cultural, or social elites. Populists favour recall votes to remove unfaithful public officials, plebiscites and referendums, short terms of office and term limits for public officials, and citizen initiatives to force action on an issue or policy proposal. They oppose party discipline.

Positive state A state that is active in attempting to shape society and influence its direction. It was championed by liberal intellectuals such as John Dewey in the United States (*The Public and Its Problems*, 1927), socialist thinkers in the United Kingdom, most prominently the members of the Fabian Society, and in Canada by Progressive movement intellectuals early in the twentieth century.

Post-materialism An ideological view emphasizing human needs for belonging, self-esteem, and personal fulfillment. Consequently, high value is placed on quality-of-life issues such as the environment, group equality, and human rights.

Postmodernism A world view that rejects absolute truths of any kind and conceives of state–society relations as contingent and relative but of the state as nonetheless oppressive. This oppression may be targeted at groups based on their race, gender, ethnicity, sexual preference, or some other trait that places them outside the dominant group in control of the levers of state power.

Poverty lines "Low-income cut-offs" (LICOs) established by Statistics Canada that are routinely referred to by journalists, politicians, academics, and others as "poverty lines." These cut-offs or poverty lines represent a relative measure of low income, currently defined to mean that the amount a households spends on food, clothing, and shelter is 20 percentage points above the median. For example, the LICO for a family of four persons in a medium-size city in 2017 was $33,575. In May 2003 Statistics Canada and Human Resources Development Canada introduced a "market basket measure" for determining poverty, geared to the cost of living in communities across the country. This measure was adopted as the Official Poverty Line by the Liberal government in 2018.

Power The ability to influence what happens. It may assume various forms, including *coercion*, *influence* (persuasion), and *authority*.

Prime ministerial government The argument that the concentration of power in the hands of the prime minister and his advisers has reached unprecedented levels and that both Parliament and cabinet have been relegated to the margins of the policy-making process. While some commentators attribute this to the personal styles of prime ministers going back at least to Jean Chrétien, more fundamental and enduring factors have contributed to this concentration of power.

Privy Council Essentially the cabinet, under the leadership of the prime minister. Formally, however, anyone who has ever been a member of cabinet retains the title of privy councillor, but only those who are members of the government of the day exercise the constitutional and legal powers associated with the Privy Council.

Propaganda The organized use of selected information (true or not) and publicity to promote a particular political or social view.

Proportional representation System of political representation, variants of which exist in many European countries, under which the number of seats a party receives in the legislature is based roughly on the share of the popular vote cast for that party.

Protest parties Political parties that have arisen out of dissatisfaction with the operation of brokerage politics in Canada and what has been seen, particularly in western Canada, as the inability of the Liberal and Conservative parties to represent certain regional interests. The *Reform Party*, created in 1987, was a prominent example of such a party. Others have included the Progressives, Social Credit, the Western Canada Concept, and the early *Co-operative Commonwealth Federation*.

Province-building The phenomenon of powerful provincial governments creating large and competent bureaucracies and using the various constitutional, legal, taxation, and public opinion levers available to them to increase their control over activities and interests within their provincial borders and, in consequence, vis-à-vis Ottawa. Province-building is most often associated with Alberta in the 1970s and Quebec during the 1960s and 1970s, but some students of Canadian federalism argue that the concept continues to be relevant in explaining intergovernmental relations.

Public agenda The issues, concepts, and ideas current in a society's politics at a given point in time. The capacity to get an issue onto the agenda or framed in a particular way may be an indication of political influence, but the ability to keep an issue off the public agenda may also be a sign of a group's influence.

Purchasing power parities (PPPs) A measure of average real purchasing power that takes into account both average nominal incomes and what a standardized currency unit can purchase in a country. Although average nominal incomes are much higher in many countries than in Canada, when PPPs are used to measure standardized purchasing power Canadians are among the most affluent people in the world.

Quality of life (QOL) Concept referring to the level of satisfaction with life that members of a society experience, based on their material well-being, their level of health, the state of their environment, the level of equality between groups, or some combination of these. The United Nations annually ranks countries according to its Human Development Index, which combines various factors, including literacy, infant mortality, average life expectancy, average income, and average years of formal education. This UN index is accepted by some as a measure of QOL.

Québécois de souche Quebecers, and more specifically francophone Quebecers, whose roots in the province go back many generations. The term is used to distinguish what in English might be called old-stock Quebecers from more recent arrivals whose first language usually is not French and whose cultural heritage is not French Canadian. A similar term is "*québécois pure laine*" (pure-wool Quebecers). This distinction between old-stock Quebecers and others is objected to by some as being fundamentally discriminatory, but others maintain that the attachment of immigrants to the French language and Quebec's distinctive culture has often been weak.

Quiet Revolution The early 1960s in Quebec when the provincial Liberal government of Jean Lesage transformed the Quebec state in order to play a greater role in education, social services, and the economy. During the Lesage years (1960–6) the conservative traditional nationalism was swept away by a more aggressive Quebec nationalism that turned to the Quebec state as the chief instrument for the modernization of Quebec society and the advancement of francophone interests.

Rattrapage French for "catching up," one of the key goals of the anti-establishment challenge to the conservative ideology and elites that dominated Quebec during the 1940s and 1950s. *Rattrapage* involved bringing Quebec's society, economy, and government up to the level of development that existed in the rest of Canada, a goal that required a larger and more interventionist provincial government.

Realignment election An election (or series of elections) that produces a durable change in the political parties' bases of support within a region or regions of a country.

Reasonable limits Section 1 of the Charter of Rights and Freedoms states that the rights and freedoms guaranteed by the Charter are subject to "such reasonable limits prescribed by law as can be demonstrably justified in a free and democratic society." See also *Oakes test*.

Receptive bilinguals People who are capable of responding to French communication but do not themselves initiate conversations in French, consume French-language media, or seek out opportunities to live in their acquired second language.

Red Toryism The belief system associated with Canadian conservatives who believe that government has a responsibility to act as an agent for the collective good and that this responsibility goes far beyond maintaining law and order. Red Tories have supported the creation of public enterprises to achieve a range of cultural and economic goals and are generally supportive of Canadian nationalism.

Reform Party Founded in 1987 under the slogan "The West wants in," it became the Canadian Alliance Party in 2000. The Reform Party emerged out of the feelings of alienation that peaked in western Canada during the 1980s, triggered by the Conservative government's 1987 decision to award a major defence contract to Quebec instead of Manitoba and the widespread view that whether the Liberal or Progressive Conservative Party was in power federally, western interests would continue to be sacrificed to those of central Canada.

Regionalism A political identity based on a shared sense of place. It may be linked to a variety of cultural, economic, institutional, and historical factors that tend to distinguish the inhabitants of one region of a country from those of other regions.

Representative bureaucracy The practice of hiring and promotion so that the composition of the bureaucracy reflects in fair proportion some of the demographic characteristics of society. In Canada, the concept and practice of representative bureaucracy were first applied to increase the share of francophones in the public service. Since the 1980s it has been expanded to include women, Indigenous people, visible minorities, and disabled persons.

Representative democracy A form of democracy in which citizens delegate law-making authority to elected representatives, holding them responsible for their actions through periodic elections.

Reserves Territories set aside under treaties between the federal government and First Nations for the members of such communities; the vast majority of those residing on reserves are status Indians.

Responsible government The constitutional principle according to which the prime minister and cabinet require the support of a majority of members in the House of Commons in order to govern. If the government can no longer maintain majority support in the House, in other words, if it loses the confidence of the House, it is compelled by constitutional convention to resign.

Revanche des berceaux, la A French term meaning "revenge of the cradles." This refers to the exceptionally high birth rate among French-speaking Canadians for about a century after Confederation, enabling them to maintain numerical strength against an English-speaking population to which most immigrants assimilated linguistically.

Revenue budget A budget presented from time to time in Parliament, announcing changes to the taxation system. Whereas the expenditure budget (*estimates*) is tied to a regular cycle of decision-making, a new revenue budget may be tabled at any time when, in the government's view, conditions require.

Revolutionary origins and counter-revolutionary origins American sociologist Seymour Martin Lipset argues in *Revolution and Counter-Revolution* (1960) that the political histories and ideological development of the United States and Canada have been significantly marked by the American Revolution of 1776. The political values, symbols, and institutions of the United States have been based on the liberal ideas of the Revolution while, historically, those in Canada have been based on a rejection of what the Revolution stood for and a greater tendency to trust and embrace the state.

Right, left, and centre Labels that signify a range of ideological beliefs from collectivist (left) at one end of the spectrum to individualistic (right) at the other, with those in the middle ground (centre) embracing elements from both extremes.

Royal Commission on Aboriginal Peoples Commission established by the federal government in 1991 and chaired by Georges Erasmus and René Dussault; its 1996 *Report* included about 440 recommendations for the reform of Aboriginal policy. The fundamental premise of the *Report* was that the original sovereignty of Indigenous peoples and their ownership of the land to which they laid historic claim should be acknowledged and their right to self-government should be embedded in the Constitution.

Royal Commission on Bilingualism and Biculturalism Federal Royal Commission created in 1963 in response to the new assertive nationalism of the Quiet Revolution. The B&B Commission recommended numerous reforms aimed at protecting the rights of the francophone minority outside Quebec and transforming the federal government into a more bilingual institution. The Official Languages Act of 1969 embodied some of the recommendations made by the B&B Commission, as did the federal policy of *multiculturalism* announced in 1971.

Royal Proclamation of 1763 Proclamation of King George III dealing with the North American territories that were formally surrendered by France to England under the terms of the Treaty of Paris that included detailed provisions regarding relations between the British and the Indigenous inhabitants of these territories, whereby unsettled lands were reserved for the "Indians" and could be alienated only by the Crown, as occurred in much of Canada through the treaty process in the last half of the nineteenth century and in the first decades of the twentieth century.

Rule of law A vital principle of democratic government that the actions of governments and their agents must be based on the authority of law and that all persons, the governed and those who govern, are subject to the same laws.

Separation of powers A constitutional principle, supported by s. 24 of the Charter, that guarantees the special role of the judiciary, without interference from the legislature or the executive, to interpret what the law and the Constitution mean when disputes arise.

Sexism Term coined during the 1960s as a label for behaviour that treats males and females unequally for no other reason than the fact of being male or female.

Shared-cost programs Provincially administered programs, such as those in the field of health care, to which Ottawa contributes money earmarked for a particular purpose. During the 1960s and 1970s it was common for Ottawa's contribution to be determined by how much a province spent on such a program. Since the late 1970s successive federal governments have abandoned this model in favour of *block funding*.

Single-member constituency A voting system under which each member of the legislature is elected to represent a particular *constituency* or riding, receiving this right when he or she receives more votes than any other single candidate in the election held in that constituency. It is not necessary to receive a majority of the votes cast in a constituency and under Canada's multi-party system most successful candidates do not.

Social capital A concept that refers to norms of interpersonal trust, a sense of civic duty, and a belief that one's political participation matters. Contemporary theorists like Robert Putnam argue that the successful functioning of democracies depends on a high level of social capital among the general population that is reflected in social networks, such as work, church groups, community associations, clubs, and the like.

Socialism An ideology based on the principle of equality of condition. Historically, socialists led the fight for a greater state role in managing the economy, better working conditions and rights for workers, and the egalitarian and redistributive policies associated with the welfare state. Modern socialists, or social democrats, often temper their advocacy of an egalitarian society with an acceptance of market norms and institutions, while remaining highly critical of the inequalities generated by modern capitalism.

Socio-economic mobility The ability of individuals, families, and groups to move from one social or economic position to another. Where socio-economic mobility is high, movement up and down the social ladder is relatively common and the barriers to entry into high-paying occupations, prestigious status groups, or powerful elites are relatively low.

Soft power Term coined by American scholar Joseph Nye to describe forms of international influence based on culture, values, and the perceived legitimacy of a nation's international aims, rather than on armaments, sanctions, and coercion. Soft power is associated with an "idealist" as opposed to "realist" world view and with *multilateralism* and support for international structures of governance and problem resolution such as the UN and the International Criminal Court.

Sovereignty-association A term generally understood to mean that a politically sovereign (independent) Quebec would continue to be linked to Canada through some sort of commercial union, free trade agreement, and shared currency. Sovereignty-association was the option proposed to Quebecers in the 1980 referendum.

State The structures through which public authority is exercised, including the legislature, bureaucracy, courts, police, armed forces, and other publicly owned or controlled institutions, such as schools and hospitals. See also Box 1.2.

Substantive equality An approach to the interpretation of equality rights and s. 15 of the Charter premised on the idea that individuals may experience advantages or disadvantages as a result of belonging to a particular group and that their equality rights claims should be judged against the reality of these group-based inequalities in society. This approach rejects the concept of *formal equality*, whereby all individuals are identical under the law, on the grounds that this cannot overcome the social roots of inequality.

Suffragists Advocates of the right to vote for women. Many of the early suffragists supported female enfranchisement on the grounds that women voters would inject a morally uplifting element into politics. Nellie McClung was Canada's best-known suffragist.

Survivance, la French for "survival." *La survivance* captures the conservative character of traditional French-Canadian nationalism, focused as it was on preserving the religious and linguistic heritage of French Canada in the face of assimilationist pressures.

Systemic discrimination Discrimination without conscious individual intent. Systemic discrimination inheres in traditions, customary practices, rules, laws, and institutions that have the effect of placing the members of one or more ascriptive groups at a disadvantage compared to other groups.

"The higher, the fewer" Canadian political scientist Sylvia Bashevkin's characterization of the fact that, although female participation levels in politics are about the same as men's for activities like voting and campaigning, the proportion of women tends to decrease as the political activity becomes more demanding, such as holding office in a political party or being a candidate for public office.

Totalitarianism A system of government that suppresses all dissent in the name of some supreme goal.

Two-nations theory Canada, viewed from this perspective, as fundamentally a partnership between two ethnolinguistic communities or nations, one French-speaking and the other English-speaking. This premise underlies such constitutional proposals as a Quebec right of veto over constitutional reform and recognition of Quebec as a distinct society. Although the two-nations theory continues to enjoy popularity among Quebec nationalists and some English-Canadian intellectuals, it appears to have much less public support in English-speaking Canada, especially as the historical and contemporary political significance of Indigenous peoples within Canada is better understood.

Tyranny of the majority Term used by Alexis de Tocqueville in *Democracy in America* (1835) to refer to the danger that majoritarian democracy might oppress the rights of minorities.

Ultra vires From the Latin, meaning "beyond its strength"; a judicial ruling of ultra vires means that a legislative act is beyond or outside the constitutional power or authority of that legislature. In contrast, an intra vires judicial ruling means that a legislature has acted within its constitutional competence.

Unholy alliance The term that critics sometimes applied to the three pillars of the conservative Quebec establishment during the 1940s and 1950s: the Catholic Church, anglophone capital, and the Union Nationale under the leadership of *le chef*, Maurice Duplessis.

Universal Declaration of Human Rights A declaration passed by the United Nations in 1948 that provides the basis for various international covenants to which Canada is a signatory, such as the International Covenant on Civil and Political Rights and the International Covenant on Economic, Social and Cultural Rights.

Visible minority A term that refers to people who belong to a minority that is non-white in colour or race, but that does not include Indigenous Canadians. This is the definition used in the federal Employment Equity Act and by Statistics Canada. The term entered the Canadian political lexicon in the 1980s. It is not commonly used in such countries as the United States or France to refer to non-white minorities.

Western alienation A belief held over the years by many in western Canada, but particularly in Alberta and British Columbia, that Ottawa and the mainstream political parties are by and large insensitive to the interests and preferences of western Canadians. The roots of this sentiment go back to the high tariff policies and freight rates of the federal government from the late nineteenth century. Regional parties of protest such as the Progressives after World War I and the *Reform Party* in 1987 have emerged from this sense of regional grievance.

Whistleblowing When a public servant brings attention to government actions or policies that he or she believes endanger public health or safety. Such actions are protected by law, but in deciding to go public with information acquired in the course of his or her job, a public servant must be mindful of his or her duty of loyalty to the government and take care to get the facts right.

White Paper (1969) An ambitious set of reforms to Indigenous policy proposed by the Liberal government that would have ended the system of Indian reserves and abolished different status for Indians under law. It was strongly opposed by most Indigenous spokespersons and was soon abandoned.

Women's liberation Term that came into widespread use during the 1960s to refer to the struggle for equal rights for women. Feminist intellectuals such as Betty Friedan, Germaine Greer, and Gloria Steinem were among the leaders of the women's liberation movement.

Notes

Part I   Introduction

1   An Introduction to Political Life

1. Insights West, "Nurses, Doctors and Scientists Are Canada's Most Respected Professionals," https://insightswest.com/news/nurses-doctors-and-scientists-are-canadas-most-respected-professionals/.
2. World Values Survey, Wave 6, 2000–2014.
3. Wislawa Szymborska, "Children of Our Era," *People on a Bridge, with Adam Czerniawski.* London: Forest Books, 1990.
4. Jill Vickers, *Reinventing Political Science* (Halifax: Fernwood, 1997), 113–14.
5. See the full exchange between Prime Minister Trudeau and CBC journalist Tim Ralfe online at http://www.cbc.ca/archives/entry/1970-pierre-trudeau-says-just-watch-me-during-october-crisis.
6. Revisions to the Anti-Terrorism Act were proposed in late 2017 by Bill C-59, An Act Respecting National Security Matters. The bill received royal assent in June 2019. Bill C-59 was widely criticized by civil liberties advocates, including the Canadian Civil Liberties Association.
7. Leo Panitch, "State," in *The Canadian Encyclopedia,* http://www.thecanadianencyclopedia.ca/en/article/state/.
8. Quoted in Vickers, *Reinventing Political Science,* 42.
9. Ta-Nehisi Coates, "Barack Obama, Ferguson, and the Evidence of Things Unsaid: Violence Works. Nonviolence Does Too," https://www.theatlantic.com/politics/archive/2014/11/barack-obama-ferguson-and-the-evidence-of-things-unsaid/383212/?single_page=true.
10. Allison Jones, "Idle No More: Judge Slams Ontario Police for Not Ending First Nations Protest near Kingston," 7 Jan. 2013, www.ctvnews.ca/canada/judge-slams-ontario-police-for-not-ending-first-nations-rail-blockade-1.1103669.
11. Howard Zinn, *Declarations of Independence: Cross-Examining American Ideology* (New York: Harper Perennial, 1991).
12. Noam Chomsky and Edward S. Herman, *Manufacturing Consent: The Political Economy of the Mass Media* (New York: Pantheon Books, 1988).
13. Victor Davis Hanson, talk at Woodrow Wilson Center, 2 June 2005, Washington, DC.
14. Non-Canadian readers may not be familiar with Tim Hortons, a chain of coffee shops that is both ubiquitous and iconic in Canada.
15. Economist Intelligence Unit, https://www.eiu.com/public/topical_report.aspx?campaignid=DemocracyIndex2017.
16. Gabriel A. Almond and Sidney Verba, *The Civic Culture* (Princeton, NJ: Princeton University Press, 1963).
17. The Legatum Institute, *The 2017 Legatum Prosperity Index,* at: http://www.prosperity.com/about/methodology.
18. Amy Crawford, "For the People, by the People," *Slate,* 22 May 2013, www.slate.com/articles/news_and_politics/politics/2013/05/new_england_town_halls_these_experiments_in_direct_democracy_do_a_far_better.html.
19. Swiss Confederation, https://www.bk.admin.ch/ch/d/pore/va/vab_2_2_4_1.html#.
20. Quoted in Henry Steele Commager, *Living Ideas in America* (New York: Harper, 1951), 556.
21. Neil Postman, *Amusing Ourselves to Death* (New York: Viking, 1985), 107.
22. Pew Research Center, *Globally, Broad Support for Representative and Direct Democracy,* http://assets.pewresearch.org/wp-content/uploads/sites/2/2017/10/17102729/Pew-Research-Center_Democracy-Report_2017.10.16.pdf.
23. *Federalist Papers,* No. 10
24. Arthur Lupia and John G. Matsusaka, "Direct Democracy: New Approaches to Old Questions," *Annual Review of Political Science* 7 (2004): 463–82. doi: 10.1146/annurev.polisci.7.012003.104730.
25. Eugene Forsey, *How Canadians Govern Themselves,* 9th edn (Ottawa: Library of Parliament, Public Information Office, 2016), 30.
26. Robert B. Reich, *Supercapitalism: The Transformation of Business, Democracy and Everyday Life* (New York: Knopf, 2007), 18.
27. Julie Cazzin, "Why Everyone Feels Like They're in the Middle Class," 16 June 2017, http://www.macleans.ca/economy/why-everyone-feels-like-theyre-in-the-middle-class/.
28. See www.worldvaluessurvey.org.
29. Ronald F. Inglehart, "Changing Values among Western Publics from 1970 to 2006," *West European Politics* 31, 1–2 (2008): 130–46.
30. Quoted in PBS, "Up for Debate: Globalization and Poverty," http://www.pbs.org/wgbh/commandingheights/shared/minitext/ufd_poverty_full.html.

Part II   The Societal Context of Politics

2   Political Culture

1. "In Search of the Canadian Dream," *The Atlantic* (Dec. 2004).
2. Russell Kirk, *The Conservative Mind* (London: Faber & Faber, 1953).
3. Daniel Bell, *The End of Ideology* (New York: Free Press, 1962), 402–3.
4. CROP, https://www.crop.ca/en/blog/2017/207/, 20 Nov. 2017.

5. *The Internet Encyclopedia of Philosophy*, "John Stuart Mill, 1806–1873," https://www.iep.utm.edu/milljs/.

6. David Bell and Lorne Tepperman, *The Roots of Disunity* (Toronto: McClelland & Stewart, 1979), 23.

7. Fernand Ouellet, *Histoire économique et sociale du Québec, 1760–1850* (Paris: Fides, 1966).

8. Bell and Tepperman note that the estimated number of anglophones in what are now the Maritimes, Quebec, and Ontario at the time of the American Revolution was about 15,000. Between 30,000 and 50,000 Loyalists immigrated to these British colonies in the years during and immediately after the American War of Independence. They were followed by probably twice or even three times that number of non-Loyalist Americans in the years from about 1790 to the War of 1812, the vast majority of whom settled in Ontario. According to historian Fred Landon, by 1812 people born in the United States accounted for about 80 per cent of Ontario's population of roughly 136,000. He estimates that only one in four of these immigrants from the United States were Loyalists. This post-Loyalist wave of immigration came in search of cheap land and economic prospects, not because they preferred to live under the British Crown.

9. William Christian and Colin Campbell, *Political Parties and Ideologies in Canada*, 2nd edn (Toronto: McGraw-Hill Ryerson, 1982), 23–5; Gad Horowitz, "Conservatism, Liberalism, and Socialism in Canada: An Interpretation," *Canadian Journal of Economics and Political Science* 32 (1966): 143–71.

10. Kenneth McRae, "The Structure of Canadian History," in Louis Hartz, ed., *The Founding of New Societies* (New York: Harcourt, Brace & World, 1964), 235.

11. Bell and Tepperman, *The Roots of Disunity*, 76–7.

12. Horowitz, "Conservatism, Liberalism, and Socialism."

13. Seymour Martin Lipset, *Continental Divide* (Montreal: C.D. Howe Institute, 1989), 1.

14. Bell and Tepperman, *The Roots of Disunity*, 61–2.

15. George Grant, *Lament for a Nation: The Defeat of Canadian Nationalism* (Montreal and Kingston: McGill-Queen's University Press, 2015). First published in 1965.

16. Jocelyn Létourneau, Raphaël Gani, et Stéphane Lévesque, "Tout a commencé par la défaite. La guerre de Sept Ans dans la mémoire et la conscience historiques des Québécois," in *Laurent Veyssière, ed., La Nouvelle-France en héritage* (Montreal: Armand Collin, 2013), 311.

17. James Mahoney, "Path Dependence in Historical Sociology," *Theory and Society* 29 (2000): 507–8.

18. Patricia Marchak, *Ideological Perspectives on Canada* (Toronto: McGraw-Hill Ryerson, 1975), 115.

19. Prime Minister Justin Trudeau quoted in Guy Lawson, "Trudeau's Canada, Again," *New York Times Magazine*, 8 Dec. 2015, https://www.nytimes.com/2015/12/13/magazine/trudeaus-canada-again.html?_r=0.

20. Quoted in Charles Foran, "The Canadian Experiment: Is This the World's First Post-National Country?" *The Guardian*, 4 Jan. 2017, https://www.theguardian.com/world/2017/jan/04/the-canada-experiment-is-this-the-worlds-first-postnational-country.

21. Will Kymlicka, "Being Canadian," *Government & Opposition* 38, 3 (2003): 385.

22. W.L. Morton, "The Dualism of Culture and the Federalism of Power," in Richard Abbott, ed., *A New Concept of Confederation*, Proceedings of the Seventh Seminar of the Canadian Union of Students (Ottawa, 1965), 121.

23. Donald Smiley, *The Canadian Political Nationality* (Toronto: Methuen, 1967).

24. En collaboration, *Québec: Un pays incertain: Réflexions sur le Québec post-référendaire* (Montréal: Québec/Amérique, 1980), 170–2.

25. Roper Center, "The Quebec Referendum on Sovereignty, and the Future of Canada," *The Public Perspective* (Dec.–Jan. 1996), https://ropercenter.cornell.edu/public-perspective/ppscan/71/71021.pdf.

26. P. Whitney Lackenbauer and Yale Deron Belanger, eds, *Blockades or Breakthroughs? Aboriginal Peoples Confront the Canadian State* (Montreal and Kingston: McGill-Queen's University Press, 2014).

27. Chiefs of Ontario, "Understanding First Nations Sovereignty," http://www.chiefs-of-ontario.org/first-nations/sovereignty/.

28. John Farthing, *Freedom Wears a Crown* (Toronto: Kingswood, 1957). Farthing, a Canadian conservative, argued that in a world divided between American-style democracy and the Marxist models represented by the Soviet Union and Communist China, Canada and the other Commonwealth democracies represented a preferable political model.

29. Lipset, *Continental Divide*, 136.

30. Pierre Berton, *Why We Act Like Canadians* (Toronto: McClelland & Stewart, 1982), 16.

31. Mollie J. Cohen et al., *The Political Culture of Democracy in the Americas, 2016/17*, Latin American Public Opinion Project, Vanderbilt University, https://www.vanderbilt.edu/lapop/ab2016/AB2016-17_Comparative_Report_English_V2_FINAL_090117_W.pdf.

32. Lipset, *Continental Divide*, 90.

33. Nick Baxter-Moore, Munroe Eagles, Dupinder Aheer, Racquel Maxwell, Lisa-Anne Pilkey, and Kimmy Samra, "Explaining Canada–US Differences in Attitudes toward Crime and Justice: An Empirical Test of S.M. Lipset's Account," *American Review of Canadian Studies* 46, 4 (2017): 430–51. doi:10.1080/02722011.2016.1265567, p. 17.

34. Miles Corak, "Chasing the Same Dream, Climbing Different Ladders: Economic Mobility in the United States and Canada," Economic Mobility Project of the Pew Charitable Trusts, Jan. 2010, www.economicmobility.org.

35. In fairness to such a remarkably astute observer as Tocqueville, he certainly was not blind to slavery in the United States, nor did he think it of little consequence. Indeed, one of the least cited but most insightful sections of *Democracy in America* deals with what Tocqueville recognized as the unequal and unjust treatment of the black and Indigenous segments of the American population.

36. S.D. Clark, *The Canadian Community* (Toronto: University of Toronto Press, 1962); Seymour Martin Lipset, "The Value Patterns of Democracy: A Case Study in Comparative Analysis," *American Sociological Review* 28, 4 (1963): 515–31.

37. Many examples of this could be cited. A recent high-profile example of this genre of praise from the American left for the Canadian model is found in Stephen Rodrick, "Justin Trudeau: North Star," *Rolling Stone*, 26 July 2017, https://www.rollingstone.com/politics/features/justin-trudeau-canadian-prime-minister-free-worlds-best-hope-w494098.

38. Ipsos Affairs, "Public Perspectives: Basic Universal Income," 2017, https://www.ipsos.com/sites/default/files/2017-06/public-perspectives-basic-universal-income-2017-06-13-v2.pdf.

39. Lipset, *Continental Divide*, 156.

40. Pew Research Center, *Economies of Emerging Markets Better Rated during Difficult Times*, 23 May 2013, www.pewglobal.org/files/2013/05/Pew-Global-Attitudes-Economic-Report-FINAL-May-23-20131.pdf.

41. Corak, "Chasing the Same Dream," 3.

42. Ibid., 14.

43. Constitution Act, 1982, s. 27.

44. Constitution Act, 1982, s. 15(2).

45. Raymond Breton and Jeffrey Reitz, *The Illusion of Difference* (Toronto: C.D. Howe Institute, 1994), 133.

46. Martin Turcotte, "Passing on the Ancestral Language," *Canadian Social Trends* no. 80 (Spring 2006): 20–7.

47. Lloyd L. Wong and Annette Tézli, "Measuring Social, Cultural, and Civic Integration in Canada: The Creation of an Index and Some Applications," *Canadian Ethnic Studies* 45, 3 (2013): 27.

48. World Economic Forum, *The Global Gender Gap Report 2017*, http://reports.weforum.org/global-gender-gap-report-2017/dataexplorer/#economy=USA.

49. Catalyst, *Women on Corporate Boards Globally*, http://www.catalyst.org/knowledge/women-corporate-boards-globally.

50. Gallup International, "Global Values: Religion, Race, Culture," Oct.–Dec. 2016, http://www.gallup-international.com/wp-content/uploads/2017/11/2016_Religion_Race_Culture.pdf.

51. Association for Canadian Studies, *A Four-Country Survey of Opinions on Racism and Prejudice in 2010: Canada, the United States, Germany and Spain*, 21 Jan. 2011.

52. Feng Hou, Zheng Wu, Christoph Schimmele, and John Myles, "Group Size and Social Interaction: A Canada–US Comparison of Interracial Marriage," *Canadian Labour Market and Skills Researcher Network Working Paper*, No. 151, July 2015, http://www.clsrn.econ.ubc.ca/workingpapers/CLSRN%20Working%20Paper%20no.%20151%20-%20Hou%20et%20al.pdf.

53. OECD, stats.oecd.org/Index.aspx?QueryId=4549.

54. Tax Policy Center, *Briefing Book*, https://www.taxpolicycenter.org/briefing-book/how-do-us-taxes-compare-internationally.

55. Charles Taylor, "Deep Diversity and the Future of Canada," in David M. Hayne, ed., *Can Canada Survive? Under What Terms and Conditions?* (Toronto: University of Toronto Press, 1997), 29–36.

56. Neil Nevitte, *The Decline of Deference: Canadian Value Change in Cross-National Perspective* (Peterborough, ON: Broadview Press, 1996); Nevitte, "The Decline of Deference Revisited: Evidence after 25 Years," Mar. 2011, https://www.democracy .uci.edu/files/docs/conferences/2011/Decline_Revisited_%20Evidence_after_25_Years_Neil_Nevitte.pdf.

3 The Social and Economic Setting

1. World Bank, http://databank.worldbank.org/data/download/GNIPC.pdf.

2. Environics Institute, *Focus Canada 2012*, p. 10, www.environics institute.org/uploads/institute-projects/environics%20institute%20-%20focus%20canada%202012%20final%20report.pdf; Abacus Data, 21 Nov. 2016, http://abacusdata.ca/what-keeps-us-awake-top-national-issues/.

3. OECD, www.oecd-ilibrary.org/sites/factbook-2013-en/07/02/02/ltunemp_g1.html?contentType=&itemId=/content/chapter/factbook-2013-58-en&containerItemId=/content/serial/181473 64&accessItemIds=&mimeType=text/html; for 2007–16, *OECD Economic Outlook*, No. 102, Nov. 2017, and Statistics Canada, CANSIM tables 282-0087 and 282-0089, 9 Mar. 2018.

4. OECD, https://read.oecd-ilibrary.org/employment/oecd-labour-force-statistics-2018/international-comparisons_oecd_lfs-2018-2-en#page30.

5. This debate is taken up in Michael Spence, "Globalization and Unemployment," *Foreign Affairs* (July–Aug. 2011), www.foreignaffairs.com/articles/67874/michael-spence/globalization-and-unemployment, and Richard Katz and Robert Lawrence, "Manufacturing Globalization," *Foreign Affairs* (Nov.–Dec. 2011), www.foreignaffairs.com/articles/136594/richard-katz-robert-z-lawrence-michael-spence/manufacturing-globalization#. The case for the continuing importance of manufacturing and the negative consequences for developed economies of globalization is also made by Louis Uchitelle, *Making It: Why Manufacturing Still Matters* (New York: New Press, 2017).

6. Claire Cain Miller, "The Long-Term Jobs Killer Is Not China. It's Automation," *New York Times*, 21 Dec. 2016, https://www.nytimes.com/2016/12/21/upshot/the-long-term-jobs-killer-is-not-china-its-automation.html.

7. René Morissette, "Planning for Canada's Future Labour Market," *Policy Options*, 30 Oct. 2017, http://policyoptions.irpp.org/magazines/october-2017/planning-for-canadas-future-labour-market/.

8. CBC, "Generation Jobless," http://www.cbc.ca/doczone/episodes/generation-jobless.

9. Léo Charbonneau, "This Is Not 'Generation Jobless'," *University Affairs*, 13 Feb. 2013, https://www.universityaffairs.ca/opinion/margin-notes/this-is-not-generation-jobless/.

10. Ross Finnie et al., "Barista or Better? New Evidence on the Earnings of Post-Secondary Education Graduates: A Tax Linkage Approach," *Education Policy Research Initiative*, University of Ottawa, 26 July 2016, p. 17.

11. Richard Fry, "Young Adult Households Are Earning More Than Most Older Americans Did at the Same Age," Pew Research Center, 11 Dec. 2018, http://www.pewresearch.org/fact-tank/2018/12/11/young-adult-households-are-earning-more-than-most-older-americans-did-at-the-same-age/.

12. Stephanie Levitz, "Canadians Appear Pessimistic about Their Economic Futures, Poll Suggests," *Globe and Mail*, 9 Oct. 2017,

https://www.theglobeandmail.com/news/national/canadians-appear-pessimistic-about-their-economic-futures-poll-suggests/article36526629/.

13. Julie Cazzin, "Why Everyone Feels Like They're in the Middle Class," *Maclean's*, 16 June 2017, https://www.macleans.ca/economy/why-everyone-feels-like-theyre-in-the-middle-class/.

14. Nanos/Bloomberg, "The Majority of Canadians Are Concerned about the Gap between the Rich and Poor and Housing Affordability," http://www.nanos.co/wp-content/uploads/2017/11/2017-1106-Bloomberg-OMNI-Populated-report-with-Tabulations.pdf.

15. Environics, *Americas Barometer: Canada 2017*, p. 56: http://environicsresearch.com/wp-content/uploads/2017/06/AmericasBarometer-2017-Canada-Report-EMBARGOED-FINAL-June-28-20171.pdf.

16. Statistics Canada, http://www5.statcan.gc.ca/cansim/a26?lang=eng&retrLang=eng&id=2040001&&pattern=&stByVal=1&p1=1&p2=31&tabMode=dataTable&csid=.

17. Statistics Canada, https://www150.statcan.gc.ca/n1/daily-quotidien/180322/t002b-eng.htm.

18. CTV News/Nanos Survey, "Canadians' Opinions on Possible Key Priorities for the Federal Budget," http://www.nanos.co/wp-content/uploads/2017/07/Mar-6-Canadians%E2%80%99-opinions-on-possible-key-priorities-for-the-federal-budget.pdf.

19. Statistics Canada, https://www150.statcan.gc.ca/t1/tbl1/en/tv.action?pid=1110024101. The low-income measure and market basket measure used by Statistics Canada to measure the incidence of low incomes are explained at https://www12.statcan.gc.ca/census-recensement/2016/ref/dict/fam021-eng.cfm and https://www12.statcan.gc.ca/census-recensement/2016/ref/dict/pop165-eng.cfm.

20. Statistics Canada, https://www.canada.ca/en/employment-social-development/programs/poverty-reduction/backgrounder.html#h2.1.

21. Anne Tweddle, Ken Battle, and Sherri Torjman, *Canada Social Report Welfare in Canada 2016*, Caledon Institute of Social Policy, Nov. 2017, https://maytree.com/wp-content/uploads/1119ENG.pdf.

22. Statistics Canada: https://www150.statcan.gc.ca/n1/daily-quotidien/171025/dq171025a-eng.htm; "Canada: Degree of Urbanization from 2007 to 2017," https://www.statista.com/statistics/271208/urbanization-in-canada/.

23. Miles Corak, "Should We Worry about the Top 1%, or Praise Them?" 27 Nov. 2016, https://milescorak.com/2016/11/27/should-we-worry-about-the-top-1-or-praise-them/.

24. Ibid.

25. Statistics Canada, "Income and Mobility of Immigrants 2015," https://www.statcan.gc.ca/daily-quotidien/171127/dq171127a-eng.htm.

26. On happiness, see http://worldhappiness.report/. On life satisfaction, see the OECD's measure, which forms part of its Better Life Index, at http://stats.oecd.org/index.aspx?DataSetCode=BLI.

27. *US News and World Report*, "Best Countries 2018," https://www.usnews.com/news/best-countries.

28. Gallup, "Coming to America," 28 June 2017, http://news.gallup.com/opinion/gallup/212687/coming-america.aspx.

29. C.P. Barrington-Leigh and S. Sloman, "Life Satisfaction among Aboriginal Peoples in the Canadian Prairies: Evidence from the Equality, Security and Community Survey," *International Indigenous Policy Journal*, 7, 2 (2016), http://ir.lib.uwo.ca/iipj/ vol7/iss2/2; doi: 10.18584/iipj.2016.7.2.2.

30. Conference Board of Canada, *How Canada Performs: A Report Card on Canada*, http://www.conferenceboard.ca/hcp/default.aspx; OECD, *Better Life Initiative: Measuring Well-Being and Progress*, http://www.oecd.org/statistics/better-life-initiative.htm.

31. All of these figures are from the Canadian Institute for Health Information, based mainly on OECD data, in *How Canada Compares Internationally: A Health Spending Perspective* (2017), https://www.cihi.ca/en/canadas-health-system-international-comparisons.

32. Statistics Canada, "Health-Adjusted Life Expectancy in Canada," http://www.statcan.gc.ca/pub/82-003-x/2018004/article/54950-eng.htm; Simon Iain Hay et al., "Global, Regional, and National Disability-Adjusted Life-Years (DALYs) for 333 Diseases and Injuries and Healthy Life Expectancy (HALE) for 195 Countries and Territories, 1990–2016: A Systematic Analysis for the Global Burden of Disease Study 2016," *The Lancet*, 390 (16 Sept. 2017), https://www.thelancet.com/pdfs/journals/lancet/PIIS0140-6736(17)32130-X.pdf.

33. Statistics Canada, "Canada's Crime Rate: Two Decades of Decline," http://www.statcan.gc.ca/pub/11-630-x/11-630-x2015001-eng.htm.

34. International Crime Victim Survey, http://wp.unil.ch/icvs/.

35. Environics Institute, Americas Barometer, *Canada Report 2012*, 48, 50.

36. Statistics Canada, "Police Reported Crime Statistics in Canada, 2016," http://www.statcan.gc.ca/pub/85-002-x/2017001/article/54842-eng.htm.

37. Stephen Easton, *The Cost of Crime in Canada* (Vancouver: Fraser Institute, Oct. 2014), https://www.fraserinstitute.org/sites/default/files/cost-of-crime-in-canada.pdf.

38. Jeffrey Sachs, *World Happiness Report 2012*, https://worldhappiness.report/ed/2012/; Ronald Inglehart, "Ron Inglehart Discusses How Economic Growth, Democratization and Social Tolerance Lead to Happiness," https://nsf.gov/news/news_videos.jsp?cntn_id=111725&media_id=62521; Philip Greenspun, "The Secret to Danish Happiness," https://philip.greenspun.com/blog/2013/06/18/the-secret-to-danish-happiness/.

39. Statistics Canada, http://www5.statcan.gc.ca/cansim/a47.

40. Statistics Canada, https://www.statcan.gc.ca/pub/89-653-x/89-653-x2016008-eng.htm.

41. "To Combat Loneliness, Promote Social Health," https://www.scientificamerican.com/article/to-combat-loneliness-promote-social-health1/?WT.mc_id=send-to-friend.

42. Cited in *CBC News*, "Loneliness: A Major Public Health Risk?" http://www.cbc.ca/news/thenational/loneliness-a-major-public-health-risk-1.4250709.

43. Manfred E. Beutel et al., "Loneliness in the General Population: Prevalence, Determinants and Relations to

Mental Health," *BMC Psychiatry* 17 (2017): 97, doi:10.1186/s12888-017-1262-x.

44. Chris Allen, "How the Digitalisation of Everything Is Making Us More Lonely," *The Conversation*, https://theconversation.com/how-the-digitalisation-of-everything-is-making-us-more-lonely-90870.

45. Bruce Alexander, *The Globalization of Addiction* (London: Oxford University Press, 2010).

46. Jason Connor and Wayne Hall, "Thresholds for Safer Alcohol Use Might Need Lowering," *The Lancet* 391, 10129 (14 Apr. 2018): 1460–1.

47. Canadian Centre on Substance Abuse and Addiction, "Alcohol," Fall 2017, https://www.ccsa.ca/sites/default/files/2019-04/CCSA-Canadian-Drug-Summary-Alcohol-2017-en.pdf, p. 7.

48. Canadian Institute for Health Information, *Alcohol Harm in Canada, 2017,* https://www.cihi.ca/sites/default/files/document/report-alcohol-hospitalizations-en-web.pdf.

49. Øyvind Horverak, "Alcohol and Economics: Research, Politics or Industry?" *Nordic Studies on Alcohol and Drugs* 27 (2010), http://www.nopus.org/PageFiles/4867/Horverak.pdf.

50. Canadian Observatory on Homelessness, *The State of Homelessness in Canada 2016*, http://www.homelesshub.ca/sites/default/files/SOHC16_final_20Oct2016.pdf.

51. Employment and Social Development Canada, *The National Shelter Study 2005–2014* (2017), p. 18, http://publications.gc.ca/collections/collection_2017/edsc-esdc/Em12-17-2017-eng.pdf.

52. Based on CBC News, "Over Half of Vancouver's Homeless Population Have Been Homeless for Less Than a Year, Count Finds," 1 May 2018, http://www.cbc.ca/news/canada/british-columbia/vancouver-homeless-count-2018-1.4644233.

53. Food Banks Canada, *Hunger Count 2016*, https://www.foodbankscanada.ca/getmedia/6173994f-8a25-40d9-acdf-660a28e40f37/HungerCount_2016_final_singlepage.pdf.aspx?ext=.pdf.

54. OECD, *Better Life Index: Canada*, http://www.oecdbetterlifeindex.org/countries/canada/.

4 Diversity and Multiculturalism

1. Joe Clark, as cited in Desmond Morton and Morton Weinfeld, eds, *Who Speaks for Canada?* (Toronto: McClelland & Stewart, 1998). In fact, as so often is the case, criticisms of Clark's campaign statement did not report the full and thoughtful context within which he made a remark that some called divisive.

2. Gerald Walton Paul, "Thoughts on Canadian Values," *Kingston Whig-Standard,* 13 Apr. 2017, http://www.thewhig.com/2017/04/13/thoughts-on-canadian-values.

3. John Porter, *The Vertical Mosaic* (Toronto: University of Toronto Press, 1965).

4. All of these data are from Statistics Canada, "Ethnic and Cultural Origins of Canadians: Portrait of a Rich Heritage," Oct. 2017, https://www12.statcan.gc.ca/census-recensement/2016/as-sa/98-200-x/2016016/98-200-x2016016-eng.cfm.

5. Association for Canadian Studies, "Soccer & Turbans," 14 June 2013, www.acs-aec.ca/en/social-research/?limit=10&start=70&csort=&order=#?limit=10&start=0&csort=&order=.

6. Angus Reid Institute, "What Makes Us Canadian? A Study of Values, Beliefs, Priorities and Identity," 3 Oct. 2016, http://angusreid.org/canada-values/; CROP/Radio-Canada, "Les Canadiens, le populisme et la xénophobie," Feb. 2017 [published in French only, all translations in this chapter are mine], http://ici.radio-canada.ca/nouvelles/special/2017/03/sondage-crop/Sondage%20CROP-Radio-Canada.pdf; Pew Research Center, "What It Takes to Truly Be 'One of Us'," Feb. 2017, http://assets.pewresearch.org/wp-content/uploads/sites/2/2017/04/14094140/Pew-Research-Center-National-Identity-Report-FINAL-February-1-2017.pdf.

7. *Multani v. Commission scolaire Marguerite-Bourgeoys*, [2006] 1 S.C.R. 256.

8. CBC News, "Sikhs with Kirpan Not Allowed in Que. Legislature," 18 Jan. 2011, www.cbc.ca/canada/montreal/story/2011/01/18/sikhs-denied-entry-nat-ass-quebec.html.

9. Leslie A. Pal, *Interests of State: The Politics of Language, Multiculturalism, and Feminism in Canada* (Montreal and Kingston: McGill-Queen's University Press, 1993).

10. Ibid., 281.

11. R. Brian Howe and David Johnson, *Restraining Equality: Human Rights Commissions in Canada* (Toronto: University of Toronto Press, 2000), 35.

12. CRTC, "Offering Cultural Diversity on TV and Radio," https://crtc.gc.ca/eng/info_sht/b308.htm.

13. From a speech by Premier Jean Charest, 22 May 2008, at: www.premier-ministre.gouv.qc.ca/salle-de-presse/discours/2008/mai/2008-05-22-en.shtml.

14. Information on a parliamentarian's religious affiliation was once included in the *Canadian Parliamentary Handbook*.

15. Erin Tolley, "Visible Minority and Indigenous Members of Parliament," in Alex Marland and Thierry Giasson, eds, *Canadian Election Analysis 2015: Communication, Strategy, and Democracy*, 51. Accessed at http://www.ubcpress.ca/CanadianElectionAnalysis2015.

16. Andrew Griffith, "Diversity in the Senate," *Policy Options*, 14 Feb. 2017, http://policyoptions.irpp.org/magazines/february-2017/diversity-in-the-senate/.

17. Andrew Griffith, "Diversity among Federal and Provincial Judges," *Policy Options*, 4 May 2016, http://policyoptions.irpp.org/2016/05/04/diversity-among-federal-provincial-judges/.

18. Aaron Wherry, "How the Federal Government Is Slowly Becoming as Diverse as Canada," http://www.cbc.ca/news/politics/trudeau-appointments-diversity-analysis-wherry-1.4448740.

19. Treasury Board of Canada, "Employment Equity in the Public Service of Canada 2015–2016," https://www.canada.ca/en/treasury-board-secretariat/services/values-ethics/diversity-equity/employment-equity-annual-reports/employment-equity-public-sevice-canada-2015-2016.html.

20. Andrew Griffith, "Diversity among Canadian Heads of Mission: Two Years In," Canadian International Council, 8 Nov. 2017, https://thecic.org/hom-diversity/.

21. Rich Morin, "The Most (and Least) Culturally Diverse Countries in the World," Pew Research Center, http://www.pewresearch.org/fact-tank/2013/07/18/the-most-and-least-culturally-diverse-countries-in-the-world/.

22. Jon Sharman, "Sweden Ranked the World's Best Country for Immigrants to Live In," *The Independent*, 11 July 2017, https://www.independent.co.uk/News/world/europe/sweden-world-best-country-immigrants-live-canada-switzerland-australia-germany-job-market-stability-a7834791.html.

23. Alberto F. Alesina, William Easterly, Arnaud Devleeschauwer, Sergio Kurlat, and Romain T. Wacziarg, "Fractionalization," (Jan. 2003), *NBER Working Paper* No. w9411, https://ssrn.com/abstract=366448.

24. Paul Sniderman and Louk Hagendoorn, *When Ways of Life Collide: Multiculturalism and Its Discontents* (Princeton, NJ: Princeton University Press, 2007), 15.

25. Willem Huijnk and Jaco Dagevos, *Closer Together? The Socio-cultural position of Non-Western Migrants in the Netherlands*, 20 Dec. 2012, www.scp.nl/english/Publications/Summaries_by_year/Summaries_2012/Closer_together.

26. Paul Sniderman and Louk Hagendoorn, *When Ways of Life Collide: Multiculturalism and Its Discontents* (Princeton, NJ: Princeton University Press, 2007), 15.

27. National Council for the Social Studies, *National Curriculum Standards for Social Studies: Introduction*, https://www.socialstudies.org/standards/introduction.

28. Gallup, "Migrant Acceptance in Canada, U.S. Follows Political Lines," 26 Apr. 2018, http://news.gallup.com/poll/233147/migrant-acceptance-canada-follows-political-lines.aspx.

29. National Council for the Social Studies, *National Curriculum Standards for Social Studies: Introduction*. https://www.socialstudies.org/standards/introduction.

30. Guillaume Gendron, "France 'diverse' mais pas 'multiculturelle': à quoi joue Macron dans 'Causeur'?" *Libération*, 14 avril 2017, http://www.liberation.fr/politiques/2017/04/14/france-diverse-mais-pas-multiculturelle-a-quoi-joue-macron-dans-causeur_1562655.

31. Statistics Canada, *Focus on Geography Series*, 2016 Census, https://www12.statcan.gc.ca/census-recensement/2016/as-sa/fogs-spg/Facts-pr-eng.cfm?Lang=Eng&GK=PR&GC=24&TOPIC=7.

32. See municipalite.herouxville.qc.ca/Standards.pdf.

33. See the discussion of these concepts in Mirian Chiasson, "A Clarification of Terms: Canadian Multiculturalism and Quebec Interculturalism," a report prepared for the Centaur Jurisprudence Project, Centre for Human Rights and Legal Pluralism, McGill University, Aug. 2012, 1–3, http://canadianicon.org/wp-content/uploads/2014/03/TMOD Part1-Clarification.pdf.

34. CBC News, "Minority Report 'Misses the Point' PQ Says," 23 May 2008, www.cbc.ca.

35. http://www.assnat.qc.ca/en/travaux-parlementaires/projets-loi/projet-loi-62-41-1.html.

36. Catherine Lévesque, "Les Québécois en faveur de la neutralité religieuse de l'État," *Huffpost*, 4 Oct. 2017, https://quebec.huffingtonpost.ca/2017/10/04/les-quebecois-en-faveur-de-la-neutralite-religieuse-de-l-etat_a_23232670/.

37. Statistics Canada, "Population Growth: Migratory Increase Overtakes Natural Increase," https://www.statcan.gc.ca/pub/11-630-x/11-630-x2014001-eng.htm.

37. Statistics Canada, *Educational and Labour Market Outcomes of Childhood Immigrants by Admission Class*, 25 Apr. 2016, http://www.statcan.gc.ca/pub/11f0019m/11f0019m2016377-eng.htm.

39. Tracey M. Derwing and Erin Waugh, *"Language Skills and the Social Integration of Canada's Adult Immigrants,"* Institute for Research on Public Policy, 31 May 2012, http://irpp.org/research-studies/study-no31/.

40. Derrick Thomas, "The Impact of Working in a Non-Official Language on the Occupations and Earnings of Immigrants in Canada," *Canadian Social Trends* (2009), www.statcan.gc.ca/pub/11-008-x/2009001/article/10771-eng.htm.

41. American Immigration Council, "The RAISE Act: What Lies Beneath the Proposed Points System?" 11 Aug. 2017, https://www.americanimmigrationcouncil.org/research/raise-act.

42. Statistics Canada, "Longitudinal Survey of Immigrants to Canada: Progress and Challenges of New Immigrants in the Workforce" (Ottawa, 2003), www.statcan.gc.ca/pub/89-615-x/2005001/4079178-eng.htm; Statistics Canada, "National Portrait of Immigrant Outcomes: 2001–2008 Employment Earnings," 15 May 2012, https://www.canada.ca/en/immigration-refugees-citizenship/corporate/reports-statistics/research/imdb-2008-core-report-national-portrait-immigrant-outcomes-2001-2008-employment-earnings/overview.html#outcomes.

43. Jeffrey Reitz, "Economic Opportunity, Multiculturalism, and the Roots of Popular Support for High Immigration in Canada," 2013, munkschool.utoronto.ca/ethnicstudies/files/2013/02/Reitz-Economic-Opportunity-Multiculturalism-and-the-Roots-of-Popular-Support-CISAN-UNAM-Mexico-City-2012.pdf.

44. Environics Research Group, "New Directions for Foreign Credentials Recognition: Final Report," a study commissioned by Employment and Social Development Canada, 2014, p. 16.

45. Ibid., p. xvi.

46. Sandra Elgersma, "Recognition of the Foreign Qualifications of Immigrants, Background Paper," Library of Parliament, Apr. 2012, https://lop.parl.ca/Content/LOP/ResearchPublications/2004-29-e.pdf.

47. Jackie Dunham, "'The Last Cheerful Nation': Does Pro-Multiculturalism Canada Stand Alone?" CTV News, 27 Dec. 2016, https://www.ctvnews.ca/canada/the-last-cheerful-nation-does-pro-multiculturalism-canada-stand-alone-1.3197035.

48. OECD, *Indicators of Immigrant Integration 2015*, http://www.oecd.org/els/mig/Indicators-of-Immigrant-Integration-2015.pdf.

5 Regionalism and Canadian Politics

1. Matthew Mendelsohn and J. Scott Matthews, "The New Ontario: The Shifting Attitudes of Ontarians toward the Federation," Mowat Centre for Policy Innovation, Feb. 2010,

https://mowatcentre.ca/wp-content/uploads/publications/
1_the_new_ontario.pdf. The Mowat Centre, in co-operation with the Centre d'analyse politique: Constitution et
Fédéralisme, based at UQAM, carried out a somewhat similar survey in 2017 (https://mowatcentre.ca/portraits-2017/).
Unfortunately, it surveyed only residents of Ontario and
Quebec.

2. Cited in *The Economist*, "Special Survey of Canada," 15 Feb.
1986, 16.

3. Pierre Fortin, "Tout à l'Alberta, rien pour les autres?"
L'Actualité, 5 Oct. 2005, 50–2.

4. Richard Simeon and David Elkins, "Regional Political
Cultures in Canada," *Canadian Journal of Political Science* 7, 3
(1974): 397–437.

5. Michael Ornstein and Michael Stevenson, *Politics and
Ideology in Canada* (Montreal and Kingston: McGill-Queen's
University Press, 1999), ch. 5.

6. Ibid., 206.

7. Canadian Constitution Foundation and Abacus, http://
theccf.ca/wp-content/uploads/2017/03/Constitution-
Day-27-32.pdf.

8. Ekos, "The Return of Ideology?" 16 Mar. 2012, http://
www.ekospolitics.com/wp-content/uploads/full_report_
march_16_2012.pdf.

9. Environics Institute, *AmericasBarometer 2017*, 15, https://
www.environicsinstitute.org/docs/default-source/project-
documents/americasbarometer-2017/americasbarometer---
canada-2017---data-tables---canada.pdf?sfvrsn=e3f34459_2.

10. Abacus Data, "How Big Are Canadian Regional Differences
on Questions of Morality?" 10 July 2016, http://abacusdata
.ca/how-big-are-canadian-regional-differences-on-questions-
of-morality/.

11. Statistics Canada, *Canadian Identity 2013*, https://www150
.statcan.gc.ca/n1/en/pub/89-652-x/89-652-x2015005-eng
.pdf?st=V5V5mJz_.

12. Ekos, "The Trust Deficit: What Does It Mean?" 14 May 2013,
http://www.ekospolitics.com/wp-content/uploads/full_
report_may_14_2013.pdf.

13. Statistics Canada, "Public Confidence in Canadian
Institutions," https://www150.statcan.gc.ca/n1/pub/89-652-
x/2015007/t/tbl04-eng.htm.

14. Association for Canadian Studies, "In God We Canadians
Trust?" http://www.acs-aec.ca/pdf/polls/In%20God%20
Canadians%20Trust%20II.pdf.

15. CROP, "Religious Beliefs in Continuous Decline for
Almost 20 Years!" 10 Apr. 2017, https://www.crop.ca/en/
blog/2017/169/.

16. David McGrane and Loleen Berdahl, "'Small Worlds'
No More: Reconsidering Provincial Political Cultures in
Canada," *Regional and Federal Studies* (2013): 9, dx.doi.org/1
0.1080/13597566.2013.794415.

17. Maxime Héroux-Legault. "Substate Variations in Political
Values in Canada," *Regional & Federal Studies* 26, 2 (2016):
171–97, doi: 10.1080/13597566.2016.1161612.

18. Nelson Wiseman, *In Search of Canadian Political Culture*
(Vancouver: University of British Columbia Press, 2007), 3,
https://www.ubcpress.ca/asset/9386/1/9780774813884.pdf.

19. Debora VanNijnatten, *The Emergence of Cross-Border Regions
between Canada and the United States: Final Report*. Nov. 2008.
http://publications.gc.ca/collection_2009/policyresearch/
PH4-31-2-2008E.pdf.

20. To learn more about how environmental governance works
in these cross-border regions, see Stephen Brooks and Andrea
Olive, eds, *Transboundary Governance across the World's
Longest Border* (East Lansing: Michigan State University Press,
2019).

21. Mirielle Paquet, *Province Building and the Federalization of
Immigration in Canada* (Toronto: University of Toronto Press,
2018).

22. Matt Wilder and Michael Howlett, "Bringing the Provinces
Back In: Re-evaluating the Relevance of Province-Building to
Theories of Canadian Federalism and Multi-Level Governance,"
Canadian Political Science Review 9, 3 (2015–16): 1–34.

23. Roger Gibbins and Sonia Arrison, *Western Visions: Perspectives
on the West in Canada*, 2nd edn (Toronto: University of
Toronto Press, 2003), 45.

24. W.L. Morton, "The Bias of Prairie Politics," *Transactions of the
Royal Society of Canada* series 3, 49 (June 1955): 66.

25. Barry Cooper, "Western Political Consciousness," in Stephen
Brooks, ed., *Political Thought in Canada: Contemporary
Perspectives* (Toronto: Irwin, 1984), 230.

26. Barry Cooper, "Fresh News from Laurentian Canada,"
Reviews from the Frontier No. 2 (Apr. 2013), Frontier Centre
for Public Policy, 7, www.fcpp.org/files/1/RW02Laurentian_
AP22F1.pdf.

27. Patrick Boyer, *Direct Democracy in Canada: The History and
Future of Referendums* (Toronto: Dundurn Press, 1992).

28. Loleen Berdahl, "Whither Western Alienation? Shifting
Patterns of Western Canadian Discontent with the Federal
Government" (Calgary: Canada West Foundation, Oct.
2010), 3–6.

29. Angus Reid Institute, "What Unites & Defines the 'West'?
In a Complicated Confederation, Less Than One Might
Think," 30 Jan. 2019, p. 7, http://angusreid.org/wp-content/
uploads/2019/01/2019.01.10-Identity-Release.pdf.

30. Antoine Bilodeau, Stephen White, and Neil Nevitte, "The
Development of Dual Loyalties: Immigrants' Integration to
Canadian Regional Dynamics," *Canadian Journal of Political
Science* 43, 3 (Sept. 2010): 515–44.

31. Statistics Canada, "Recent Changes in Demographic Trends
in Canada," chart 5, https://www150.statcan.gc.ca/n1/
pub/75-006-x/2015001/article/14240-eng.htm.

32. Gary Mason, "Jason Kenney Taps into Deep Well of
Alienation," *Globe and Mail*, 29 Mar. 2018, https://www
.theglobeandmail.com/opinion/article-jason-kenney-taps-
into-deep-well-of-western-alienation/.

33. Jack M. Mintz, "Canada's Catalonia? Careful Ottawa,
Western Alienation Is Beginning to Rear Its Head Again," 13
Oct. 2017, *Financial Post*, http://business.financialpost.com/
opinion/jack-mintz-pipeline-antagonism-and-lopsided-
equalization-stir-catalonian-feelings-in-alberta.

34. Ernest R. Forbes, *The Maritime Rights Movement, 1919–1927
A Study in Canadian Regionalism* (Montreal and Kingston:
McGill-Queen's University Press, 1979).

35. In the case of Newfoundland and Labrador, which does not receive equalization payments from Ottawa, this is in large part through the agreement on oil royalties that the province has with the federal government. Royalties from this industry account for about one-quarter of the province's revenues.

36. Darrell Bricker and John Ibbitson, *The Big Shift* (Toronto: HarperCollins, 2013).

Part III The Structures of Governance

6 The Constitution

1. Canadian Constitutional Foundation, press releases archived under "News," at http://theccf.ca/.
2. Constitution Act, 1982, s. 16(1).
3. Pierre Trudeau, *Federalism and the French Canadians* (Toronto: Macmillan, 1968), 187.
4. *Commissions des gouverneurs et intendants du Canada, 1612*, eco.canadiana.ca/view/oocihm.40524/34?r=0&s=1.
5. Constitution of Brazil, 1988, https://www.constituteproject.org/constitution/Brazil_2014.pdf.
6. Constitution Act, 1867, preamble.
7. Ibid., s. 121.
8. Ibid., s. 145 (repealed in 1893).
9. Constitution Act, 1982, s. 36.
10. *Reference re Secession of Quebec*, Aug. 1998, at p. 18 of online decisions.
11. *OPSEU v. A.G. of Ontario*, [1987] 2 S.C.R. 2, S7.
12. *Reference re Secession of Quebec*, 19.
13. Ibid., 20.
14. Ibid., 21.
15. Ibid., 22.
16. *R. v. Oakes*, [1986] 1 S.C.R. 103, 136.
17. *Reference re Secession of Quebec*, 22.
18. Ibid., 23.
19. Ibid.
20. Ibid., 25.
21. Constitution Act, 1982, s. 6(3)(6).
22. Ibid., s. 6(4).
23. Library of Parliament, "Mobility Rights and the Charter of Rights and Freedoms," Aug. 1998, http://publications.gc.ca/Collection-R/LoPBdP/CIR/904-e.htm#D.%20%20Marketingtxt.
24. *Morgentaler, Smoling and Scott v. The Queen* (1988), 37 C.C.C. (3rd) 449.
25. Constitution Act, 1982, s. 15(1).
26. Ibid., s. 15(2).
27. Samara, *Samara's MP Exit Interviews: Volume II*, 12 June 2018, https://www.samaracanada.com/research/political-leadership/mp-exit-interviews/volume-ii/flip-the-script/.
28. Eugene Forsey, *How Canadians Govern Themselves*, 9th edn, at https://lop.parl.ca/About/Parliament/senatoreugeneforsey/book/assets/pdf/How_Canadians_Govern_Themselves9.pdf.
29. See the discussion at www.parliament.uk/about/how/sovereignty/.
30. Canada, Commission of Inquiry into the Sponsorship Program and Advertising Activities, *Final Report: Who Is Responsible?* (Ottawa, 1 Feb. 2006), 18–19; emphasis added.
31. Max Paris, "The New Ministerial Responsibility: Punish the Underlings," *CBC News*, 27 Jan. 2014, https://www.cbc.ca/news/politics/the-new-ministerial-responsibility-punish-the-underlings-1.2510068.
32. Constitution Act, 1867, ss. 96–100.
33. *The Queen v. Beauregard, [1986]* 2 S.C.R. 56. This was the basis of a 1986 court action brought against the Quebec government by several Provincial Court judges and the Chief Justice of the Quebec Superior Court.
34. Justice Ian Binnie, "Judicial Independence in Canada," World Conference on Constitutional Justice, Rio de Janeiro, 16–18 Jan. 2011, p. 28.
35. Peter Harder, "On Cannabis Bill, Senate Must Defer to Canadians' Democratic Will," *Policy Options*, 5 Apr. 2018, http://policyoptions.irpp.org/magazines/april-2018/cannabis-bill-senate-must-defer-canadians-democratic-will/.
36. Comparative Constitutions Project, "Constitution Rankings," http://comparativeconstitutionsproject.org/ccp-rankings/.
37. Section 91(1). Repealed by the Constitution Act, 1982.
38. Section 92(1). Repealed by the Constitution Act, 1982.
39. *Re Constitution of Canada* (1981), 125 D.L.R. (3rd) 1.
40. *Re Attorney General of Quebec and Attorney General of Canada* (1982), 140 D.L.R. (3rd) 385.
41. Cited in Paul Gérin-Lajoie, *Constitutional Amendment in Canada* (Toronto: University of Toronto Press, 1950), 241.
42. Cited ibid., 234.
43. *Reference re Secession of Quebec*, 26.
44. Ibid., 19.
45. Ibid., 27.
46. Ibid., 35.
47. Ibid., 4.

7 Rights and Freedoms

1. *Schenck v. United States*, 249 U.S. 47 (1919).
2. These are the words used in the "anti-hate" section of Canada's Criminal Code.
3. *Nova Scotia (Workers' Compensation Board) v. Martin; Nova Scotia (Workers' Compensation Board) v. Laseur*, [2003] 2 S.C.R. 504, 2003 SCC 54.
4. Justice Rosalie Abella, "Constitutions and Judges: Changing Roles, Rules and Expectations," lecture delivered at University College London, 7 July 2011, www.ucl.ac.uk/constitution-unit/events/judicial-independence-events/Justice_Abella_Lecture_to_JIP_07-07-11.pdf.
5. University of Calgary, *Charter Database*.
6. Supreme Court of Canada, *Statistics Reports*, https://www.scc-csc.ca/case-dossier/stat/years-annees-eng.aspx.
7. Harry Arthurs and Brent Arnold, "Does the Charter Matter?" *Review of Constitutional Studies* 1, 1 (2005): 38.
8. Walter S. Tarnopolsky, "Human Rights," in *The Canadian Encyclopedia*, 2nd edn (Edmonton: Hurtig, 1988), vol. 2, 1024.

9. United States Constitution, 14th amendment, 1868.

10. Justin Brake, "Constitutionalize Our Right to a Clean Environment: David Suzuki," *The Independent*, 24 Sept. 2014, https://theindependent.ca/2014/09/24/constitutionalize-our-right-to-a-clean-environment-david-suzuki/; emphasis added.

11. Reginald Bibby, "Ethos versus Ethics: Canada, the U.S. and Homosexuality," paper presented at the annual meeting of the Pacific Sociological Association, San Francisco, Apr. 2004, 9.

12. Reginald Bibby, "Homosexuality in Canada: A National Reading," 13 May 2002, 2, www.reginaldbibby.com/images/PCReleaseHomosexualityMay02.pdf.

13. Jenkins Research Inc., "The Dynamics of Gay Marriage Support," http://jenkinsresearch.ca/2013/03/an-historic-evolution-of-public-opinion-a-look-back-at-same-sex-marriage-in-canada/.

14. Episcopal Commission for Social Affairs, Canadian Conference of Catholic Bishops, "Pastoral Letter on Immigration and the Protection of Refugees," 15 Jan. 2006, http://www.cccb.ca/site/Files/PastoralLetter_Immigration.html.

15. Michael Ignatieff, *Human Rights as Politics, Human Rights as Idolatry*, The Tanner Lectures on Human Values, Princeton University, 4–7 Apr. 2000.

16. R. MacGregor Dawson, *Constitutional Issues in Canada, 1900–1931* (London: Oxford University Press, 1933).

17. R. MacGregor Dawson, *The Government of Canada* (Toronto: University of Toronto Press, 1947).

18. J.A. Corry and J.E. Hodgetts, *Democratic Government and Politics* (Toronto: University of Toronto Press, 1946).

19. Quoted in Richard Gwyn, "Bill of Rights No Simple Issue," *Ottawa Citizen*, 9 Oct. 1980, 12.

20. *Reference re Alberta Statutes, [1938]* S.C.R. 100.

21. *Saumur v. Quebec and Attorney General of Quebec, [1953]* 2 S.C.R. 299.

22. *Switzman v. Elbing and Attorney General of Quebec, [1957]* S.C.R. 285.

23. *Attorney General of Canada and Dupond v. Montreal, [1978]* 2 S.C.R. 770.

24. Quoted in Peter H. Russell, *Leading Constitutional Decisions*, 4th edn (Ottawa: Carleton Library Series, 1987), 390.

25. Diefenbaker Canada Centre, "Voter Concern for Personal Liberties Declines in Decade but One in Five Still Feels Civil Rights are Endangered," www.usask.ca/diefenbaker/galleries/virtual_exhibit/bill_of_rights/sanders_letter_to_dief.php.

26. Norman Ward, *The Government of Canada* (Toronto: University of Toronto Press, 1987), 84.

27. Corry and Hodgetts, *Democratic Government and Politics*, 462.

28. *Robertson and Rosetanni v. The Queen* (1963), quoted in Russell, *Leading Constitutional Decisions*, 399.

29. Quoted in Walter S. Tarnopolsky, *The Canadian Bill of Rights*, 2nd edn (Toronto: McClelland & Stewart, 1975), 132.

30. *R. v. Drybones, [1970]* S.C.R. 282.

31. *Attorney General of Canada v. Lavell, [1974]* S.C.R. 1349.

32. *Hogan v. The Queen, [1975]* 2 S.C.R. 574.

33. On s. 93, see *City of Winnipeg v. Barrett, [1892]* A.C. 445; *Ottawa Roman Catholic Separate School Trustees v. Mackell,* *[1917]* A.C. 62; *Protestant School Board of Greater Montreal v. Minister of Education of Quebec* (1978), 83 D.L.R. (3d) 645.

34. Quoted in Sanjeev Anand, "The Truth about Canadian Judicial Activism," *Constitutional Forum constitutionnel* 15, 2 (2006): 87.

35. Beverley McLachlin, "Respecting Democratic Roles," *Constitutional Forum constitutionnel* 14, 3 (2005): 19.

36. Ian Burns, "Supreme Court Shaped Charter into What It Is Today: McLachlin," *The Lawyer's Daily*, 9 Apr. 2018, https://www.thelawyersdaily.ca/articles/6273/supreme-court-shaped-charter-into-what-it-is-today-mclachlin.

37. *R. v. Oakes* (1986), 26 D.L.R. (4th) 20.

38. *Ford v. Attorney General of Quebec, [1988]* 2 S.C.R. 712.

39. Quoted in Peter Russell, F.L. Morton, and Rainer Knopff, *Federalism and the Charter* (Ottawa: Carleton University Press, 1989), 578.

40. Ibid., 579.

41. Quoted in "Tobacco Ad Ban Struck Down," *Globe and Mail*, 22 Sept. 1995, A1, A11.

42. *Carter v. Canada*, [2015] 1 SCR 331, paras 102–13, https://scc-csc.lexum.com/scc-csc/scc-csc/en/item/14637/index.do?r=AAAAAQAGQ0FSVEVSAQ.

43. James Stribopoulos, "Top 10 Charter Cases: As Revealed at the Symposium on the 25th Anniversary of the Charter, A Tribute to Chief Justice Roy McMurtry," theCourt.ca, http://www.thecourt.ca/top-10-charter-cases-as-revealed-at-the-symposium-on-the-25th-anniversary-of-the-charter-a-tribute-to-chief-justice-roy-mcmurtry/.

44. Roy Romanow et al., *Canada . . . Notwithstanding: The Making of the Constitution 1976–1982* (Toronto: Carswell, 1984), 211.

45. Borovoy, *When Freedoms Collide*, 211–12.

46. *Alliance des Professeurs de Montréal et al. v. Attorney General of Quebec* (1983), 9 C.C.C. (3d) 268.

47. F.L. Morton, "The Political Impact of the Canadian Charter of Rights and Freedoms," *Canadian Journal of Political Science* 20, 1 (Mar. 1987): 47.

48. Russell, Knopff, and Morton, *Federalism and the Charter*, 446.

49. *Singh v. Canada (Minister of Employment and Immigration)* (1985), 17 D.L.R. (4th) 469.

50. *Reference re Section 94(2) of the Motor Vehicle Act (B.C.), [1985]* S.C.R. 486.

51. *Hunter et al. v. Southam Inc., [1984]* 2 S.C.R. 145.

52. *Attorney General of Quebec v. Quebec Protestant School Boards* (1984), 10 D.L.R. (4th) 321.

53. *Reference re Public Service Employee Relations Act, Labour Relations Act and Police Officers Collective Bargaining Act* (1987), 38 D.L.R. (4th) 161.

54. *Operation Dismantle Inc. et al. v. The Queen* (1985), 18 D.L.R. (4th) 481.

55. *Retail, Wholesale & Department Store Union, Local 580 et al. v. Dolphin Delivery Ltd.* (1986), 33 D.L.R. (4th) 174.

56. Quoted in Michael Mandel, *The Charter of Rights and the Legalization of Politics in Canada*, 2nd edn (Toronto: Thompson Educational Publishing, 1994), 204.

57. *R. v. N.S.*, 2012 SCC 72, [2012] 3 S.C.R. 726, scc.lexum.org/decisia-scc-csc/scc-csc/scc-csc/en/12779/1/document.do, p. 4.

58. Jessie Park, "The Charter at 35: The Police Reined in by Rights," *Ipolitics*, 17 Apr. 2017, https://ipolitics.ca/2017/04/17/the-charter-at-35-the-police-reined-in-by-rights/.

59. *R. v. Keegstra*, [1990] 3 S.C.R. 697.

60. *Saskatchewan (Human Rights Commission) v. Whatcott*, [2013] 1 S.C.R. 467.

61. *Harper v. Canada*, [2004] 1 S.C.R. 827.

62. *WIC Radio Ltd. v. Simpson, 2008 SCC* 40.

63. Martha Jackman, "Constitutional Castaways: Poverty and the McLachlin Court," *Supreme Court Law Review* 50 (2010): 297–328, https://ssrn.com/abstract=2304524.

64. Harry Arthurs and Brent Arnold, "Does the Charter Matter?" *Review of Constitutional Studies* 1, 1 (2005): 37–117; Elizabeth McIsaac, "Bringing Human Rights Back into Balance: The case for Social and Economic Rights in the Charter," Mowat Centre, 30 May 2017, https://mowatcentre.ca/bringing-human-rights-back-into-balance/.

65. *Reference Re An Act to Amend the Education Act (Ontario)* (1987), 40 D.L.R. (4th) 18.

66. Before the law was passed, provincial support to Roman Catholic schools ended after Grade 10.

67. *Law v. Minister of Human Resources Development*, [1999] 1 S.C.R. 497.

68. Ibid.

69. Linda MacKay-Panos, "The Charter of Rights and Homeless Persons," *LawNow: Relating Law to Life in Canada*, 6 Mar. 2018, https://www.lawnow.org/charter-of-rights-and-homeless-persons/.

70. Jutta Brunnee and Stephen J. Toope, "A Hesitant Embrace: The Application of International Law by Canadian Courts," *Canadian Yearbook of International Law* 40 (2002): 5.

71. *Citizens United v. Federal Election Commission*, 558 U.S. 310 (2010).

72. Christopher Manfredi and Mark Rush, "Electoral Jurisprudence in the Canadian and U.S. Supreme Courts: Evolution and Convergence," *McGill Law Journal* 52 (2007): 460–1.

73. Christopher L. Eisgruber and Mariah Zeisberg, "Religious Freedom in Canada and the United States," *International Journal of Constitutional Law* 4, 2 (1 Apr. 2006): 244–68, https://doi.org/10.1093/icon/mol004. Several of the articles in this issue of the *International Journal of Constitutional Law* compare the interpretation of various rights and freedoms in Canada and the United States.

74. Mary Ann Glendon, *Rights Talk: The Impoverishment of Political Discourse* (New York: Free Press, 2008), 14.

8 Federalism

1. William S. Livingston, *Federalism and Constitutional Change* (Oxford: Clarendon Press, 1956), 2.

2. Ibid., 4.

3. In *Democracy in America*, Alexis de Tocqueville states that the cultural differences between communities separated by very short distances in Europe were far greater than any that he observed between the different states of the United States. As *The Federalist Papers* and the deliberations of the American founders at the Philadelphia convention of 1787 make clear, accommodating cultural diversity was not an important factor in the decision to choose a federal constitution.

4. An analysis of the theoretical and conceptual shortcomings of the sociological approach to federalism may be found in Michael Burgess, *Comparative Federalism: Theory and Practice* (New York: Routledge, 2006), 140–4.

5. Pierre Elliott Trudeau, "Federalism, Nationalism and Reason," in Trudeau, *Federalism and the French Canadians* (Toronto: Macmillan, 1968), 195.

6. Burgess, *Comparative Federalism*, 97.

7. Donald Smiley, *The Canadian Political Identity* (Toronto: Methuen, 1967), 30–1.

8. Peter Waite, *The Life and Times of Confederation 1864–1867* (Toronto: University of Toronto Press, 1962), 96.

9. The diversity of expectations was reflected in newspaper accounts of the Confederation agreement. See ibid., 111.

10. There are some exceptions. In *Citizens Insurance Co. v. Parsons; Queen Insurance Co. v. Parsons* (1881), the Judicial Committee of the Privy Council ruled that Ottawa's trade and commerce power did not take pre-eminence over enumerated provincial powers. In explaining why, Sir Montague Smith stated that the founders "could not have intended that the powers exclusively assigned to the provincial legislature should be absorbed in those given to the dominion parliament." Reproduced in Peter H. Russell, ed., *Leading Constitutional Decisions*, 4th edn (Ottawa: Carleton University Press, 1987), 35.

11. Ibid., 527, *Re Constitution of Canada* (1981).

12. Government of Quebec, *Quebecers: Our Way of Being Canadian*, June 2017, https://www.sqrc.gouv.qc.ca/documents/relations-canadiennes/politique-affirmation-en.pdf.

13. Karine Richer, "The Federal Spending Power," Library of Parliament, 2007, https://lop.parl.ca/content/lop/Research Publications/prb0736-e.htm; Hamish Telford, "The Federal Spending Power in Canada: Nation-Building or Nation-Destroying?" Institute for Intergovernmental Relations, Queen's University, Working Paper Series, 1999 (4), www.queensu.ca/iigr/WorkingPapers/Archive/1999/1999-4HamishTelford.pdf.

14. *Attorney General of Ontario v. Attorney General of Canada* (Local Prohibition case), 1896, in Russell, ed., *Leading Constitutional Decisions*, 59.

15. *Re Board of Commerce Act and Combines and Fair Prices Act*, 1919, 1922, ibid., 75.

16. *Co-operative Committee on Japanese Canadians v. A.G. Canada*, [1947] A.C. 87; *Reference re Validity of Wartime Leasehold Regulations*, [1950] S.C.R. 124.

17. *Attorney General of Canada v. Attorney General of Ontario* (Employment and Social Insurance Act Reference), 1937.

18. See Peter Russell, "The Anti-Inflation Case: The Anatomy of a Constitutional Decision," *Canadian Public Administration* 10, 4 (Winter 1977).

19. *Johannesson v. West St. Paul*, [1952] 1 S.C.R. 292, [1951] 4 D.L.R. 609; *Munro v. National Capital Commission*, [1966] S.C.R. 663, 57 D.L.R. (3d) 753; *R. v. Crown Zellerbach Can. Ltd.*, [1988] 1 S.C.R. 401.

20. Constitution Act, 1867, s. 91(2).

21. Ibid., s. 92(13).

22. Russell, ed., *Leading Constitutional Decisions*, 39.
23. *The King v. Eastern Terminal Elevator Co.*, [1925] S.C.R. 434; *A.G. of British Columbia v. A.G. of Canada* (Natural Products Marketing Reference), [1937] A.C. 377; *Canadian Federation of Agriculture v. A.G. of Quebec* (Margarine Reference), [1951], A.C. 179.
24. *Ontario Farm Products Marketing Reference*, [1957] S.C.R. 198; *R. v. Klassen* (1959), 20 D.L.R. (2nd) 406 (Manitoba Court of Appeal); *Caloil v. A.G. of Canada*, [1971] S.C.R. 543.
25. *Caloil*, 551.
26. Russell, ed., *Leading Constitutional Decisions*, 194.
27. Ibid., 199.
28. *General Motors of Canada Ltd. v. City National Leasing*, [1989] 1 S.C.R. 641.
29. *Reference Re Securities Act*, 2011 SCC 66.
30. Harvey Naglie, "Not Ready for Prime Time: Canada's Proposed New Securities Regulator," C.D. Howe Institute, Sept. 2017, https://www.cdhowe.org/sites/default/files/attachments/research_papers/mixed/Commentary_489.pdf.
31. Trudeau, "Federalism, Nationalism and Reason," 198.
32. Henri Bourassa, "The French Language and the Future of Our Race," in Ramsay Cook, ed., *French Canadian Nationalism* (Toronto: Macmillan, 1969), 141.
33. See Richard Simeon, *Federal–Provincial Diplomacy* (Toronto: University of Toronto Press, 1972), 115–22.
34. Government of Quebec, *Quebecers: Our Way of Being Canadian*.
35. Alan Cairns, "The Governments and Societies of Canadian Federalism," in Cairns, *Constitution, Government, and Society in Canada* (Toronto: McClelland & Stewart, 1988), 153–4.
36. Kendrick Lo, "Constitutional Turf Wars: A Quick Look at Federalism Issues in Securities Regulation," *CanLII Connects*, 28 Aug. 2017, http://canliiconnects.org/en/commentaires/46533.
37. See R.A. Young, Philippe Faucher, and André Blais, "The Concept of Province-Building: A Critique," *Canadian Journal of Political Science* 17, 4 (Dec. 1984): 785. Two of the major works using this concept are John Richards and Larry Pratt, *Prairie Capitalism* (Toronto: McClelland & Stewart, 1979), and Kenneth McRoberts, *Quebec: Social Change and Political Crisis*, 3rd edn (Toronto: Oxford University Press, 1993).
38. Matt Wilder and Michael Howlett, "Bringing the Provinces Back In: Re-evaluating the Relevance of Province-Building to Theories of Canadian Federalism and Multi-Level Governance," *Canadian Political Science Review* 9, 3 (2015–16): 28.
39. Ibid., 2.
40. Privy Council Office, Canadian Intergovernmental Conference Secretariat, http://www.scics.ca/en/publication/departmental-results-report-2017-18/.
41. Constitution Act, 1867, s. 118 (repealed).
42. Ibid., s. 111.
43. Based on data from Canada, Department of Finance, *Fiscal Reference Tables, 2017*, and Statistics Canada, *Canadian Economic Observer*, Historical Statistical Supplement 1994–95, Catalogue no. 11-210.
44. These transfers to persons include Employment Insurance, the Canada Pension Plan, and Old Age Security. All of these data may be found in Library of Parliament, *Distribution of Federal Revenues and Expenditures by Province*, 10 Jan. 2017, https://lop.parl.ca/Content/LOP/ResearchPublications/2017-01-e.html?cat=economics.
45. *Reference re Canada Assistance Plan (B.C.)*, [1991] 2 S.C.R. 525.
46. Howard Pawley, *Opinion Canada* 7, 10 (17 Mar. 2005).
47. Marcelin Joanis, "The Politics of Chequebook Federalism: Can Electoral Considerations Affect Federal–Provincial Transfers?" School of Public Policy, University of Calgary, *SPP Research Papers*, 7:25, Sept. 2014, p. 1, https://www.policyschool.ca/wp-content/uploads/2016/03/joanis-equalization.pdf.
48. Daniel Béland, André Lecours, Gregory P. Marchildon, Haizhen Mou, and M. Rose Olfert, *Fiscal Federalism and Equalization Policy in Canada* (Toronto: University of Toronto Press, 2017).
49. *Schneider v. The Queen*, [1982] 2 S.C.R. 112.
50. Marlisa Teidemann, "The Federal Role in Health and Health Care," 20 Oct. 2008, Parliament of Canada, www.parl.gc.ca/Content/LOP/ResearchPublications/prb0858-e.htm.
51. See www.cbc.ca/news/politics/story/2012/01/12/pol-cp-pbo-health-transfers-cut.html.
52. Office of the Parliament Budget Office, *Renewing the Canada Health Transfer: Implications for Federal and Provincial–Territorial Fiscal Sustainability*, 12 Oct. 2012, www.pbo-dpb.gc.ca/files/files/Publications/Renewing_CHT.pdf.
53. Office of the Parliamentary Budget Officer, *Fiscal Sustainability Report: Provincial–Territorial Health Care Cost Drivers*, 20 Nov. 2017, http://www.pbo-dpb.gc.ca/en/blog/news/FSR2017_Health-Care_drivers.
54. Trudeau, "Federalism, Nationalism and Reason," 195.
55. Amy Gutmann, ed., *Multiculturalism: Examining the Politics of Recognition* (Princeton, NJ: Princeton University Press, 1994); Charles Taylor, *Reconciling the Solitudes: Essays on Canadian Federalism and Nationalism* (Montreal and Kingston: McGill-Queen's University Press, 1993); James Tully, *Strange Multiplicity: Constitutionalism in an Age of Diversity* (Cambridge: Cambridge University Press, 1995).
56. Daniel J. Elazar, "Federalism," *International Encyclopedia of the Social Sciences* (New York: Macmillan, 1968), 356–61.
57. John Porter, *The Vertical Mosaic* (Toronto: University of Toronto Press, 1965), 385.
58. For example, Brooke Jeffrey, *Dismantling Canada: Stephen Harper's New Conservative Agenda* (Montreal and Kingston: McGill-Queen's University Press, 2010), ch. 9.
59. https://www.eiu.com/topic/democracy-index.

9   The Machinery of Government

1. "The Executive Government and Authority of and over Canada is hereby declared to continue and be vested in the Queen." Constitution Act, 1867, s. 9.
2. In the provinces, the Crown's authority is exercised through the lieutenant-governors, who are formally appointed by the Governor General to serve five-year terms. In fact, the selection is made by the Prime Minister with the advice, since 2012, of the Advisory Committee on Vice-Regal Appointments.

3. James R. Mallory, *The Structure of Canadian Government*, rev. edn (Toronto: Gage, 1984), 42–3.

4. Eric Grenier, "Why the Senate Is Unpredictable—And Its Independents Not So Independent," *CBC News*, 19 June 2017, https://www.cbc.ca/news/politics/grenier-senators-votes-1.4162949. See also Paul Thomas, "The 'New' Improved Senate," *Policy Options*, 25 Jan. 2018, http://policyoptions.irpp.org/magazines/january-2018/the-new-improved-senate/.

5. Thomas Hockin, *The Apex of Power: The Prime Minister and Political Leadership in Canada* (Toronto: Prentice-Hall, 1977).

6. Constitution Act, 1867, s. 54.

7. A good explanation of the annual budget cycle is found in Alex Smith, "A Guide to the Estimates," Library of Parliament, www.parl.gc.ca/Content/LOP/ResearchPublications/prb0925-e.htm.

8. Prime Minister's Office, "Cabinet Committee Mandate and Membership," https://pm.gc.ca/eng/cabinet-committee-mandate-and-membershiphttps://pm.gc.ca/eng/cabinet-committee-mandate-and-membership.

9. Donald Savoie, *Governing from the Centre: The Concentration of Power in Canadian Politics* (Toronto: University of Toronto Press, 1999), ch. 4. See also Savoie, *Power: Where Is It?* (Montreal and Kingston: McGill-Queen's University Press, 2010), ch. 6.

10. Donald Savoie, *Whatever Happened to the Music Teacher? How Government Decides and Why* (Montreal and Kingston: McGill-Queen's University Press, 2013).

11. Savoie, *Governing from the Centre*, 4.

12. Doug Owram, *The Government Generation: Canadian Intellectuals and the State 1900–1945* (Toronto: University of Toronto Press, 1986).

13. Savoie, *Governing from the Centre*, 109.

14. Alex Smith, "The Roles and Responsibilities of Central Agencies," Library of Parliament, 23 Apr. 2009, revised 22 Apr. 2015, https://lop.parl.ca/Content/LOP/ResearchPublications/2009-01-e.html?cat=government.

15. Donald Savoie, *Power: Where Is It?* (Montreal and Kingston: McGill-Queen's University Press, 2013), 204–5.

16. Brooke Jeffrey, "The Parliamentary Budget Officer Two Years Later: A Progress Report," *Canadian Parliamentary Review* (Winter 2010): 43.

17. Savoie, *Power: Where Is It?*, 208.

18. Smith, "The Roles and Responsibilities of Central Agencies," Library of Parliament, 23 Apr. 2009, revised 22 Apr. 2015, at: https://lop.parl.ca/Content/LOP/ResearchPublications/2009-01-e.html?cat=government.

19. Savoie, *Governing from the Centre*, 109.

20. Ibid., 121.

21. *The Hill Times*, "Top 100 Most Influential Powerful & Influential People in Government & Politics," published annually, https://www.hilltimes.com/2018/01/08/list-100-powerful-influential-people-federal-government-politics-2018/129936.

22. Donald J. Savoie, *Court Government and the Collapse of Accountability in Canada and the United Kingdom* (Toronto: University of Toronto Press, 2008).

23. Ibid., 195.

24. Ibid.

25. Smith, "The Roles and Responsibilities of Central Agencies," Library of Parliament, 2.

26. Savoie, *Governing from the Centre*, 101.

27. Some of these criticisms and a rebuttal to them may be found in Ian Brodie, "In Defense of Political Staff," *Canadian Parliamentary Review* 35, 3 (2012), http://www.revparl.ca/english/issue.asp?param=212&art=1493.

28. Alex Marland, "Strategic Management of Media Relations: Communications Centralization and Spin in the Government of Canada," *Canadian Public Policy* 43, 1 (2017), https://www.utpjournals.press/doi/full/10.3138/cpp.2016-037.

29. Donald Savoie, in *Governing from the Centre* and *Court Government and the Collapse of Accountability*, and Jeffrey Simpson in *The Friendly Dictatorship* (Toronto: McClelland & Stewart, 2001), make this argument.

30. Savoie, *Governing from the Centre*, 260.

31. Simpson, *The Friendly Dictatorship*, 248.

32. CBC, full text of interview with Peter Mansbridge, https://www.cbc.ca/news/politics/canada-election-2015-justin-trudeau-interview-peter-mansbridge-full-transcript-1.3219779.

33. Charlie Gillis, "The Case for Decentralizing Power in the PMO: In Conversation with Donald Savoie, author of What Is Government Good At?", *Maclean's*, 18 Sept. 2015, https://www.macleans.ca/politics/ottawa/the-case-for-decentralizing-power-in-the-pmo/.

34. Donald Savoie, "The Federal Cabinet: Revisiting Court Government in Canada," in Luc Bernier, Keith Brownsey, and Michael Howlett, eds, *Executive Styles in Canada: Cabinet Structures and Leadership Practices in Canadian Government* (Toronto: University of Toronto Press, 2005), 17–46.

35. Donald J. Savoie, "Power at the Apex: Executive Dominance," in Alain-G. Gagnon and James Bickerton, eds, *Canadian Politics*, 6th edn (Toronto: University of Toronto Press, 2014), 135–51.

36. David Pond, "The Impact of Parliamentary Officers on Canadian Parliamentary Democracy: A Study of the Commissioner of the Environment and Sustainable Development and the Environmental Commissioner of Ontario," Canadian Study of Parliament Group, p. 3, www.studyparliament.ca/English/pdf/PondPaperFinal-2010-e.pdf.

37. Supreme Court of Canada, *Reference Re Senate Reform* (2014), https://scc-csc.lexum.com/scc-csc/scc-csc/en/item/13614/index.do.

38. Savoie, *Governing from the Centre*, 91.

39. Ibid., 92.

40. Samara Centre for Democracy, *It's My Party: Parliamentary Dysfunction Reconsidered*, 2010, pp. 12–13, www2.samaracanada.com/downloads/ItsMyParty.pdf.

41. Andrea Ulrich, "A Question of Accountability: Is Question Period in Canada Working?" *Queen's Policy Review* 2, 2 (Fall 2011): 2.

42. David C. Docherty, *Mr. Smith Goes to Ottawa: Life in the House of Commons* (Vancouver: University of British Columbia Press, 1998), 234.

43. Samara Centre for Democracy, "MP Exit Interviews," 2010, www.samaracanada.com/What-We-Do/MP-Exit-Interviews.

44. CPAC (Cable Public Affairs Channel) is a required part of the basic package provided by virtually every cable or satellite service in Canada. Even ardent supporters of CPAC, including the nationalist Friends of Canadian Broadcasting, concede that its audience is "modest in comparison with other channels." That is probably an understatement. In any event, those who do watch CPAC programming on a regular basis are much more likely than most Canadians to be politically knowledgeable and active. Thus, CPAC's influence may be greater than its modest audience share might suggest.

45. Samara, *It's My Party*, 12.

46. Paul Thomas, "The 'New' Improved Senate," *Policy Options*, 25 Jan. 2018, http://policyoptions.irpp.org/magazines/january-2018/the-new-improved-senate/.

47. House of Commons, Compendium of Procedure, Auditor General of Canada, https://www.ourcommons.ca/About/Compendium/FinancialProcedures/c_d_auditorgeneralcanada-e.htm.

48. Lee Berthiaume, "Senate Report Shows the Growing Power of the Auditor General," *Ottawa Citizen*, 12 June 2015, https://ottawacitizen.com/news/politics/senate-report-shows-the-growing-power-of-the-auditor-general.

49. C.E.S. Franks, "Debate and Question Period," in *The Parliament of Canada* (Toronto: University of Toronto Press, 1987), 156.

50. Ulrich, "A Question of Accountability," 1–16.

51. Samara Centre for Democracy, *Samara's MP Exit Interviews: Volume II*, https://www.samaracanada.com/research/political-leadership/mp-exit-interviews/volume-ii/flip-the-script.

52. A full description of MPs' budgetary entitlements may be found at https://www.ourcommons.ca/MarleauMontpetit/DocumentViewer.aspx?Sec=Ch04&Seq=14&Language=E.

53. Docherty, *Mr. Smith Goes to Ottawa*, 204.

54. Ibid., 206.

55. See the Constitution Act, 1867, s. 99(1). This phrase, or reference to "misbehaviour," is found in the federal and provincial statutes that govern the removal of judges.

56. Allan McEachern, "Report to the Canadian Judicial Council of the Inquiry Committee Established Pursuant to Subsection 63(1) of the Judges Act at the Request of the Attorney General of Nova Scotia," 1990.

57. Judges of county courts and all higher courts are appointed by Ottawa. Provincial court judges are appointed by the provinces. See Figure 9.3 in the text.

58. Richard H. Sander, "Class in American Legal Education," *Denver University Law Review* 88, 4 (2011): 631–82.

59. Michael Ornstein, *The Changing Face of the Ontario Legal Profession*, Report to the Law Society of Upper Canada, Oct. 2004, rc.lsuc.on.ca/pdf/equity/ornsteinReport.pdf.

60. Glenn Kauth, "B.C. Legal Profession Far Behind Other Fields on Diversity," *Canadian Lawyer*, 9 July 2012, http://www.canadianlawyermag.com/legalfeeds/author/glenn-kauth/bc-legal-profession-far-behind-other-fields-on-diversity-4621/.

61. Law Society of Upper Canada, "Statistical Snapshot of Lawyers in Ontario," 2014, https://www.lsuc.on.ca/uploadedFiles/Equity_and_Diversity/Members2/TAB%207.3.1%20-%20Snapshot-Lawyers16_apr13.pdf.

62. Wendy Cukier, *Improving Representation in the Judiciary: A Diversity Strategy* (Toronto: Ryerson University, Diversity Institute, 27 June 2012). See also Kirk Makin, "Of 100 New Federally Appointed Judges 98 Are White, Globe Finds," *Globe and Mail*, 17 Apr. 2012.

63. See Marie-Claire Belleau and Rebecca Johnson, "Les femmes juges feront-elles véritablement une différence? Réflexions sur leur présence depuis vingt ans à la Cour suprême du Canada," *Canadian Journal of Women and the Law* 17, 1 (2005): 27–39.

64. Joel Bakan, *Just Words: Constitutional Rights and Social Wrongs* (Toronto: University of Toronto Press, 1997), 3.

65. Norman Ward, "The Formative Years of the House of Commons, 1867–1891," *Canadian Journal of Economics and Political Science* 18: 431–51.

66. Adam Przeworski, *Sustainable Democracy* (London: Cambridge University Press, 1995).

10 The Administrative State

1. These figures are from Jacques DesRoches, "The Evolution of the Organization of Federal Government in Canada," *Canadian Public Administration* 5, 4 (1962): 408–27.

2. A list of these organizations may be found at www.canada.gc.ca/depts/major/depind-eng.html.

3. Readers wanting a good overview of the structural characteristics and activities of these other levels of government will find this in Andrew Sancton, *Canadian Local Government* (Toronto: Oxford University Press, 2011), and Christopher Dunn, ed., *Provincial Politics, 3rd edn.* (Toronto: University of Toronto Press, 2015).

4. Henry David Thoreau, "A Yankee in Canada" (1850), p. 38, www.thoreau-online.org.

5. Susanna Moodie, *Roughing It in the Bush* (1852).

6. Royal Commission to Enquire into and Report on the Operation of the Civil Service Act and Kindred Legislation, *1908—Report of the Commissioners*, p. 13, www.psc-cfp.gc.ca/plcy-pltq/rprt/impart/chapter4-chapitre4-eng.htm.

7. Max Weber, *The Protestant Ethic and the Spirit of Capitalism* (New York: Charles Scribner, 1958 [1904–5]), 182.

8. *Fraser v. PSSRB*, [1985] 2 S.C.R. 455, para. 41.

9. *Osborne v. Canada (Treasury Board)*, [1991] 2 S.C.R. 69.

10. *Haydon v. Canada (Treasury Board)*, [2004] FC 749. See Office of the Commissioner for Federal Judicial Affairs Canada, reports.fja.gc.ca/eng/2005/2004fc749.html. Reproduced with the permission of the Minister of Public Works and Government Services Canada, 2011.

11. Quoted in Carl Berger, *The Writing of Canadian History*, 2nd edn (Toronto: University of Toronto Press, 1986), 24.

12. Public Service Alliance of Canada, "Expressing Political Opinions on Social Media: Your Rights," http://psacunion.ca/expressing-political-opinions-social-media-your.

13. Government of Canada, "Values and Ethics Code for the Public Sector," https://www.tbs-sct.gc.ca/pol/doc-eng.aspx?id=25049.

14. John Porter, *The Vertical Mosaic* (Toronto: University of Toronto Press, 1965), 611.

15. Ibid., 435.

16. Doug Owram, *The Government Generation: Canadian Intellectuals and the State, 1900–1945* (Toronto: University of Toronto Press, 1986).

17. All figures in this section are based on F.H. Leacy, ed., *Historical Statistics of Canada*, 2nd edn (Ottawa: Statistics Canada, 1983).

18. Lance W. Roberts et al. *Recent Social Trends in Canada: 1960–2000* (Montreal and Kingston: McGill-Queen's University Press, 2005), 441.

19. Jason Clemens and Milagros Palacios, *Prime Ministers and Government Spending: A Retrospective*, May 2017, Fraser Institute, https://www.fraserinstitute.org/sites/default/files/prime-ministers-and-government-spending-retrospective.pdf.

20. *Financial Post*, "The Trudeau Liberals Make History for the Highest per Person Spending outside a War or Recession," 24 May 2017, https://business.financialpost.com/opinion/the-trudeau-liberals-make-history-for-the-highest-per-person-spending-outside-a-war-or-recession.

21. David Held and Anthony McGrew, "Globalization," in Joel Krieger, ed., *The Oxford Companion to Politics of the World*, 2nd edn (New York: Oxford University Press, 2001), 324–7.

22. International Monetary Fund, http://data.imf.org/?sk=061a17b2-7e6a-4b58-9b17-042af9e59a3d&sId=1409151544549.

23. Livio di Matteo, "An Analysis of Public and Private Sector Employment Trends in Canada, 1990–2013," Fraser Institute, https://www.fraserinstitute.org/sites/default/files/analysis-of-public-and-private-sector-employment-trends-in-canada.pdf.

24. Philip Cross, *Estimating the True Size of Government: Adjusting for Regulation*, Macdonald-Laurier Institute, https://www.macdonaldlaurier.ca/files/pdf/MLIPCrossSizeOfGovernmentPaper0514.pdf.

25. Data from the National Survey of Nonprofit and Voluntary Organizations, "The Nonprofit and Voluntary Sector in Canada," *Imagine Canada*, 2006, http://www.imaginecanada.ca/sites/default/files/www/en/nsnvo/sector_in_canada_factsheet.pdf, and David Lasby and Emily Cordeaux, "Sector Monitor," *Imagine Canada*, Oct. 2016, http://sectorsource.ca/sites/default/files/resources/files/sector_monitor_public_policy_activity_2016.pdf.

26. This is an approximate figure because of the inconsistencies between provinces in the formal status of these organizations, contributing to difficulty in determining what is and is not a Crown corporation. These problems and a good analysis of the universe of Crown corporations in Canada may be found in Daria Crisan and Kenneth J. McKenzie, "Government-Owned Enterprises in Canada," University of Calgary, School of Public Policy, *SPP Research Paper* No. 6-8, Feb. 2013, 1–30.

27. David Mitchell and Ryan Conway, "From the Deputy Shuffle to the Deputy Churn: Keeping the Best and Brightest in Ottawa," *Policy Options*, May 2011.

28. James Lahey and Mark Goldenberg, *Assistant Deputy Ministers in the Canadian Public Service*, Centre on Public Management and Policy, University of Ottawa, 15 Nov. 2014, https://socialsciences.uottawa.ca/public-management-policy/sites/socialsciences.uottawa.ca.public-management-policy/files/report_adm_study_2014_e.pdf.

29. Donald Savoie, *Governing from the Centre: The Concentration of Power in Canadian Politics* (Toronto: University of Toronto Press, 1999), 248.

30. A good summary of the literature on representative bureaucracy may be found in Carol Agocs, "Representative Bureaucracy? Employment Equity in the Public Service of Canada," https://www.cpsa-acsp.ca/papers-2012/Agocs.pdf.

31. Porter, *The Vertical Mosaic*.

32. Employment Equity Act, S.C. 1995, c. 44, section 2.

33. Andrew Griffith, "Diversity in the Public Service's Executive Ranks," *Policy Options*, 16 Oct. 2017, http://policyoptions.irpp.org/magazines/october-2017/diversity-in-the-public-services-executive-ranks/.

34. The latest was Bill C-220, An Act to Amend the Financial Administration Act, introduced by NDP member Sheila Malcolmson in 2016. It would have established a minimum number of men and women on the boards of federal Crown corporations.

35. House of Commons, Hansard, 7 June 2017, http://www.ourcommons.ca/DocumentViewer/en/42-1/house/sitting-189/hansard.

36. Griffith, "Diversity in the Public Service's Executive Ranks."

37. Statutes of Canada, An Act to amend the Canada Business Corporations Act, the Canada Cooperatives Act, the Canada Not-for-profit Corporations Act and the Competition Act, 1 May 2018.

38. B.G. Peters, "Bureaucracy and Democracy," *Public Organization Review* 10 (2010): 209.

Part IV   Participation in Politics

11   Parties and Elections

1. Eugene A. Forsey, *How Canadians Govern Themselves,* 9th edn (Ottawa: Library of Parliament, 2016), 35–6, https://lop.parl.ca/About/Parliament/SenatorEugeneForsey/book/chapter_6-e.html#6_4.

2. Leon Epstein, *Political Parties in Western Democracies* (New Brunswick, NJ: Transaction Books, 1980 [1967]), 9.

3. In the 2015 general election, for example, the Animal Protection Party ran eight candidates and the Libertarian Party ran 72.

4. John Meisel and Matthew Mendelsohn, "Meteor? Phoenix? Chameleon? The Decline and Transformation of Party in Canada," in Hugh G. Thorburn and Alan Whitehorn, eds, *Party Politics in Canada*, 8th edn (Toronto: Pearson Education Canada, 2001).

5. This section on the early history of the Liberal and Conservative parties was co-authored by Professor A. Brian Tanguay, Wilfrid Laurier University.

6. George M. Hougham, "The Background and Development of National Parties," in Hugh G. Thorburn, ed., *Party Politics in Canada* (Toronto: Prentice-Hall, 1963), 13.

7. Escott Reid, "The Rise of National Parties in Canada," in Hugh G. Thorburn, ed., *Party Politics in Canada*, 5th edn

(Scarborough, ON: Prentice-Hall, 1985), 12. See also Norman Ward, *The Canadian House of Commons* (Toronto: University of Toronto Press, 1950), 157–62.

8. Stephen Wolinetz, "Patronage and Theories of Party Organization: Canada in Comparative Context," paper delivered at the ECPR Joint Workshop on Political Parties and Patronage, Nicosia, Cyprus Apr. 2006, 16–17.

9. André Siegfried, *The Race Question in Canada* (Toronto: McClelland & Stewart, Carleton Library Edition, 1966 [English translation first published 1907]), 114.

10. J.A. Corry, *Democratic Government and Politics*, 2nd edn (Toronto: University of Toronto Press, 1951), 22. Variations on this theme can be found in R.M. Dawson and Norman Ward, *The Government of Canada*, 5th edn (Toronto: University of Toronto Press, 1987), 430–3, and Hugh G. Thorburn, "Perspectives on the Structure and Dynamics of the Canadian Party System," in Thorburn and Alan Whitehorn, eds., *Party Politics in Canada*, 8th edn (Scarborough, ON: Pearson, 2001), 20–40.

11. R. Kenneth Carty and William Cross, "Political Parties and the Practice of Brokerage Politics," in John C. Courtney and David E. Smith, eds, *The Oxford Handbook of Canadian Politics* (New York: Oxford University Press, 2010), 193.

12. Janine Brodie and Jane Jenson, *Crisis, Challenge and Change: Party and Class Revisited* (Ottawa: Carleton University Press, 1988).

13. Janine Brodie and Jane Jenson, "Piercing the Smokescreen: Brokerage Parties and Class Politics," in Alain-G. Gagnon and A. Brian Tanguay, eds, *Canadian Parties in Transition: Discourse, Organization, and Representation* (Scarborough, ON: Nelson, 1989), 28.

14. Christopher Cochrane, "Left/Right Ideology and Canadian Politics," *Canadian Journal of Political Science* 43, 3 (Sept. 2010): 583–4.

15. Ibid., 584.

16. The references to King's "medium" and "ruins" may require an explanation. King occasionally consulted mediums and believed that via them he was able to communicate with his deceased mother and dog Pat. He also collected the ruins from various sites in Europe that may now be found on what was once his estate in Gatineau National Park, a short distance north of Ottawa.

17. Walter Young, *The Anatomy of a Party: The National CCF, 1932–61* (Toronto: University of Toronto Press, 1969), 298, 300.

18. Robert M. Campbell and Leslie A. Pal, *The Real Worlds of Canadian Politics* (Peterborough, ON: Broadview Press, 1989), 5.

19. Canadian Institute of Public Opinion, *The Gallup Report*, "Confidence in Political Parties Declines," 1 Feb. 1989, and "Government Increasingly Becoming Object of Scorn among Canadians," 20 Feb. 1991.

20. The Progressive Conservative Party of Canada and the Canadian/Reform Alliance Party merged in 2003 to become the Conservative Party of Canada. The Progressive Conservative Party and some of its most prominent figures,

particularly those such as former Prime Minister Joe Clark, a red Tory, had opposed this unite-the-right merger for several years.

21. Canada, Royal Commission on Electoral Reform and Party Financing, *Reforming Electoral Democracy*, vol. 7 (Ottawa: Supply and Services Canada, 1991), 221.

22. The huge vote swings that occurred in 1958 and 1984, when Quebecers massively shifted their support to the Progressive Conservative Party, proved not to be durable.

23. Richard Johnston, *The Canadian Party System: An Analytic History* (Vancouver: University of British Columbia Press, 2017), 92.

24. Richard Fidler, "The NDP, Poised for Power but to What Effect?" *Canadian Dimension*, 4 Mar. 2013, https://canadian dimension.com/articles/view/the-ndp-poised-for-power-but-to-what-effect.

25. I am not counting the 1921 election, a rather unusual exception to the pre-1935 party system that saw the Progressive Party run candidates and emerge as the second largest party in the House of Commons.

26. John C. Courtney, *Do Conventions Matter? Choosing National Party Leaders in Canada* (Montreal and Kingston: McGill-Queen's University Press, 1995), 61–4.

27. Ofer Kenig, "The Democratization of Party Leaders' Selection Methods: Canada in Comparative Perspective," p. 11: https://www.cpsa-acsp.ca/papers-2009/Kenig.pdf.

28. Paul E.J. Thomas, "Measuring the Effectiveness of a Minority Parliament," *Canadian Parliamentary Review*, Spring 2007, http://revparl.ca/30/1/30n1_07e_PaulE.J.Thomas.pdf.

29. Josep Colomer, "The More Parties, the Greater Policy Stability," *Journal of European Political Science* 11 (2012): 229. https://doi.org/10.1057/eps.2011.34.

30. *CBC News*, "Liberal Fears of Proportional Representation and a Referendum Killed Trudeau's Reform Promise," 3 Feb. 2017, https://www.cbc.ca/news/politics/trudeau-reform-promise-referendum-1.3963533.

31. Alan Cairns, "The Electoral System and the Party System in Canada, 1921–1965," *Canadian Journal of Political Science* 1, 1 (Mar. 1968): 55–80.

32. William P. Irvine, *Does Canada Need a New Electoral System?* (Kingston, ON: Institute of Intergovernmental Relations, Queen's University, 1979), 14.

33. Jennifer L. Merolla and Laura B. Stephenson, "Strategic Voting in Canada: A Cross Time Analysis," *Electoral Studies* 26 (2007): 235–46.

34. André Blais, Elisabeth Gidengil, Richard Nadeau, and Neil Nevitte. "Measuring Party Identification: Britain, Canada, and the United States," *Political Behavior* 23, 1 (2001): 5–22.

35. Éric Grenier, "Change to Preferential Ballot Would Benefit Liberals," CBC News, 26 Nov. 2015, https://www.cbc.ca/news/politics/grenier-preferential-ballot-1.3332566.

36. André Blais, Elisabeth Gidengil, Patrick Fournier, Neil Nevitte, Joanna Everitt, and Jiyoon Kim, "Political Judgments, Perceptions of Facts, and Partisan Effects," *Electoral Studies* 29 (2010): 8.

37. Elisabeth Gidengil, "An Overview of the Social Dimension of Vote Choice," in Mebs Kanji, Antoine Bilodeau, and

Thomas J. Scotto, eds, *The Canadian Election Studies: Assessing Four Decades of Influence* (Vancouver: University of British Columbia Press, 2012), 104.

38. Sarah Wilkins-Laflamme, "The Changing Religious Cleavage in Canadians' Voting Behaviour," *Canadian Journal of Political Science* 49, 3 (Sept. 2016): 508.
39. Ibid., 510.
40. Ibid., 513.
41. Pieter Bevelander and Ravi Pendakur, "Social Capital and Voting Participation of Immigrants and Minorities in Canada," *Ethnic and Racial Studies* 32, 8 (2009): 1406–30.
42. Elisabeth Gidengil, André Blais, Richard Nadeau, and Neil Nevitte, "Women to the Left? Gender Differences in Political Beliefs and Policy Preferences," in M. Tremblay and L. Trimble eds, *Gender and Elections in Canada* (Toronto: Oxford University Press, 2001), 140–59.
43. J. Matthew Wilson and Michael Lusztig, "The Spouse in the House: What Explains the Marriage Gap in Canada?" *Canadian Journal of Political Science* 37, 4 (2004): 979–96.
44. Zack Taylor, Phil Triadafilopoulos, and Christopher Cochrane, "On the Backs of Immigrants? Conservative Politics and New Canadian Voters," paper presented at the annual meeting of the Canadian Political Science Association, Edmonton, 2012, 11, Table 2.
45. Nelson Wiseman observes that Green Party leader Elizabeth May spent no time whatsoever in the Prairie provinces or in Newfoundland and Labrador during the 2015 election campaign. See his piece, "Regional Sensibilities and Regional Voting," in Alex Marland and Thierry Giasson, eds, *Canadian Election Analysis, Communication, Strategy, and Democracy* (Vancouver: University of British Columbia Press, 2015), 98–99, http://www.ubcpress.ca/asset/1712/election-analysis2015-final-v3-web-copy.pdf.
46. See Figure 2 in Andre Barnes and Erin Virgint, "Youth Voter Turnout in Canada: 1. Trends and Issues," Parliament of Canada, Legal and Legislative Affairs Division, 7 Apr. 2010, revised 9 Aug. 2013, http://www.lop.parl.gc.ca/content/lop/researchpublications/2010-19-e.htm#a5.
47. Elections Canada, "Voter Turnout by Age Group," http://www.elections.ca/content.aspx?section=res&dir=rec/eval/pes2015/vtsa&document=table1&lang=e.
48. André Blais et al., "Where Does Turnout Decline Come From?" *European Journal of Political Research* 43 (2004): 221–2.
49. Ibid., 224.
50. Ibid., 225.
51. Ibid., 227.
52. Henry Milner, *Civic Literacy: How Informed Citizens Make Democracy Work* (Boston: Tufts University Press, 2002); Milner, *The Informed Political Participation of Young Canadians and Americans*, May 2008, www.civicyouth.org/PopUps/WorkingPapers/WP60Milner.pdf.
52. Martin Turcotte, "Civic Engagement and Political Participation in Canada," Statistics Canada, https://www150.statcan.gc.ca/n1/pub/89-652-x/89-652-x2015006-eng.htm#a22.
54. Ibid., Table 7. These non-electoral forms of civic engagement are discussed in Paul Howe, *Citizens Adrift: The Democratic*

Disengagement of Young Canadians (Vancouver: University of British Columbia Press, 2010), ch. 2.
55. Brenda O'Neill, "Indifferent or Just Different? The Political and Civic Engagement of Young People in Canada," *CPRN Research Report*, June 2007, 20, http://citeseerx.ist.psu.edu/viewdoc/download?doi=10.1.1.516.3596&rep=rep1&type=pdf.
56. See Khayyam Paltiel, *Political Party Financing in Canada* (Toronto: McGraw-Hill Ryerson, 1970), 19–75.
57. These services are discussed by Reg Whitaker, *The Government Party: Organizing and Financing the Liberal Party of Canada, 1930–1958* (Toronto: University of Toronto Press, 1977), 204–6, 216–63.
58. According to Khayyam Paltiel, "For the 1972 [national] election half the funds raised in Ontario by the Liberal Party were collected personally by the chairman of the party's Treasury Committee from 90 large corporations." Paltiel, "Campaign Financing in Canada and Its Reform," in Howard R. Penniman, ed., *Canada at the Polls: The General Election of 1974* (Washington: American Enterprise Institute, 1975), 182.
59. See A.B. Stevenson, *Canadian Election Reform: Dialogue on Issues and Effects* (Toronto: Ontario Commission on Election Contributions and Expenses, 1982); Whitaker, *The Government Party.*
60. Candidates are now eligible to be reimbursed for 60 per cent of their campaign expenses if they receive at least 10 per cent of the vote.
61. The number of hours per network and the division of time between the parties are determined by the CRTC. In deciding how much time each party receives the CRTC is guided by a formula weighted according to each party's share of the seats and popular vote in the previous election. See CRTC, "Election Campaigns and Political Advertising," https://crtc.gc.ca/eng/television/publicit/pol.htm.
62. See Larry Sabato, *The Rise of Political Consultants* (New York: Basic Books, 1981), especially ch. 4.
63. Dalton Camp, *Points of Departure* (Toronto: Deneau and Greenberg, 1979), 91.
64. Zoë Knowles and Fraser Lockerbie, "Part 1: New Political Advertising Rules under the Elections Modernization Act," Sussex Strategy Group, 1 Aug. 2019, http://sussex-strategy.com/posts/part-1-new-political-advertising-rules-under-the-elections-modernization-act.
65. Environics Institute, "Confidence in Democracy and the Political System," *AmericasBarometer 2012*, p. 27, https://www.environicsinstitute.org/docs/default-source/project-documents/americasbarometer-2012/confidence-in-democracy-and-the-political-system.pdf?sfvrsn=cb010ff5.

12 Interest Groups

1. V.O. Key, *Politics, Parties, and Pressure Groups*, 4th edn (New York, 1958), 23.
2. James Madison, *The Federalist Papers*, no. 10 (New York: New American Library, 1961 [1787]).
3. *Associations Canada* (Toronto: Grey House Publishing, 2018).
4. Estimates based on ibid.

5. E.E. Schattschneider, *The Semi-Sovereign People* (New York: Holt, Rinehart and Winston, 1960), 35.

6. Ibid.

7. Ibid.

8. Mancur Olson Jr, *The Logic of Collective Action: Public Goods and the Theory of Groups* (Cambridge, MA: Harvard University Press, 1965).

9. Éric Montpetit, "The Deliberative and Adversarial Attitudes of Interest Groups,"" in John C. Courtney and David E. Smith, eds, *The Oxford Handbook of Canadian Politics* (New York: Oxford University Press, 2010), 247.

10. Charles E. Lindblom, *Politics and Markets* (New York: Basic Books, 1977), especially chs 13–16.

11. Jason Markusoff, "Alberta's Handful of Anti-Pipeline Protesters Wage a Lonely War," *Maclean's*, 26 May 2018, https://www.macleans.ca/news/canada/albertas-handful-of-anti-pipeline-protestors-wage-a-lonely-war/.

12. Dean Bennett, "Rachel Notley Pulls Alberta out of Federal Climate Plan after Pipeline Decision," *Financial Post*, 30 August 2018, https://business.financialpost.com/pmn/business-pmn/cp-newsalert-notley-pulling-alberta-out-of-federal-climate-plan-2.

13. Michael Bliss, *Northern Enterprise: Five Centuries of Canadian Business* (Toronto: McClelland & Stewart, 1987), 578.

14. Geoffrey Hale, *Uneasy Partnership: The Politics of Business and Government in Canada*, 2nd edn (Toronto: University of Toronto Press, 2018), 94.

15. David Vogel, *Fluctuating Fortunes: The Political Power of Business in America* (New York: Basic Books, 1989), 193.

16. David Vogel, *Kindred Strangers: The Uneasy Relationship between Politics and Business in America* (Princeton, NJ: Princeton University Press, 1996).

17. Neil J. Mitchell, *The Conspicuous Corporation: Business, Public Policy, and Representative Democracy* (Ann Arbor: University of Michigan Press, 1997).

18. Examples of this neo-institutional approach include, among others, Michael M. Atkinson and William D. Coleman, "Strong States and Weak States: Sectoral Policy Networks in Advanced Capitalist Economies," *British Journal of Political Science* 19 (1989): 47–67; Michael M. Atkinson and William D. Coleman, *The State, Business, and Industrial Change in Canada* (Toronto: University of Toronto Press, 1989); Leslie Pal, *Interests of State: The Politics of Language, Multiculturalism, and Feminism in Canada* (Montreal and Kingston: McGill-Queen's University Press, 1993).

19. Earl Latham, *The Group Basis of Politics* (New York: Octagon Books, 1965), 35.

20. Arthur F. Bentley, *The Process of Government* (Evanston, Ill., 1935), 208.

21. David B. Truman, *The Governmental Process* (New York: Alfred Knopf, 1951); Robert Dahl, *Who Governs?* (New Haven, CT: Yale University Press, 1961); John Kenneth Galbraith, *American Capitalism: The Concept of Countervailing Power* (Boston: Houghton Mifflin, 1952).

22. Theodore Lowi, *The End of Liberalism* (New York: W.W. Norton, 1969).

23. P. Bachrach and M. Baratz, "Two Faces of Power," *American Political Science Review* 56, 4 (1962): 948.

24. This is true of Nicos Poulantzas, *Political Power and Social Classes* (London: New Left Books, 1973); Fred Block, *Revising State Theory* (Philadelphia: Temple University Press, 1987); Bob Jessop, *The Capitalist State* (New York: New York University Press, 1982). Interest groups are given some passing mention in James O'Connor, *The Fiscal Crisis of the State* (New York: St Martin's Press, 1973); Claus Offe, *Contradictions of the Welfare State* (Cambridge, MA: MIT Press, 1984). Among the leading Marxist intellectuals of his generation, it is perhaps fair to say that only Ralph Miliband had very much to say on interest groups; see Miliband, *The State in Capitalist Society* (London: Quartet Books, 1973).

25. The term "political economy" includes three separate streams or meanings today: the Canadian tradition of political economy which, after Harold Innis's early work, moved squarely to the left; the political economy in the economics and organization theory fields, whose major early figures were Anthony Downs and James Buchanan, with a pro-market orientation; and the political economy work among those in international relations, whose focus is globalization and its discontents and whose orientation is more often than not on the left.

26. *Studies in Political Economy*, https://www.tandfonline.com/action/journalInformation?show=aimsScope&journalCode=rsor20&.

27. Miriam Smith, "Introduction: Theories of Group and Movement," *Group Politics and Social Movements in Canada*, 2nd edn (Toronto: University of Toronto Press, 2014), xiv.

28. Peter John, *Analysing Public Policy*, 2nd edn (New York: Routledge, 2012), 92.

29. William D. Coleman and Grace Skogstad, "Introduction," in Coleman and Skogstad, eds, *Policy Communities and Public Policy in Canada* (Toronto: Copp Clark Pitman, 1990), 2.

30. Some of the classics of this literature include Anthony Downs, *An Economic Theory of Democracy* (New York: Harper and Row, 1957); Olson, *The Logic of Collective Action*; James M. Buchanan and Gordon Tullock, *The Calculus of Consent* (Ann Arbor: University of Michigan Press, 1965); Anthony Downs, *Inside Bureaucracy* (Boston: Little, Brown and Company, 1967).

31. Michael Atkinson, "How Do Institutions Constrain Policy?" paper delivered at the conference "Governing Canada: Political Institutions and Public Policy," McMaster University, 25 Oct. 1991, 8. A good introduction to this approach and its application to politics is provided by Queen's University economist Dan Usher in *Political Economy* (London: Blackwell, 2003).

32. Alan Cairns, "The Governments and Societies of Canadian Federalism," *Canadian Journal of Political Science* 10, 4 (1977): 695–725.

33. These works include James G. March and Herbert Simon, *Organizations* (New York: John Wiley, 1958); James G. March, *Decisions and Organizations* (Oxford: Blackwell, 1988); James G. March and Johan P. Olsen, "The New Institutionalism: Organizational Factors in Political Life," *American Political Science Review* 78 (1984): 734–49; James G. March and Johan P. Olsen, *Rediscovering Institutions: The Organizational Basis of Politics* (New York: Free Press, 1989).

34. Charles Perrow, *Complex Organizations: A Critical Essay*, 3rd edn (New York: Random House, 1986), 260.

35. James Q. Wilson, *Political Organizations* (New York: Basic Books, 1973), 3–4.

36. These definitions are the ones used in Coleman and Skogstad, "Introduction." They are not, however, agreed upon by everyone who mines this vein.

37. Coleman and Skogstad, "Introduction," 25.

38. Figure 12.1 is a generic diagram of how a policy community may be represented. For an example of how this may be applied to a specific case, see Stephen Brooks, "Uncertain Embrace: The Rise and Fall of Canadian Studies Abroad as a Tool of Foreign Policy," in Brooks, ed., *Promoting Canadian Studies Abroad: Soft Power and Cultural Diplomacy* (New York: Palgrave Macmillan, 2018), 26, Figure 1.1.

39. Wolfgang Streeck and Philippe C. Schmitter, "Community, Market, State—And Associations? The Prospective Contribution of Interest Governance to Social Order," *European Sociological Review* 1, 2 (Sept. 1985): 119–38.

40. Coleman and Skogstad, "Introduction," 23.

41. J.L. Granatstein, *The Ottawa Men* (Toronto: Oxford University Press, 1982).

42. O. Mary Hill, *Canada's Salesman to the World: The Department of Trade and Commerce, 1892–1939* (Montreal and Kingston: McGill-Queen's University Press, 1977), 172.

43. Pal, *Interests of State*, ch. 6.

44. A. Paul Pross, *Group Politics and Public Policy* (Toronto: University of Toronto Press, 1986), 68–9.

45. Voices-voix, "Women's Legal Education and Action Fund," 15 Nov. 2012, voices-voix.ca/en/facts/profile/womens-legal-education-and-action-fund-leaf.

46. See, for example, Ian Brodie, *Friends of the Court: The Privileging of Interest Group Litigants in Canada* (Albany: State University of New York Press, 2012); F. Leslie Seidle, ed., *Equity & Community: The Charter, Interest Advocacy and Representation* (Montreal: Institute for Research on Public Policy, 1993).

47. Pross, *Group Politics and Public Policy*, 114–16.

48. Larry Pynn, "Recession Hits Environmental Organizations as Funding Slides," *Vancouver Sun*, 18 Dec. 2008, www.sierraclub.bc.ca/.../recession-hits-environmental-organizations-as-funding-slides.

49. John W. Kingdon, *Agendas, Alternatives, and Public Policies* (Boston: Little, Brown and Company, 1984), 54–7.

50. See the data provided in the various waves of the World Values Survey, http://www.worldvaluessurvey.org/WVSOnline.jsp.

51. Michael Woods, "Assembly of First Nations Head Shawn Atleo Calls for Aboriginal Unity as Challenge to Authority Mounts," *Postmedia News*, 16 July 2013, accessed online.

52. Olson, *The Logic of Collective Action*.

53. Wilson, *Political Organizations*, 36–8.

54. Schattschneider, *The Semi-Sovereign People*, 37.

55. Ibid., 38.

56. Timothy Werner and Graham Wilson, "Business Representation in Washington, DC," in David Coen et al., *The Oxford Handbook of Business and Government* (New York: Oxford University Press, 2010), 271

57. See Cristin Schmitz, "No Changes Planned for Two-Way Costs Rule Despite Pleas from Groups," *The Lawyer's Daily*, 24 Nov. 2016, https://www.thelawyersdaily.ca/articles/3646/no-changes-planned-for-two-way-costs-rule-despite-pleas-from-groups.

58. In a class action case brought against Inco, a Canadian nickel mining company, the Ontario Court of Appeals awarded the company $1.7 million in costs, to be paid by the Law Foundation of Ontario, which had financed the plaintiffs. Inco claimed that its total legal costs amounted to $5.3 million: http://www.cela.ca/blog/2014-06-16/dollars-and-sense-who-pays-costs-public-interest-cases.

59. Gordon Hamilton, "Enbridge Launches Multimillion-Dollar Ad Campaign to Combat B.C. Pipeline Opposition," *Vancouver Sun*, 30 May 2012, http://www.vancouversun.com/business/2035/Enbridge+launches+multimillion+dollar+campaign+combat+pipeline+opposition/6698138/story.html.

60. Mike Gaworecki and M. Fernanda Tomaselli, "Do Environmental Advocacy Campaigns Drive Successful Forest Conservation?" 29 Mar. 2018, part 6 in a series entitled Conservation Effectiveness, carried out for Mongabay: https://news.mongabay.com/2018/03/do-environmental-advocacy-campaigns-drive-successful-forest-conservation/.

61. Wharton School of Business, "To Boycott or Not: The Consequences of a Protest," University of Pennsylvania, 9 June 2010, http://knowledge.wharton.upenn.edu/article/to-boycott-or-not-the-consequences-of-a-protest/.

62. See, for example, Kenneth Kollman, *Outside Lobbying: Public Opinion and Interest Group Strategies* (Princeton, NJ: Princeton University Press, 1998).

63. Robert Benzie, "Canadians Rank Politicians among Least Trusted Professionals: Poll," *Toronto Star*, 5 Nov. 2014, https://www.thestar.com/news/queenspark/2014/11/05/canadians_rank_politicians_among_least_trusted_professionals_poll.html.

64. McCarthy Tétrault, "Lobbying in Canada after *R. v. Carson*," 28 Mar. 2018, https://www.mccarthy.ca/en/insights/articles/lobbying-canada-after-r-v-carson.

65. Peter Mazereeuw, "Canadian Lobbying Goes Digital," *The Hill Times*, 28 June 2017, https://www.hilltimes.com/2017/06/28/canadian-lobbying-goes-digital/111828.

66. All of these data may be found under "Lobbying Statistics" at the website of the Office of the Commissioner of Lobbying of Canada, ocl-cal.gc.ca.

13 The Media

1. Neil Postman, *Amusing Ourselves to Death: Public Discourse in the Age of Show Business* (New York: Penguin, 1985).

2. Walter Lippmann, *Public Opinion* (New York: Harcourt, Brace and Company, 1922), 13.

3. Thomas Carlyle, *On Heroes and Hero-Worship in History*, "Lecture V. The Hero as a Man of Letters: Johnson, Rousseau, Burns," 19 May 1840, www.gutenberg.org/files/1091/1091-h/1091-h.htm#link2H_4_0006.

4. GroupM, *The State of Digital*, Apr. 2018, http://eaca.eu/wp-content/uploads/2018/05/State-of-Digital_2018_single_pgs.pdf.

5. Numeris, "TV Weekly Top 30," http://en.numeris.ca/media-and-events/tv-weekly-top-30.

6. CRTC, *Communications Monitoring Report 2017*, 160, Table 4.2.14, based on data provided by Numeris: https://crtc.gc.ca/eng/publications/reports/PolicyMonitoring/2017/cmr2017.pdf.

7. A 2016 survey that asked Canadians their reasons for watching television found that entertainment and relaxation were by far the two reasons most commonly cited, news and current affairs coming in a distant third. See Reality Mine, "Touch Points and Media Engagement in French Quebec—10 Important Things to Know," Nov. 2016, slide 10, https://static1.squarespace.com/static/5810b3479f74561bfcd6361b/t/583cc21bf7e0ab6135203442/1480376905777/November+2+2016+Quebec+Presentation.pdf.

8. The data reported in this and the next three paragraphs may be found in Public Policy Forum, *The Shattered Mirror: News, Democracy and Trust in the Digital Age*, Ottawa, Jan. 2017, https://shatteredmirror.ca/wp-content/uploads/theShatteredMirror.pdf.

9. Quoted ibid., 20.

10. https://scc-csc.lexum.com/scc-csc/scc-csc/en/item/7837/index.do.

11. Quoted in Anthony King, "Citizen Journalism: A Phenomenon That Is Here to Stay," *EuroScientist*, 13 July 2017, https://www.euroscientist.com/citizen-journalism-phenomenon-stay/.

12. Pew Research Center, 11 Jan. 2018, http://www.pewglobal.org/2018/01/11/detailed-tables-global-media-habits/.

13. Ken Goldstein, "Canada's Digital Divides," Communications Management Inc., 20 Aug. 2015, 11, http://media-cmi.com/downloads/CMI_Discussion_Paper_Digital_Divides_082015.pdf.

14. Pamela J. Shoemaker, *Gatekeeping* (Newbury Park, CA: Sage, 1991), 1.

15. http://ocean.otr.usm.edu/~w304644/ch5.html#N_76_.

16. Stuart N. Soroka, "The Gatekeeping Function: Distributions of Information in Media and the Real World," *Journal of Politics* 74, 2 (Apr. 2012): 516.

17. S. Robert Lichter, "Theories of Media Bias," in Kate Kenski and Kathleen Hall Jamieson, eds, *The Oxford Handbook of Political Communication* (New York: Oxford University Press, 2017).

18. Pew Research Center, 11 Jan. 2018, http://www.pewglobal.org/2018/01/11/publics-around-the-world-follow-national-and-local-news-more-closely-than-international/.

19. J-Source, "Politico Pro Tests Canadian Market with New Newsletter Offering," 28 Sept. 2018, http://j-source.ca/article/politico-pro-tests-canadian-market-with-new-newsletter-offering/.

20. Public Policy Forum, "Mind the Gaps: Quantifying the Decline of News Coverage in Canada," 25 Sept. 2018, https://www.ppforum.ca/publications/mind-the-gaps/.

21. William Watson, "Let's Not Subsidize Journalism," Fraser Institute, 16 Feb. 2018, https://www.fraserinstitute.org/blogs/let-s-not-subsidize-journalism.

22. Abacus Data, "Newspapers in Peril? . . . Canadians Unworried," 16 June 2017, http://abacusdata.ca/newspapers-in-peril-canadians-unworried/.

23. Quoted in Laura Payton, "One-third of Canadians Watch TV Online, CRTC Says," *CBC News*, 26 Sept. 2013, accessed online.

24. Peter Menzies, "Will the CRTC Ever Join the 21st Century?" *Globe and Mail*, 4 June 2018, https://www.theglobeandmail.com/business/commentary/article-will-the-crtc-ever-join-the-21st-century/.

25. Steven Globerman, "Netflix Becomes More Canadian—But You'll Pay for It," Fraser Institute, 5 Oct. 2017, https://www.fraserinstitute.org/blogs/netflix-becomes-more-canadian-but-you-ll-pay-for-it.

26. Stanley Rothman and S. Robert Lichter, "Personality, Ideology and World View: A Comparison of Media and Business Elites," *British Journal of Political Science* 15, 1 (1984): 36, 46.

27. Lars Willnat and David H. Weaver. *The American Journalist in the Digital Age: Key Findings* (Bloomington, IN: School of Journalism, Indiana University, 2014), 11, http://archive.news.indiana.edu/releases/iu/2014/05/2013-american-journalist-key-findings.pdf.

28. Lydia Miljan and Barry Cooper, *Hidden Agendas: How the Beliefs of Canadian Journalists Influence the News* (Vancouver: University of British Columbia Press, 2003). Also see Barry Cooper, *Sins of Omission: Shaping the News at CBC TV* (Toronto: University of Toronto Press, 1994).

29. Marsha Barber and Ann Rauhala, "The Canadian News Directors Study: Demographics and Political Leanings of Television Decision-Makers," *Canadian Journal of Communication* 30, 2 (2005), https://www.cjc-online.ca/index.php/journal/article/view/1543/1685.

30. Neil Nevitte, André Blais, Elisabeth Gidengil, and Richard Nadeau, *Unsteady State: The 1997 Canadian Federal Election* (Toronto: Oxford University Press, 1999).

31. Observatory on Media and Public Policy, *2006 Federal Election Newspaper Content Analysis*, McGill University, 2006, www.ompp.mcgill.ca.

32. Ken Boessenkool, "What Can a Little Birdie Tell Us about the Parliamentary Press Gallery?" *Policy Options*, 4 May 2015, http://policyoptions.irpp.org/magazines/is-it-the-best-of-times-or-the-worst/boessenkool/.

33. Heather Rollwagen, Ivor Shapiro, Lindsay Fitzgerald, Geneviève Bonin, and Lauriane Tremblay, "Journalists in Canada," Worlds of Journalism Study, 18 Oct. 2016, https://epub.ub.uni-muenchen.de/29701/1/Rollwagen_Shapiro_Fitzgerald_Bonin_Tremblay_Country_report_Canada.pdf.

34. Surveys carried out by Angus Reid on religion in 2015 and the police in 2016, and by Forum Research on the military in 2014, provide the basis for the comparison to the Ryerson/Ottawa 2016 poll of journalists.

35. Amy Mitchell et al., "Political Polarization and Media Habits," Pew Research Center, 2014, http://www.journalism.org/2014/10/21/political-polarization-media-habits/.

36. Richard Fletcher, "Polarisation in the News Media," Reuters Institute for the Study of Journalism, University of Oxford, 2017, http://www.digitalnewsreport.org/survey/2017/polarisation-in-the-news-media-2017/.

37. Charles Taylor, *Multiculturalism and the Politics of Recognition* (Princeton, NJ: Princeton University Press, 1992), 25.

38. Arthur Siegel, *A Content Analysis: The Canadian Broadcasting Corporation—Similarities and Differences of French and English News.* Background research paper for the Committee of Inquiry into the National Broadcasting Service (Ottawa: CRTC, 1977), 42.

39. David Taras, "The Mass Media and Political Crisis: Reporting Canada's Constitutional Struggles," *Canadian Journal of Communications* 18, 2 (1993), https://www.cjc-online.ca/index .php/journal/article/view/741/647%20Taras,%20coverage%20 of%20Meech%20Lake%20and%20Charlottetown.

40. Kyle Conway, *Everyone Says No: Public Service Broadcasting and the Failure of Translation* (Montreal and Kingston: McGill-Queen's University Press, 2011).

41. Thomas Jefferson, Letter to Charles Yancey, 6 Jan. 1816, http://tjrs.monticello.org/letter/327.

42. Quoted in Tim Knight, "Watching the Watchdog: Why Citizen Bloggers Aren't Journalists," *HuffPost Canada*, 23 Jan. 2014, https://www.huffingtonpost.ca/tim-knight/citizen-journalists_b_4045334.html.

43. IPSOS, "Trust and Confidence in News Sources," 25 May 2018, https://www.ipsos.com/en-ca/news-polls/RTNDA-Trust-and-Confidence-in-News-Sources-May-25-2018.

44. Insights West, "Nurses, Doctors and Scientists Are Canada's Most Respected Professionals," https://insightswest.com/news/nurses-doctors-and-scientists-are-canadas-most-respected-professionals/.

45. IPSOS-Mori, 29 Nov. 2017, https://www.ipsos.com/ipsos-mori/en-uk/politicians-remain-least-trusted-profession-britain.

46. Gallup, "Americans' Trust in Mass Media Sinks to New Low," 14 Sept. 2016, https://news.gallup.com/poll/195542/americans-trust-mass-media-sinks-new-low.aspx.

47. *Edelman Trust Barometer 2019: Canada*, https://www.edelman .ca/sites/default/files/edelman-trust/2019-Canadian-Trust-Barometer-Edelman.pdf.

48. See Douglas Fetherling, *The Rise of the Canadian Newspaper* (Toronto: Oxford University Press, 1949); W.H. Kesterton, *A History of Journalism in Canada* (Toronto: McClelland and Stewart, 1967).

49. Senate of Canada, *The Report of the Special Senate Committee on Mass Media*, Vol. 1, 67.

50. Ibid., *71;* emphasis in original.

51. Government of Canada, *Report of the Royal Commission on Newspapers,* 1980, 177.

52. Ibid.

53. Aldous Huxley, *Brave New World Revisited* (New York: Harper & Brothers, 1958), 44.

54. *The Economist*, "How Are Social Media Changing Democracy? *The Economist* Explains," London, online edition, 28 Mar. 2016.

55. Postman, *Amusing Ourselves to Death*, 86; emphasis added.

56. Hossein Derakhshan, "Television Has Won," http://www .niemanlab.org/2017/12/television-has-won/.

57. Research Co., "Few Canadians Willing to Pay as News Content Shifts Online," 2 Aug. 2018, https://researchco .ca/2018/08/02/content-shifts-online/.

58. Canadian Association of Journalists, "Ethics Guidelines," last revised June 2011, http://caj.ca/content.php?page=ethics-guidelines.

Part V Contemporary Issues in Canadian Political Life

14 Language Politics

1. CTV Montreal, "Quebec Poll Shows CAQ Maintaining Lead over Liberals," 3 May 2018, https://montreal.ctvnews.ca/quebec-poll-shows-caq-maintaining-lead-over-liberals-1.3913170.

2. Hugh MacLennan, *Two Solitudes* (Toronto: New Canadian Library, 2008 [1945]).

3. Information on mother tongue was first collected with the census of 1931. Before then, the census only asked about ethnic origin. Demographer Jacques Henripin suggests that French ethnic origin was probably a good surrogate measure for language group at the time of Confederation.

4. In fact, Jacques Henripin predicted that by 2001, over 40 per cent of Montrealers would be anglophone. This prediction was based on census data from 1971. See *L'Immigration et le déséquilibre linguistique* (Ottawa: Main d'oeuvre et immigration, 1974), 31, tableau 4.7.

5. Henripin estimated that at the rate of decline experienced in the early 1970s, Quebec would still be 77 per cent French-speaking by 2001. His prediction proved to be fairly accurate.

6. Marian Scott, "Census 2016: English Is Making Gains in Quebec," *Montreal Gazette*, 2 Aug. 2017, https://montrealgazette .com/news/local-news/census-2016-bilingualism-hits-all-time-high-in-quebec-across-canada.

7. Statistics of Canada, *Census of Canada*, 2016.

8. Richard Joy, *Languages in Conflict* (Toronto: McClelland & Stewart, 1972), 58, Table 25.

9. René Houle and Jean-Pierre Corbeil, "Language Projections for Canada, 2011 to 2036," 25 Jan. 2017, p. 34, https://www150 .statcan.gc.ca/n1/en/pub/89-657-x/89-657-x2017001-eng. pdf?st=6WRj8_R9.

10. Ibid., 60–1.

11. The first experience with immersion education was in 1975 in St Lambert, Quebec.

12. Jean-François Lepage and Jean-Pierre Corbeil, "The Evolution of English–French Bilingualism in Canada from 1961 to 2011," Statistics Canada (May 2013), www.statcan.gc.ca/pub/75-006-x/2013001/article/11795-eng.pdf. This finding is confirmed in Statistics Canada, "English–French Bilingualism Reaches New Heights," 2 Aug. 2017: "In Canada outside Quebec, people with English as their mother tongue who develop the ability to conduct a conversation in French generally do so in school, when they are between 5 and 19 years of age. Bilingualism rates then gradually decline from one age group to the next." https://www12.statcan.gc.ca/census-recensement/2016/as-sa/98-200-x/2016009/98-200-x2016009-eng.cfm.

13. All of the statistics in this paragraph are from Statistics Canada, "English–French Bilingualism Reaches New Heights."

14. See Peter C. Waite, *Pre-Confederation* (Toronto: Prentice-Hall, 1965), 54–5.

15. Louis Hemon, *Maria Chapdelaine*, trans. Sir Andrew Macphail (Toronto: Oxford University Press, 1921), 212–13.

16. Henri Bourassa, *La langue, guardienne de la foi* (Montréal: Bibliothèque de l'action française, 1918).

17. Henri Bourassa, "The French Language and the Future of Our Race," in Ramsay Cook, ed., *French Canadian Nationalism* (Toronto: Macmillan, 1969), 133.

18. Marcel Rioux, "Sur l'evolution des ideologies au Quebec," English translation in Richard Schultz et al., eds, *The Canadian Political Process*, 3rd edn (Toronto: Holt, Rinehart and Winston, 1979), 99–102.

19. Denis Monière, *Ideologies in Quebec* (Toronto: University of Toronto Press, 1981), esp. ch. 2.

20. These voices included such figures as Gonzalve Doutre, Errol Bouchette, and Olivar Asselin, and the activities of the Institut Canadien.

21. F.H. Leacy, ed., *Historical Statistics of Canada* (Ottawa: Supply and Services Canada, 1983), R1–22, R81–97.

22. The numbers were about 390,000 in manufacturing compared to 249,000 in agriculture. The figure for the agricultural labour force counts only males.

23. Quoted by Pierre Trudeau in "Quebec on the Eve of the Asbestos Strike," in Cook, ed., *French Canadian Nationalism*, 35–6.

24. Victor Barbeau, *Mesure de notre taille* (1936); Barbeau, *Avenir de notre bourgeoisie* (Montréal: Editions de l'action canadienne française, 1939); Jacques Melançon, "Retard de croissance de l'entreprise canadienne-francaise," *L'actualité économique* (jan.–mars 1956): 503–22.

25. Rioux, "Sur l'évolution," 105–8.

26. Ibid., 105.

27. See Melançon, "Retard de croissance."

28. Lois du Quebec, 1974, c. 6.

29. Lois du Quebec, 1977, c. 5.

30. See sections 23–29.1 of the Charter of the French Language, www2.publicationsduquebec.gouv.qc.ca/dynamicSearch/telecharge.php?type=2&file=/C_11/C11_A.html.

31. *Ford v. Attorney General of Quebec*, [1988] 2 S.C.R. 712.

32. Charter of the French Language, s. 58.

33. Ibid., s. 73.

34. Eric Waddell, "State, Language and Society: The Vicissitudes of French in Quebec and Canada," in Alan Cairns and Cynthia Williams, eds, *The Politics of Gender, Ethnicity and Language in Canada*, vol. 34 of the research studies for the Royal Commission on the Economic Union and Development Prospects for Canada (Toronto: University of Toronto Press, 1985), 97.

35. Raymond Breton, "The Production and Allocation of Symbolic Resources: An Analysis of the Linguistic and Ethnocultural Fields in Canada," *Canadian Review of Sociology and Anthropology* 21, 2 (1984): 129.

36. Commissioner of Official Languages, *Annual Report 1985* (Ottawa: Supply and Services Canada, 1986), 50.

37. Government of Canada, Privy Council Office, "The Next Level: Normalizing a Culture of Inclusive Linguistic Duality in the Federal Public Service Workplace," 2017, https://www.canada.ca/en/privy-council/corporate/clerk/publications/next-level/next-level.html.

38. Ibid.

39. Ibid.

40. Treasury Board Secretariat, Annual Report on Official Languages 2015–16, 2017, https://www.canada.ca/en/treasury-board-secretariat/services/values-ethics/official-languages/reports/annual-report-official-languages-2015-2016.html#toc3-4.

41. *Attorney General of Manitoba v. Forest* (1979), 101 D.L.R. (3d) 385; *Reference re Language Rights under the Manitoba Act, 1870* (No. 1) (1985), 19 D.L.R. (4th) 1.

42. *Attorney General of Quebec v. Quebec Protestant School Boards* (1984), 10 D.L.R. (4th) 321; *Ford v. Attorney General of Quebec.*

43. *Mahe v. Alberta* (1990), https://scc-csc.lexum.com/scc-csc/scc-csc/en/item/580/index.do; *Arsenault-Cameron v. Prince Edward Island* (2000), https://scc-csc.lexum.com/scc-csc/scc-csc/en/item/1762/index.do.

44. Canadian Parents for French, "French as a Second Language Enrolment Statistics, 2012–2013 to 2016–2017," https://cpf.ca/en/files/Enrolement-Stats-2018-web-1.pdf. Based on Provincial and Territorial Ministries of Education.

45. Waddell, "State, Language and Society," 101; Sharon Lapkin, ed., *French as Second Language Education in Canada: Recent Empirical Studies* (Toronto: University of Toronto Press, 1998); Sheryl Ubelacher, "Few Chances to Use French Immersion Skills," *Toronto Star*, 4 Dec. 2007.

46. E.S. Yoon and K. Gulson, "School Choice in the Stratilingual City of Vancouver, British Columbia," *Journal of the Sociology of Education* 31, 6 (2010): 703–18.

47. Statistics Canada, "Languages Used in the Workplace in Canada," 29 Nov. 2017, https://www12.statcan.gc.ca/census-recensement/2016/as-sa/98-200-x/2016031/98-200-x2016031-eng.cfm.

48. *CBC News*, "Majority of Quebecers Believe Question of Independence Is Settled: Poll," 3 Oct. 2016, https://www.cbc.ca/news/canada/montreal/quebec-angus-reid-canada-indepdence-1.3788110. Already, several years earlier, polls had indicated that an increasing number of Quebecers no longer believed that separatism was necessary: "Survey: 30 Years after the 1980 Referendum, Quebeckers Believe That Issue Is Outmoded," 18 May 2010, www.ideefederal.ca.

49. Karel Maynard, "Lettre à Jean-François Lisée: Montréal sur l'autoroute de l'anglicisation," *Huffington Post*, 1 Feb. 2014, https://quebec.huffingtonpost.ca/karel-mayrand/lettre-a-jean-francois-lisee-montreal-anglicisation_b_4373663.html?utm_hp_ref=qc-anglicisation-montreal. My translation.

50. All of the statistics in this paragraph are from René Houle and Jean-Pierre Corbeil, "Language Projections for Canada, 2011 to 2036," 25 Jan. 2017, https://www150.statcan.gc.ca/n1/en/pub/89-657-x/89-657-x2017001-eng.pdf?st=6WRj8_R9.

15 Women and Politics

1. See Kristina Zosuls et al., "Gender Development Research in Sex Roles: Historical Trends and Future Directions," *Sex Roles: A Journal of Research* 64, 11–12 (June 2011): 826–42.

2. Nellie McClung, "Hardy Perennials," in McClung, *In Times Like These* (Toronto: University of Toronto Press, 1972), 43–58.

3. Simone de Beauvoir, *The Second Sex*, trans. H.M. Parshley (London: Jonathan Cape, 1970), 273.

4. John Stuart Mill, *On the Subjugation of Women* (1869), www.fordham.edu/halsall/mod/jsmill-women.html.

5. Ibid.

6. Friedrich Engels, *The Origin of Family, Private Property and the State* (1884), www.marxists.org/archive/marx/works/1884/origin-family/index.htm#intro.

7. See Margaret Mead, *Sex and Temperament in Three Primitive Societies* (New York: Dell, 1969 [1935]); Mead, *Male and Female* (New York: William Morrow, 1950).

8. See Anthony Thomson, *The Making of Social Theory: Order, Reason, and Desire*, 2nd edn (Toronto: Oxford University Press, 2010), 54–5.

9. Sheila Rowbotham, *Hidden from History* (London: Pluto Press, 1974), 47.

10. American Psychological Association, "Men and Women: No Big Difference," 20 Oct. 2005, https://www.apa.org/research/action/difference.aspx.

11. Janet Shibley Hyde, "The Gender Similarities Hypothesis," *American Psychologist* 60, 6 (2005).

12. Rong Su and James Rounds, "All STEM Fields Are Not Created Equal: People and Things Interests Explain Gender Disparities across STEM Fields," *Frontiers in Psychology*, 25 Feb. 2015, https://www.frontiersin.org/articles/10.3389/fpsyg.2015.00189/full.

13. Diane F. Halpern, *Sex Differences in Cognitive Abilities*, 4th edn (New York: Psychology Press, 2011); Halpern, "A Cognitive-Process Taxonomy for Sex Differences in Cognitive Abilities," *Current Directions in Psychological Research* 13, 4 (2004): 135–9.

14. Larry Cahill, "An Issue Whose Time Has Come: Sex/Gender Influences on Nervous System Function," *Journal of Neuroscience Research* 95, 1–2 (Jan./Feb. 2017), 12.

15. Halpern, "A Cognitive-Process Taxonomy," 139.

16. Terry Copp, *Anatomy of Poverty* (Toronto: McClelland & Stewart, 1974), 43.

17. The statement was made by Montreal's Chief Inspector of Factories in the late 1800s. Quoted ibid., 49.

18. Nellie McClung, "Hardy Perennials," in McClung, *In Times Like These* (Toronto: University of Toronto Press, 1972), 56.

19. A. Richard Allen, "Social Gospel," in *The Canadian Encyclopedia*, 2nd edn (Edmonton: Hurtig, 1988), vol. 3, 2026.

20. See Richard Allen, *The Social Passion* (Toronto: University of Toronto Press, 1971).

21. See the discussion in Penney Kome, *Women of Influence* (Toronto: Doubleday Canada, 1985), ch. 2.

22. Quoted ibid., 32.

23. This was the title of a retrospective article that Macphail wrote in 1949, after having served five terms as an MP for Ontario's South Grey constituency.

24. Quoted in Sylvia Bashevkin, *Toeing the Lines: Women and Party Politics in English Canada,* 2nd edn (Toronto: University of Toronto Press, 2003), 16.

25. See, for example, ibid., 20–3.

26. Betty Friedan, *The Feminine Mystique* (New York: Norton, 1963).

27. Ibid., 32.

28. Statistics Canada, "The Surge of Women in the Workforce," https://www150.statcan.gc.ca/n1/pub/11-630-x/11-630-x2015009-eng.htm.

29. Pat Armstrong and Hugh Armstrong, *The Double Ghetto: Canadian Women and Their Segregated Work*, 3rd edn (Toronto: Oxford University Press, 2010), 42–3.

30. Warren Clark, "Education," *Canadian Social Trends* 59 (Winter 2000): 6, http://publications.gc.ca/Collection-R/Statcan/11-008-XIE/0030011-008-XIE.pdf.

31. Barbara Frum, "Why There Are So Few Women in Ottawa," *Chatelaine* 44 (Oct. 1971): 33, 110.

32. Bashevkin, *Toeing the Lines*, 110–19.

33. This was true in *Murdoch* (1973), *Canard* (1975), and *Bliss* (1979).

34. Michael Mandel, *The Charter of Rights and the Legalization of Politics in Canada* (Toronto: Wall and Thompson, 1995), 389–99.

35. *Re Casagrande and Hinton Roman Catholic Separate School District* (1987), 38 D.L.R. (4th) 382.

36. Canadian Advisory Council on the Status of Women, *Canadian Charter and Equality Rights for Women: One Step Forward or Two Steps Back?* (Sept. 1989), 19.

37. *Law Society of British Columbia v. Andrews and Kinersley*, [1989] 1 S.C.R. 143.

38. Christopher P. Manfredi, *Judicial Power and the Charter: Canada and the Paradox of Liberal Constitutionalism*, 2nd edn (Toronto: Oxford University Press, 2001), 123–4.

39. Penney Kome, *The Taking of Twenty-Eight: Women Challenge the Constitution* (Toronto: Women's Press, 1983).

40. Jacquetta Newman and Linda Smith, *Women, Politics and Public Policy*, 2nd edn (Toronto: Oxford University Press, 2012), 133–44.

41. Cheryl Collier, "Neo-Liberalism and Violence against Women: Can Retrenchment Convergence Explain the Path of Provincial Anti-Violence Policy, 1985–2005?" *Canadian Journal of Political Science* 41, 1 (2008): 19–42.

42. Kathleen Mahoney, "A Charter of Rights: The Canadian Experience," Parliament of Australia, *Papers on Parliament*, No. 23 (Sept. 1994), https://www.aph.gov.au/~/~/link.aspx?_id=A3510D1C29DD48CEBC5B7DDBD621C1EF&_z=z.

43. R. Claire Snyder, "What Is Third-Wave Feminism? A New Directions Essay," *Signs: Journal of Women in Culture and Society* 34, 1 (Autumn 2008): 177.

44. Rebecca Walker, "'Being Real: An Introduction,' from *To Be Real: Telling the Truth and Changing the Face of Feminism*," in Leslie L. Heywood, ed., *The Women's Movement Today: An Encyclopedia of Third-Wave Feminism*, vol. 2, *Primary Documents* (Westport, CT: Greenwood, 2005), 22.

45. Leslie L. Heywood, ed., *The Women's Movement Today: An Encyclopedia of Third-Wave Feminism*, vol. 1, *A–Z* (Westport, CT: Greenwood, 2005), xx.

46. Snyder, "What Is Third-Wave Feminism? A New Directions Essay," 184.

47. Quoted in Jennifer C. Nash, "'Home Truths' on Intersectionality," *Yale Journal of Law & Feminism* 23, 2 (2011): 451.

48. Kimberlé Crenshaw, "Demarginalizing the Intersection of Race and Sex: A Black Feminist Critique of Antidiscrimination Doctrine, Feminist Theory, and Antiracist Politics," *University of Chicago Legal Forum* 139 (1989).

49. Judy Rebick, "Fighting Racism," *Feminist Action* 6, 2 (June 1992).

50. Cheryl N. Collier, "Not Quite the Death of Organized Feminism in Canada: Understanding the Demise of the National Action Committee on the Status of Women," *Canadian Political Science Review* 8, 2 (2014).

51. See Leslie Grimard, "The Feminine Mystique at Fifty: Time for a New Feminism," *Public Discourse*, 7 Mar. 2013, www.thepublicdiscourse.com/2013/03/9230/.

52. Jill Filipovic, "What's with Hillary's Woman Problem?", *Politico*, Sept./Oct., 2016, https://www.politico.com/magazine/story/2016/09/hillary-clinton-feminism-white-house-2016-women-214217.

53. Nielsen, "When It Comes to Gender Equality, Millennial Women Are More Optimistic about Closing the Gap," 8 Mar. 2017, https://www.nielsen.com/us/en/insights/news/2017/when-it-comes-to-gender-equality-millennial-women-are-more-optimistic-on-closing-the-pay-gap.html.

54. Anna North, "The #MeToo Generation Gap Is a Myth," *Vox*, 20 Mar. 2018, https://www.vox.com/2018/3/20/17115620/me-too-sexual-harassment-sex-abuse-poll.

55. YouGov, "Sexual Harassment: How the Genders and Generations See the Issue Differently," 1 Nov. 2017, https://yougov.co.uk/topics/lifestyle/articles-reports/2017/11/01/sexual-harassment-how-genders-and-generations-see-; *The Economist*, "Over-Friendly, or Sexual Harassment? It depends partly on whom you ask," 17 Nov. 2017, https://www.economist.com/graphic-detail/2017/11/17/over-friendly-or-sexual-harassment-it-depends-partly-on-whom-you-ask.

56. Margaret Atwood, "Am I a Bad Feminist?" *Globe and Mail*, 13 Jan. 2018, https://www.theglobeandmail.com/opinion/am-i-a-bad-feminist/article37591823/.

57. YouGov, "Sexual Harassment Reports May Be Just the Tip of the Iceberg," https://today.yougov.com/topics/politics/articles-reports/2017/11/17/sexual-harassment-reports-may-just-be-tip-iceberg.

58. Snyder, "What Is Third-Wave Feminism? A New Directions Essay," 6.

59. Alice Hines, "Bitch Magazine Turns Twenty," *The New Yorker*, 23 May 2016, https://www.newyorker.com/culture/culture-desk/bitch-magazine-turns-twenty; Alix Strauss, "Bust Magazine Is on a Mission," *New York Times*, 31 Oct. 2018, https://www.nytimes.com/2018/10/31/nyregion/bust-womens-feminist-magazine.html.

60. Brenda O'Neill, "Continuity and Change in the Contemporary Canadian Feminist Movement," *Canadian Journal of Political Science* 50, 2 (June 2017): 450.

61. Ibid., 456.

62. Jessica Fortin-Rittberger, "Cross-National Gender Gaps in Political Knowledge: How Much Is Due to Context?" *Political Research Quarterly* 69, 3 (Sept. 2016): 391–402, https://www.ncbi.nlm.nih.gov/pmc/articles/PMC4968032/.

63. Bashevkin, *Toeing the Lines*.

64. Pippa Norris and Joni Lovenduski, "'If Only More Candidates Came Forward': Supply-Side Explanations of Candidate Selection in Britain," *British Journal of Political Science* 23, 3 (July 1993): 373–408; Joni Lovenduski, "The Supply and Demand Model of Candidate Selection: Some Reflections," *Government and Opposition* 51, Special Issue 3 (July 2016): 513–28.

65. Melissa Moyser and Amanda Burlock, "Time Use: Total Work Burden, Unpaid Work, and Leisure," Statistics Canada, 30 July 2018, https://www150.statcan.gc.ca/n1/pub/89-503-x/2015001/article/54931-eng.htm.

66. Brenda O'Neill, "Unpacking Gender's Role in Political Representation in Canada," *Canadian Parliamentary Review* (Summer 2015): 27, http://revparl.ca/38/2/38n2e_15_ONeill.pdf.

67. Elizabeth Goodyear-Grant, "Crafting a Public Image: Women MPs and the Dynamics of Media Coverage," in Sylvia Bashevkin, ed., *Are Doors Opening Wider? Studies of Women's Political Engagement in Canada* (Vancouver: University of British Columbia Press, 2009), 147–66; Miki Caul Kittilson and Kim Fridkin, "Gender, Candidate Portrayals and Election Campaigns: A Comparative Perspective," *Politics & Gender* 4, 3 (2008) 371–92.

68. Louise Carbert, "Are Cities More Congenial? Tracking the Rural Deficit of Women in the House of Commons," in Baskevkin, ed., *Are Doors Opening Wider?*, 70–90.

69. Sylvia Bashevkin, "When Do Outsiders Break In? Institutional Circumstances of Party Leadership Victories by Women in Canada," *Commonwealth and Comparative Politics* 48, 1 (2010): 72–90; see also the discussion in O'Neill, "Unpacking Gender's Role," 25–6.

70. United Nations Development Programme, http://hdr.undp.org/sites/default/files/2018_human_development_statistical_update.pdf; Georgetown Institute for Women, Peace and Security, https://giwps.georgetown.edu/the-index/; World Economic Forum, http://www3.weforum.org/docs/WEF_GGGR_2018.pdf; *U.S News & World Report*, https://www.usnews.com/news/best-countries/women-full-list.

71. Ipsos Public Affairs, "Feminism and Gender Equality around the World," https://www.ipsos.com/sites/default/files/2017-03/global-advisor-feminism-charts-2017.pdf.

72. Randstad, "Men Are Favored in Management Positions, but Employees Prefer Working in Gender-Diverse Teams," *Workmonitor Q3*, Sept. 2016, https://cdn2.hubspot.net/hubfs/481927/Randstad%20Workmonitor_global%20report_Q32016.pdf?submissionGuid=a5af7837-450c-423f-9a25-9a9be0c37a3a.

73. Angus Reid Institute, "#MeToo: Moment or Movement?" 9 Feb. 2018, https://www.rosenzweigco.com/media-1/the-13th-annual-rosenzweig-report-on-women-at-the-top-levels-of-corporate-canada.

74. Statistics from Melissa Moyser, "Women and Paid Work," in Statistics Canada, *Women in Canada: A Gender-based Statistical Report*, 8 Mar. 2017, https://www150.statcan.gc.ca/n1/pub/89-503-x/2015001/article/14694-eng.htm; Solomon Israel, "StatsCan on Gender Pay Gap: Women Earn 87¢ to Men's $1," *CBC News*, 8 Mar. 2017, https://www.cbc.ca/news/business/statistics-canada-gender-pay-gap-1.4014954.

75. All statistics and quotations in the following section are from Moyser, "Women and Paid Work."

76. Claire Cain Miller, "Children Hurt Women's Earnings, but Not Men's (Even in Scandinavia)," *New York Times*, 5 Feb. 2018, https://www.nytimes.com/2018/02/05/upshot/even-in-family-friendly-scandinavia-mothers-are-paid-less.html.

77. Jon Erlichman, "One in 100: Canada's 'Embarrassing' Lack of Female CEOs among Top TSX Companies," BNN Bloomberg, 6 July 2018, https://www.bnnbloomberg.ca/female-ceos-noticeably-absent-from-canada-s-c-suite-1.1103584.

78. Dan Fox and Melissa Moyser, "Women in Canada: A Gender-based Statistical Report: The Economic Well-Being of Women in Canada," Statistics Canada, 16 May 2018, https://www150.statcan.gc.ca/n1/pub/89-503-x/2015001/article/54930/c-g/c-g05-eng.htm.

79. Rosenzweig and Company, "The 13th Annual Rosenzweig Report," 2018, https://www.rosenzweigco.com/media-1/the-13th-annual-rosenzweig-report-on-women-at-the-top-levels-of-corporate-canada.

80. Heidrick & Struggles, "Route to the Top 2017," 2017, https://www.heidrick.com/Knowledge-Center/Publication/Route-to-the-top-2017.

81. OECD Stat, https://stats.oecd.org/index.aspx?queryid=54753.

82. OECD Stat, https://stats.oecd.org/index.aspx?queryid=54757.

83. Anne-Marie Slaughter, "Why Women Still Can't Have It All," *Atlantic Monthly*, July/Aug. 2012, https://www.theatlantic.com/magazine/archive/2012/07/why-women-still-cant-have-it-all/309020.

84. Oxfam Canada, "Oxfam Scorecard Tracking Liberal Government Action on Women's Rights Shows Progress—But More Needed to Turn Feminist Words into Action," 6 Mar. 2017, https://www.oxfam.ca/news/oxfam-scorecard-tracking-liberal-government-action-on-women%E2%80%99s-rights.

16 Aboriginal Politics

1. UN Human Rights Council, *Universal Periodic Review: Canada*, "Compilation of UN Information," 11 May 2018, 9, https://www.ohchr.org/EN/HRBodies/UPR/Pages/CAIndex.aspx.

2. Liam Stack, "Wave of Indigenous Suicides Leaves Canadian Town Appealing for Help," *New York Times*, 18 Mar. 2016, https://www.nytimes.com/2016/03/19/world/americas/canada-youth-suicide.html.

3. Selena Randhawa, "'Our Society Is Broken': What Can Stop Canada's First Nations Suicide Epidemic?" *The Guardian*, 30 Aug. 2017, https://www.theguardian.com/inequality/2017/aug/30/our-society-is-broken-what-can-stop-canadas-first-nations-suicide-epidemic.

4. National Aboriginal Economic Development Board, *The Aboriginal Economic Progress Report*, 2015, 19, table 6, http://www.naedb-cndea.com/reports/NAEDB-progress-report-june-2015.pdf.

5. Frank Trovato and Anatole Romaniuk, eds, *Aboriginal Populations: Social Demographic and Epidemiological Perspectives* (Edmonton: University of Alberta Press, 2014).

6. Tom Flanagan, *Incentives, Identity, and the Growth of Canada's Indigenous Population* (Vancouver: Fraser Institute, 2017), https://www.fraserinstitute.org/sites/default/files/incentives-identity-and-the-growth-of-canadas-indigenous-population.pdf.

7. Data based on the 2016 census data, reported by Statistics Canada.

8. The word "aboriginality" is sometimes used, and in a non-derogatory way, in Canada, as in Tom Jackson and Dominique Keller's 2007 NFB documentary, *Aboriginality*. https://www.nfb.ca/film/aboriginality/.

9. Chiefs of Ontario, "Disconcerting Use of the Term 'Aboriginal' Unveiled in Announcement of New Federal Cabinet," www.chiefs-of-ontario.org/node/189.

10. See the definitions at Indigenous Foundations, https://indigenousfoundations.arts.ubc.ca/terminology/.

11. Graeme Hamilton, "Mohawk Community's Law against Mixed Couples on Reserve Ruled Unconstitutional," *National Post*, 30 Apr. 2018, https://nationalpost.com/news/canada/mohawk-communitys-law-against-mixed-couples-on-reserve-ruled-unconstitutional.

12. *Reference whether "Indians" includes "Eskimo,"* [1939] S.C.R. 104.

13. The Labrador Métis, or Inuit-Métis, are an interesting case. These are people of mixed Inuit–European heritage living in central and southern Labrador who, for reasons of geography and birthplace, did not qualify as beneficiaries of the Nunatsiavut land claim agreement in northern Labrador. See John C. Kennedy, ed., *History and Renewal of Labrador's Inuit-Métis* (St. John's: ISER Books, 2014), esp. 1–37.

14. *Daniels v. Canada (Indian Affairs and Northern Development)*, 2016 SCC 12, [2016] 1 S.C.R. 99.

15. Sandro Contenta, "In Newfoundland, Too Many Want Recognition as Mi'kmaq Indians, Federal Government Says," *Toronto Star*, 5 May 2013, www.thestar.com/news/insight/2013/05/05/in_newfoundland_too_many_want_recognition_as_mikmaq_indians_federal_government_says/html.

16. See Chris Andersen, *"Métis": Race, Recognition, and the Struggle for Indigenous Peoplehood* (Vancouver: University of British Columbia Press, 2015).

17. Olive Patricia Dickason, with David T. McNab, *Canada's First Nations: A History of Founding Peoples from Earliest Times*, 4th edn (Don Mills, Ont.: Oxford University Press, 2009), 517, n. 27.

18. Christopher Alcantara, "Individual Property Rights on Canadian Indian Reserves: The Historical Emergence and Jurisprudence of Certificates of Possession," *Canadian Journal of Native Studies* 23, 2 (2003): 391–424, http://www3.brandonu.ca/cjns/23.2/cjnsv23no2_pg391-424.pdf.

19. Indian and Northern Affairs Canada, *Resolving Aboriginal Claims*, 2003, 2, www.aadnc-aandc.gc.ca/DAM/DAM-INTER-HQ/STAGING/texte-text/rul_1100100014175_eng.pdf. More recently, Statistics Canada has placed the number of reserves at 3,100. This much higher number and the discrepancy between the two numbers appear to be due to the inclusion in the Statistics Canada estimate of First Nations villages and communities that do not have the legal status of reserves.

20. Harvey McCue, updated by Zach Parrot, "Reserves," *The Canadian Encyclopedia*, last updated 12 July 2018, https://www.thecanadianencyclopedia.ca/en/article/aboriginal-reserves/.

21. Cole Harris, *Making Native Space: Colonialism, Resistance, and Reserves in British Columbia* (Vancouver: University of British Columbia Press, 2002, reprinted 2011), 291–2.

22. Statistics Canada, *Language Highlight Tables, 2016 Census*, https://www12.statcan.gc.ca/census-recensement/2016/dp-pd/hlt-fst/lang/Table.cfm?Lang=E&T=41&Geo=01.

23. For a valuable discussion of Indigenous languages in contemporary Canada, see James S. Frideres, *First Nations in the Twenty-First Century,* 2nd edn (Toronto: Oxford University Press, 2016), ch. 6.

24. G.F.G. Stanley, "The First Indian 'Reserves' in Canada," *Revue d'histoire de l'Amérique française* (1950): 168, 209–10.

25. Francis Parkman, *The Jesuits in North America in the Seventeenth Century* (Toronto: George N. Morang, 1907 [1867]), 131.

26. Quoted in Royal Commission on Aboriginal Peoples, *Report,* vol. 2, *Restructuring the Relationship* (Ottawa, 1996), 531–2.

27. A good documentary explaining the origins and history of the American Indian Movement was produced by PBS in 2009. See *What was the American Indian Movement?* at https://www .pbs.org/video/american-experience-what-was-american-indian-movement/.

28. Harold Cardinal, *The Unjust Society* (Edmonton: Hurtig, 1969), 1.

29. Mary Hurley, "Aboriginal Self-Government," 15 Dec. 2009, www.parl.gc.ca/content/lop/researchpublications/prb0923-e.htm.

30. Indian leader James Gosnell, quoted in Michael Asch, *Home and Native Land: Aboriginal Rights and the Canadian Constitution* (Vancouver: University of British Columbia Press, 1993), 29.

31. *Delgamuukw v. British Columbia,* [1997] 3 S.C.R. 1010 at para. 128.

32. Ibid., para. 122.

33. Assembly of First Nations 2018 Special Chiefs Assembly, Gatineau, Quebec, Resolution no. 02/2018.

34. Georges Erasmus and Joe Sanders, "Canadian History: An Aboriginal Perspective," in Diane Engelstad and John Bird, eds, *Nation to Nation: Aboriginal Sovereignty and the Future of Canada* (Concord, ON: House of Anansi Press, 1992), 6.

35. Ibid., 8.

36. Quoted in David De Brou and Bill Waiser, eds, *Documenting Canada: A History of Modern Canada in Documents* (Saskatoon: Fifth House Publishers, 1992), 572.

37. Ibid., 665.

38. *Tsilhqot'in Nation v. British Columbia,* 2014 SCC 44 at para. 76.

39. *Delgamuukw v. British Columbia,* para. 83.

40. Ibid., para. 86.

41. *Ktunaxa Nation v. British Columbia,* 2017 SCC 54. For discussion of the issues and political machinations involved in the *Ktunaxa Nation* case, see Joyce Green, "Enacting Reconciliation," in Gina Starblanket and David Long with Olive Patricia Dickason, eds, *Visions of the Heart: Issues Involving Indigenous Peoples in Canada,* 5th edn (Toronto: Oxford University Press, 2020), ch. 14.

42. Erasmus and Sanders, "Canadian History," 3.

43. Ibid., 4.

44. A map of historical treaties of Canada may be seen at https://www.aadnc-aandc.gc.ca/DAM/DAM-INTER-HQ/STAGING/texte-text/htoc_1100100032308_eng.pdf; a map of modern treaties and self-government agreements is found at https://www.aadnc-aandc.gc.ca/DAM/DAM-INTER-HQ-AI/STAGING/texte-text/mprm_pdf_modrn-treaty_1383144351646_eng.pdf.

45. Menno Boldt, *Surviving as Indians: The Challenge of Self-Government* (Toronto: University of Toronto Press, 1993).

46. Bob Rae, "The Gap between Historic Treaty Peoples and Everyone Else," University of Regina, 30 Oct. 2014, http://oktlaw.com/drive/uploads/2016/10/BRRegina.pdf.

47. Quoted in Peter A. Cumming and Neil H. Mickenberg, eds, *Native Rights in Canada* (Toronto: General Publishing, 1972), 61–2.

48. *Nowegijick v. The Queen,* [1983] 1 S.C.R. 29.

49. *R. v. Marshall,* [1999] 3 S.C.R. 456.

50. *R. v. Marshall,* 2005 SCC 43 (case no. 30063).

51. Sally Weaver, "The Joint Cabinet/National Indian Brotherhood Committee: A Unique Experiment in Pressure Group Politics," *Canadian Public Administration* 25 (Summer 1982): 211–39.

52. J. Hugh Faulkner, "Pressuring the Executive," *Canadian Public Administration* 25 (Summer 1982): 248.

53. Ninth annual presidential address to the National Indian Brotherhood, Fredericton, New Brunswick, Sept. 1978.

54. Rick Ponting and Roger Gibbins, *Out of Irrelevance: A Socio-Political Introduction to Indian Affairs in Canada* (Toronto: Butterworths, 1980), 124.

55. Quoted in Canadian Press, "Rival Meetings Hint at Aboriginal Divisions," 15 July 2013, www.ipolitics.ca/2013/07/15/rival-meetings-hint-at-aboriginal-divisions/.

56. APTN National News, "Relevancy of AFN and Election of National Chief Put InFocus," 23 May 2018, http://aptnnews .ca/2018/05/23/relevancy-of-afn-and-election-of-national-chief-put-infocus/.

57. Robert Jago, "Budget 2017 Sets the Stage for a Nation-to-Nation Partnership with Indigenous People, but Fails to Mention the Role of Individual Bands," *Policy Options,* 29 Mar. 2017, http://policyoptions.irpp.org/magazines/march-2017/the-fatal-flaw-in-the-nation-to-nation-agenda/.

58. Gary Granzberg et al., "New Magic for Old: TV in Cree Culture," *Journal of Communication* 27, 4 (1977): 155–77; Gary Granzberg, "Television as Storyteller: The Algonkian Indians of Central Canada," *Journal of Communication* 32, 1 (1982): 43–52.

59. "Idle No More Founders Distance Themselves from Chiefs," *National Post,* 1 Jan. 2013, https://nationalpost.com/news/politics/idle-no-more-founders-distance-themselves-from-chiefs.

60. *CBC News,* "Iconic First Nations Protests," 18 Oct. 2013, https://www.cbc.ca/news/canada/iconic-first-nations-protests-1.2125374.

61. Jill Mahoney, "Canadians' Attitudes Hardening on Aboriginal Issues: New Poll," *Globe and Mail,* 15 Jan. 2013, https://www.theglobeandmail.com/news/national/canadians-attitudes-hardening-on-aboriginal-issues-new-poll/article7408516/.

62. Angus Reid Institute, "Truths of Reconciliation: Canadians Are Deeply Divided on How Best to Address Indigenous Issues," 7 June 2018, http://angusreid.org/indigenous-canada/.

63. Ken Coates, "Government Isn't Only Key to Progress for Aboriginal People," *Toronto Star,* 16 May 2014, https://www .thestar.com/opinion/commentary/2014/05/16/government_isnt_only_key_to_progress_for_aboriginal_people.html.

17 Canada in the World

1. Marvin McInnis, "Canadian Economic Development in the Wheat Boom Era: A Reassessment," Department of Economics, Queen's University, n.d., http://qed.econ.queensu.ca/faculty/mcinnis/Cdadevelopment1.pdf.

2. The idea that America and in particular its influence abroad are in decline has been popular over the past decade. A summary of some of this debate may be found in Stephen Brooks, *American Exceptionalism in the Age of Obama* (New York: Routledge, 2013), ch. 1. The 2016 election of Donald Trump as president was followed by a significant spike in the declinist literature on America in the world. As has occurred during past cycles of predictions and analysis of decline, not everyone agreed. See, for example, Robert Kagan, *The Jungle: America and Our Imperiled World* (New York: Knopf, 2018), and Michael Beckley, *Why America Will Remain the World's Sole Superpower* (Ithaca, NY: Cornell University Press, 2018).

3. Mark Kingwell, "What Distinguishes Us from the Americans," *National Post*, 5 Mar. 2003, A16.

4. John Ralston Saul, *Reflections on a Siamese Twin: Canada at the End of the Twentieth Century* (Toronto: Penguin, 1997), 171.

5. Michael Adams, *Sex in the Snow: Canadian Social Values at the End of the Millennium* (Toronto: Penguin, 1997), 171.

6. See, for example, the annual surveys of Reputation Institute, www.reputationinstitute.com/thought-leadership/country-reptrak; *US News & World Report*, "Overall Best Countries Ranking," 2018, https://www.usnews.com/news/best-countries/overall-full-list; Amarendra Bhushan Dhiraj, "Results Are In: The 80 Best Countries in the World for 2018," *CEOWorld Magazine*, 24 Jan. 2018, https://ceoworld.biz/2018/01/24/80-best-countries-in-the-world-for-2018/.

7. Globescan, "Sharp Drop in World Views of US, UK: Global Poll," 4 July 2017, https://globescan.com/sharp-drop-in-world-views-of-us-uk-global-poll/.

8. Stephen Brooks, ed., *Promoting Canadian Studies Abroad: Soft Power and Cultural Diplomacy* (London: Palgrave MacMillan, 2019).

9. https://www.theguardian.com/commentisfree/2017/apr/17/stop-swooning-justin-trudeau-man-disaster-planet.

10. https://fr.metrotime.be/2018/11/19/actualite/monde/canada-russie-et-chine-menent-a-un-rechauffement-de-5c/ (my translation).

11. https://www.lemonde.fr/energies/article/2018/05/29/le-controverse-oleoduc-trans-mountain-nationalise-par-le-canada_5306519_1653054.html (my translation).

12. https://www.theguardian.com/law/2016/jun/02/chinese-foreign-minister-canada-angry-human-rights-question.

13. "Bankrupt Canada?" *Wall Street Journal*, 12 Jan. 1995.

14. Published as Michael Ignatieff, "Canada in the Age of Terror: Multilateralism Meets a Moment of Truth," *Policy Options* (Feb. 2003), www.irpp.org.

15. The self-perceptions that Ignatieff attributed to Canadians are confirmed by a 2018 Environics Institute survey: "Canada's World Survey 2018: Final Report," Apr. 2018, https://www.environicsinstitute.org/docs/default-source/canada's-world-2018-survey/canada's-world-survey-2018---final-report.pdf?sfvrsn=17208306_2.

16. Abacus Data, "Diplomatic, Tolerant & Ethical. How Canadians Think the Rest of the World Sees Our Country," 4 June 2018, http://abacusdata.ca/diplomatic-tolerant-ethical-how-canadians-think-the-rest-of-the-world-sees-our-country/.

17. Environics Institute, "Canada's World Survey 2018," Apr. 2018, https://www.environicsinstitute.org/docs/default-source/canada's-world-2018-survey/canada's-world-survey-2018---final-report.pdf?sfvrsn=17208306_2.

18. David Haglund, "The Paradigm That Dare Not Speak Its Name," *International Journal* 72, 2 (2017): 230–42.

19. Remarks by Lawrence Schembri, Deputy Governor of the Bank of Canada, Atlantic Institute for Market Studies, Halifax, NS, 8 Nov. 2016, Chart 1, https://www.bankofcanada.ca/wp-content/uploads/2016/11/remarks-081116.pdf.

20. Robert Wolfe and Giancarlo Acquaviva, "Recent Polls of Americans and Canadians Have Found Widespread Support for Free Trade, but These Preferences Are Volatile. How Does It Affect the NAFTA Talks?" *Policy Options*, 19 Apr. 2018, http://policyoptions.irpp.org/magazines/april-2018/public-sit-nafta/.

21. Robbie Robertson, *The Three Waves of Globalization: A History of a Developing Global Consciousness* (Chicago: University of Chicago Press, 2003).

22. World Bank, https://data.worldbank.org/indicator/NE.TRD.GNFS.ZS.

23. World Bank: https://data.worldbank.org/indicator/BX.KLT.DINV.CD.WD.

24. Swiss Federal Institute of Technology Zurich, KOF Index of Globalization, globalization.kof.ethz.ch/.

25. Quoted in Nikil Saval, "Globalisation: The Rise and Fall of an Idea That Swept the World," *The Guardian*, 14 July 2017, https://www.theguardian.com/world/2017/jul/14/globalisation-the-rise-and-fall-of-an-idea-that-swept-the-world.

26. David A. Green, W. Craig Riddel, and France St-Hilaire, "Income Inequality in Canada: Driving Forces, Outcomes and Policy," Institute for Research on Public Policy, 23 Feb. 2017, http://irpp.org/research-studies/income-inequality-in-canada/.

27. Steven Pressman, "Defining and Measuring the Middle Class," 2017, http://www.lisdatacenter.org/wp-content/uploads/s41.pdf.

28. *Canada's State of Trade: Trade and Investment Update—2018*, Table 5-3, http://www.international.gc.ca/gac-amc/publications/economist-economiste/state_of_trade-commerce_international-2018.aspx?lang=eng#1.0.

29. Statistics Canada, *Historical Statistics of Canada*, "Canadian International Investment Position," https://www150.statcan.gc.ca/n1/pub/11-516-x/sectiong/4147439-eng.htm#2.

30. Statistics Canada, "Canada's Merchandise Trade with the United States by State," 19 June 2017, https://www150.statcan.gc.ca/n1/daily-quotidien/170619/dq170619b-eng.htm.

31. Jocelyn Coulon, *Un Selfie avec Justin Trudeau* (Montreal: Québec/Amérique, 2018).

32. The scale of this asymmetry is demonstrated in a series of animated trade maps created by data journalist Max Hartshorn: "These Animated Maps Show Canada Has So Much More to Lose in a Trade War than the U.S.," Global News, 4 July

2018, https://globalnews.ca/news/4297411/canada-us-trade-war-animated-maps/.

33. These calculations are based on data provided by the Alberta government and the US Energy Information Administration: http://economic.alberta.ca/documents/US-AB.pdf and https://www.eia.gov/tools/faqs/faq.php?id=727&t=6.

34. Renamed the Alliance of Manufacturers & Exporters Canada in 1996 and Canadian Manufacturers & Exporters in 2000.

35. Alexander Moens and Nachum Gabler, *What Congress Thinks of Canada*, May 2011, Fraser Institute, 48, www.fraserinstitute.org/uploadedFiles/fraser-ca/Content/research-news/research/publications/whatcongressthinksofcanada.pdf; Tom Blackwell, "Canada Is Counting on Its Allies in the U.S. Congress to Curb Trump's Trade War—But Do They Have the 'Guts'?" *National Post*, 12 July 2018, https://nationalpost.com/news/canada-is-counting-on-its-allies-in-the-u-s-congress-to-curb-trumps-trade-war-but-do-they-have-the-guts.

36. Allan Gotlieb, "Getting Attention," *National Post*, 17 May 2002, A17.

37. For an interesting revisionist view of the Pearson legacy in foreign affairs, which takes to task those on both the right and the left for using Lester Pearson in support of their ideological stances, see Mark Neufeld, "'Happy Is the Land That Needs No Hero': The Pearsonian Tradition and the Canadian Intervention in Afghanistan," in J. Marshall Beier and Lana Wylie, eds, *Canadian Foreign Policy in Critical Perspective* (Toronto: Oxford University Press, 2010), 126–38.

38. Ignatieff, "Canada in the Age of Terror."

39. Ibid.

40. In *The Politics of Linkage: Power, Interdependence, and Ideas in Canada–US Relations* (Vancouver: University of British Columbia Press, 2009), Brian Bow examines four cases of conflict between the Canadian and American governments, explaining why, despite Canadian refusal to comply with the preferences of the US administration, Canada did not experience hard-power punishment.

41. President John F. Kennedy, "Speech to the Canadian Parliament," 17 May 1961, www.presidency.ucsb.edu/ws/index.php?pid=8136.

42. Center for Global Development, https://www.cgdev.org/commitment-development-index-2018.

43. Data from OECD, http://www.oecd.org/els/mig/keystat.htm.

44. Data from Canadian Bureau for International Education, https://cbie.ca/media/facts-and-figures/.

45. AUCC, *Canada's Universities in the World AUCC Internationalization Survey, 2014*, https://www.univcan.ca/wp-content/uploads/2015/07/internationalization-survey-2014.pdf.

46. Canadian Bureau for International Education, https://cbie.ca/media/facts-and-figures/.

47. Migration Policy Institute, "International Students in the United States," 9 May 2018, https://www.migrationpolicy.org/article/international-students-united-states.

48. Quoted in CBC Radio, "Should Canada Risk Soldiers' Lives in Its Peacekeeping Mission in Mali?" 20 Mar. 2018, https://www.cbc.ca/radio/thecurrent/the-current-for-march-20-2018-1.4583785/should-canada-risk-soldiers-lives-in-its-peacekeeping-mission-in-mali-1.4583883.

49. *CBC News*, "Michael Ignatieff on Canada's New Peacekeeping Role," 23 Sept. 2016, https://www.cbc.ca/news/politics/michael-ignatieff-on-canada-s-new-peacekeeping-role-1.3777134.

50. NATO, Public Diplomacy Division, "Defence Expenditure of NATO Countries (2010–2017)," 15 Mar. 2018, https://www.nato.int/nato_static_fl2014/assets/pdf/pdf_2018_03/20180315_180315-pr2018-16-en.pdf.

51. "Address by Minister Freeland on Canada's Foreign Policy Priorities," 6 June 2017, https://www.canada.ca/en/global-affairs/news/2017/06/address_by_ministerfreelandoncanadasforeignpolicypriorities.html.

52. Thomas L. Friedman, *Thank You for Being Late: An Optimist's Guide to Thriving in the Age of Accelerations* (New York: Farrar, Straus and Giroux, 2016).

53. Giancarlo Acquaviva, Eliane Hamel Barker, and Robert Wolfe, "Over the Past Two Decades Canadians Have Become Less Concerned about Trade and Globalization, but a Drift toward Populism Cannot Be Ruled Out," *Policy Options*, 9 Oct. 2018, Figure 1, http://policyoptions.irpp.org/magazines/october-2018/what-do-canadians-think-about-trade-and-globalization/.

Index